Eternal Japan

Eternal Japan

Nicolas Wauters

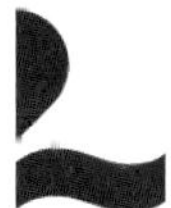

Lannoo

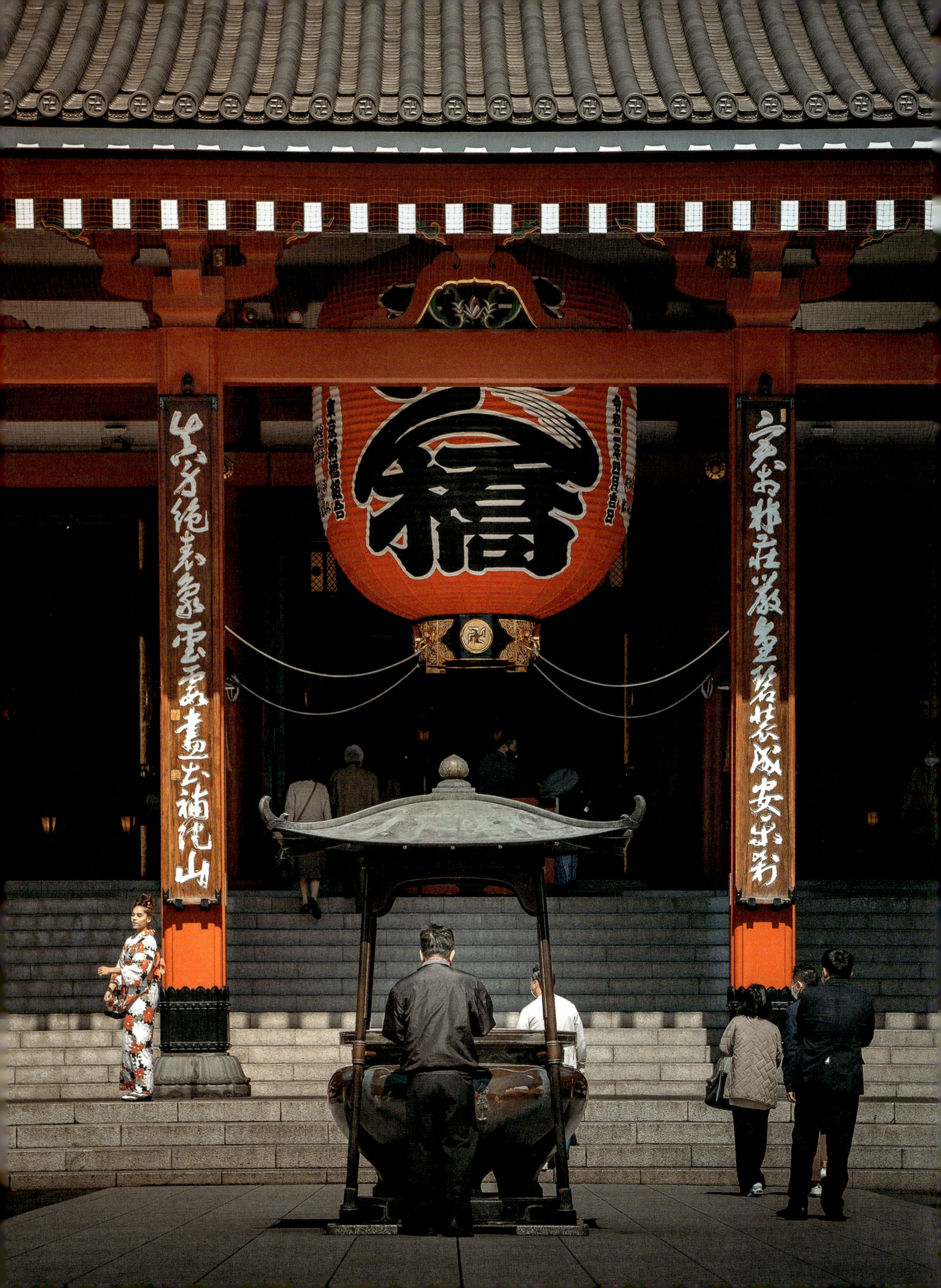
東京新橋組合
令和二年四月吉日

Sensō-ji Temple
in Tokyo.

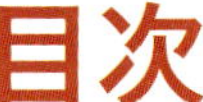

序文
Foreword
6

北海道
Hokkaidō
Japan's Untamed Wilderness
8

東北
Tōhoku
A Wild Jewel
and Spiritual Heritage
34

関東
Kantō
A Blend of History and Modernity
62

中部
Chūbu
A Land of Beauty
and Diversity
126

関西
Kansai
The Cradle of History
and the Heart of Japan
160

中国地
Chūgoku
The Perfect Balance Between
History and Nature
208

四国
Shikoku
The Island of Four Kingdoms
232

九州 / 沖縄
Kyūshū and Okinawa
Japan's Southern Soul
254

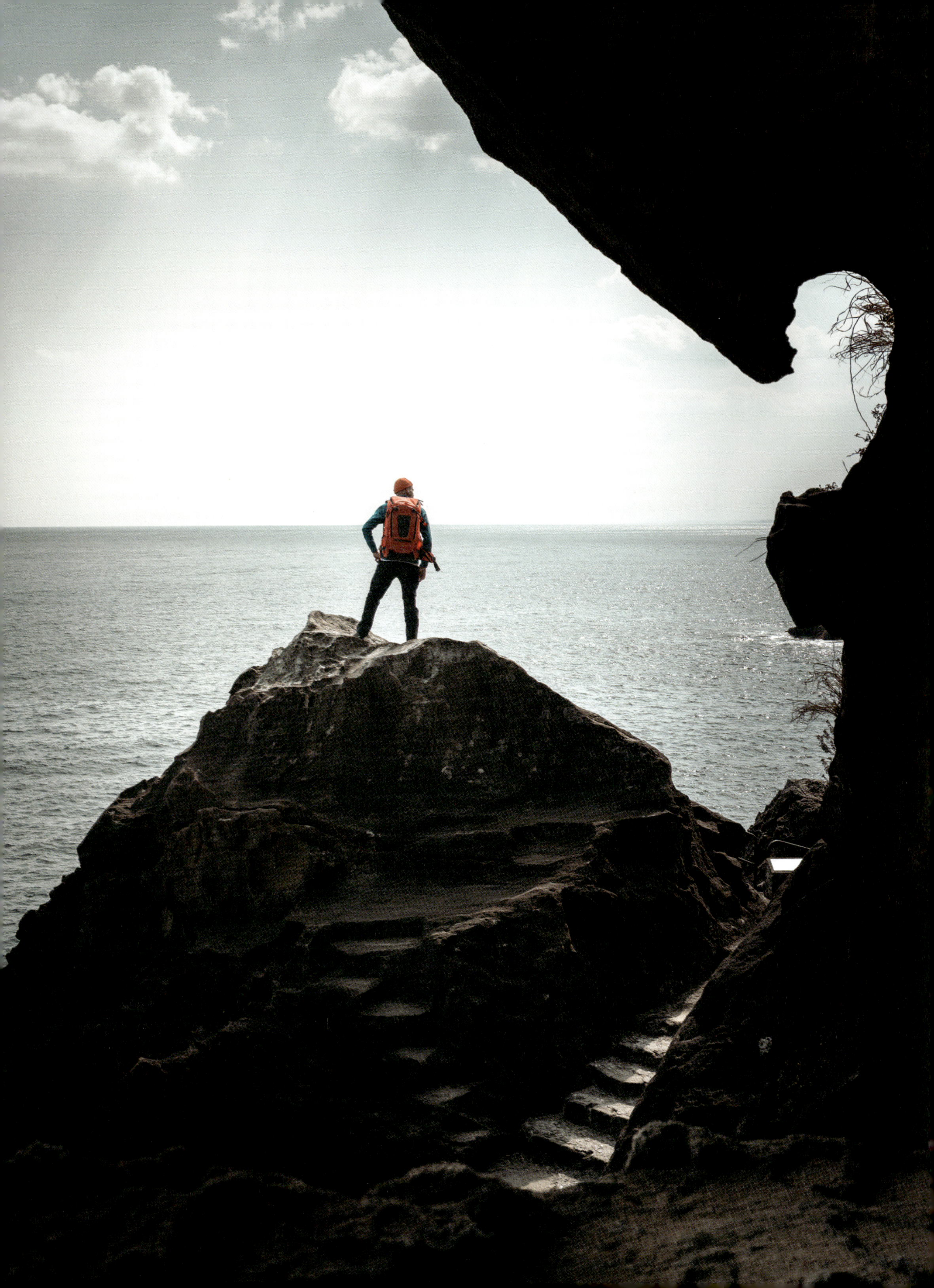

序文

Foreword

This book is a personal journey in which every image tells a story and each street corner unveils a world of its own. It is a celebration of the creativity born from the meeting of two cultures and a heartfelt tribute to the country that welcomed me as its own.

My passion for Japan began long before I ever set foot there — it all started when I was three years old, in front of the glowing screen of a video game console. The vibrant pixels of the '80s and '90s were my first glimpse into Japanese pop culture. What began as a fascination with imagined worlds soon blossomed into a deep love for a real country — rich, complex, and endlessly captivating.

In 2009, this passion took an unexpected turn when I met a young Japanese woman in Brussels — an encounter that would change my life. After several years of a long-distance relationship, marked by travel and mutual discovery, I made the bold decision to leave everything behind and move to Tokyo in 2013. It was as much a leap into the unknown as a return to a place that, in many ways, already felt strangely familiar.

A few months after arriving in this vast metropolis, one thing became clear: many foreign visitors seemed overwhelmed — if not completely lost — by the sheer scale of the city and the complexity of its transport system. With that in mind, I founded Tokyo Trip, a tour guide company aimed at providing travellers with a more personal and accessible experience.

At the same time, eager to promote my business through visuals, I began wandering the streets of Tokyo with a modest camera in hand, gradually teaching myself how to work with light, compose a shot, and capture the city's unique energy. What started as a practical necessity soon blossomed into a deep and lasting passion.

Photography provided me with the perfect opportunity to explore Tokyo — and eventually the entirety of Japan. Each walk transformed into an adventure, with every photo representing a new discovery. Since 2013, I have had the chance to document Japan in all its richness — from the narrow alleyways of Tokyo to the breathtaking landscapes of the countryside — always aiming to move beyond clichés. My goal is to tell diverse stories and reveal an authentic, vibrant, and multifaceted Japan.

Though I am in awe of Japan's majestic mountains and dramatic waterfalls, it is the urban landscapes — the concrete, the glass, the glow of electric lights — that truly captivate me. These places are where people and technology coexist in fascinating harmony. Through my images, I strive to capture this urban soul and reveal the hidden beauty in the details of everyday life.

For me, Tokyo is much more than just a city — it is an endless playground, a living, breathing organism in constant flux. Its streets shift, its buildings evolve, and its neighbourhoods continuously reinvent themselves.

Whether you are passionate about Japan, a photography enthusiast, or simply curious and seeking a bit of escapism, I invite you to explore these images with the eye of an adventurer. Tokyo and Japan are much more than their most famous landmarks — it is the overlooked corners, the unexpected angles, and the fleeting moments that give the country its true depth and magic.

I hope this visual journey evokes in you the same sense of wonder and emotion that it has in me.

Wauters Nicolas

Nicolas Wauters

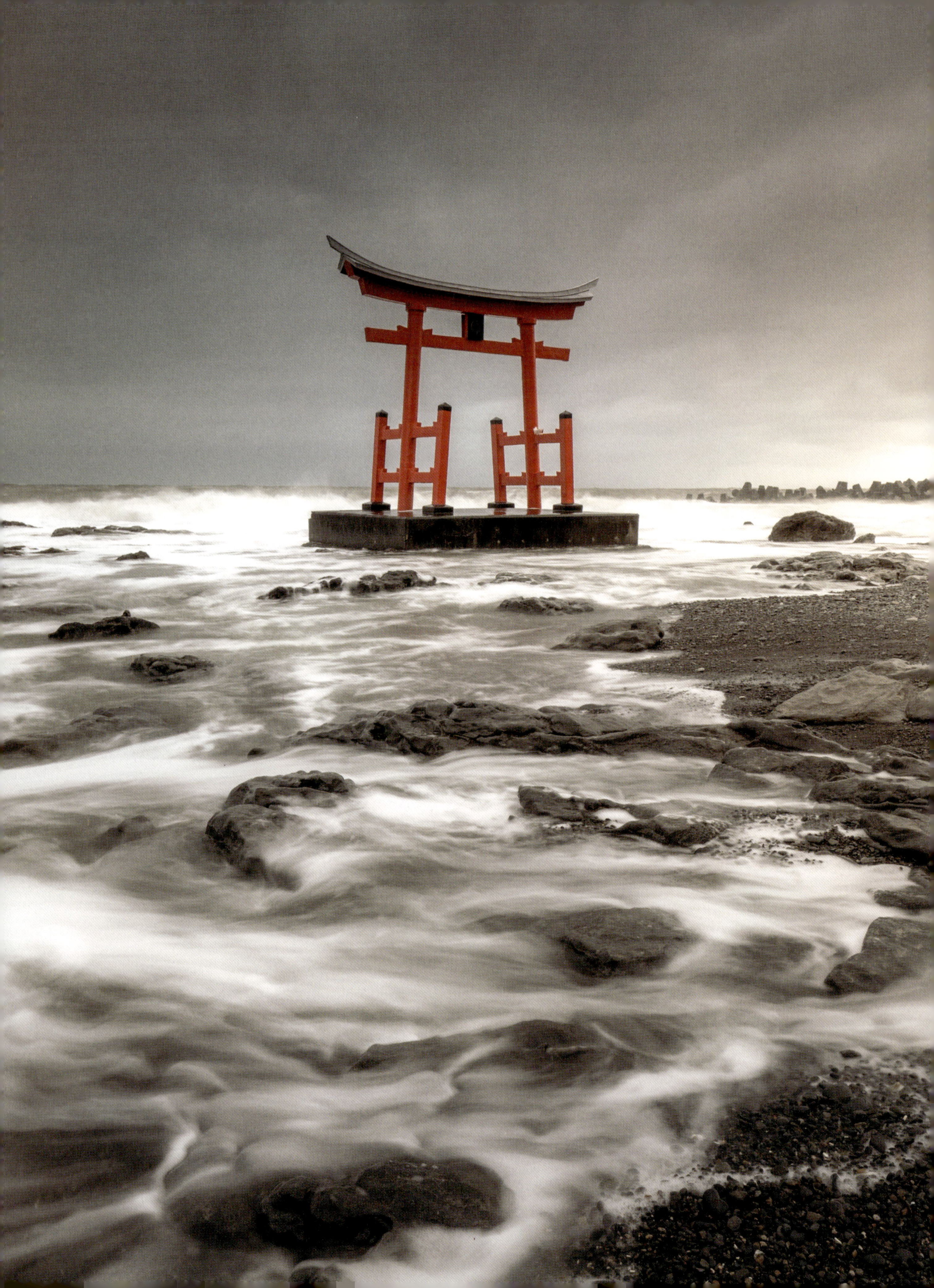

Toyosaki Konpira Shrine.
Perched on the coast of Hokkaido, the Toyosaki Konpira Shrine is renowned for its iconic red *torii* standing in the water. The shrine exemplifies traditional Japanese architecture beautifully. These wooden gates, marking the entrance to Shinto shrines, symbolise the boundary between the sacred and the profane, with their red hue thought to ward off evil spirits and disasters.

北海道
Hokkaidō
Japan's Untamed Wilderness

In the northernmost reaches of the Japanese archipelago, where nature reveals its full grandeur, lies Hokkaidō – an island that is both wild and captivating. Japan's second-largest island after Honshū, it is a haven for those who crave open spaces and adventure. With its rugged mountains, dense forests, crystal-clear lakes, and vast green plains, the landscape here showcases pristine and raw beauty. Hokkaidō is also a land rich in traditions, home to the Ainu, its indigenous people, and steeped in a history that stands in stark contrast to the modern urban vibe of Sapporo, its bustling capital.

Area.
Hokkaidō is the second-largest island in Japan, covering an area of approximately 83,456 km².

Demographics and Population.
As of 2020, Hokkaidō's population was estimated to be around 5.3 million, with a relatively low population density compared to other regions of Japan.

Geographical Location.
Located north of the Japanese archipelago, Hokkaidō is separated from the main island of Honshū by the Tsugaru Strait. It is bordered by the Sea of Japan to the west, the Pacific Ocean to the east, and the Sea of Okhotsk to the north. The regional capital is Sapporo.

Climate and Seasons.
Hokkaidō has a humid continental climate, characterised by long, harsh winters with heavy snowfall, and short, cool summers. Winter temperatures can plunge well below freezing, while summers remain pleasantly cool, providing a sharp contrast to the rest of Japan.

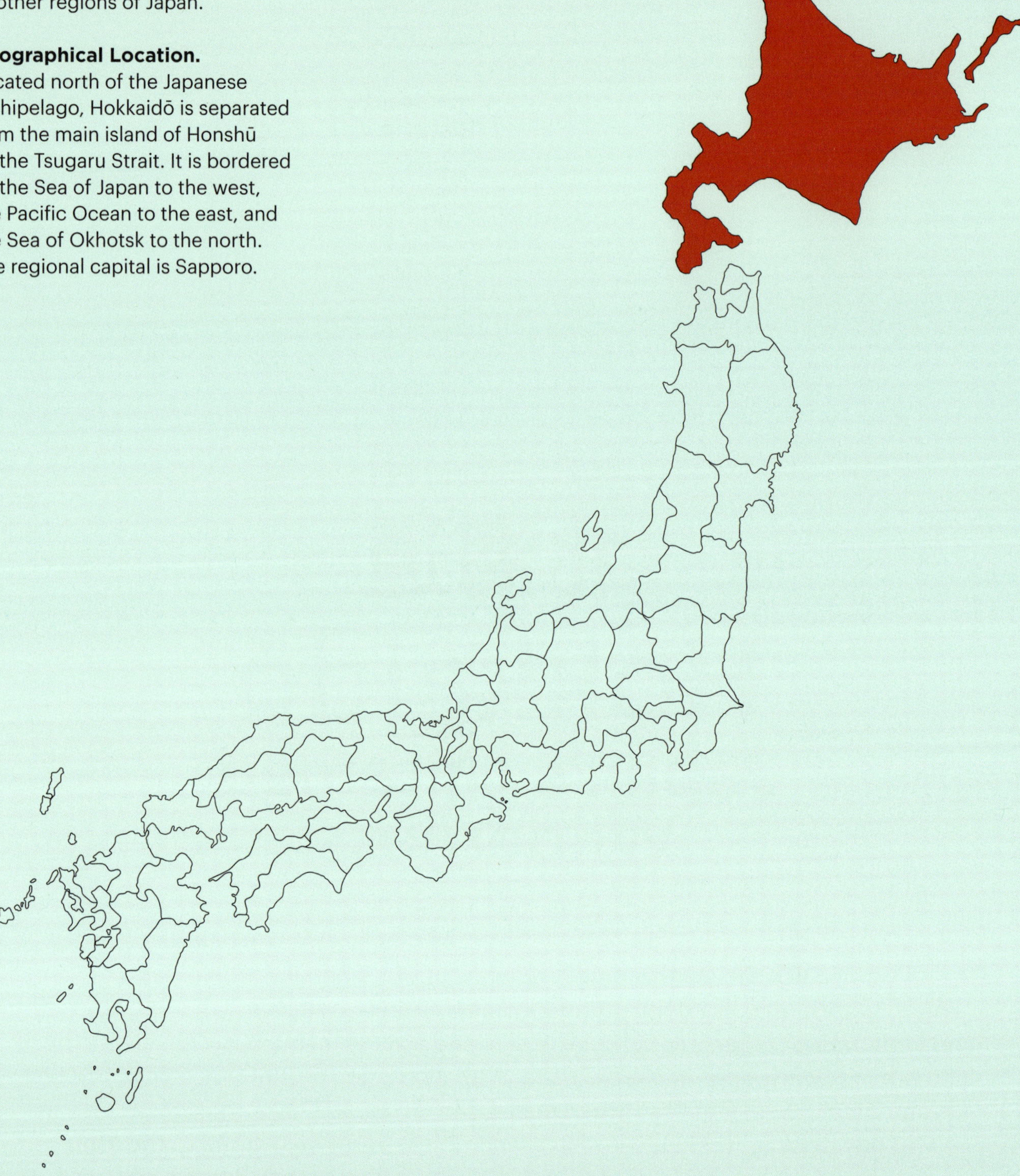

北海道

Sapporo,
the Vibrant Heart of the Island

Sapporo, the largest city in Hokkaidō, is a modern metropolis nestled among stunning natural landscapes. Renowned for hosting the 1972 Winter Olympics, it perfectly balances the island's energy with a deep respect for its natural surroundings.

In winter, Sapporo transforms into the stage for the iconic Snow Festival (*Yuki Matsuri*), where towering ice and snow sculptures attract visitors from around the globe. Odori Park, the heart of the festival, sparkles with enchanting lights, while the Mount Moiwa ski resort presents a breathtaking panorama of the snow-covered city below.

In summer, Sapporo captivates with its lively festivals, lush green parks, and bustling markets. A visit to Nijo Market is essential for tasting local delicacies such as crab, sea urchins, and fresh salmon. And let's not forget Sapporo beer – one of Japan's oldest and most beloved brews – celebrated at the Sapporo Beer Museum.

The Natural Splendour
of Furano and Biei

In central Hokkaidō, the towns of Furano and Biei reveal landscapes reminiscent of an impressionist painting. During summer, the vast lavender fields of Furano create a breathtaking sea of purple, while the gentle hills of Biei, adorned with vibrant flowers, captivate photographers and those seeking peace and tranquillity.

In winter, this region transforms into a paradise for winter sports. The Furano resorts are renowned for their impeccably maintained slopes and pristine powder snow, making them a haven for both skiers and snowboarders.

Hakodate,
Historic Charm

Situated in the southern part of the island, Hakodate is a port city abundant in history and culture. It was among the first Japanese cities to open to foreign trade during the Meiji period, giving it a unique cosmopolitan flair.

Mount Hakodate, which is accessible by cable car, offers a breathtaking view of the city at night and is often ranked among the top three most beautiful night views in Japan. In the morning, visiting the Asaichi Market (Morning Market) is a must for tasting fresh seafood, particularly *donburi* – rice bowls topped with raw fish.

The Motomachi district, featuring colonial-era buildings and churches, bears witness to Western influence. Meanwhile, Goryōkaku Fort, a star-shaped fortress encircled by cherry trees, serves as an iconic landmark, particularly popular during the spring.

Daisetsuzan National Park,
Nature in Its Purest Form

Daisetsuzan, Japan's largest national park, is a haven for hiking and exploration enthusiasts. Known as "the roof of Hokkaidō", this mountain range features towering peaks like Mount Asahi, glacial valleys, and hidden hot springs.

The hiking trails, accessible in summer and autumn, showcase a variety of flora and fauna, where brown bears, deer and foxes rub shoulders with forests of birch, pine, Japanese maple and vast alpine meadows. In winter, the park transforms into a pristine wonderland, attracting adventurers in search of breathtaking scenery.

The Shikotsu-Tōya Lakes, Mirrors of Tranquillity

In the southwest of Hokkaidō, the lakes of Shikotsu and Tōya offer a serene and picturesque escape. Lake Shikotsu, a lake of volcanic origin, is renowned for the extraordinary purity of its waters, which remain unfrozen even in winter. Visitors can kayak, fish, or simply relax in the nearby *onsen*.

Lake Tōya, surrounded by mountains, is famous for its summer fireworks and the central island accessible by boat. Nearby, Mount Usu, an active volcano, provides stunning views of the area, along with remnants of past eruptions.

Abashiri and the Drifting Ice

Located on the northeast coast of Hokkaidō, Abashiri is among the best spots to witness the drifting ice that floats in from the Sea of Okhotsk each winter. Visitors can board icebreakers for an up-close view of this breathtaking natural spectacle, which is unique to Japan.

The Drift Ice Museum offers an intriguing look into polar ecosystems and their ecological significance. The area is also known for its historic prison, which recounts the story of the settlers who endured harsh conditions while working to develop Hokkaidō.

Kushiro and the Eastern Marshes

To the east of Hokkaidō, the town of Kushiro serves as the gateway to the Kushiro Marshes, Japan's largest wetlands. This rich ecosystem is home to remarkable wildlife, including the Japanese crane, which symbolises good fortune and longevity.

Panoramic views of the vast marshes can be enjoyed from observatories such as *Kushiro Shitsugen*, while canoe trips provide the opportunity to navigate the winding rivers and experience nature up close.

Wakkanai, The Far North

Nestled in the far north of Hokkaidō, Wakkanai is a remote town dominated by nature. On clear days, you can catch a glimpse of the Russian island of Sakhalin in the distance. Cape Sōya, Japan's northernmost point, is steeped in symbolism.

Nearby, Cape Noshappu offers breathtaking sunsets, while the island of Rebun, often referred to as the *Island of Flowers*, enchants visitors with its vibrant flower-filled landscapes and scenic hiking trails.

Noboribetsu and Its Hot Springs

Noboribetsu is renowned for its *onsen*, particularly Hell Valley (*Jigokudani*), a volcanic landscape where sulphurous fumes rise from rocky cracks. The town's thermal baths, celebrated for their therapeutic properties, attract those seeking both relaxation and rejuvenation.

Ainu Culture

Hokkaidō is also home to the Ainu people, the island's indigenous inhabitants. In the village of Ainu Kotan, near Lake Akan, you can explore their traditional crafts, songs, and dances – testaments to a culture that has endured the challenges of history.

北海道

Best Times to Visit

– Winter (December to February).
Perfect for winter sports lovers, featuring ski resorts with excellent powder snow.

– Spring (May).
Cherry blossoms create stunning landscapes, although the season is slightly later than in other regions of Japan.

– Summer (July to August).
Ideal for escaping the oppressive heat found in other parts of the country, offering comfortable temperatures and fields filled with blooming flowers.

– Autumn (September to October).
Autumn foliage paints the landscape in vivid colours, providing opportunities for hiking and photography.

Top 5 Must-See destinations

1. Shiretoko National Park.
UNESCO World Heritage Site, this park features pristine and untouched landscapes that are ideal for hiking and wildlife observation.

2. Sapporo.
The regional capital, renowned for its modern architecture, vibrant festivals such as the Snow Festival, and an exciting culinary scene.

3. Furano and Biei.
Famous for their stunning lavender fields and charming rural scenery, these areas are particularly magical in the summer months.

4. Lake Toya.
A picturesque caldera lake that offers tranquil views, soothing hot springs, and a variety of outdoor activities.

5. Hakodate.
A historic port city with strong western influences, celebrated for its breathtaking night view from Mount Hakodate and its bustling morning market.

北海道

Gastronomy

Hokkaidō is a region rich in culinary specialities, shaped by its cold climate and abundant natural resources. Below is a list of the region's culinary highlights, organised by city, complete with detailed descriptions for each dish.

札幌
Sapporo

[札幌味噌ラーメン]
Sapporo Miso Rāmen
This rāmen is renowned for its thick, umami-rich miso broth. It is frequently topped with corn, butter, *chāshū* (braised pork), and sautéed vegetables, which together create a unique and comforting flavour.

[スープカレー]
Soup Curry
A spicy, light curry featuring a fragrant, fluid broth. It's typically garnished with fresh vegetables such as potatoes, pumpkin, and peppers, and is often served with chicken or pork.

[ジンギスカン]
Jingisukan
A lamb barbecue grilled on a domed cast-iron plate, accompanied by vegetables like cabbage and onions. This dish is popular in Sapporo's *izakayas* and specialised restaurants.

函館
Hakodate

[函館塩ラーメン]
Hakodate Shio Rāmen
Unlike Sapporo's *miso rāmen*, Hakodate's version features a clear, salty broth, often made with seafood. It's light, subtle, and perfect for showcasing the local ingredients.

[いかめし]
Ikameshi
A signature dish from the nearby city of Mori, *Ikameshi* is a squid stuffed with glutinous rice and simmered in a sweet soy sauce. It's commonly sold as ekiben (train station bento).

[塩焼きそば]
Shio Yakisoba
This is a lighter version of yakisoba, in which the noodles are stir-fried with seafood and seasoned with salt rather than the usual thick sauce.

旭川
Asahikawa

[旭川醤油ラーメン]
Asahikawa Shōyu Rāmen
A soy sauce-based *rāmen*, often enriched with a thin layer of pork fat to keep the broth hot. It's loved for its balance of intense shōyu and the richness of pork.

[旭川大雪ビール]
Asahikawa Taisetsu Beer
A craft beer brewed in Asahikawa, known for its purity and refreshing taste, thanks to the region's crystal-clear water.

帯広
Obihiro

[豚丼]
Buta Don
A rice bowl topped with grilled pork slices lacquered in a sweet soy-based sauce, this dish originates from Obihiro and offers a local alternative to *gyūdon* (beef rice bowl).

釧路
Kushiro

[勝手丼]
Kattedon
A rice bowl where you can select your fresh seafood at the Washo Market. Customers can create their donburi with salmon sashimi, tuna, shrimp, scallops, and ikura (salmon roe).

[釧路秋刀魚]
Kushiro Sanma
Sanma (Japanese mackerel pike) is an iconic fish in Kushiro, often grilled whole and served with grated daikon radish and lemon

根室
Nemuro

[根室サンマ寿司]
Nemuro Sanma Zushi
A unique sushi made with the region's fish, *sanma* (Japanese mackerel pike), marinated in vinegar and served on rice.

稚内
Wakkanai

[稚内カニ飯]
Wakkanai Kanimeshi
A rice bowl topped with crab meat, often seasoned with soy sauce and served with wasabi and pickled ginger.

石狩
Ishikari

[石狩鍋]
Ishikari Nabe
A hot pot made with fresh salmon, simmered with miso, cabbage, mushrooms, and tofu. This dish is inspired by recipes from Ishikari's fishermen, who used freshly caught salmon as an everyday fare.

夕張
Yubari

[夕張メロン]
Yubari King Melon
Yubari melons are renowned across Japan for their exceptional sweetness. They are often eaten as they are or used in desserts and ice creams.

富良野
Furano

[富良野チーズ]
Furano Cheese
Made with fresh milk from Hokkaidō's meadows, *Furano* cheese is famous for its high quality.

[オムカレー]
Omu-Curry
A Japanese curry topped with a fluffy omelette. This Furano speciality blends Japanese curry with omelette, offering a creamy and delicious texture.

紋別
Monbetsu

[紋別タラバガニ]
Monbetsu Tarabagani
Monbetsu's royal crab is one of the region's most excellent delicacies. It's often enjoyed grilled, boiled, or as sashimi.

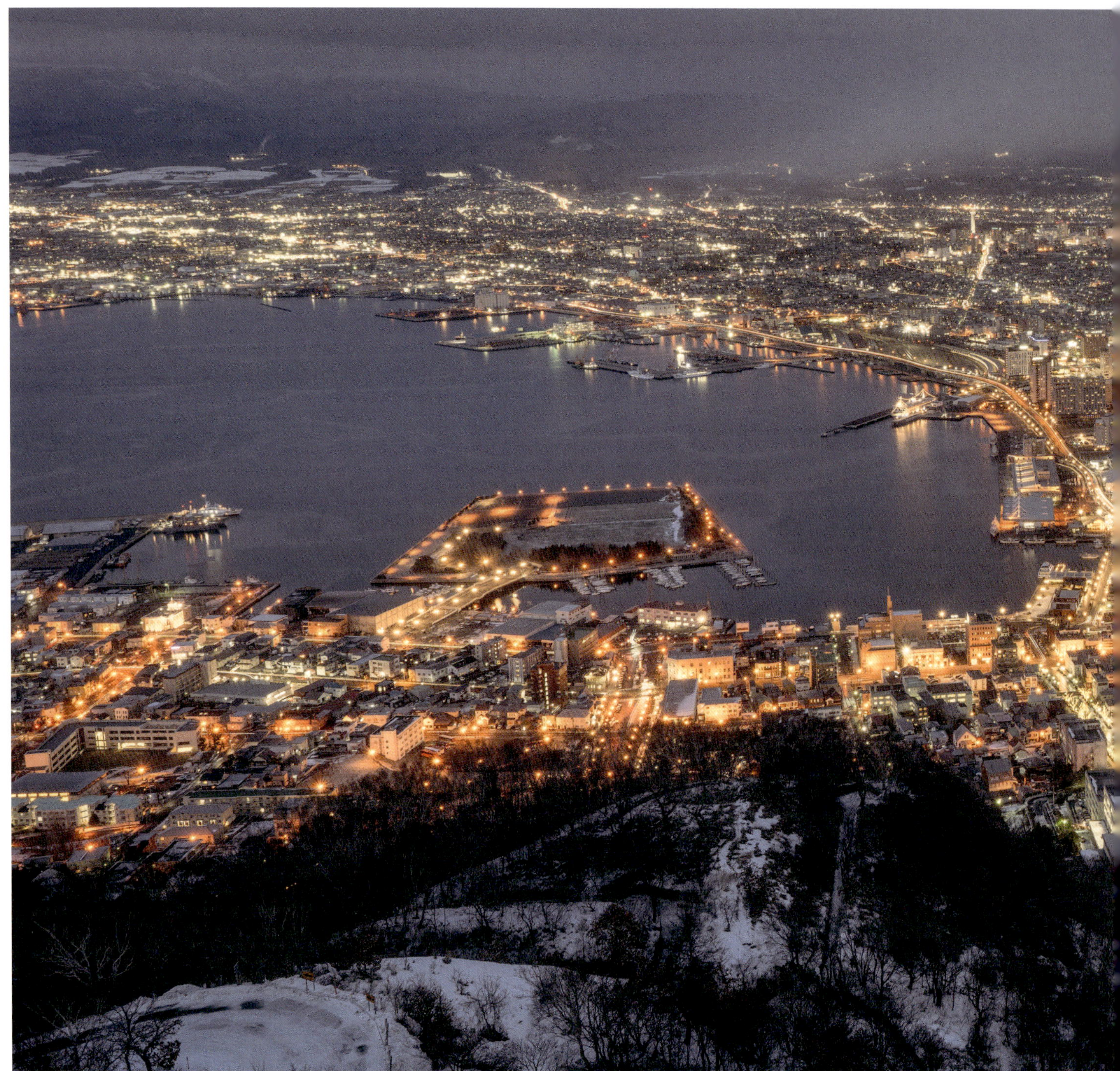

Hakodate.

The Hakodate region, located at the southern tip of Hokkaido, captivates with its blend of rich history and stunning landscapes. From the Mount Hakodate observatory, visitors can take in one of the world's most beautiful night views, where the city sparkles between the mountains and the sea.

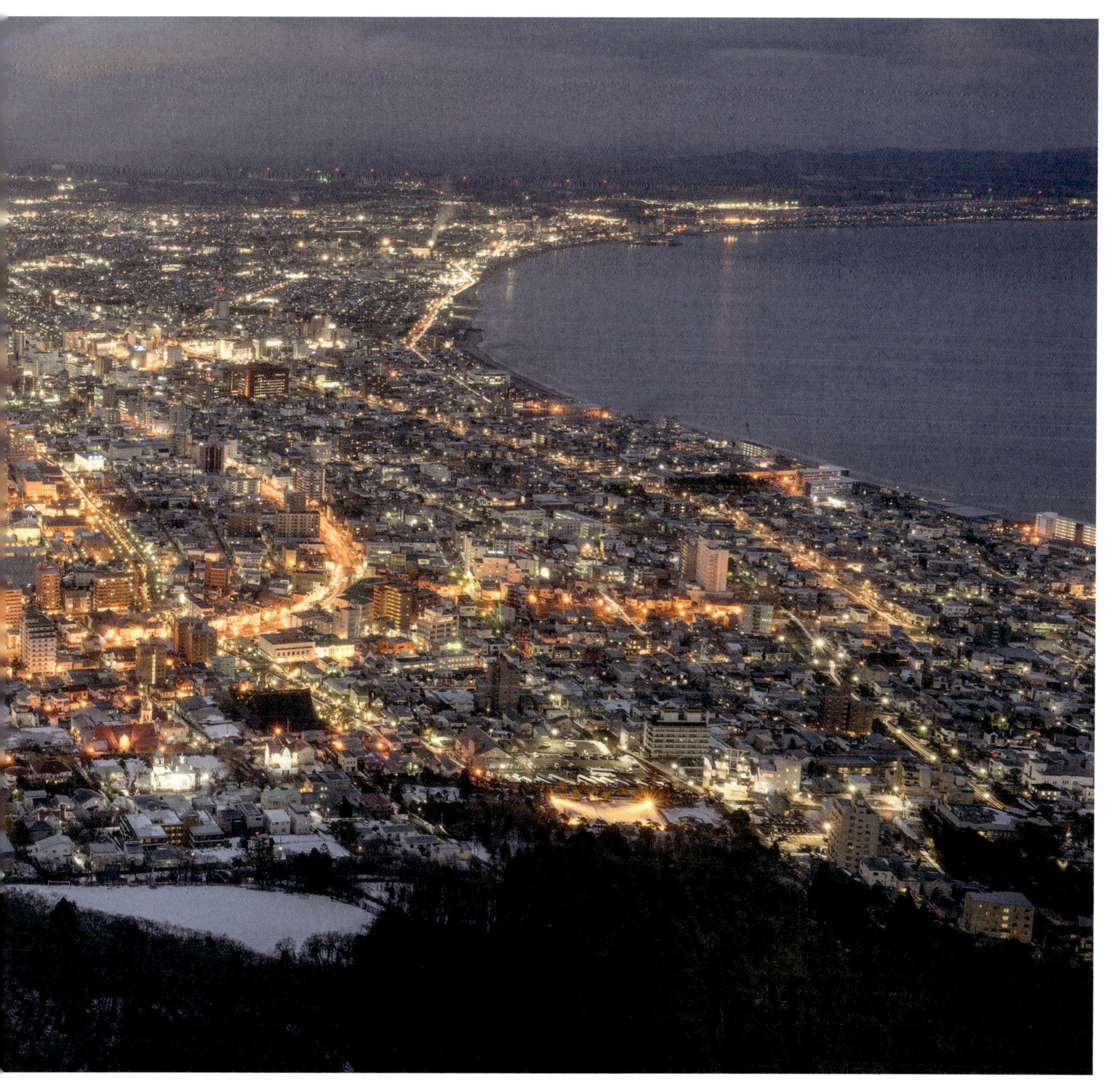

Goryokaku.

Located in Hakodate, Goryokaku is a star-shaped fortress renowned for its unique Vauban-inspired architecture and pivotal role in the Boshin War. Now a public park, it offers beautiful scenery, especially in winter when the moat freezes or in spring when the cherry blossoms are in full bloom. >

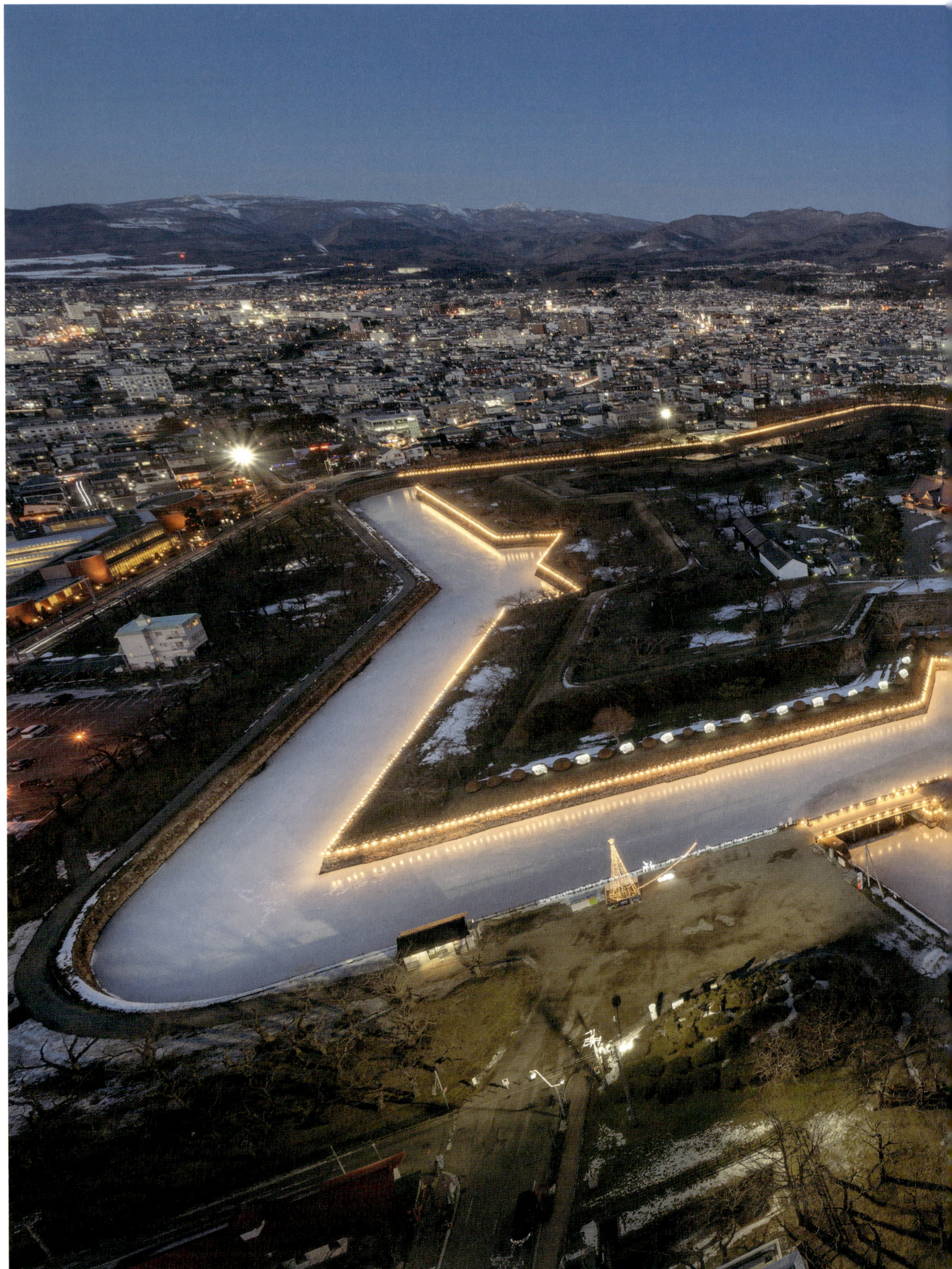

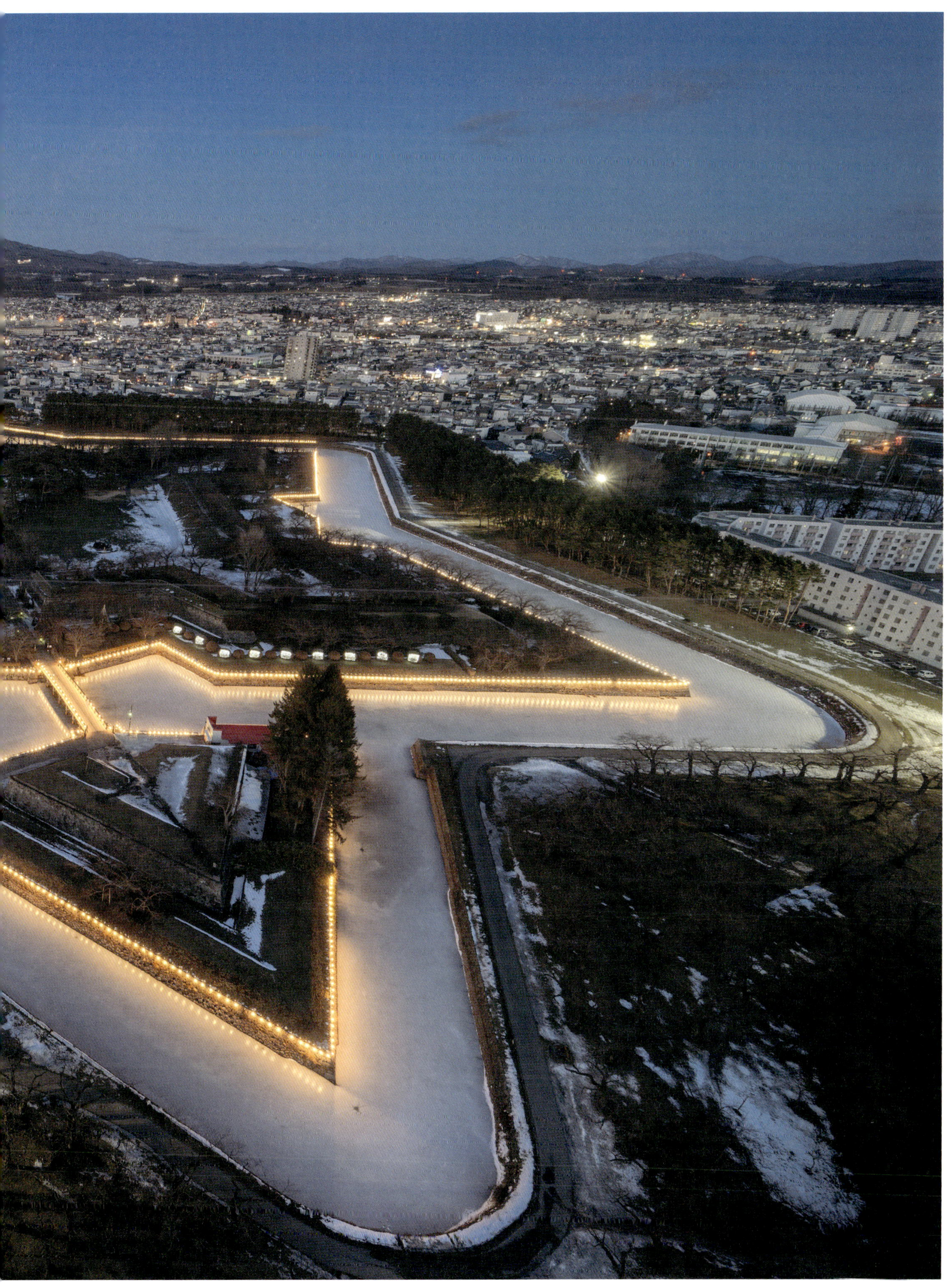

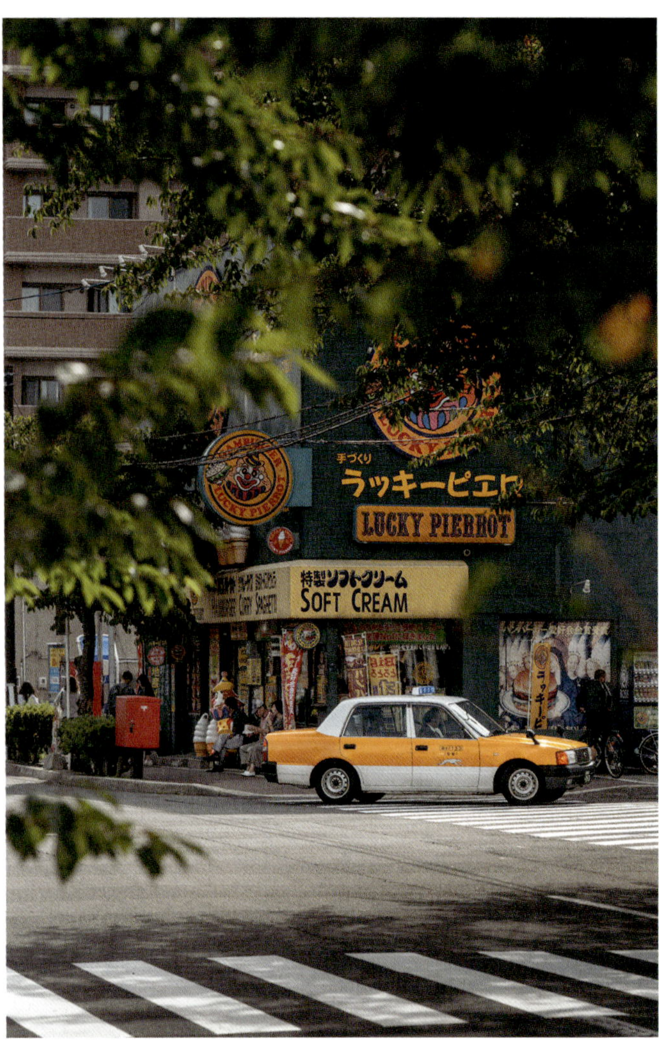

Lucky Pierrot.
In Hakodate, the beloved Lucky Pierrot restaurant is a local legend, famed for its quirky vibe and iconic burgers. With its brightly coloured signs and delightfully kitsch décor, it attracts both locals and curious travellers.

Susukino Crossing.
In the heart of one of the world's snowiest cities, the iconic Asahi billboard – promoting the famous Japanese beer – overlooks the intersection, starkly contrasting with the frozen ground where trams and pedestrians navigate the cold.

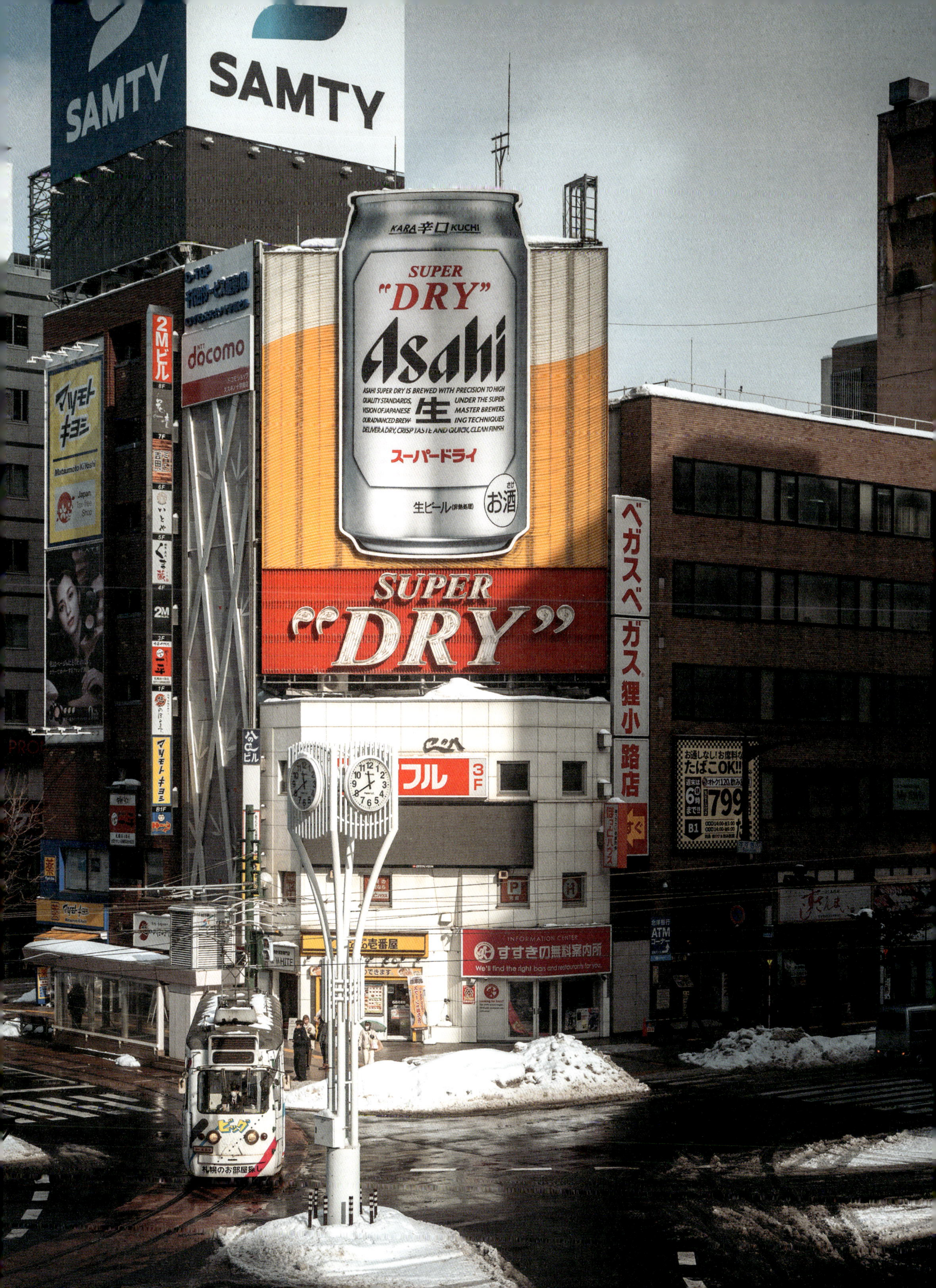
SAMTY
SAMTY
KARA 辛口 KUCHI
SUPER "DRY"
Asahi
ASAHI SUPER DRY IS BREWED WITH PRECISION TO HIGH QUALITY STANDARDS, UNDER THE SUPER-VISION OF JAPANESE MASTER BREWERS. OUR ADVANCED BREWING TECHNIQUES DELIVER A DRY, CRISP TASTE AND QUICK, CLEAN FINISH
生
スーパードライ
生ビール
お酒
SUPER "DRY"
docomo
2Mビル
マツモトキヨシ
ベガスベガス狸小路店
フル 3F
たばこOK!!
799
ATM
INFORMATION CENTER
すすきの無料案内所
We'll find the right bars and restaurants for you.

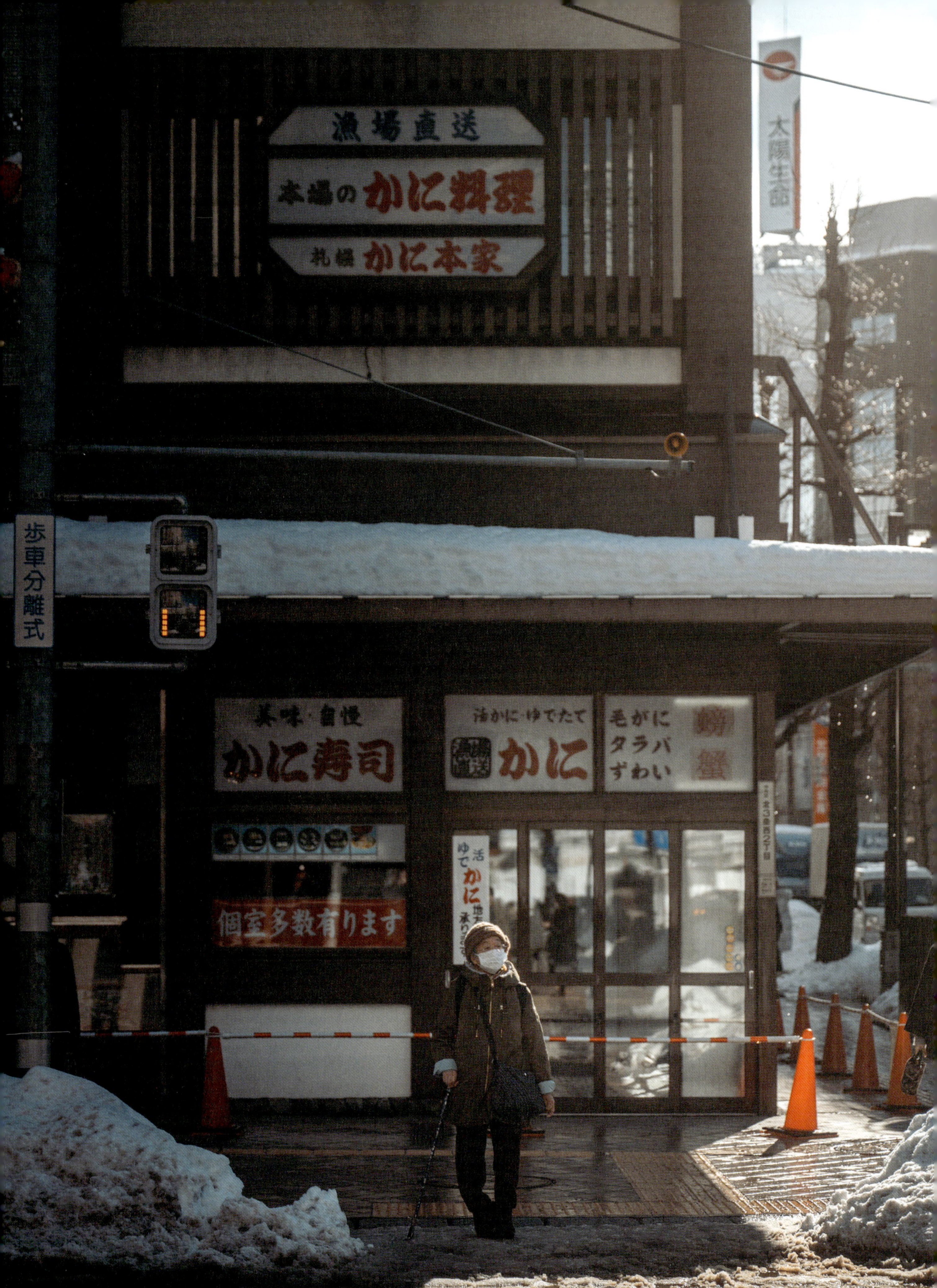
漁場直送
本場のかに料理
札幌かに本家
太陽生命
歩車分離式
美味・自慢
かに寿司
活かに・ゆでたて
かに
毛がに
タラバ
ずわい
個室多数有ります

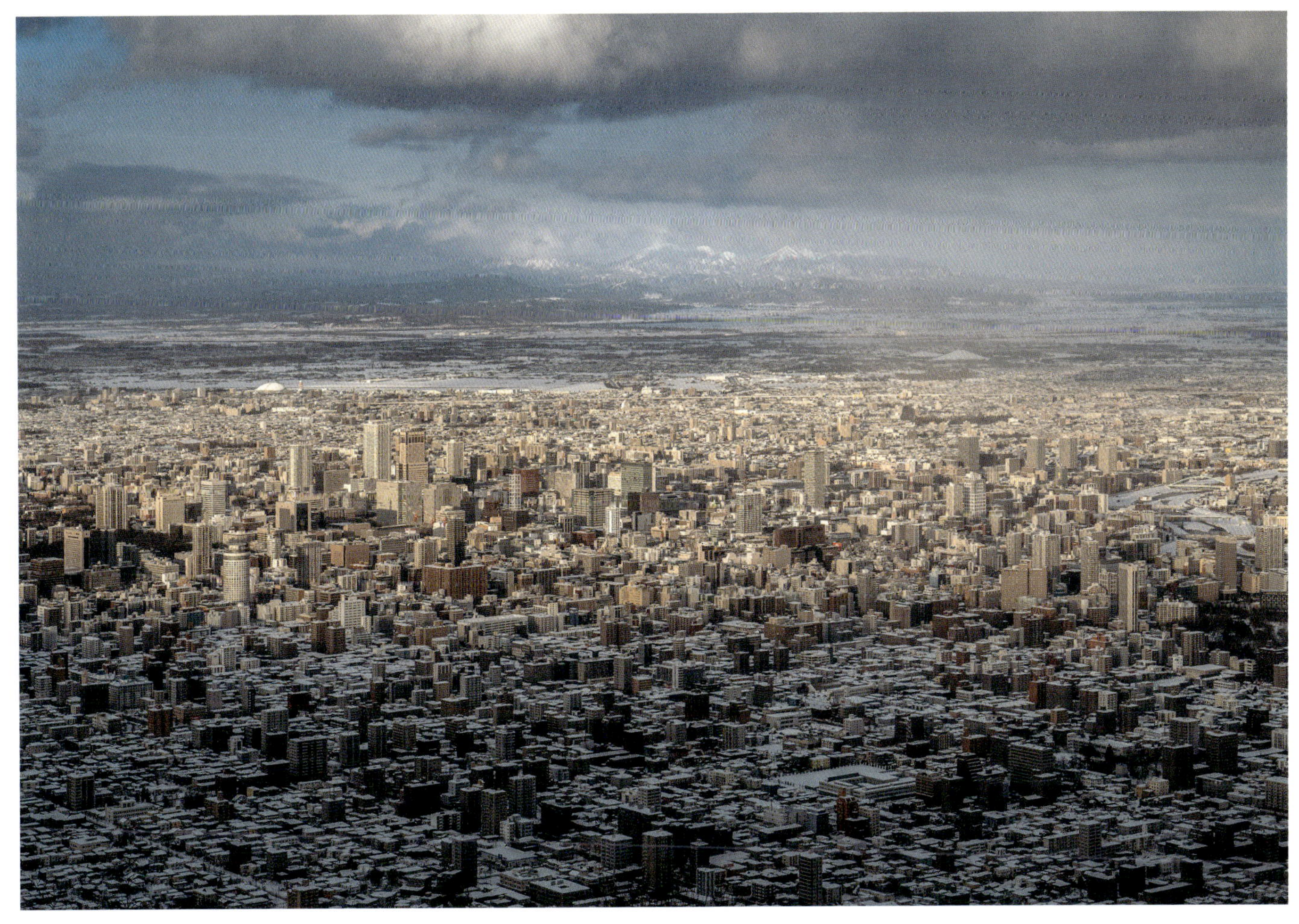

Mount Moiwa.
Just outside Sapporo in Hokkaido, Mount Moiwa provides breathtaking panoramic views of the city and its surroundings. Easily accessible by cable car, its summit is a popular spot for enjoying the snow-dusted urban landscape, which is widely regarded as one of the most stunning vistas in all of Japan.

Sapporo.
Sapporo, the capital of Hokkaido, is a vibrant city renowned for its snow festival, iconic beer, and delicious local dishes such as rāmen and Genghis Khan. Nestled among mountains, it seamlessly integrates modernity with nature, making it an ideal gateway for exploring the island.

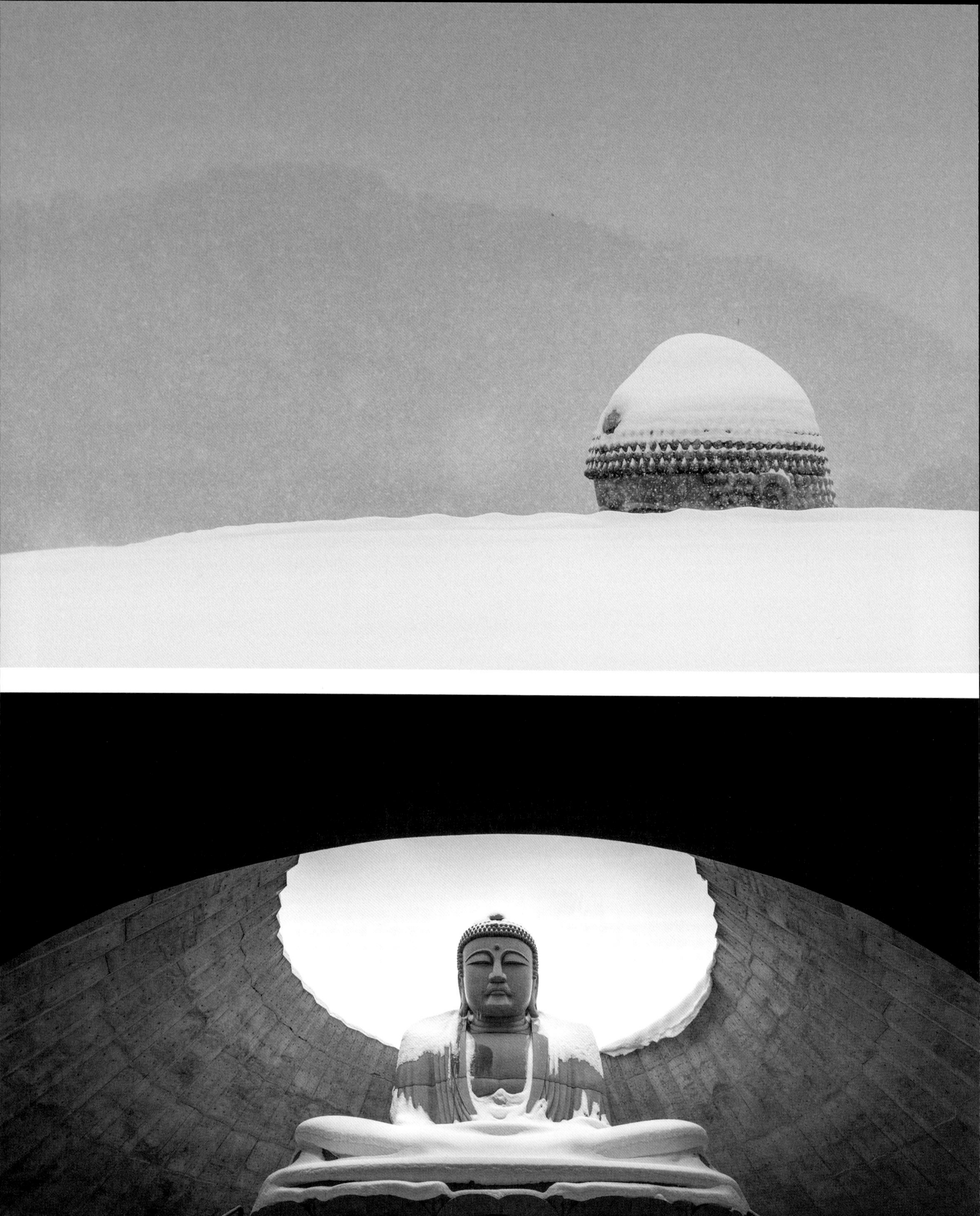

Hill of the Buddha.

Just outside Sapporo, the Hill of the Buddha is a stunning architectural masterpiece, featuring a towering 13-metre-high stone Buddha perched atop a hill blanketed in snow during winter and adorned with lavender in spring. Designed by architect Tadao Ando, this site combines spirituality with modernity, offering a peaceful sanctuary for reflection and tranquillity.

Cap Kamui.

Located at the western tip of Hokkaido's Shakotan Peninsula, Cape Kamui is a stunning natural wonder that offers panoramic views of the Sea of Japan. Its dramatic cliffs and scenic pathways invite visitors to explore a rugged landscape rich in mystery and local legend. >

Shirahige Falls.

The Shirahige Falls, located near Biei in Hokkaido, are famous for their vibrant blue waters, fed by underground springs. These unique waterfalls cascade down moss-covered cliffs, offering an enchanting natural display, especially stunning in winter under the snow. >>

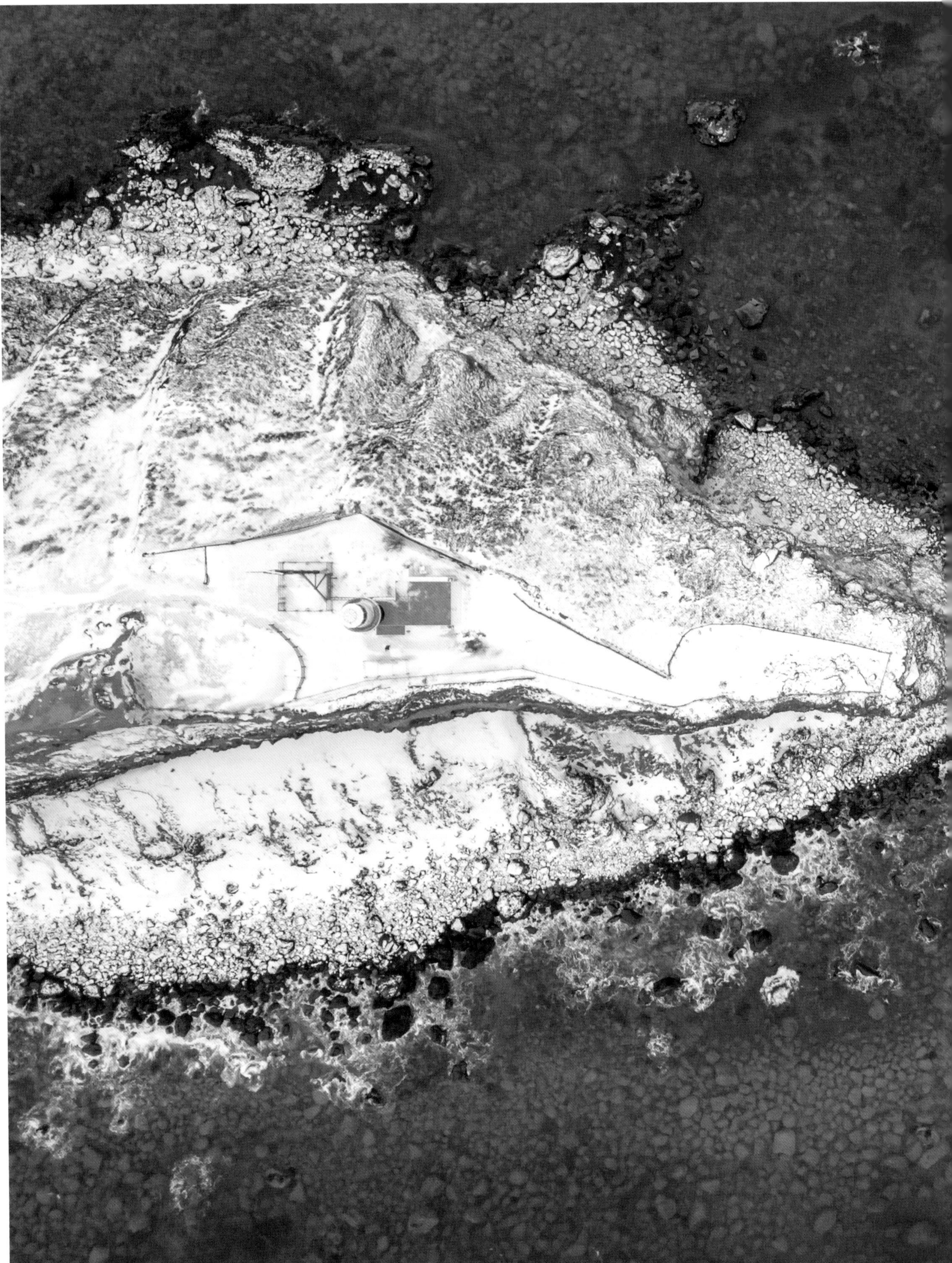

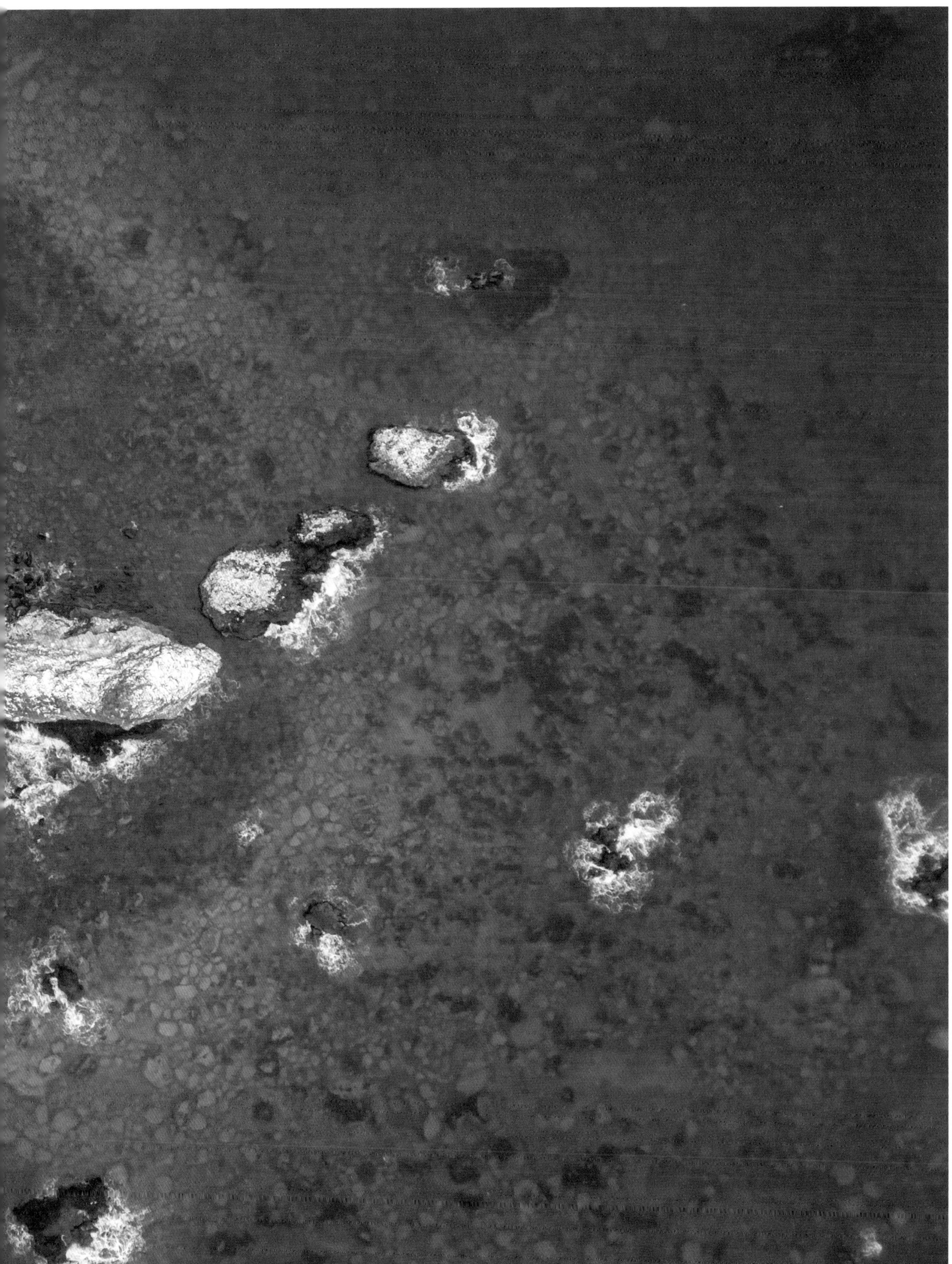

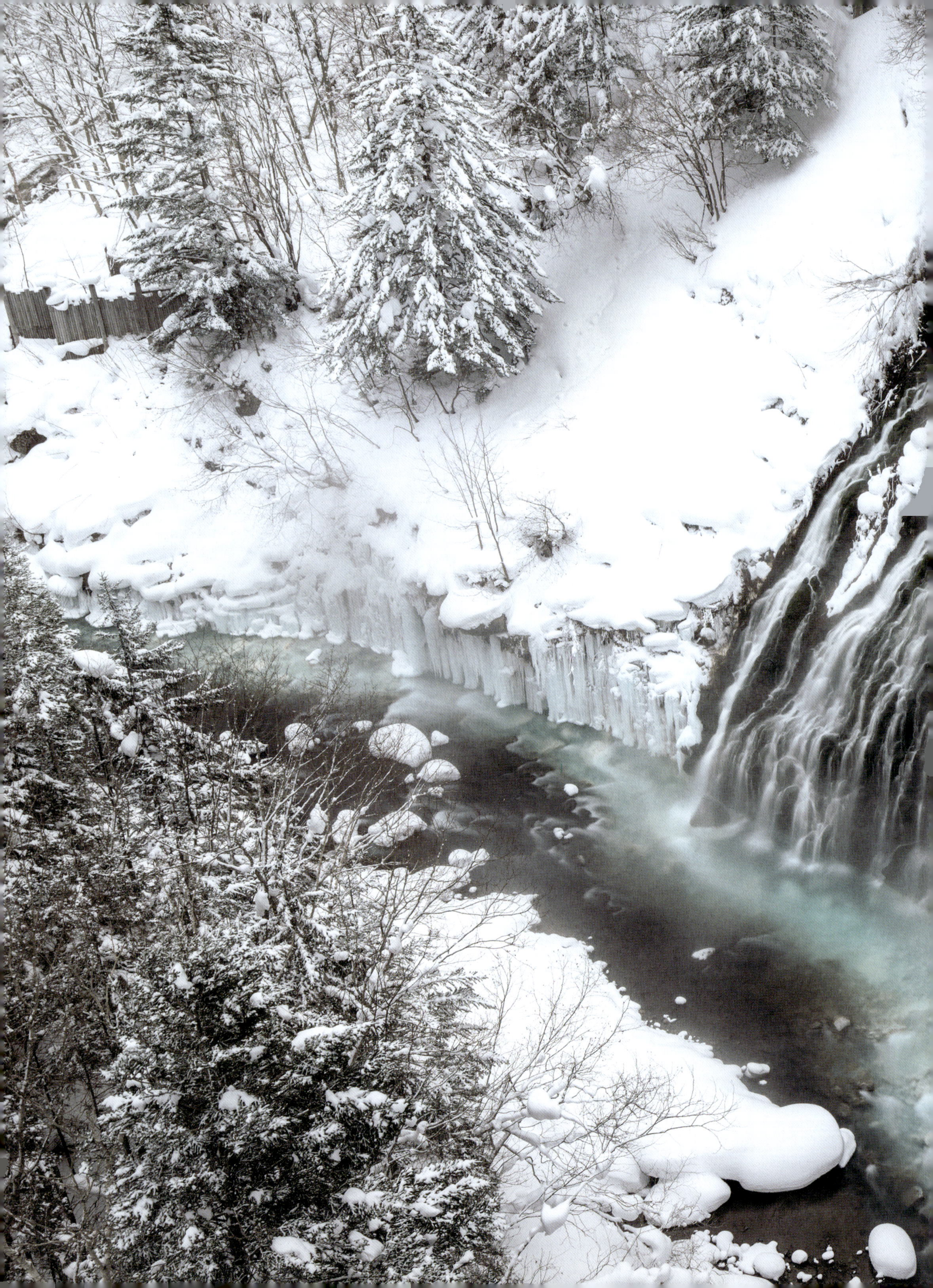

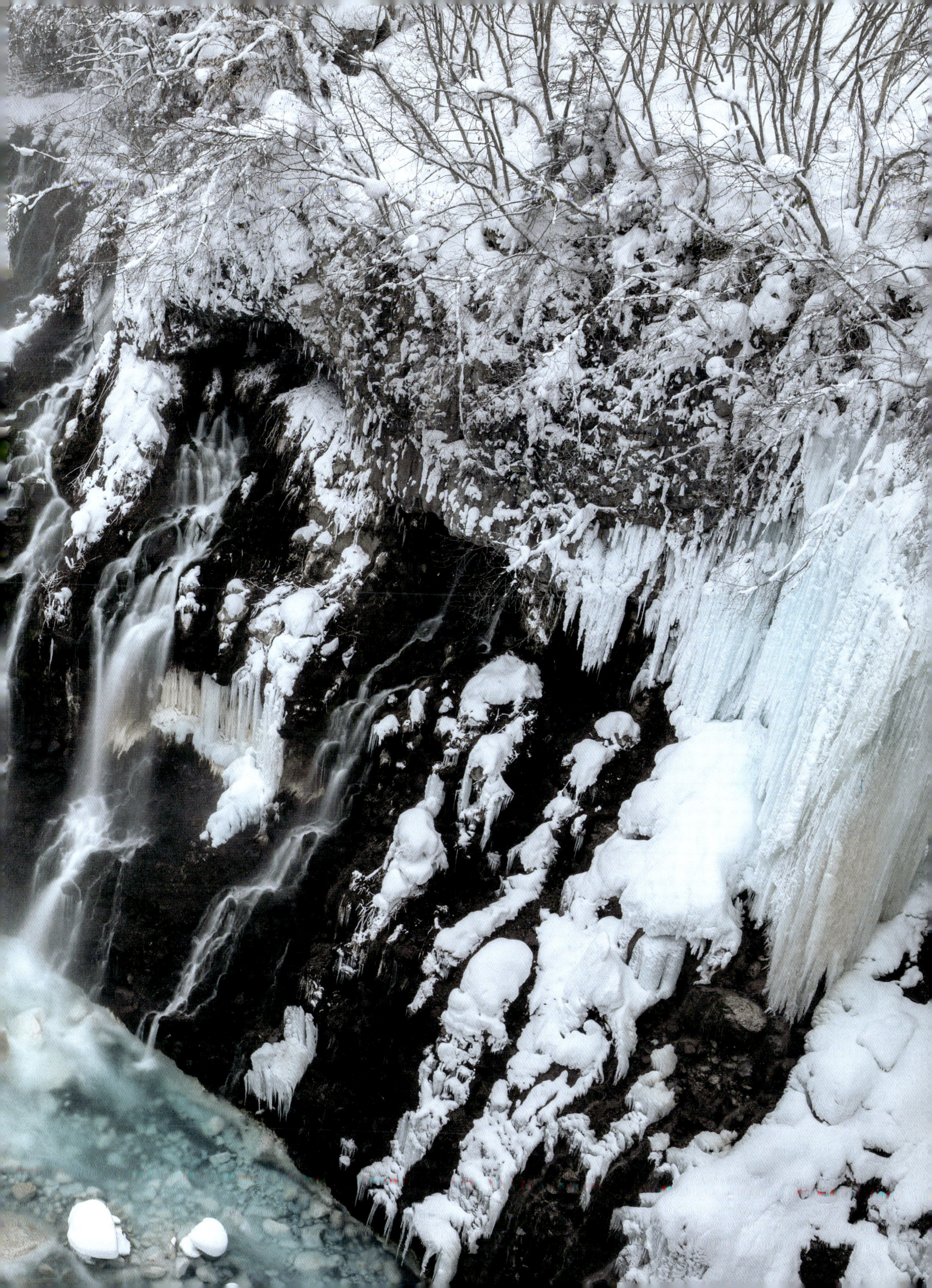

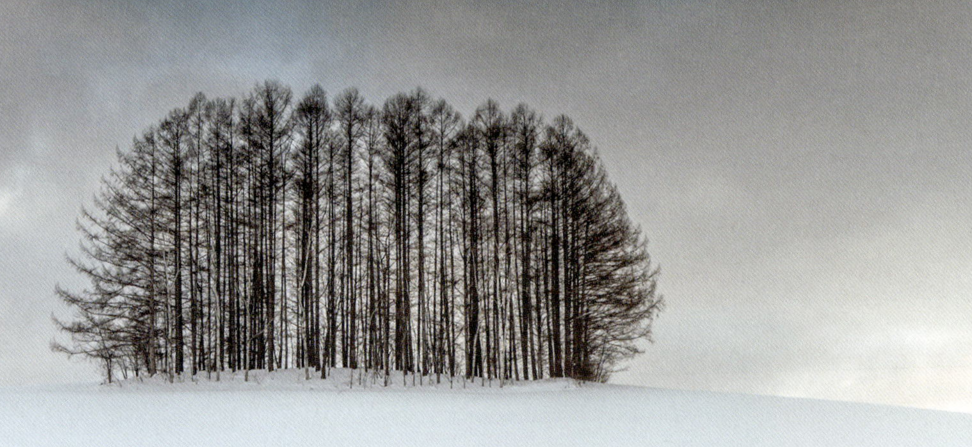

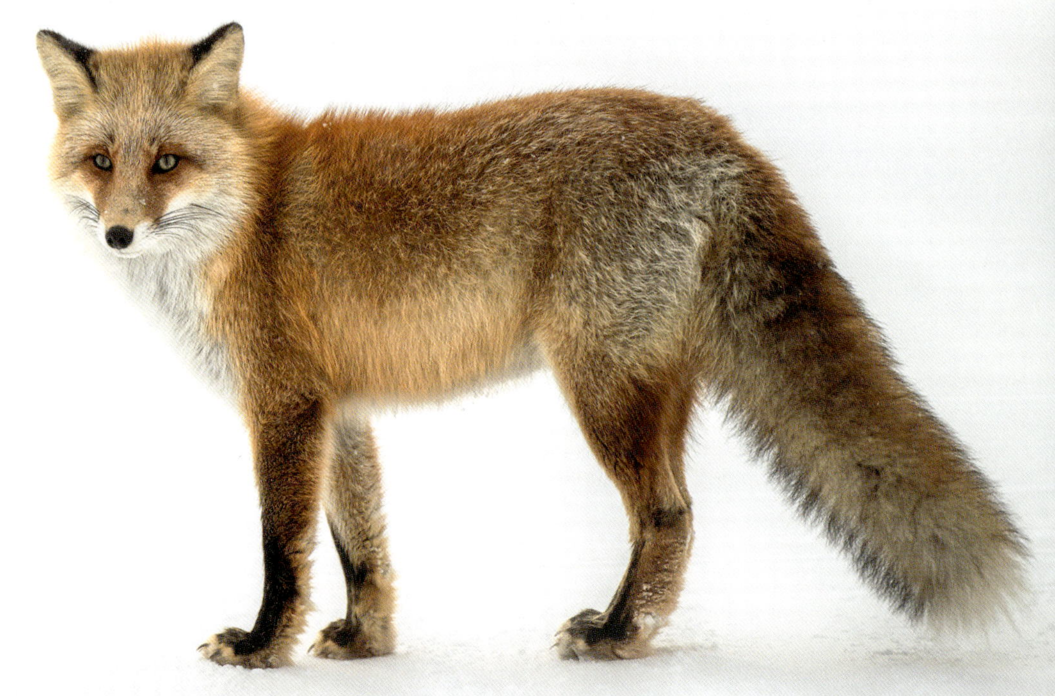

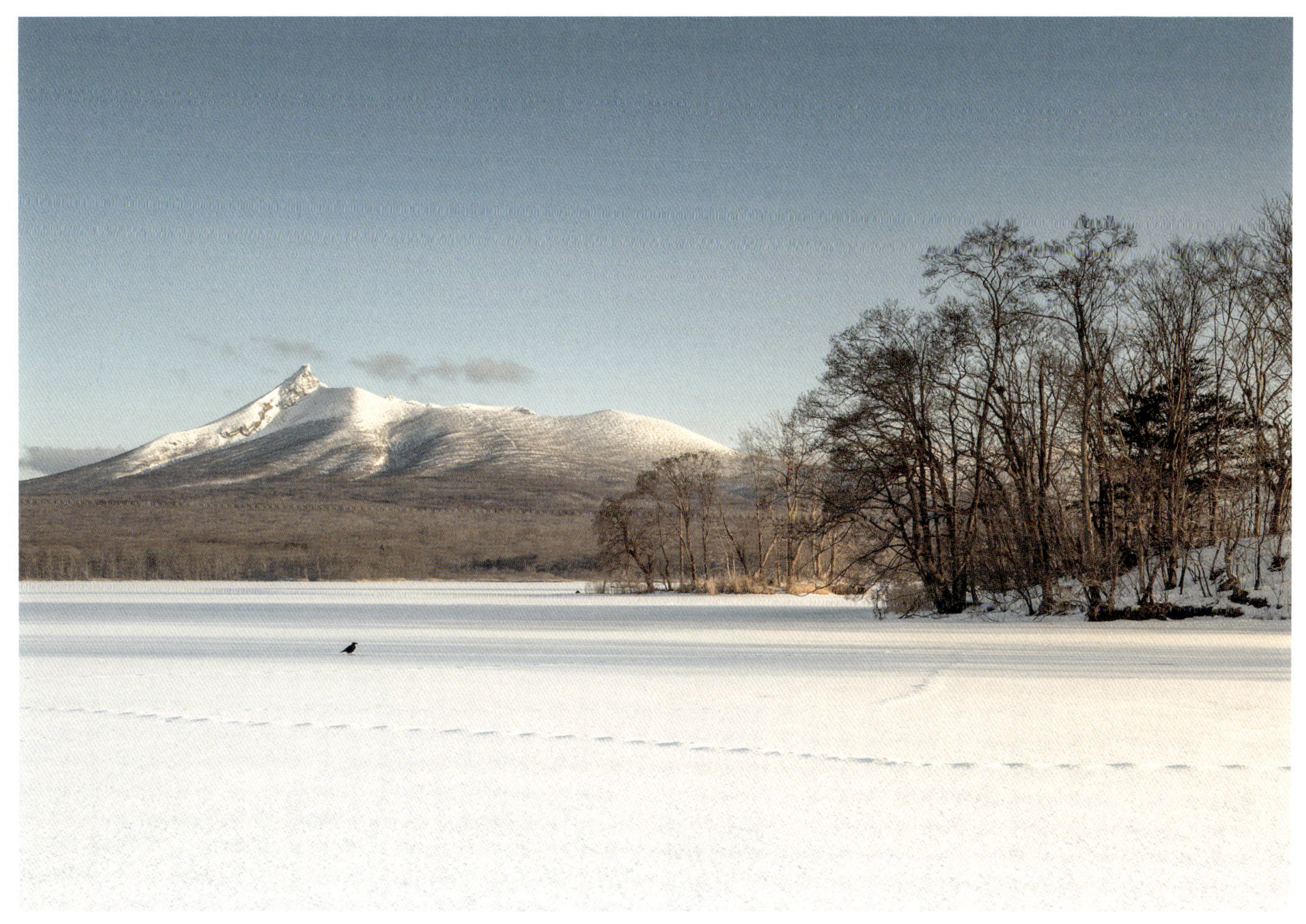

Komagatake.
This majestic volcano in Hokkaido towers over the surrounding landscape from its snow-capped summit. With various hiking trails, it is celebrated for its breathtaking views and enchanting atmosphere.

Biei Mild Seven Hills.
In winter, the Mild Seven Hills in Biei transform into a breathtaking landscape, where endless snowy slopes stretch out in all directions. Solitary trees rise majestically against the pure white expanse, creating a poetic and minimalist scene – perfect for capturing the serene beauty of Hokkaido.

Hokkaido fox.
Wild Hokkaido foxes, also known as *kitsune*, are truly mesmerising creatures. The fox plays an essential role in Japanese culture and is often regarded as the God's messenger and a protective spirit.

Ebisu Rocks.
The Ebisu Rocks, located on Hokkaido's southeast coast near Samani, are a striking group of rock formations that rise dramatically from the sea. The area is renowned for its breathtaking scenery, especially in winter when it is blanketed in pristine snow.

>

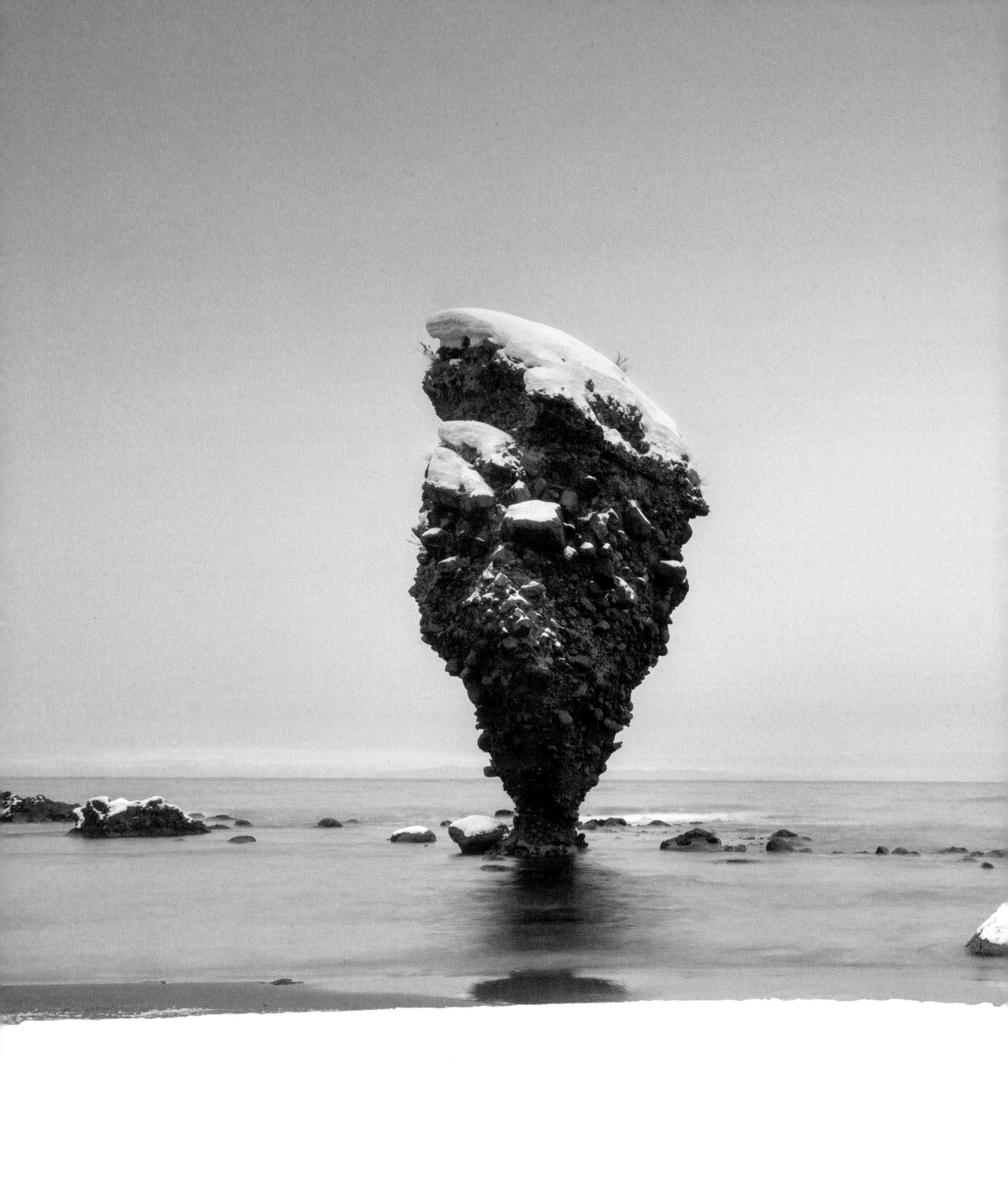

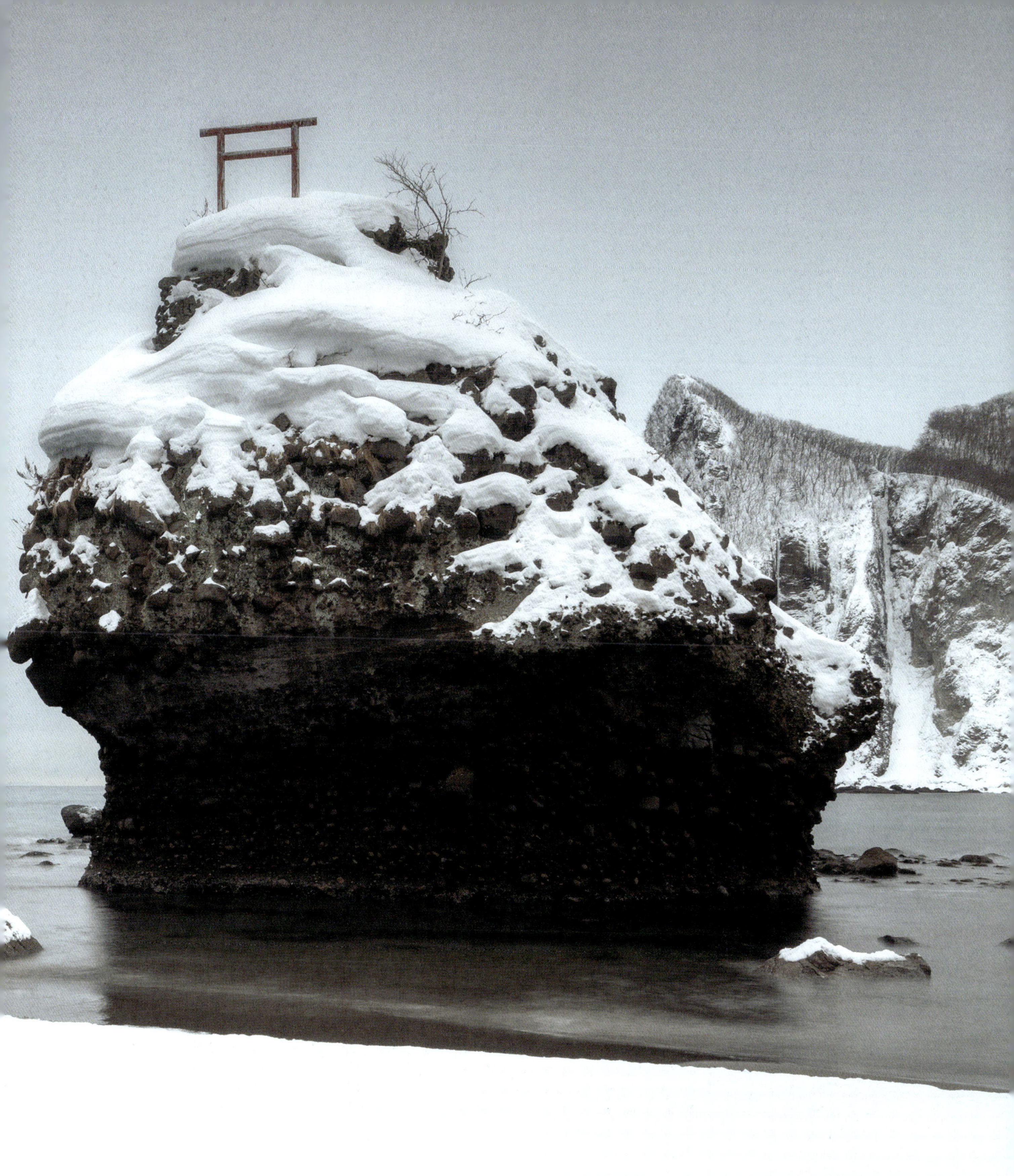

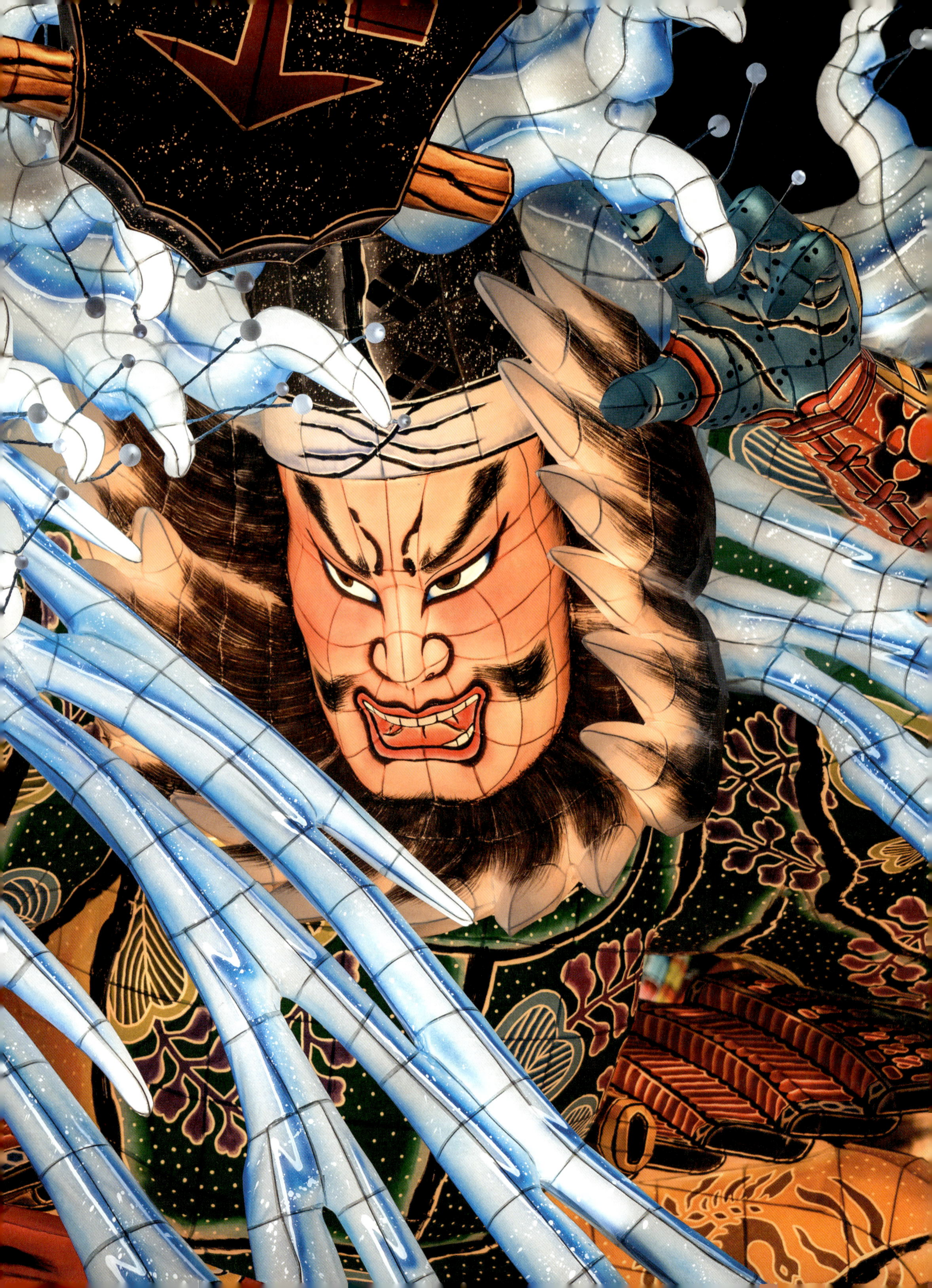

Aomori Nebuta Matsuri.
The *omikoshi* on display at Aomori's Nebuta Festival Museum is a striking illuminated papier-mâché float that brings to life mythological and historical figures. The vibrant parade features these impressive floats – called nebuta – which can reach up to 9 metres in length and 5 metres in height, lighting up the streets with their bold, colourful designs.

東北

Tōhoku

A Wild Jewel and Spiritual Heritage

In the northeast of Honshū, Japan's main island, lies the Tōhoku region, which comprises six prefectures: Aomori, Akita, Iwate, Miyagi, Yamagata, and Fukushima. In Tōhoku, nature reigns supreme, with the seasons transforming the landscape into living works of art while ancient traditions find their place in the modern world. Its sacred mountains, vibrant festivals, and timeless shrines captivate the souls of all who venture there.

Area.
Tōhoku covers about 30% of Honshū, with an area of roughly 66,889 km².

Demographics and Population.
The region is home to approximately 9 million inhabitants.

Geographical Location.
The Sea of Japan borders the Tōhoku region to the west and the Pacific Ocean to the east. This mountainous area is traversed from north to south by the Ōu mountain range, featuring coastlines that are generally rocky and rugged. It encompasses six prefectures: Aomori, Iwate, Miyagi, Akita, Yamagata, and Fukushima.

Climate and Seasons.
Tōhoku has a humid continental climate, characterised by cold, snowy winters, particularly in the mountainous regions, and hot, humid summers. The transitional seasons of spring and autumn provide pleasant temperatures.

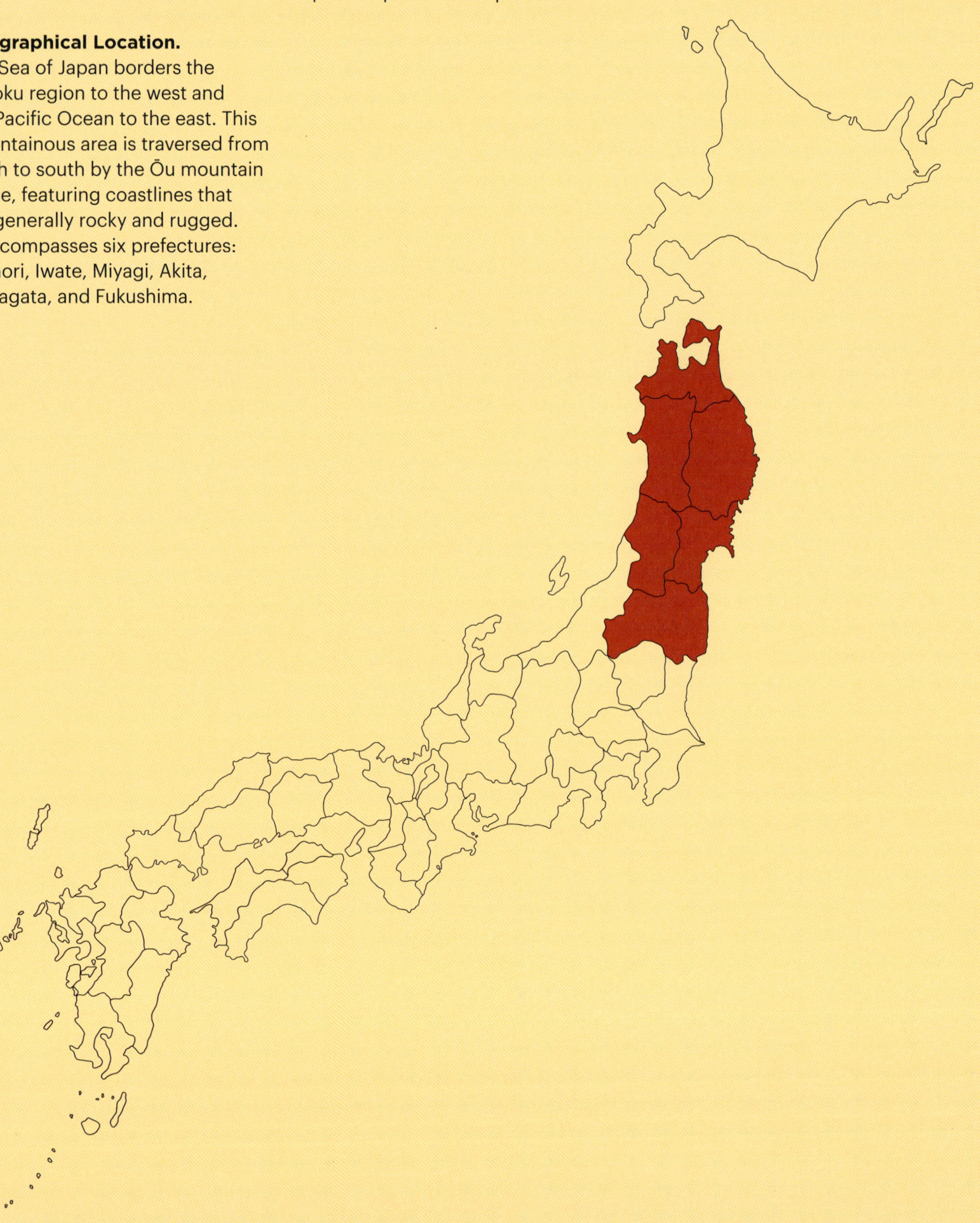

東北

Aomori,
Gateway to the North

At the northern tip of Honshū, Aomori is a land of mystery and dramatic landscapes. The Hakkōda Mountains, often shrouded in mist, are popular destinations for hikers. Lake Towada, nestled in a volcanic crater, offers deep blue waters surrounded by forests that burst into fiery colours each autumn.

Every summer, the city of Aomori comes alive with the *Nebuta Matsuri Festival*, where illuminated floats depicting warriors and mythological scenes parade to the beat of drums and flutes. The Osorezan Temple, located on the shores of Lake Usori, is a sacred site steeped in mysticism, often referred to as the "Gate to Hell" due to its sulphurous vapours and association with the spirit world.

Akita,
Untouched Beauty

The Akita prefecture is renowned for its pristine landscapes and centuries-old traditions. Lake Tazawa, Japan's deepest lake, captivates visitors with its clear waters and the legend of Princess Tatsuko, who was transformed into a dragon after seeking immortality. The Nyūtō Onsen hot springs, nestled in the heart of the mountains, provide a peaceful retreat where guests can rejuvenate in outdoor baths surrounded by forests.

Akita is also famous for the Kanto Matsuri, where performers balance massive bamboo poles adorned with lanterns on their shoulders in a stunning display of strength and skill. The Kakunodate district, known as "Little Kyoto", preserves samurai residences in a picturesque setting, especially enchanting in spring when cherry blossoms create a pink tunnel.

Iwate,
Echoes of History

Iwate, a vast prefecture with diverse landscapes, is rich in history and spirituality. The city of Hiraizumi, a UNESCO World Heritage Site, was once a thriving cultural and political centre. Today, visitors can admire the remnants of this ancient capital of the northern Fujiwara clan, including the Chūson-ji Temple, with its Konjiki-dō Hall covered in gold leaf, representing the pinnacle of Heian-period Buddhist art.

Additional gems of the region are the Takkoku-no-Iwaya Temple, carved into rock, and the Mōtsū-ji Temple, symbolising the Buddhist paradise.

The Geibikei Gorge, listed among Japan's 100 most beautiful sites, offers a tranquil boat cruise along cliffs that tower over 100 metres, famous for their remarkable rock formations, such as the "Lion's Nose", and abundant wildlife. Further east, the Sanriku coastline reveals its untamed natural beauty, featuring rugged cliffs, secret coves, and the famous rock formations of Jōdogahama, which evoke an earthly vision of paradise.

Miyagi,
Between Ocean and Spirituality

Miyagi Prefecture is where Shinto and Buddhist traditions blend with coastal landscapes. Matsushima, an archipelago of more than 260 islands scattered across the bay, is one of Japan's "three most scenic views". The pine-clad islets, reflected in the calm waters of the bay, offer a serene vision immortalised in the poems of Matsuo Bashō.

Sendai, known as "the City of Trees", is the region's heart. Founded by the feudal lord Date Masamune, it is home to the Zuihō-den Mausoleum, a brilliant example of Momoyama architecture. The *Tanabata* Festival, which lights up the city in summer with colourful decorations, is one of the most famous festivals in Japan.

To the south, the active Zao Volcano attracts visitors with its emerald green crater lake, known as "Okama". In winter, the famous "snow monsters", trees covered in ice, transform the slopes of Mount Zao into a surreal landscape.

Yamagata, The Serenity of the Mountains

Yamagata is a prefecture where sacred mountains and hot springs harmonise. Mount Haguro, one of the Three Mountains of Dewa, is a revered site for *shugendō*, an ancient spiritual practice that combines Buddhism and nature worship. A five-story pagoda, surrounded by giant cedars, welcomes pilgrims and travellers seeking meditation.

The Yamadera Temple, literally "Mountain Temple", is perched on a cliff, offering breathtaking views of the valley. Its steps, climbed in solemn silence, lead to pavilions that seem to be suspended between heaven and earth.

Yamagata is renowned for its cherries, considered the best in Japan, and its *onsen*, particularly those in Ginzan. In this charming hot spring village, wooden buildings illuminated by lanterns create a timeless atmosphere.

Fukushima, Resilience and Beauty

Fukushima, the southernmost prefecture of Tōhoku, is a land characterised by profound resilience. Severely impacted by the 2011 tsunami and the resulting nuclear disaster, local communities continue to rebuild while preserving their cultural heritage.

Lake Inawashiro, known as the "Heavenly Mirror Lake", is a tranquil place where migrating swans find refuge. Mount Bandai, sometimes called the "Mount Fuji of Aizu", dominates the region, its slopes dotted with lakes and marshes, like the five lakes of Goshikinuma, whose colours change with the seasons.

The city of Aizuwakamatsu, known as "the Samurai City", is a living testament to the feudal era. The beautifully reconstructed Tsuruga Castle recalls the heroic battles of the Boshin War. Nearby, with its thatched houses and streets lined with craft shops, the traditional village of Ouchi-juku transports visitors back to the Edo period.

The Sanriku Coast, The Power of the Sea

Stretching across several Tōhoku prefectures, the Sanriku Coast is a stunning example of the power and beauty of the sea. The cliffs of Kitayamazaki, towering at 200 metres, offer spectacular views, while boat trips reveal sea caves and natural arches shaped by the waves.

東北

Best Times to Visit

– Spring (April to June).
Cherry blossoms create stunning landscapes and offer comfortable Temperatures.

– Summer (July to August).
To attend the many traditional festivals and explore the mountains.

– Autumn (September to November).
Perfect for admiring colourful autumn leaves and agricultural crops.

– Winter (December to February).
Ideal for winter sports and the snowy landscapes.

Top 5 Places to Visit

1. Matsushima.
A picturesque bay with over 200 pine-clad islands, considered one of Japan's three most beautiful landscapes.

2. Hiraizumi.
A historic city home to UNESCO World Heritage Sites, including Chūson-ji and Mōtsū-ji Temples.

3. Geibikei Gorge.
Spectacular rock formations along the Satetsu River, offering traditional boat cruises.

4. Lake Towada and Oirase Gorge.
Popular natural sites renowned for their magnificent landscapes, particularly in autumn.

5. Aizu-Wakamatsu.
A historic city known for its Tsuruga Castle and well-preserved samurai district.

東北

Gastronomy

Located in the northern part of Honshū, the Tōhoku region is known for its hearty, comforting cuisine influenced by its cold climate. Below is a list of culinary specialities from each prefecture and city in the Tōhoku region, with detailed descriptions.

青森
Aomori

[八戸せんべい汁]
Hachinohe Senbei-jiru – Hachinohe
A traditional stew made with vegetables, meat (usually chicken), and pieces of *senbei* (rice crackers) that soften as they absorb the broth. This dish originates from Hachinohe and is particularly popular in winter.

[大間マグロ]
Oma Maguro – Oma
The bluefin tuna from Oma is considered among the best in Japan. It is often enjoyed as sashimi or sushi and is highly prized at tuna auctions in Tokyo.

[アップルパイ]
Apple Pie – Hirosaki
Hirosaki is famous for its apples. Local apple pies are made using sweet and juicy varieties, often served with whipped cream or ice cream.

岩手
Iwate

[盛岡冷麺]
Morioka Reimen – Morioka
Cold noodles served in a mildly spicy broth, often accompanied by beef and a slice of watermelon. This dish, influenced by Korean cuisine, is very popular in summer.

[じゃじゃ麺]
Jajamen – Morioka
Thick noodles served with a salty miso sauce, grated cucumber, and ginger. The noodles are mixed before eating, and they can be transformed into a soup by adding an egg and hot broth after the meal.

[わんこそば]
Wanko Soba – Hanamaki
A style of eating soba where the noodles are served in small bowls that are continuously refilled by servers. The goal is to eat as many bowls as possible.

宮城
Miyagi

[牛タン]
Gyūtan – Sendai
Grilled beef tongue is a speciality of Sendai, often served with barley rice and oxtail soup. The texture is tender and juicy, with a slightly smoky flavour.

[ずんだ餅]
Zundamochi – Sendai
A slightly sweet dessert made with mochi (glutinous rice cake), covered in a paste of crushed green soybeans (*zunda*).

[牡蠣料理]
Kaki Ryōri – Matsushima
Matsushima oysters are renowned for their rich taste and creamy texture. They are eaten grilled, deep-fried as kaki fry, or raw with a squeeze of lemon.

秋田
Akita

[きりたんぽ]
Kiritanpo – Akita
Rice sticks that are mashed, skewered, and grilled, often added to a *nabe* (Japanese hot pot) with chicken, vegetables, and soy broth. This dish is a winter classic.

[稲庭うどん]
Inaniwa Udon – Yuzawa
Fine, smooth udon noodles handmade using a traditional method. Unlike regular udon, these noodles are more delicate and slightly translucent.

[ハタハタ寿司]
Hata-hata Zushi – Noshiro
A fermented sushi made with *hata-hata* (a local fish), often consumed during the New Year festivities in the region.

山形
Yamagata

[芋煮]
Imoni – Yamagata
A traditional soup made with taro root, beef (or pork, depending on the region), mushrooms, and soy sauce. This dish is central to many autumn festivals called "imoni-kai," where locals cook the soup outdoors.

[米沢牛]
Yonezawa Gyū – Yonezawa
Yonezawa beef is one of Japan's most prized wagyū varieties. It is often enjoyed as steak, sukiyaki, or *shabu-shabu*.

[どんどん焼き]
Dondon-yaki – Yamagata
A popular snack resembling a savoury pancake wrapped around a skewer and topped with sauce, often sold during festivals.

福島
Fukushima

[喜多方ラーメン]
Kitakata Rāmen – Kitakata
This *rāmen* is known for its clear soy-based broth and thick, wavy noodles. It is often topped with *chāshū*, bamboo shoots, and green onions.

[会津ソースカツ丼]
Aizu Sauce Katsu-don – Aizu-Wakamatsu
A bowl of rice topped with *tonkatsu* (breaded pork) drizzled with a thick, slightly sweet sauce. Unlike the traditional katsudon (which is served with eggs), this version highlights the savoury sauce.

[もも]
Momo – Fukushima
Fukushima is famous for its juicy and sweet peaches, often eaten fresh or used in desserts like parfaits and pies.

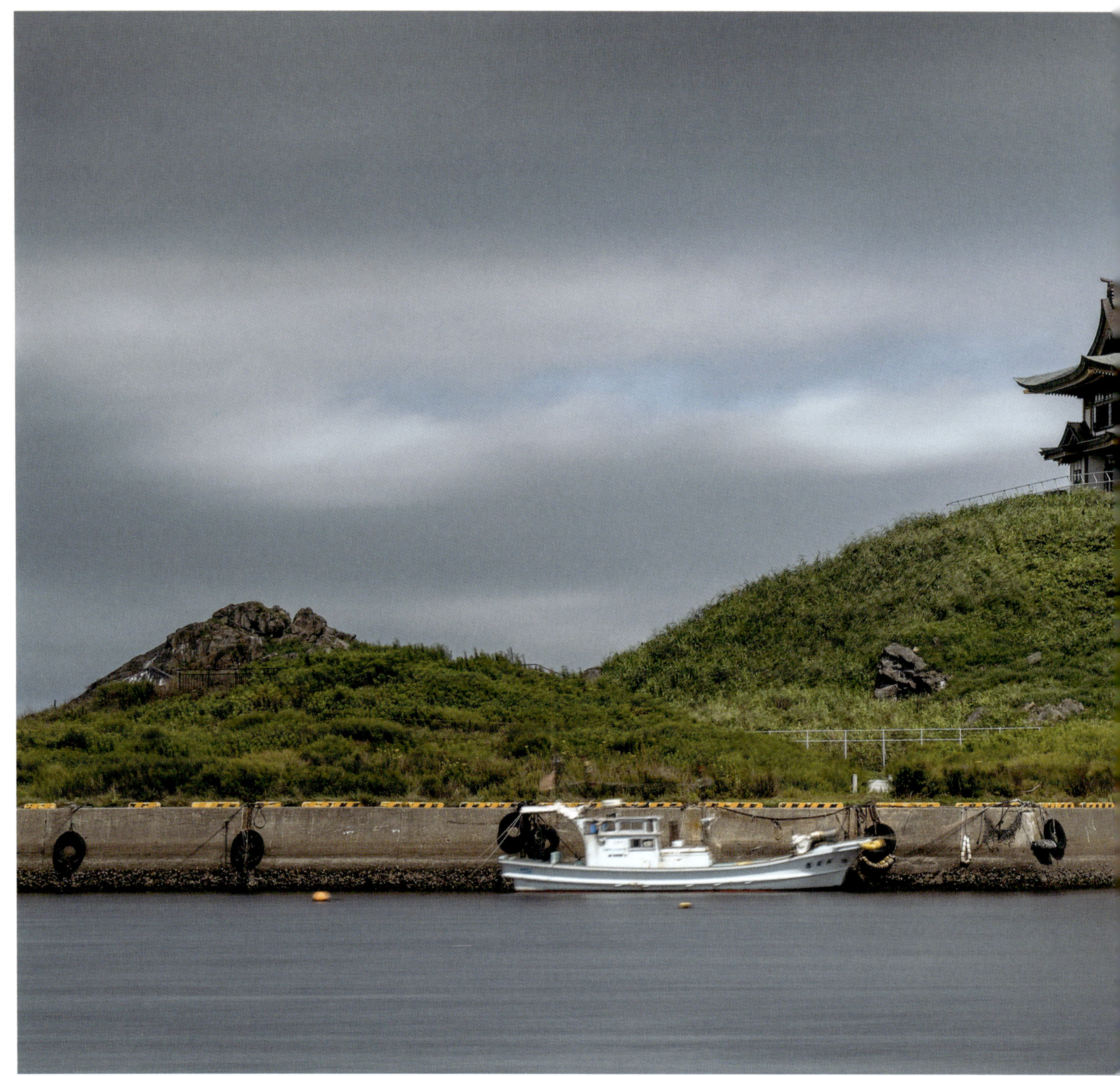

Kabushima Shrine.
Perched on a hill overlooking the sea, the Kabushima Shrine in Hachinohe is dedicated to black-tailed gulls, symbols of fortune and prosperity. It comes alive in spring, when thousands of gulls nest on its grounds, creating a vibrant atmosphere.

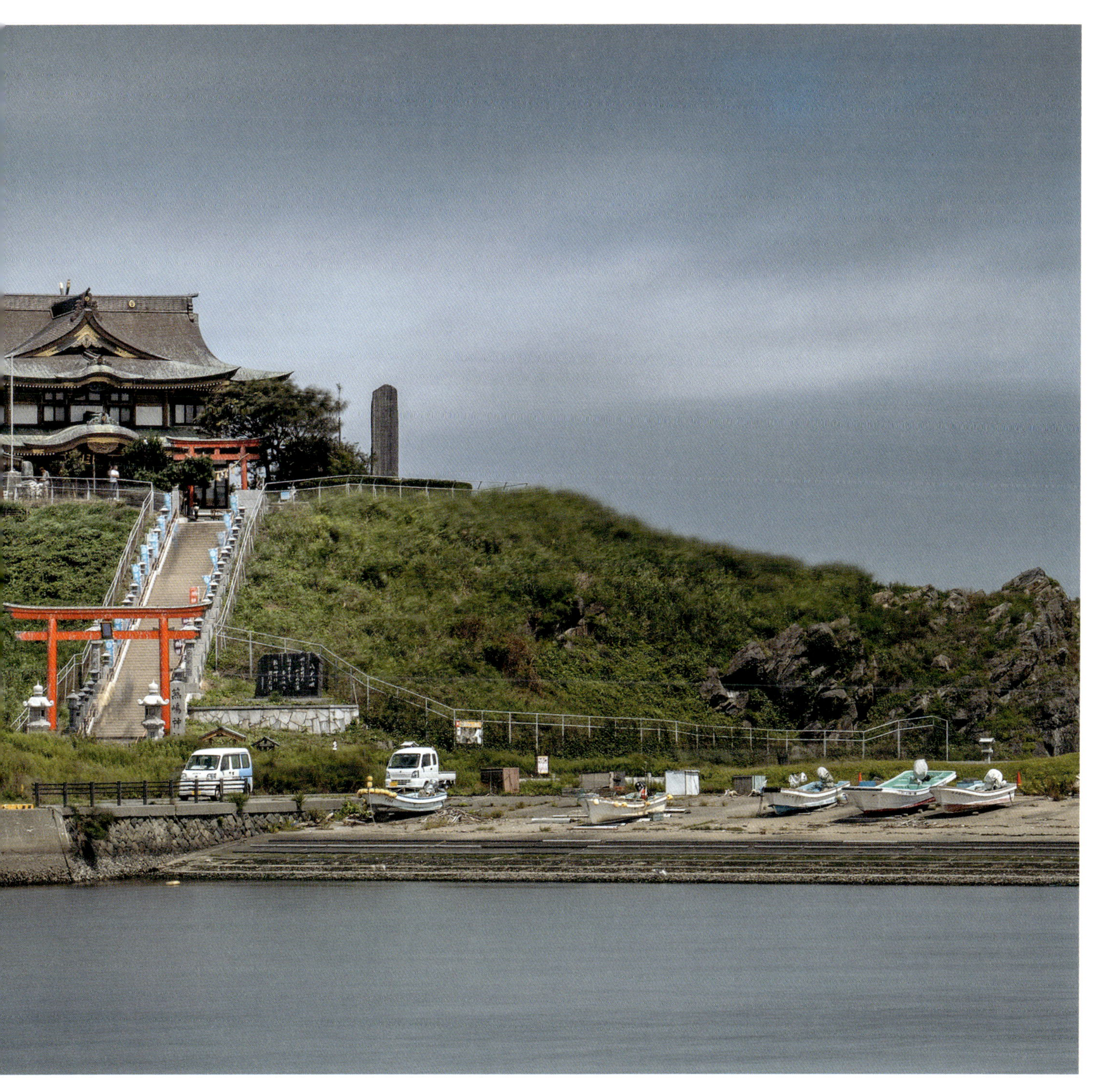

The Tsugaru Railway Line.
Winding through the heart of the Tohoku region, the Tsugaru Line offers a journey through untouched countryside. As the train glides through natural tunnels of dense foliage, it connects quaint rural towns to the rugged landscapes of Aomori. Its charm lies in its gentle pace, inviting travellers to slow down and immerse themselves in the understated beauty of northern Japan.

Tsuru No Mai Bashi.
Stretching gracefully over Lake Tsugaru Fujimi, the Tsuru no Mai Bridge in north-eastern Tohoku is Japan's longest wooden bridge.

>

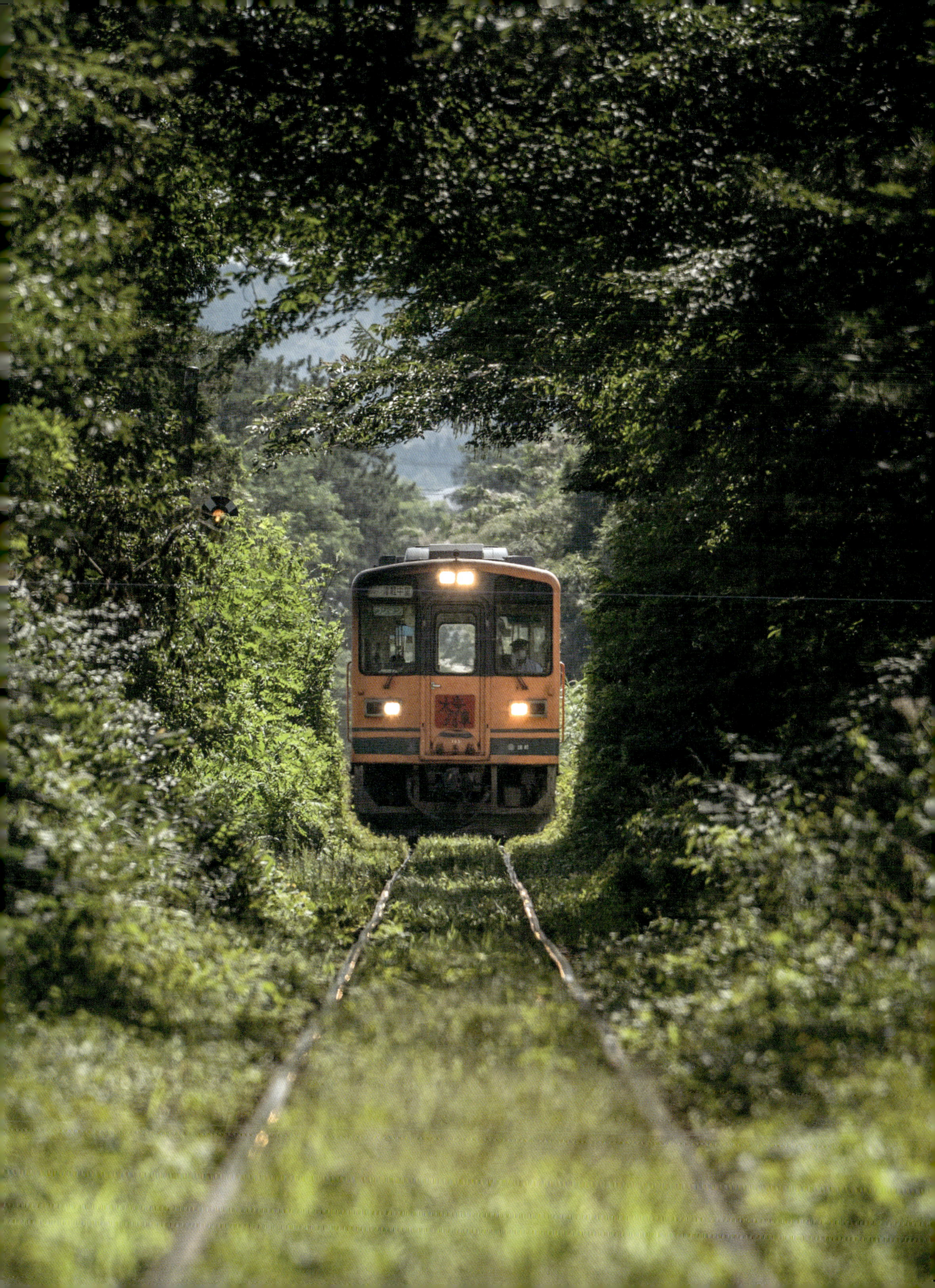

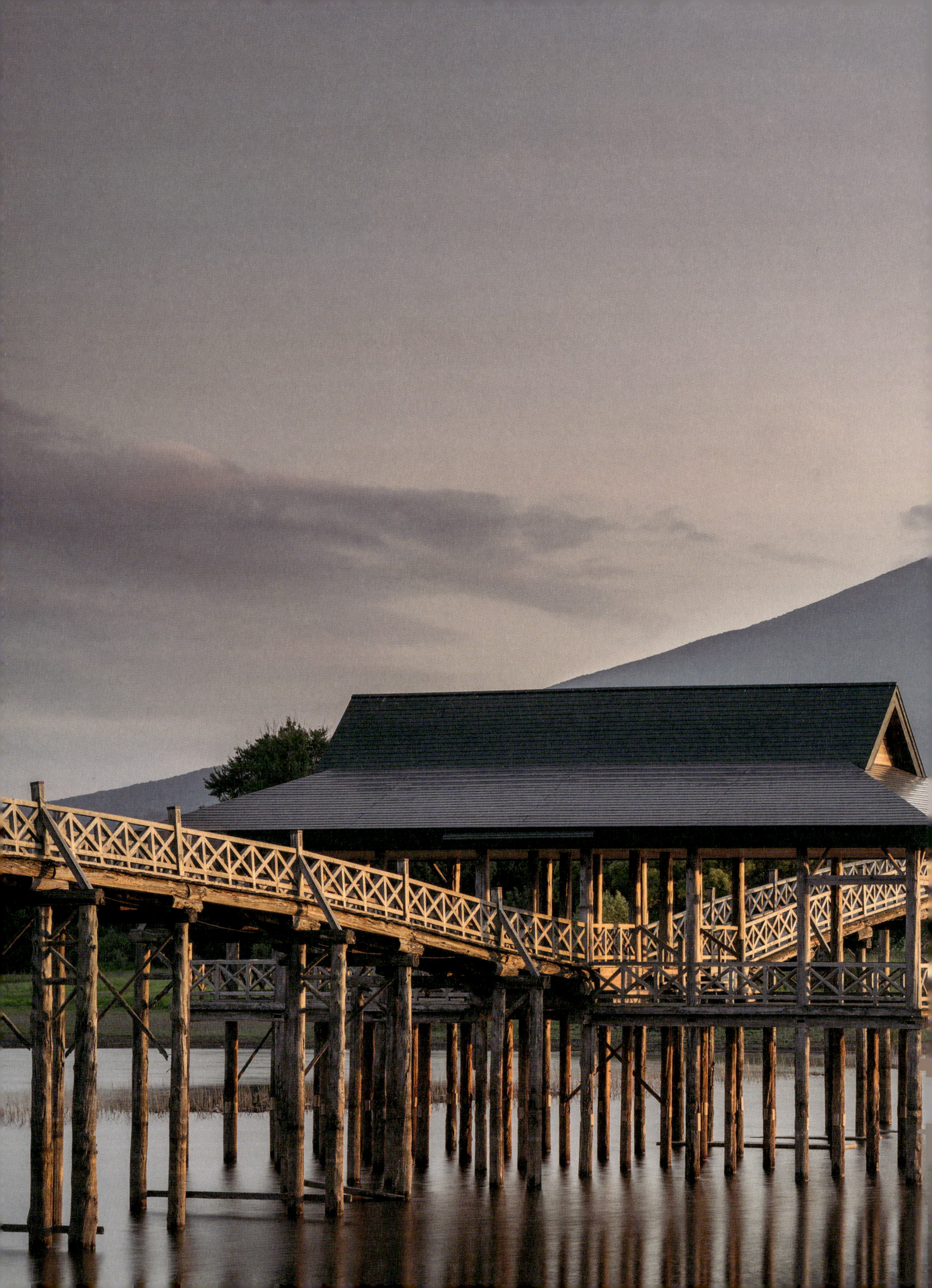

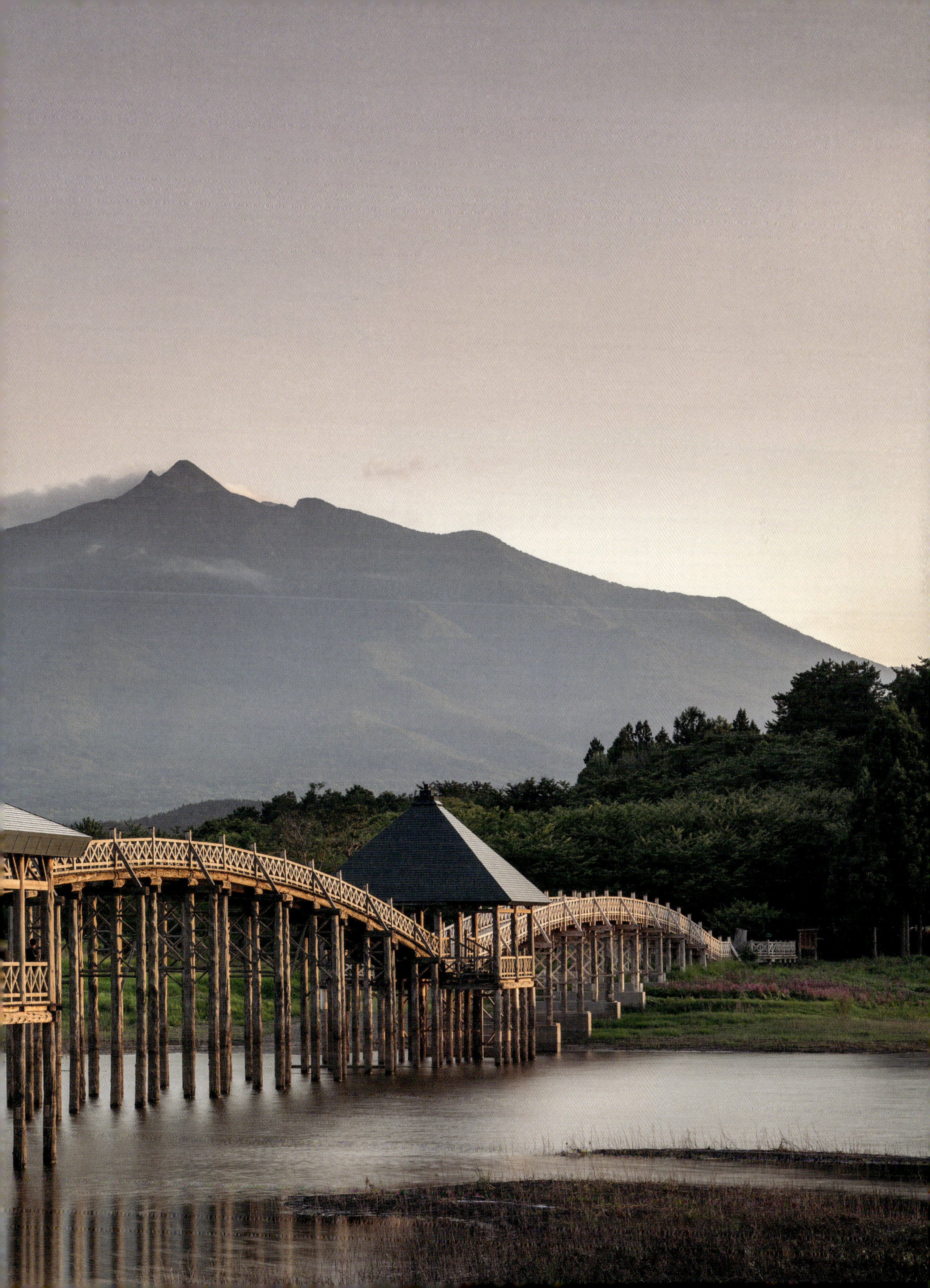

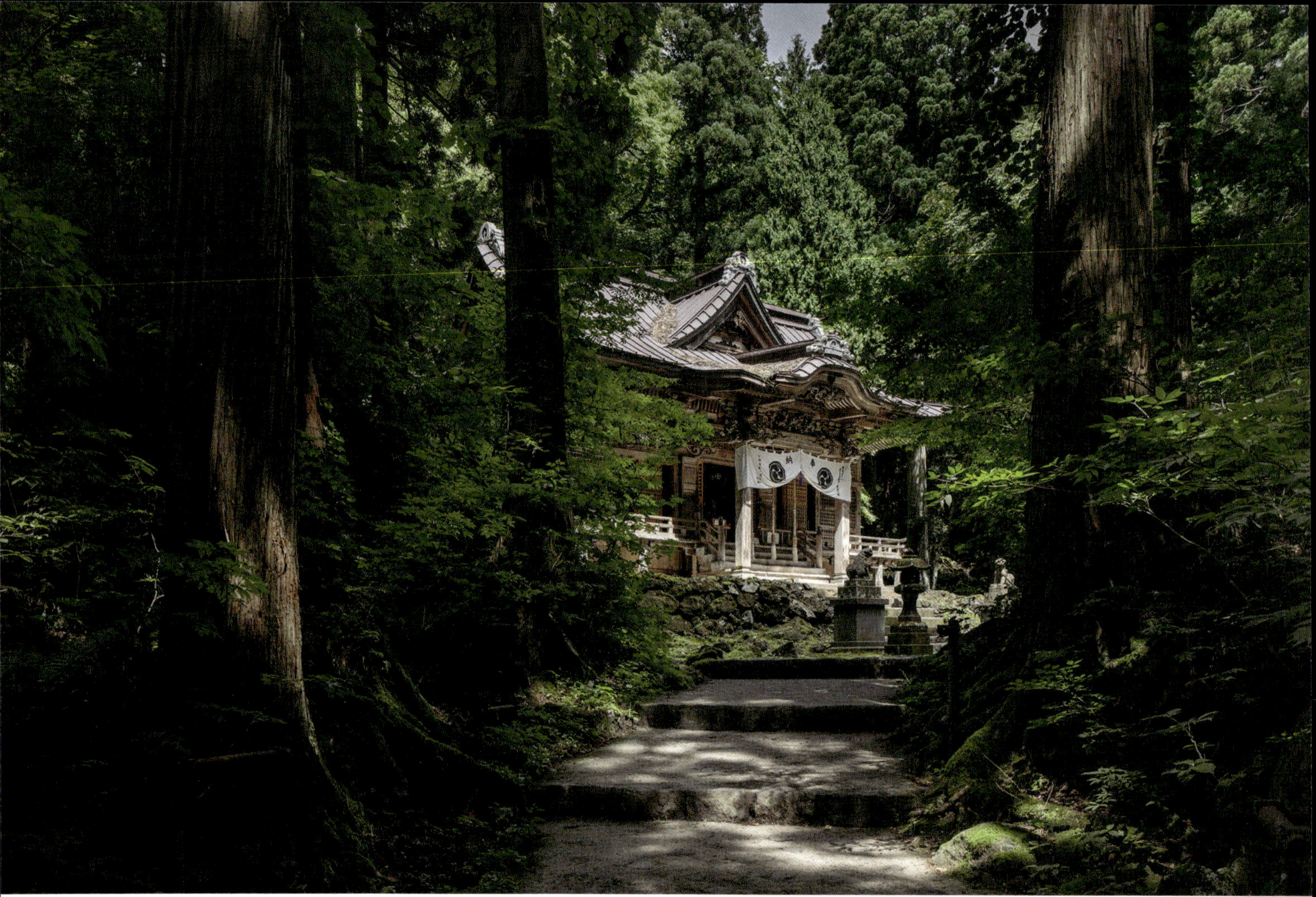

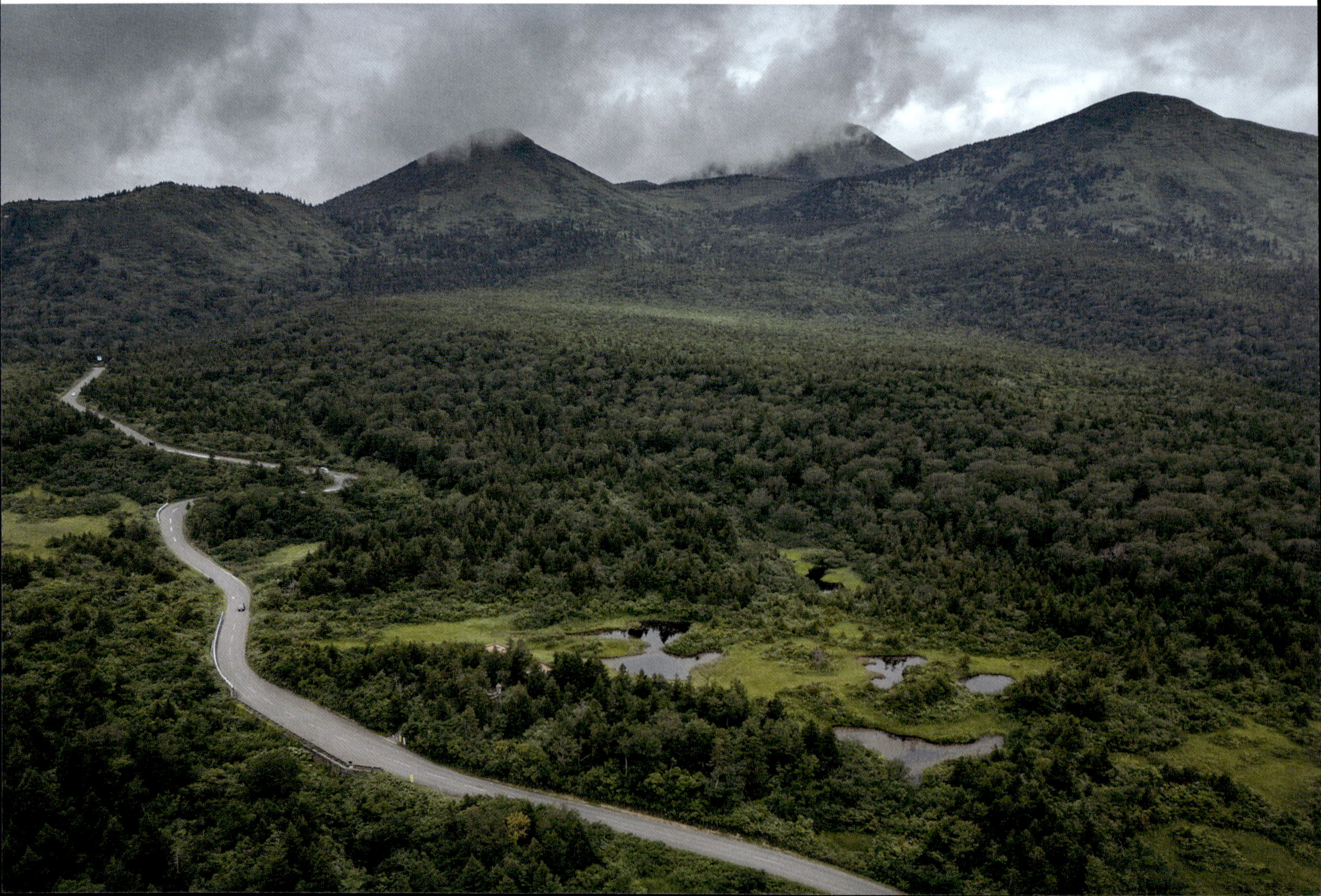

東北

Towada Shrine.
Nestled along the shores of the tranquil Towada Lake, Towada Shrine is enveloped by ancient forests.

Hakkoda Mountains.
Nestled in the heart of the lush Hakkoda Mountains, the Suiren-numa ponds serve as a captivating hiking destination for nature lovers.

Takayama Inari Shrine.
Nestled deep within the lush forests of Tōhoku, the 17th-century Takayama Inari Shrine unveils a winding path lined with vibrant vermilion *torii* gates.

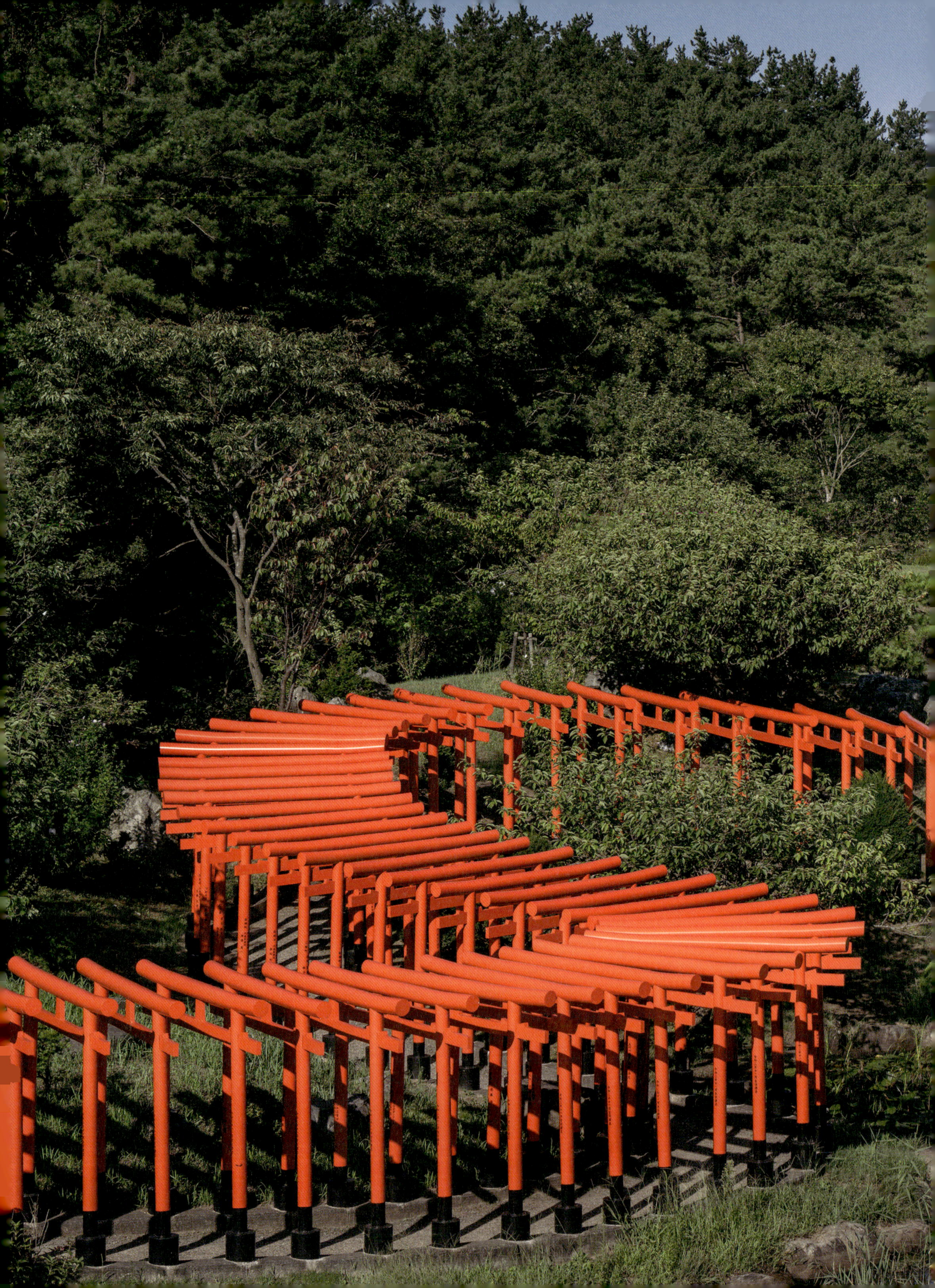

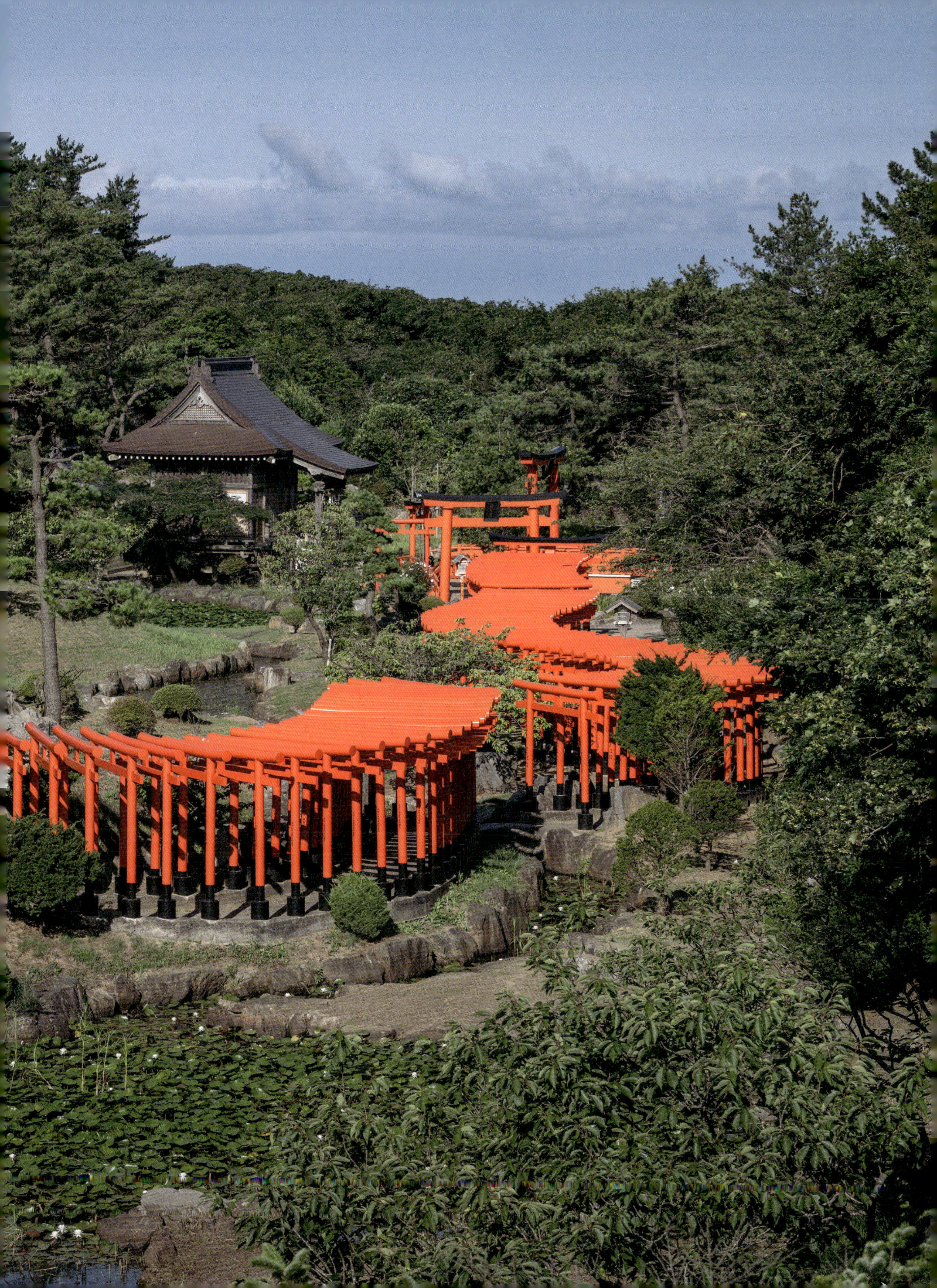

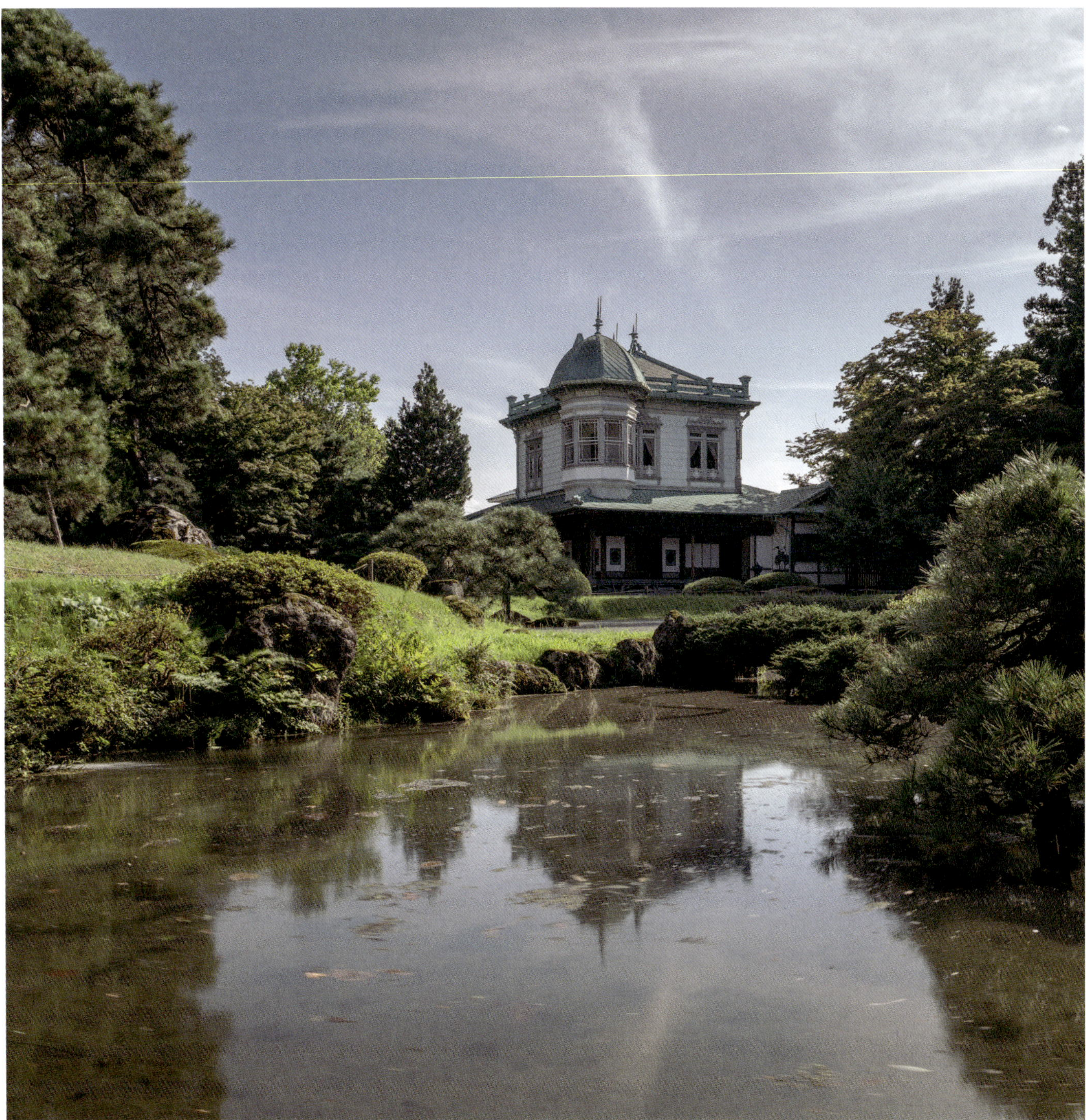

Seibi-en.
Nestled in the heart of Hirakawa, Seibi-en is a Japanese garden of exceptional elegance, crafted between 1902 and 1911. Its lush landscapes frame a villa that blends traditional Meiji-era (1868-1912) Japanese architecture with Western influences, symbolising Japan's transformation from a rural nation to a modern industrial power. This tranquil haven inspired Studio Ghibli's beloved animated film *The Secret World of Arrietty*, where its enchanting atmosphere breathes life into the world of miniature creatures.

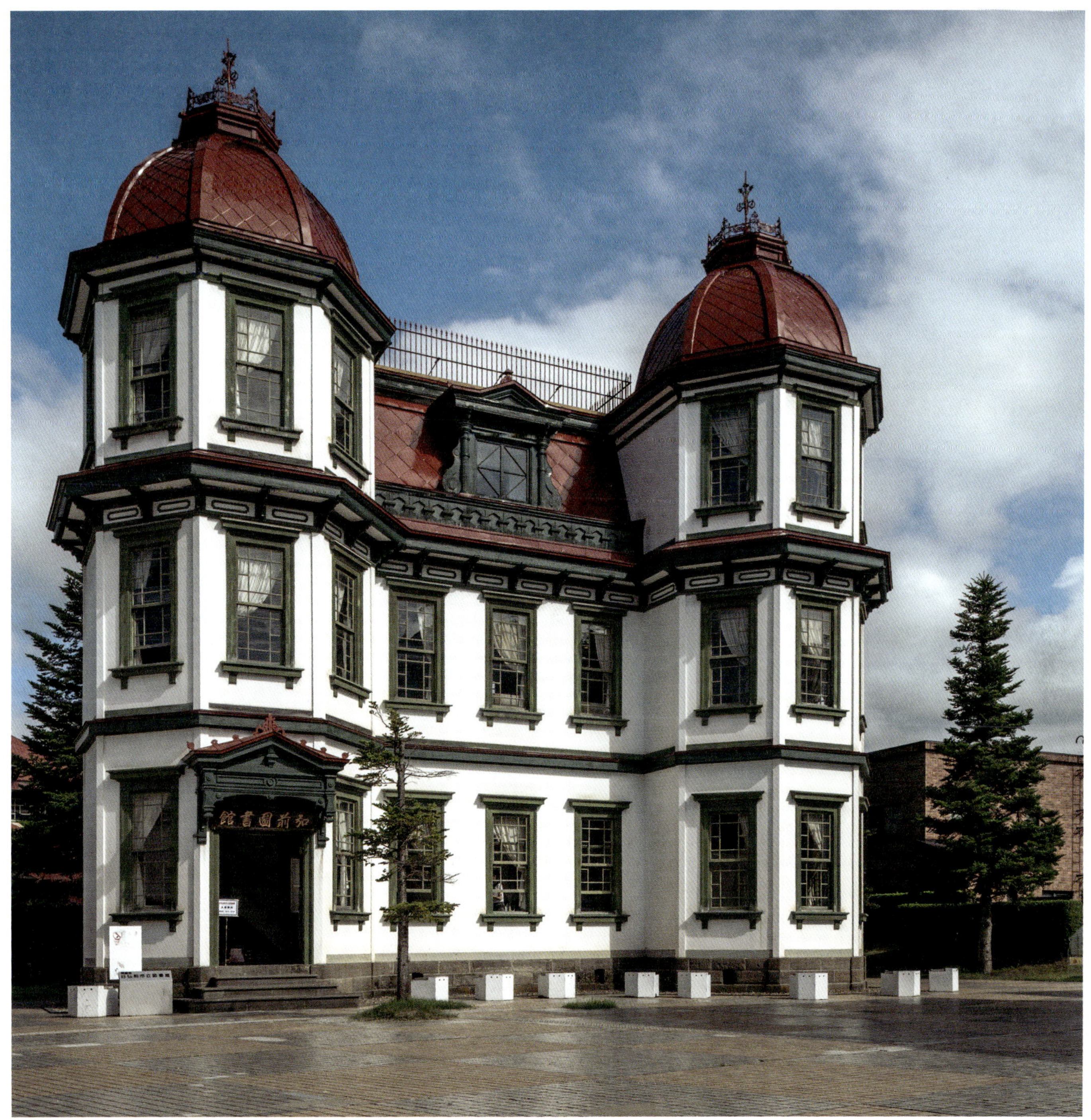

Hirosaki City Library.
The former Hirosaki City Library, with its stately Western-style architecture, reflects the profound influence of the Meiji era on the region. Its pristine white facade, adorned with green and dark red roofs, imparts a regal air.

Bunka Yokocho.
Tucked away in the heart of Sendai, the narrow alleyways of Bunka Yokocho are alive with the buzz of small stalls and lively *izakayas*. At night, the red lanterns glow softly in front of these small traditional bars, where locals and travellers gather to enjoy *sake* and *shōchū*.

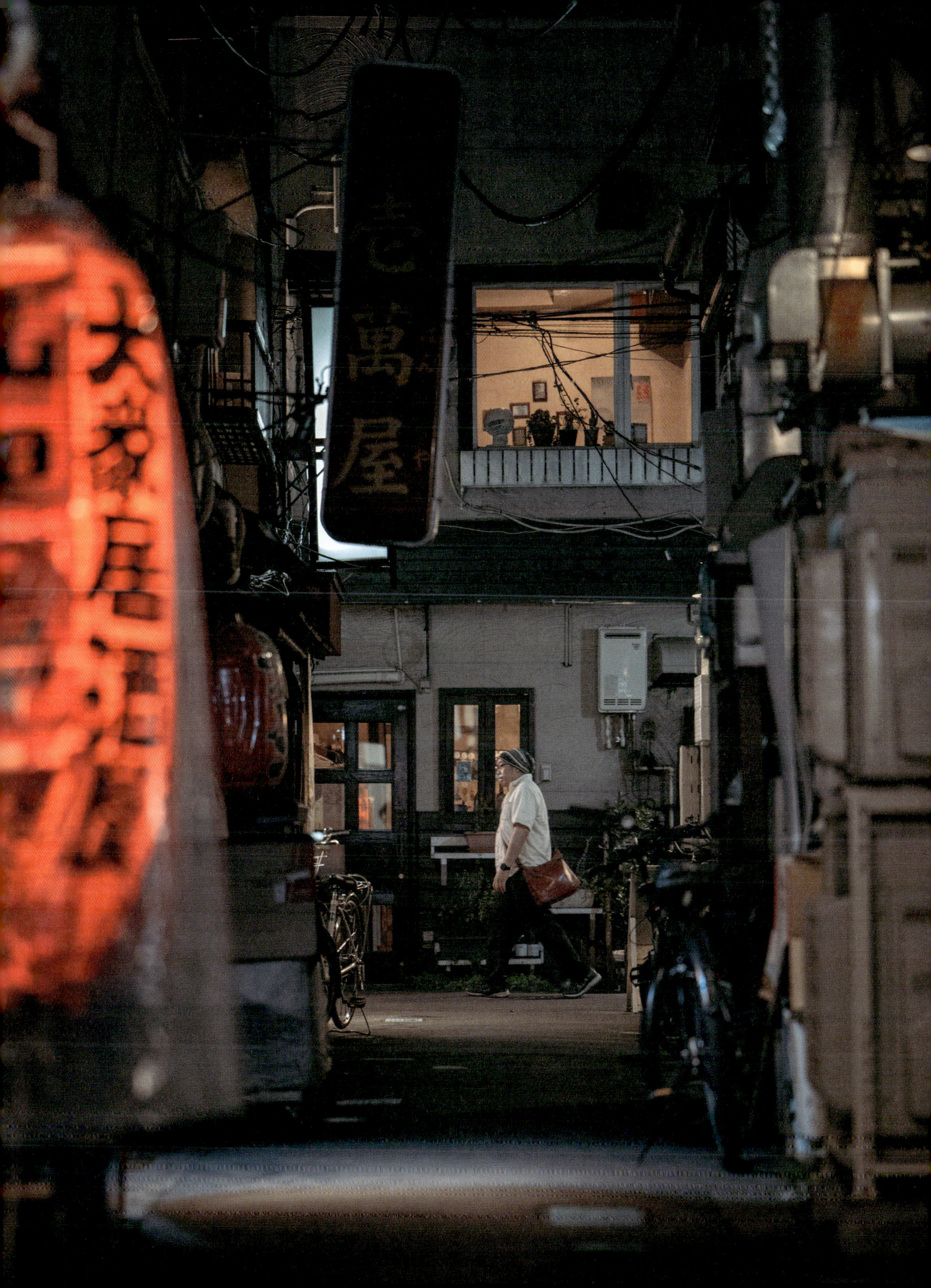
萬屋

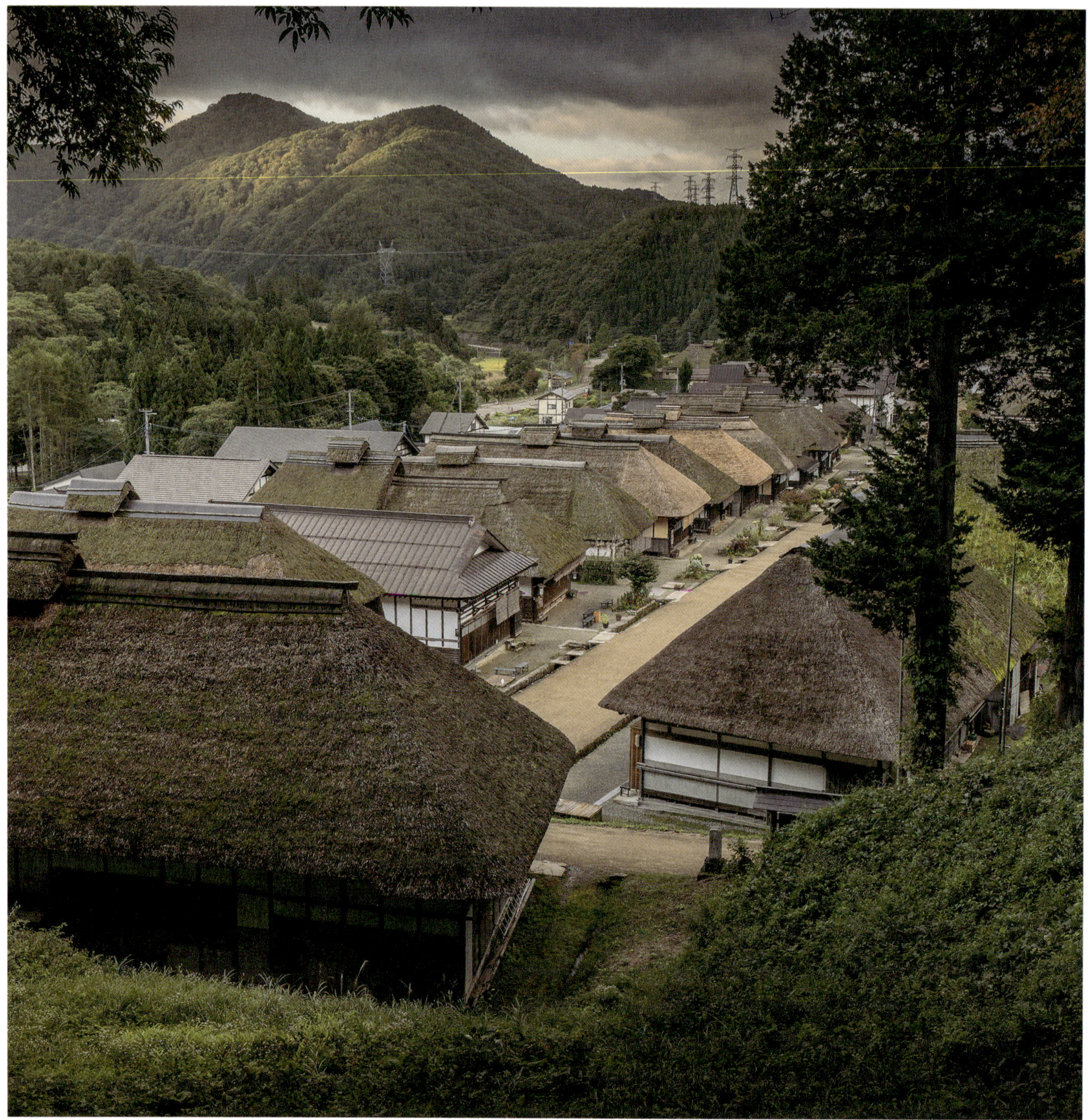

Ouchi-Juku Village.
The village of Ouchi-juku, once a key stop on the Aizu Nishi Kaido trade route, transports visitors to a bygone era. With its 300-year-old thatched-roof houses and charming cobblestone alleys, Ouchi-juku offers an authentic glimpse into the Edo period (1603-1868).

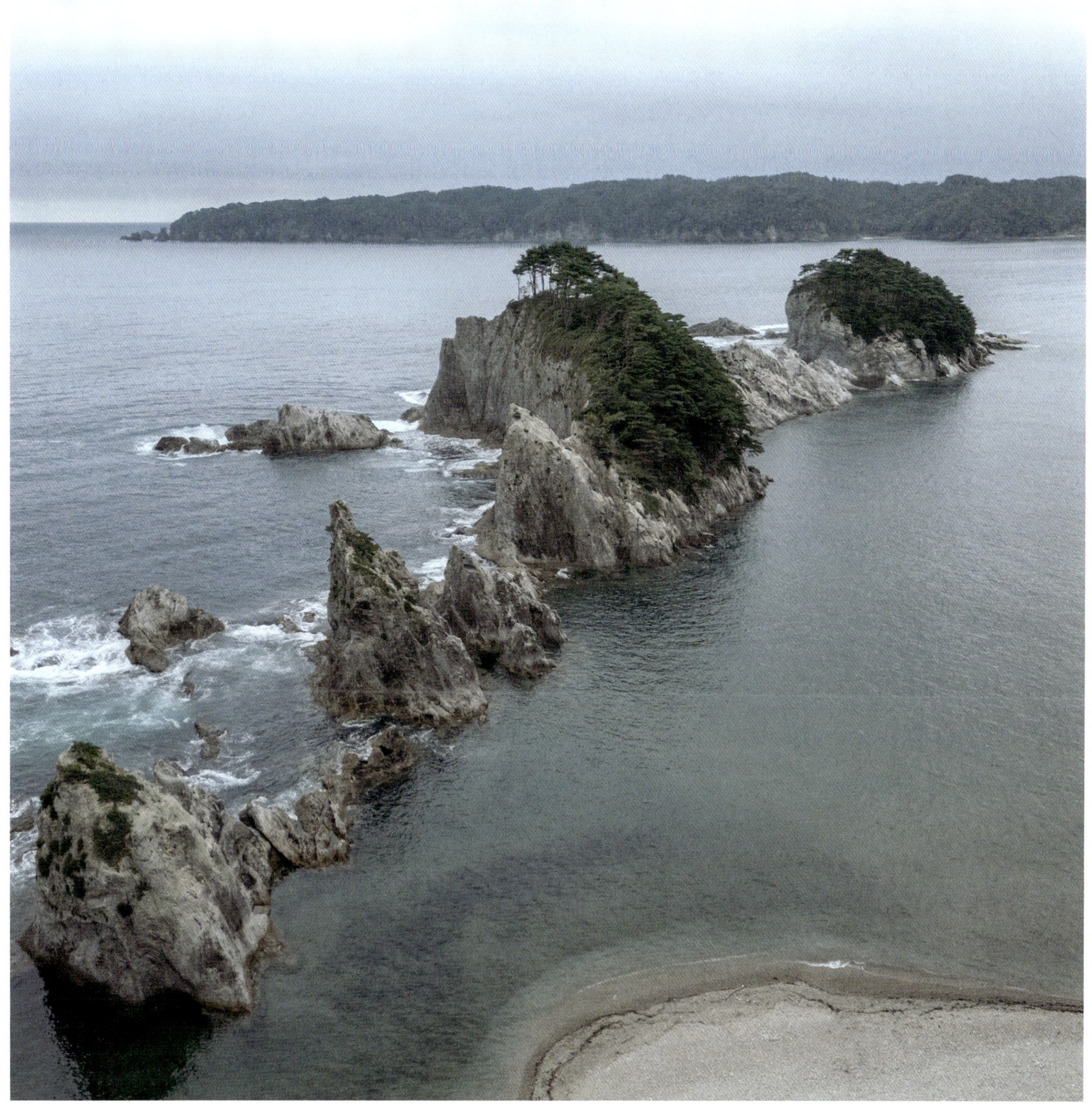

Jodogahama Beach.
Beneath a soft winter sky, Jodogahama Beach unveils its dramatic landscape, where wave-carved rocks stretch along the shoreline.

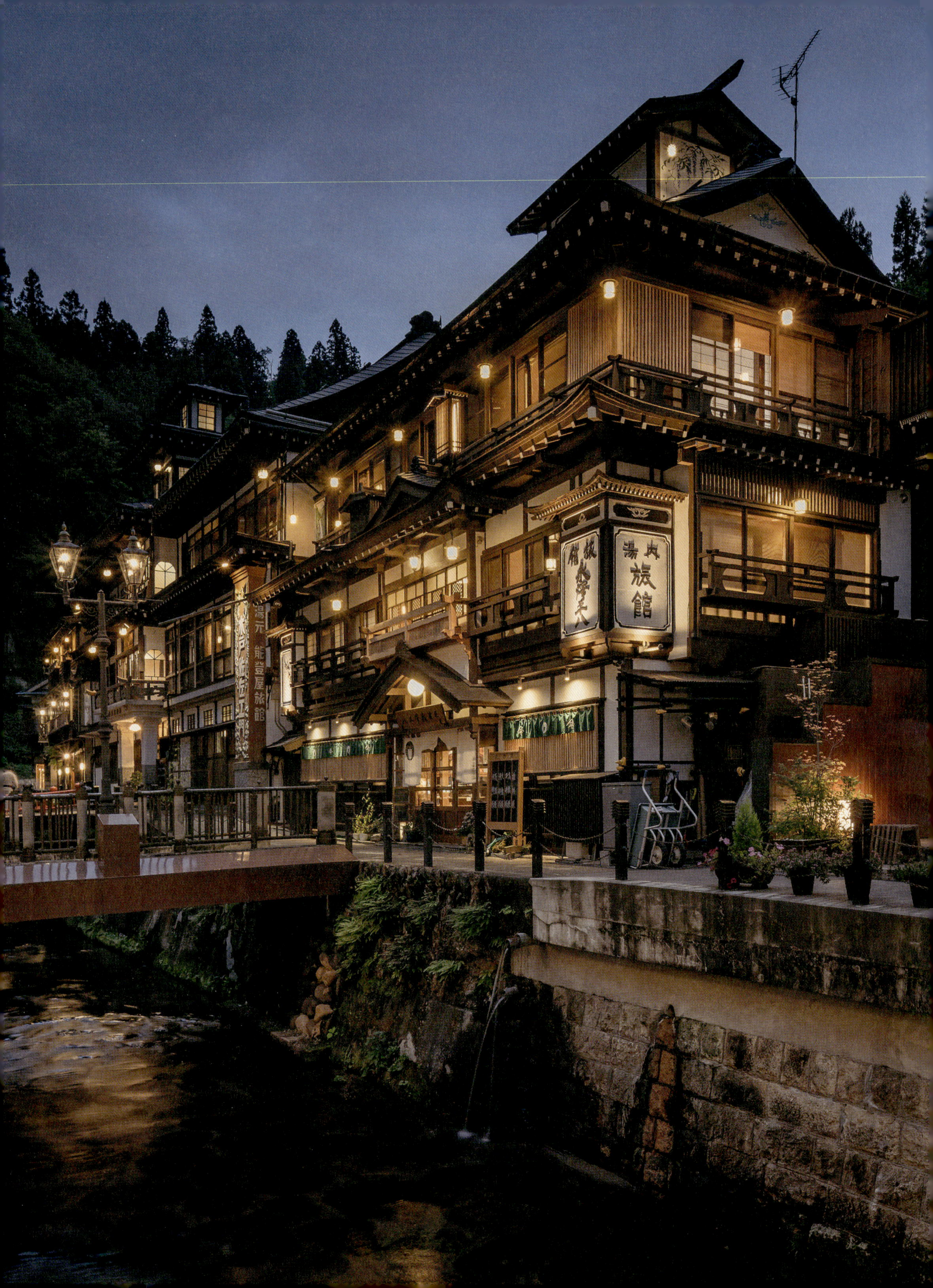

湯元 能登屋旅館
旅館
永澤平八
内湯
旅館

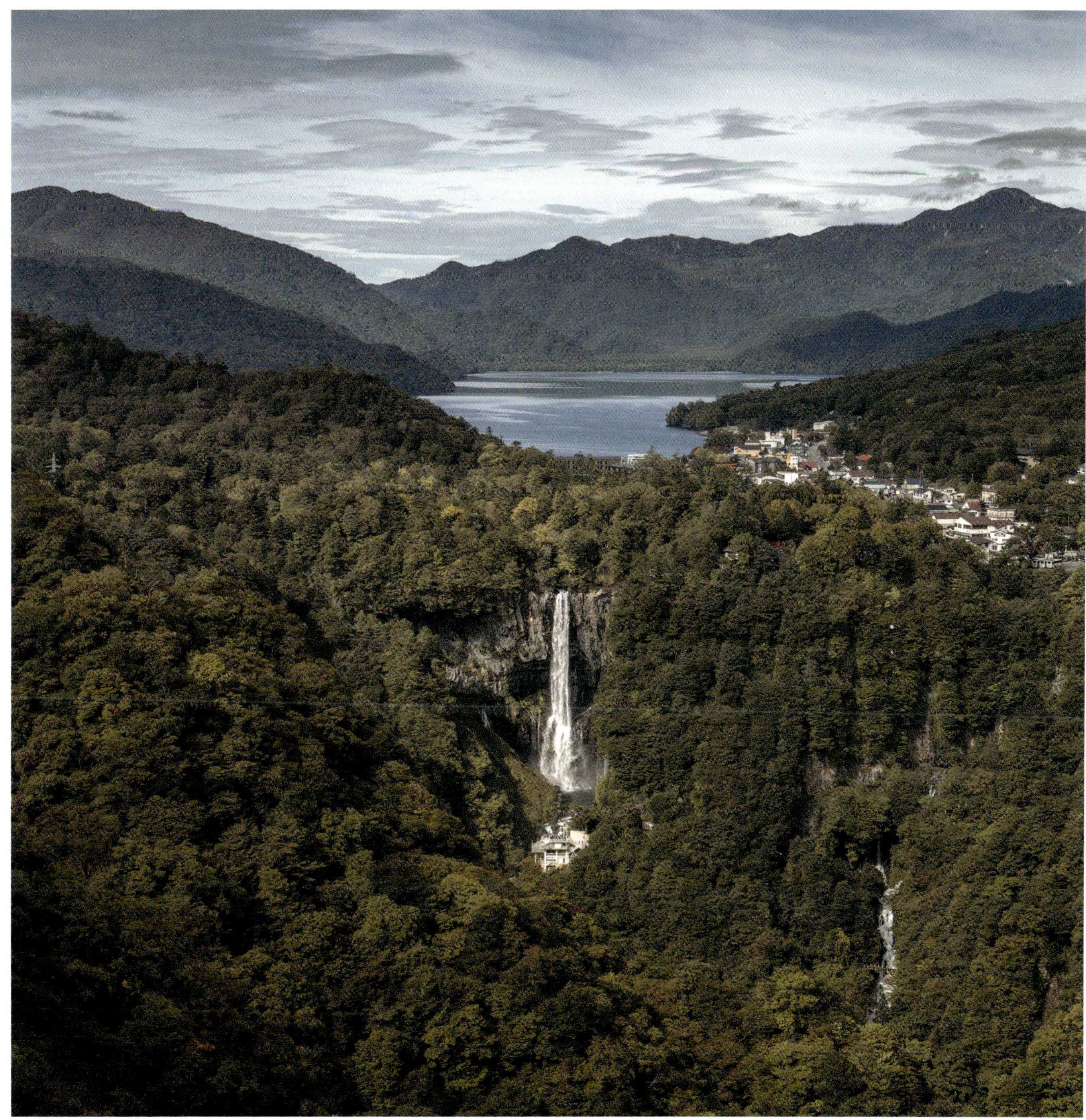

Ginzan Onsen.

Nestled in a picturesque valley, the village of Ginzan *Onsen* is a charming gem of traditional Japan. Famous for its thermal baths and wooden ryokan – quintessential Japanese inns – it exudes a nostalgic atmosphere, especially in the evening, when the streets glow with the soft light of lanterns.

Tadami Line.

Nestled deep within the mountains of Fukushima, the Tadami railway line is one of Japan's most scenic routes. >

Akechidaira Observatory.

Perched at 1,373 metres above sea level, the Akechidaira Observatory offers a panoramic view of Kegon Falls, Lake Chuzenji, and the surrounding mountains.

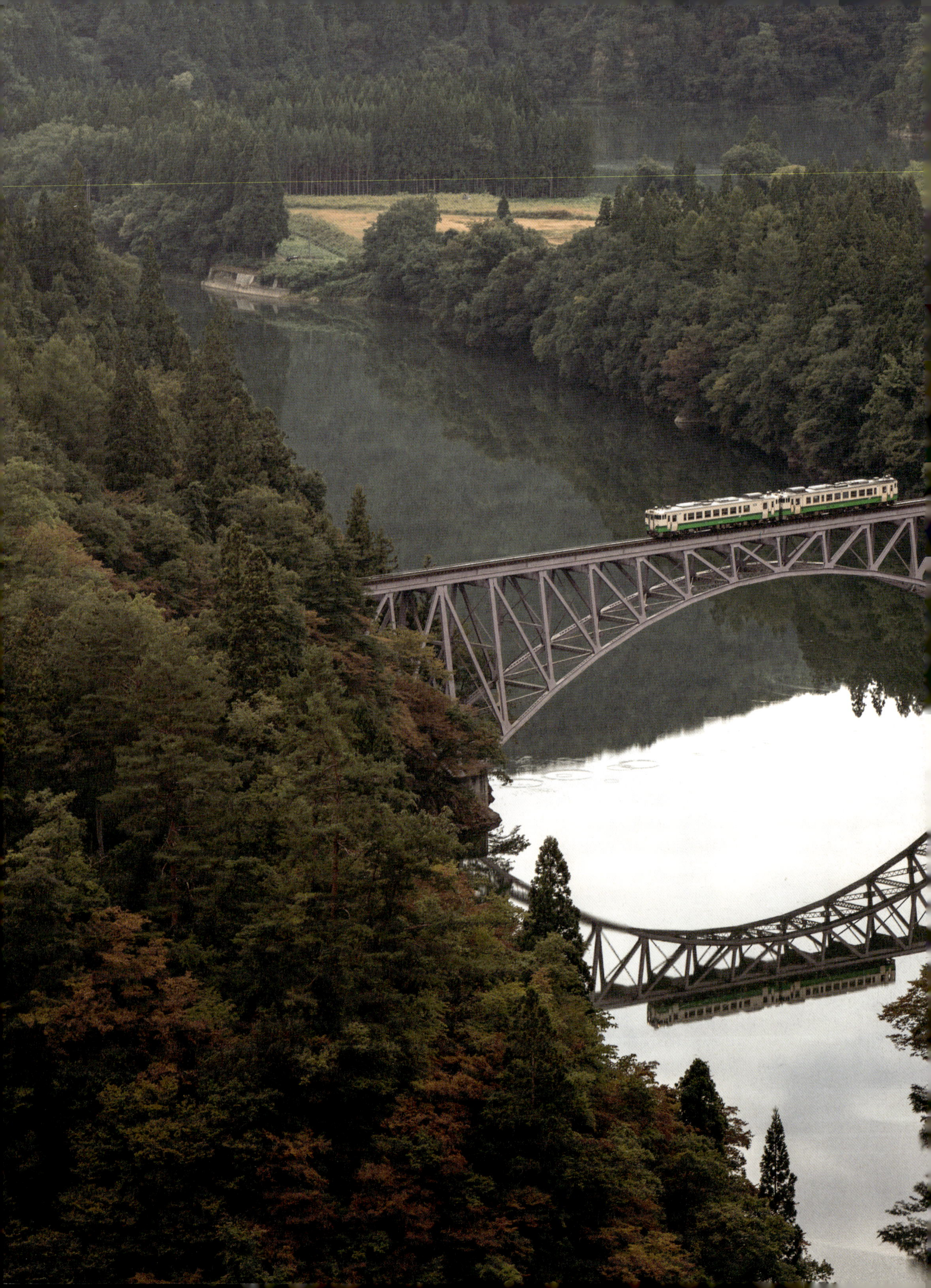

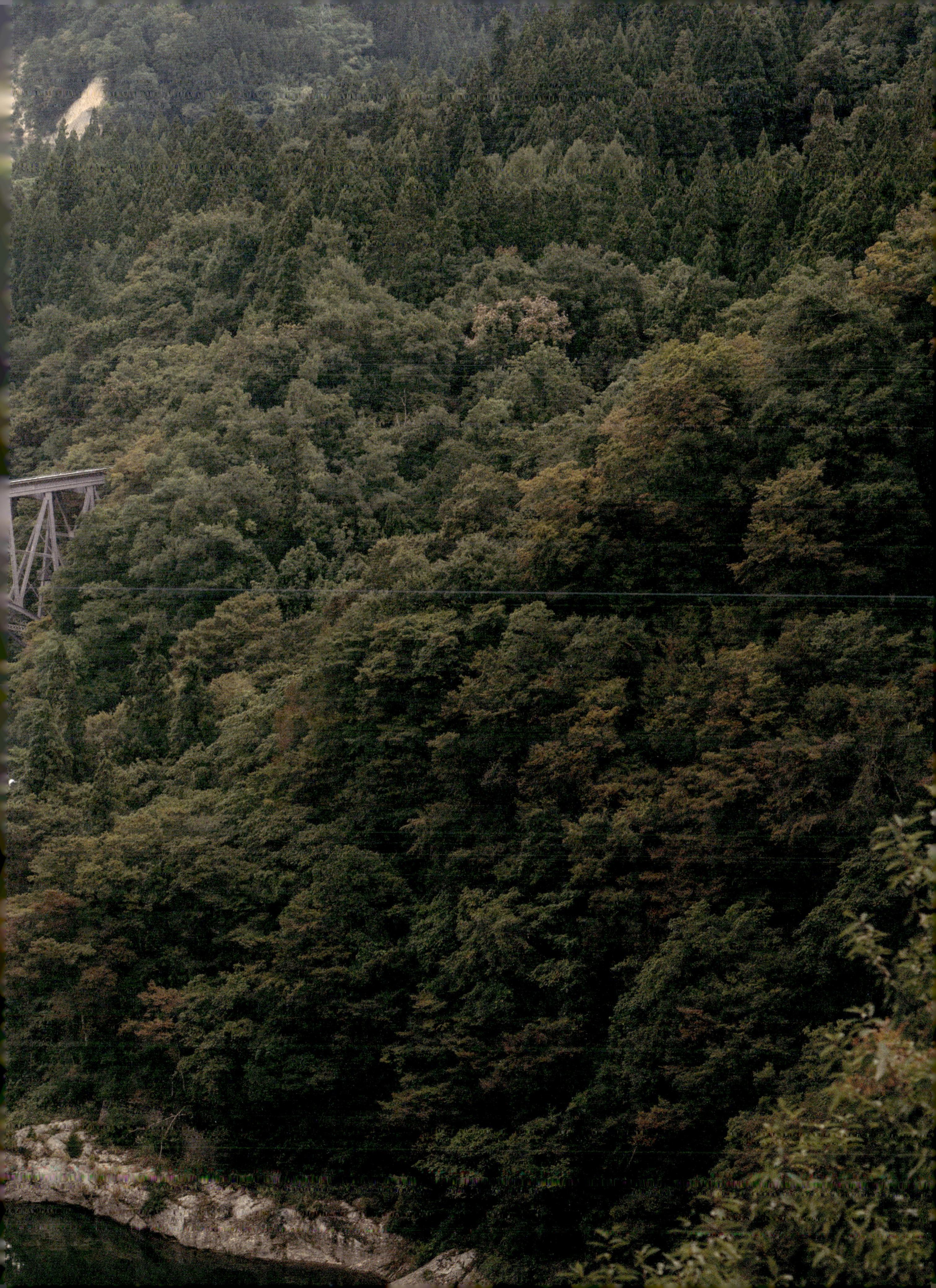

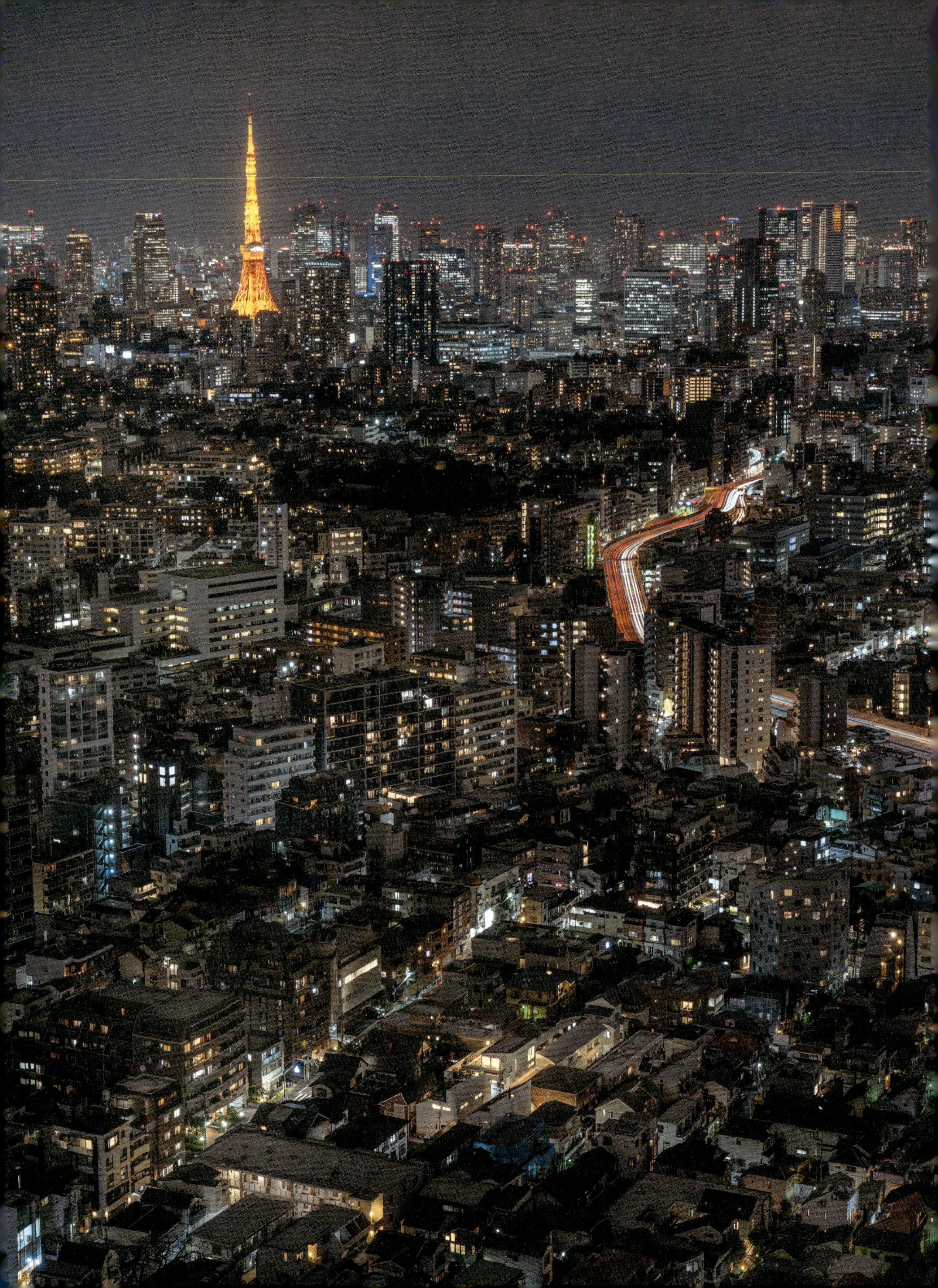

View of Tokyo.
A sea of lights stretches to the horizon, outlining the endless expanse of the metropolis. At the heart of this sprawling urban landscape. Tokyo Tower rises dramatically, its red and orange lights bursting into the night and dominating the cityscape from its lofty perch.

関東
Kantō
A Blend of History and Modernity

Situated on the main island of Honshū, the Kantō region is a place where the past and present intertwine, balancing ancient traditions with bold innovations. As the beating heart of Japan, it spans approximately 32,000 square kilometres and includes seven prefectures: Tokyo, Kanagawa, Saitama, Chiba, Gunma, Tochigi, and Ibaraki. This vast area offers a rich variety of landscapes, from fertile plains and Pacific coastlines to towering mountains.

Area.
Kantō spans roughly 70,821 km², accounting for 18.7% of Japan's total area.

Demographics and Population.
The region is home to approximately 52 million people, accounting for about 41% of Japan's population. The average population density is 733 people per km², with a higher concentration in Tokyo, Kanagawa, Saitama, and Chiba prefectures.

Geographical Location.
Kantō is bordered by the Pacific Ocean to the east and comprises seven prefectures: Tokyo, Chiba, Kanagawa, Saitama, Gunma, Tochigi, and Ibaraki. The region features vast plains, notably the Kantō Plain, surrounded by mountains to the west and north.

Climate and Seasons.
The climate of Kantō is temperate, with hot and humid summers alongside cool, dry winters. The region experiences a rainy season in June and is susceptible to typhoons in September and October. Springs are pleasant, showcasing cherry blossoms in full bloom, while autumn brings mild temperatures and colourful foliage.

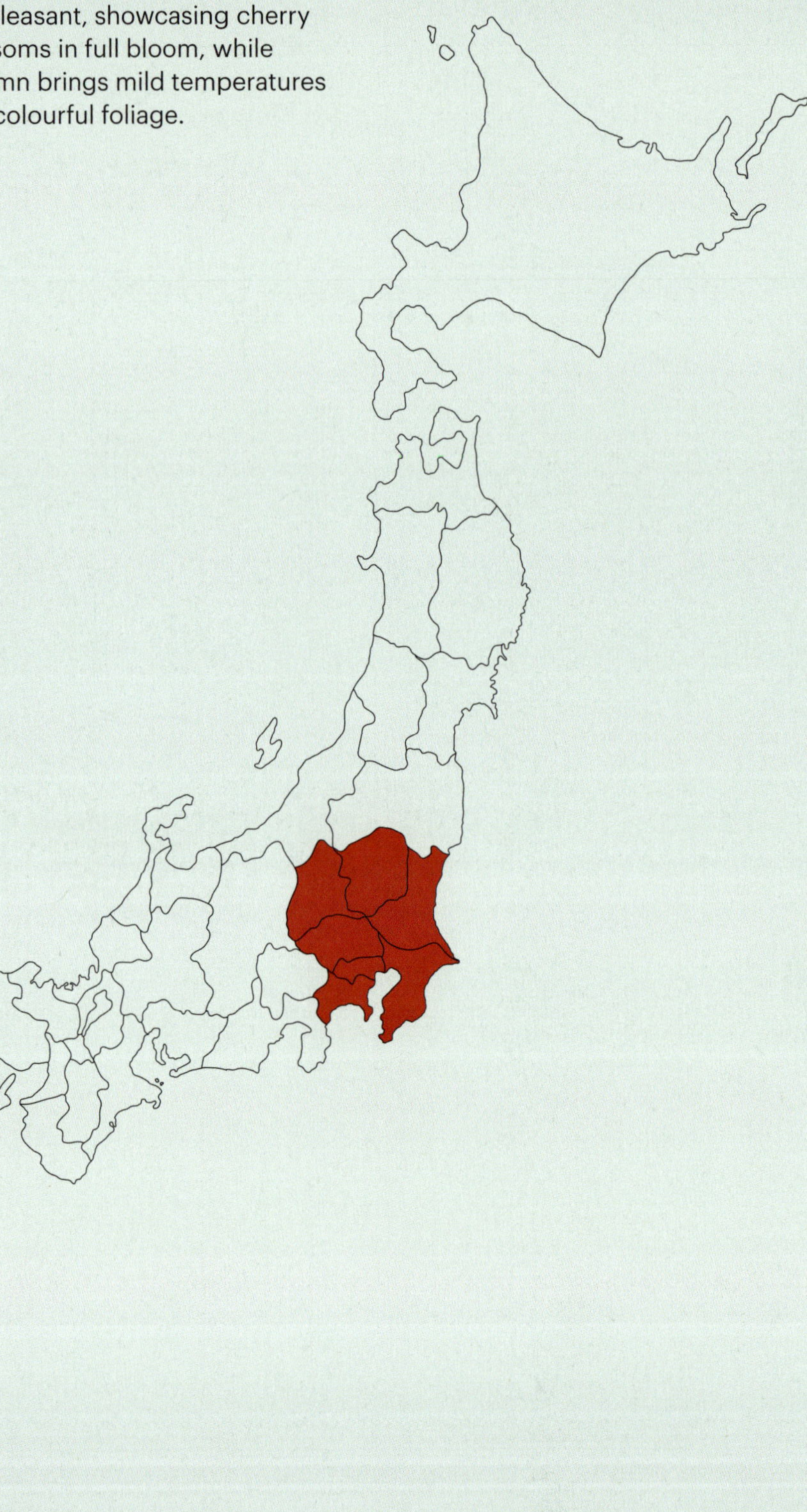

Tokyo, The capital of Infinite Possibilities

Tokyo, the vibrant heart of Kantō, is a city of striking contrasts. Its various neighbourhoods throb with unique energy, each showcasing a distinct aspect of Japanese culture. In Shinjuku, the neon lights of towering skyscrapers and the bustle of shopping streets contrast sharply with the serenity of Shinjuku Gyoen National Garden, where cherry blossoms draw crowds each spring. Shibuya, with its iconic crossing, epitomises urban vibrancy, while Harajuku serves as a mecca for fashion and unbridled creativity.

In Asakusa, the *Sensō-ji* temple, Tokyo's oldest, stands proudly in a traditional setting, surrounded by cobblestone streets lined with shops selling handcrafted souvenirs and treats like *dorayaki*. Akihabara, known as the "Electric Town", is a haven for manga, anime, and gadget enthusiasts. Not far off, the Tokyo Tower and Tokyo Skytree stand as bold symbols of the technological ambition behind this sprawling metropolis.

Kanagawa and its thousand Faces

To the south of Tokyo, Yokohama, Japan's second-largest city, seamlessly blends historical heritage with cosmopolitan modernity. Its *Minato Mirai 21* district is a futuristic hub lined with skyscrapers, museums, and shopping malls, including the iconic Landmark Tower. The *Cosmo Clock 21* Ferris wheel illuminates the night with its ever-changing colours.

Yokohama's Chinatown, one of the largest in the world, is a vibrant area filled with restaurants serving such Chinese delicacies as dim sum. Conversely, *Sankei-en Garden* offers a peaceful green retreat, where historic buildings, relocated from across Japan, stand among tranquil ponds and cherry trees.

Just a few kilometres from Yokohama, Kamakura is a city steeped in spirituality. Once the capital of the shogunate, it is renowned for its bronze Great Buddha (*Daibutsu*), sitting majestically in the open air. The city is dominated by the *Tsurugaoka Hachiman-gū* shrine, dedicated to the protective deity of the samurai.

Hiking enthusiasts will relish the trails that wind around Kamakura, connecting temples like *Hasedera*, famous for its sea views and statues of *Kannon*, the goddess of compassion. The region's beaches, such as Yuigahama, also draw sunbathers and surfers.

Nestled in the mountains, Hakone is a must-visit destination renowned for its *onsen* (hot springs) and breathtaking views of Mount Fuji. *Lake Ashi*, frequently shrouded in mist, offers serene boat cruises aboard pirate-themed vessels.

Hakone's open-air museum is a delight for art enthusiasts, seamlessly blending contemporary sculptures with the natural landscape. The hot springs of Ōwakudani Valley, with their sulphurous fumaroles, lend a dramatic atmosphere to the region's sensory richness.

Tochigi, A Sanctuary of Grandeur

In the northern part of Kantō, in Tochigi Prefecture, Nikkō is a must-see for its UNESCO World Heritage treasures. The Nikkō Tōshōgū Shrine, dedicated to the shogun Tokugawa Ieyasu, is an architectural masterpiece, adorned with intricate carvings and gold leaf detailing.

Nikko's landscapes are equally breathtaking. The Kegon Falls cascade into Lake Chūzenji, offering a spectacular sight, particularly in autumn when the maple trees blaze in shades of red and gold. The Shinkyō Bridge, spanning the Daiya River, is an iconic symbol of this mystical region.

The Wonders of Ibaraki

Ibaraki Prefecture is often overlooked by visitors; however, it boasts a wealth of natural and cultural treasures. Hitachi Seaside Park is a truly magical place where millions of flowers, such as blue *nemophila* in spring and red *kochia* in autumn, transform the landscape into a vibrant sea of colour.

The Kashima Shrine, one of Japan's oldest Shinto shrines, is a testament to the region's spiritual history. Meanwhile, the wave-swept cliffs of Ōarai provide a dramatic and breathtaking sight for nature lovers.

Gunma and its Soothing Mountains

Gunma is renowned for its *onsen*, with *Kusatsu* arguably being Japan's most famous hot spring resort. The Yubatake spring, meaning "hot water field", is a striking central basin where thermal water bubbles up in a truly unique setting.

The region is also a hiker's paradise, with peaks like Mount Akagi and scenic spots such as Gunma Flower Park offering plenty of opportunities to explore and enjoy nature.

Chiba, Where Land Meets Sea

Chiba, which borders the Pacific Ocean, is a prefecture where nature seamlessly merges with modern attractions. Tokyo Disneyland and DisneySea, situated in Urayasu, attract millions of visitors each year. The Bōsō Peninsula features stunning coastal scenery and charming fishing villages that preserve their authenticity.

The Chōshi Fish Market is a must-visit for anyone wanting to sample the freshest produce, while the Naritasan Shinshōji Temple, located near Narita Airport, offers a peaceful sanctuary for travellers seeking tranquillity.

Saitama and its Hidden Treasures

Often overshadowed by its neighbours, Saitama still boasts a wealth of fascinating sites. The Saitama Railway Museum is a paradise for train enthusiasts, showcasing the rich history of Japan's railways.

Kawagoe, affectionately known as "Little Edo", captivates visitors with its traditional architecture and streets lined with buildings dating back to the Edo period. The 2,000-year-old Hikawa Shrine serves as a spiritual site steeped in mystery and history.

Best Times to Visit

– Spring (Mars to May).
Cherry blossoms create stunning landscapes and offer comfortable Temperatures.

– Autumn (September to November).
Perfect for admiring colourful autumn leaves and benefiting from a milder climat.

Top 5 Places to Visit

1. Tokyo.
Japan's capital offers a multitude of attractions, from bustling districts like Shibuya and Shinjuku to historic temples such as Sensō-ji in Asakusa.

2. Kamakura.
A coastal city famous for its Great Buddha and numerous temples and shrines.

3. Nikkō.
UNESCO World Heritage Site, famous for the Toshogu Shrine and its mountainous landscapes.

4. Hakone.
Popular for its *onsen*, views of Mount Fuji and Lake Ashi.

5. Yokohama.
Large port city with its China-town, futuristic Minato Mirai district and Sankei-en gardens.

関東

Gastronomy

The Kantō region is the most populous area in Japan and includes the capital, Tokyo. Each city boasts its unique culinary specialities, shaped by history, culture, and local produce. Here is a list of Kantō's specialities, organised by city, with detailed descriptions.

東京
Tokyo

[江戸前寿司]
Edomae Sushi
Edomae sushi originated in Tokyo during the Edo period. Originally, fish was marinated or cooked to extend its shelf life. Today, it refers to Tokyo's traditional sushi style, often made with tuna, eel, shrimp, or scallops.

[もんじゃ焼き]
Monjayaki
A more liquid version of *okonomiyaki*, where the batter is mixed with vegetables and various ingredients (seafood, cheese, meat). It is cooked on a hot plate and eaten directly with a small spatula. The Tsukishima district is renowned for its *monjayaki* restaurants.

[ちゃんこ鍋]
Chanko Nabe
A stew consumed by sumo wrestlers to gain weight. It includes chicken, tofu, vegetables, and noodles and is often served in the *heya* (sumo stables).

[深川めし]
Fukagawa Meshi
A bowl of rice topped with clams cooked in a miso broth. This dish was once a simple and nourishing meal for fishermen in Tokyo Bay.

横浜
Yokohama

[焼売]
Shūmai
Yokohama's *shūmai* are steamed dumplings inspired by Chinese cuisine, often filled with pork and onions. They are a staple in Yokohama's Chinatown (Chūkagai).

[サンマーメン]
Sanma-men
A local rāmen with a clear soy sauce-based broth, topped with sautéed vegetables and starch to give it a slightly thickened texture.

[ナポリタン]
Napolitan
A dish of spaghetti sautéed with ketchup, onions, sausages, and mushrooms. It was invented in Yokohama after World War II, inspired by the pasta served to American soldiers.

鎌倉
Kamakura

[しらす丼]
Shirasu-don
A bowl of rice topped with shirasu (tiny white sardines) served either raw or lightly cooked. This dish highlights the freshness of locally caught seafood.

[鎌倉ほうじ茶]
Kamakura Hōjicha
A roasted green tea with a mild, smoky aroma, which is highly popular in Kamakura. It is often consumed with wagashi (traditional sweets).

川崎
Kawasaki

[川崎トマトラーメン]
Kawasaki Tomato Rāmen
A modern variation of rāmen with a tomato-based broth that offers a sweet and slightly tangy flavour.

[黒豚餃子]
Kuro Buta Gyoza
Gyoza filled with high-quality black pork, usually served grilled for a crispy texture.

千葉
Chiba

[なめろう]
Namero
A fisherman's dish made from chopped fish (usually mackerel) mixed with miso, ginger, and spring onions. It is often eaten with rice or shiso leaves.

[勝浦タンタンメン]
Katsuura Tantanmen
A spicy rāmen with a soy sauce-based broth, topped with sautéed onions and a generous amount of red chilli. Unlike Chinese *tantanmen*, it does not contain sesame paste.

[ピーナッツ最中]
Peanut Monaka
Monaka is a dessert made from a wafer filled with a sweet peanut paste. As Chiba is Japan's largest peanut producer, it is a local speciality.

埼玉
Saitama

[狭山茶]
Sayama Cha
A green tea produced in the Sayama region, known for its rich and slightly sweet flavour.

[川越芋]
Kawagoe Imo
Kawagoe sweet potatoes are used to make various desserts, such as *imo yokan* (sweet potato jelly) and *karinto* (crispy fried dough).

[浦和うなぎ]
Urawa Unagi
Grilled eel is a speciality of Urawa. It is prepared using the *kabayaki* method, where the eel is grilled and glazed with a sweet soy sauce and mirin mixture.

栃木
Tochigi

[宇都宮餃子]
Utsunomiya Gyoza
The city of Utsunomiya is famous for its *gyoza*, often served grilled, boiled, or fried. They are typically eaten with a vinegar and soy sauce-based dipping sauce.

[栃木いちご]
Tochigi Strawberry
Tochigi is Japan's leading strawberry producer. It is especially known for the "Tochiotome" variety, which is prized for its sweetness and juicy texture.

群馬
Gunma

[おっきりこみ]
Okkirikomi
A traditional dish where thick noodles are simmered with vegetables and miso, creating a rustic and hearty soup.

[群馬こんにゃく]
Gunma Konnyaku
Gunma is the largest producer of *konnyaku* (a jelly-like paste made from yam). It is often served on skewers with sweet miso sauce.

茨城
Ibaraki

[あんこう鍋]
Ankō Nabe
A stew made from anglerfish, a signature fish of Ibaraki. The anglerfish's tender flesh and creamy liver are simmered with vegetables and miso, creating a rich and flavourful soup.

[納豆]
Natto
Mito's natto is one of the most renowned in Japan. It consists of fermented soybeans with a sticky texture and a strong flavour, often consumed with rice and mustard.

Ōtaki Castle and Isumi Railway Line.
Rising proudly atop a hill, Ōtaki Castle stands as a majestic reminder of Japan's feudal past, its elegant silhouette dominating the landscape. Below, the Isumi railway line winds through tranquil rural scenery, connecting the towns of Isumi and Ōtaki.

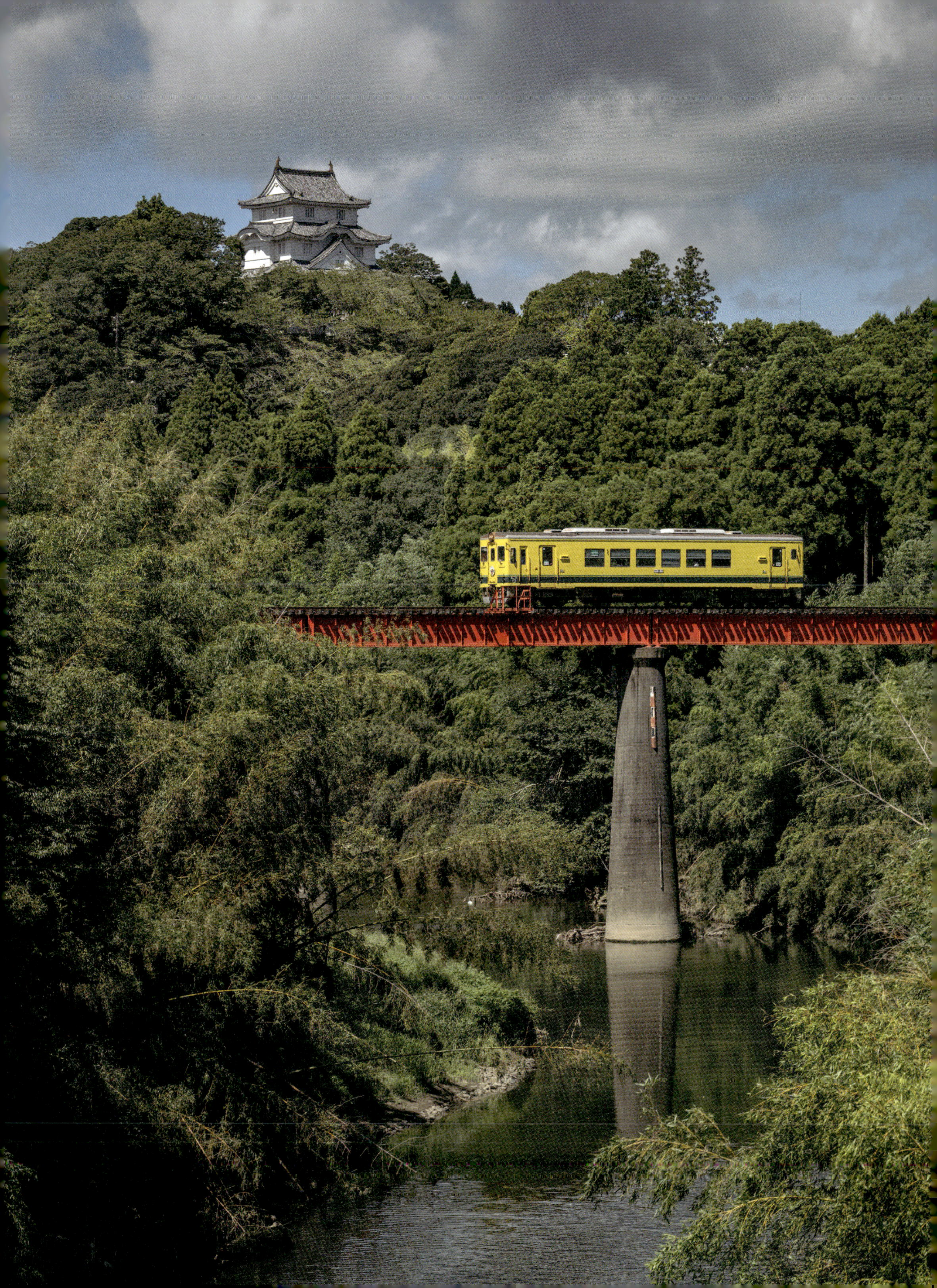

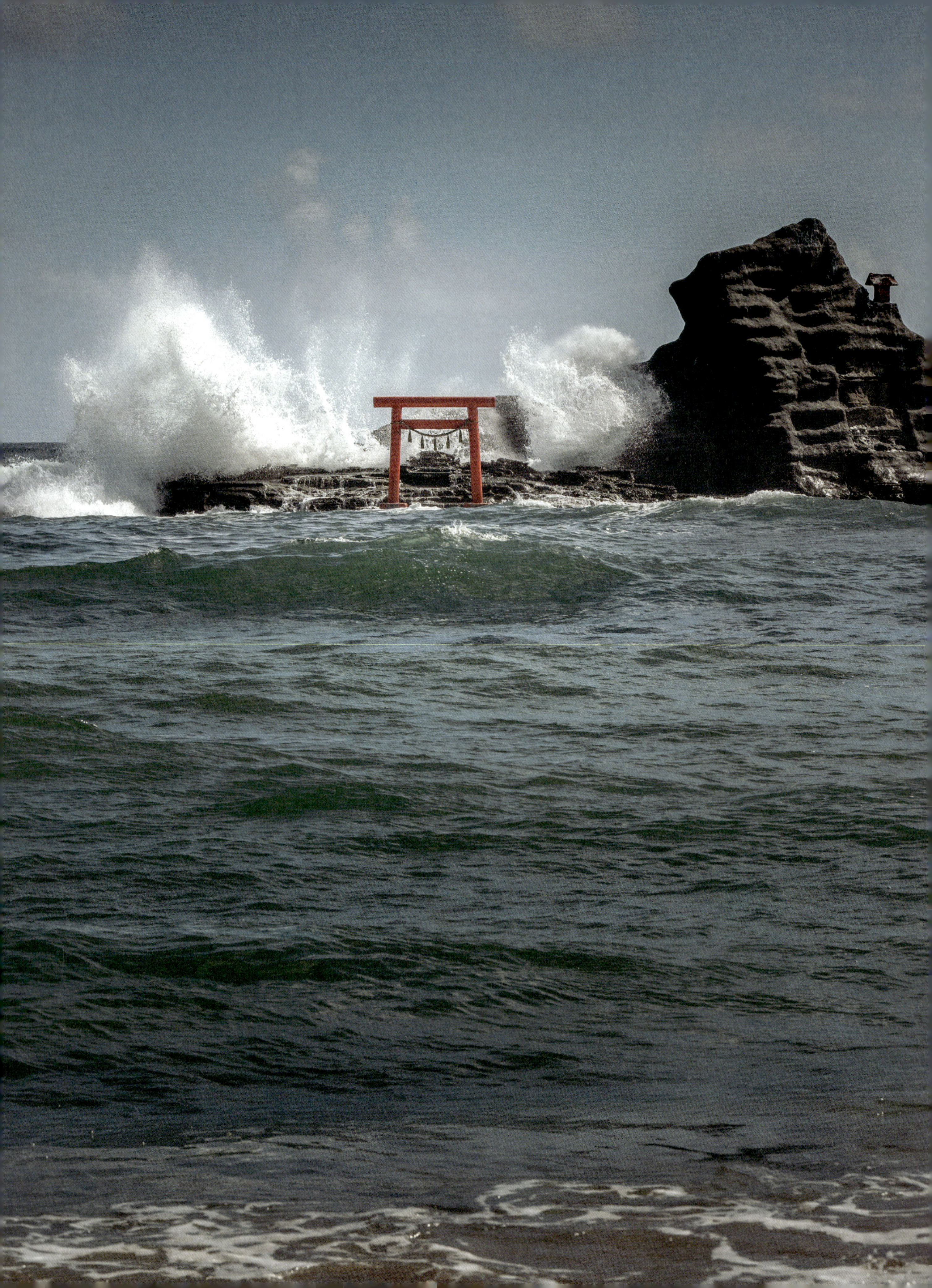

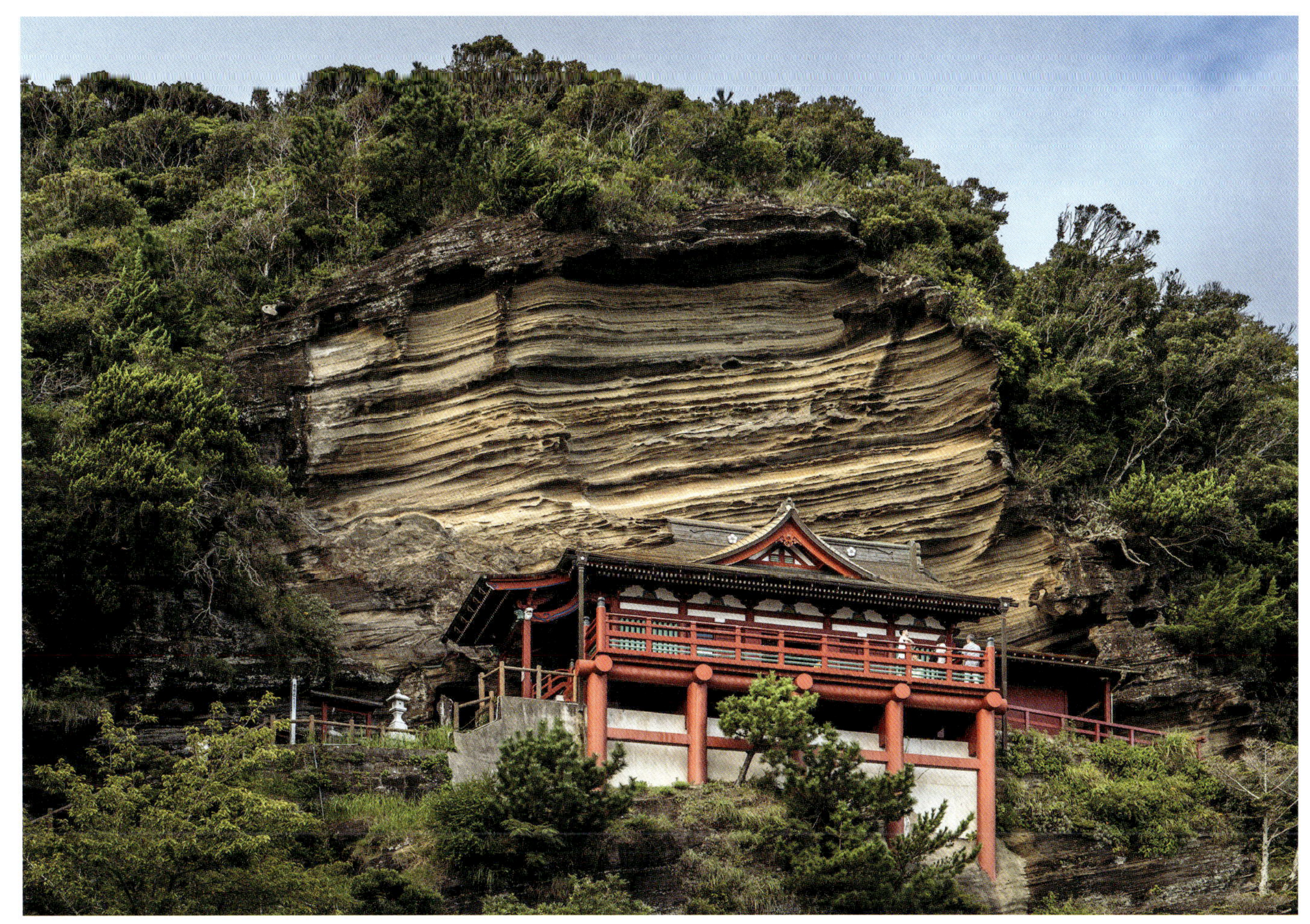

Gake Kannon Temple.
Perched dramatically on a steep cliff in Chiba Prefecture, the Gake Kannon Temple, founded in 711, captivates with its striking location and vibrant red architecture. Dedicated to the goddess Kannon, it provides a stunning panoramic view of the Pacific Ocean.

Wata Island.
Located off the coast of Chiba, Wata Island is a tranquil, isolated islet, notable for its striking red *torii* gate rising from the water.

Tokyo & Mount Fuji.
From the elevated vantage points above Tokyo, the vibrant Shinjuku district unfolds in a breathtaking panorama, where sleek skyscrapers dominate the skyline. In the distance, the iconic Mount Fuji stands majestically. >

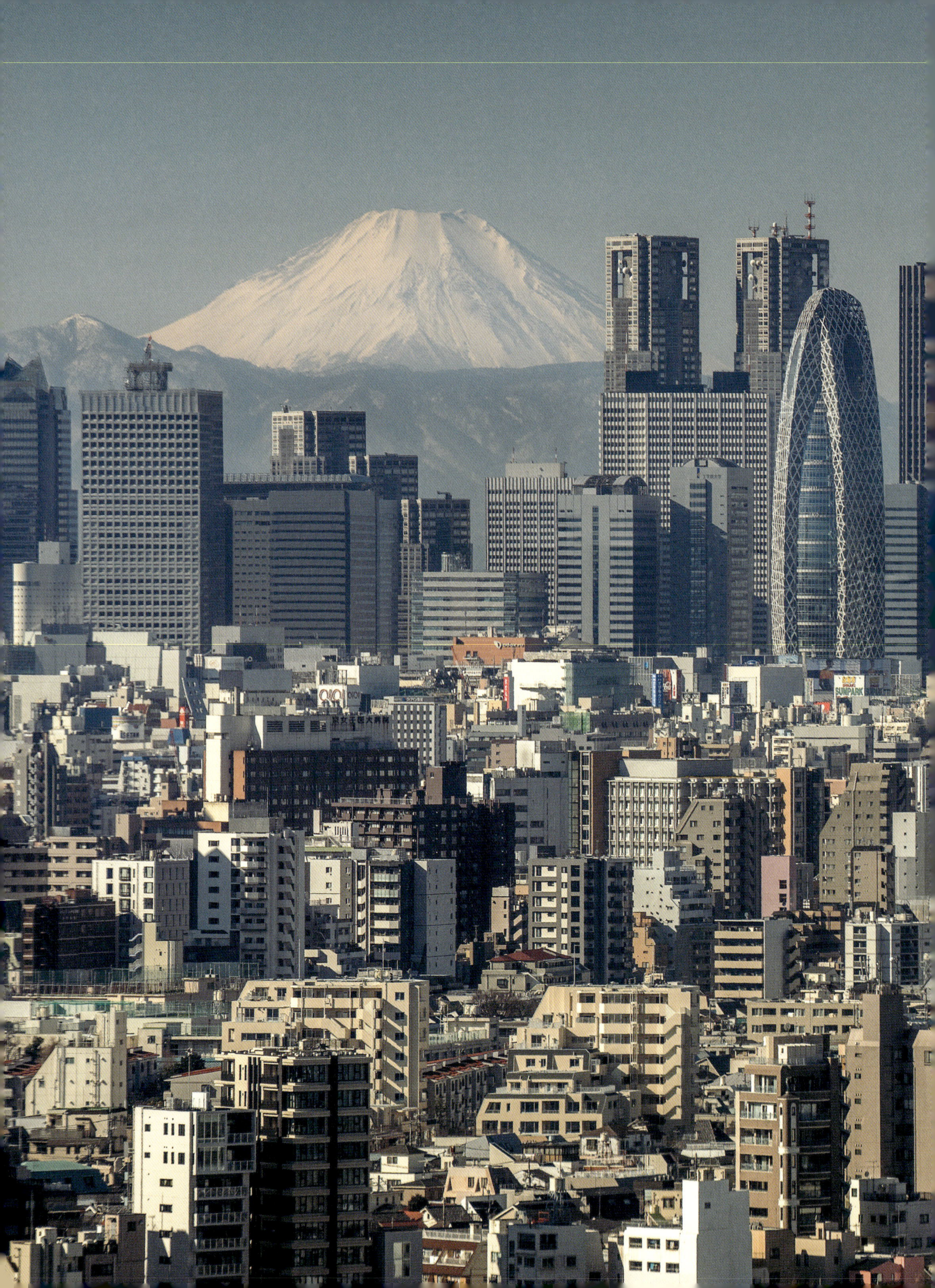

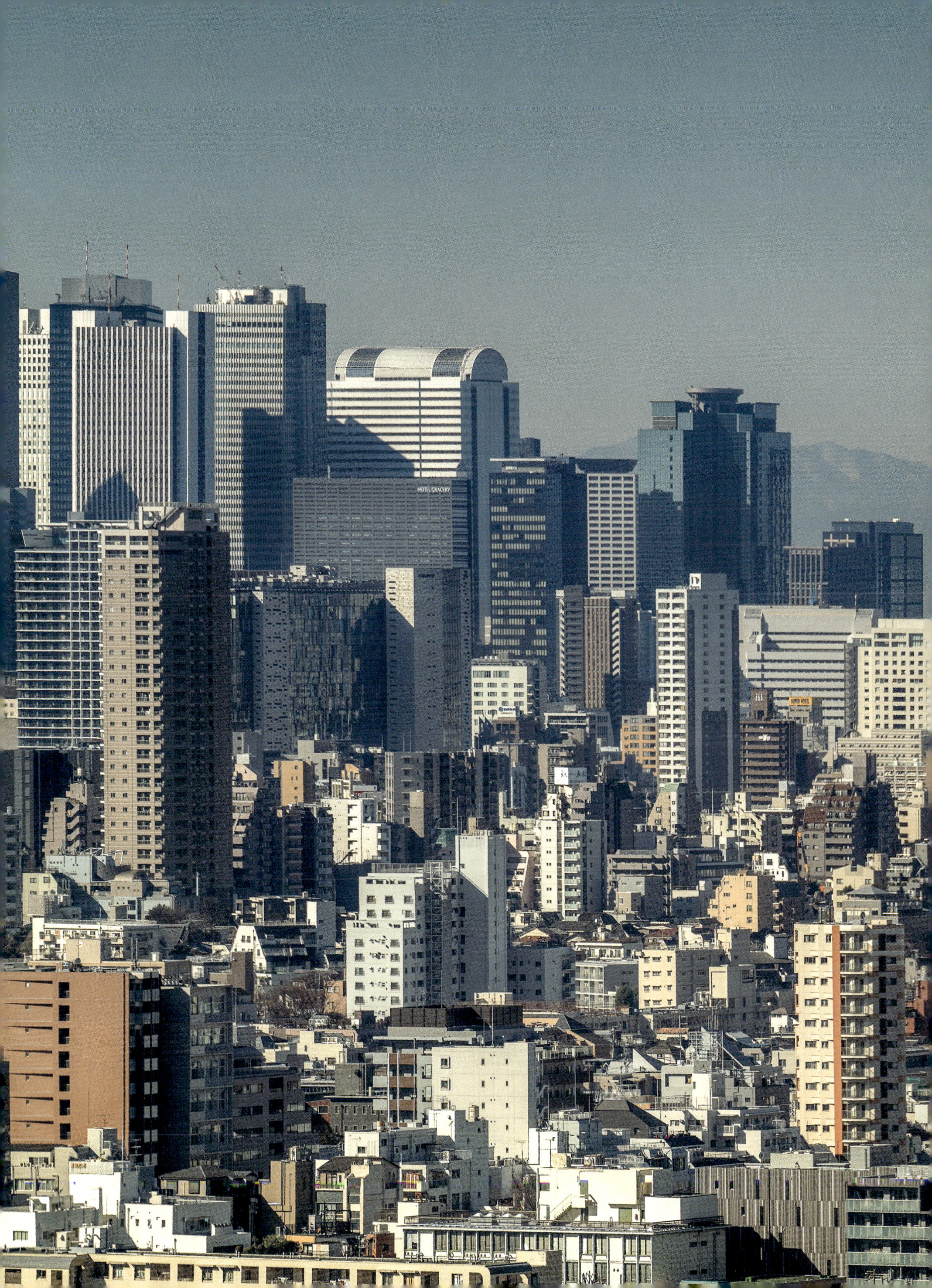
HOTEL GRACERY

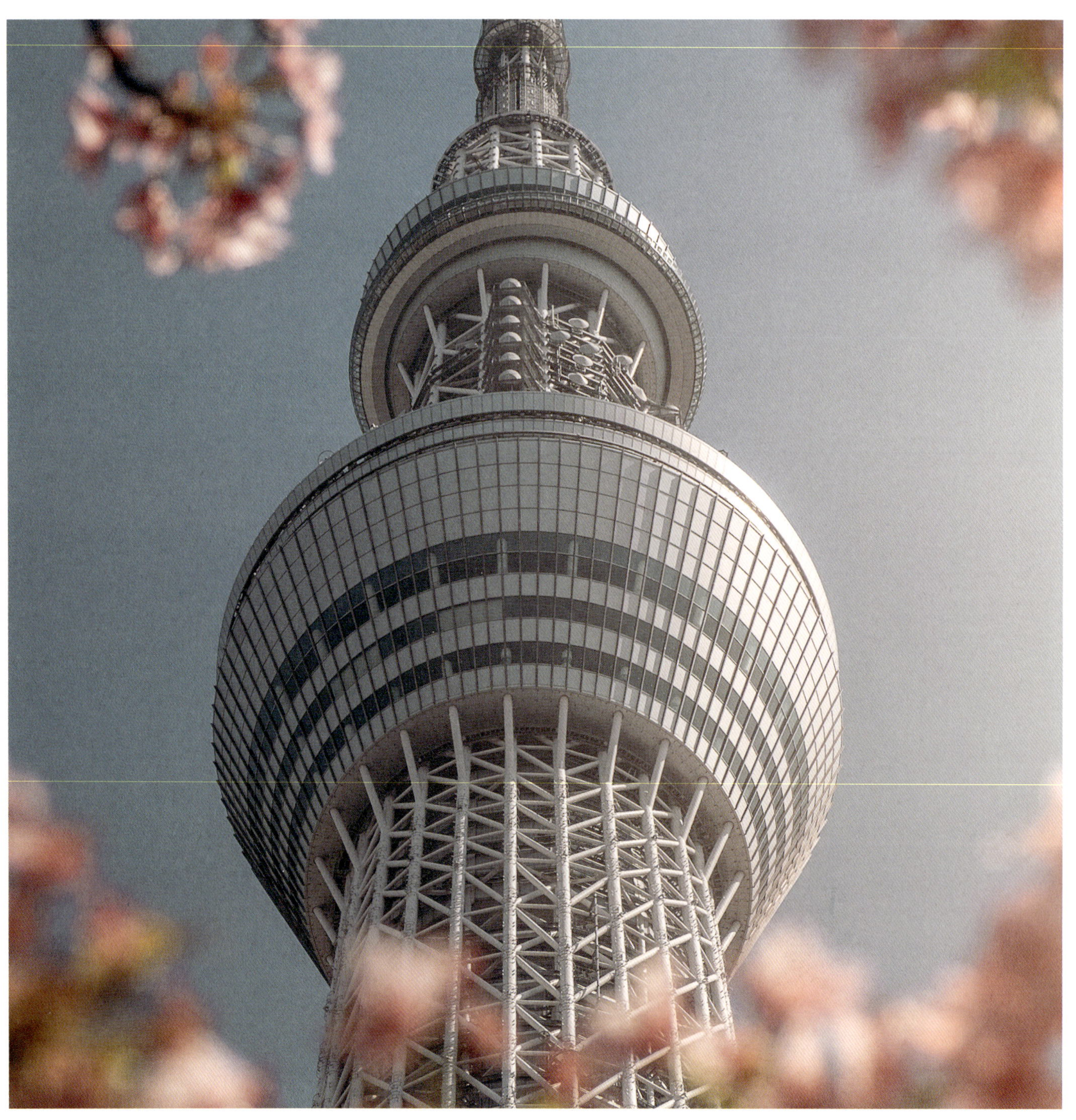

Tokyo Skytree.
Standing at 634 metres, the Tokyo Skytree is not only Japan's tallest tower but also an iconic symbol of the capital. With its futuristic design, stunning observation platforms that offer panoramic views, and a vibrant shopping mall, it has been one of Tokyo's top attractions since its grand opening in 2012.

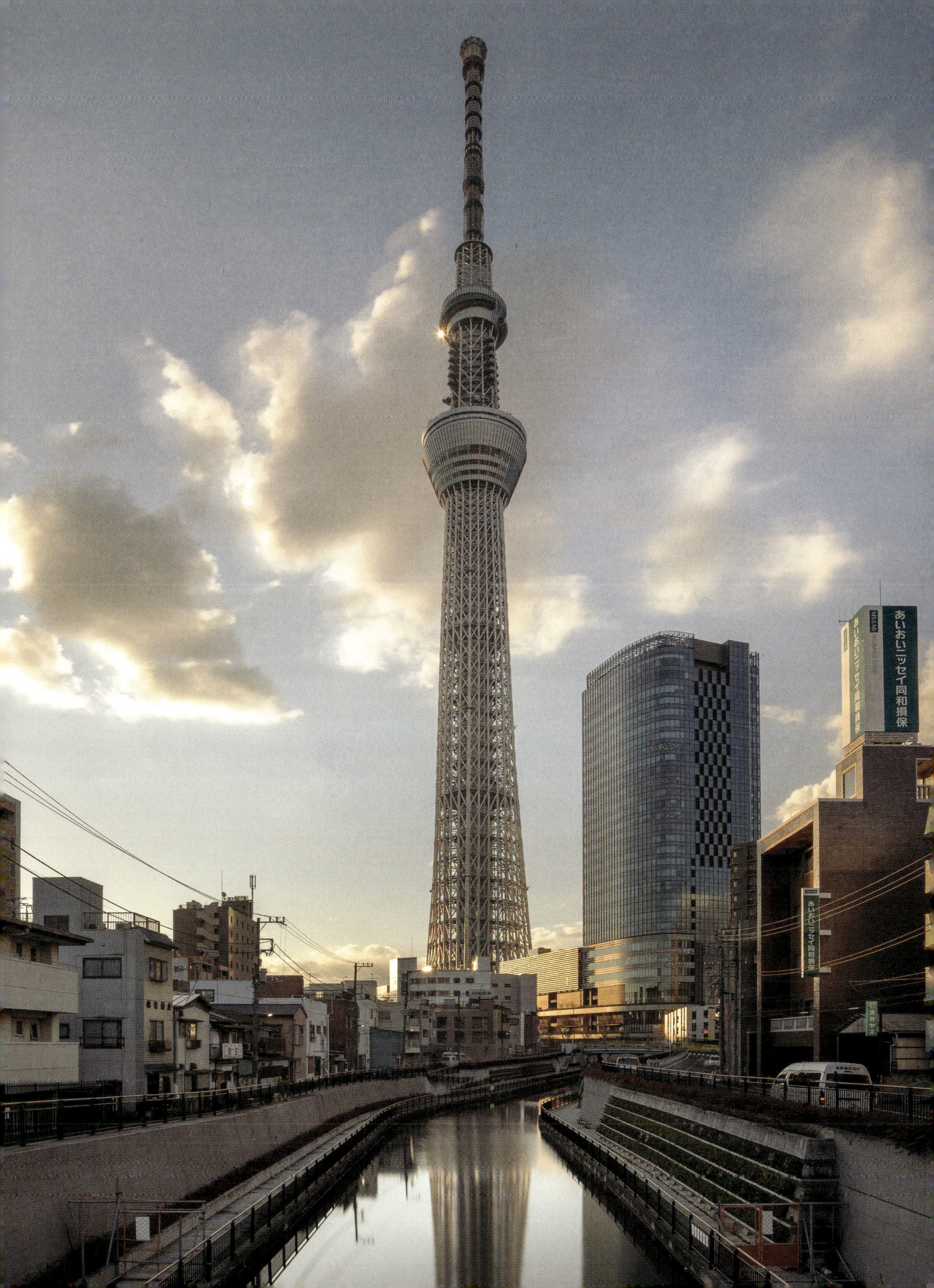

あいおいニッセイ同和損保

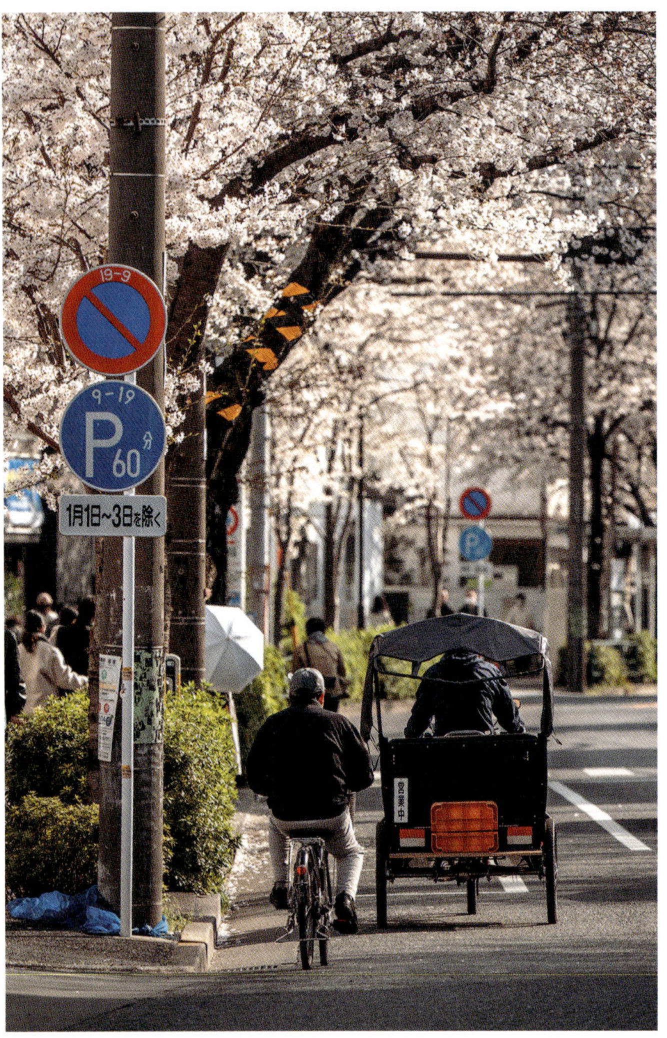

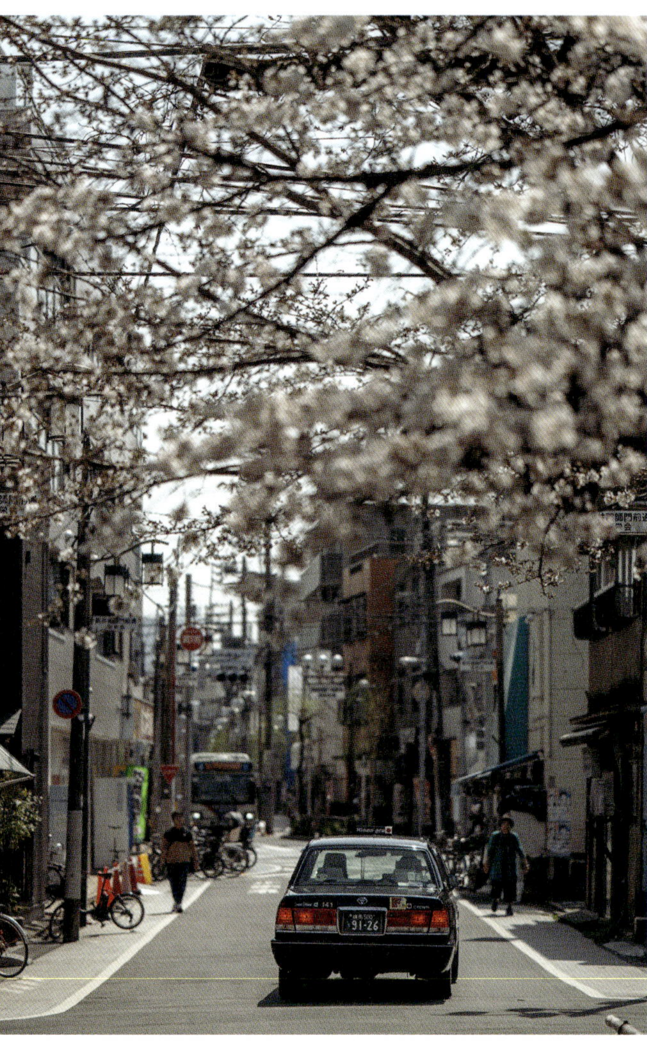

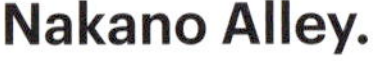

Nakano Alley.
Beneath a tunnel of cherry blossoms, a narrow lane in Tokyo comes to life at a gentle pace, with passing cyclists and traditional rickshaws contributing to its quiet charm.

Nakano.
Beneath blooming cherry trees, a classic black Tokyo taxi drives along a quiet street in Nakano. With parked bicycles and modest facades, the scene embodies the understated charm of everyday local life.

View of Nakano Rooftops and Shinjuku.
From the bustling Nakano district's rooftops, the night-time view unveils the distinctive glass roofs of Nakano Broadway, a shopping haven known for its anime, manga, and Japanese pop culture boutiques. In the distance, the illuminated towers of Shinjuku rise, providing a dazzling backdrop to the scene.

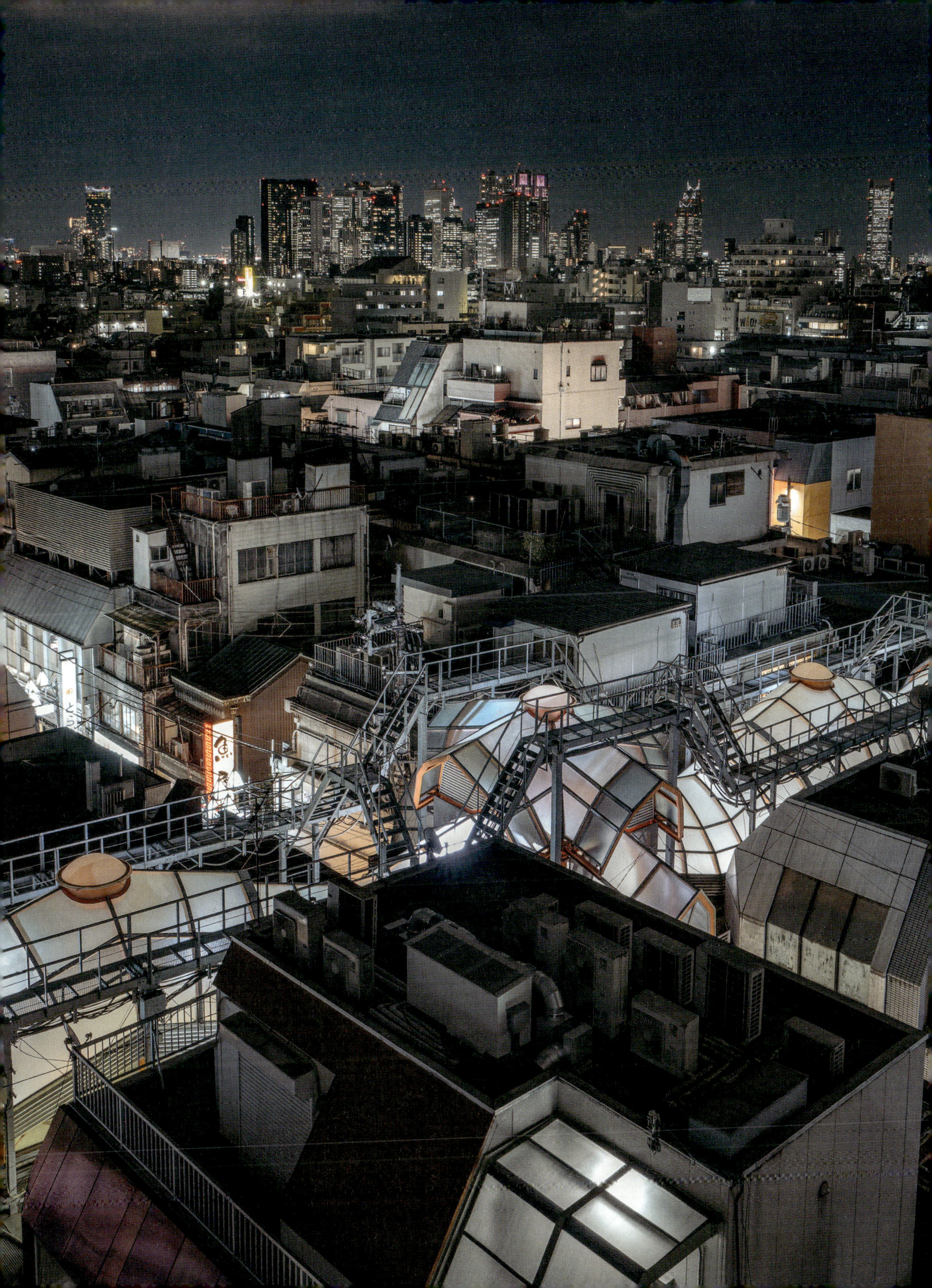

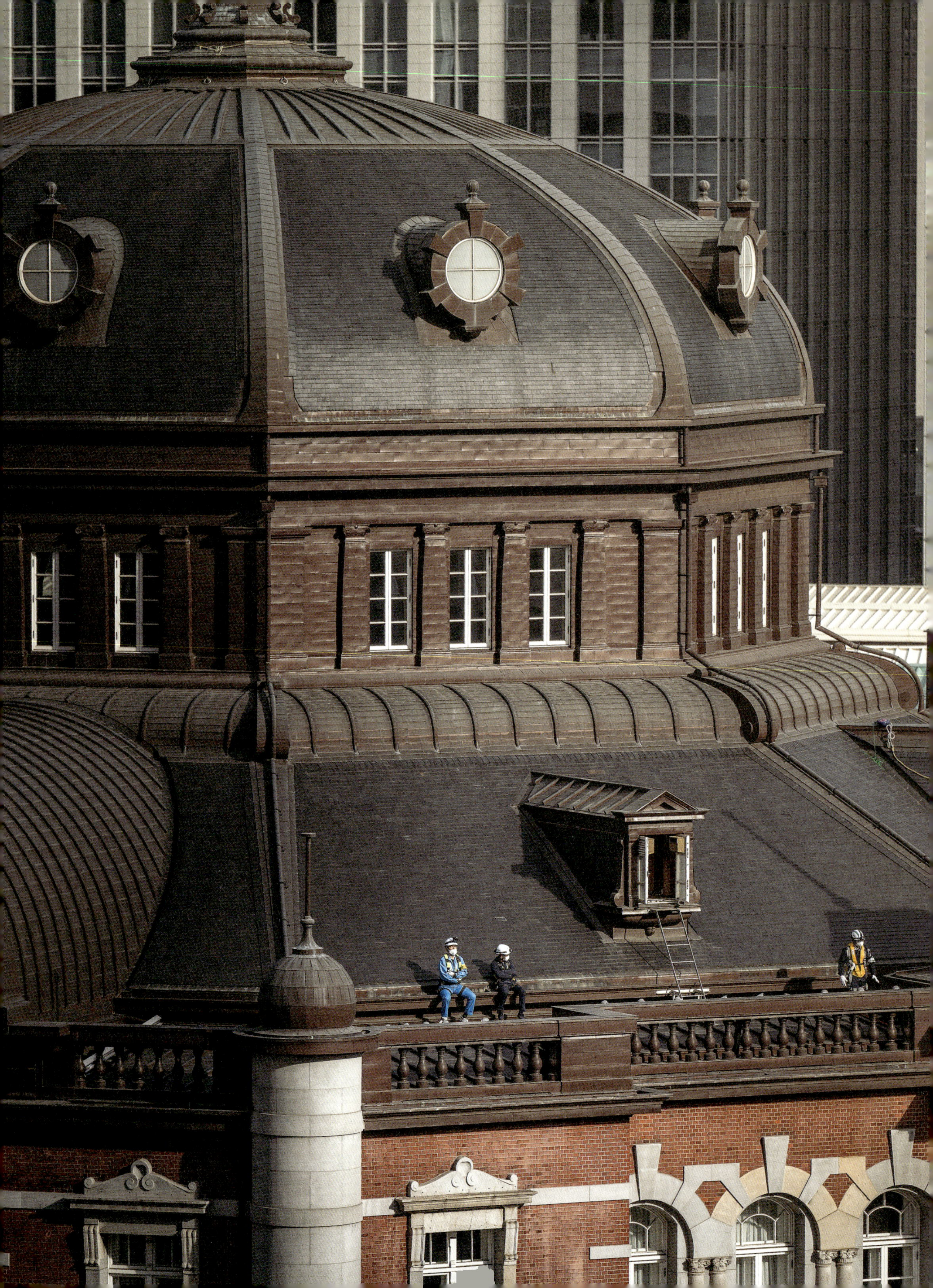

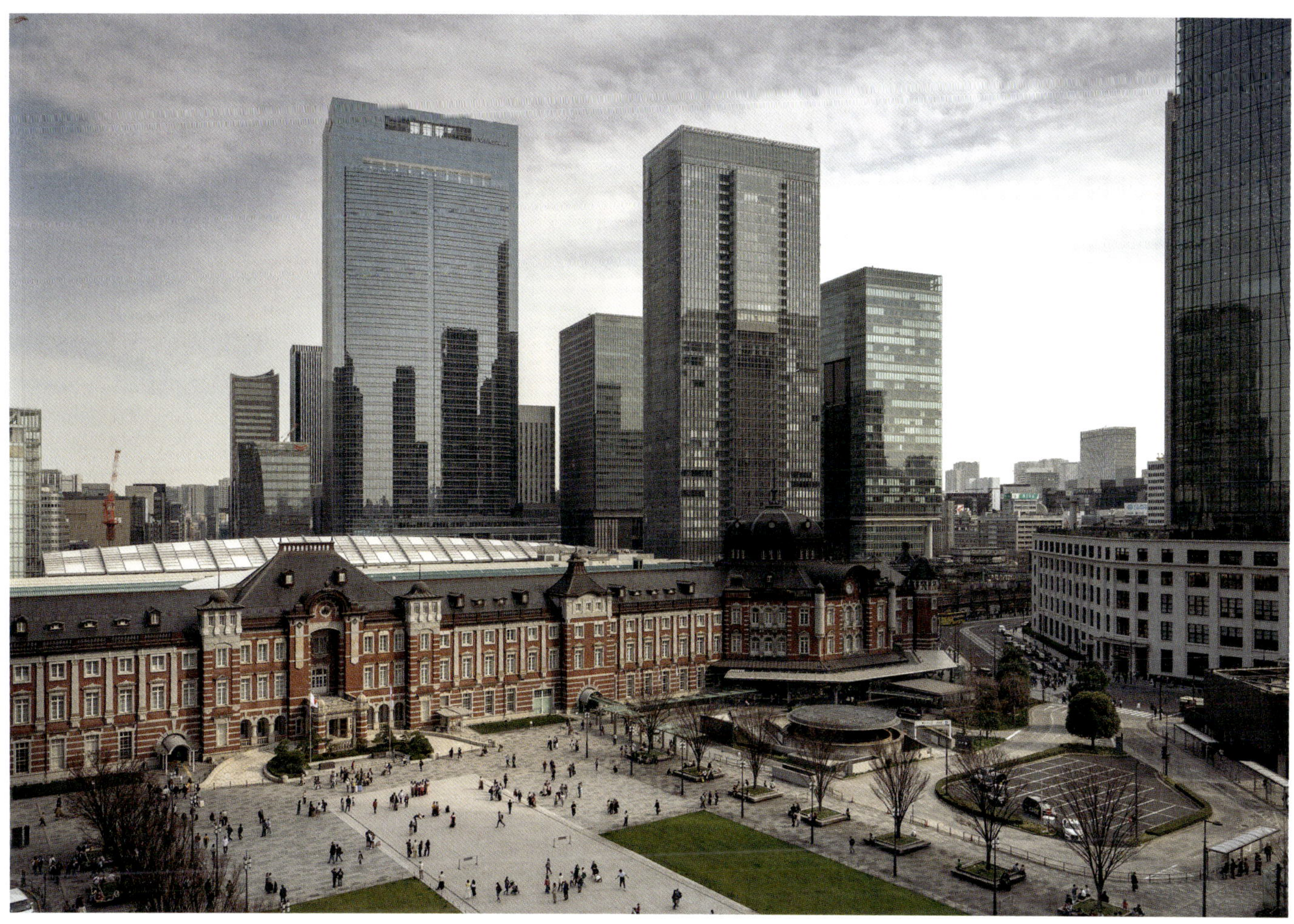

Tokyo Station.
Opened in 1914 in the Marunouchi district, Tokyo Station is a major rail hub that connects the capital to the rest of Japan via the Shinkansen. Its stately red-brick facade was meticulously restored following wartime damage.

Soho Building.
Located in the futuristic Odaiba district of Tokyo, the Soho Building is an iconic structure boasting vibrant and colourful architecture. Known for its striking multi-coloured facades and dynamic workspaces, it embodies the innovation and modern energy of this man-made island. It is a unique hub that attracts artists, start-ups, and curious visitors alike. >

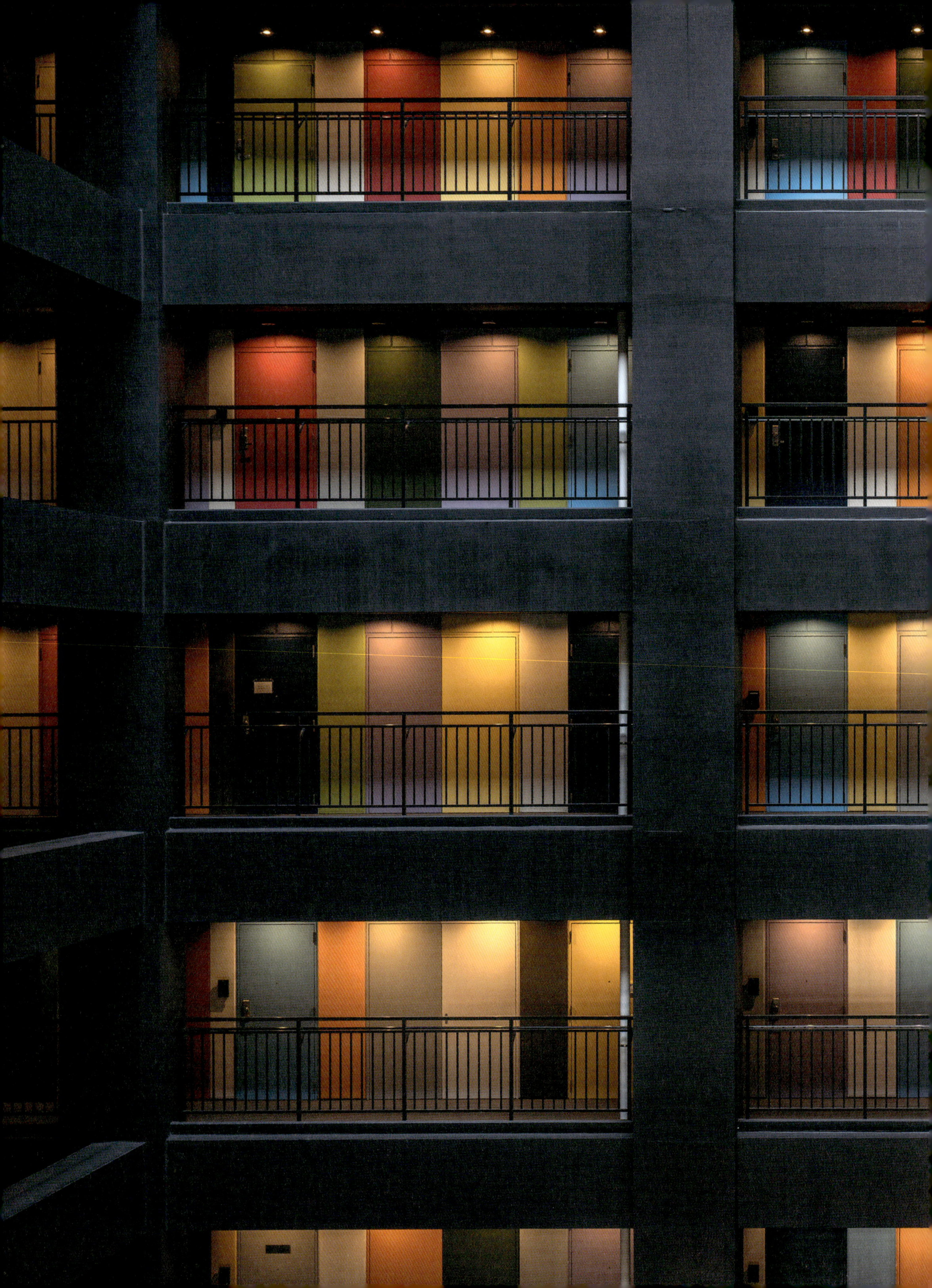

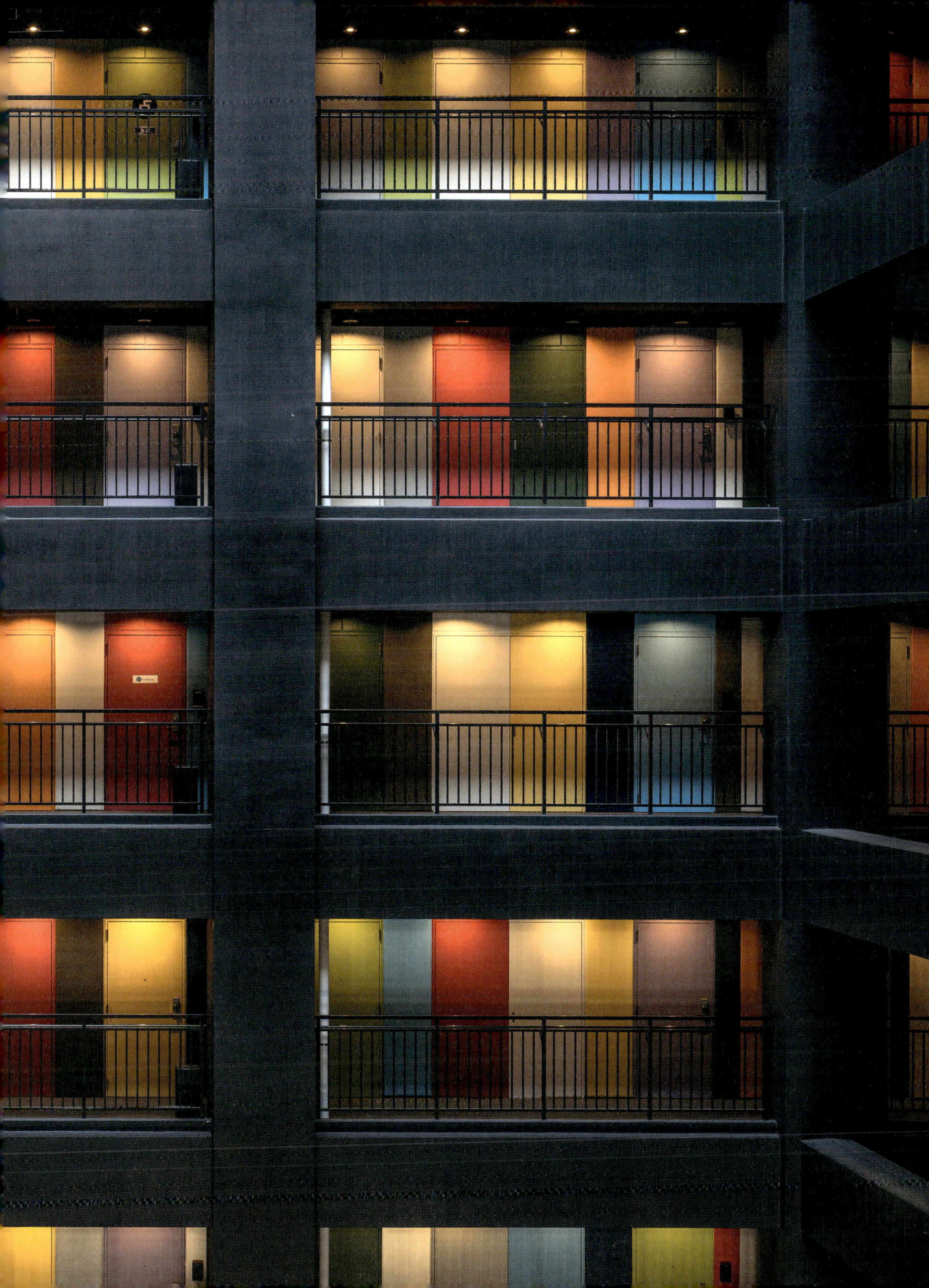

Tokyo & Shinjuku.
From the observation deck of the Bunkyo Civic Centre, Tokyo unfolds like an ocean of buildings, crowned by the skyscrapers of Shinjuku.

Aerial View of Shinjuku.
The beating heart of Tokyo, Shinjuku reveals its striking forest of skyscrapers in this aerial shot. In the distance, Shinjuku Gyoen Park emerges as a green oasis in a sea of urban energy.

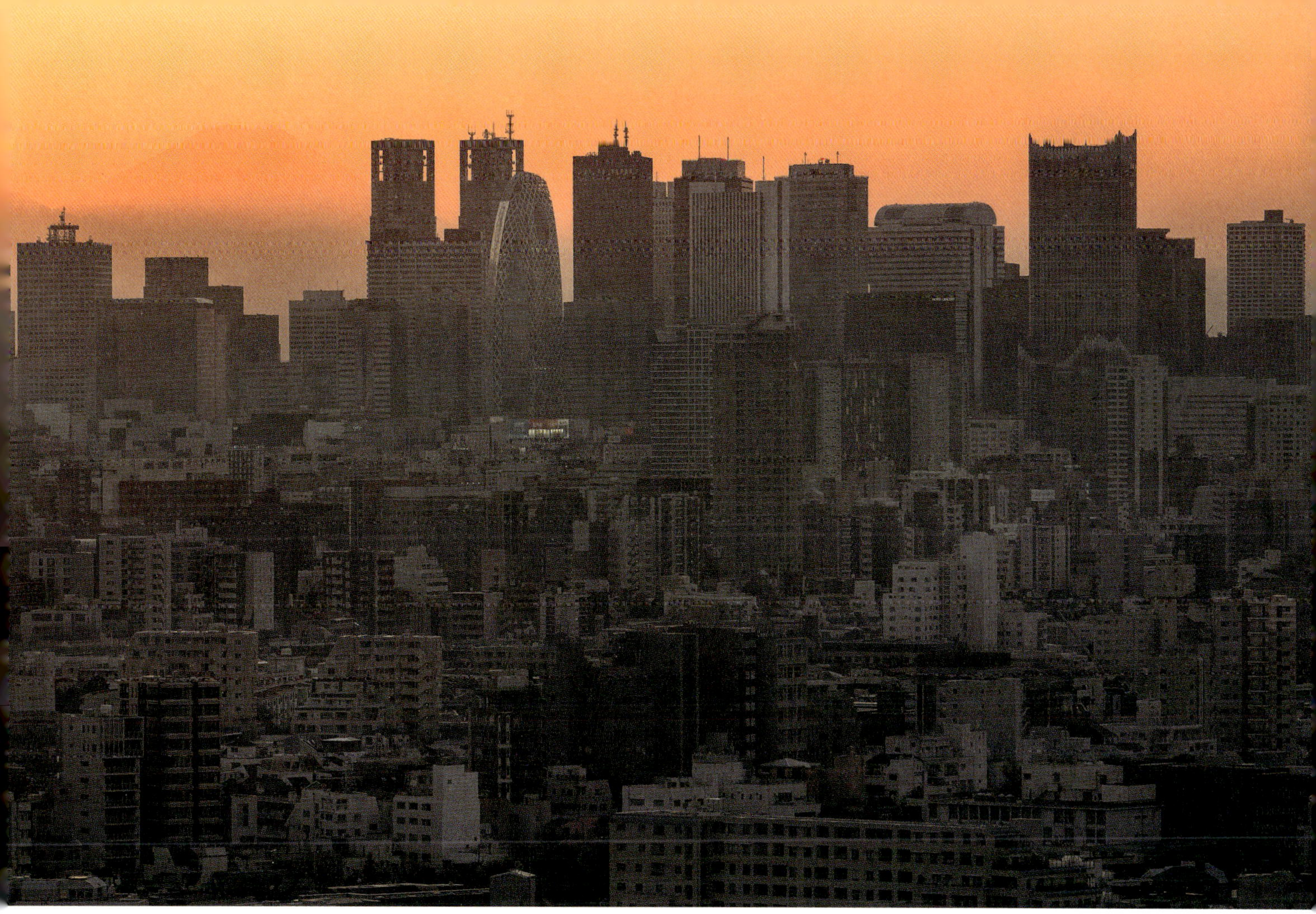

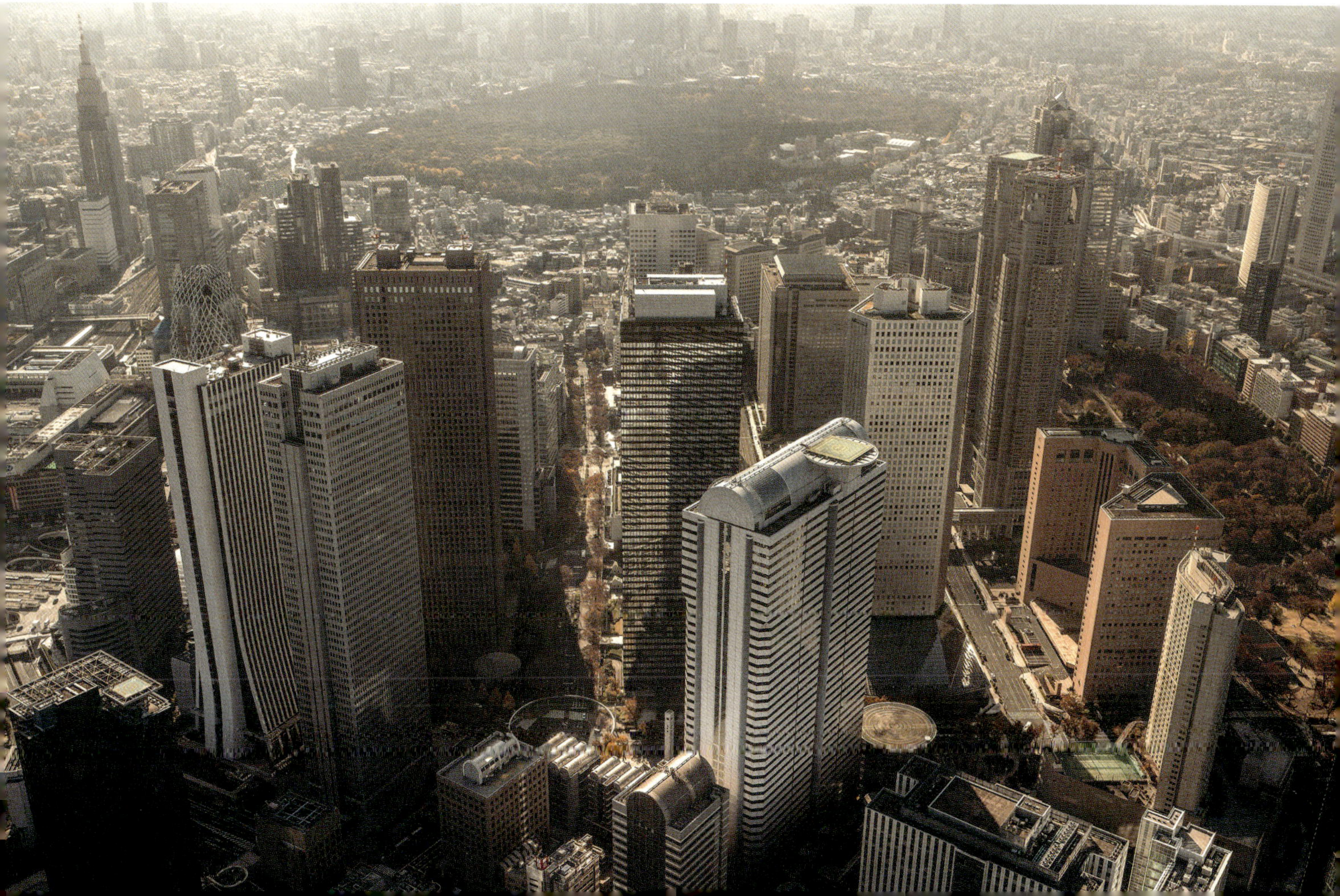

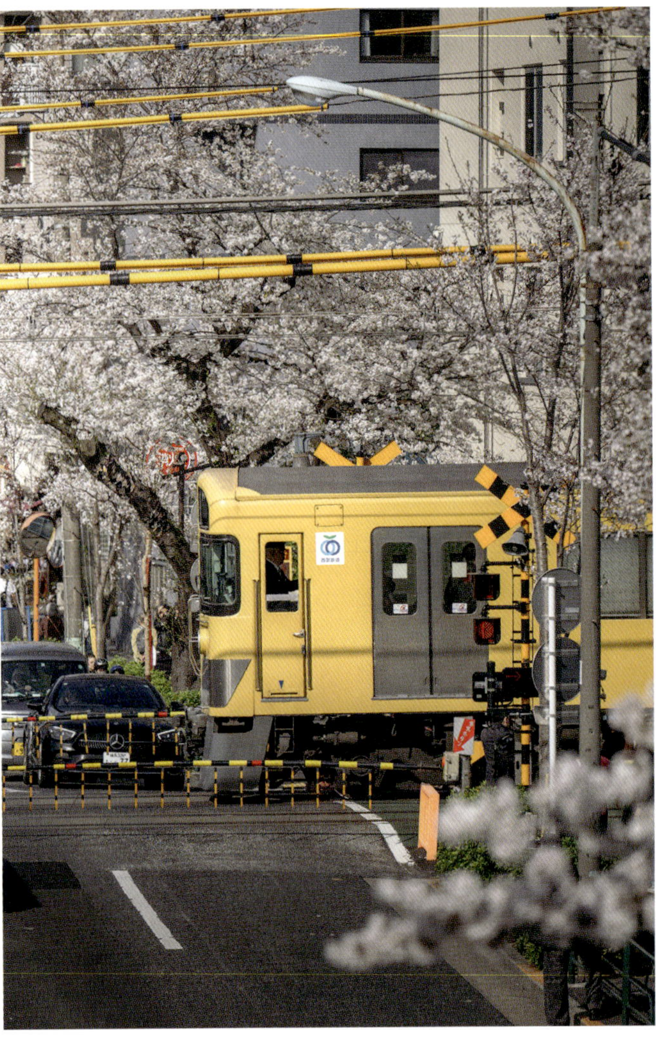

Seibu Shinjuku Line.
A bright yellow train on the Seibu Shinjuku Line passes a level crossing in central Tokyo, framed by delicate pink scatterings of cherry blossoms.

Omoide Yokocho.
Tucked away in Shinjuku, the alleys of Omoide Yokocho transport visitors into a unique retro atmosphere. Lined with red lanterns and tiny stalls serving yakitori skewers, this maze of narrow lanes, adorned with artificial maple leaves, exudes a warm, nostalgic charm.

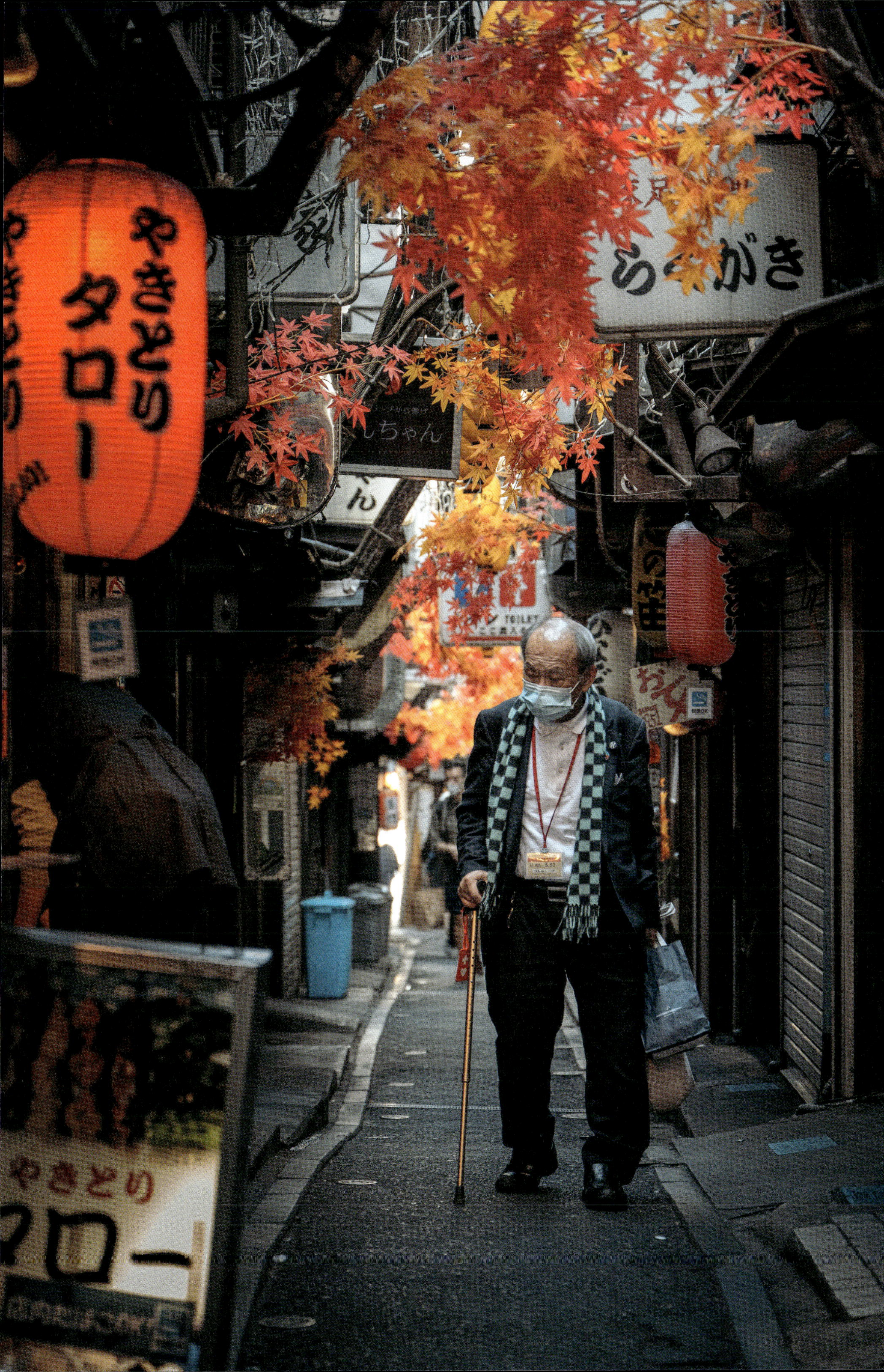
やきとり
タロー
TOILET
やきとり

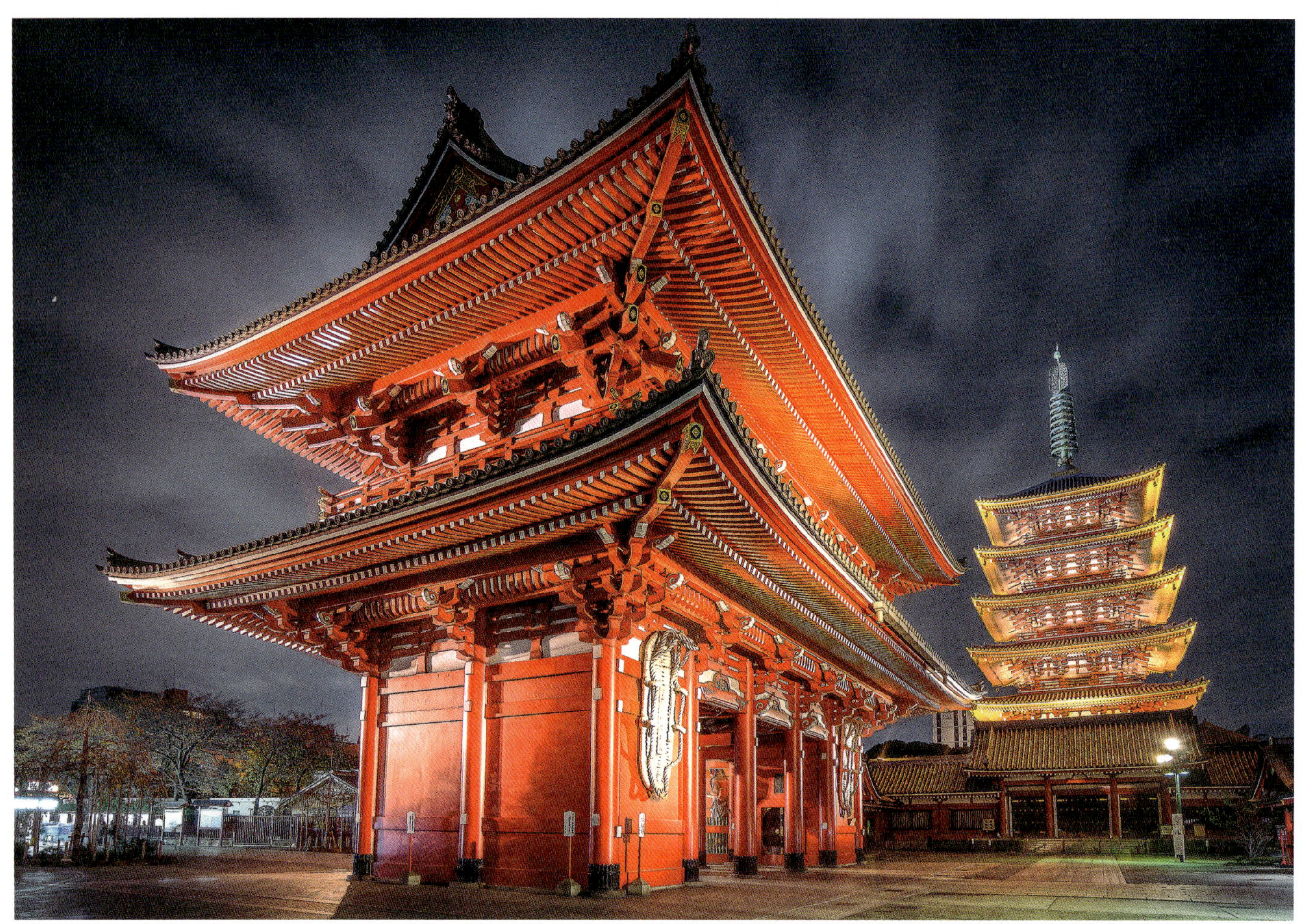

Sensō-ji.
Founded in 645, Sensō-ji is Tokyo's oldest temple. Its grand five-story pagoda and the iconic Kaminarimon gate (seen in the foreground) attract millions of visitors each year.

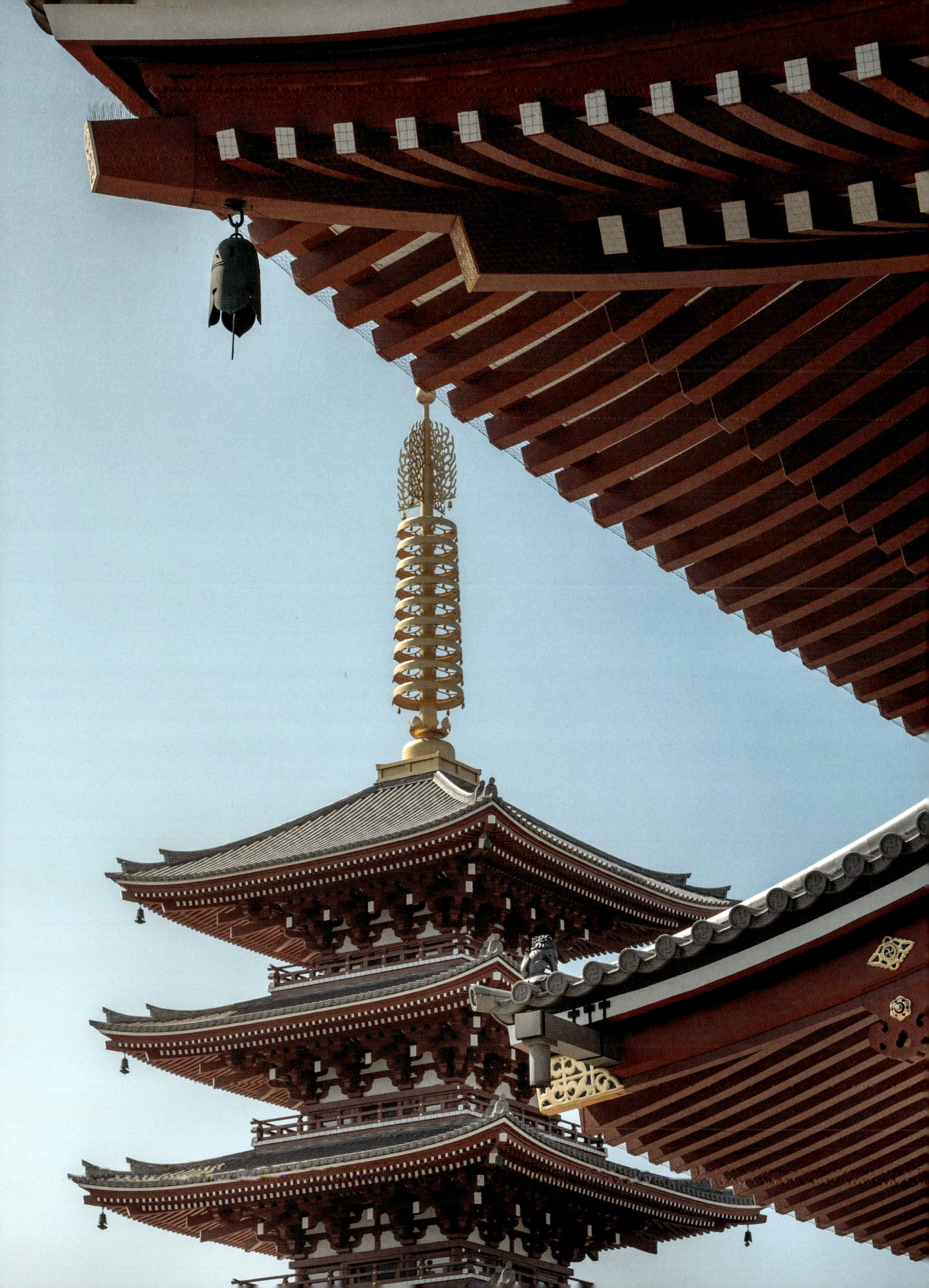

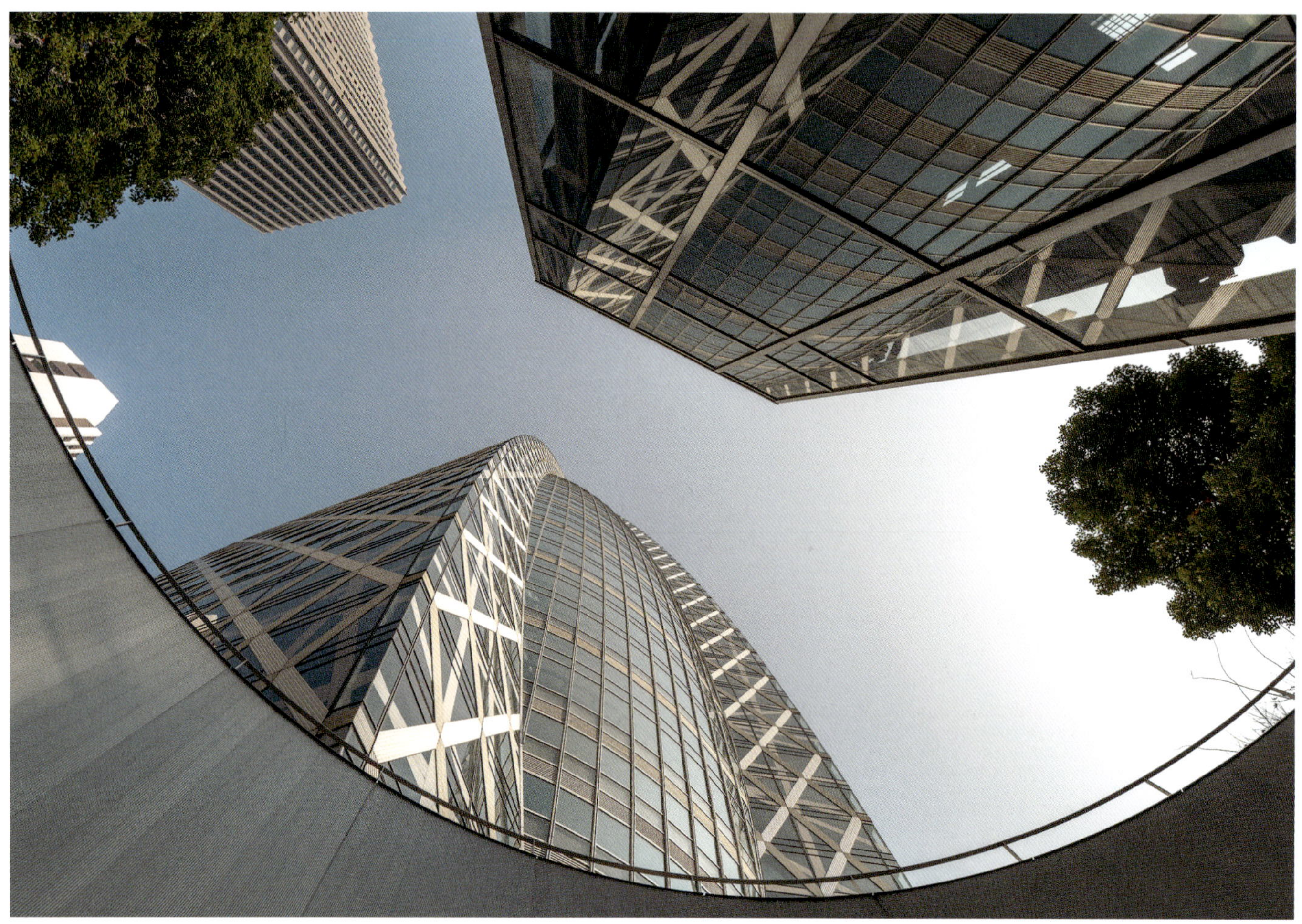

Mode Gakuen Cocoon Tower.
A prominent architectural landmark in Shinjuku, the Mode Gakuen Cocoon Tower is easily recognisable for its sleek, futuristic cocoon shape. This skyscraper houses institutions dedicated to fashion, technology, and design.

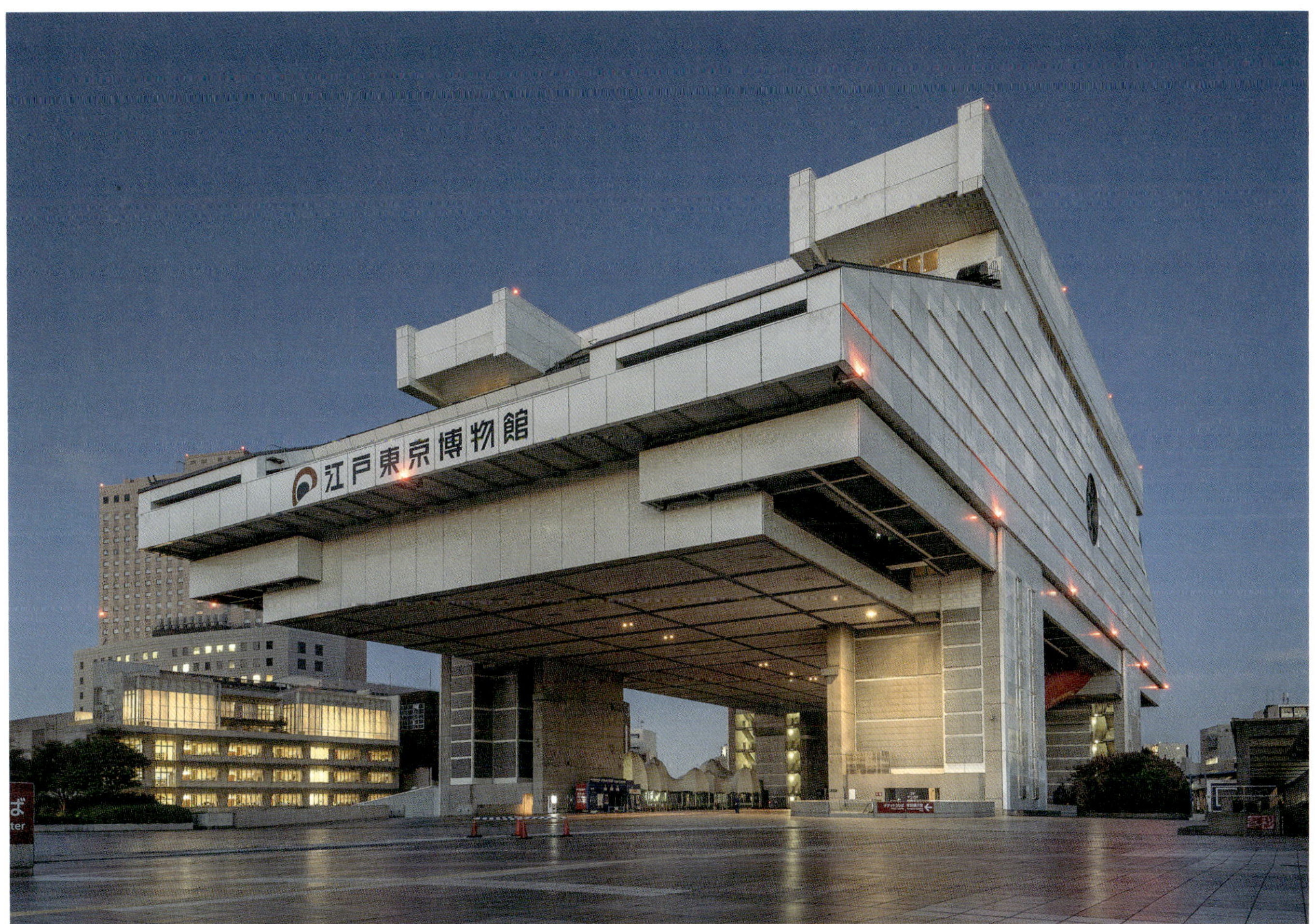

Edo Museum.
Resembling a colossal, futuristic vessel suspended in the sky, the Edo-Tokyo Museum stands as a striking landmark in the city's skyline. Inside, visitors embark on an immersive journey through Tokyo's rich history, from the bustling streets of the Edo period to the towering modern skyscrapers of today. Life-size models, artefacts, and intricate reconstructions vividly bring the city's dynamic evolution to life.

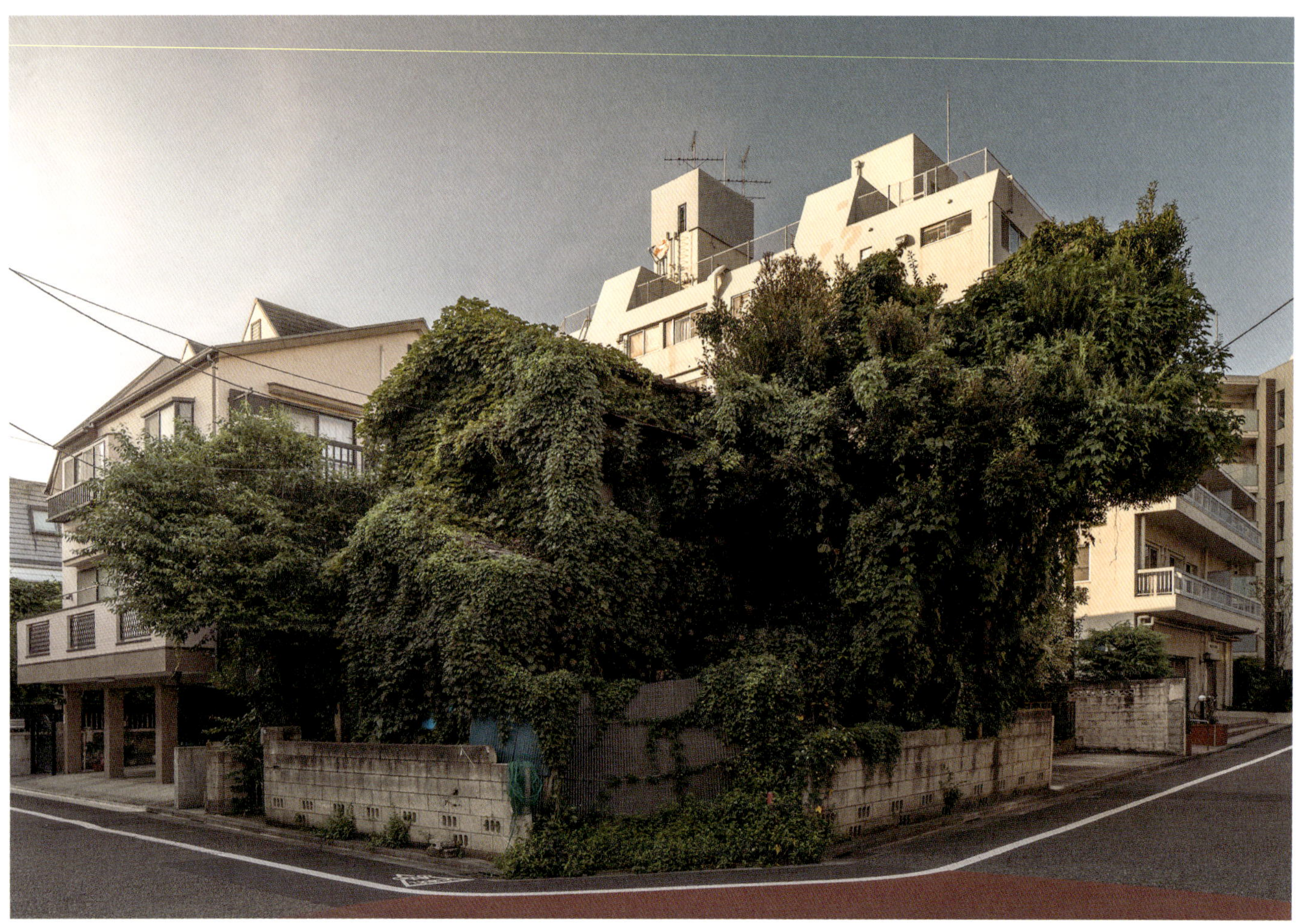

House in Kyodo.
In the peaceful residential neighbourhood of Kyodo, Tokyo's quiet streets are adorned with a unique blend of modern and traditional architecture. Here, an ivy-covered historic house represents a timeless symbol of the past, providing a serene escape from the city's fast-paced rhythm.

Kyodo Alleys.
Located in Tokyo's Setagaya Ward, the Kyodo district reminds us that the metropolis is a patchwork of vibrant neighbourhoods. Its quiet streets, lined with simple homes and criss-crossed by electric cables, reflect the everyday warmth of residential Tokyo.

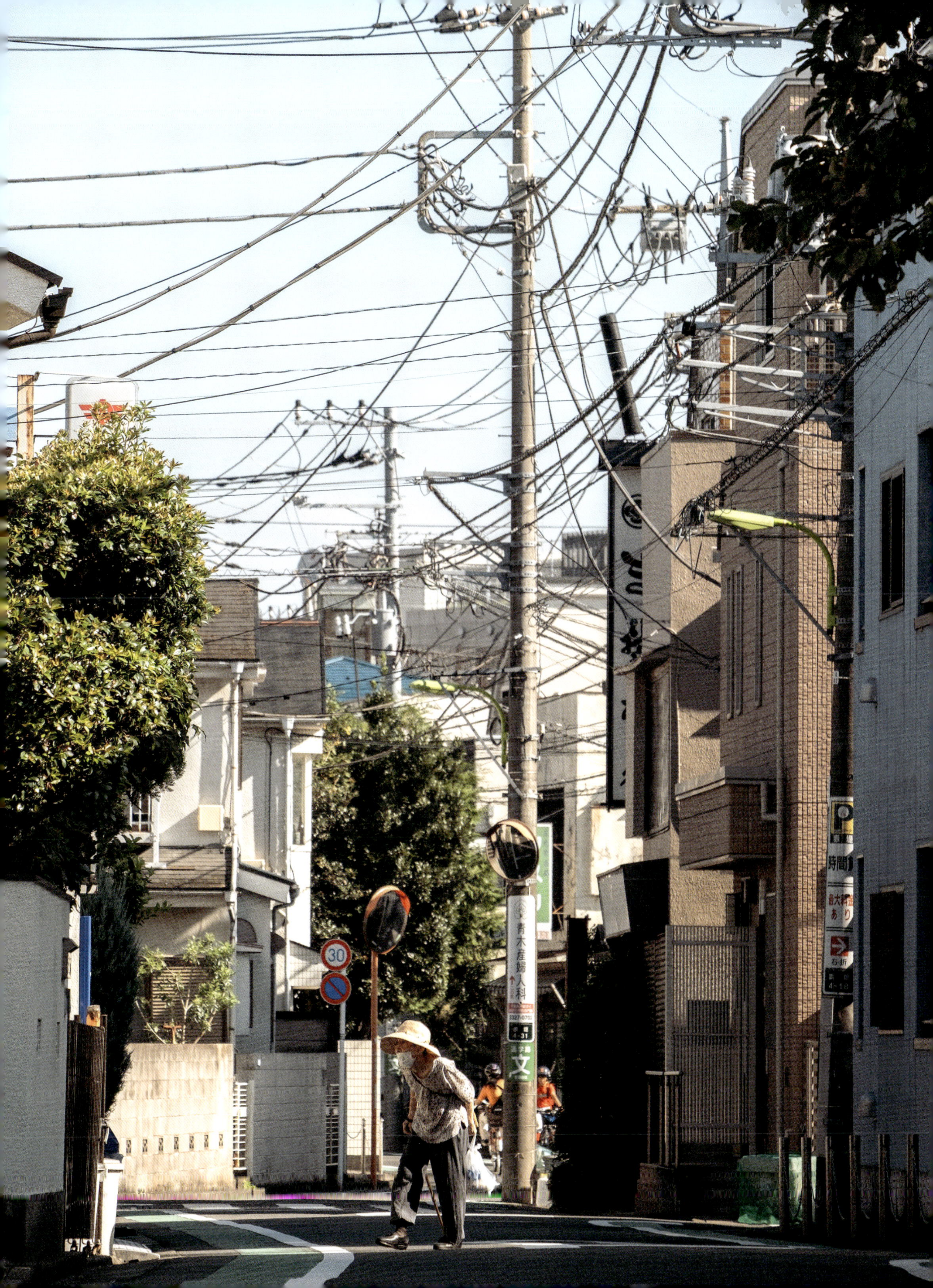

30
青木産婦人科
3327-0702
文
P
時間
最大料金
あり
右折
4-18

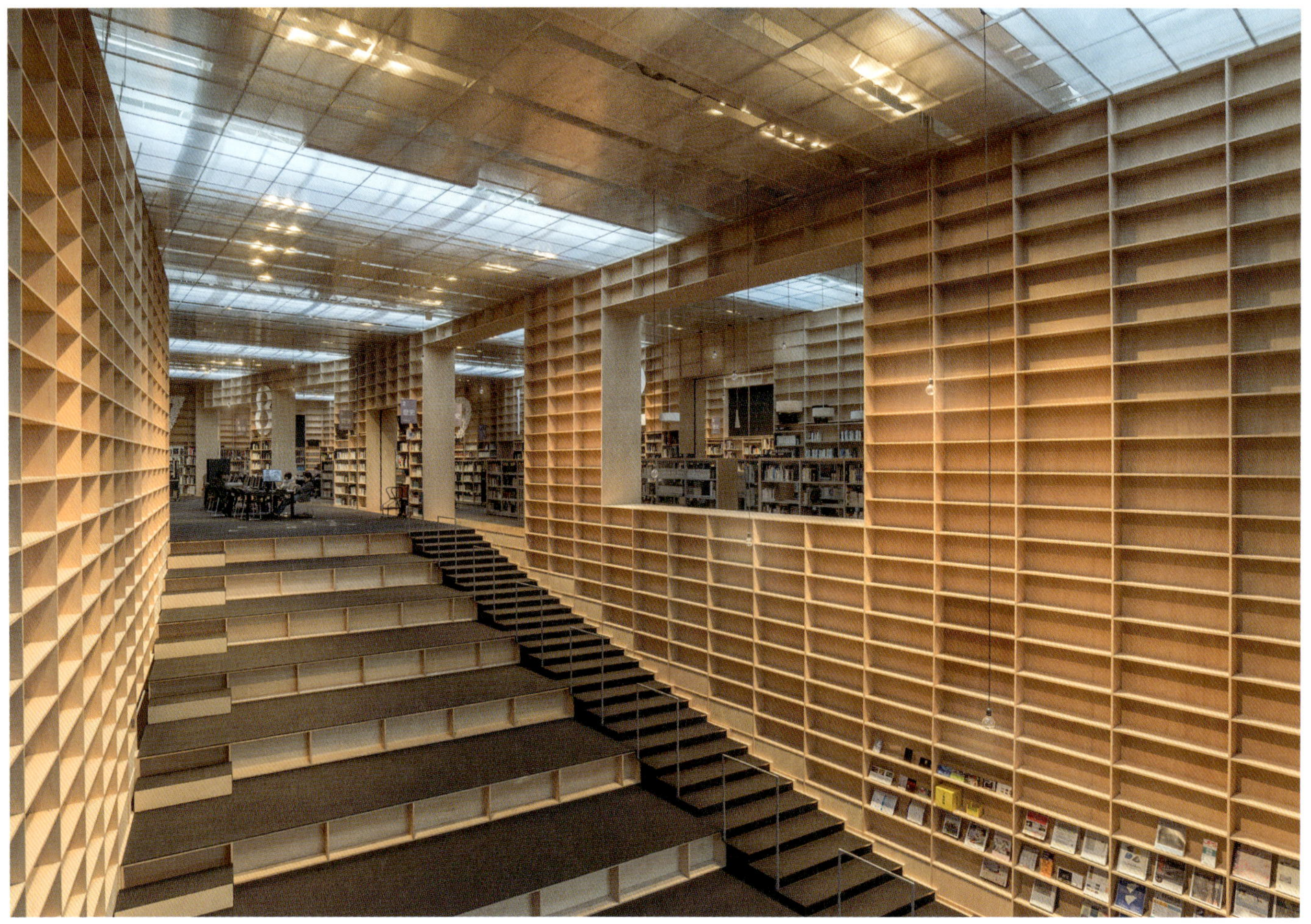

Musashino library.
The library at Tokyo's Musashino Art University is a true sanctuary for art and design enthusiasts. With its minimalist architecture and thoughtfully organised shelves, it provides a serene space to explore rare and inspiring works, all within an atmosphere that is both contemporary and welcoming.

Tokyo International Forum.
The Tokyo International Forum is a striking example of modern architecture, famous for its ship-shaped glass and steel design. This versatile venue, located in the heart of the city, offers an impressive backdrop for a range of cultural events, exhibitions, and conferences.

View of Ikebukuro.
Ikebukuro, one of Tokyo's most energetic districts, pulses with urban life. The sprawling Ikebukuro Station is, among the busiest in the world.

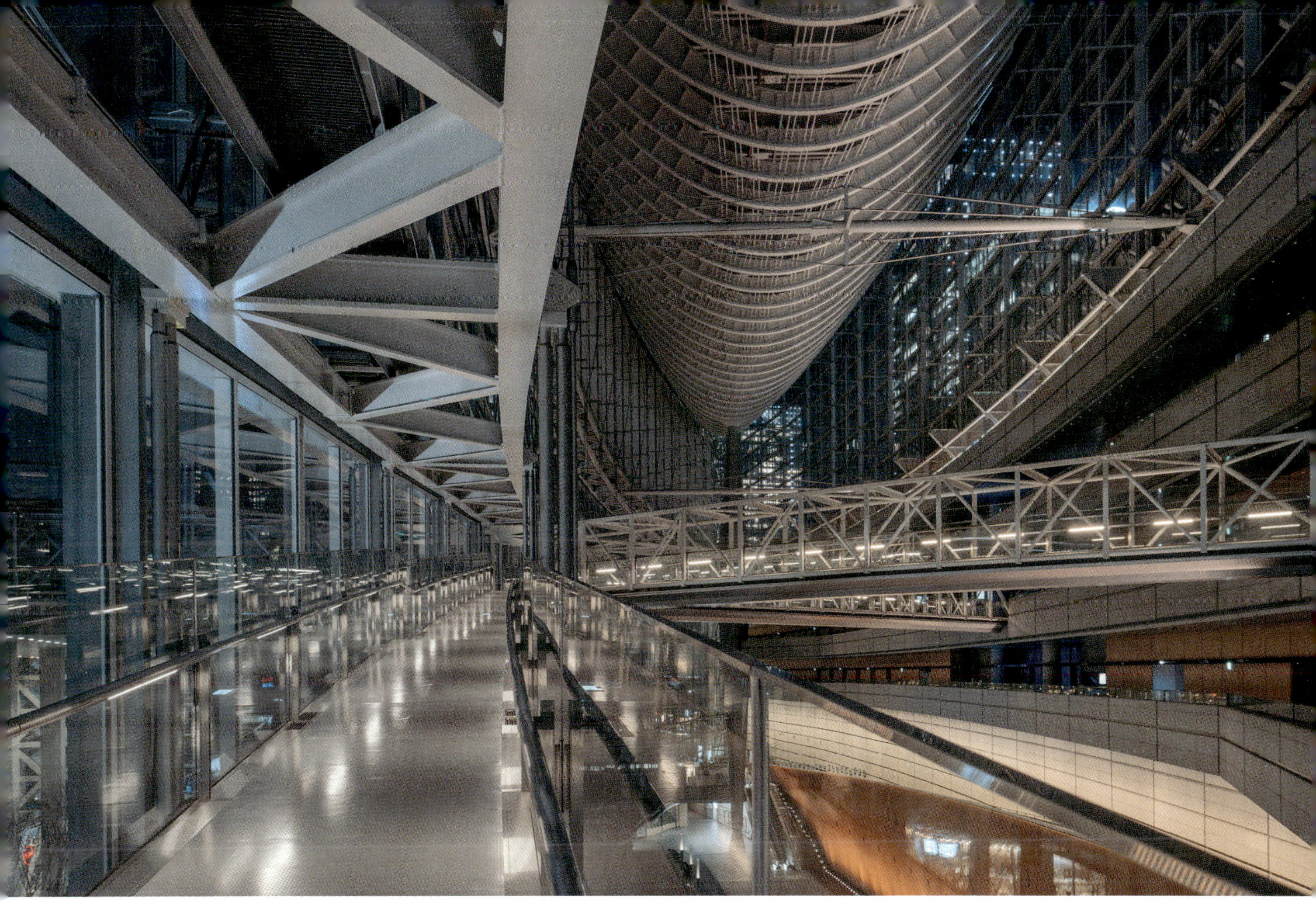

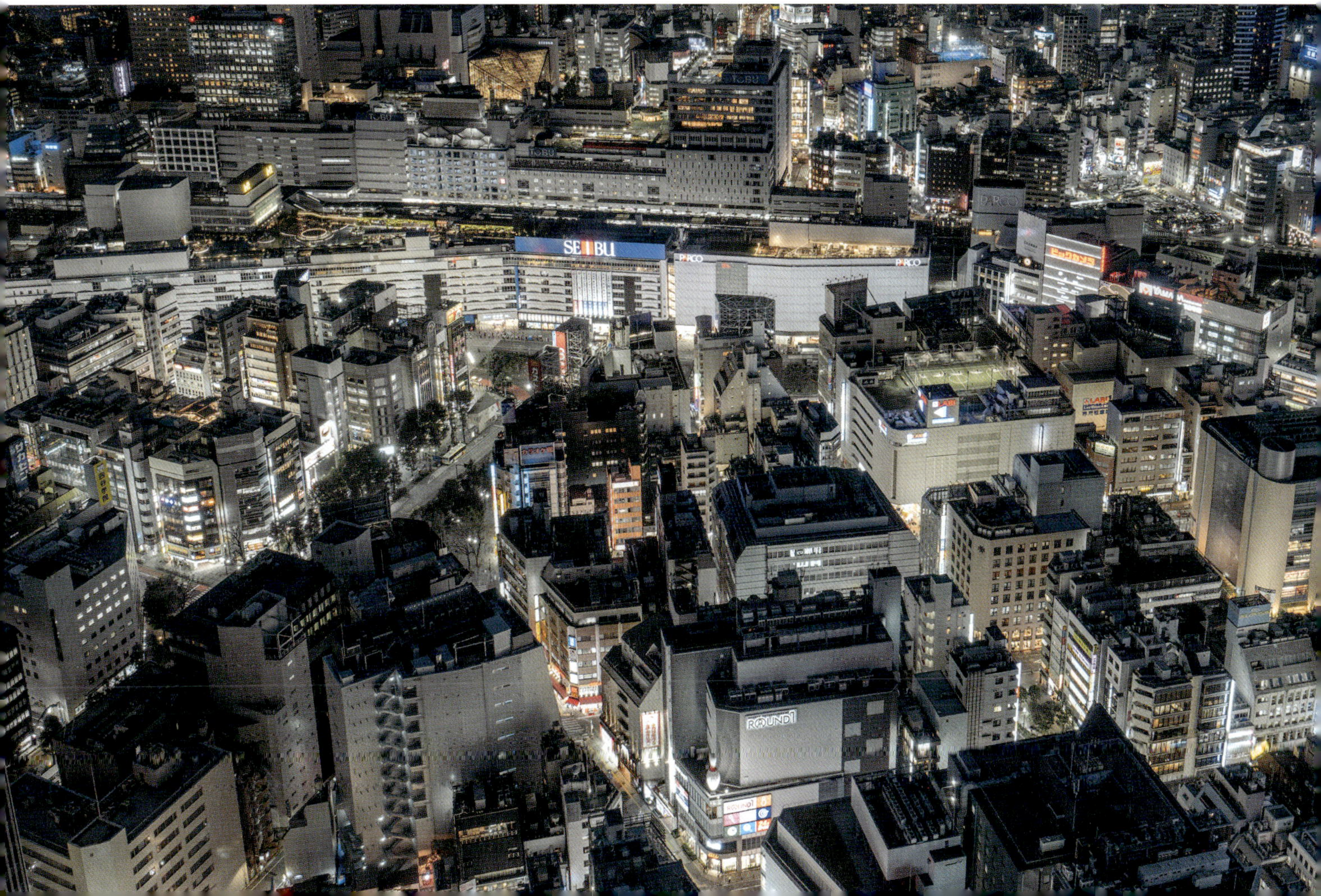

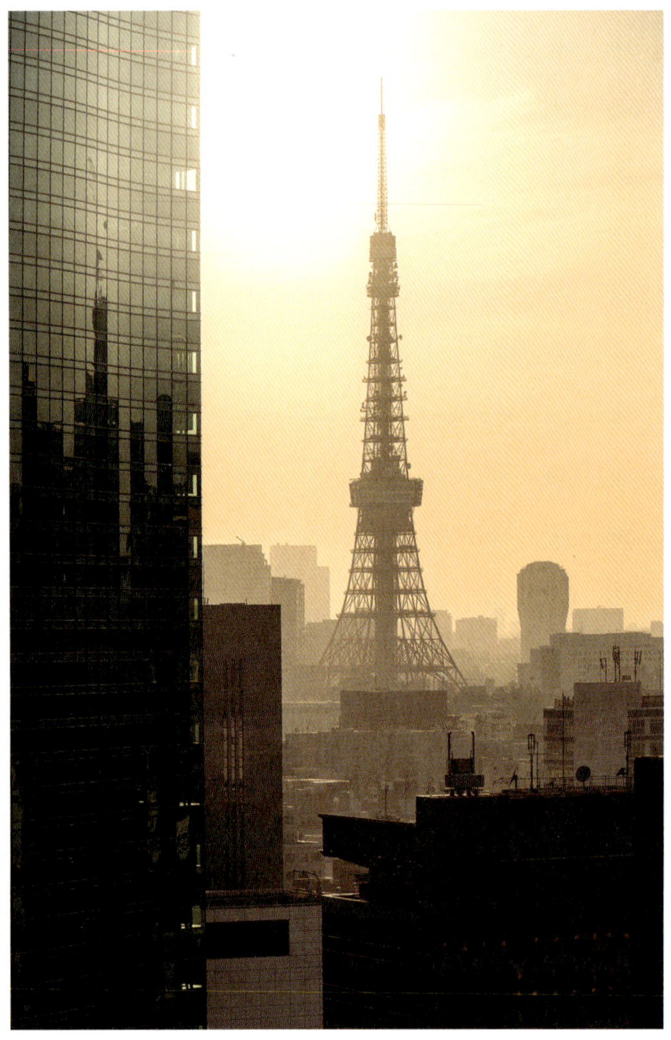

Tokyo Tower.
A quintessential symbol of the Japanese capital, Tokyo Tower proudly rises 333 metres high in the city's heart.

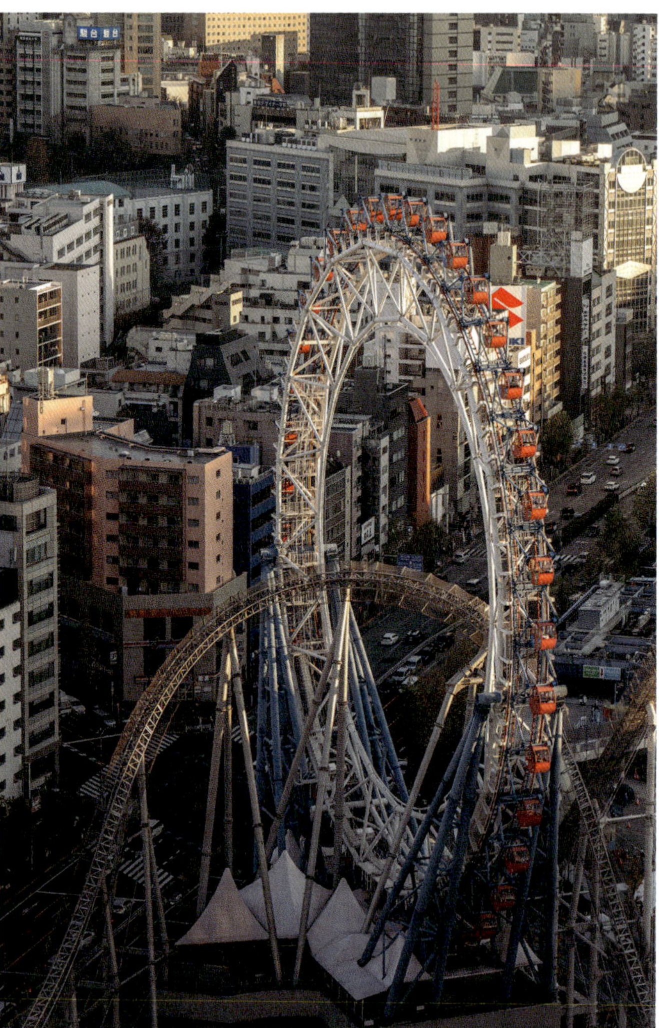

Thunder Dolphin.
Soaring high in the Suidobashi district, the *Thunder Dolphin* roller coaster zooms through the urban landscape at breathtaking speeds. This exhilarating ride, perched between towering skyscrapers, thrillingly passes through a massive hole in a Ferris wheel, offering adrenaline seekers a unique view of the city's skyline.

Shibuya by Bicycle.
Shibuya Crossing is one of the busiest pedestrian junctions in the world. As night falls, the streets are illuminated in a golden light, providing a moment of serenity in a place usually bustling with life.

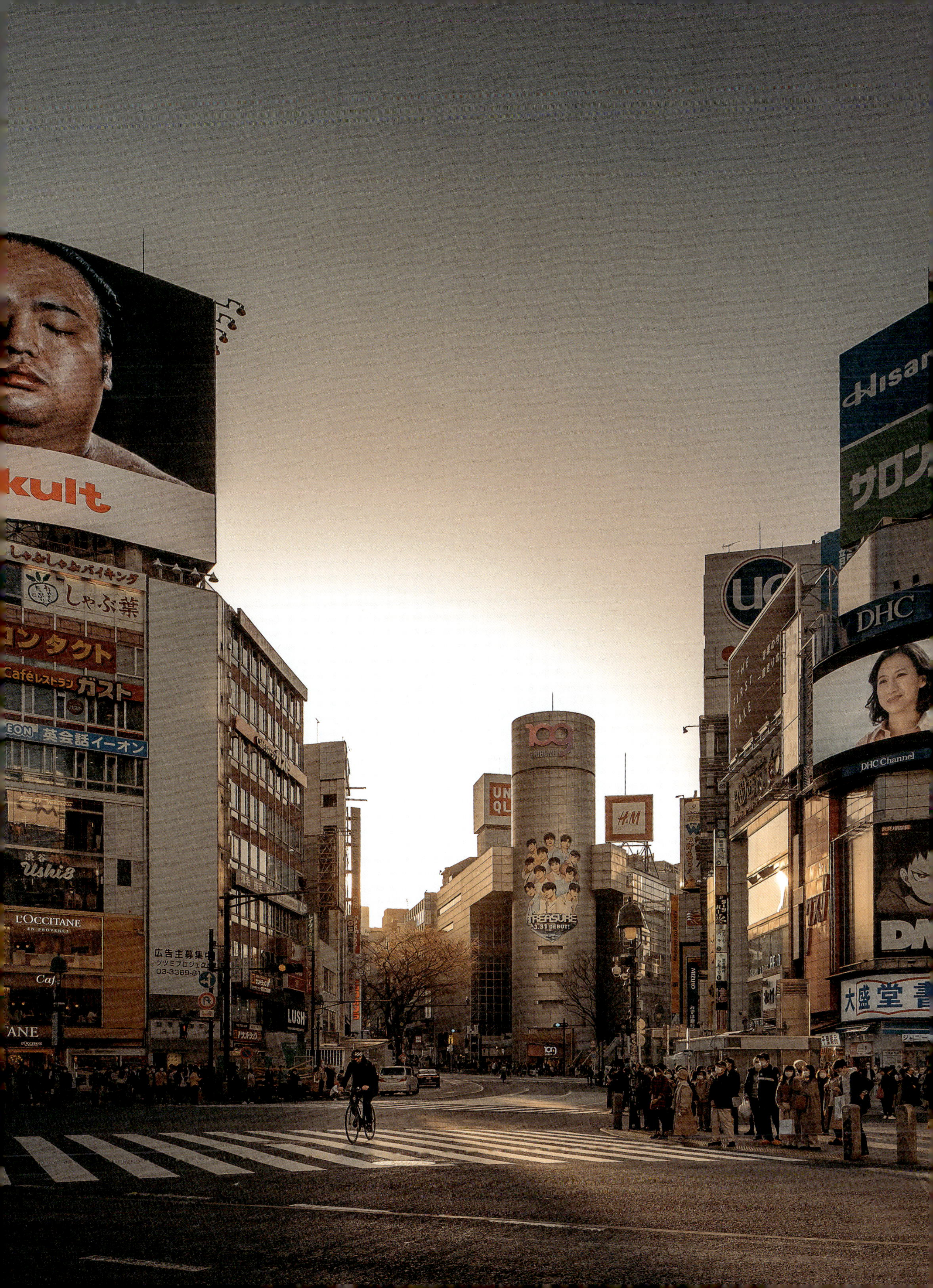

kult
しゃぶしゃぶバイキング
しゃぶ葉
コンタクト
Caféレストラン ガスト
EON 英会話イーオン
L'OCCITANE
EN PROVENCE
広告主募集中
03-3389-8
LUSH
UNI
QL
109
H&M
TREASURE
3.31 DEBUT!
Hisar
サロン
DHC
DHC Channel
大盛堂書

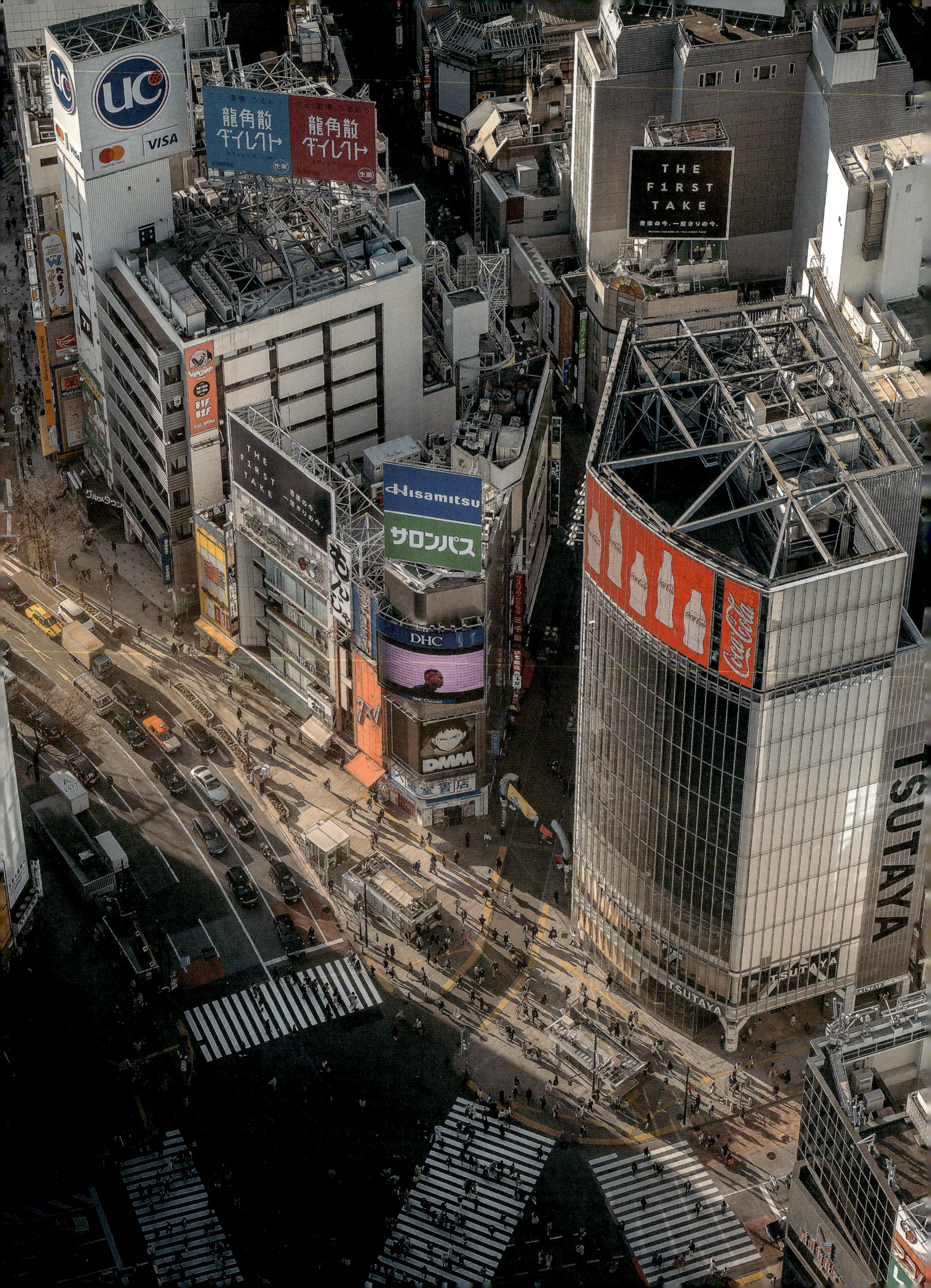
UC
VISA
龍角散
ダイレクト
龍角散
ダイレクト
THE F1RST TAKE
Hisamitsu
サロンパス
DHC
DMM
Coca-Cola
TSUTAYA
TSUTAYA

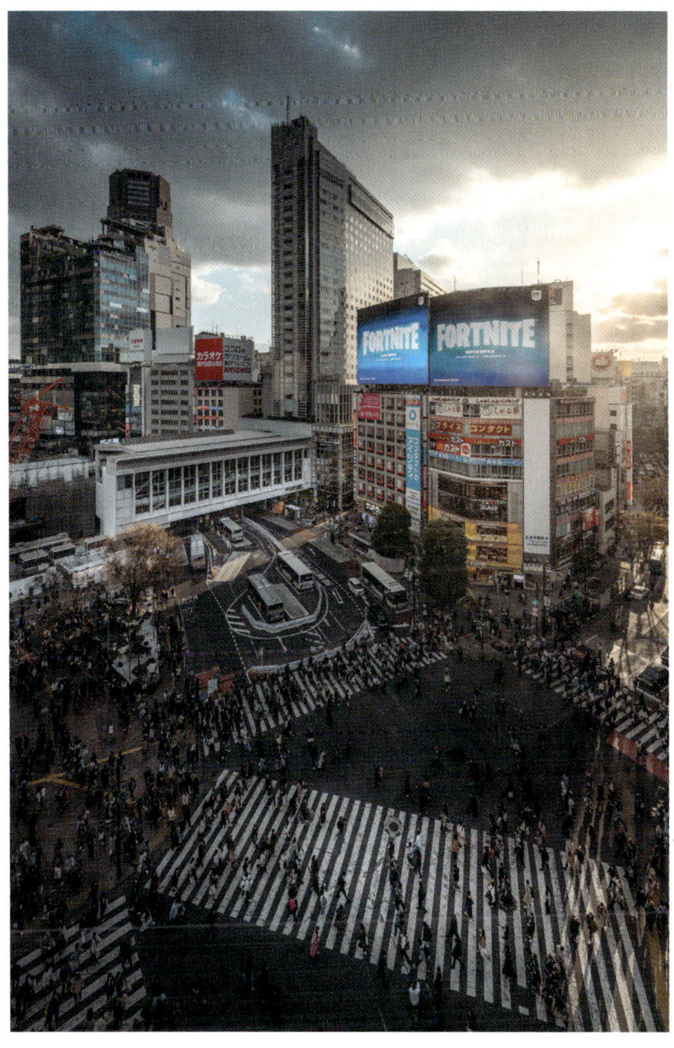

Shibuya Crossing.
From above, Shibuya Crossing resembles a fluid sea of people, perpetually in motion as thousands of pedestrians intersect with each traffic light change.

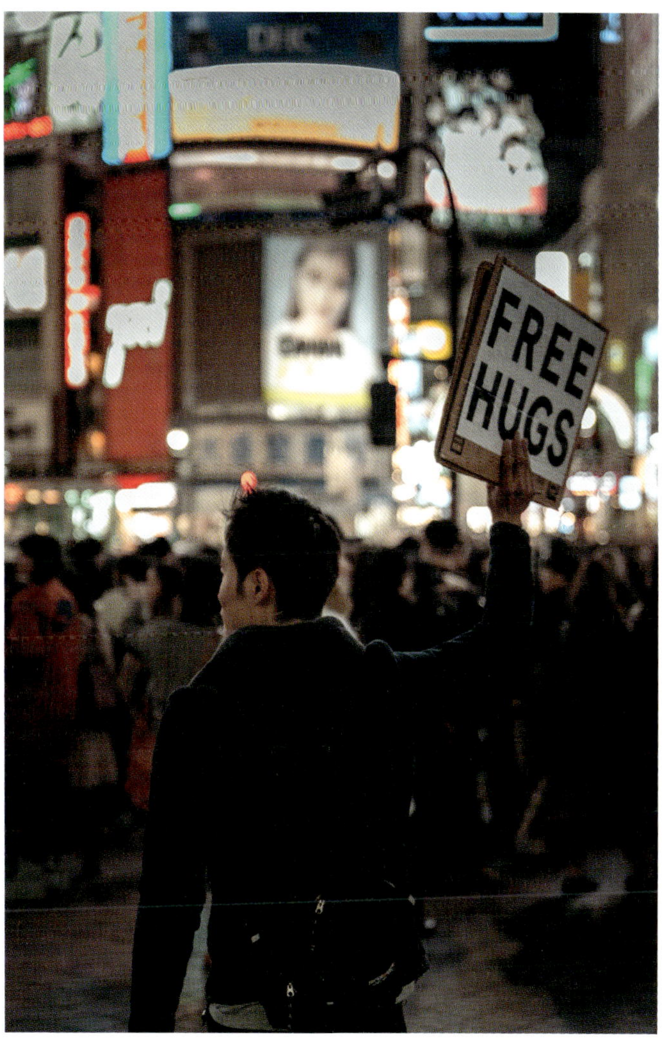

Shibuya Free Hugs.
In the vibrant chaos of Shibuya, amidst flashing neon lights and a sea of people, a young man holds up a "FREE HUGS" sign–a fleeting moment of human warmth at this bustling crossroads.

Shimotakaido.
A quiet residential district in Tokyo, Shimotakaido enchants with its down-to-earth, local atmosphere and genuine Tokyoite character.

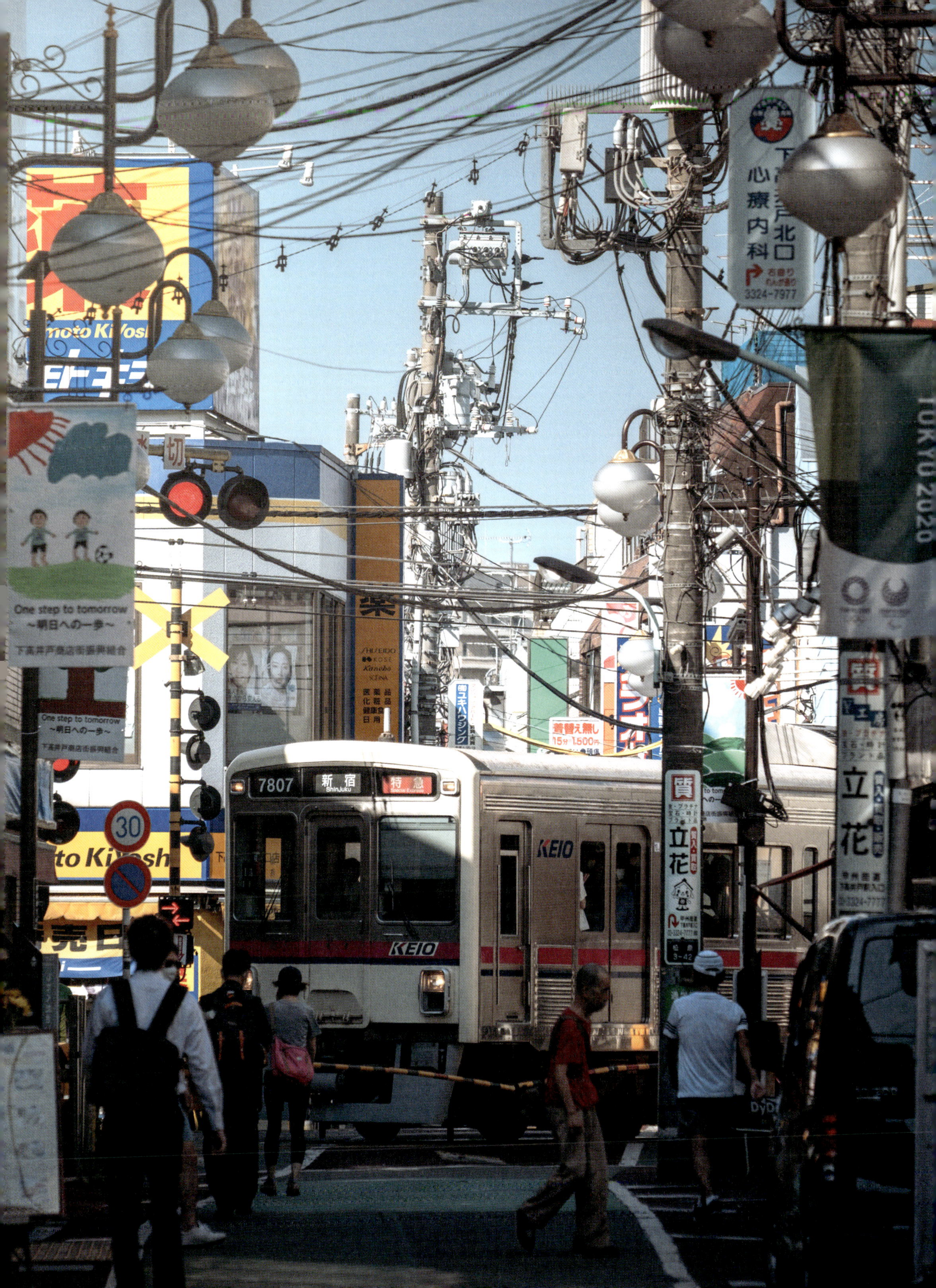

One step to tomorrow
~明日への一歩~
心療内科
3324-7977
TOKYO 2020
7807
新宿
Shinjuku
特急
KEIO
KEIO
30
質
立花
立花

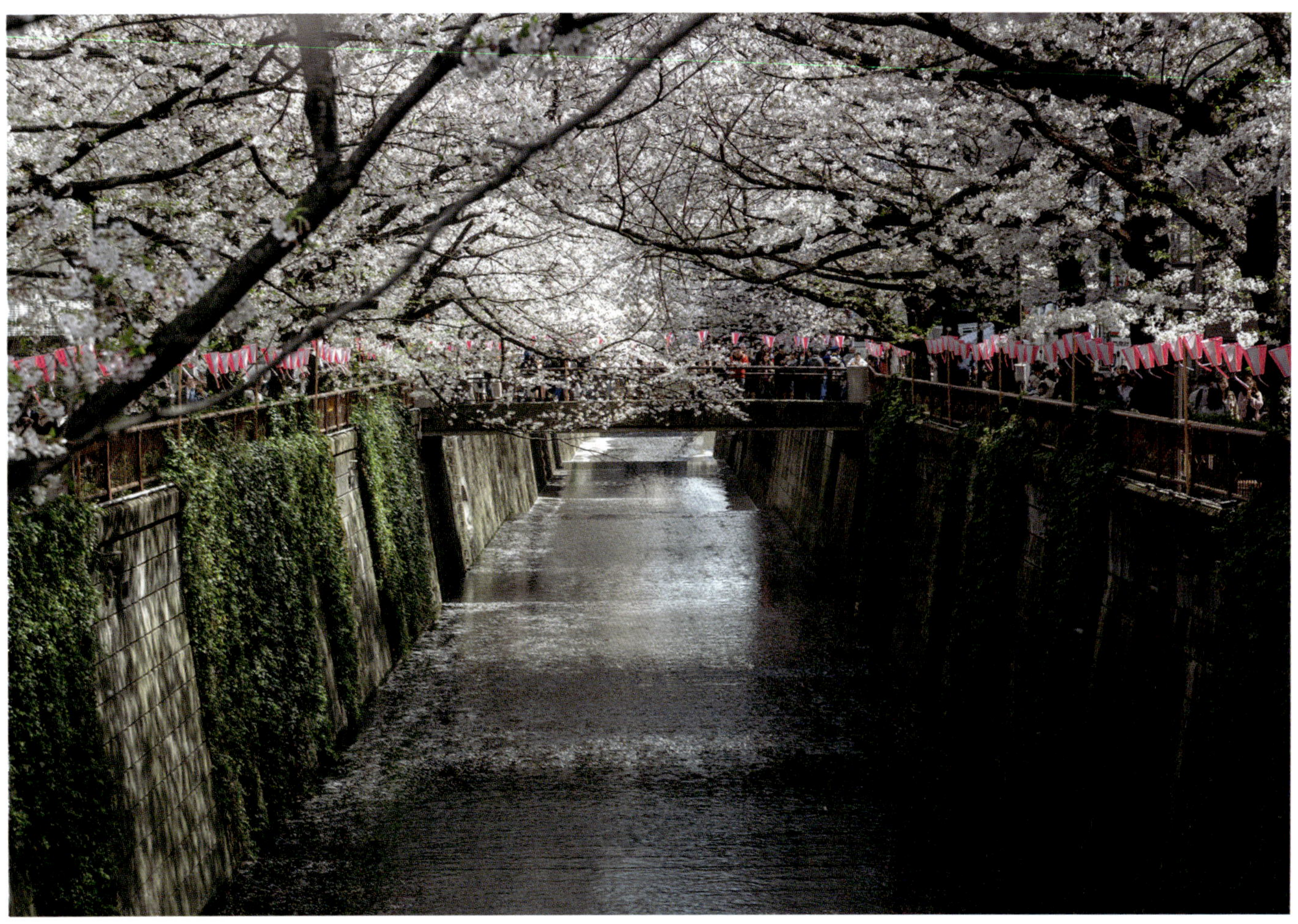

Meguro Cherry Blossoms.
In spring, the Meguro River transforms into an enchanting sight as the cherry trees bloom in soft shades of pink. Colourful lanterns add a festive touch to this iconic hanami walk. Literally meaning "flower viewing", *hanami* is a traditional Japanese custom of appreciating the fleeting beauty of blossoms.

Chidorigafuchi Park.
Renowned for its rows of cherry trees that line the Imperial Palace moat, Chidorigafuchi Park embodies the fleeting beauty of hanami in the very heart of Japan's capital. Every spring, visitors flock to admire this enchanting spectacle where boats glide peacefully on the calm waters, framed by a canopy of rose petals. This scene beautifully captures the tranquillity of *hanami*.

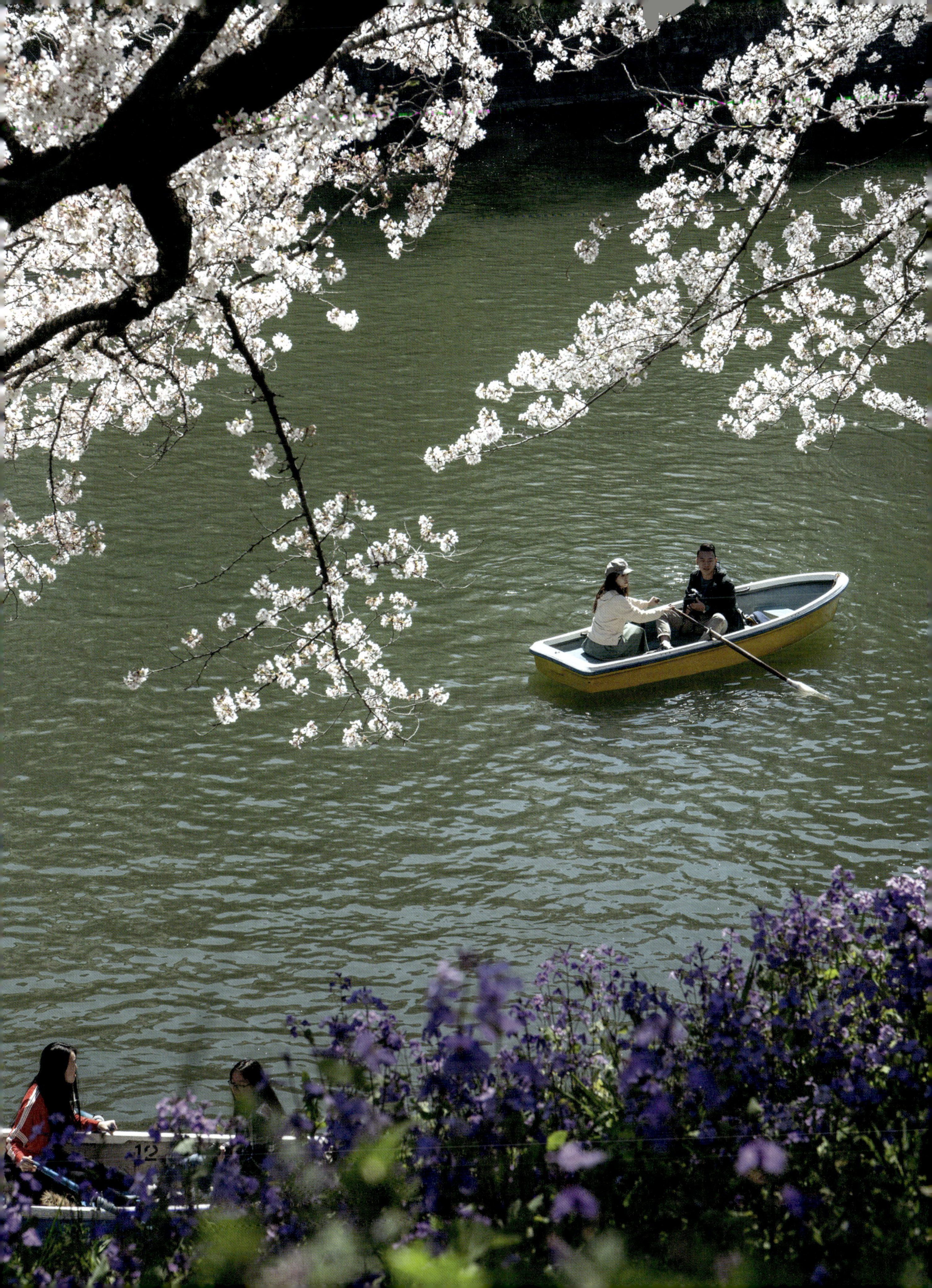
12

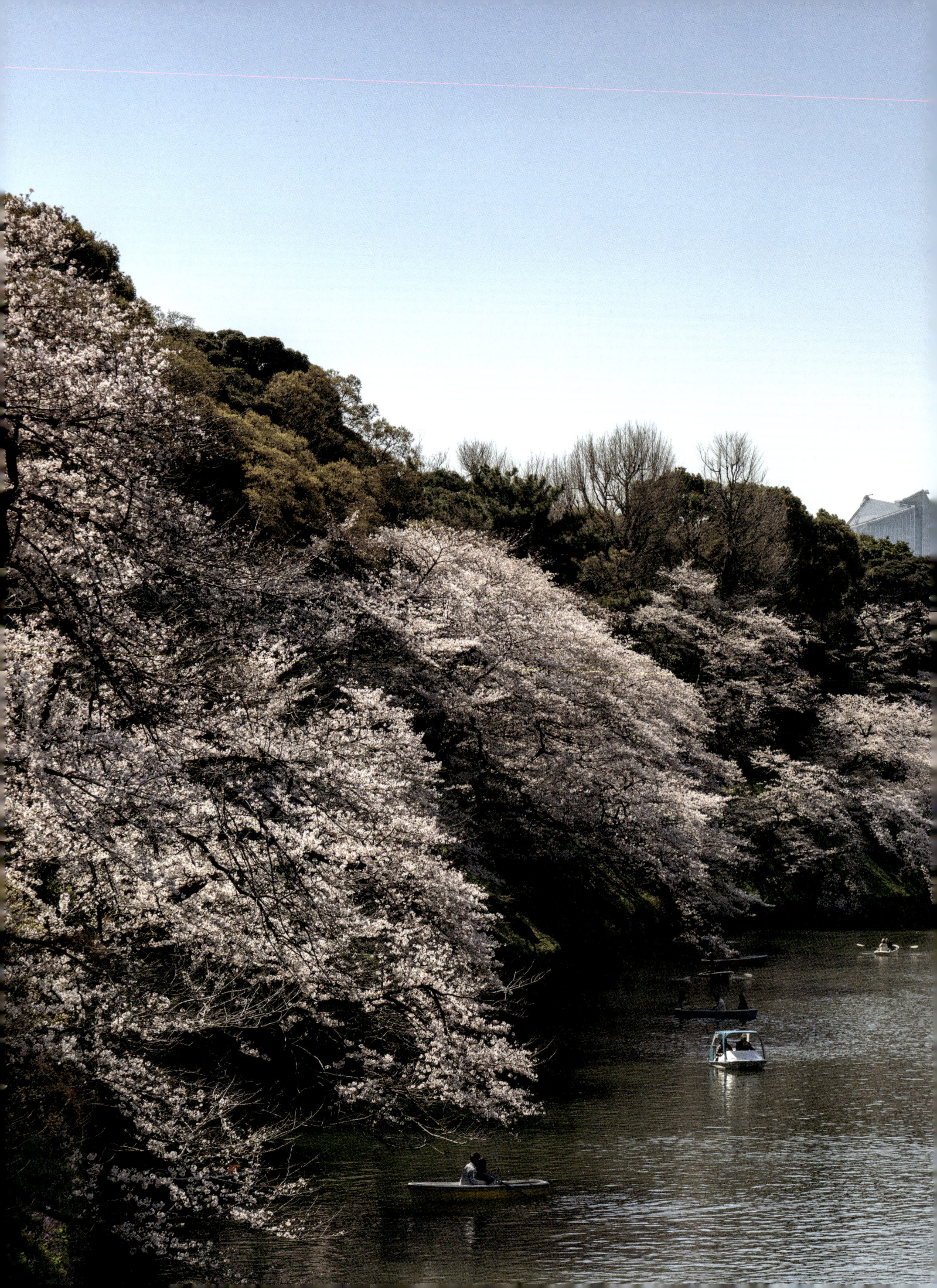

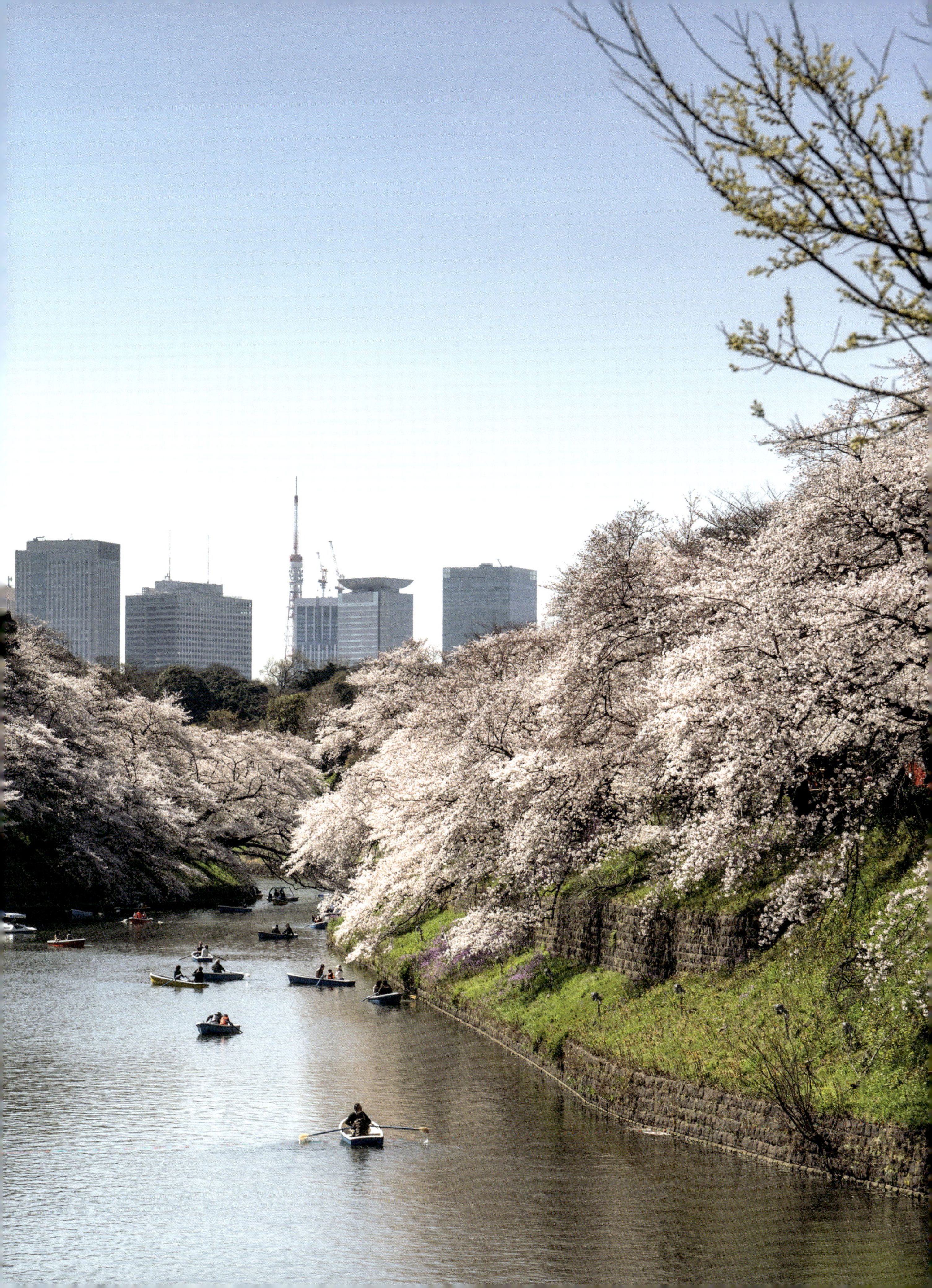

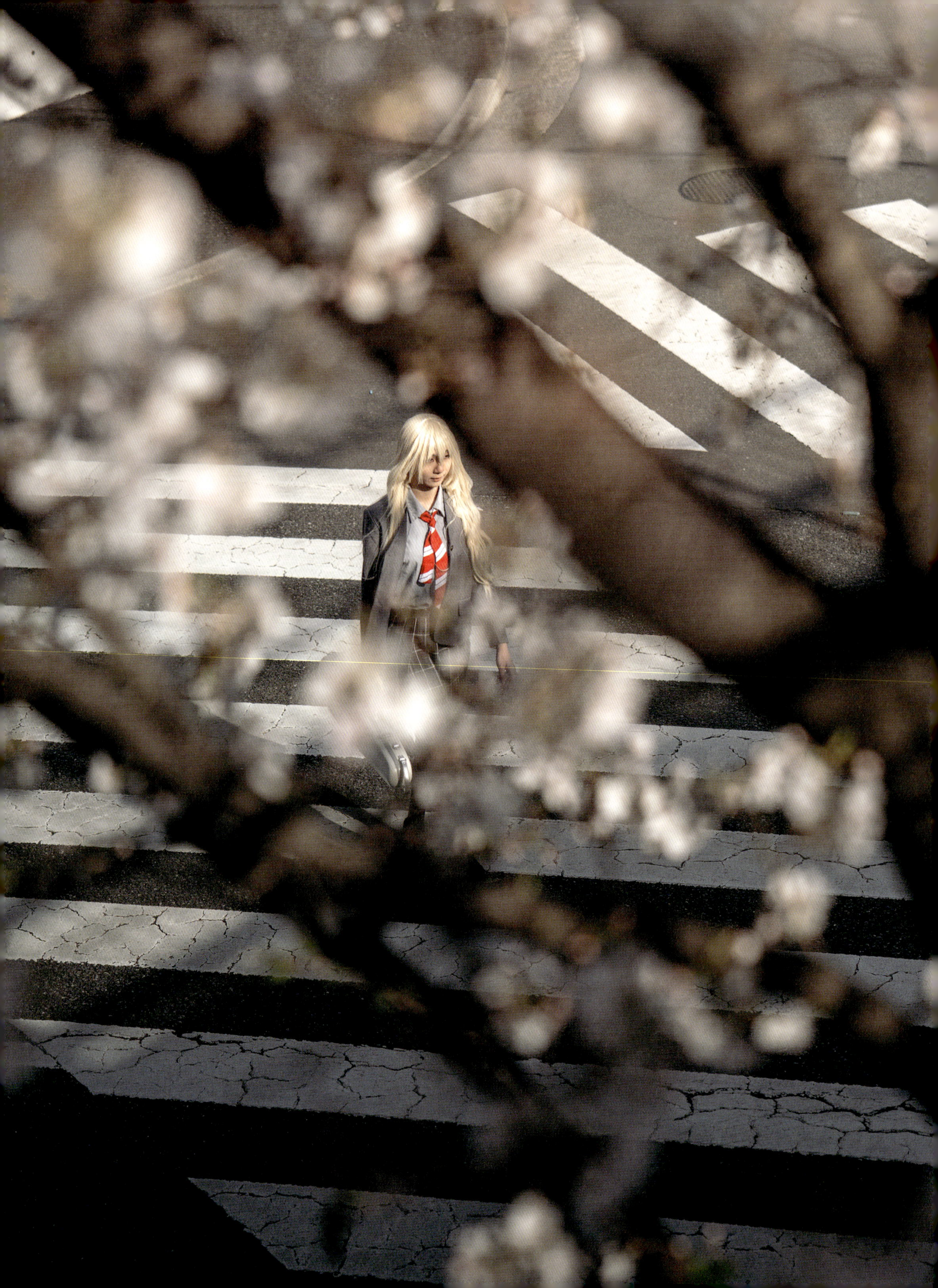

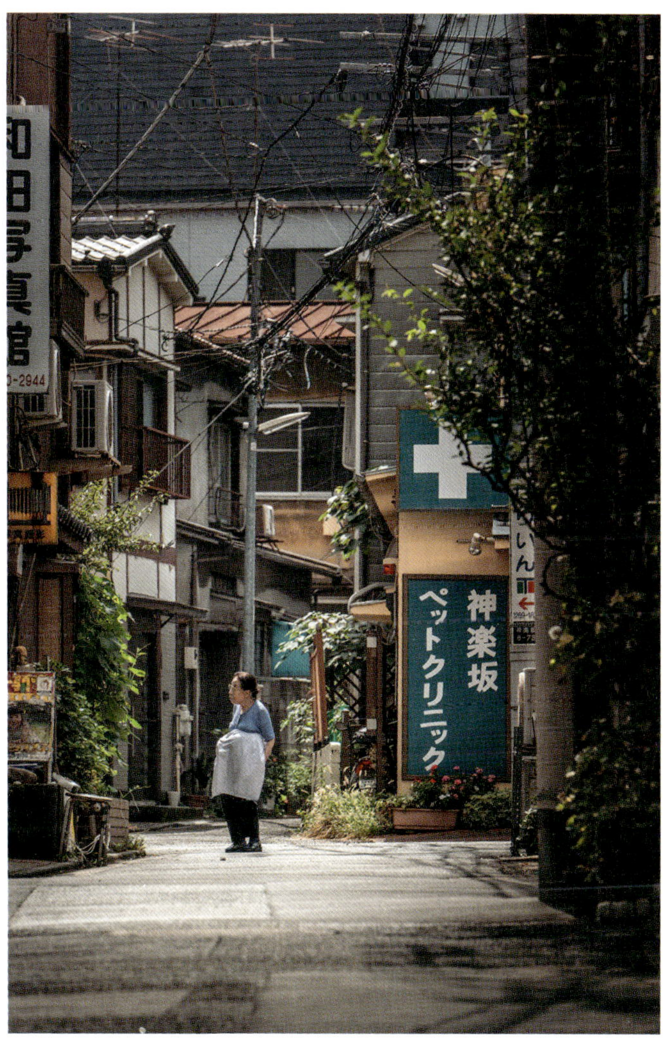

Iidabashi.
At the heart of Tokyo, the Iidabashi district reveals a more intimate side of the capital. Its peaceful lanes, dotted with small shops and a family-friendly atmosphere, perfectly capture daily life in this vibrant city.

Cosplay Under the Blossoms.
Beneath the blooming branches of a cherry tree, a young girl in cosplay wears a reimagined school uniform, featuring a vivid red tie and bright blonde hair.

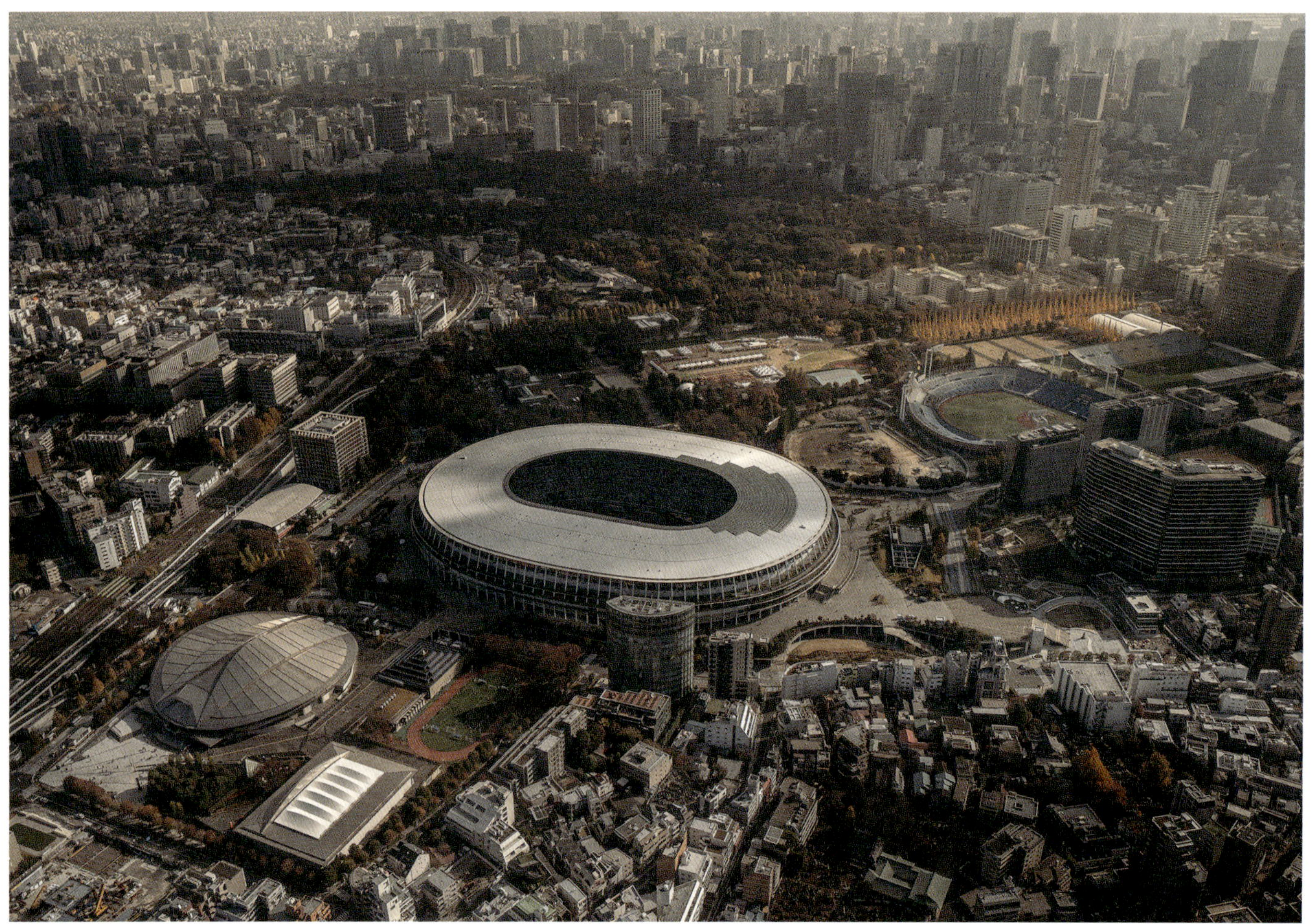

Japan National Stadium.
Designed for the 2020 Olympic Games, Japan National Stadium can host up to 68,000 spectators. Surrounded by lush greenery, the structure is crafted from cedar and pine wood sourced from all 47 prefectures of Japan.

Yurakucho Shinkansen.
Gliding with pinpoint precision over the lively streets of Yurakucho, Japan's iconic Shinkansen slices through Tokyo like a silver arrow. Travelling at over 300 km/h, the Shinkansen has embodied railway excellence since its debut in 1964.

>

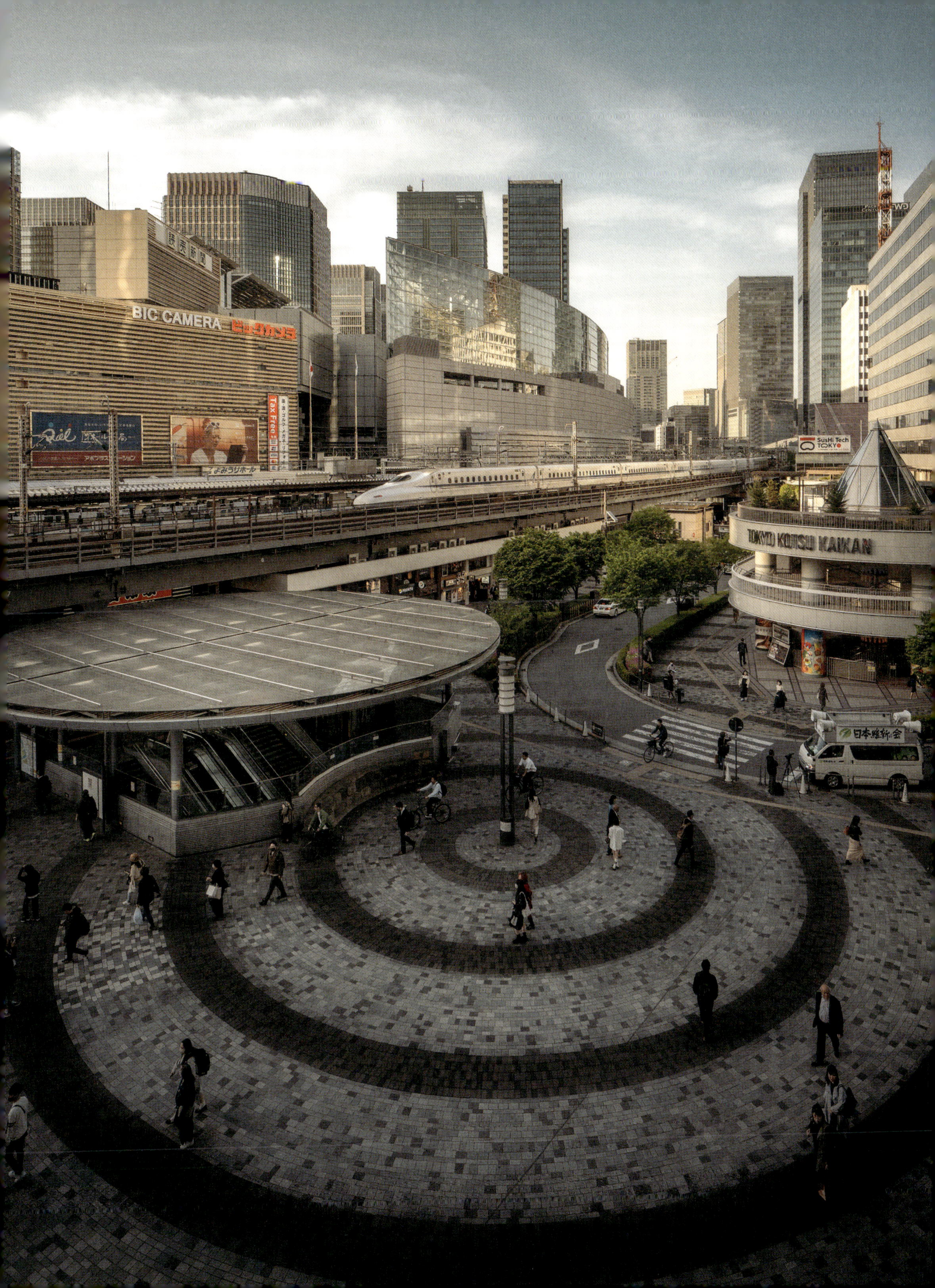
BIC CAMERA
ビックカメラ
Tax Free
よみうりホール
SusHi Tech TOKYO
TOKYO KOTSU KAIKAN

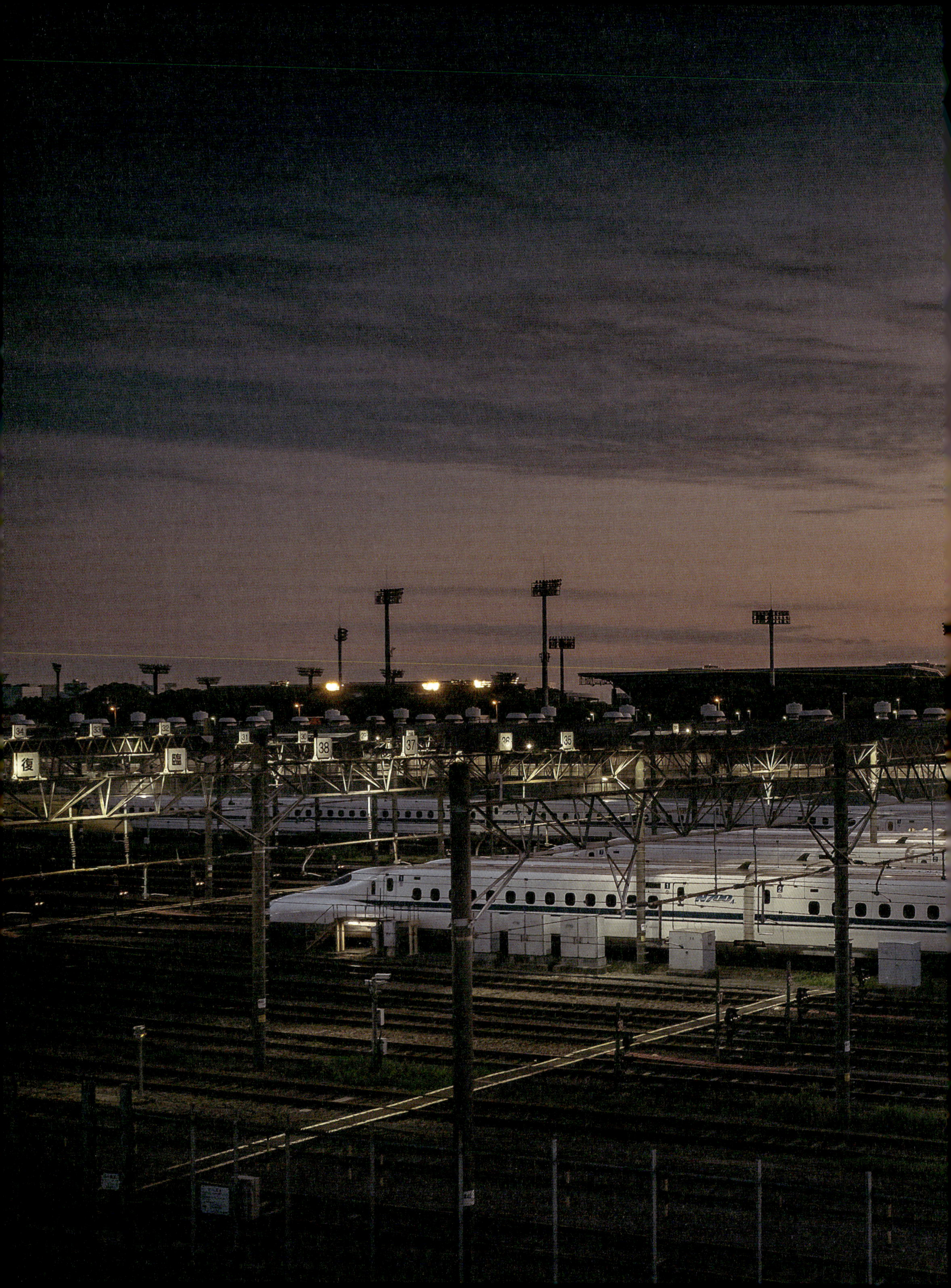
復
臨
38
37
35

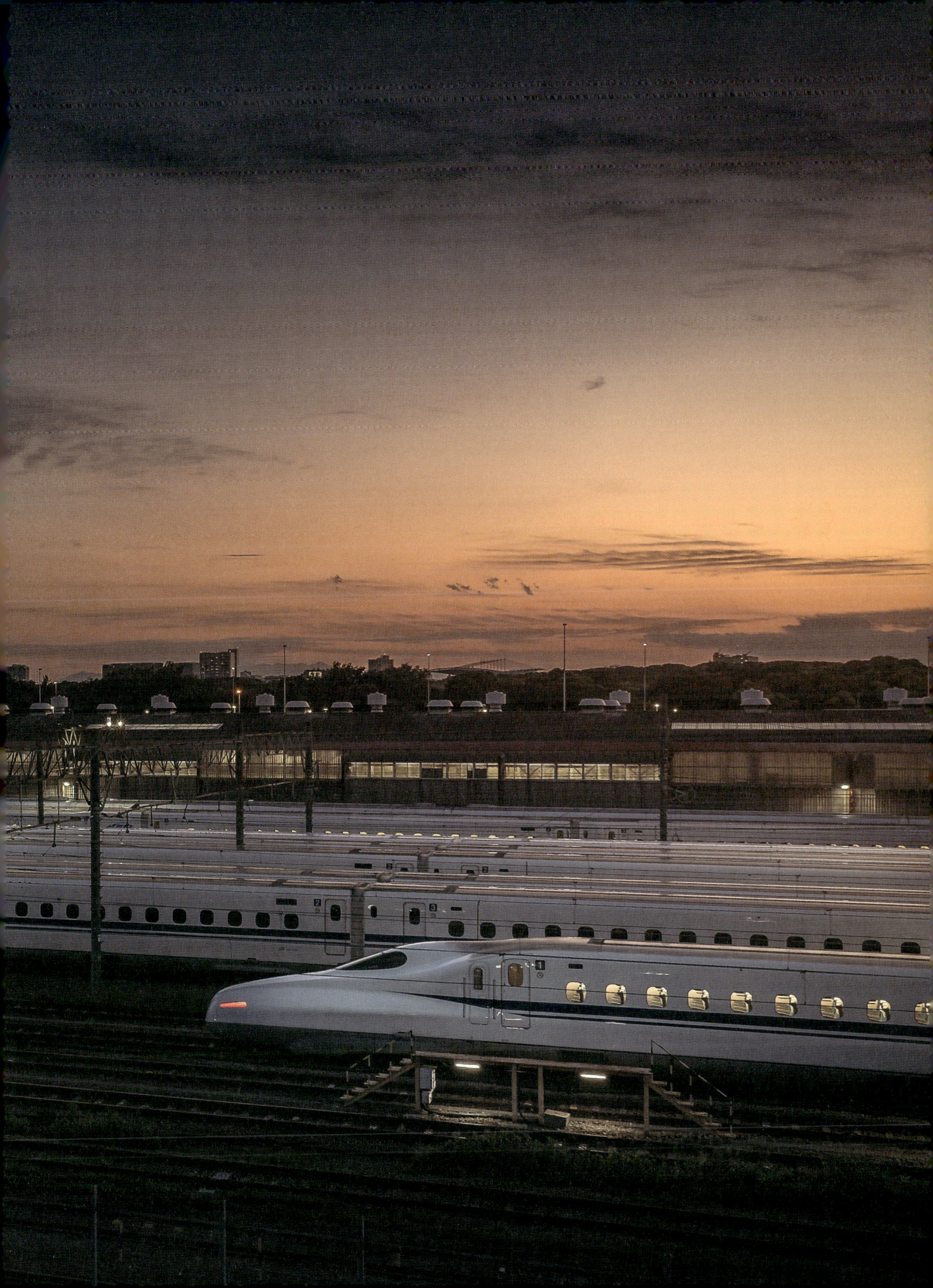

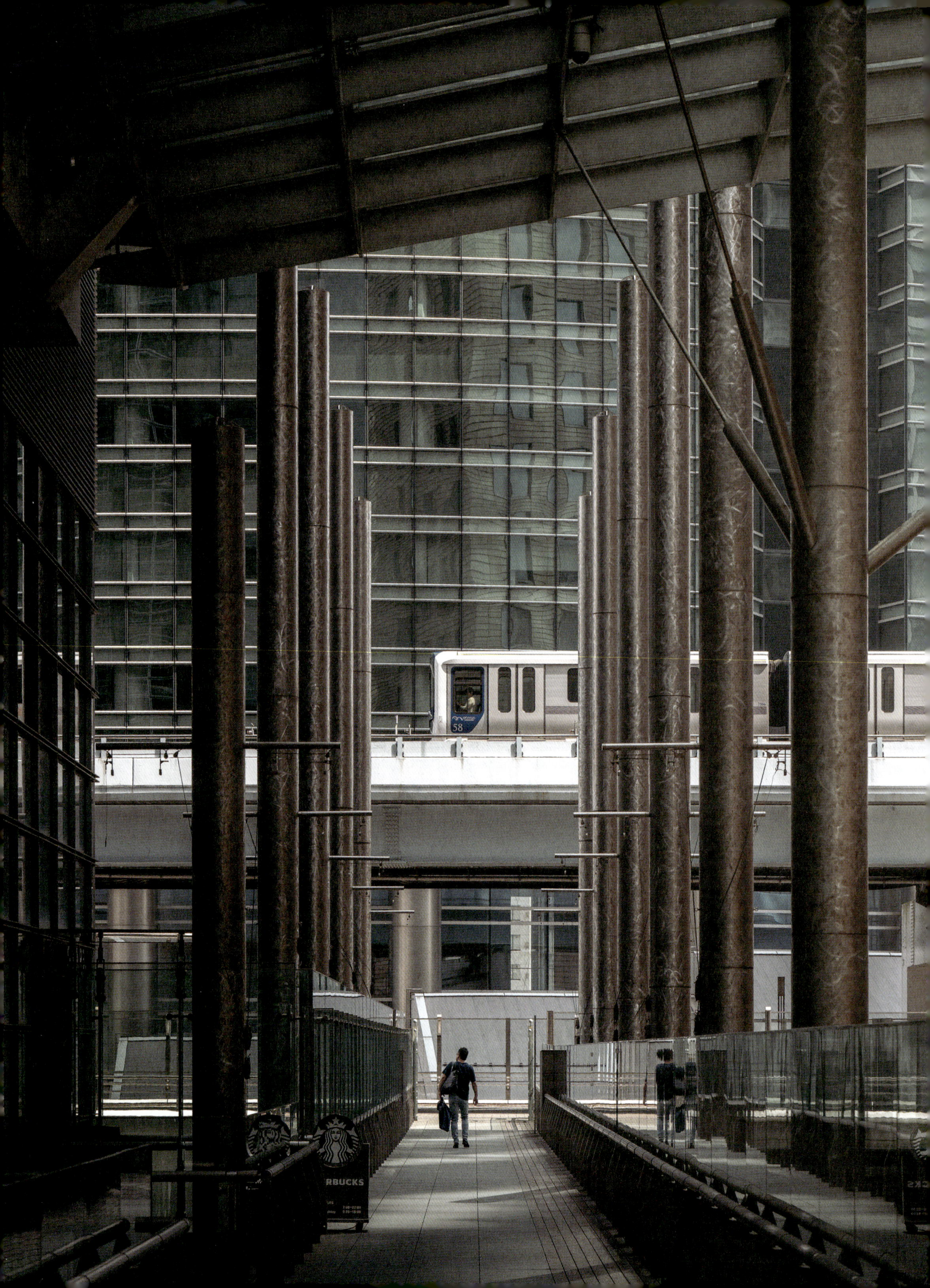
58

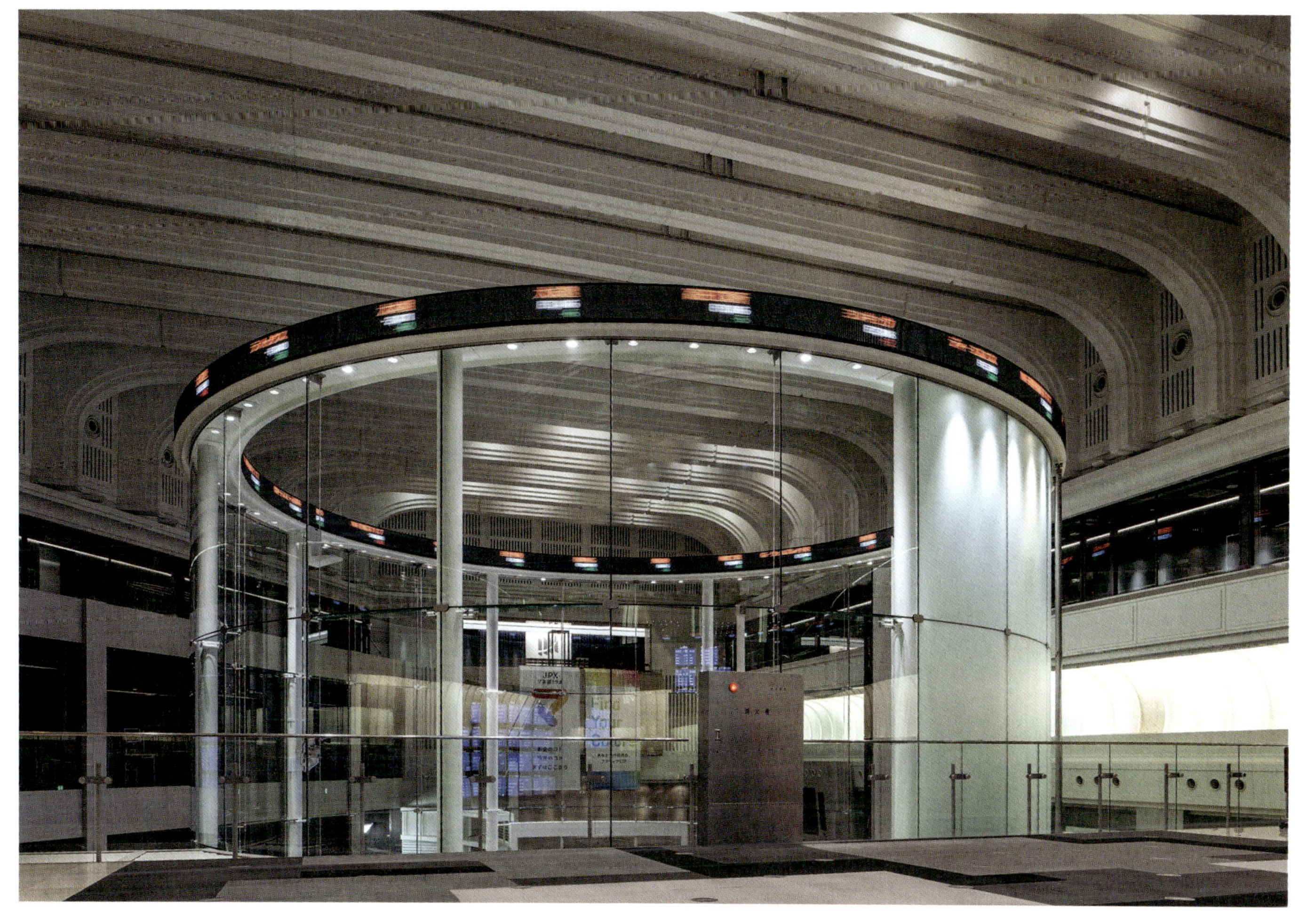

Tokyo Stock Exchange.
Located in the Nihonbashi district, the historic Tokyo Stock Exchange building is a remarkable example of architecture that showcases Japan's economic boom.

Shiodome.
The Shiodome district exemplifies Tokyo's cutting-edge urbanism, featuring sleek skyscrapers, innovative architecture, and elevated walkways. The *Yurikamome* automatic train line weaves through the area, enhancing the futuristic ambiance.

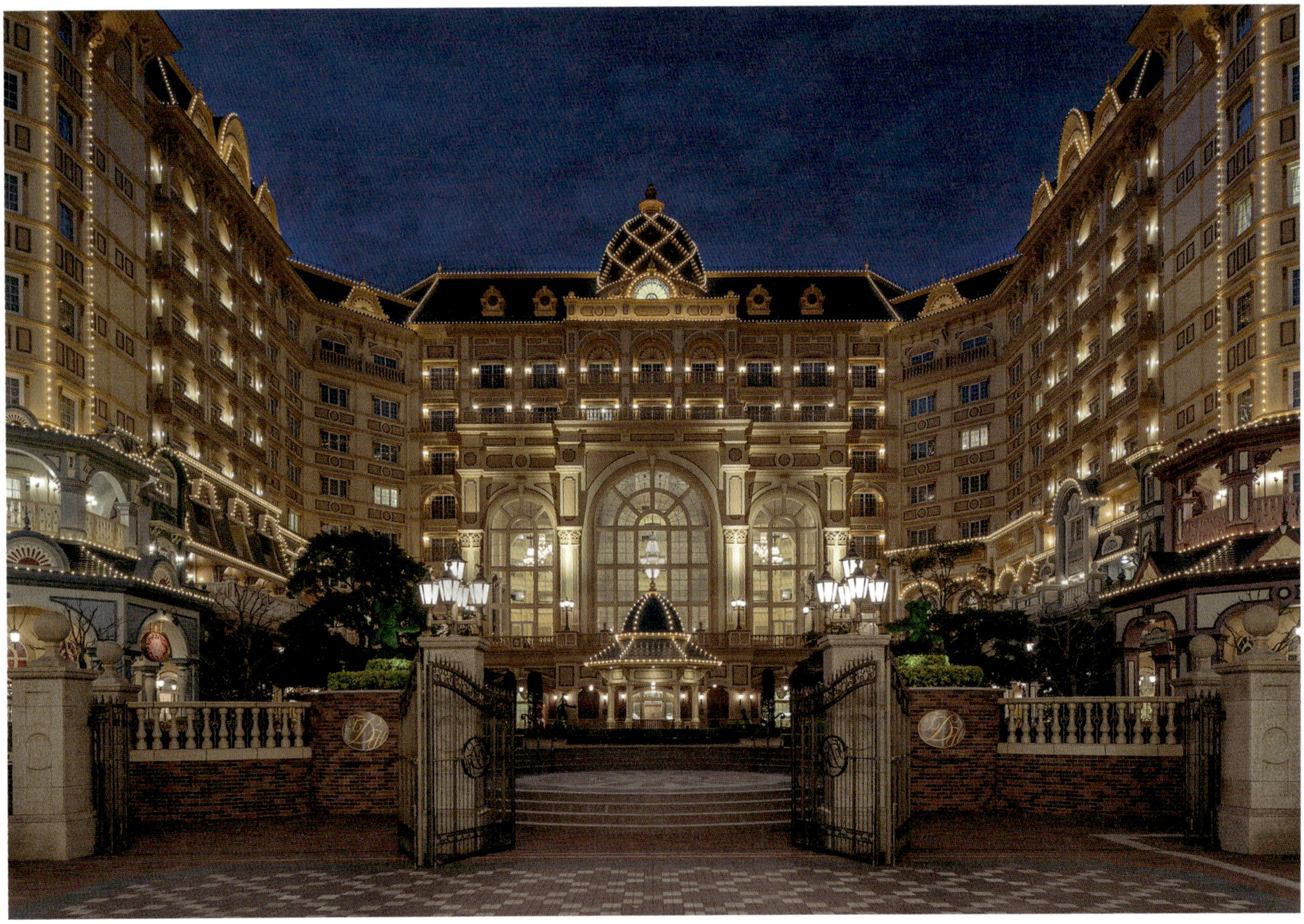

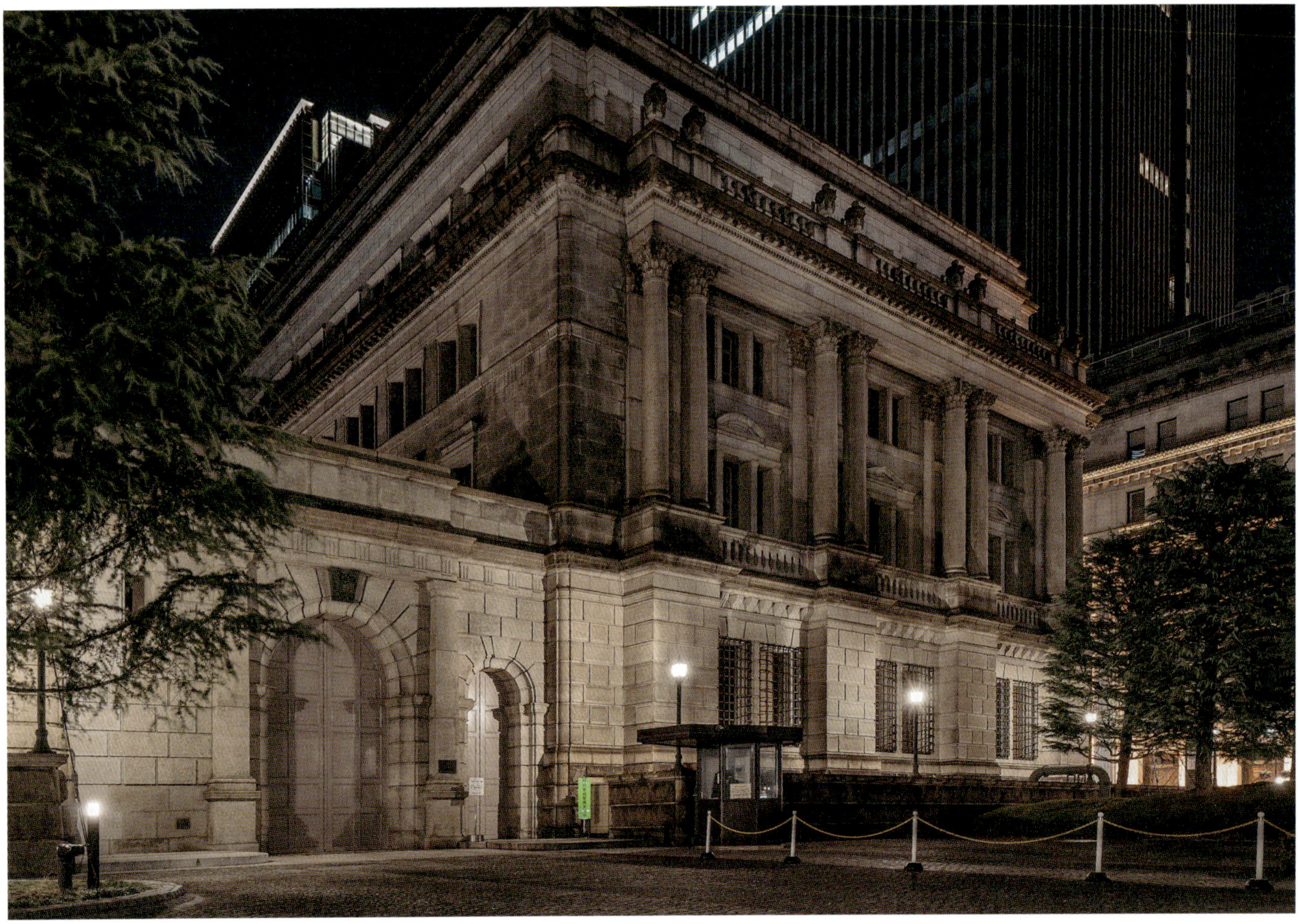

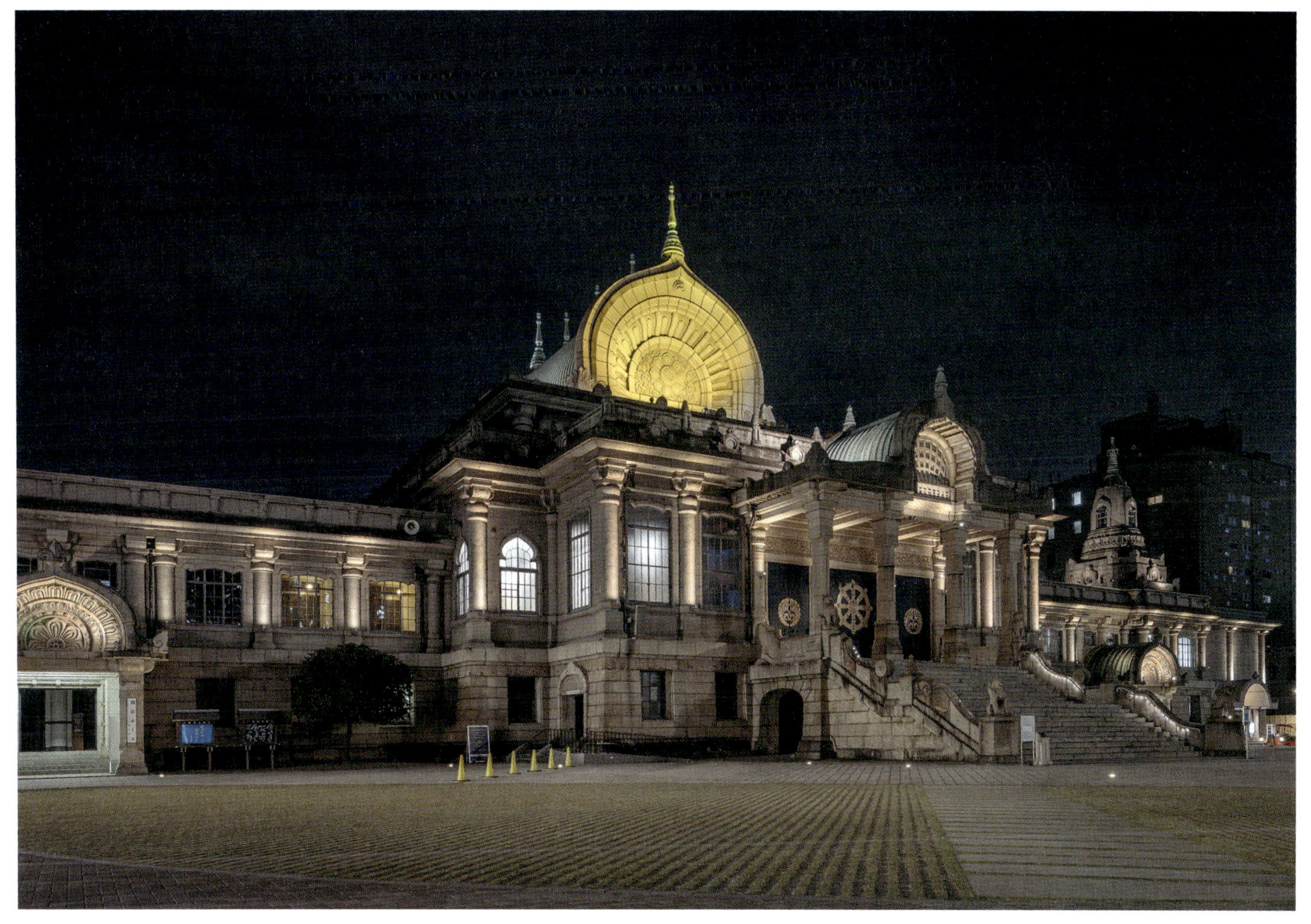

Tsukiji Hongan-ji.
Bathed in a golden glow under the night sky, the Tsukiji Hongan-ji Buddhist temple rises majestically, its curves inspired by Indian architecture.

Tokyo Disneyland Hotel.
With its ornate facade, golden accents, and grand windows, the Tokyo Disneyland Hotel invites guests into a magical world at the entrance to Tokyo DisneySea.

Bank of Japan.
The former Bank of Japan building, located in the heart of Tokyo, is a neoclassical architectural masterpiece from the Meiji era (1868-1912). A symbol of the nation's economic modernisation, its grand columns and timeless elegance are a testament to Japan's financial history.

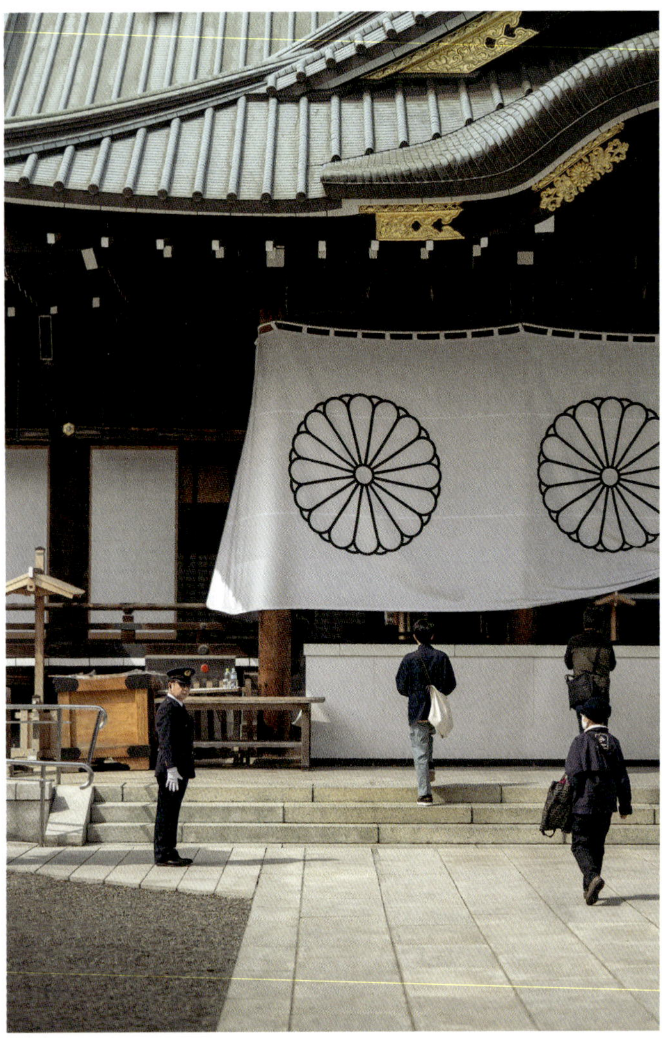

Yasukuni Shrine.
Established in 1869 to honour Japan's war dead, Yasukuni Shrine has stirred controversy since 1978 for enshrining fourteen convicted war criminals among the 2.5 million souls commemorated. Beneath gilded rooftops, chrysanthemums–the imperial emblem–adorn a grand white banner. The shrine also houses the benchmark cherry tree used to declare the start of the blooming season each spring officially.

Nezu Museum.
The gardens of the Nezu Museum in Tokyo create a magical autumn setting, ablaze with fiery maple leaves. Founded in 1941, the museum showcases the exquisite art collection of Nezu Kaichirō, one of Japan's most prominent art collectors.

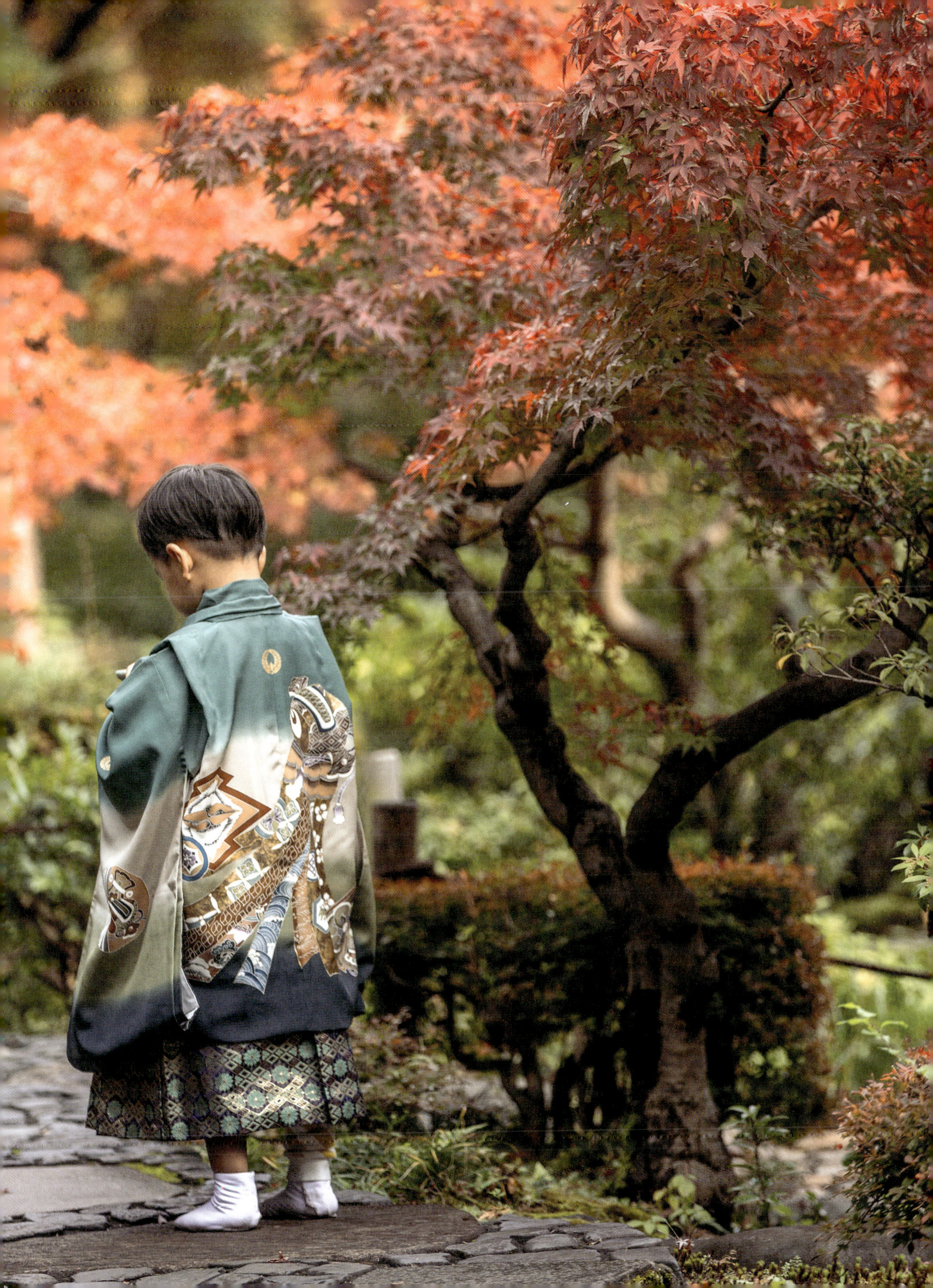

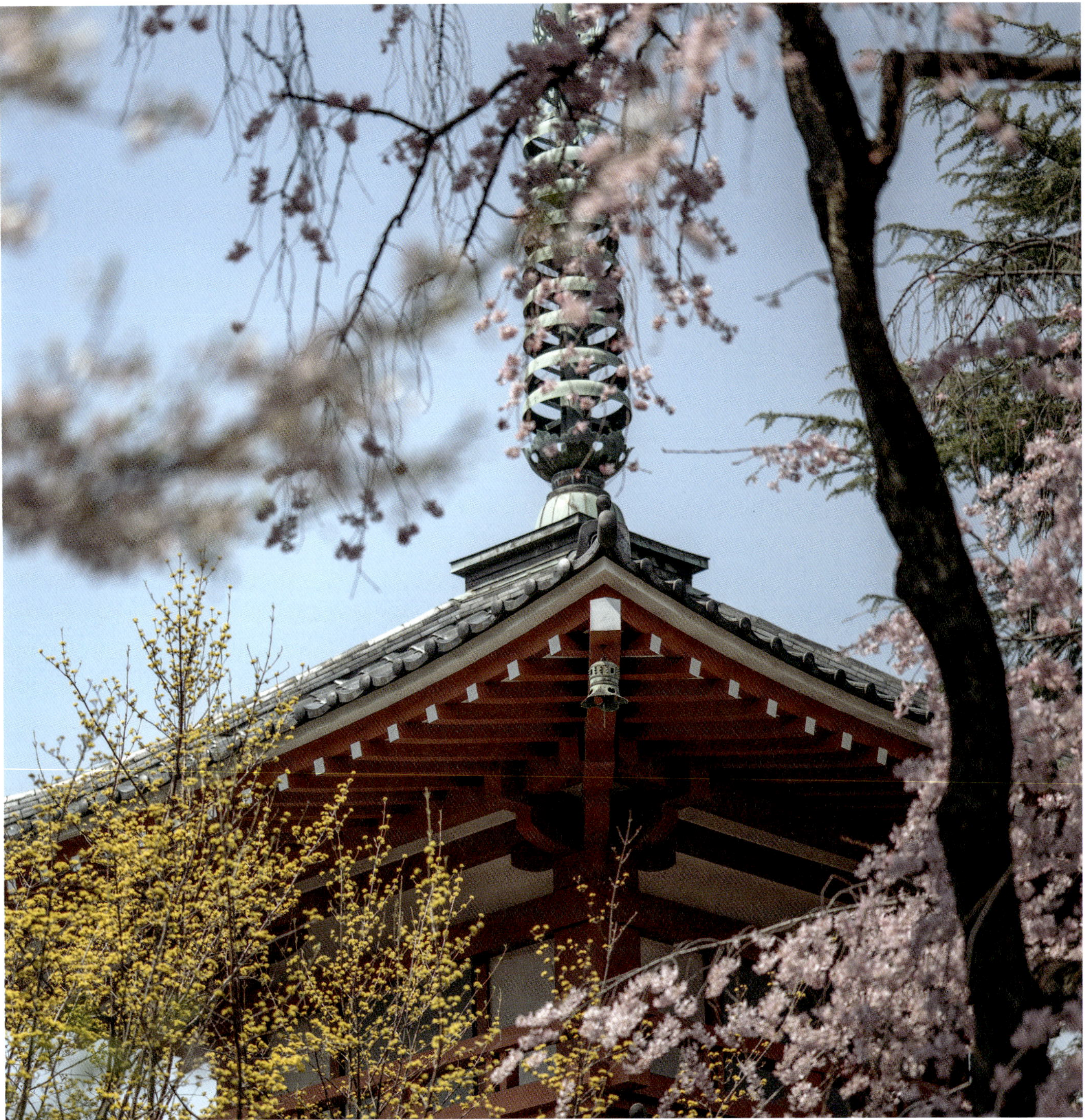

Pagoda of Araiyakushi Baishouin Temple.
The pagoda of Araiyakushi Baishouin, a Buddhist temple, stands gracefully amidst spring blooms, framed by pink cherry blossoms on the right and golden kerria flowers on the left.

Araiyakushi Baishouin Temple.
Founded in 1586, Araiyakushi Baishouin is believed to have healing powers for eye-related ailments and to support children's education.

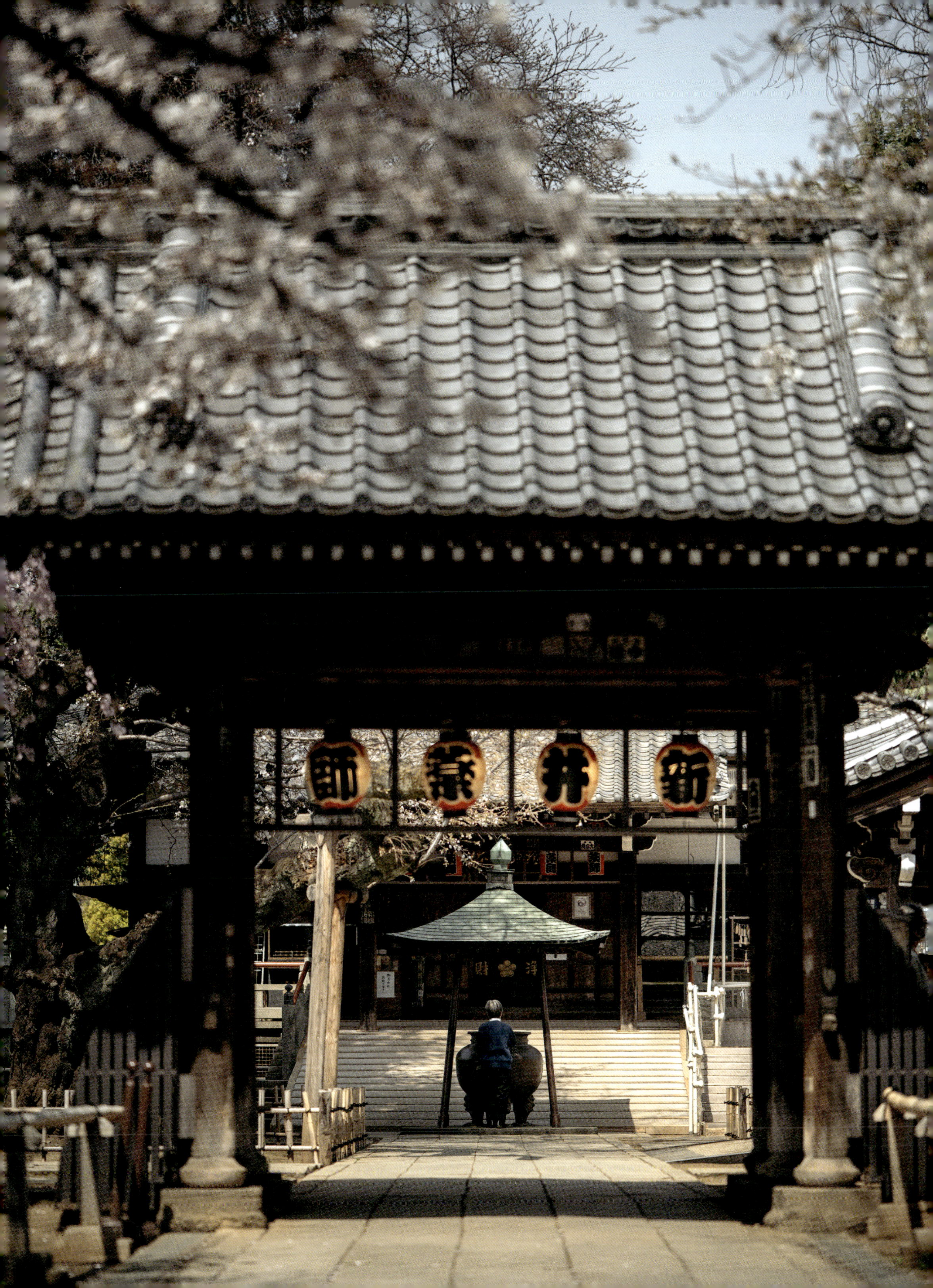
師
薬
井
新

Wedding at Meiji Jingu.
This image captures the grace and tradition of a Shinto wedding at Tokyo's Meiji Jingu Shrine. The bride, adorned in an exquisite kimono embellished with floral and golden patterns, embodies Japanese elegance, while the groom proudly dons his traditional black *hakama*.

Oarai Isosaki Shrine.
Located along the Ibaraki coast, Oarai Isosaki Shrine is famous for its majestic *torii* gate, perched on rocks and overlooking the vast Pacific Ocean. This sacred site is believed to be the earthly descent point of two Shinto deities, inspiring the shrine's establishment in 856. Facing east, it provides a breathtaking view, especially at sunrise, when the first light touches the horizon.

>

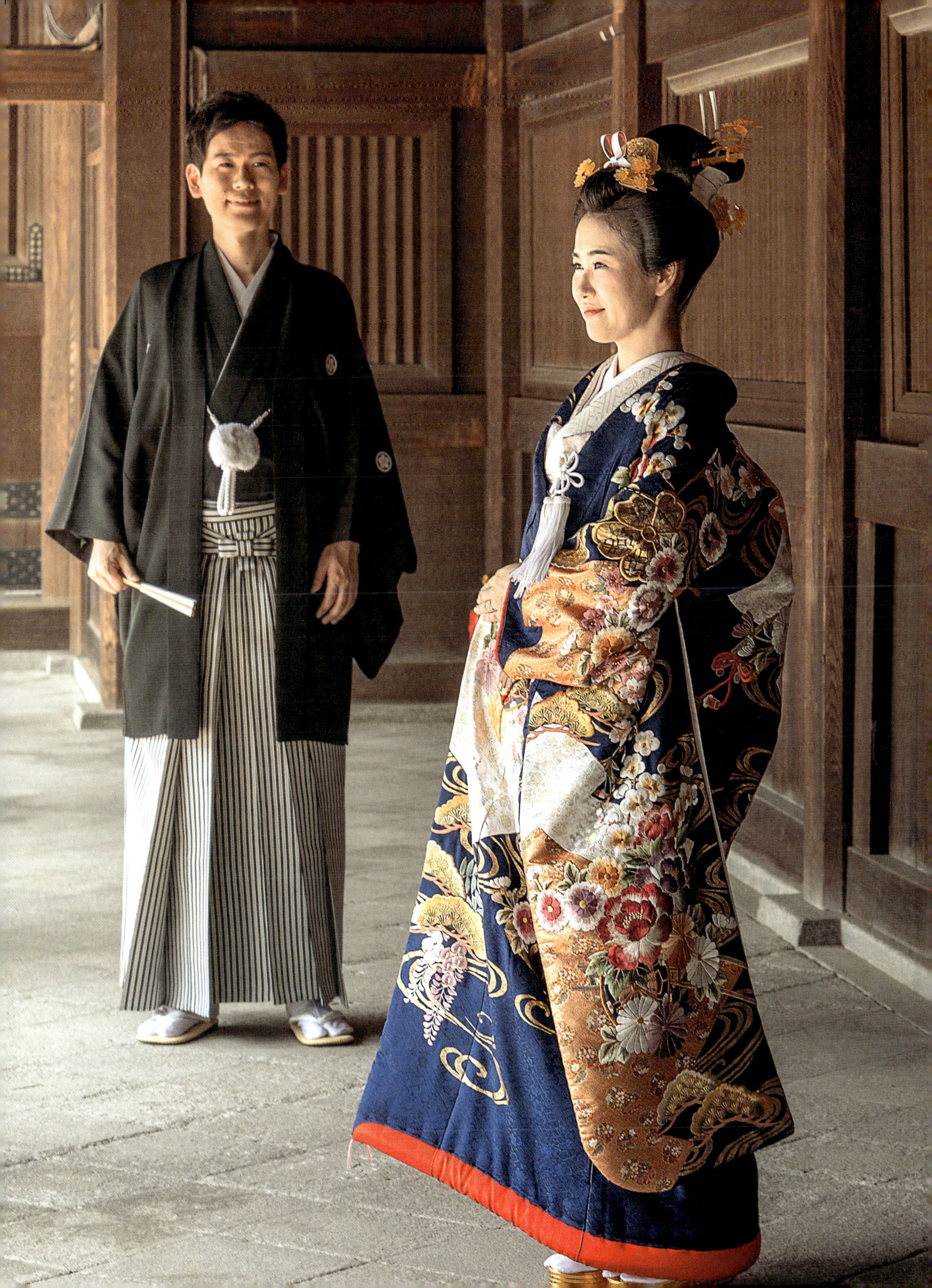

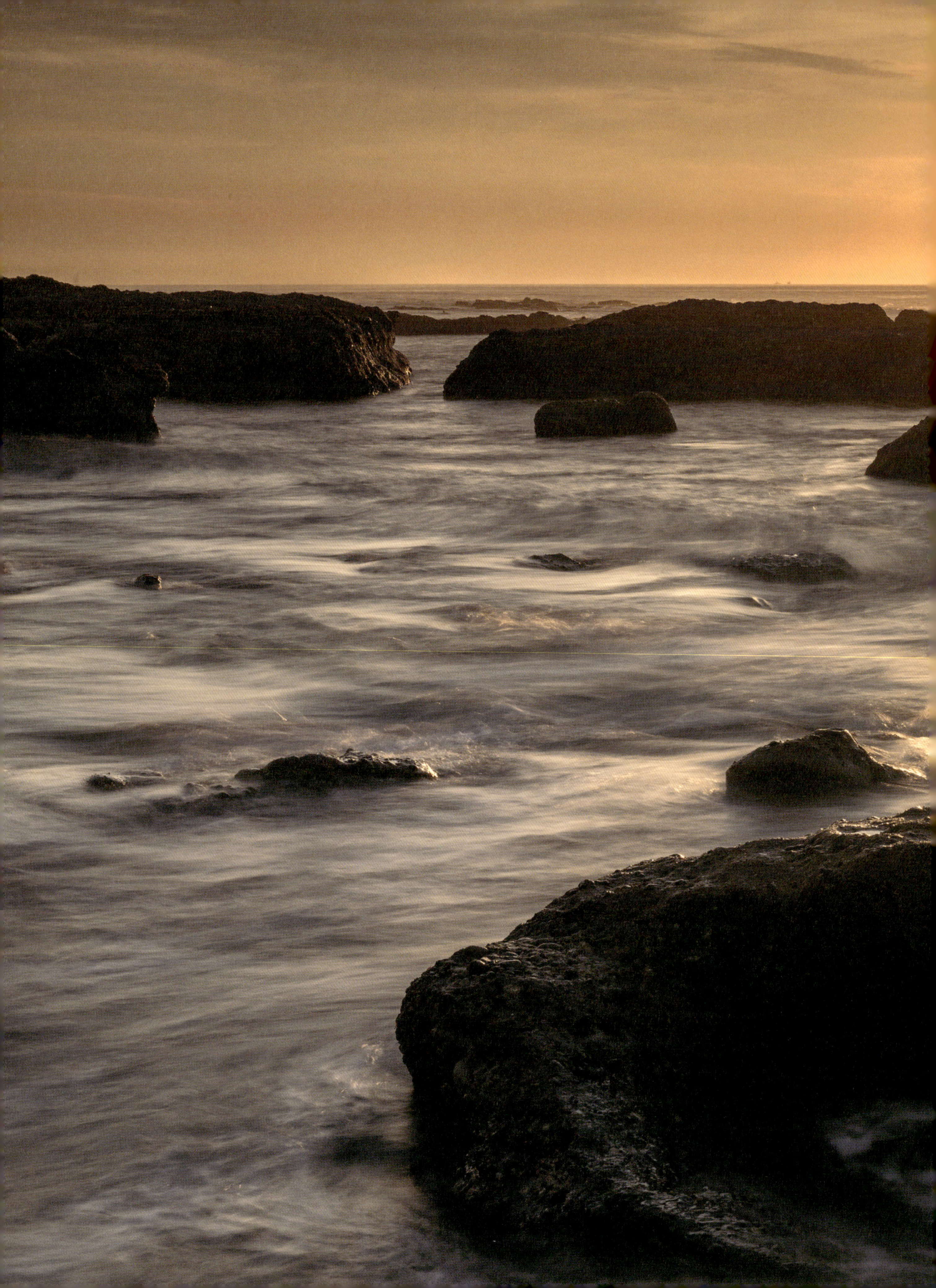

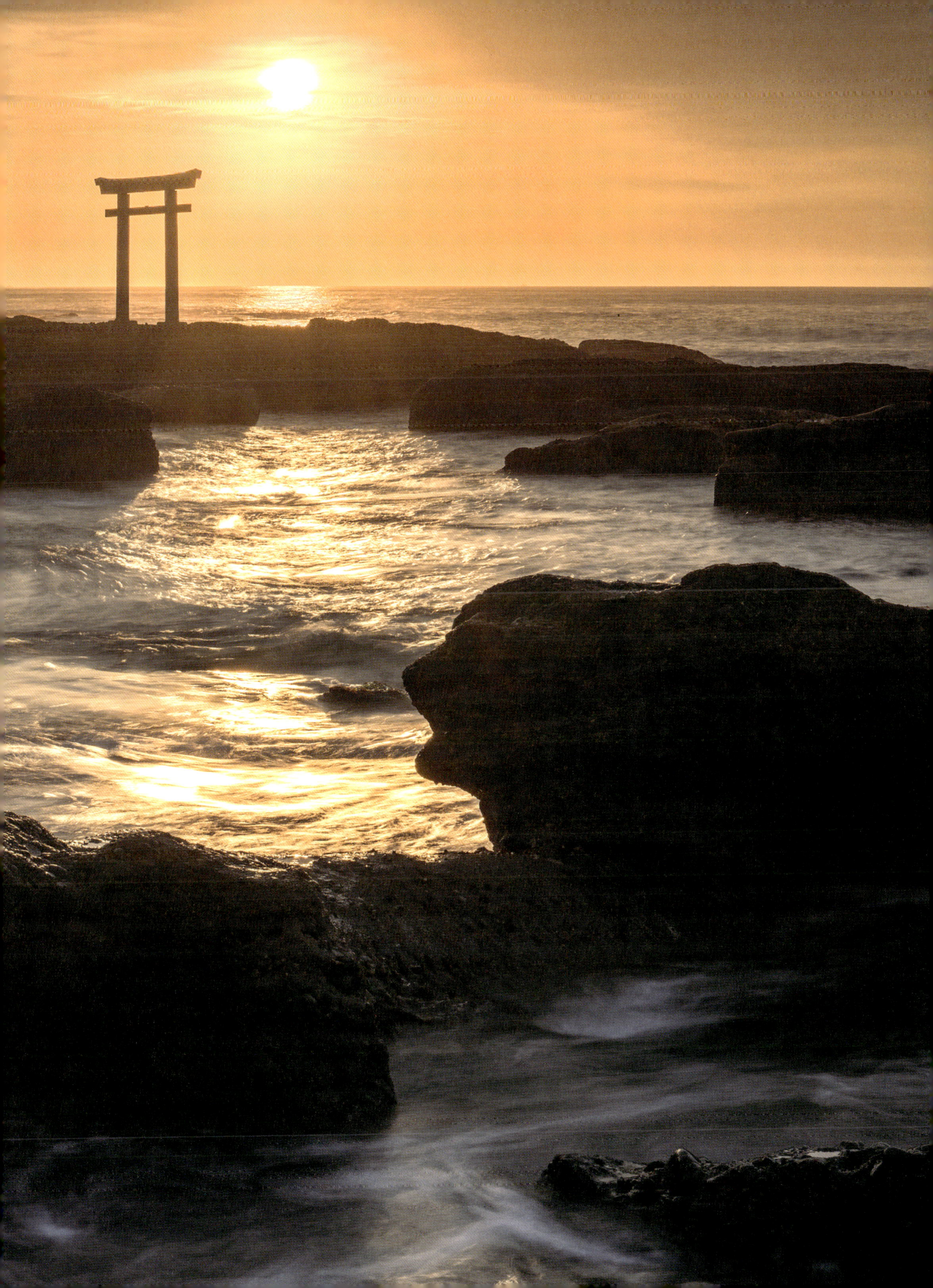

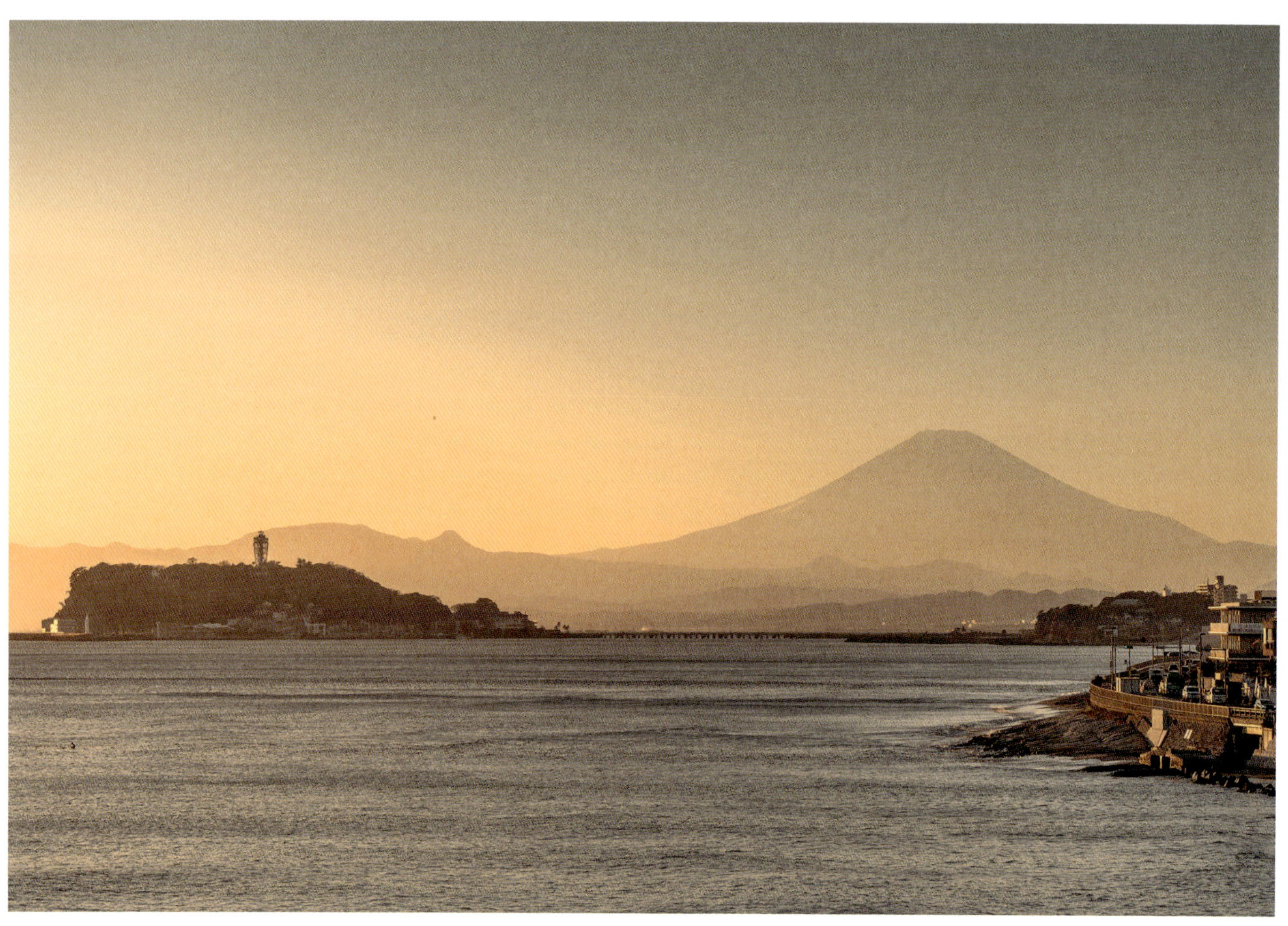

Enoshima & Mount Fuji.
Enoshima, a charming island off the coast of Kamakura, is known for its sandy beaches and palm trees; it also harbours a wealth of temples and Shinto shrines. On a clear day, the island offers a breathtaking view of Mount Fuji.

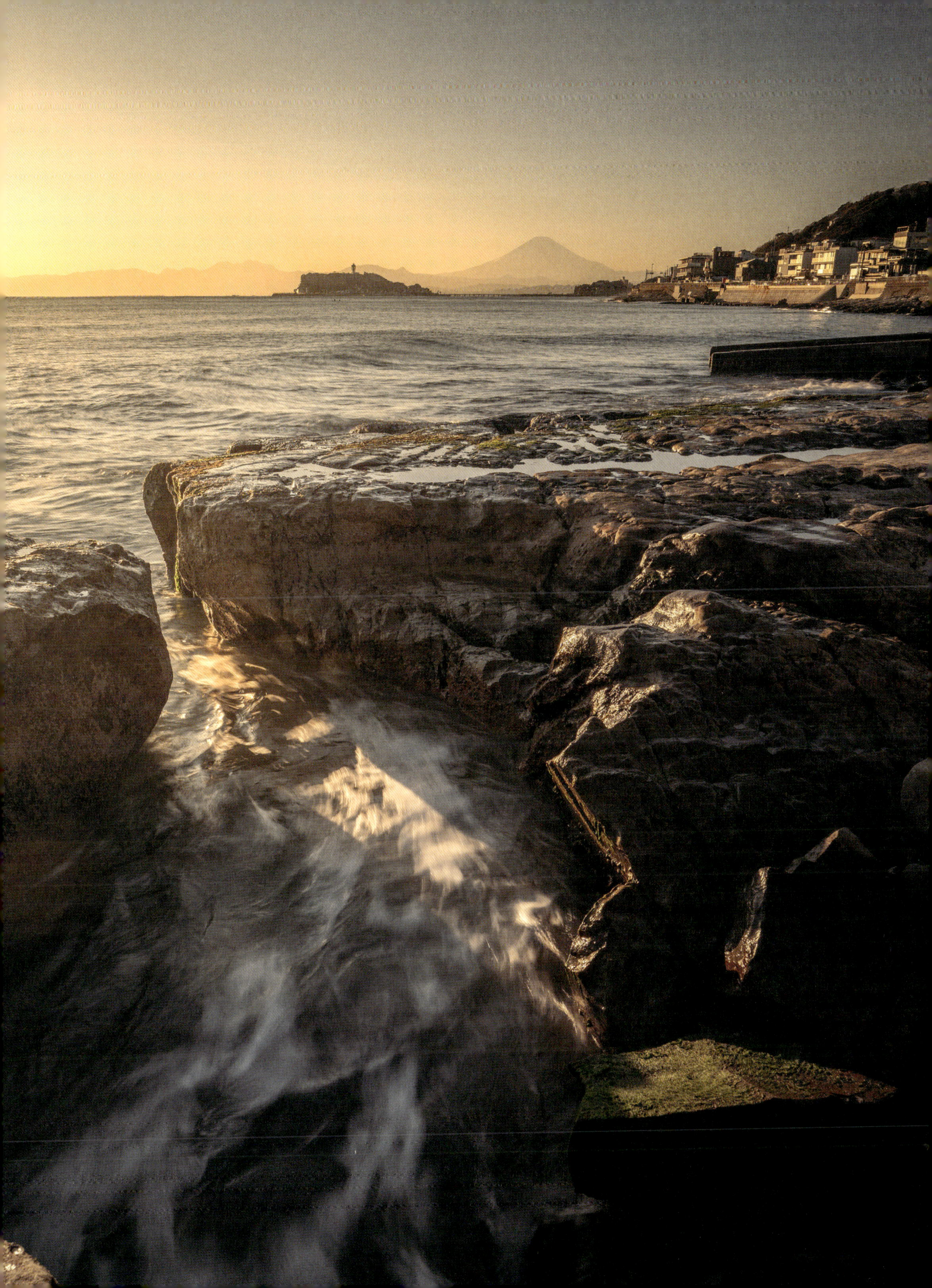

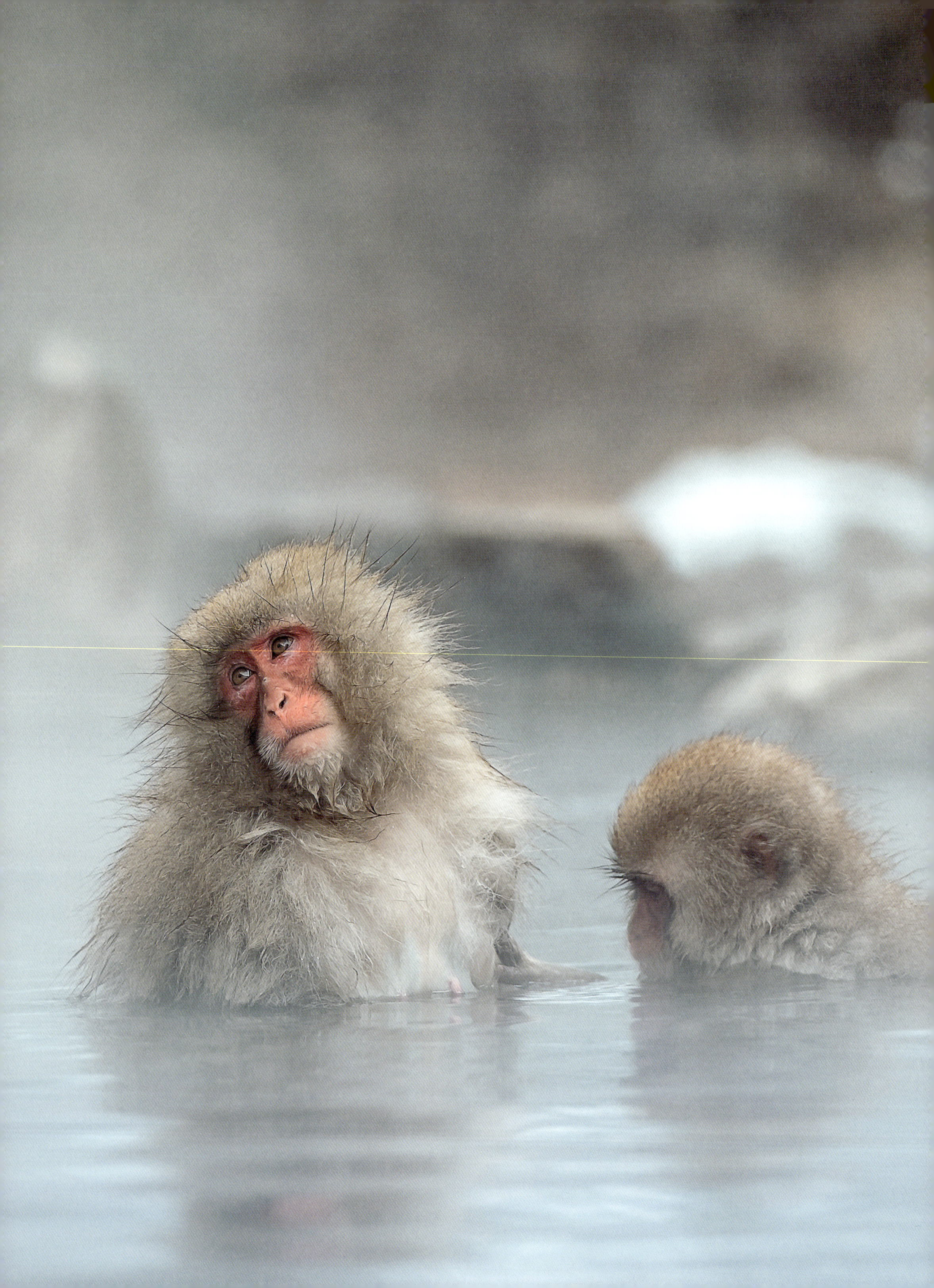

The Jigokudani Monkey Park.
Nestled in Nagano, the Jigokudani Monkey Park is famous for its Japanese macaques bathing in natural hot springs, all set against a backdrop of snow-covered winter landscapes. This unique spot offers a captivating opportunity to observe these animals in their natural environment.

中部

Chūbu

Land of Beauty and Diversity

Chūbu, nestled in the heart of Japan, is where the vibrant energy of the east meets the tranquillity of the west. Spanning across nine prefectures – Aichi, Fukui, Gifu, Ishikawa, Nagano, Niigata, Shizuoka, Toyama, and Yamanashi – Chūbu is a true kaleidoscope of nature and culture. In this region, age-old traditions are cherished and preserved, while modern innovations seamlessly blend into a timeless landscape.

Size.
Chūbu spans approximately 72,572 km², accounting for about 19% of Japan's total land area.

Demographics and Population.
The region is home to around 21.7 million people across its nine prefectures.

Geographical Location.
Chūbu comprises nine prefectures: Niigata, Toyama, Ishikawa, Fukui, Yamanashi, Nagano, Gifu, Shizuoka, and Aichi. Geographically, it lies between the Kantō region to the east and Kansai to the west, stretching from the Sea of Japan in the north to the Pacific Ocean in the south. Major cities include Nagoya, Niigata, and Nagano.

Climate and Seasons.
Thanks to its varied topography, Chūbu experiences a wide range of climates. The coast of the Sea of Japan is known for its harsh winters and heavy snowfall, while the Pacific side enjoys a milder, more temperate climate. The mountainous regions, particularly the Japanese Alps, are characterised by cool summers and snowy winters, making them a popular destination for winter sports.

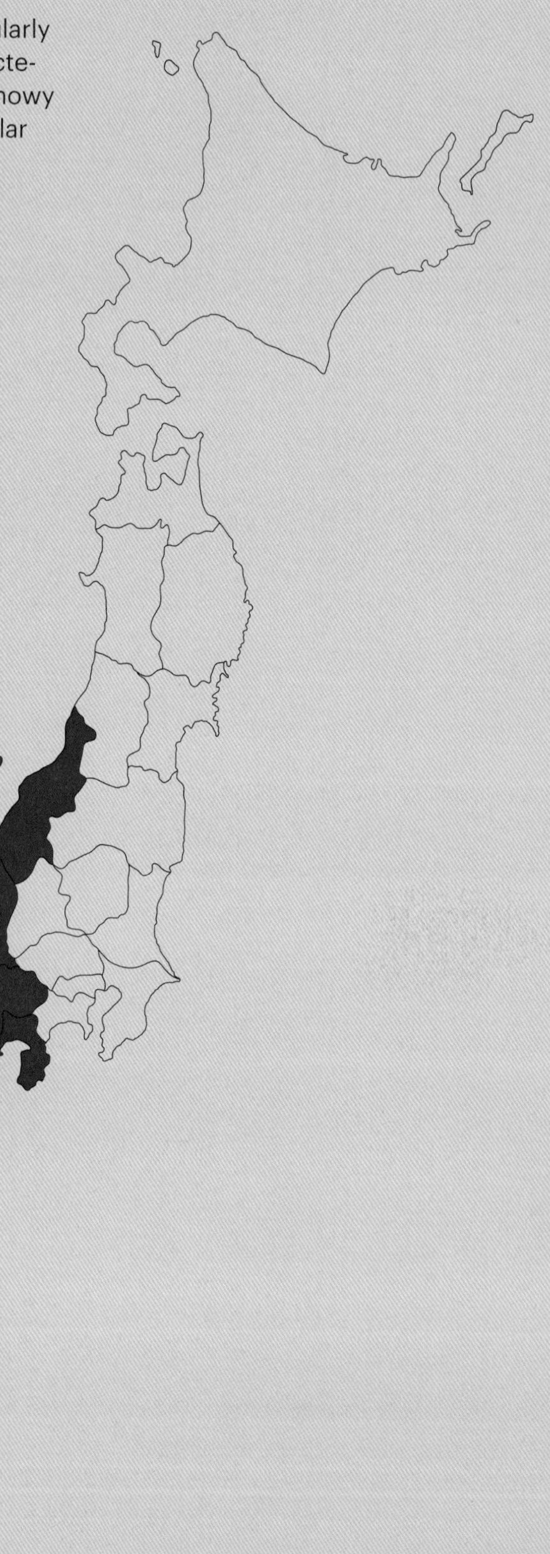

中部

Nagano, in the heart of the Japanese Alps

Nestled in the centre of the region, Nagano is a paradise for mountain and outdoor enthusiasts. Surrounded by the majestic Japanese Alps, this prefecture offers a peaceful retreat, where snow-capped peaks, lush valleys, and soothing hot springs exist in perfect harmony with nature.

The city of Nagano is renowned for its Zenkō-ji Temple, a spiritual landmark that is over 1,400 years old and home to a sacred statue of Buddha kept hidden from public view. Visitors come from far and wide to soak in the serene atmosphere and partake in the ritual of touching the "key to paradise", a symbolic gesture believed to ensure reincarnation.

Not far away, the Jigokudani Monkey Park draws travellers eager to witness snow macaques soaking in the hot springs – a charming and unique spectacle, especially in winter.

The Kamikōchi Valley, with its stunning vistas, is a haven for hikers, while Hakuba and Shiga Kōgen – both renowned ski resorts – gained worldwide recognition as the hosts of the 1998 Winter Olympics.

Shizuoka, The Kingdom of Mount Fuji

Nestled between mountains and the sea, Shizuoka is a prefecture dominated by the majestic presence of Mount Fuji, Japan's sacred peak. The Fuji-Hakone-Izu National Park, shared with the neighbouring Kantō region, offers countless vantage points from which to admire this iconic mountain, often capped with snow.

Lakes, forests, and waterfalls surround Mount Fuji, with sites such as Lake Kawaguchi – known for its stunning reflections of Fujisan – and the Shiraito Falls, a UNESCO World Heritage Site, attracting visitors from around the globe.

Shizuoka is also renowned for its green tea, grown on terraced hills that stretch to the horizon. The tea fields of Makinohara, along with tasting workshops, draw enthusiasts of this ancient beverage.

Aichi, Where Modernity Meets Tradition

Located in southeastern Chūbu, Aichi is a prefecture where history blends seamlessly with innovation. Nagoya, Japan's fourth-largest city, is a bustling industrial hub, yet it also boasts a rich historical heritage. Nagoya Castle, with its distinctive golden dolphins (shachihoko) adorning the roofs, stands as a symbol of the power once held by the Oda and Tokugawa lords.

The Atsuta Shrine – one of Japan's most revered sites – houses the Kusanagi sword, one of the nation's legendary imperial treasures. Not far from there, the Toyota Museum chronicles the evolution of Japan's automobile industry, which has deep roots in this very region.

Aichi is also famous for its traditional pottery, particularly from Seto and Tokoname, where ancient craftsmanship continues to flourish.

Gifu and the Historic Villages of Shirakawa-go

Gifu is a prefecture where tradition is still very much alive. The villages of Shirakawa-go and Gokayama, recognised as UNESCO World Heritage Sites, offer a glimpse into rural Japan from days long past. These hamlets are renowned for their *gasshō-zukuri* houses, characterised by steep, thatched roofs designed to endure the heavy winter snowfall.

The town of Takayama – often called "Little Kyoto" – is home to a picturesque street lined with traditional sake shops and breweries. Its biannual Takayama Matsuri, one of Japan's most celebrated festivals, features beautifully adorned floats parading through the charming old town.

Ishikawa and the Elegance of Kanazawa

Ishikawa is a region renowned for its refinement, where craftsmanship and culture thrive. The city of Kanazawa is home to Kenroku-en, one of Japan's three most beautifully landscaped gardens. Its serene ponds, elegant pavilions, and meticulously pruned trees create a magical atmosphere throughout the year.

Kanazawa is also renowned for its geisha district, *Higashi Chaya*, where cobblestone streets and traditional teahouses transport visitors back to the Edo period. Local crafts, such as gold leaf and *Kutani-yaki* pottery, showcase time-honoured skills passed down through generations.

Fukui and the Tōjinbō Cliffs

Fukui, which borders the Sea of Japan, is a prefecture where nature showcases its raw power. The Tōjinbō cliffs, with their dramatic basalt columns, present a stunning sight. These unique formations, sculpted by centuries of marine erosion, attract both photographers and geology enthusiasts.

Eihei-ji Temple, founded in 1244, serves as a spiritual centre for the Sōtō Zen sect. Nestled in a forest of towering cedars, it welcomes monks and visitors seeking meditation and tranquillity.

Toyama and the Tateyama Kurobe Alpine Route

Toyama is the gateway to the renowned Tateyama Kurobe Alpine Route, a marvel of engineering that traverses the mountains and offers breathtaking panoramic views. In winter, towering snow walls, sometimes reaching 20 metres high, captivate travellers, while in spring and autumn, hiking trails meander through awe-inspiring landscapes. The Kurobe Dam, one of the tallest in Japan, is an impressive sight, with water cascading dramatically against a majestic mountain backdrop.

Niigata and the Delights of the Sea of Japan

Niigata, bordered by the Sea of Japan, is a region famous for its exceptional rice, which is used to craft some of the country's finest sake. The prefecture comes alive during summer festivals, such as the *Nagaoka Fireworks Festival*, which illuminates the night sky with breathtaking displays.

Sado Island, accessible from the coast, offers a tranquil retreat, where the history of political exiles intertwines with pristine, untouched landscapes.

Yamanashi, Between Vineyards and Mount Fuji

Yamanashi, dominated by the iconic Mount Fuji, is also renowned for its vineyards. The region produces high-quality wines, particularly in Kōshū, where visitors can sample local vintages while taking in the stunning mountainous views.

Lake Kawaguchi and Arakurayama Sengen Park provide some of the most renowned views of Mount Fuji, particularly in spring when the cherry blossoms are in full bloom.

中部

Best Times to Visit

– Spring (Mars to May).
Cherry blossoms create stunning landscapes and offer comfortable Temperatures.

– Autumn (September to November).
Perfect for admiring colourful autumn leaves and benefiting from a milder climate.

– Winter (December to February).
Ideal for winter sports in the Japanese Alps.

Top 5 Must-See Destinations

1. Mount Fuji.
Japan's iconic symbol, offering a variety of hiking trails and breathtaking panoramic views.

2. -Shirakawa-go.
A UNESCO World Heritage Site, renowned for its traditional *gasshō-zukuri* thatched houses.

3. Matsumoto Castle.
One of Japan's oldest and best-preserved castles, often called "The Raven Castle".

4. Chūbu-Sangaku National Park.
A hiker's paradise, with breathtaking alpine vistas.

5. Kanazawa City.
Home to the renowned Kenroku-en garden, one of Japan's "Three Great Gardens", and a beautifully preserved geisha district.

中部

Gastronomy

The Chūbu region boasts a rich and diverse culinary heritage, shaped by its mountainous landscapes, bountiful coastal waters, and deeply rooted local traditions. Below is a town-by-town guide to Chūbu's culinary specialities, complete with detailed descriptions.

名古屋 Nagoya

[ひつまぶし] Hitsumabushi
A grilled eel (*unagi*) dish, finely chopped and served over rice. It's traditionally enjoyed in three stages: as it is, with condiments such as wasabi and spring onions, or with a ladle of hot broth poured over the top.

[味噌カツ] Miso Katsu
Nagoya's unique take on *tonkatsu* (breaded pork cutlet), featuring a rich, sweet-and-savoury miso sauce made with the region's famous red miso (*hatcho miso*) instead of the usual tonkatsu sauce.

[手羽先] Tebasaki
Deep-fried chicken wings glazed with a sweet and spicy sauce, then sprinkled with sesame seeds and black pepper. A signature dish of Nagoya's lively *izakaya* pubs.

[台湾ラーメン] Taiwan Rāmen
A fiery noodle soup inspired by Taiwanese flavours, typically topped with spicy minced pork, garlic, and Chinese chives.

[きしめん] Kishimen
Flat, wide udon noodles served in a soy-based broth, often garnished with such ingredients as tempura or seasonal vegetables.

高山 Takayama

[飛騨牛] Hida-gyū
A premium wagyū beef from the Hida region, prized for its rich marbling and melt-in-the-mouth texture. It is typically grilled as steak, in *shabu-shabu* hotpot, or as *yakiniku* (Japanese BBQ).

[朴葉味噌] Hōba Miso
A rustic mountain dish where miso paste is grilled on a magnolia leaf, often alongside vegetables and slices of meat — a warming local speciality.

[高山ラーメン]
Takayama Rāmen
A simple yet flavourful rāmen served in a clear soy sauce-based broth, with thin, slightly wavy noodles and toppings such as pork and bamboo shoots.

金沢 Kanazawa

[治部煮] Jibuni
A traditional duck or chicken stew simmered in a sweet-savoury broth of soy sauce and mirin and thickened with potato starch.

[金沢寿司]
Kanazawa Sushi
Kanazawa is famed for its fresh and refined sushi, featuring local delicacies such as snow crab, sweet prawns, and *amaebi* (raw sweet shrimp).

[ゴリ] Gori – Noto goby fry
A small fish native to the Noto Peninsula, typically fried or simmered in soy sauce and mirin — a true local delicacy.

富山 Toyama

[富山ブラックラーメン]
Toyama Black Rāmen
A bold rāmen with an intensely dark and salty soy sauce broth, often served with pork slices, chopped spring onions, and a generous dash of black pepper.

[白エビ] Shiroebi – Toyama white shrimp
Delicate, translucent prawns from Toyama Bay, enjoyed raw as sashimi, deep-fried as tempura, or even made into crispy snacks.

[鱒寿司] Masu-zushi
A type of pressed sushi made with vinegared rice and marinated trout, neatly wrapped in bamboo leaves.

福井
Fukui

[越前ガニ] Echizen Gani
Echizen crab is prized for its sweet, tender meat. It's typically grilled, raw as sashimi, or in warming crab soups.

[ソースカツ丼]
Sauce Katsu-don
A Fukui-style rice bowl topped with crispy breaded pork cutlets, drizzled with a tangy Worcestershire-style sauce.

[おろし蕎麦] Oroshi Soba
Cold soba noodles served with a refreshing grated daikon radish and a light dipping sauce made from *dashi* and soy sauce.

新潟
Niigata

[のっぺ] Noppe
A hearty, thick stew made with root vegetables, mushrooms, and occasionally seafood. Traditionally enjoyed during festivals and family gatherings.

[タレカツ]
Tare-katsu
Niigata's distinctive take on katsudon, where breaded pork cutlets are dipped in a sweet soy-based sauce before being served over a bowl of rice.

[コシヒカリ米]
Koshihikari Rice
Regarded as some of the finest rice in Japan, Niigata's *Koshihikari* is known for its soft, slightly sticky texture and naturally sweet flavour.

長野
Nagano

[信州そば] Shinshu Soba
Soba noodles from the Shinshu region are famed for their smooth texture and pronounced buckwheat taste. They can be served cold with dipping sauce or in a hot broth.

[おやき] Oyaki
Traditional dumplings made from fermented buckwheat or wheat dough, filled with savoury ingredients like vegetables, miso, or sweet red bean paste, then grilled or steamed.

[馬刺し] Basashi
– Horse Sashimi
Thin slices of raw horse meat are a local delicacy in Nagano. They are typically served with soy sauce, grated ginger, and garlic.

静岡
Shizuoka

[うなぎパイ] Unagi Pie
A crisp, buttery pastry subtly flavoured with eel extract.

[静岡おでん]
Shizuoka Oden
A darker version of oden in which ingredients are simmered in a rich, black soy sauce broth and served with a dollop of sweet miso.

[桜えび] Sakura Ebi
Tiny pink prawns fished exclusively in Suruga Bay. Valued for their delicate flavour, they are often enjoyed in tempura or served atop rice bowls (donburi).

甲府
Kōfu

[ほうとう] Hōtō
A hearty noodle stew with thick, flat wheat noodles simmered in a miso-based broth with seasonal vegetables. Widely considered Yamanashi's ultimate comfort food.

[甲州ワインビーフ]
Kōshū Wine Beef
Beef from cattle fed on grape pomace left over from local Koshu wine production, resulting in tender, richly flavoured meat with a subtle sweetness.

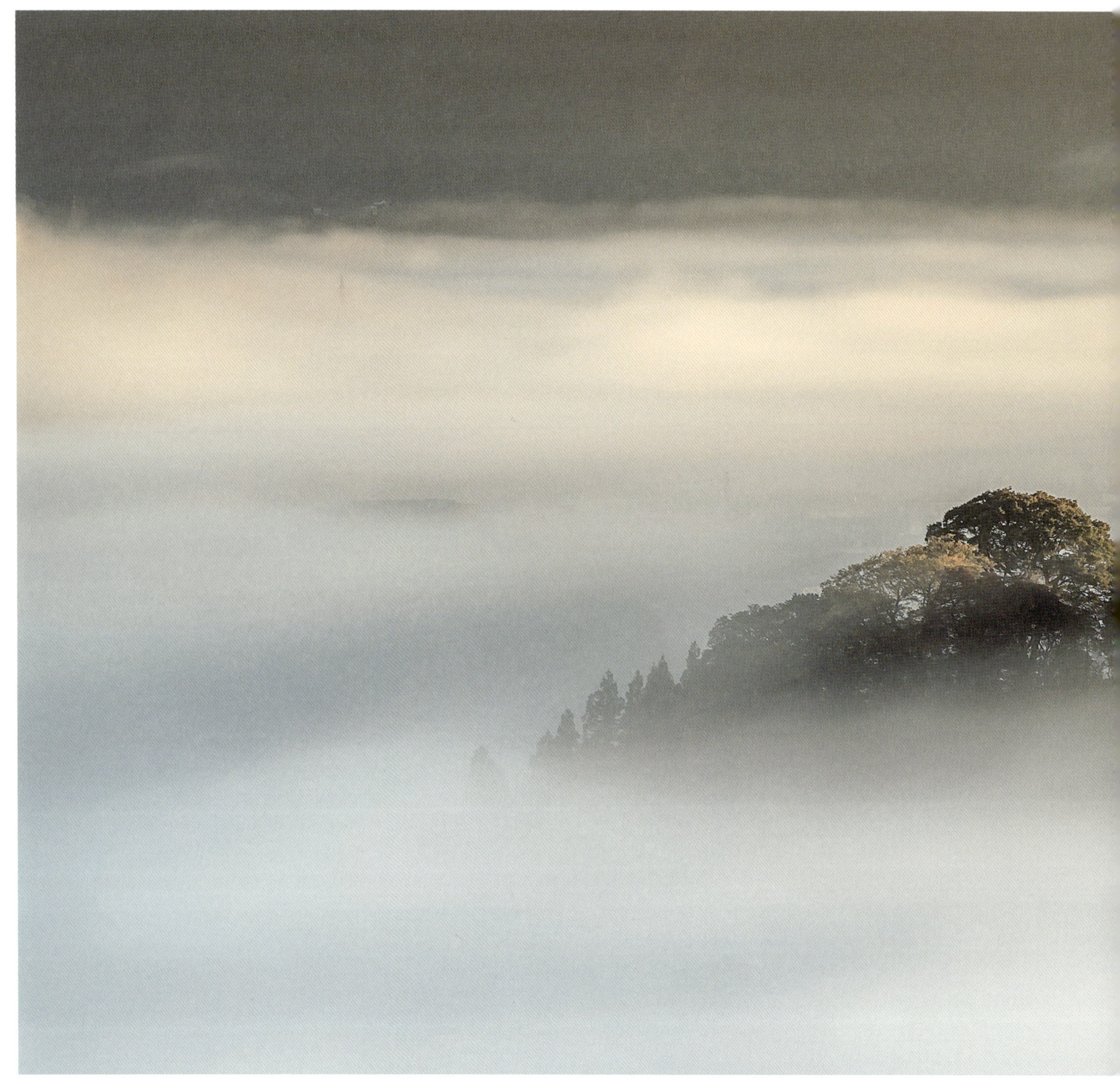

Echizen Ono Castle.
Originally constructed in 1580 and nicknamed the "Castle in the Sky", Echizen Ono Castle appears to float above the clouds on misty mornings. Situated on a hillside in Fukui, it offers a captivating, fairytale-like sight that evokes the essence of a Japanese legend.

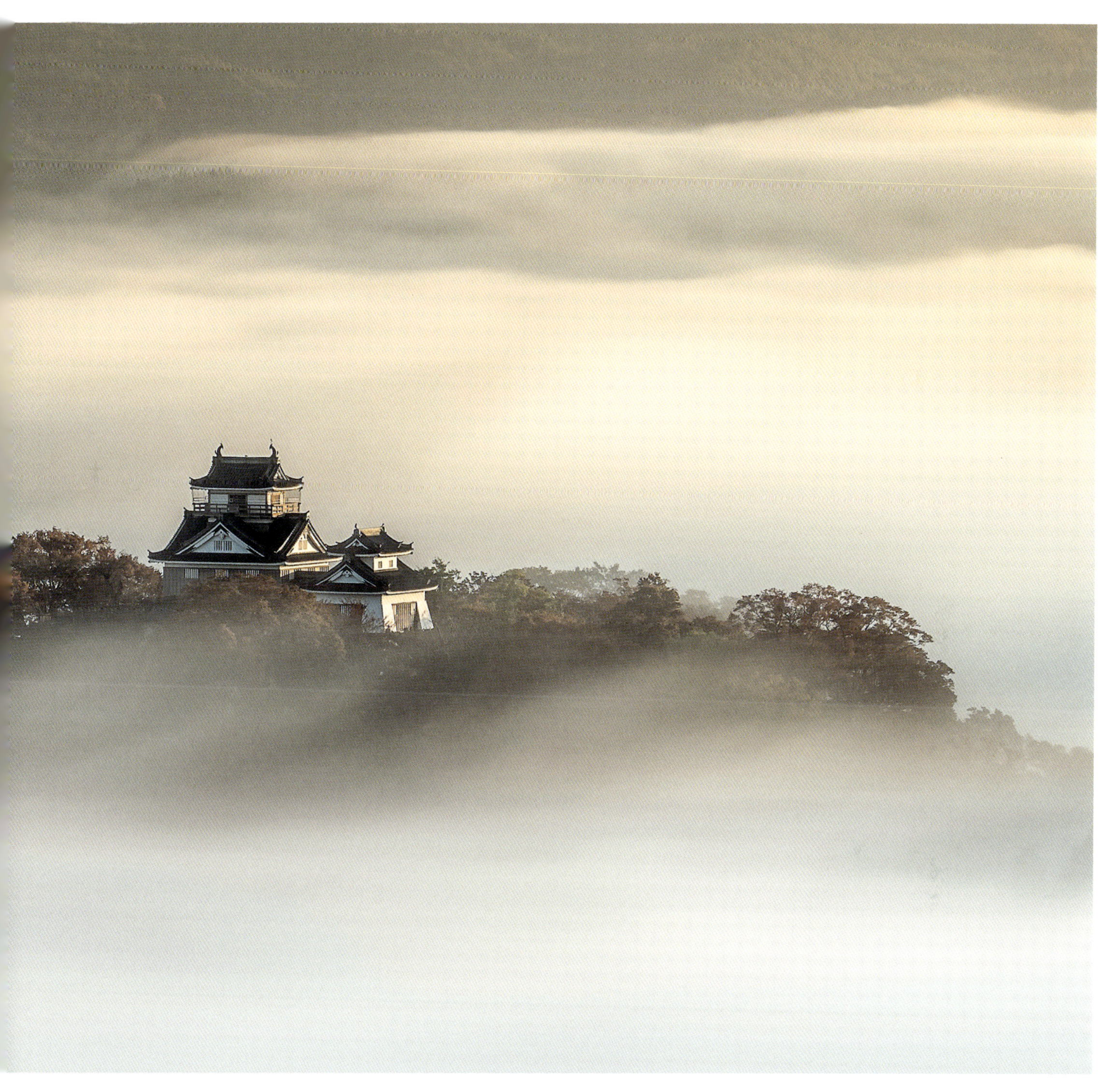

Mont-Fuji.
At dawn, Mount Fuji is unveiled in all its splendour, bathed in golden light that brushes gently against its snowy flanks. On the tranquil waters of Lake Kawaguchi, a solitary boat drifts silently, capturing the serene poetry of the moment.

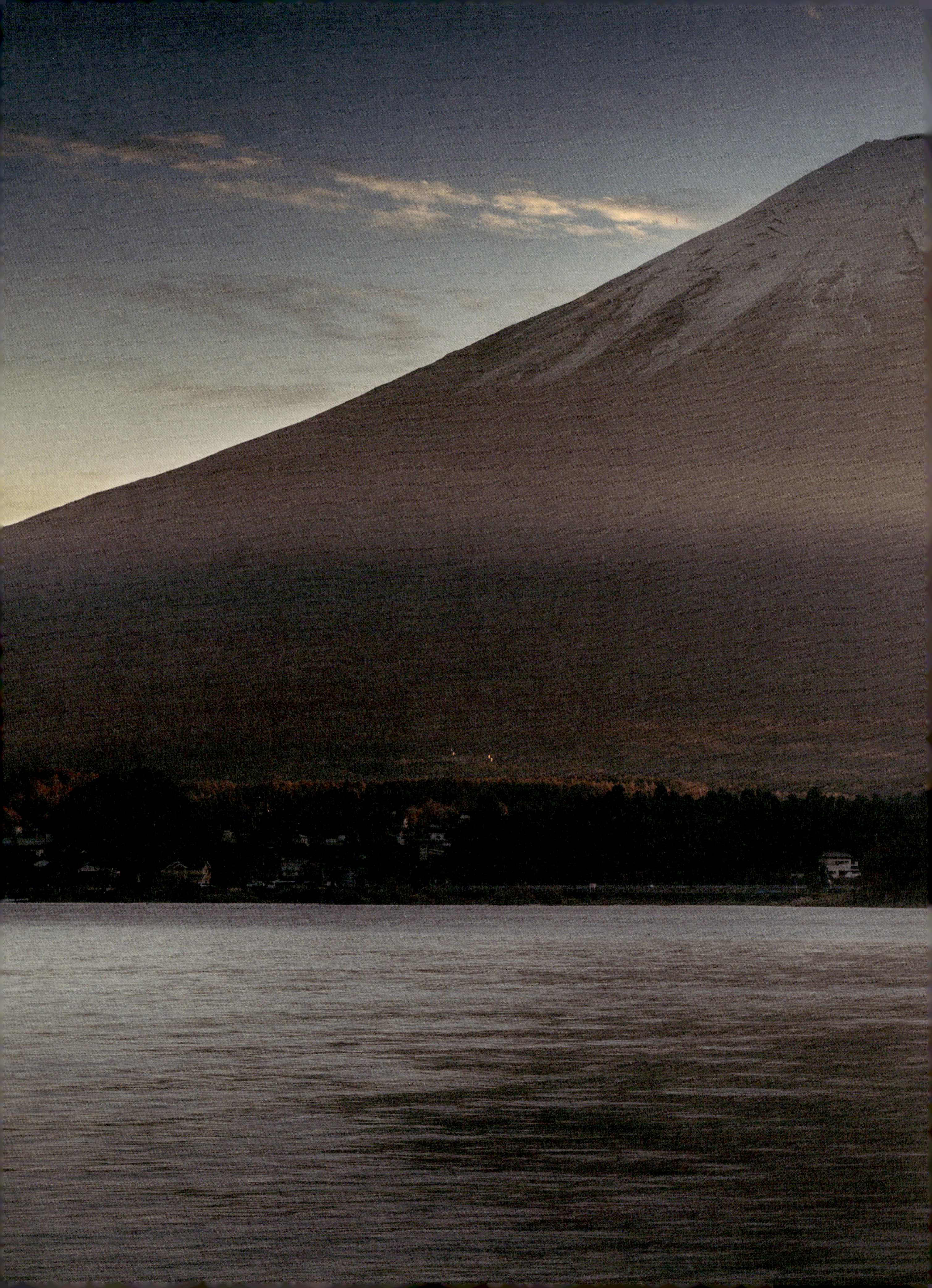

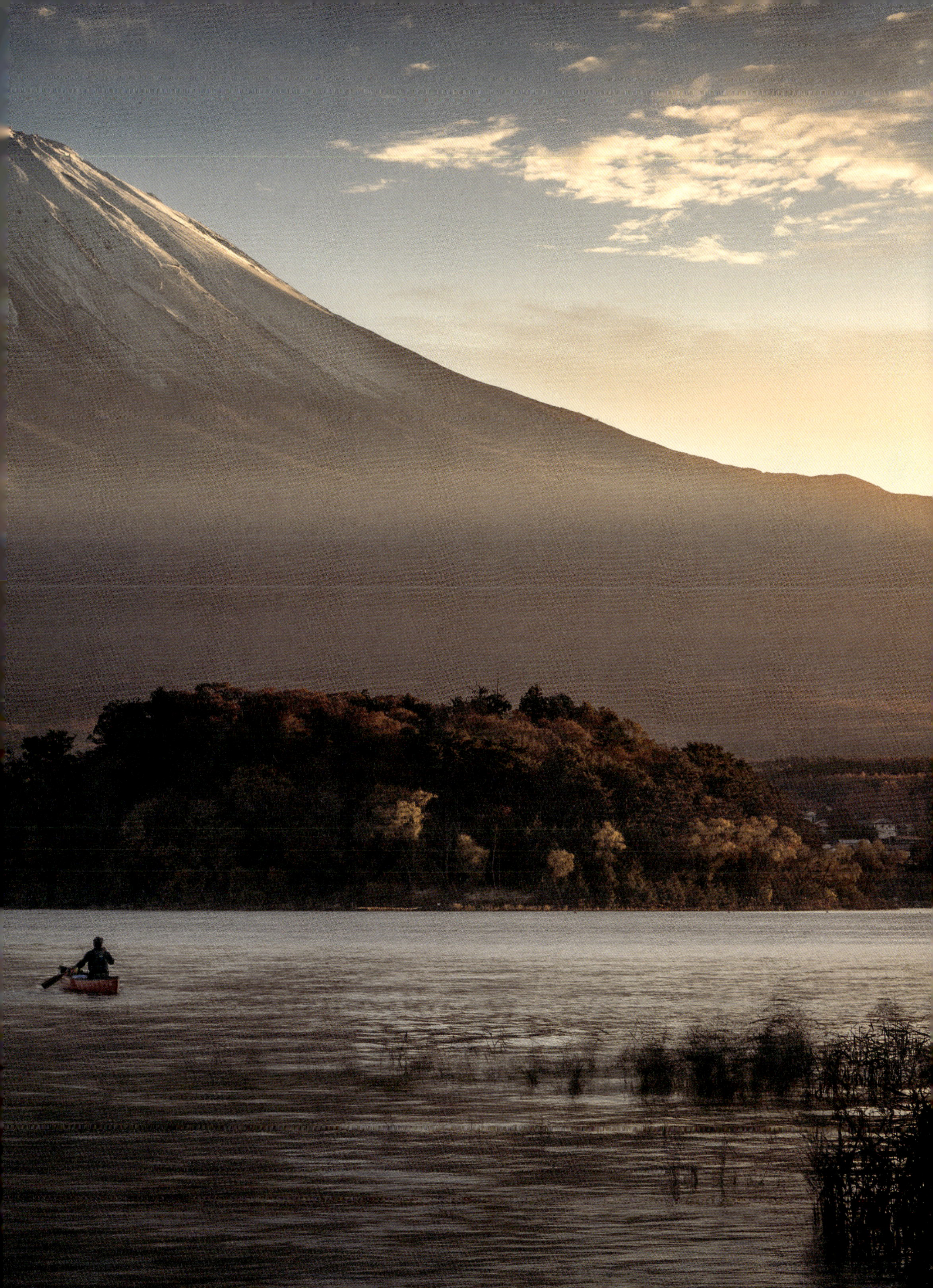

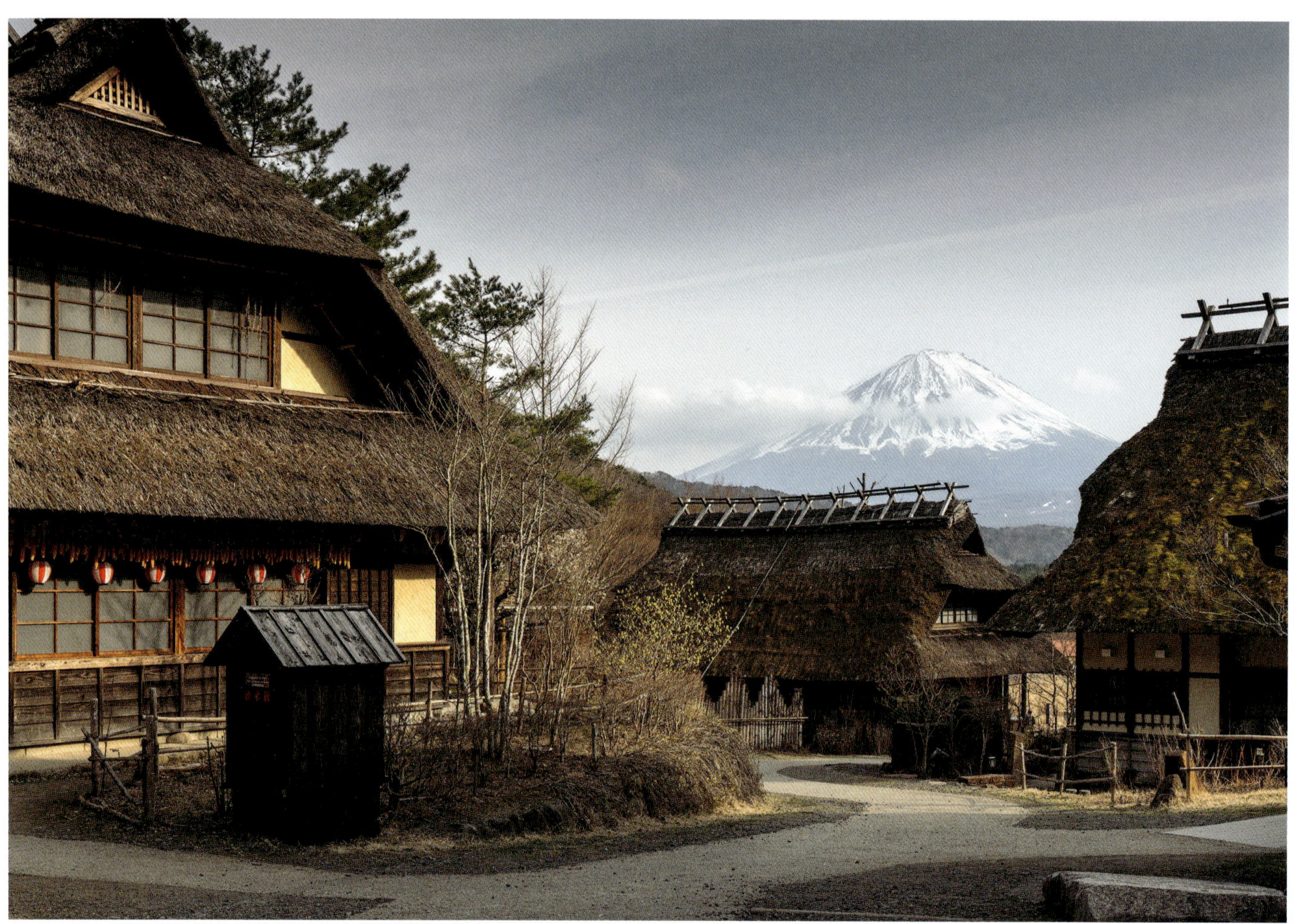

Saiko Iyashi no Sato Nenba.
Nestled at the foot of the awe-inspiring Mount Fuji, Saiko Iyashi no Sato Nenba offers a glimpse into the past. Once a farming hamlet, it has been lovingly restored as an eco-museum, allowing visitors to explore traditional thatched-roof houses and discover local crafts and Japanese culture in an authentic setting.

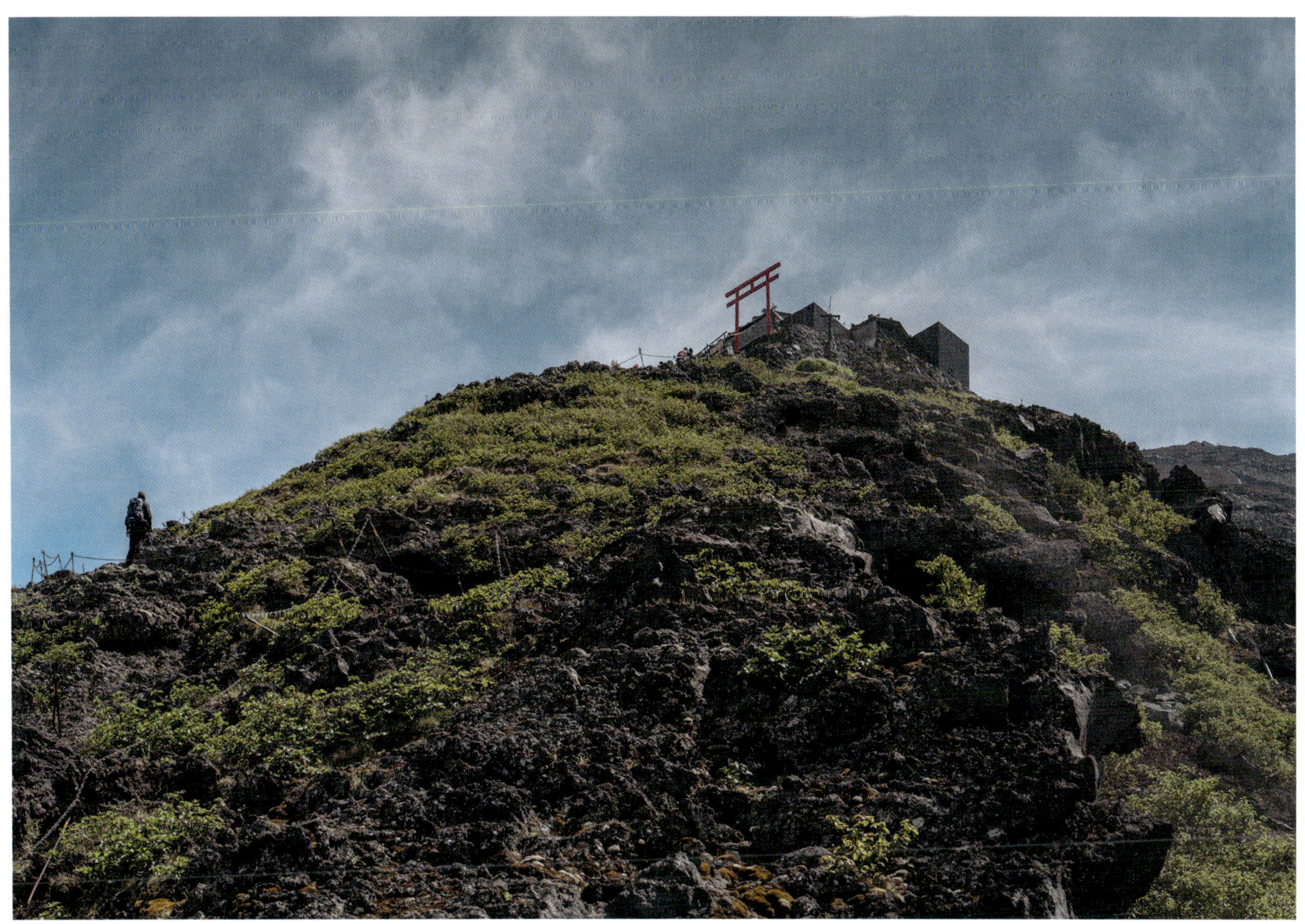

Ascent of Mount Fuji.
A sacred symbol of Japan, the mountain represents perseverance and the harmonious connection between humanity and nature. As the Japanese saying goes, "A wise man climbs Mount Fuji once, only a fool climbs it twice." The climb takes between 5 and 10 hours, a rewarding effort for the stunning views awaiting from the summit.

Shizuoka Tea Fields.
The tea fields of Shizuoka extend as far as the eye can see, presenting a lush, tranquil landscape with the majestic Mount Fuji standing proudly in the background. Renowned as the birthplace of Japanese tea, this region beautifully merges tradition and natural beauty, inviting visitors to uncover the secrets behind some of the world's finest tea.

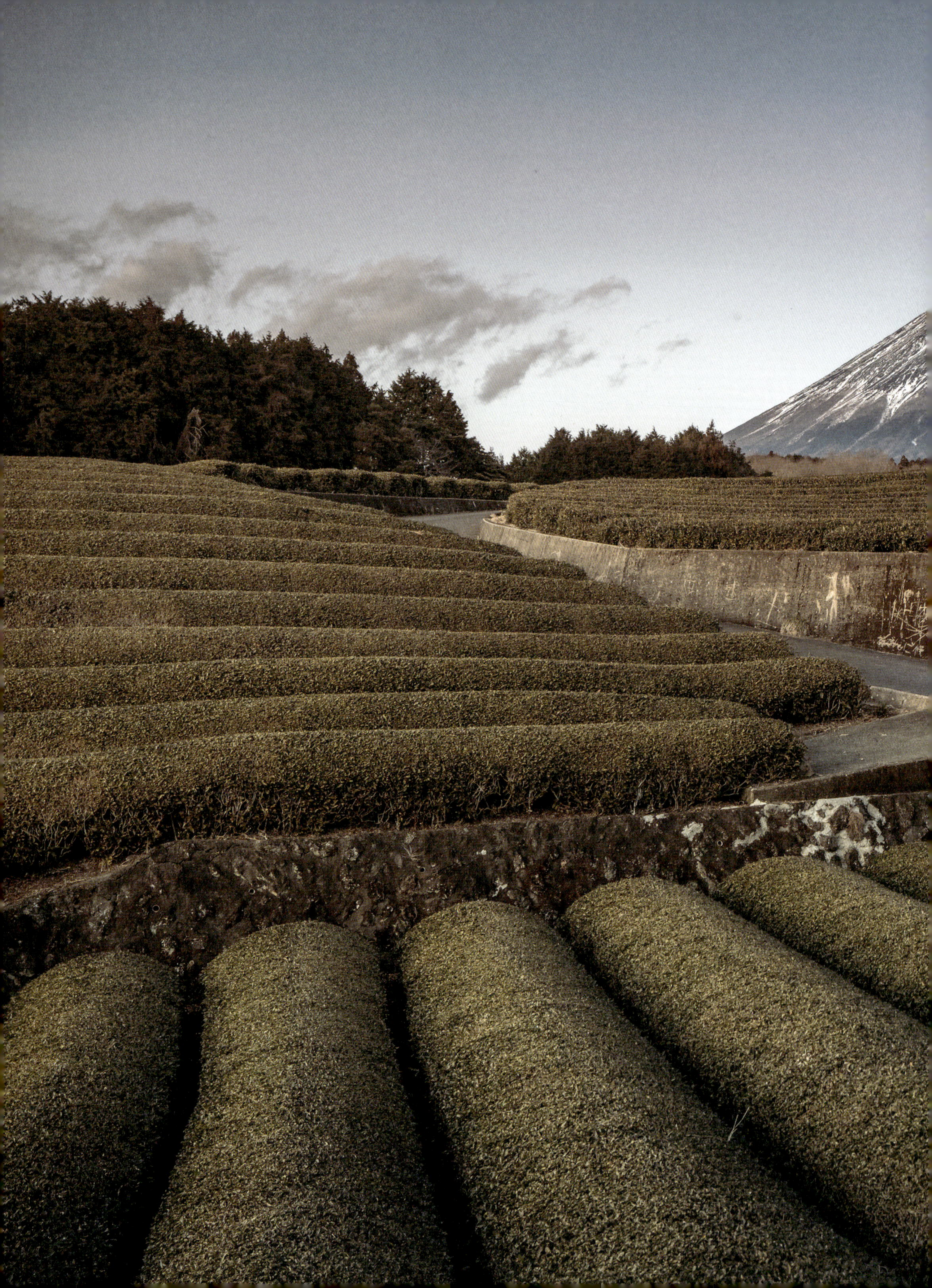

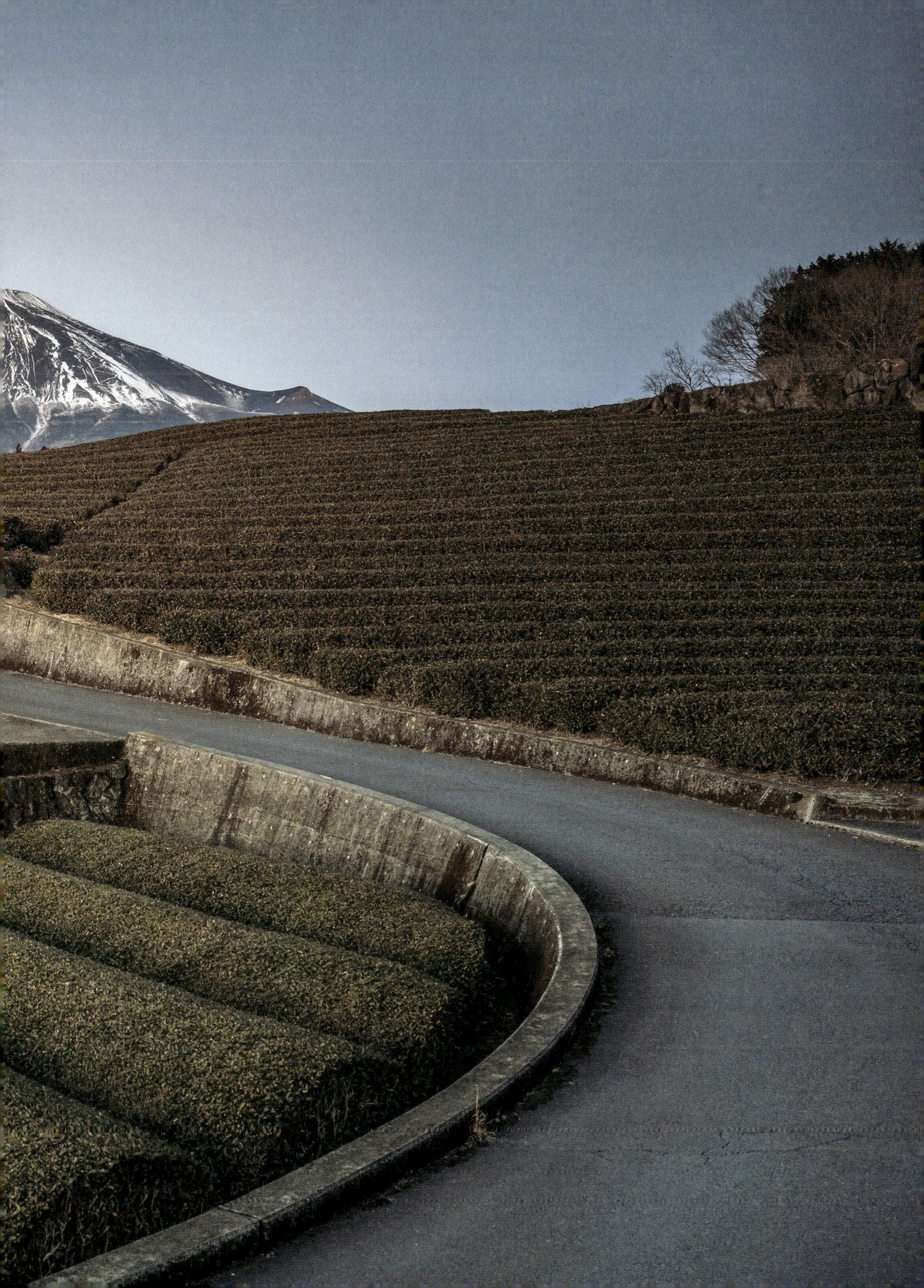

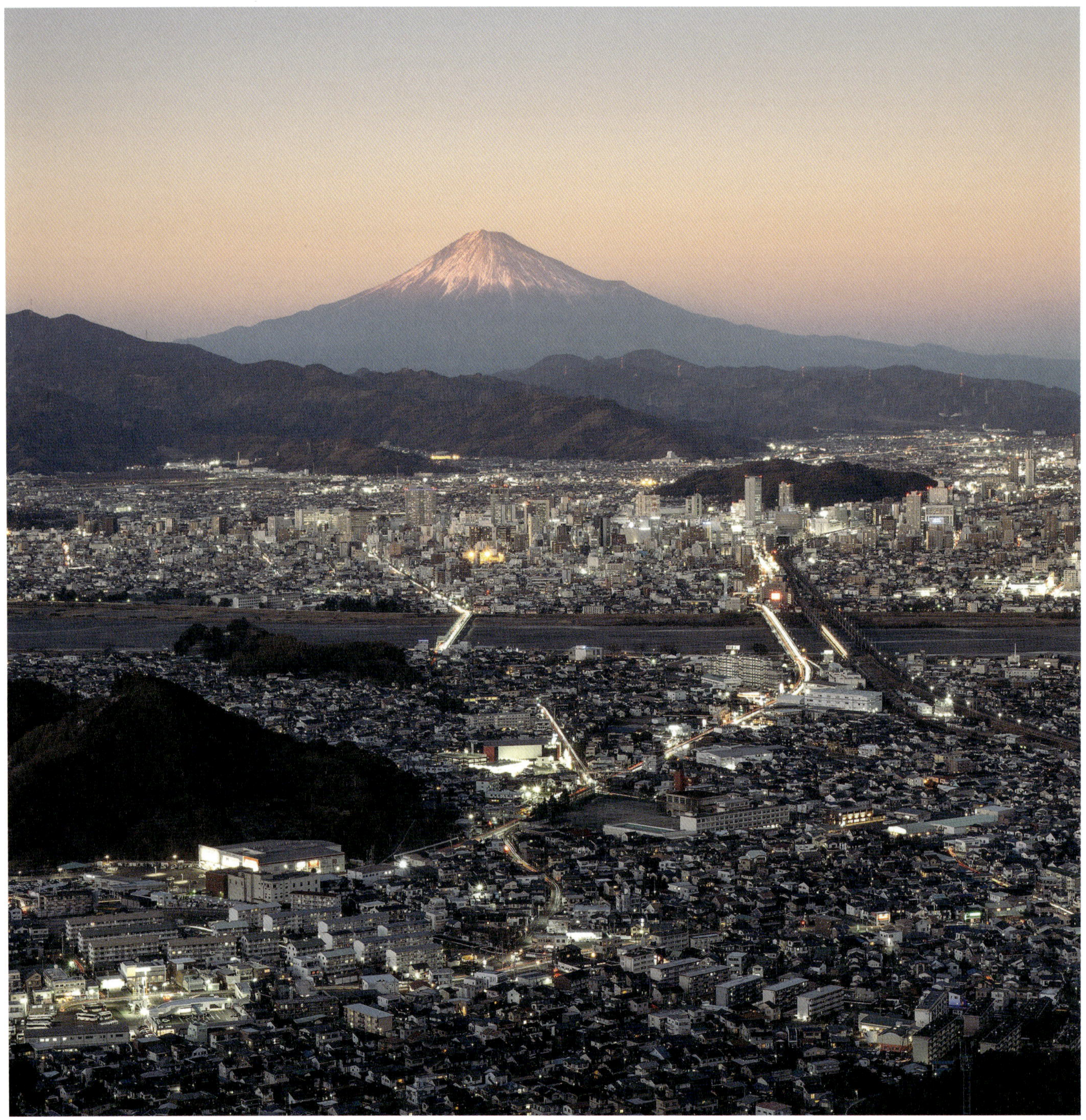

Shizuoka & Mount Fuji.
From the hills above Shizuoka, the city unfurls in a glittering tapestry of lights, set against the commanding silhouette of Mount Fuji on the horizon. As dusk falls, soft pink hues wash over the snow-capped peak, creating a scene that feels both urban and serene.

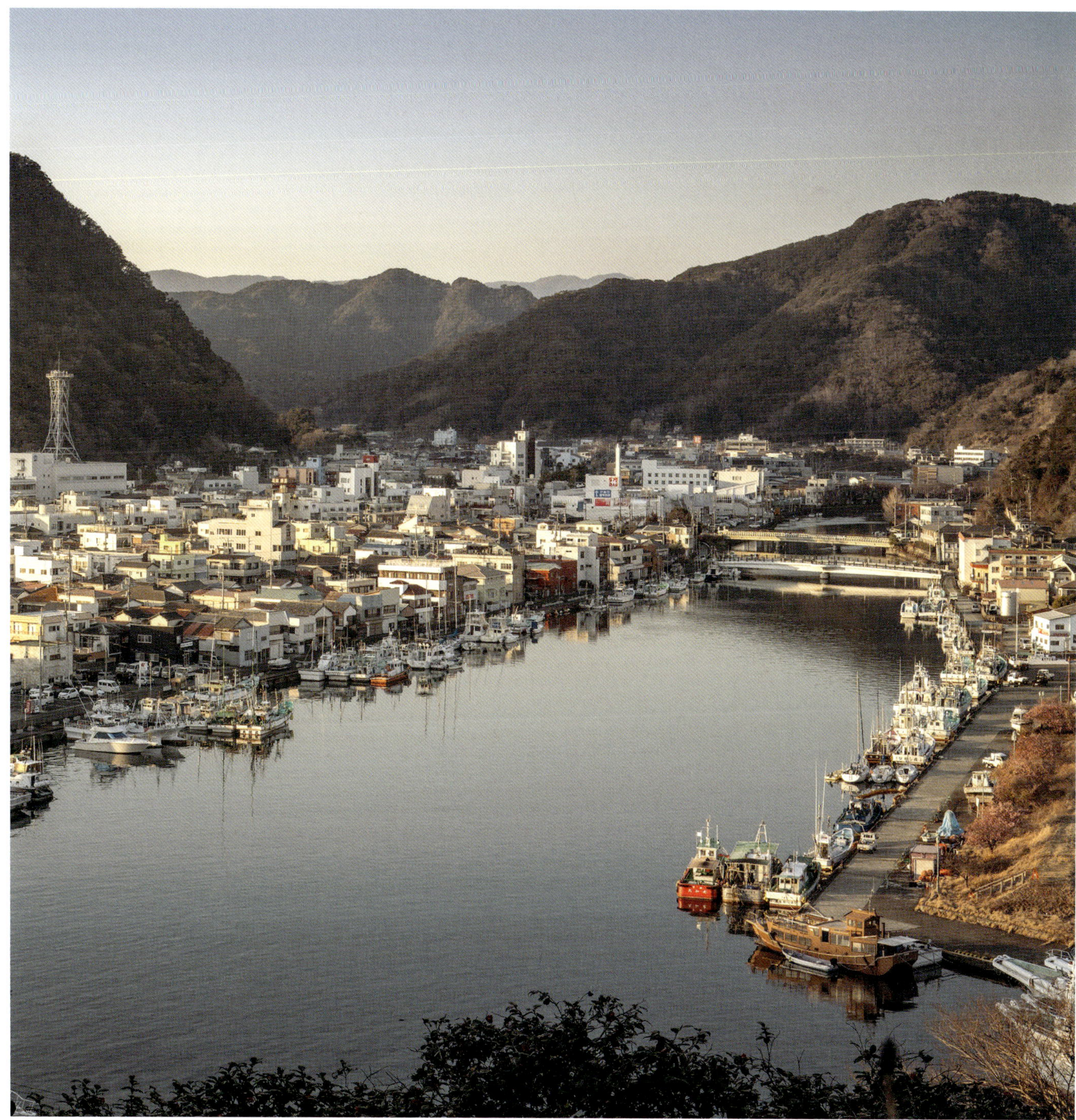

Shimoda Harbour.
Fringed by lush mountains, Shimoda Harbour holds a special place in Japanese history. It was here, in 1854, that Commodore Perry arrived with his fleet, heralding Japan's opening to the wider world. Today, this serene port, lined with fishing boats and traditional houses, offers a quiet yet vivid reminder of the country's rich maritime heritage.

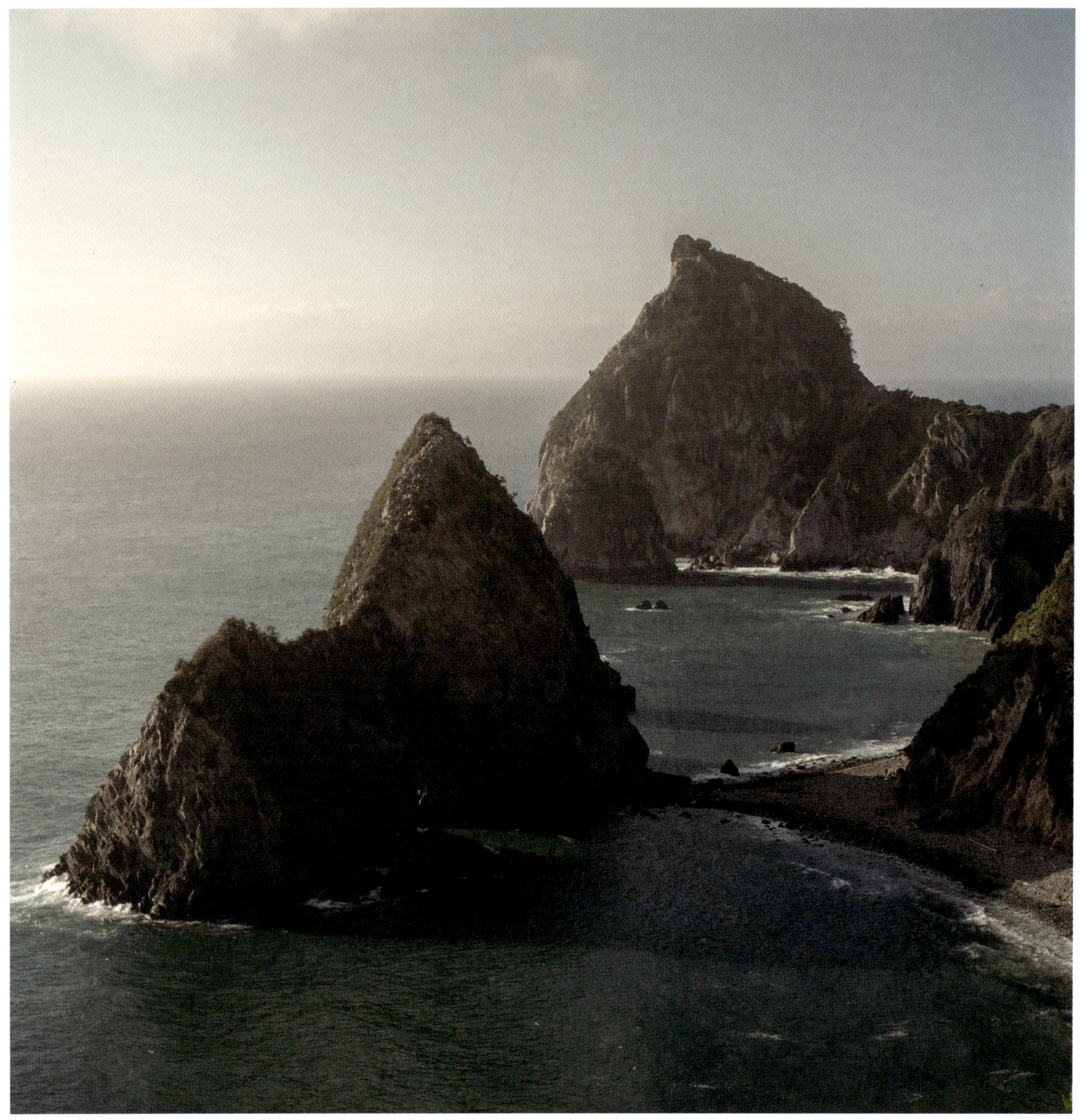

Sengamon Rocks & Mount Fuji.
The Sengamon Rocks, located along the rugged coastline of the Izu Peninsula, present a theatrical landscape. These towering rock formations, shaped over centuries by the relentless sea, give the area a wild, almost mystical atmosphere. On clear days, the distant silhouette of Mount Fuji graces the horizon, adding a majestic presence to this unforgettable coastal view.

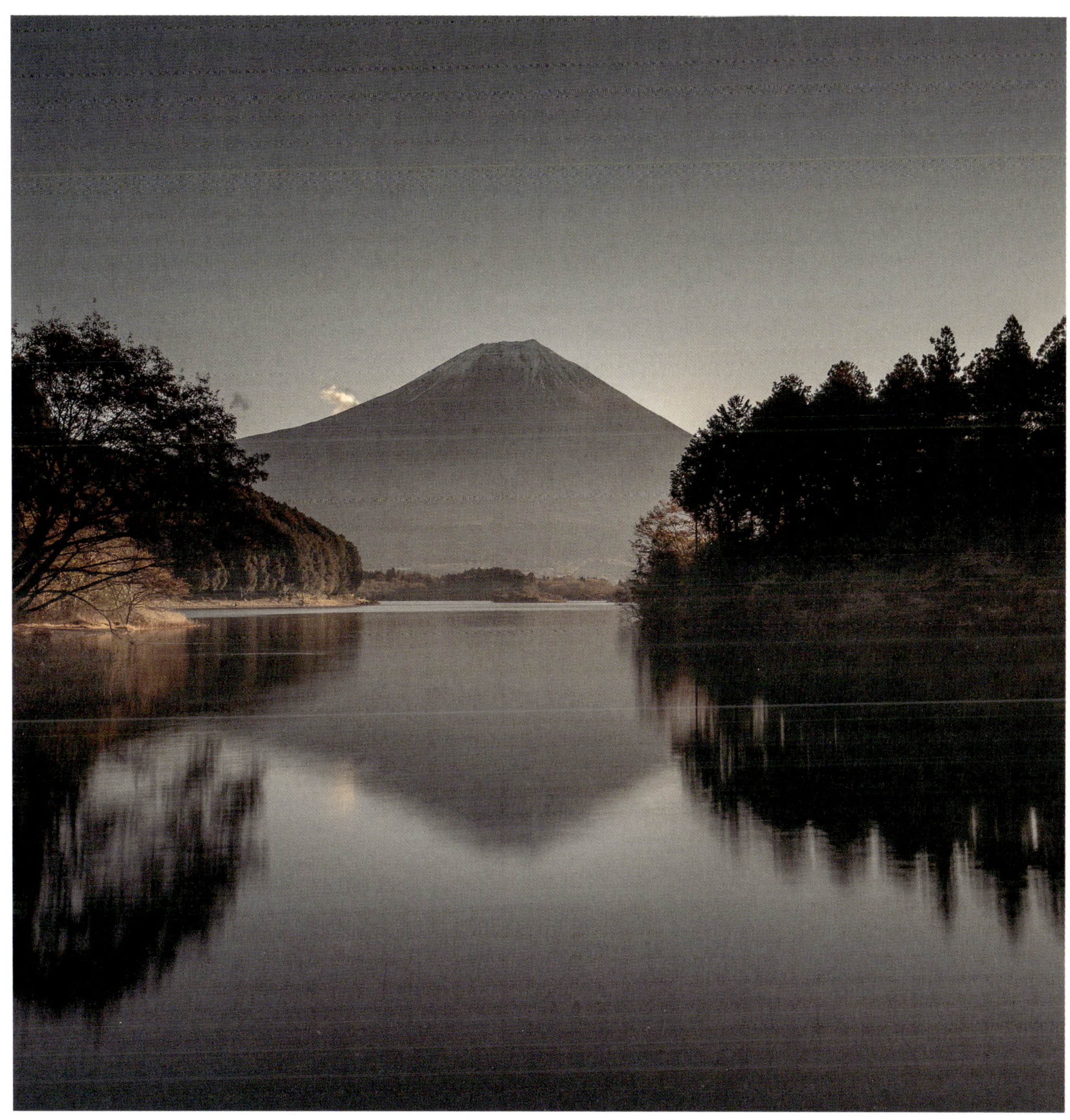

Lake Tanuki.
At daybreak, Mount Fuji rises majestically beyond the still waters of Lake Tanuki.

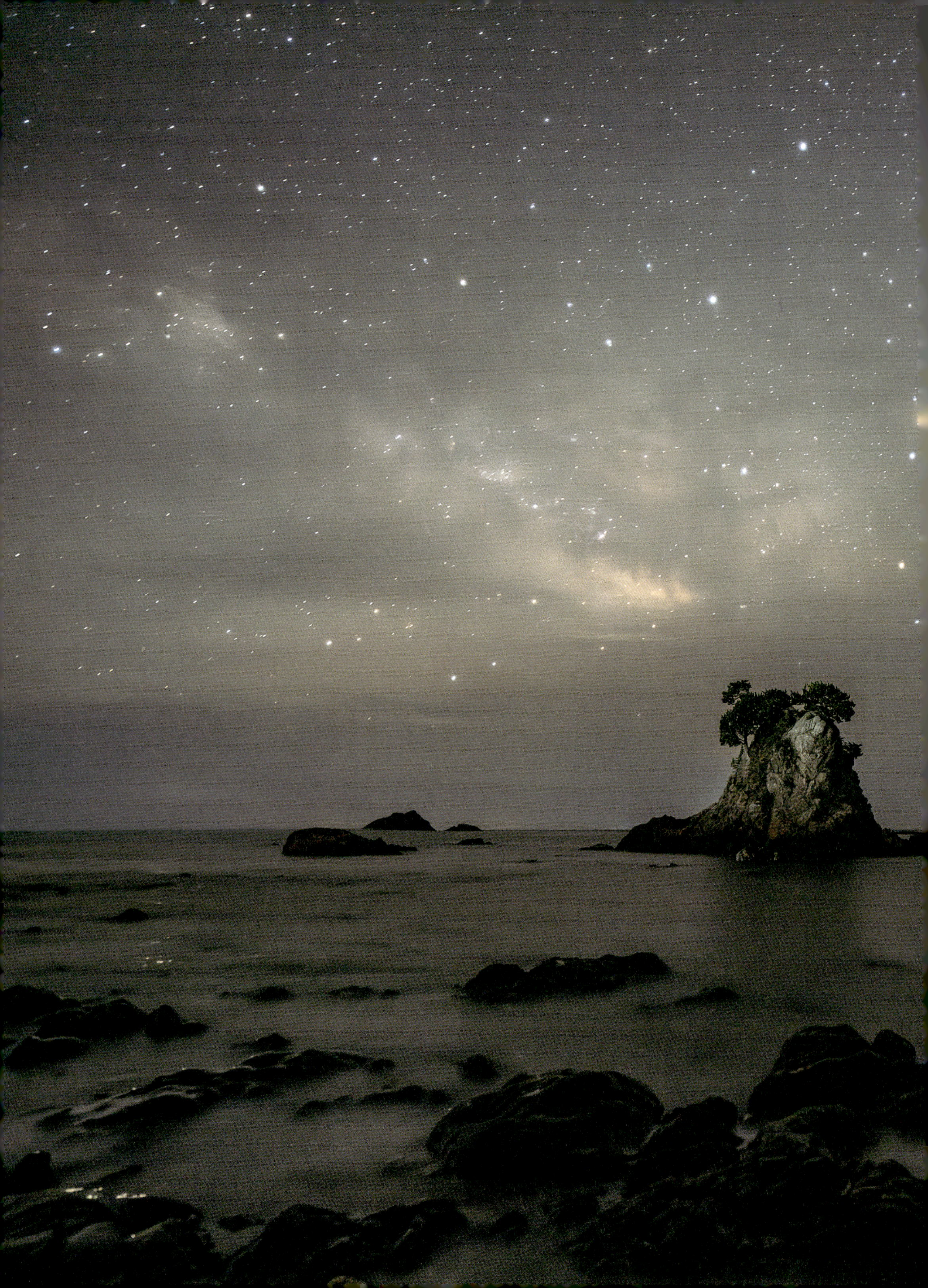

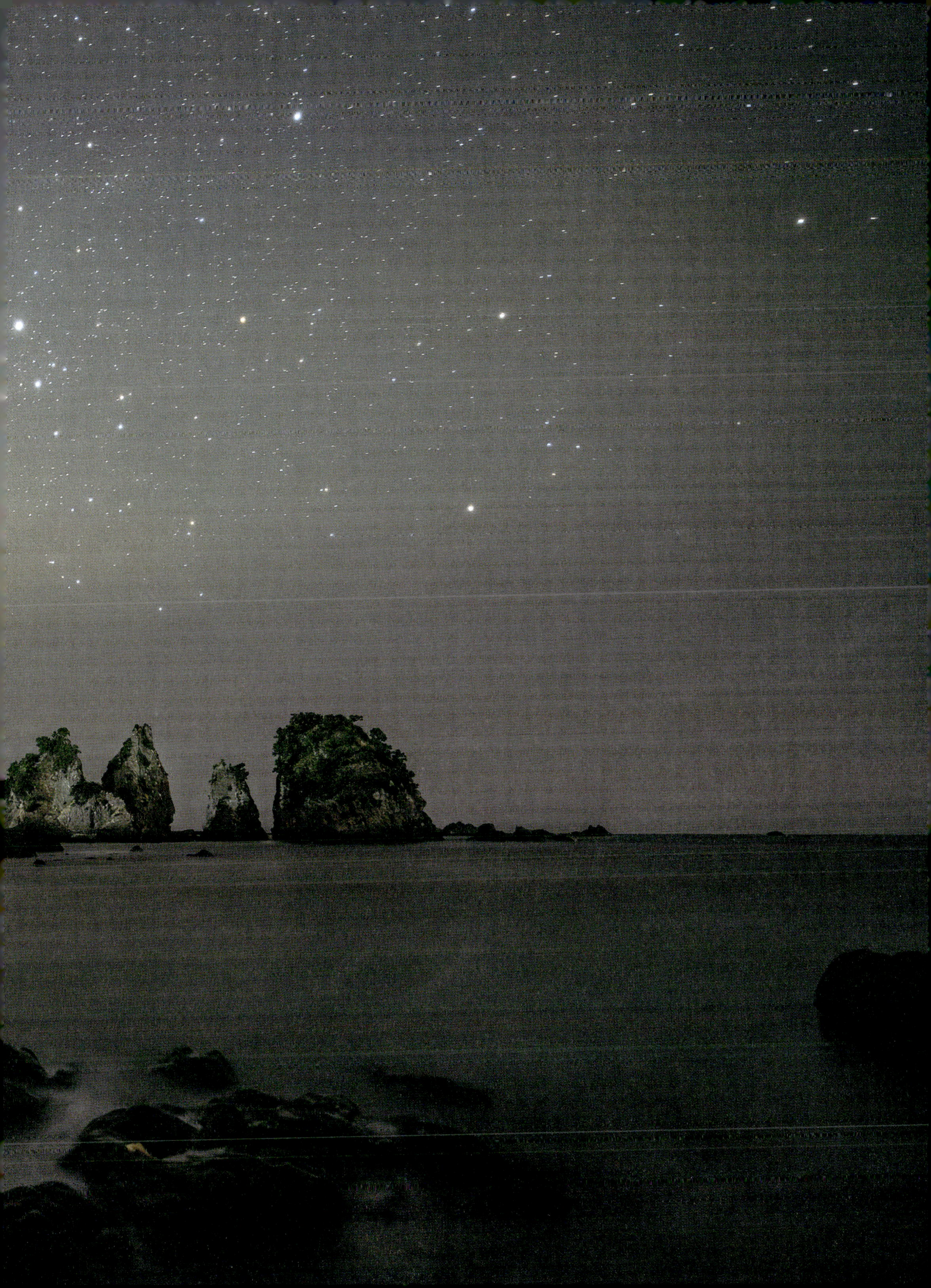

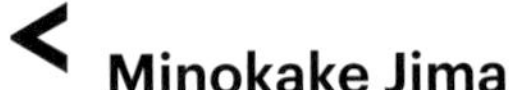

Minokake Jima.

Minokake Jima, a cluster of rocky islets rising from calm coastal waters, offers one of the clearest night skies in Japan. Far from the glow of urban lights, the Milky Way appears in all its dazzling splendour.

Matsumoto Castle.

Built between 1593 and 1594, Matsumoto Castle is one of Japan's oldest surviving wooden fortresses. Nicknamed the "Crow Castle" due to its striking black exterior, it stands with quiet grandeur above its moat, where its dark silhouette is perfectly mirrored. Designated a National Treasure in 1936, it was meticulously restored in the 20th century to preserve its distinctive feudal architecture.

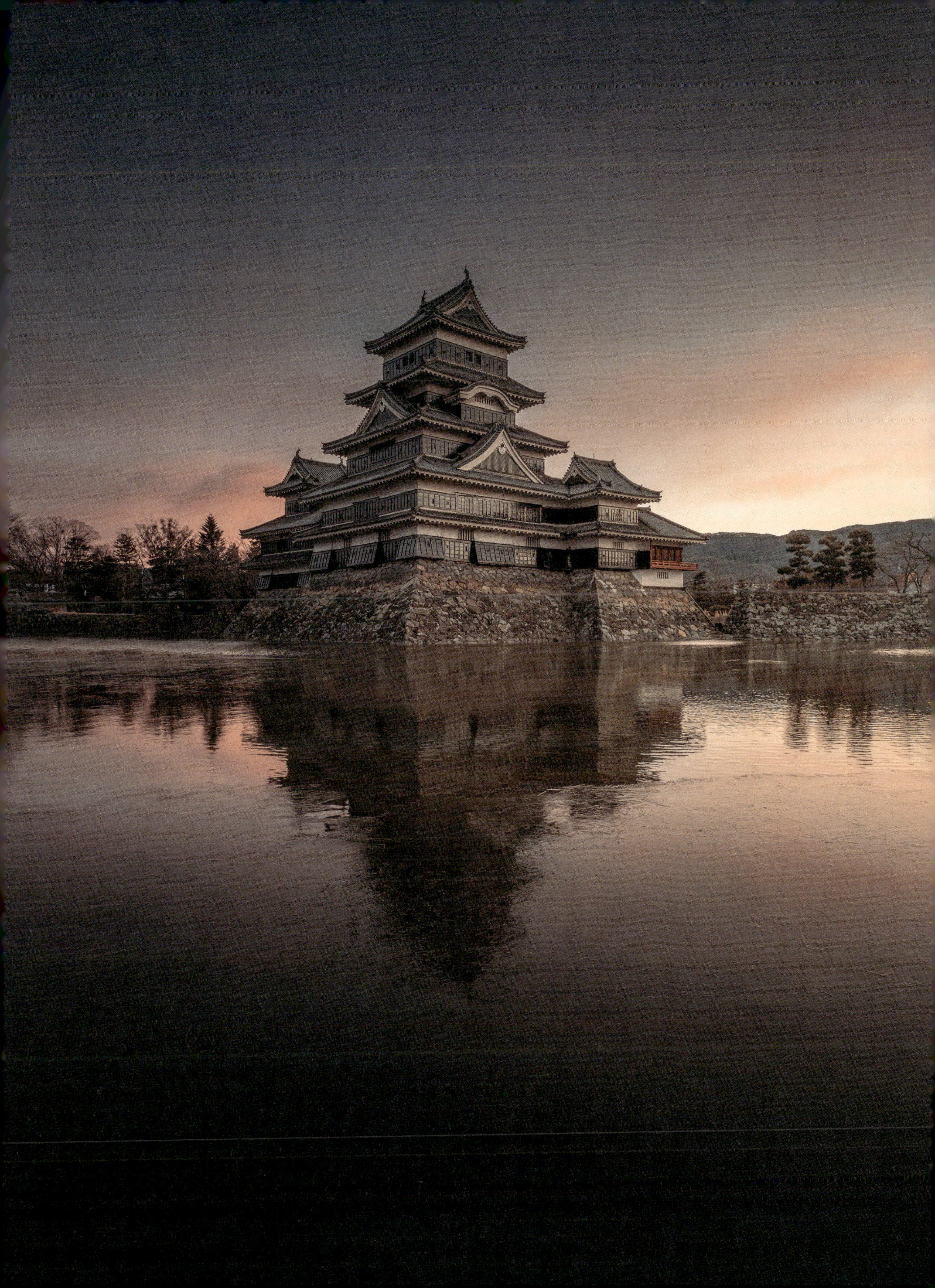

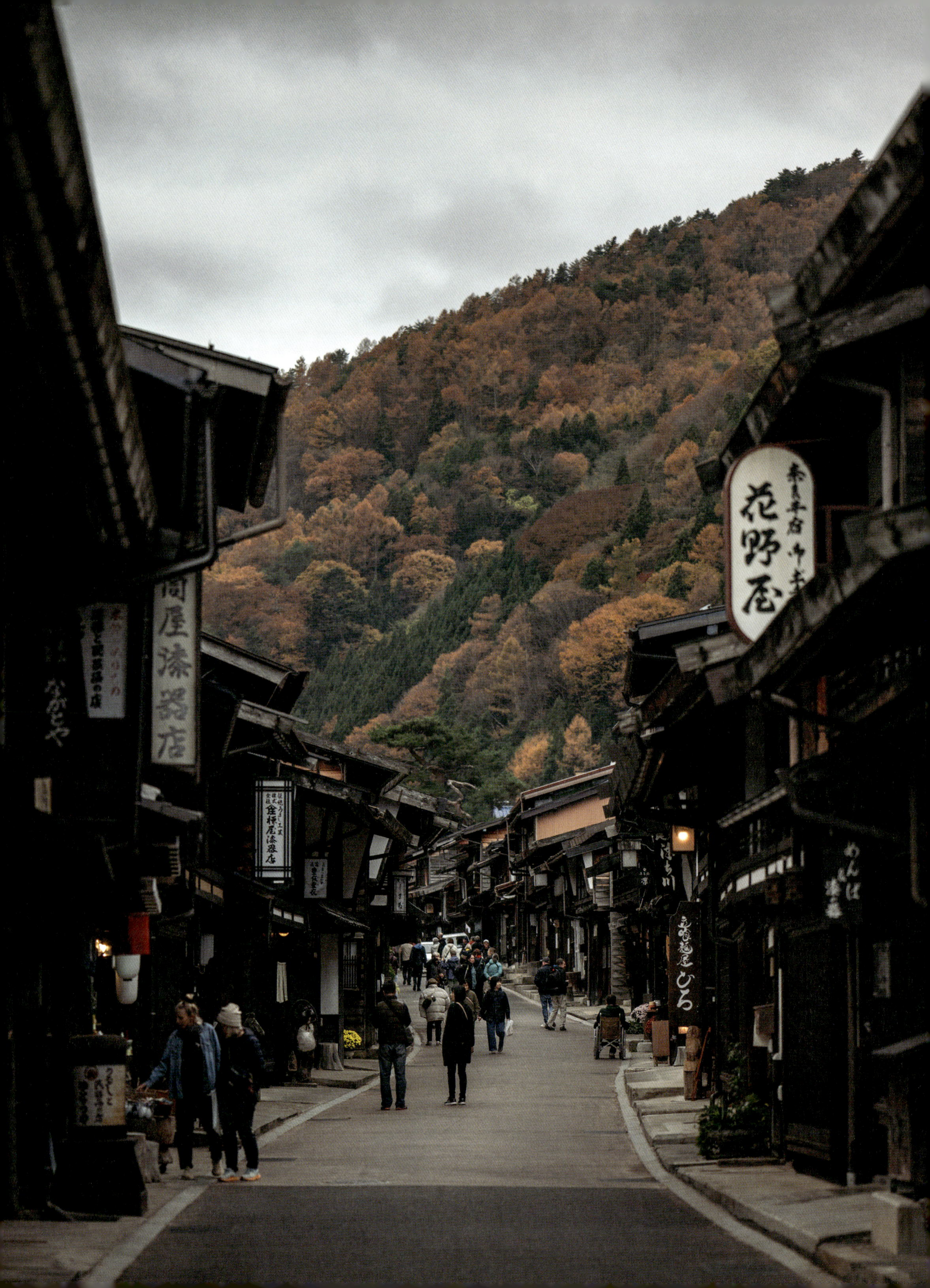
花野屋
屋漆器店
ながとや
ひろ

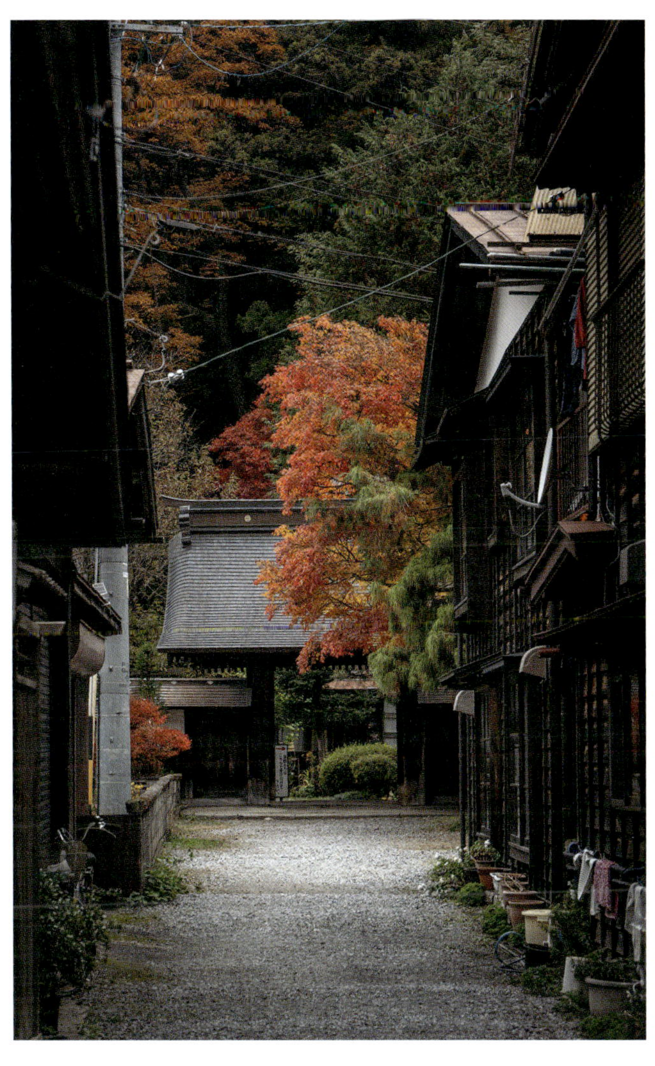

Narai-juku.
Located in Nagano Prefecture, Narai-juku was once a relay station along the Nakasendo, the historic route that connected Tokyo and Kyoto and was travelled by lords, samurai, merchants, and porters for centuries. Known as the "Narai of a thousand houses", it transports visitors to the Edo period (1603-1868) with its beautifully preserved wooden buildings.

Hoshitoge Rice Terraces.
The Hoshitoge rice terraces in Niigata present a mesmerising sight, particularly at sunrise or when shrouded in mist. >

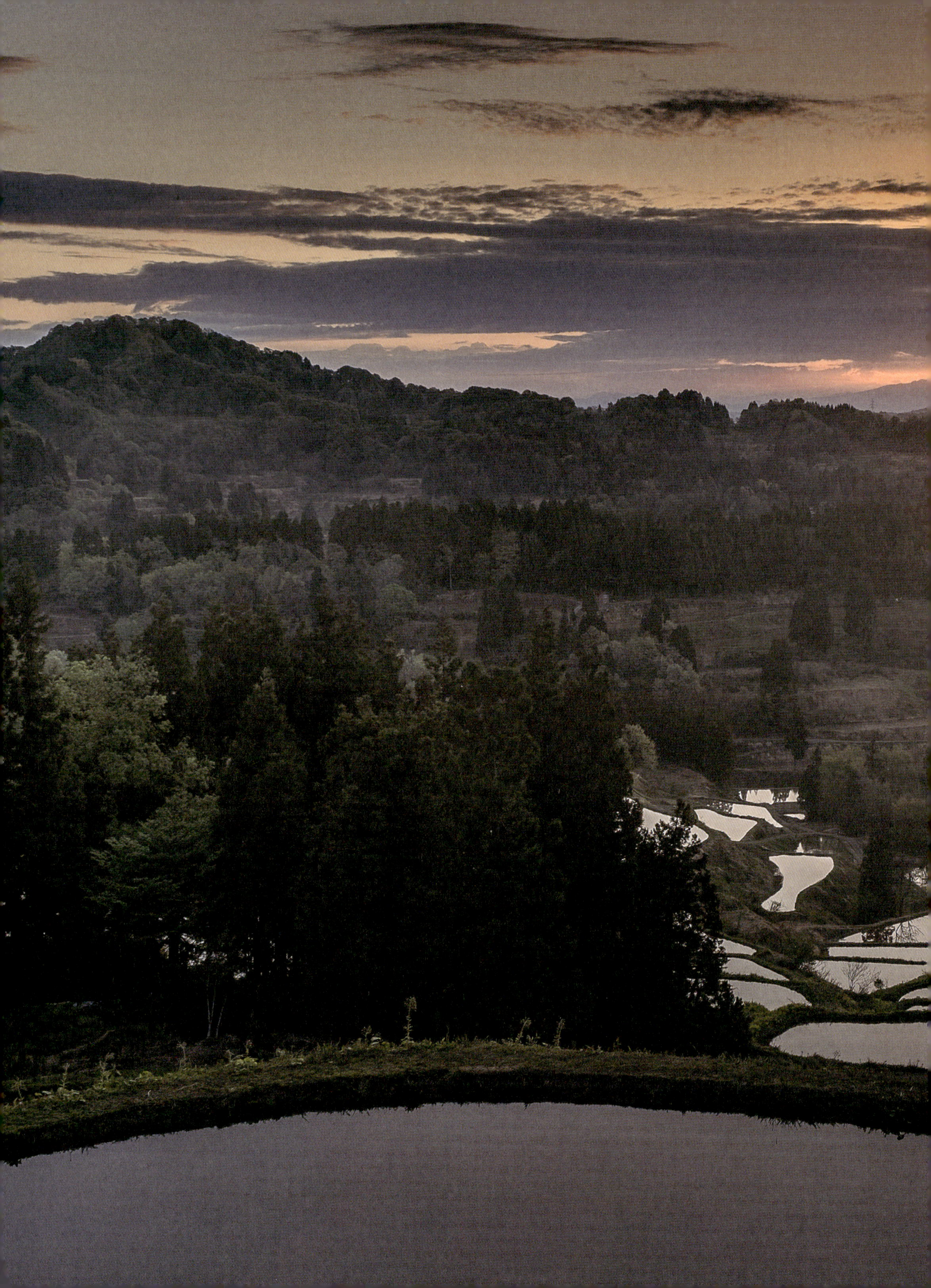

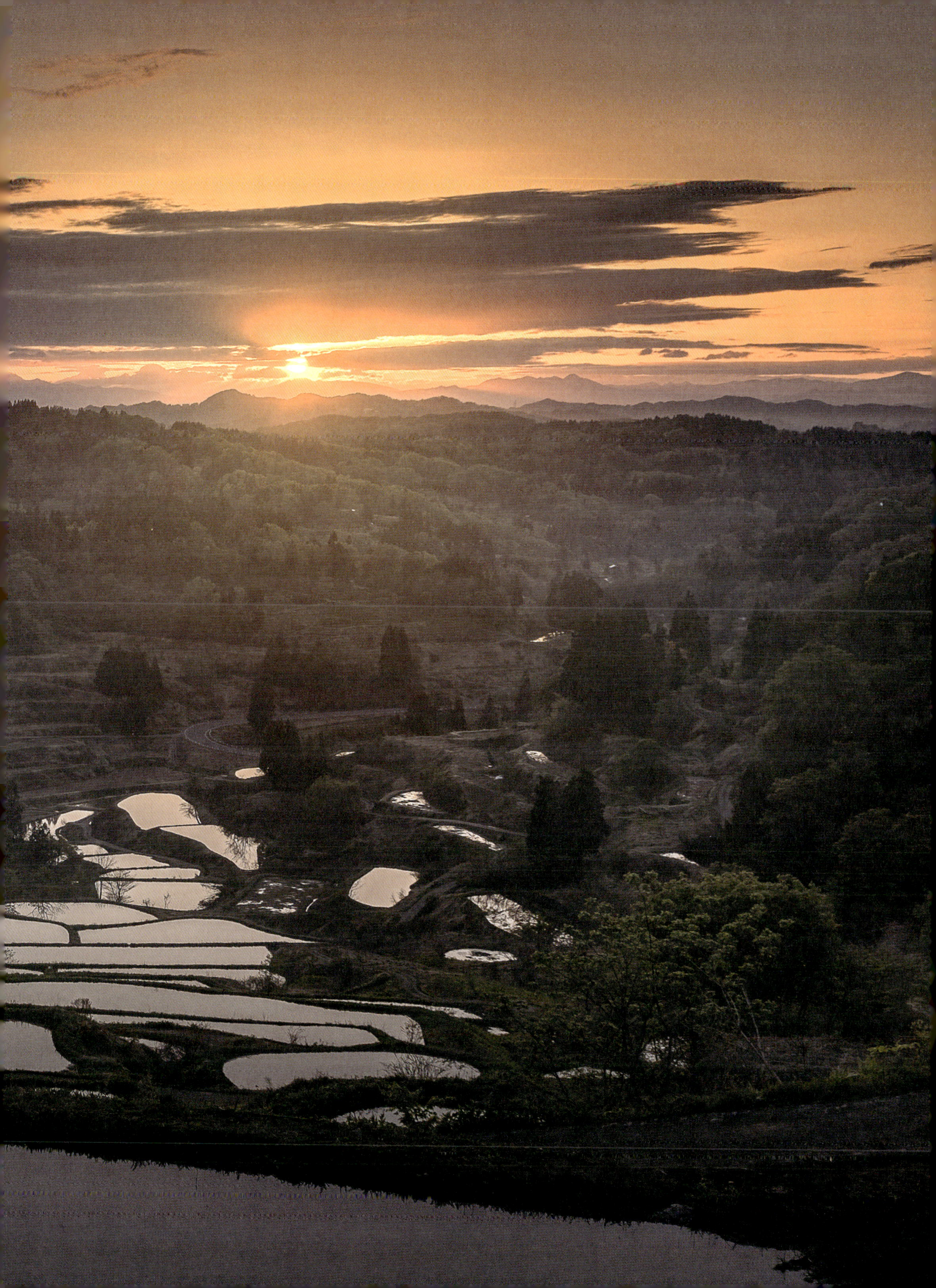

中部

Magome-juku.
The village of Magome-juku, formerly a stopover on the Nakasendo road, enchants visitors with its cobblestone streets, traditional houses, and panoramic views of the surrounding mountains.

Shirakawa-go.
A designated UNESCO World Heritage Site, the village of Shirakawa-go is renowned for its steeply pitched thatched houses, known as *gasshō-zukuri*. Nestled amidst lush mountain surroundings, these distinctive homes were ingeniously constructed to withstand heavy snowfall. Surrounded by tranquil rice paddies, they stand as a living testament to the resilience and beauty of traditional Japanese rural architecture. >

Gokayama Village.
Tucked away in the heart of the Japanese mountains, Gokayama village lies beneath a thick blanket of snow. Its traditional thatched-roof houses, known as *gasshō-zukuri*, seem frozen in time, framed by frost-covered trees and enveloped in a hushed winter stillness. >>

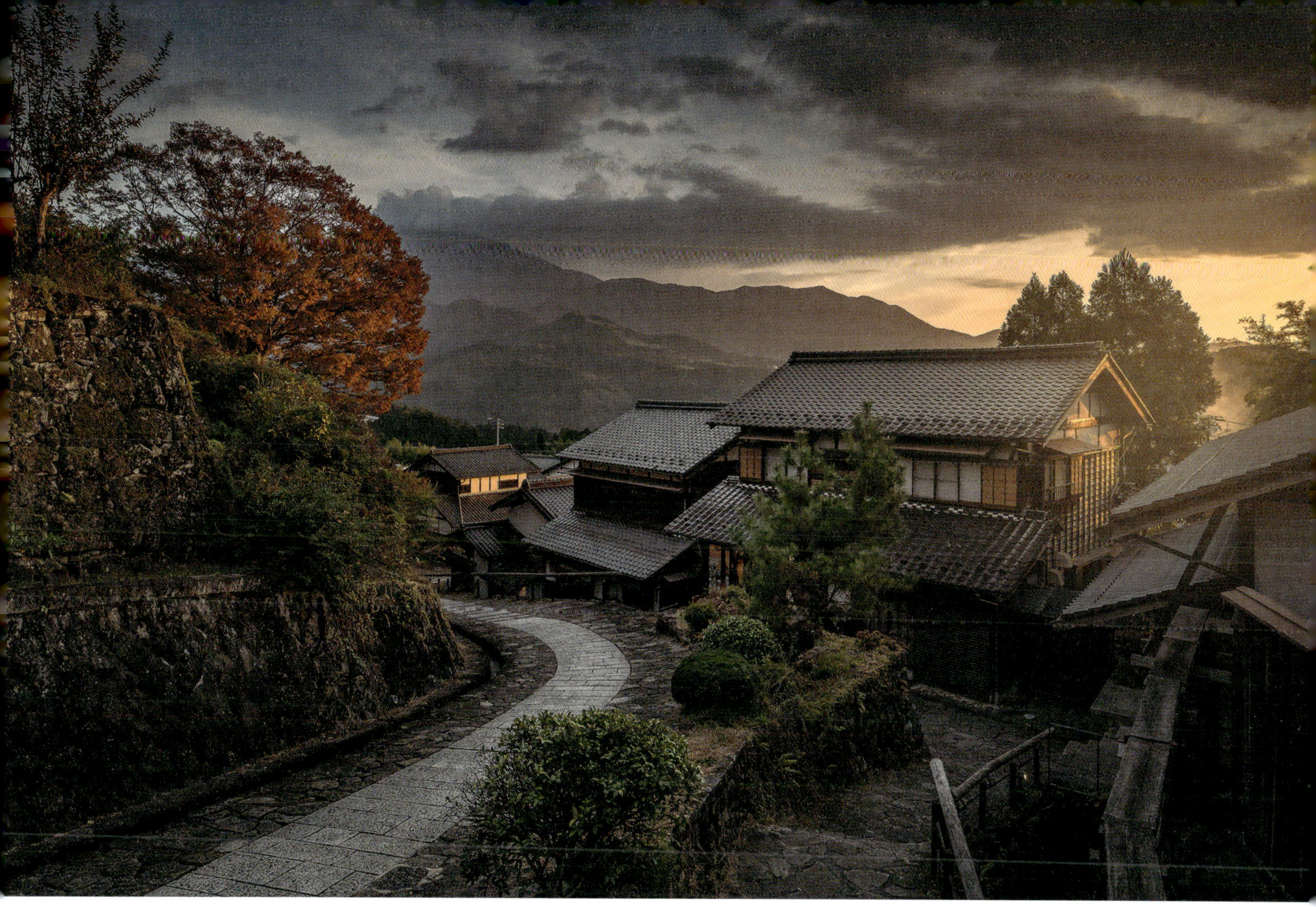

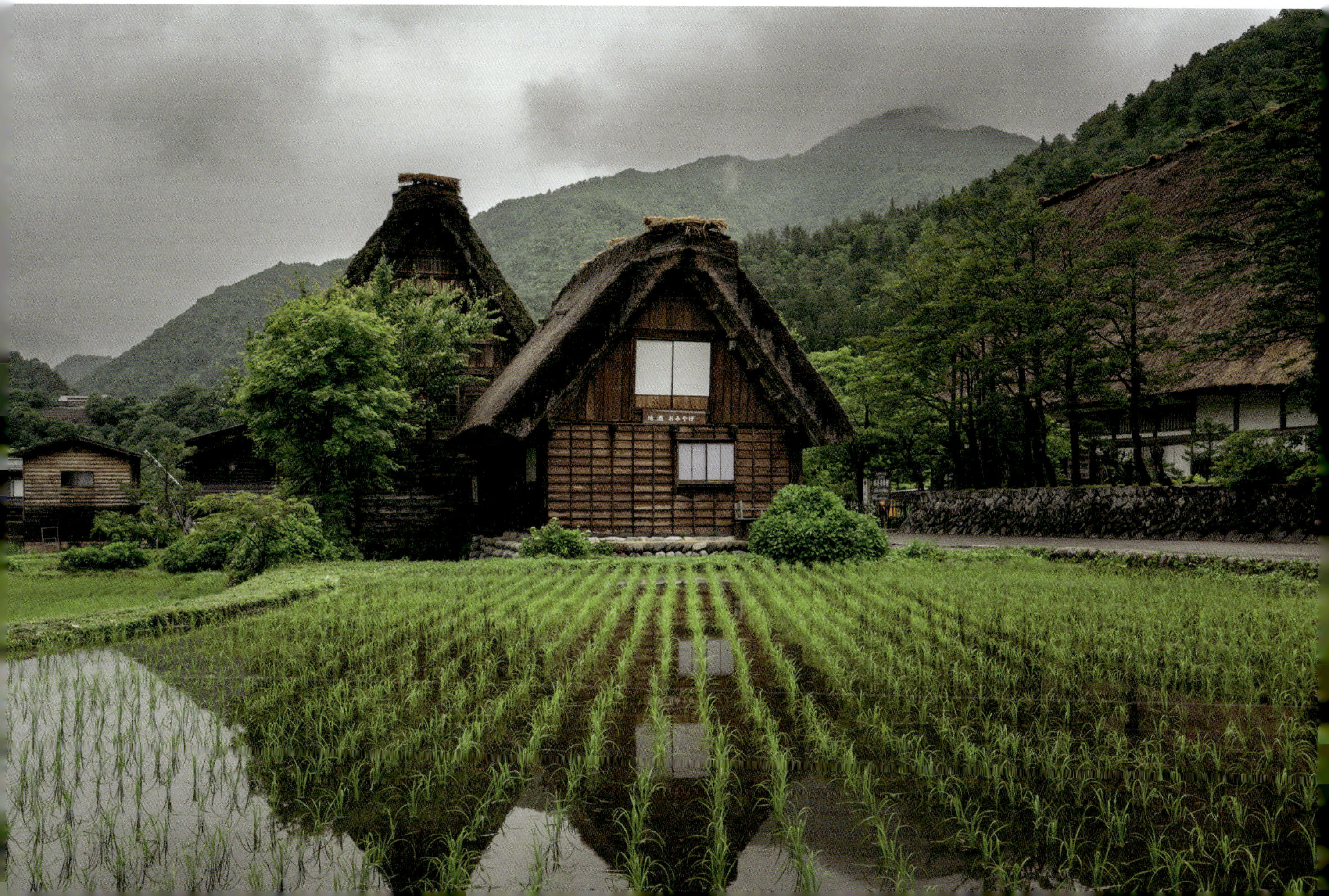

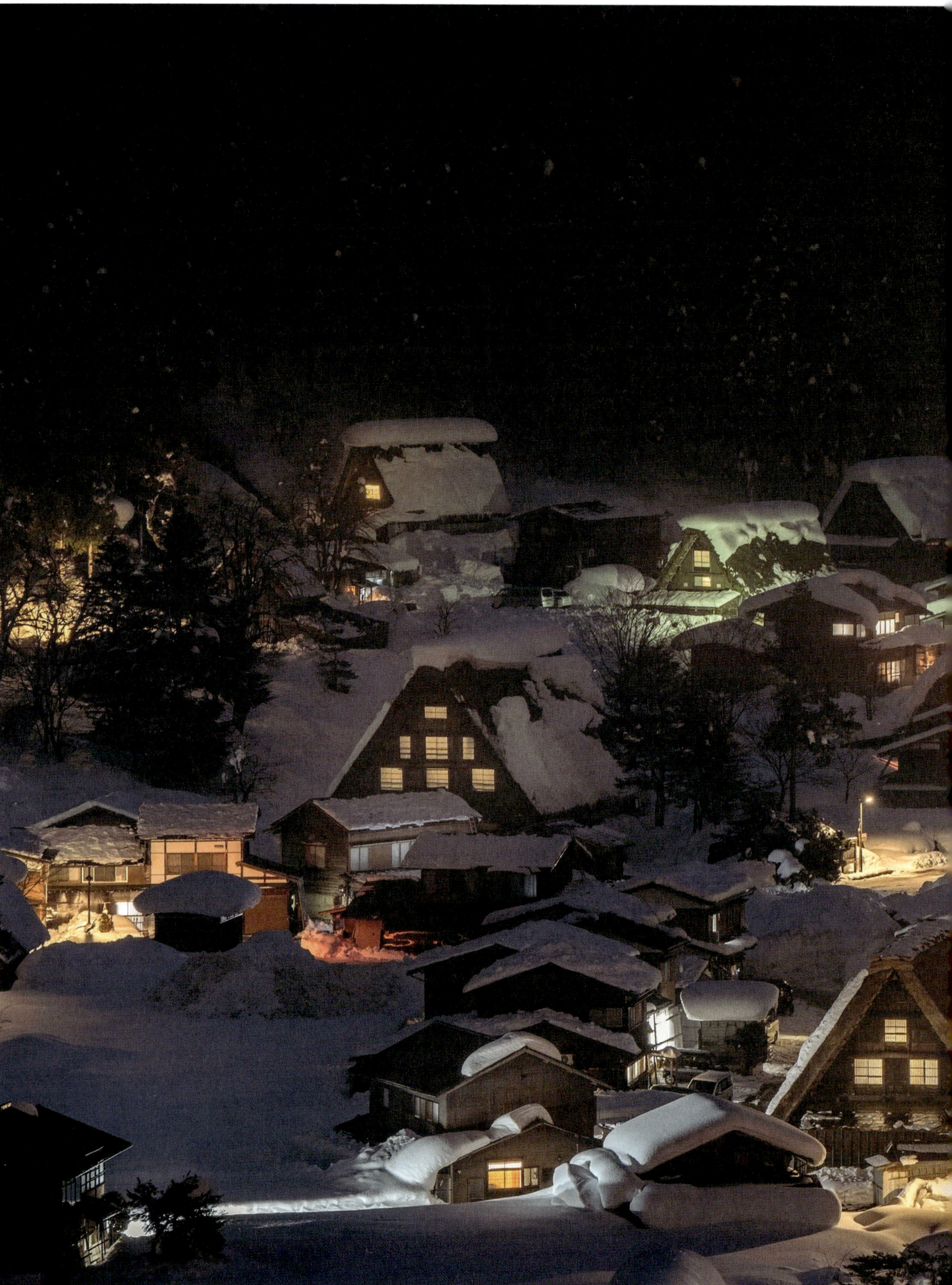

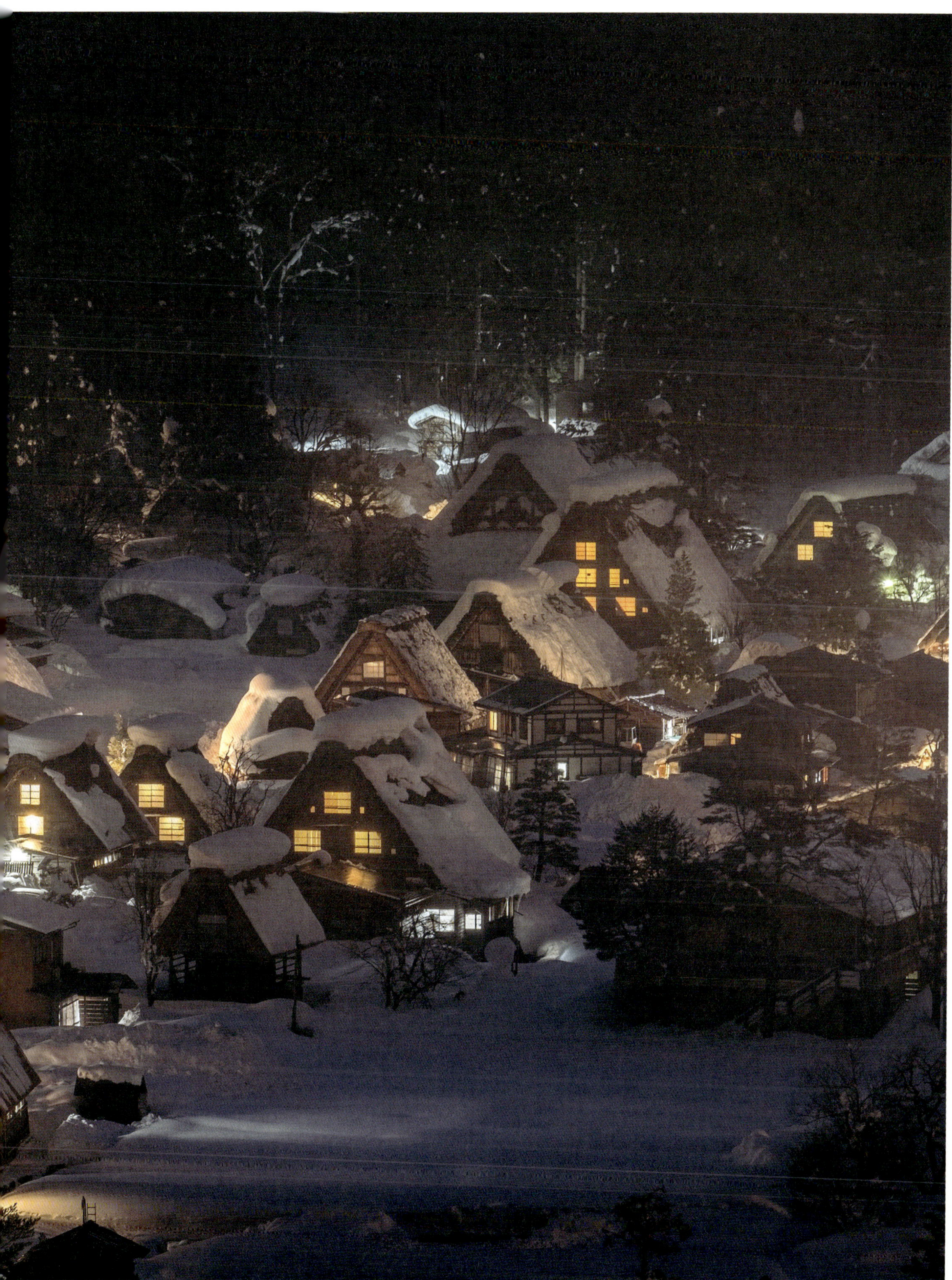

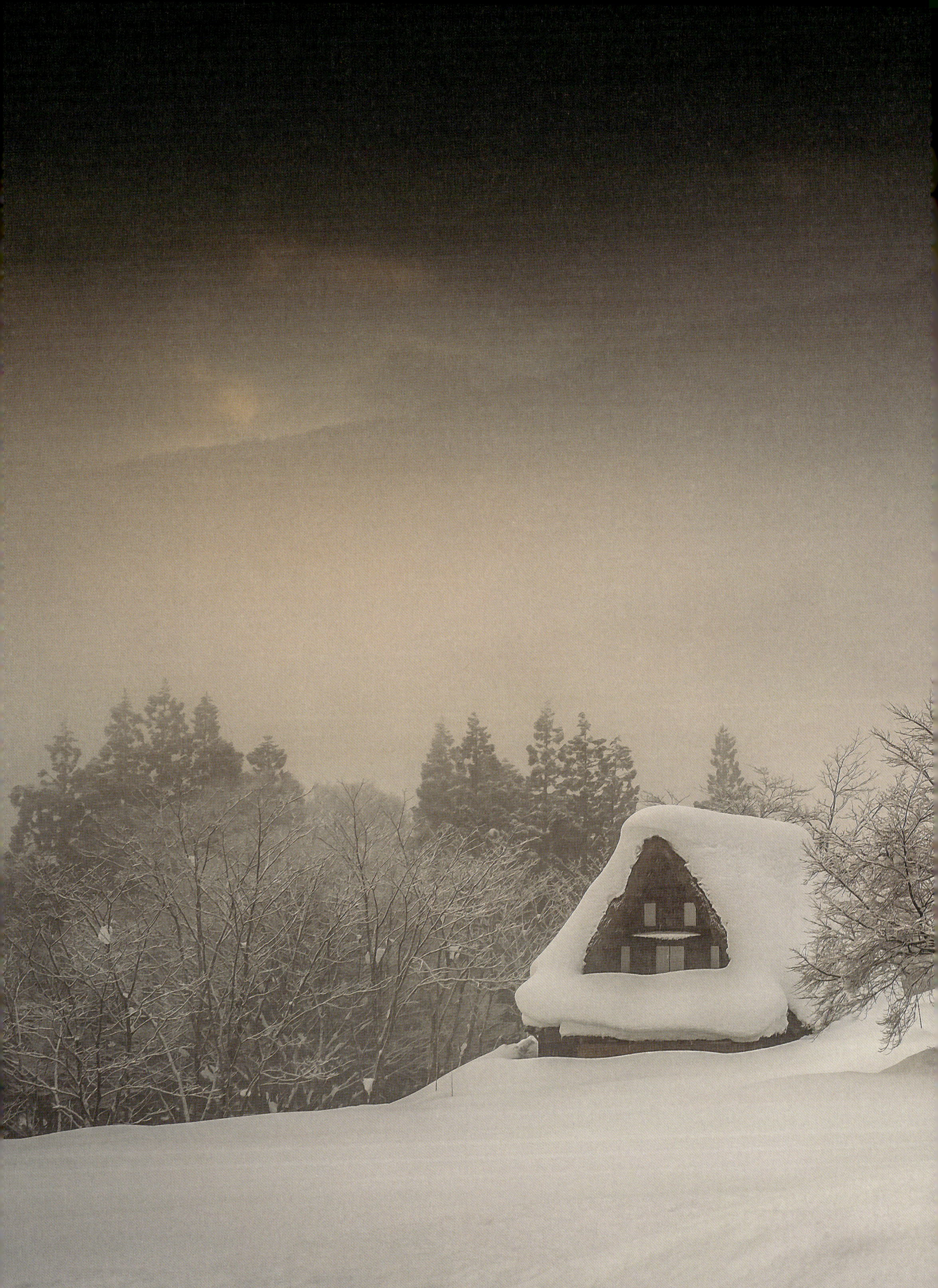

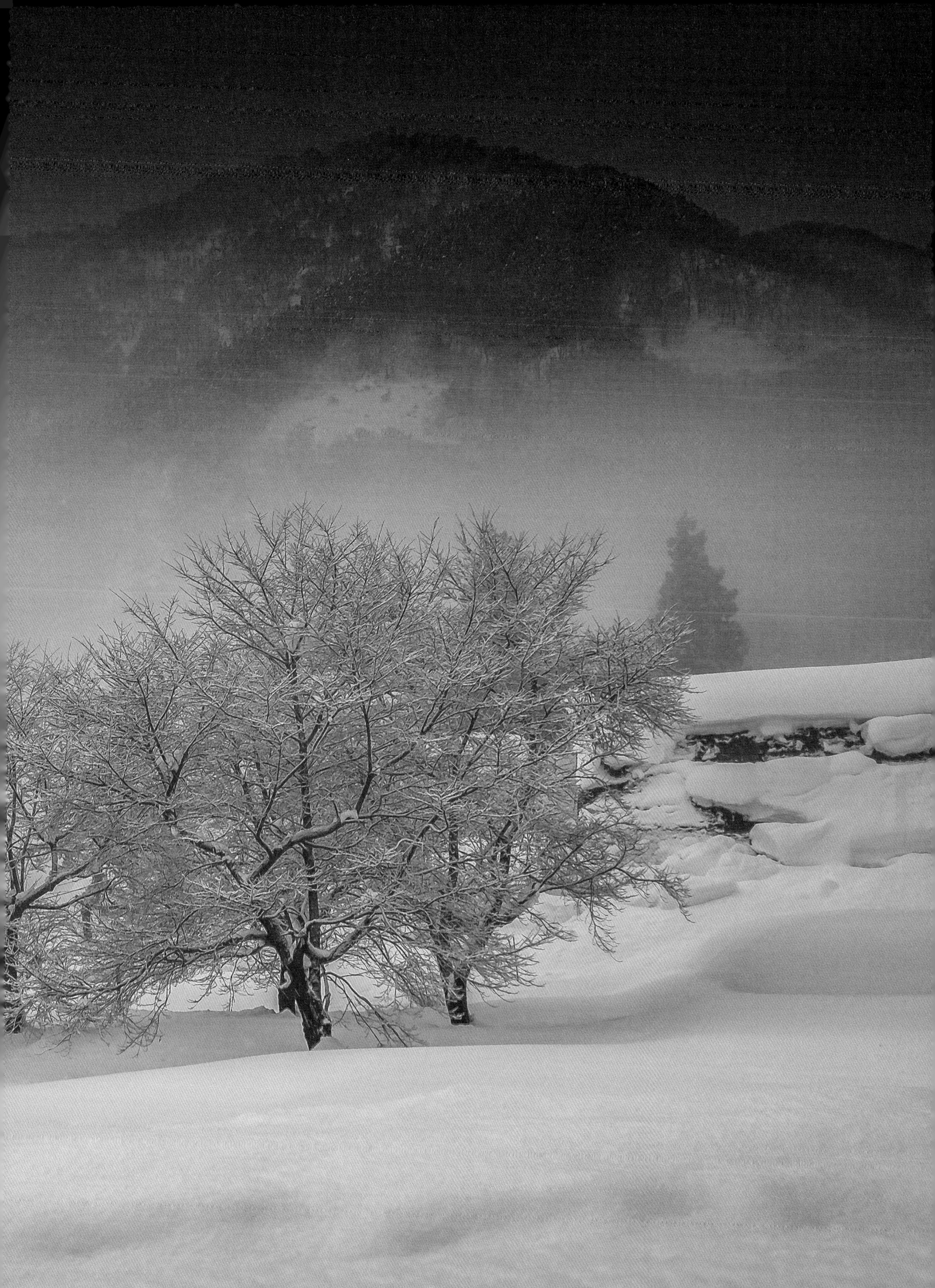

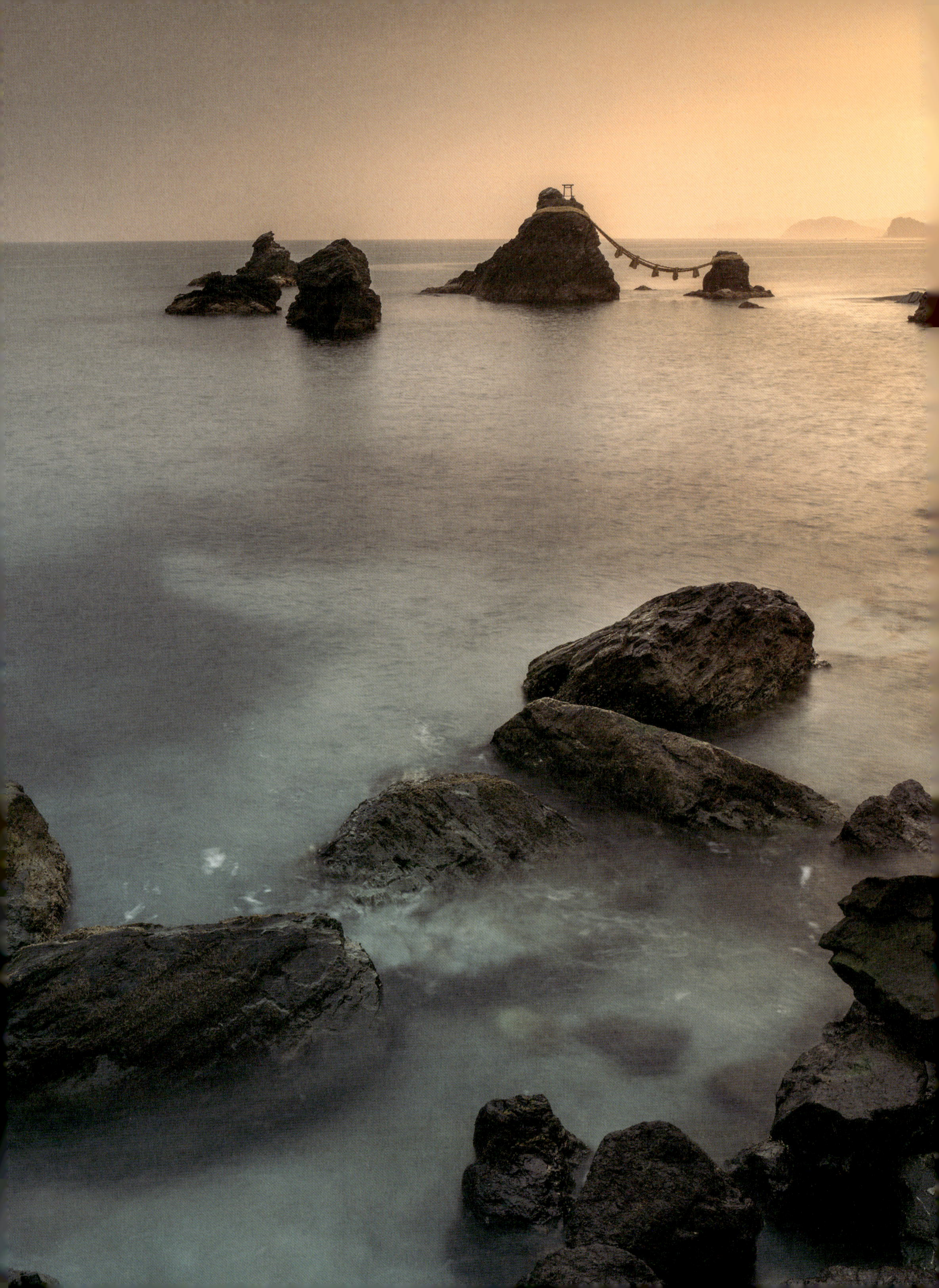

Meoto Iwa Rocks.
Rising from the tranquil waters of Ise Bay, the *Meoto Iwa* rocks, or "Wedded Rocks", stand side by side, joined by a thick sacred rope known as a *shimenawa*. Revered in Shinto tradition, they symbolise the union of Izanagi and Izanami, Japan's divine creators.

関西

Kansai

The Cradle of History and the Heart of Japan

Nestled in the heart of Japan, between lush mountains and shimmering seas, lies the Kansai region – a land rich in culture, spirituality, and ancient traditions. It is here that Japan, as we know it today, shaped its identity. Covering seven prefectures – Osaka, Kyoto, Nara, Hyōgo, Shiga, Wakayama, and Mie – Kansai is a place where ancient capitals sit alongside natural wonders, and where every stone seems to tell its own story.

Area.
Kansai encompasses an area of roughly 27,335 km², accounting for approximately 7.2% of Japan's total land area.

Demographics and Population.
The region has a population of approximately 22.8 million people, with an average density of 832.6 inhabitants per square kilometre.

Geographical Location.
The region is bordered to the east by the Chūbu region, to the west by the Chūgoku region, to the north by the Sea of Japan, and to the south by the Pacific Ocean. It includes major cities such as Kyoto, Osaka, and Kobe.

Climate and Seasons.
Kansai enjoys a temperate climate characterised by four distinct seasons. Summers are hot and humid, while winters tend to be mild, although some inland areas may experience cooler temperatures. Spring and autumn offer pleasant weather and are especially popular for cherry blossom viewing and enjoying autumn foliage.

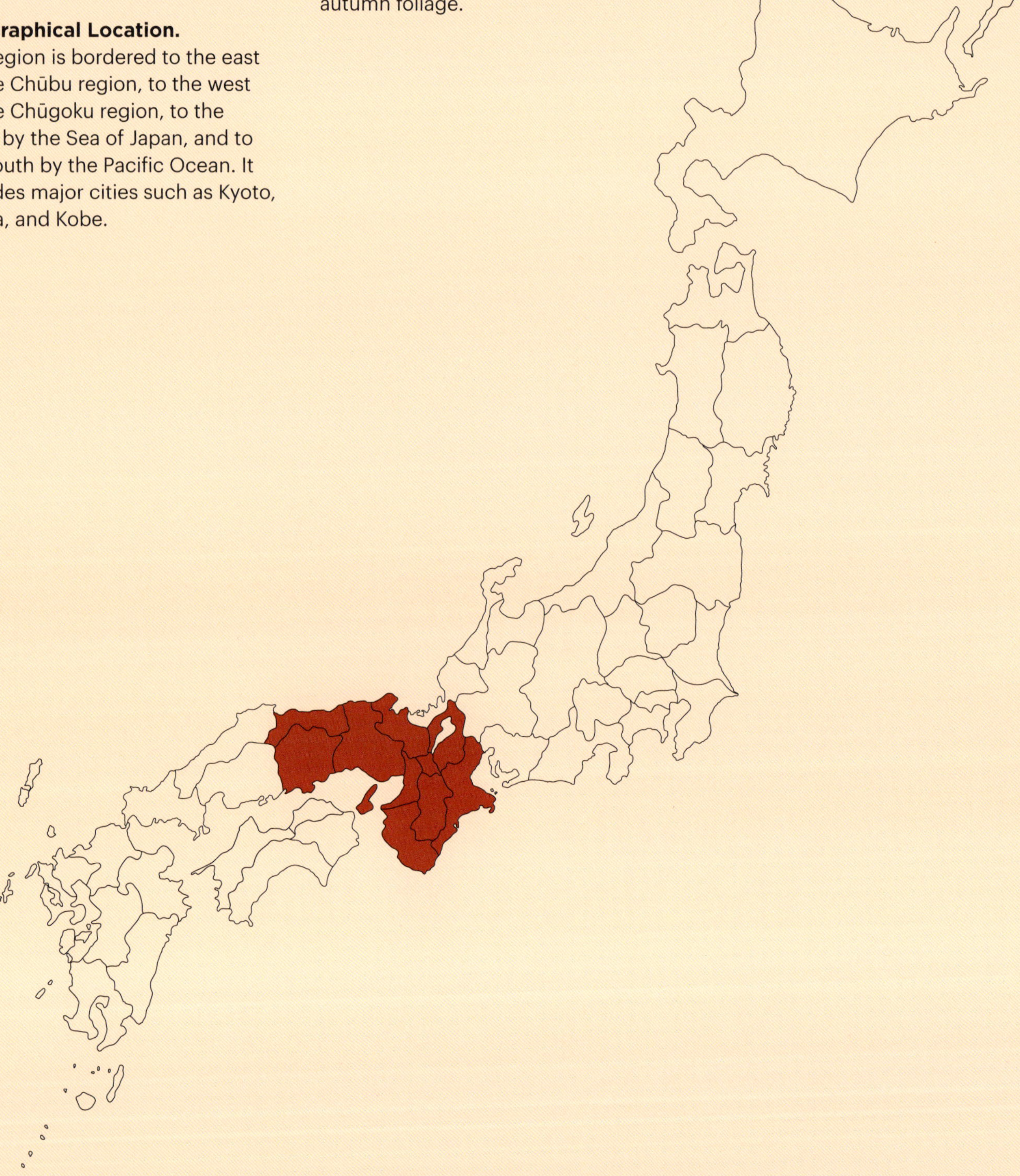

Kyoto,
The Jewel of Tradition

Once the imperial capital for over a thousand years, Kyoto embodies the essence of Japanese elegance. The city is home to more than 1,600 Buddhist temples and 400 Shinto shrines, many of which are UNESCO World Heritage Sites.

Kinkaku-ji, or the Golden Pavilion, is undoubtedly the most iconic. This gold-leaf-covered temple reflects in the serene waters of its pond, offering a scene of perfect tranquillity. To the east of the city, Kiyomizu-dera, perched high on a hill, provides a stunning panorama of Kyoto, especially in autumn when the maple trees ignite in shades of red. The Fushimi Inari Taisha shrine, with its thousands of red *torii* gates winding up the forested slopes, offers a profoundly immersive experience in Shinto spirituality. Meanwhile, the lantern-lit alleyways of the Gion district transport visitors back in time, where *geishas* and *maiko* move gracefully between the traditional teahouses. A maiko is a geisha apprentice undergoing artistic training in Kyoto. She wears colourful kimono, elaborate hairstyles and more accentuated make-up. A geisha is an accomplished artist with a more sober, refined style, specializing in traditional arts such as dance, music and conversation.

Osaka,
A Hub of Cosmopolitan Energy

Osaka, often referred to as "the kitchen of Japan", is a vibrant centre of life and modernity. Its towering skyscrapers, lively shopping streets, and bustling markets stand in stark contrast to the historic landmarks scattered throughout the city.

Osaka Castle, an imposing fortress surrounded by a moat, serves as a reminder of the samurai era and the grandeur of the shoguns. The Dotonbori district, with its dazzling neon lights and flamboyant signs, pulses with energy, filling the air with the mouth-watering aromas of *takoyaki* and *okonomiyaki*.

The Kaiyukan aquarium, one of the largest in the world, offers an intriguing look into marine ecosystems, while the Umeda Sky Building's observation deck provides a sweeping panorama of this dynamic metropolis.

Nara,
The Dawn of Civilisation

Nara, Japan's first permanent capital, is a city where history comes alive through its magnificent temples and parks filled with sacred deer.

The Tōdai-ji temple, renowned for its bronze *Daibutsu* (Great Buddha), is an architectural marvel, awe-inspiring in its size. The Kasuga Taisha shrine, adorned with thousands of stone and bronze lanterns, exudes a mystical atmosphere, especially during festivals when the lanterns are lit.

Nara Park, where deer wander freely among visitors, symbolises the harmonious relationship between humans and nature, a core value deeply embedded in Japanese culture.

Hyōgo,
Where Sea Meets Mountain

Hyōgo Prefecture is a land of contrasts, where the Seto Inland Sea meets rugged mountains. Its capital, Kobe, is a cosmopolitan city known for its vibrant port, world-renowned beef, and sophisticated charm.

Himeji Castle, often called the "White Heron Castle", is exceptionally well-preserved with its authentic wooden keep and is regarded as the most beautiful in Japan. Its impressive architecture and pristine gardens make it a must-visit for lovers of history and beauty.

Nestled in the hills, Arima Onsen is among Japan's oldest hot springs. Its mineral-rich waters offer a truly soothing experience, set against a picturesque backdrop.

Wakayama, Sanctuaries and Untamed Landscapes

Wakayama, located on the southern coast of Kansai, is a profoundly spiritual prefecture. Mount Kōya (*Kōya-san*) serves as a spiritual centre for esoteric Shingon Buddhism. This monastic complex, a UNESCO World Heritage Site, attracts both pilgrims and travellers, offering opportunities to stay in the temples and engage in meditation or ceremonies. The Okunoin Cemetery, nestled among centuries-old cedars, serves as a place of contemplation, where notable figures from Japan's history are laid to rest.

The Kumano Kodō pilgrimage trail, another UNESCO Site, meanders through forest-clad mountains, connecting sacred shrines such as Kumano Hongū Taisha. The Nachi Falls, near the Nachi Taisha shrine, present a breathtaking natural spectacle, with their waters cascading into a lush green landscape.

Shiga, Shores of Lake Biwa

Shiga is home to Lake Biwa, Japan's largest freshwater lake. This tranquil and scenic lake is surrounded by charming villages, temples, and shrines.

The sacred island of Chikubu-shima, situated in the lake, has served as a pilgrimage site for centuries. The Enryaku-ji temple, perched on Mount Hiei, dominates the landscape and provides panoramic views of the lake and the surrounding area.

The shores of Lake Biwa are ideal for a variety of activities, including cycling, sailing, and enjoying waterside picnics. The region is also famous for Hikone Castle, a national treasure that embodies the elegance of the Edo period.

Mie, A Realm of Spirituality and Natural Beauty

Though often overlooked by travellers, Mie is a prefecture where the sacred seamlessly blends with natural splendour. The Ise Shrine, dedicated to Amaterasu, the sun goddess, is regarded as the most sacred site in Shintoism. This complex, rebuilt every 20 years in accordance with ancient traditions, symbolises purity and renewal.

The Ise-Shima coast, with its rugged bays and crystal-clear waters, is a haven for seafood enthusiasts. Traditional divers, known as *ama*, still harvest pearl oysters in this region, steeped in maritime traditions.

The wedded rocks of Meoto Iwa, symbolising the union of two Shinto deities, stand proudly in the sea, connected by a sacred rope. They offer a profoundly spiritual sight, especially at sunrise.

関西

Best Times to Visit

– Spring (Mars to May).
Cherry blossoms create stunning landscapes and offer comfortable Temperatures.

– Autumn (September to November).
Perfect for admiring colourful autumn leaves and benefiting from a milder climate.

Top 5 Places to Vislt

1. Kyoto.
Former imperial capital, renowned for its temples, shrines, and traditional gardens.

2. Osaka.
A vibrant city famous for its castle, street food, and the lively Dotonbori district.

3. Nara.
Home to the Great Buddha at Tōdai-ji temple and Nara Park, where deer roam freely.

4. Himeji Castle.
Considered Japan's most beautiful castle, and a UNESCO World Heritage Site.

5. Mount Kōya (*Kōyasan*).
The spiritual heart of Shingon Buddhism, offering a unique temple stay experience.

関西

Gastronomy

The Kansai region, located in western Japan, is renowned for its refined and diverse cuisine, which differs from that of Tokyo and the Kantō region.
Below is a list of Kansai's culinary specialities, classified by city, with detailed descriptions.

大阪
Osaka

[たこ焼き]
Takoyaki
Takoyaki are small dough balls made from flour and *dashi* broth, filled with pieces of octopus and cooked in a special mould. They are served with *takoyaki* sauce, mayonnaise, *katsuobushi* (bonito flakes), and *ao-nori* (dried seaweed). This dish is iconic in Osaka and can be easily found at *yatai* (street stalls).

[お好み焼き]
Okonomiyaki
Osaka-style *okonomiyaki* is a savoury pancake made with flour, cabbage, eggs, and meat or seafood, cooked on a hot plate. It is topped with *okonomiyaki* sauce, mayonnaise, and garnished with dried bonito flakes.

[串カツ]
Kushikatsu
Kushikatsu are skewers of meat, vegetables, or seafood that are breaded and deep-fried, served with a thick, slightly sweet sauce. A golden rule in Osaka: never dip the skewer twice into the communal sauce!

[ねぎ焼き]
Negiyaki
A variant of *okonomiyaki* where cabbage is replaced with spring onions, offering a lighter, more fragrant flavour. It is often served with soy sauce instead of the traditional sweet sauce.

[ホルモン焼き]
Horumon-yaki
A dish featuring grilled offal (tripe, liver, intestines), which is very popular in Osaka's yakiniku restaurants.

京都
Kyoto

[湯豆腐]
Yudōfu
A minimalist dish of silky tofu heated in water or dashi broth, served with soy sauce and yuzu. It is especially popular in winter, particularly in the Arashiyama area.

[懐石料理]
Kaiseki Ryōri
Kaiseki cuisine is a refined multi-course meal that showcases the seasonality of ingredients. This culinary art is associated with Kyoto's traditional tea houses.

[八ツ橋] Y
Yatsuhashi
A traditional pastry shaped like a triangle, made from cinnamon-flavoured rice dough and filled with sweet red bean paste. There is also a crispy version available.

[おばんざい]
Obanzai
A style of Kyoto home-cooked cuisine, featuring seasonal vegetables, tofu, and seaweed, prepared simply yet flavourfully.

[鯖寿司]
Saba-zushi
Pressed sushi (*oshizushi*) made with marinated mackerel and vinegared rice, wrapped in kombu or bamboo leaves.

神戸
Kobe

[神戸牛]
Kobe Beef – Kōbe-gyū
Kobe beef is among the most renowned worldwide for its exceptional marbling and tenderness. It is enjoyed as steak, *sukiyaki*, or *shabu-shabu*.

[神戸ロースカツ]
Kobe Rōsu Katsu
A luxurious version of *tonkatsu*, made with Kobe beef rather than pork.

[明石焼き]
Akashiyaki
Like *takoyaki*, *akashiyaki* is a speciality from the neighbouring city of Akashi. It is lighter, contains more eggs, and is dipped into a warm *dashi* broth.

奈良
Nara

[柿の葉寿司]
Kakinoha-zushi
Pressed sushi wrapped in a persimmon leaf, which serves as a natural preservative. It is often topped with salmon or mackerel.

[茶粥]
Chagayu
A rice porridge cooked with green tea or hōjicha, offering a delicate and comforting flavour.

[三輪そうめん]
Miwa Sōmen
Very thin noodles from the Miwa region, served cold in summer with soy sauce and grated ginger.

和歌山
Wakayama

[和歌山ラーメン]
Wakayama Rāmen
A rāmen dish with soy sauce and *tonkatsu* (pork bone) broth, garnished with slices of pork and bamboo. It is often accompanied by mackerel sushi as a side dish.

[めはり寿司]
Mehari-zushi
A giant rice ball (*onigiri*) wrapped in a pickled mustard leaf. This rustic dish was once a meal for farm workers.

[梅干し]
Umeboshi
Wakayama's salted plums are some of the most famous in Japan. They are often eaten with white rice or used as an ingredient in *onigiri*.

滋賀
Shiga

[鮒寿司]
Funazushi
A type of fermented sushi made with funa (carp from Lake Biwa), preserved in fermented rice for several months. This ancient dish is one of the earliest forms of sushi in Japan.

[近江牛]
Omi Beef – Ōmi-gyū
Ōmi beef is one of the most prestigious types of *wagyū*, alongside Kobe beef. It is prized for its melt-in-your-mouth tex-ture and rich flavour.

[赤こんにゃく]
Red Konnyaku
A red version of *konnyaku*, typical of Shiga, naturally coloured by iron oxide. It is often used in stews.

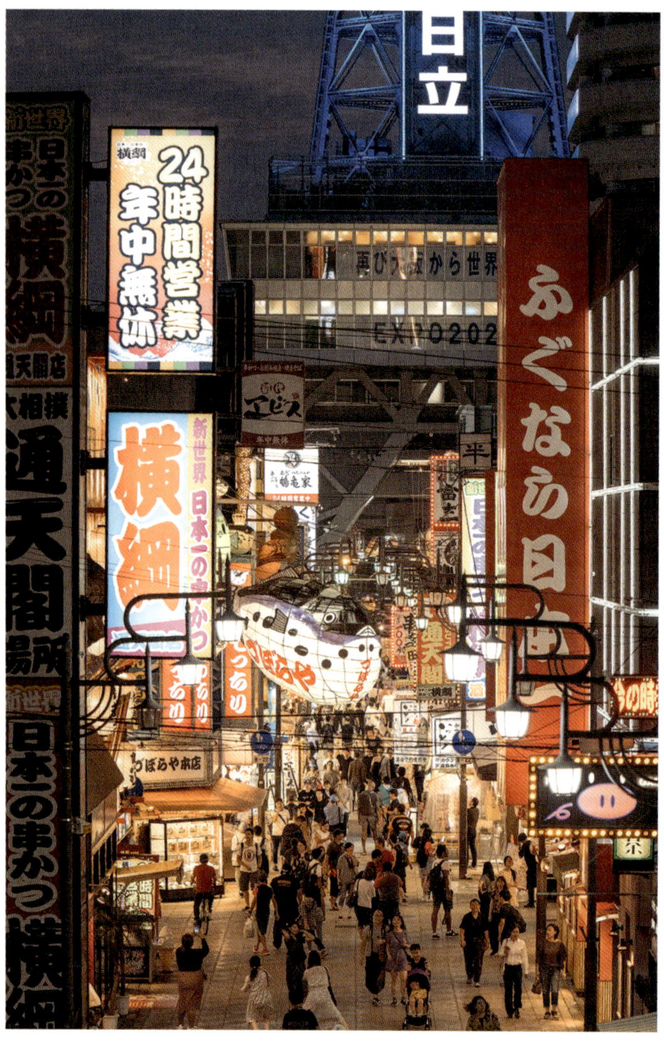

Shinsekai.
Osaka's Shinsekai district comes alive at nightfall, aglow with colourful signs and glowing lanterns. Overlooked by the iconic Tsutenkaku Tower, this vibrant area teems with traditional eateries, quirky shops, and local delights such as *kushikatsu*.

Osaka Tsutenkaku Tower.
A retro icon of Osaka's Shinsekai district, the Tsūtenkaku Tower – literally meaning "tower reaching heaven" – stands 108 metres tall. Its design, inspired by the Eiffel Tower, harks back to the Taishō era (1912-1926). Illuminated each evening, it dominates the lively streets and neon-lit alleys, offering a nostalgic glimpse into this vintage, vibrant district, which was established in the early 20th century.

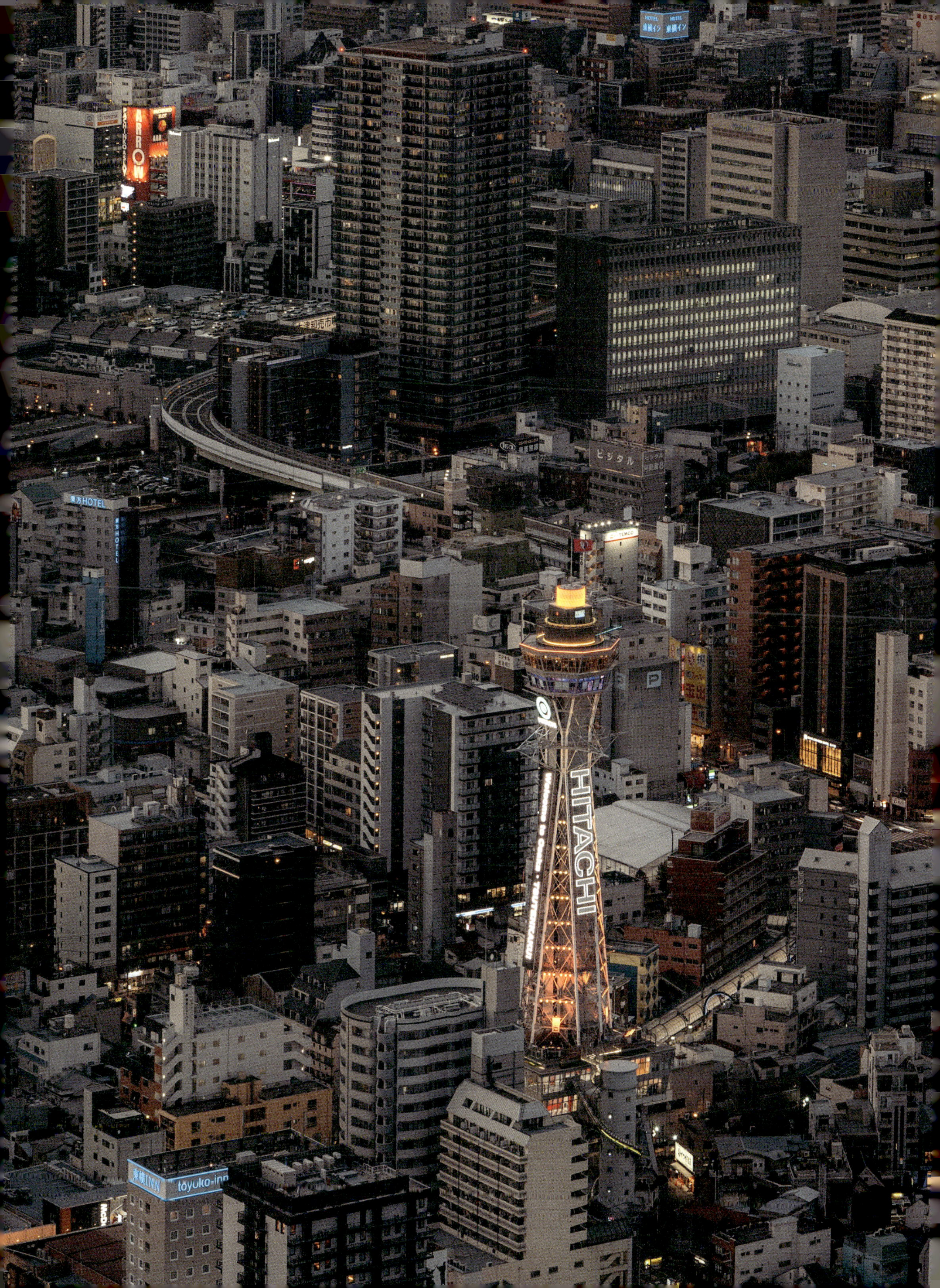
ARROW
HITACHI
toyoko-inn

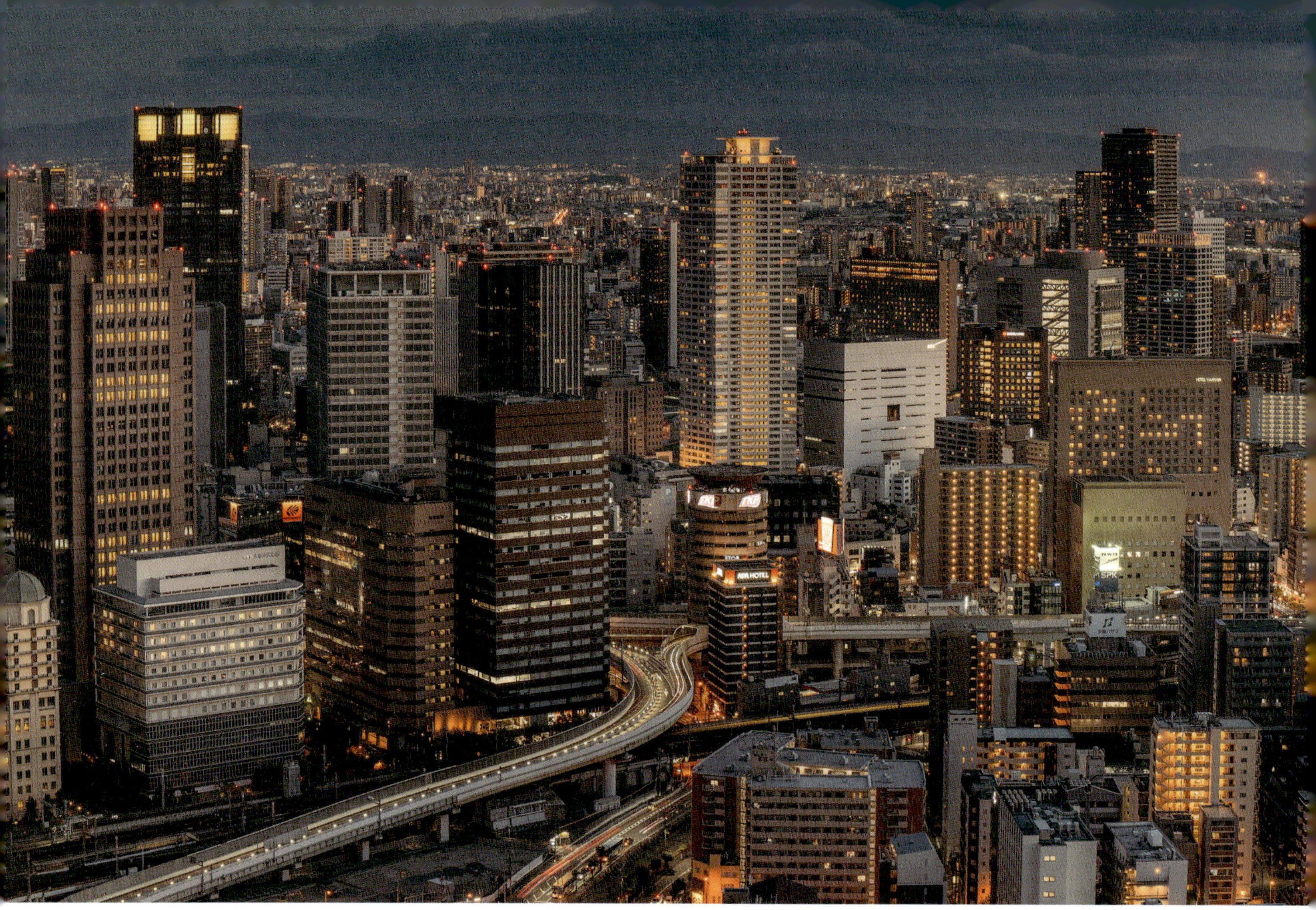

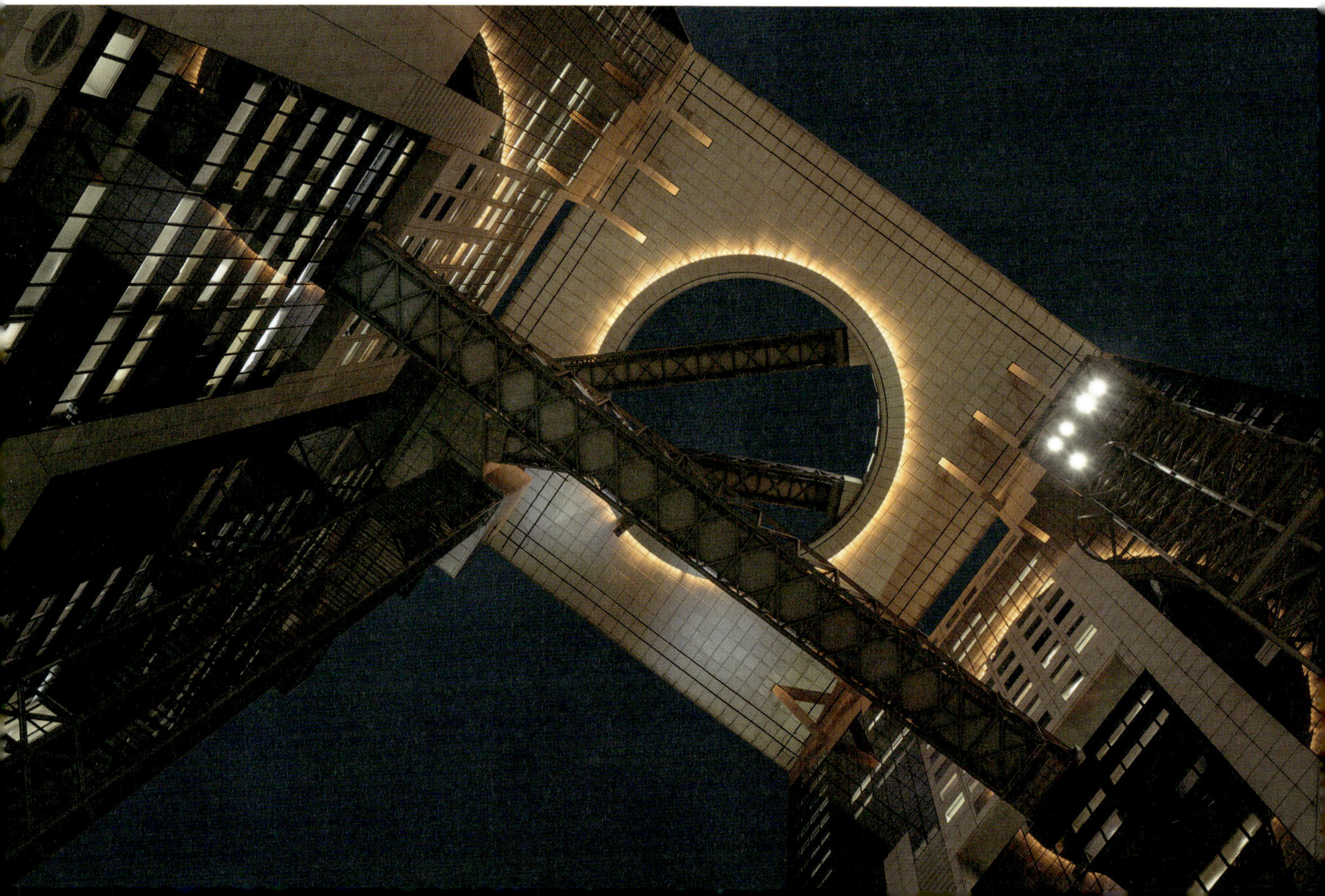

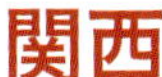

View over Osaka.

From the top of the Umeda Sky Building, Osaka gradually sparkles below, with skyscrapers rising as elegant silhouettes against the glowing cityscape.

Umeda Sky Building.

Rising with two towers connected by an aerial platform, the Umeda Sky Building stands as an architectural marvel in the heart of Osaka. Its 173-metre-high observatory offers a breathtaking panoramic view of the sprawling city below.

Dōtonbori.

Dōtonbori is a popular street for visitors, located along the eponymous canal in Osaka's southern Namba district.

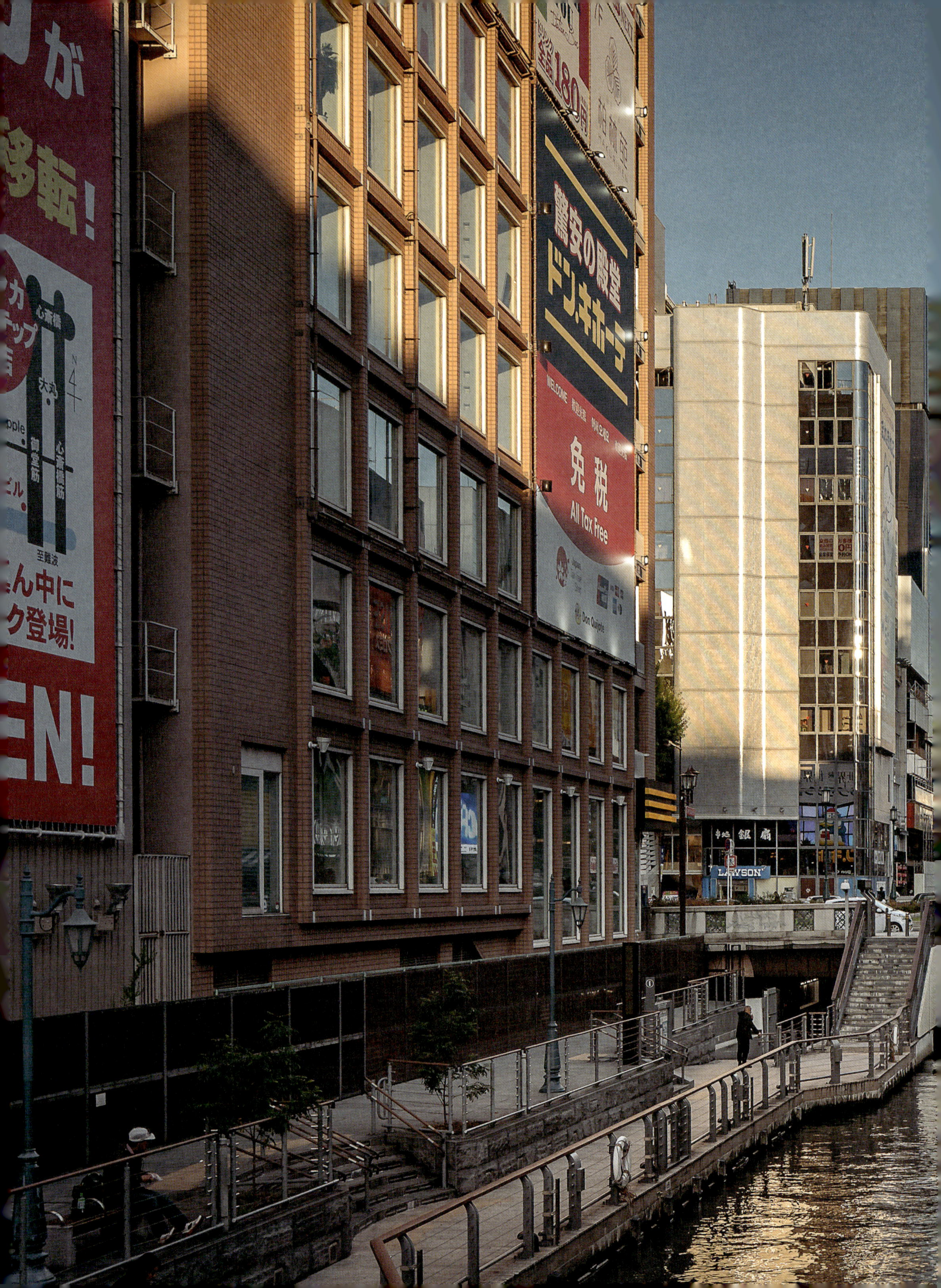

が
移転！
心斎橋
大丸
御堂筋
心斎橋筋
至難波
ん中に
ク登場!
EN!
驚安の殿堂
ドン・キホーテ
WELCOME
免税
All Tax Free
Don Quijote
LAWSON

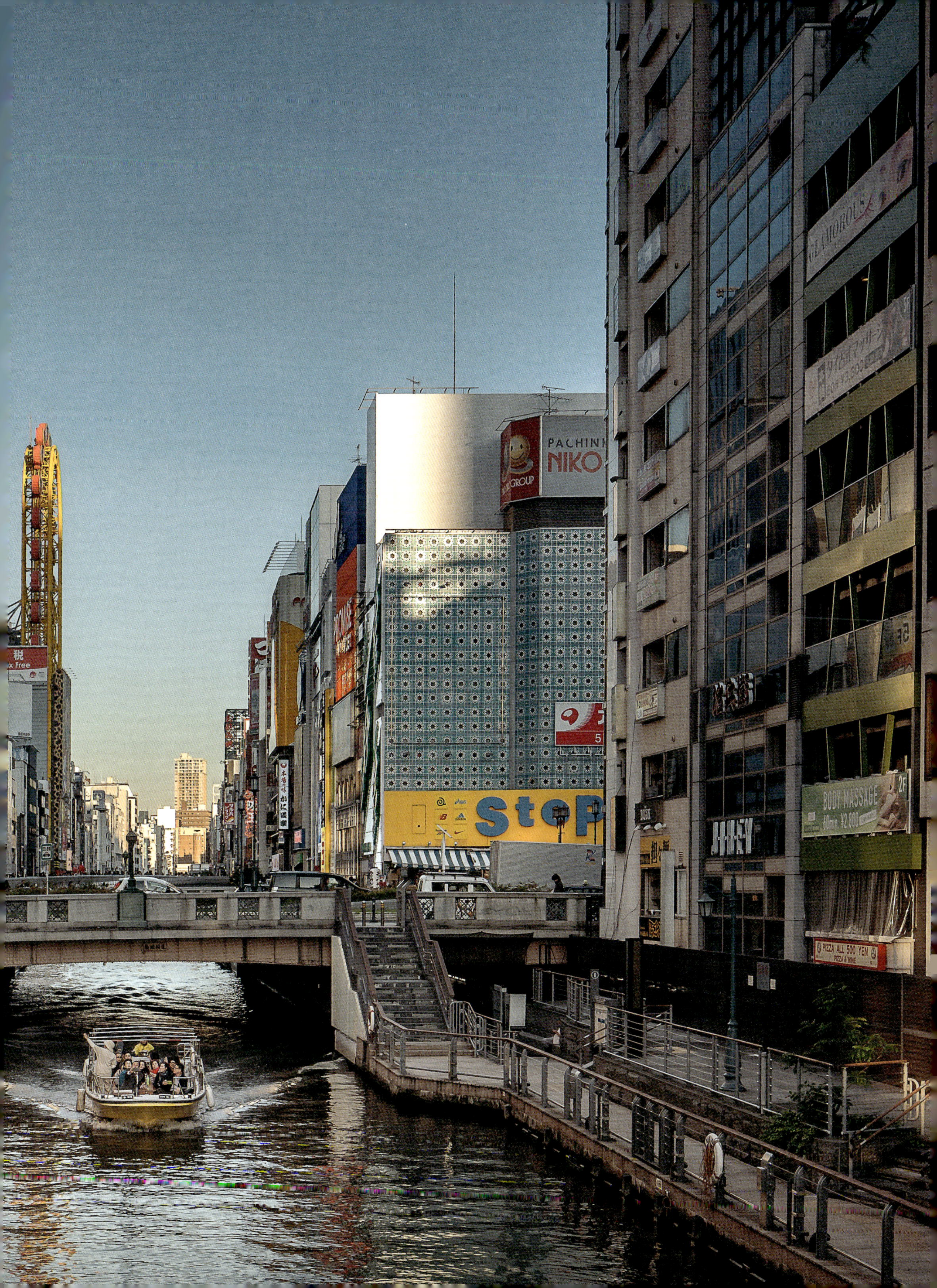
PACHINK
NIKO
BODY MASSAGE
PIZZA ALL 500 YEN

Osaka Castle.
A majestic testament to Japan's history, Osaka Castle rises at the heart of the city, encircled by a tranquil moat and lush gardens. Originally built in 1583 by Toyotomi Hideyoshi, it has been destroyed and rebuilt several times, including in 1620 and after World War II. A symbol of Japanese power and unification, its striking silhouette conveys the story of the samurai and the fierce battles that shaped the feudal era.

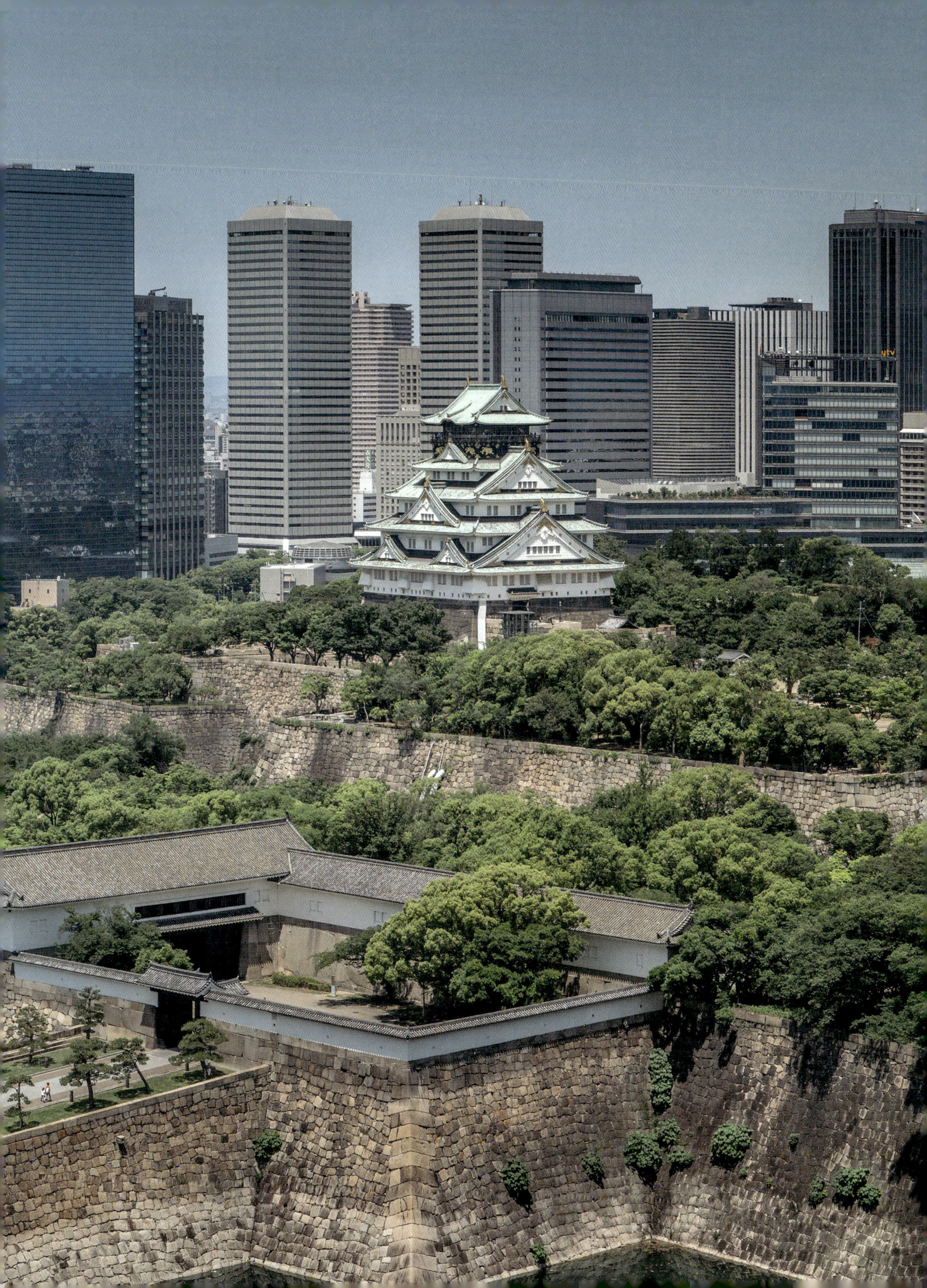

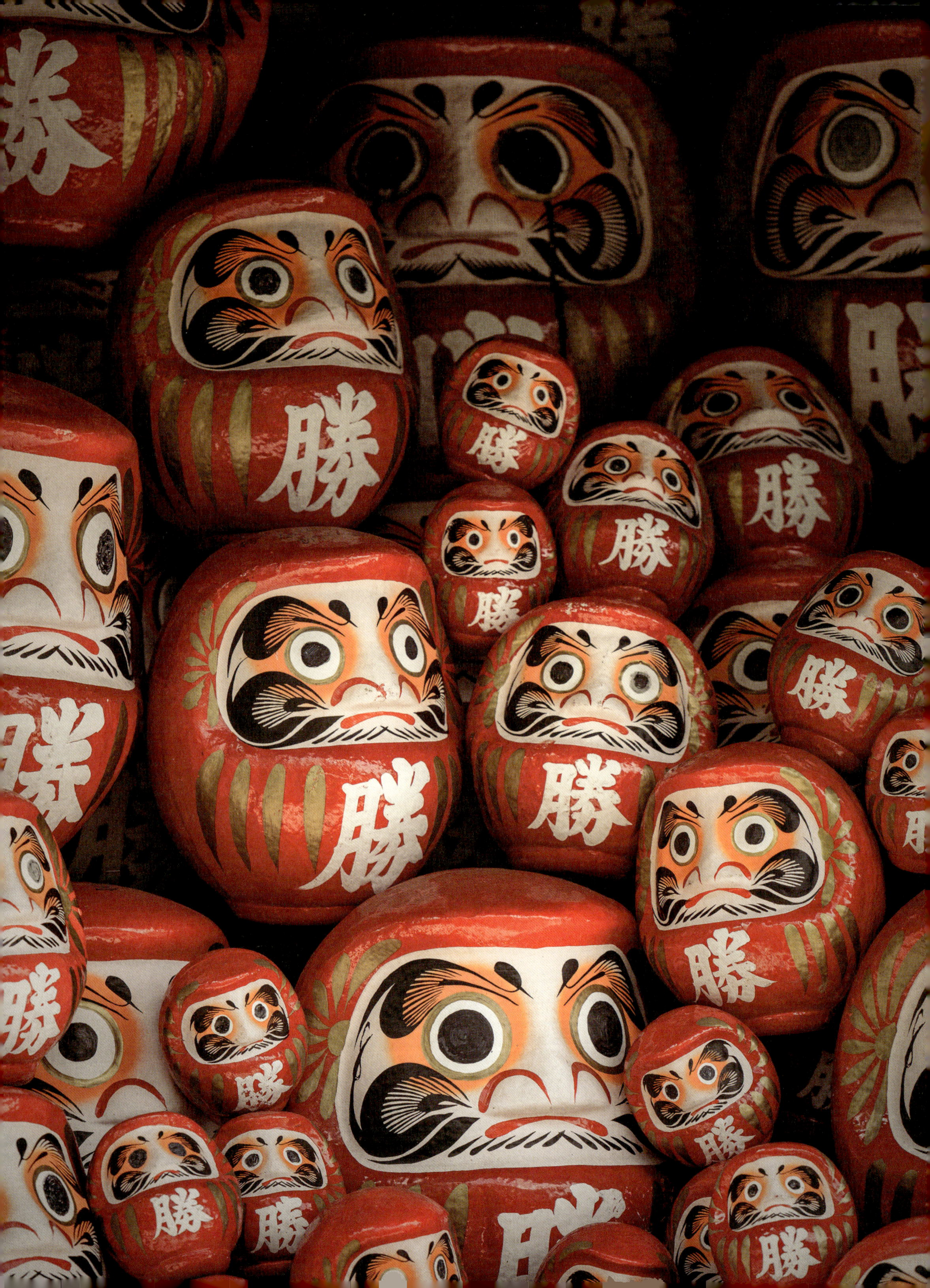

勝
勝
勝
勝
勝
勝
勝
勝
勝
勝
勝
勝
勝
勝
勝
勝

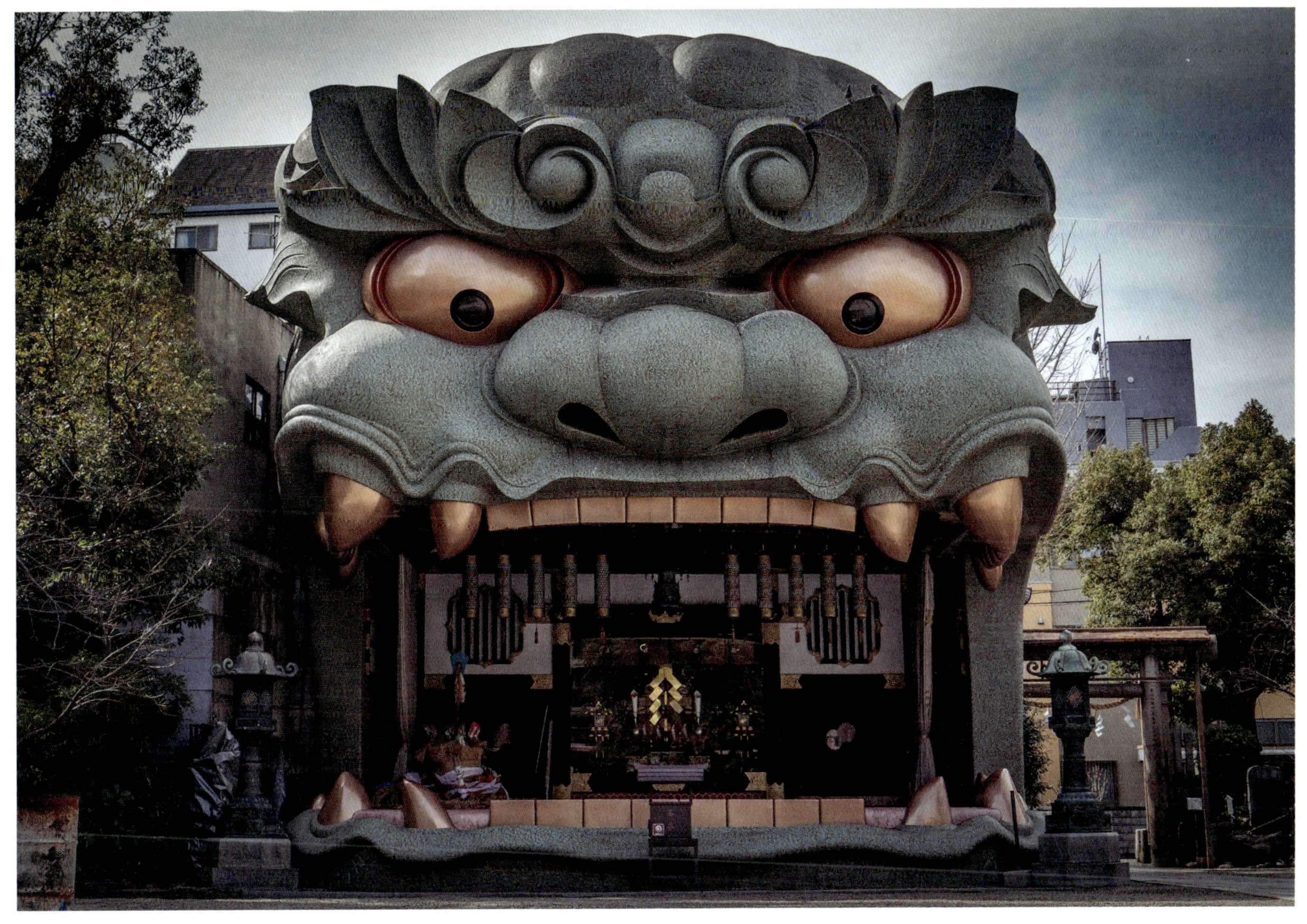

Yasaka Namba Shrine.
Nestled in the heart of Osaka, Yasaka Namba Jinja Shrine is a sanctuary of spirituality where devotees gather to pray for prosperity and protection. Revered by both shopkeepers and locals, this sacred site is easily recognised by its towering twelve-metre-high lion's head, which houses the prayer altar within its open mouth, symbolising strength and guardianship..

Daruma Dolls.
Daruma dolls, with their striking red eyes, symbolise perseverance and success in Japan. Traditionally, one eye is filled when a wish is made, and the other is coloured once the goal is achieved. Katsuo-ji Temple, known as the "Temple of Victory", is a renowned destination where visitors come to pray for success and leave their Daruma dolls as a gesture of gratitude. The stacked figurines are silent witnesses to the hopes and triumphs of those who have made their wishes here.

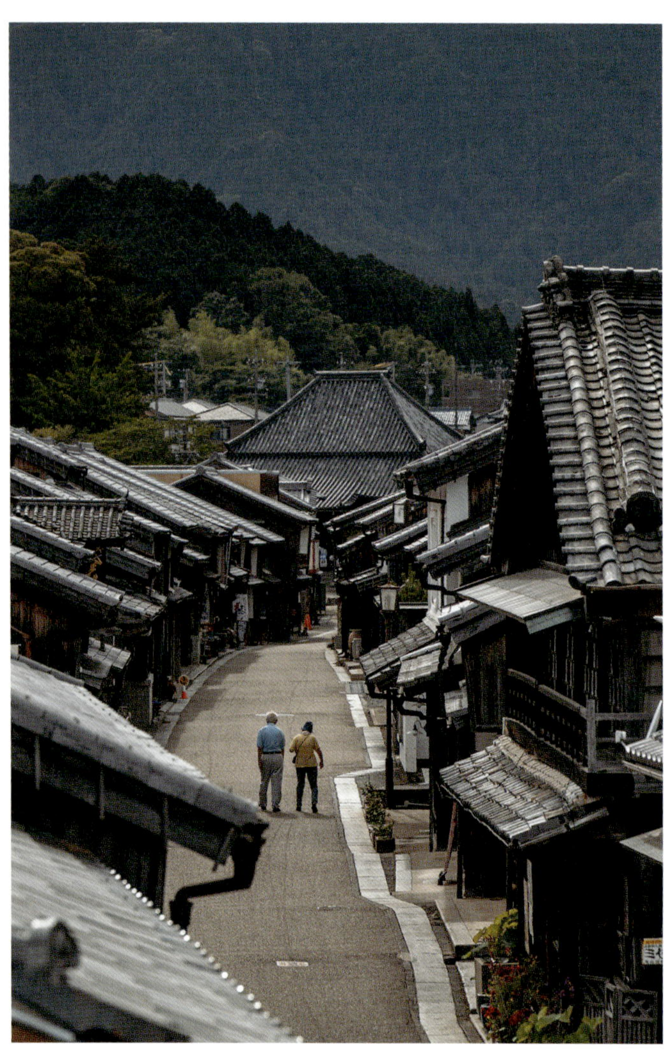

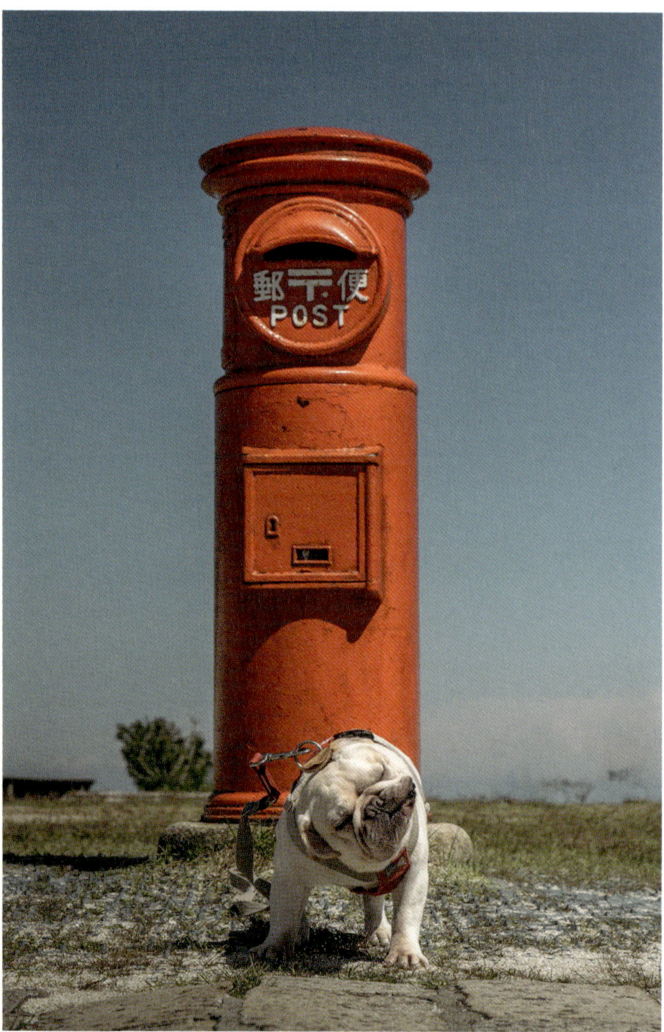

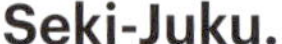

Seki-Juku.
Once a bustling station on the Tōkaidō (Eastern Sea Road) during the Edo period, Seki-juku served as a vital crossing point for travellers journeying from Edo to Kyoto. Lined with well-preserved *machiya* (traditional wooden houses), this historic route provides a vivid immersion into feudal Japan, where rest and trade once defined the rhythm of life at the post houses.

Post in the Sky.
High in the mountains of the Ise region, the "Post in the Sky" captures the imagination–a bright red letterbox seemingly suspended between earth and heaven. This whimsical landmark invites visitors to send their thoughts skyward, as if posting messages to the universe.

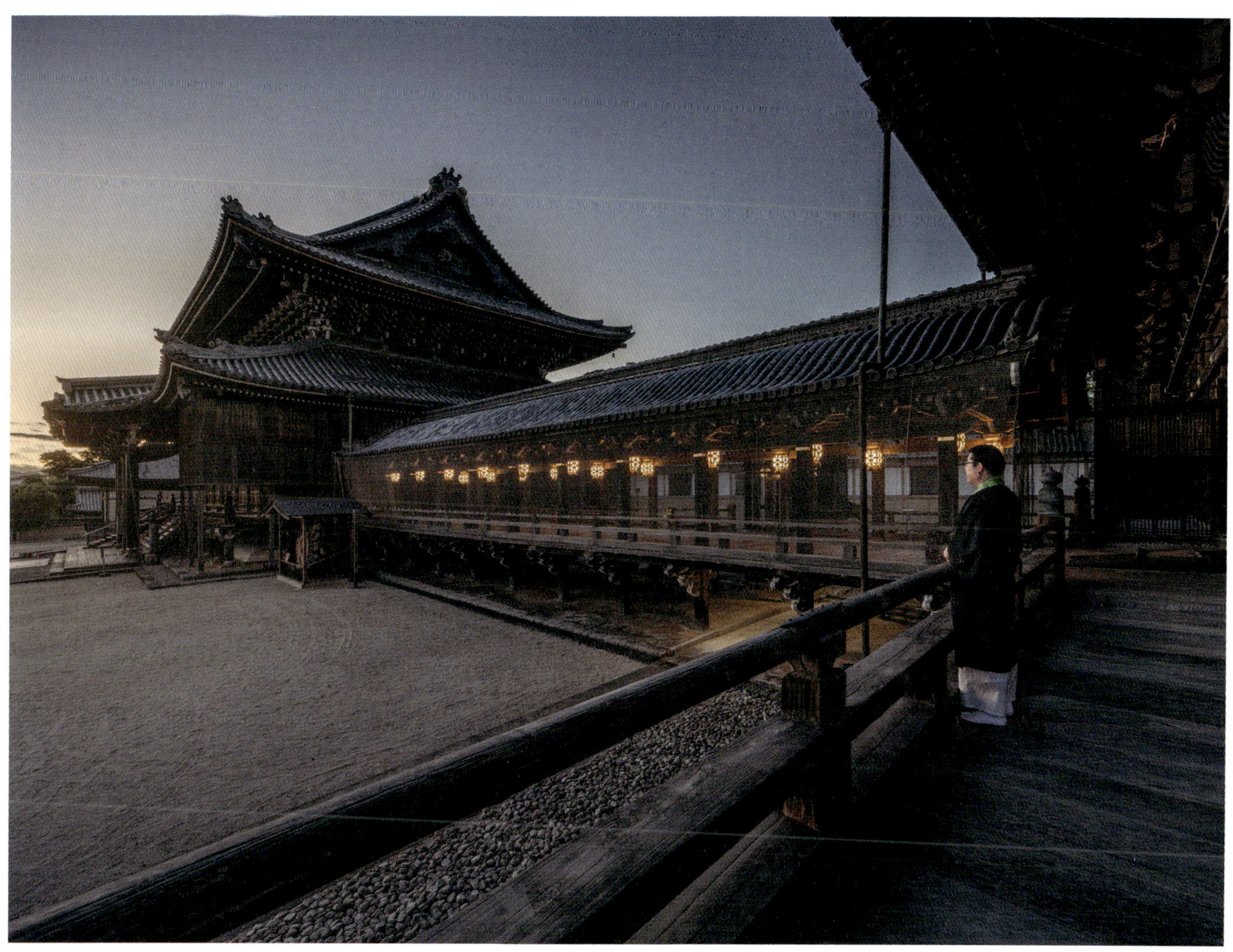

Senjuji Temple.
Founded in 1197 in Mie Prefecture, Senjuji Temple serves as a key centre of Jōdo Shinshū Buddhism. Reconstructed in 1665, it features one of Japan's largest prayer halls, reflecting its spiritual significance during the Edo period (1603-1868).

Artificial Island of Benten.
The artificial island of Benten in Katsuura is a picturesque haven of tranquillity, accessible by a small bridge that connects it to the mainland. Dominated by a shrine dedicated to Benzaiten, the goddess of music and the arts, with its iconic red *torii* standing proudly, the island offers a serene sanctuary, perfect for quiet reflection. >

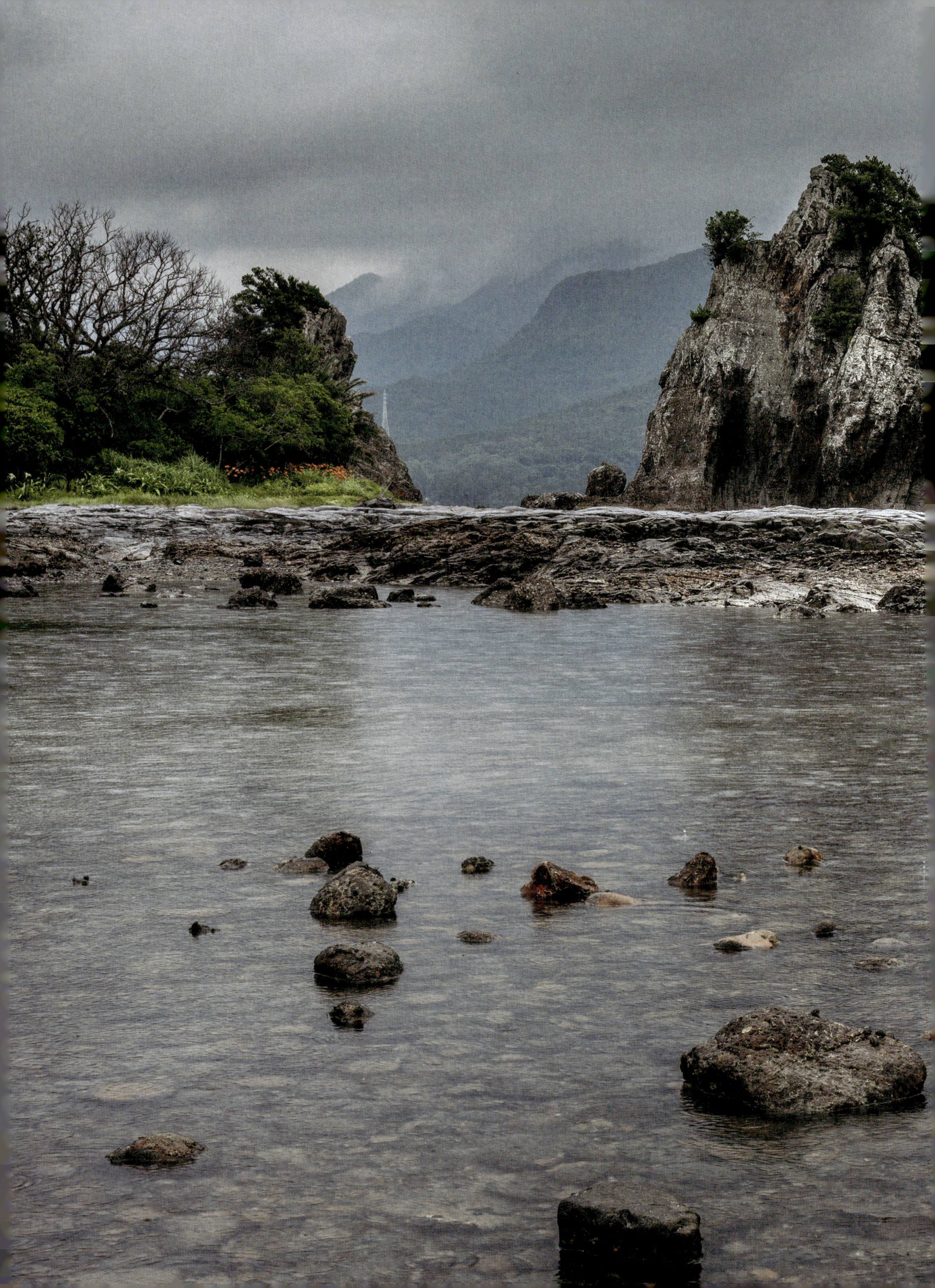

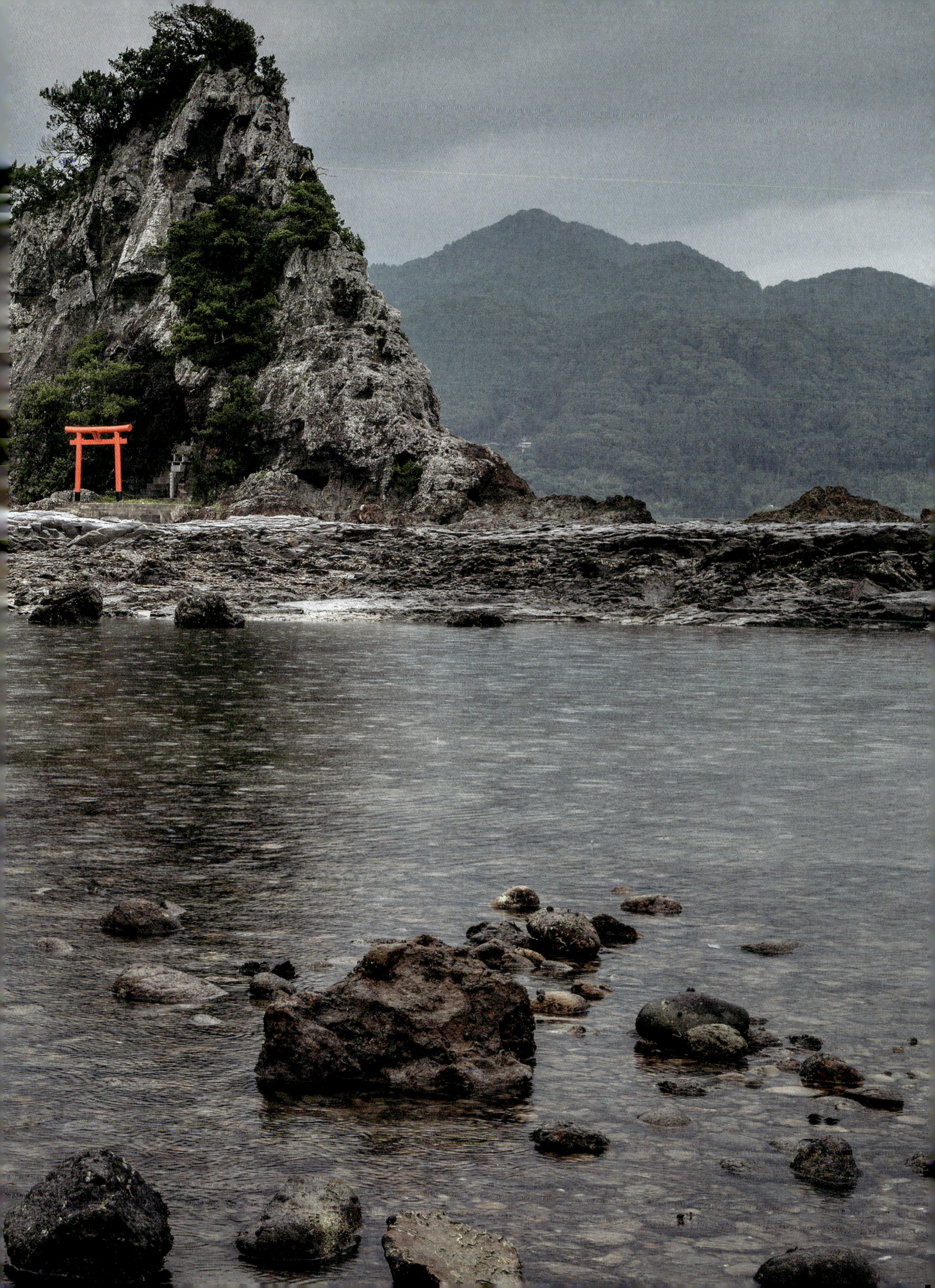

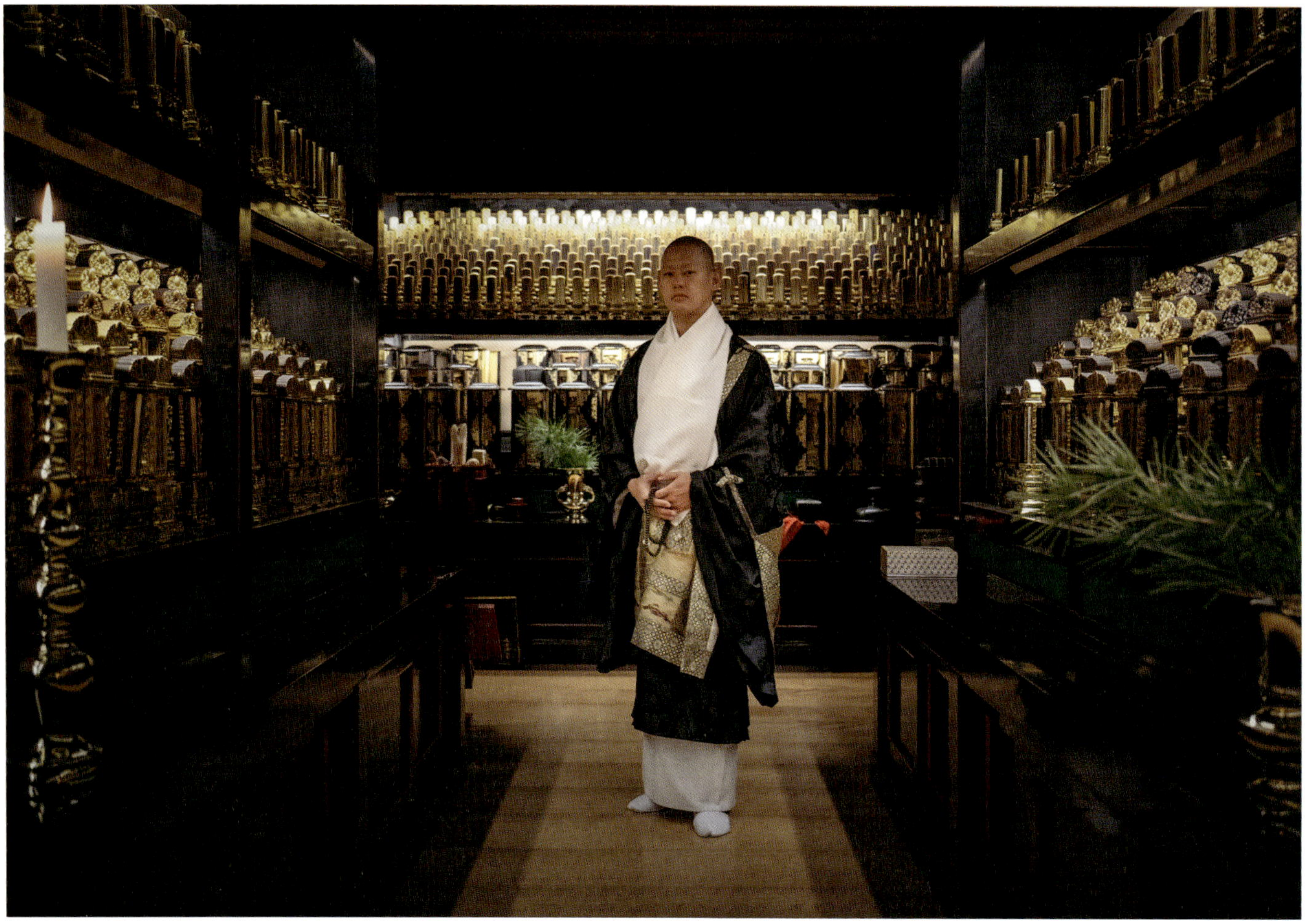

Monk on Mount Kōya.
At Ekō-in Temple, nestled in the heart of Mount Kōya, Buddhist monks continue to honour ancient rites in an atmosphere of profound serenity. Amidst morning prayers, meditation, and Goma fire ceremonies, they invite visitors to experience a unique spiritual immersion, whether for a day or two. Their way of life, rooted in simplicity and devotion, embodies the very spirit of Shingon Buddhism, which has sustained this sacred sanctuary for over a thousand years.

Danjōgaran.
The Danjōgaran is a complex comprising twenty sacred temple, among them the vivid vermilion Konpon Daitō pagoda.

Pilgrim crossing Okunoin Cemetery.

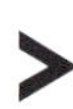

Okunoin Cemetery on Mount Kōya.
Nestled deep within a cedar forest on Mount Kōya, Okunoin Cemetery is the largest and most sacred cemetery in Japan. This mystical site is home to over 200,000 graves of monks and feudal lords, all leading to the mausoleum of Kūkai, the founder of Shingon Buddhism. Surrounded by glowing lanterns and ancient steles draped in moss, Okunoin exudes an enchanting atmosphere, making it perfect for meditation and contemplation.

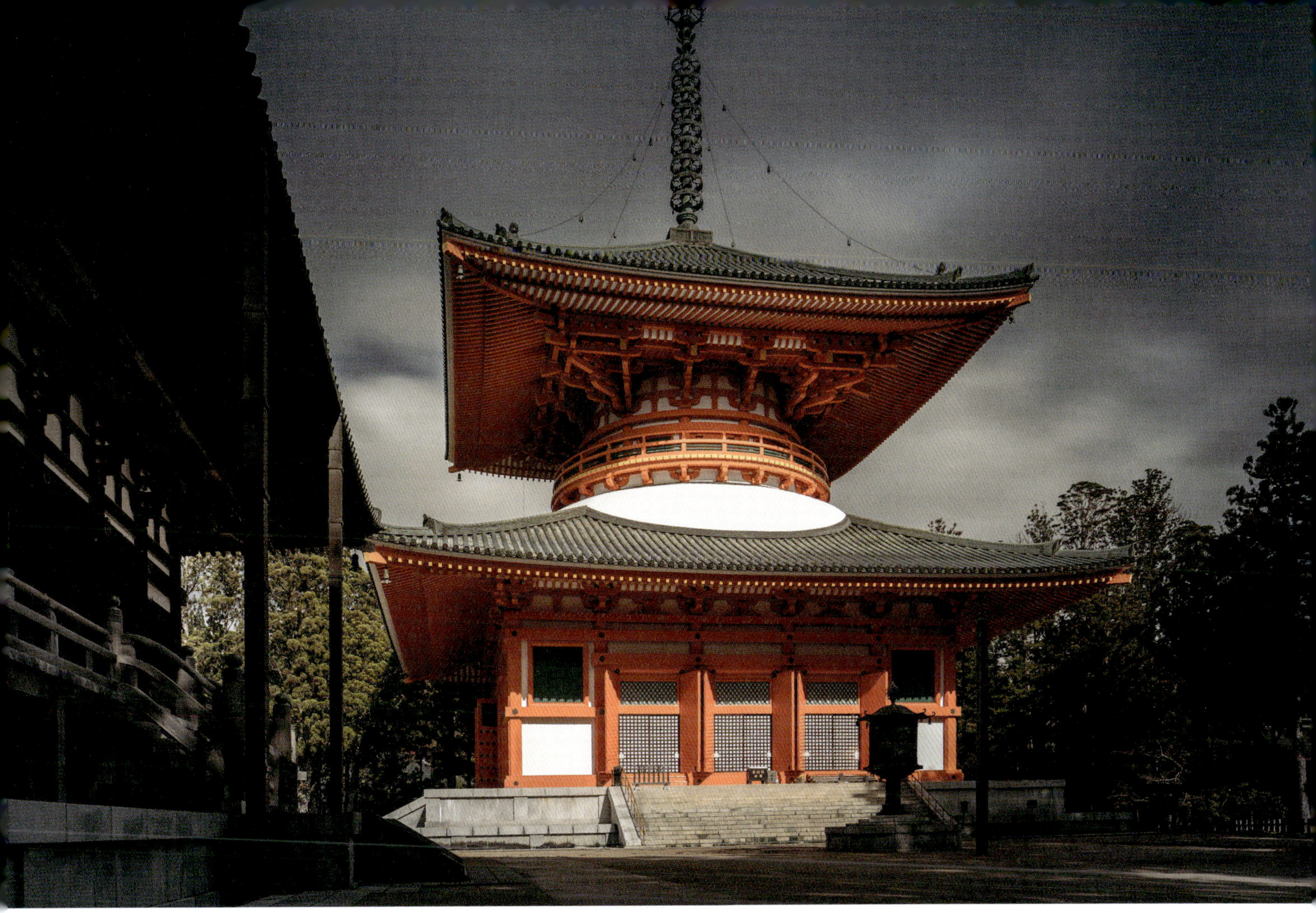

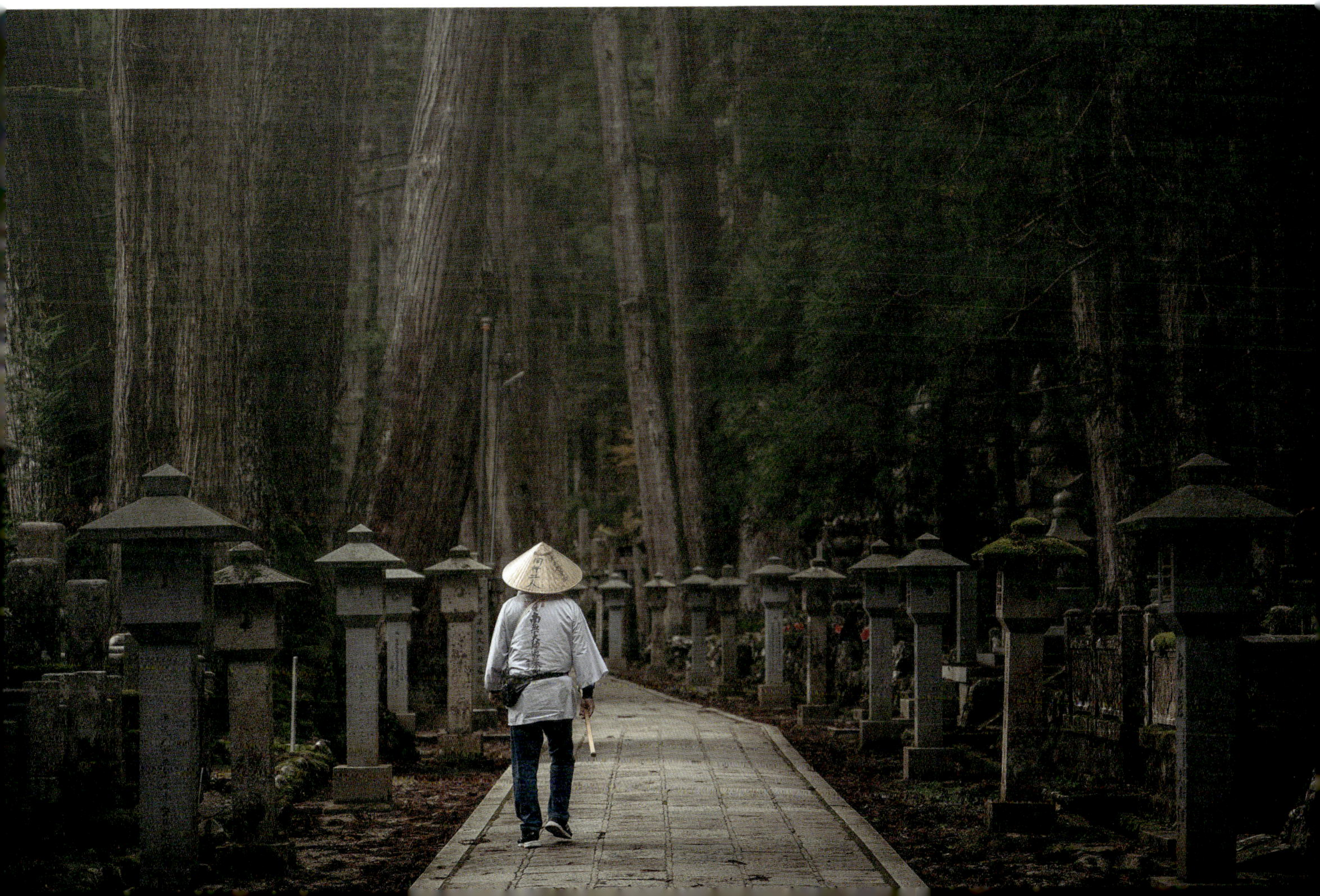

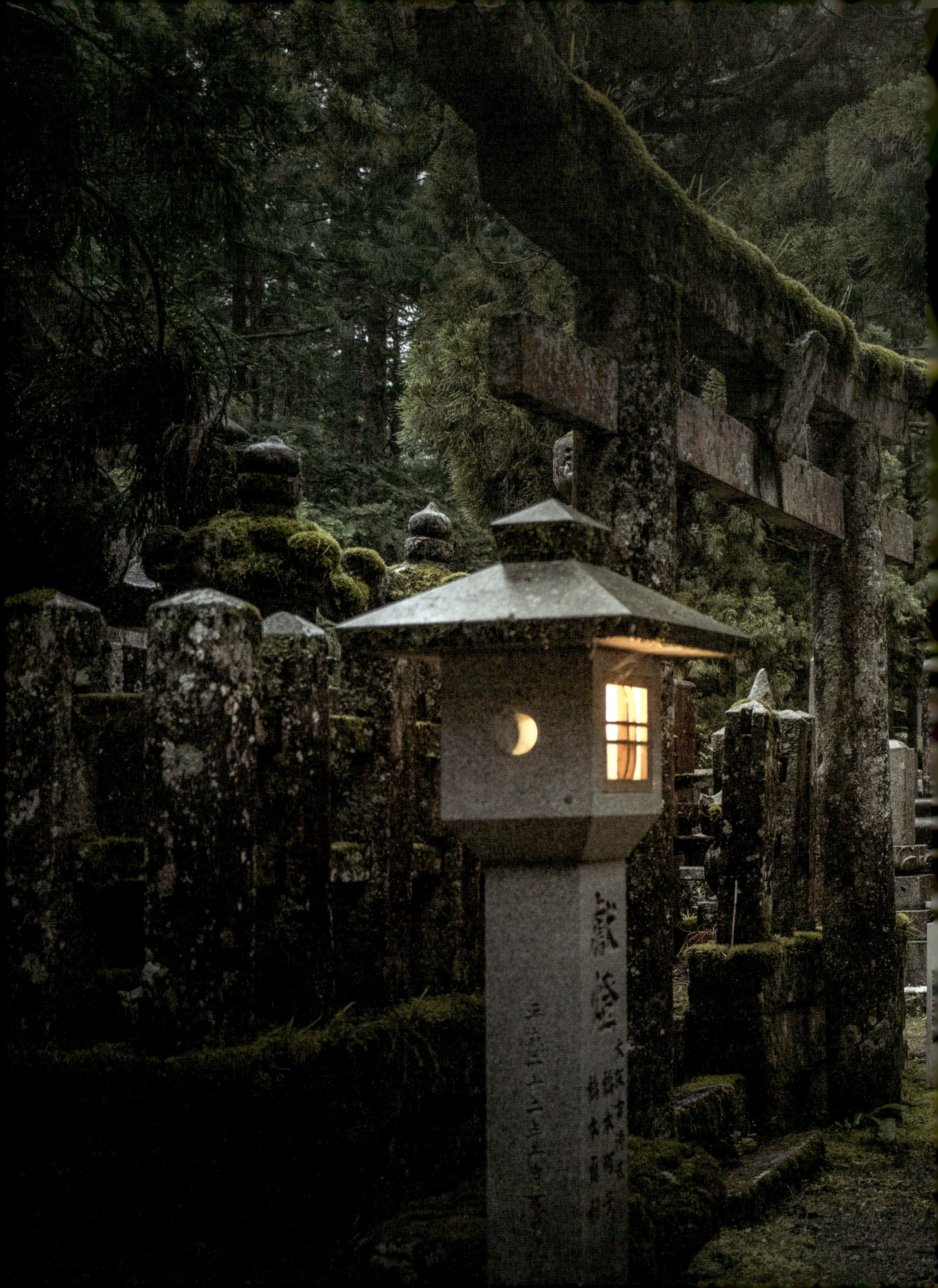

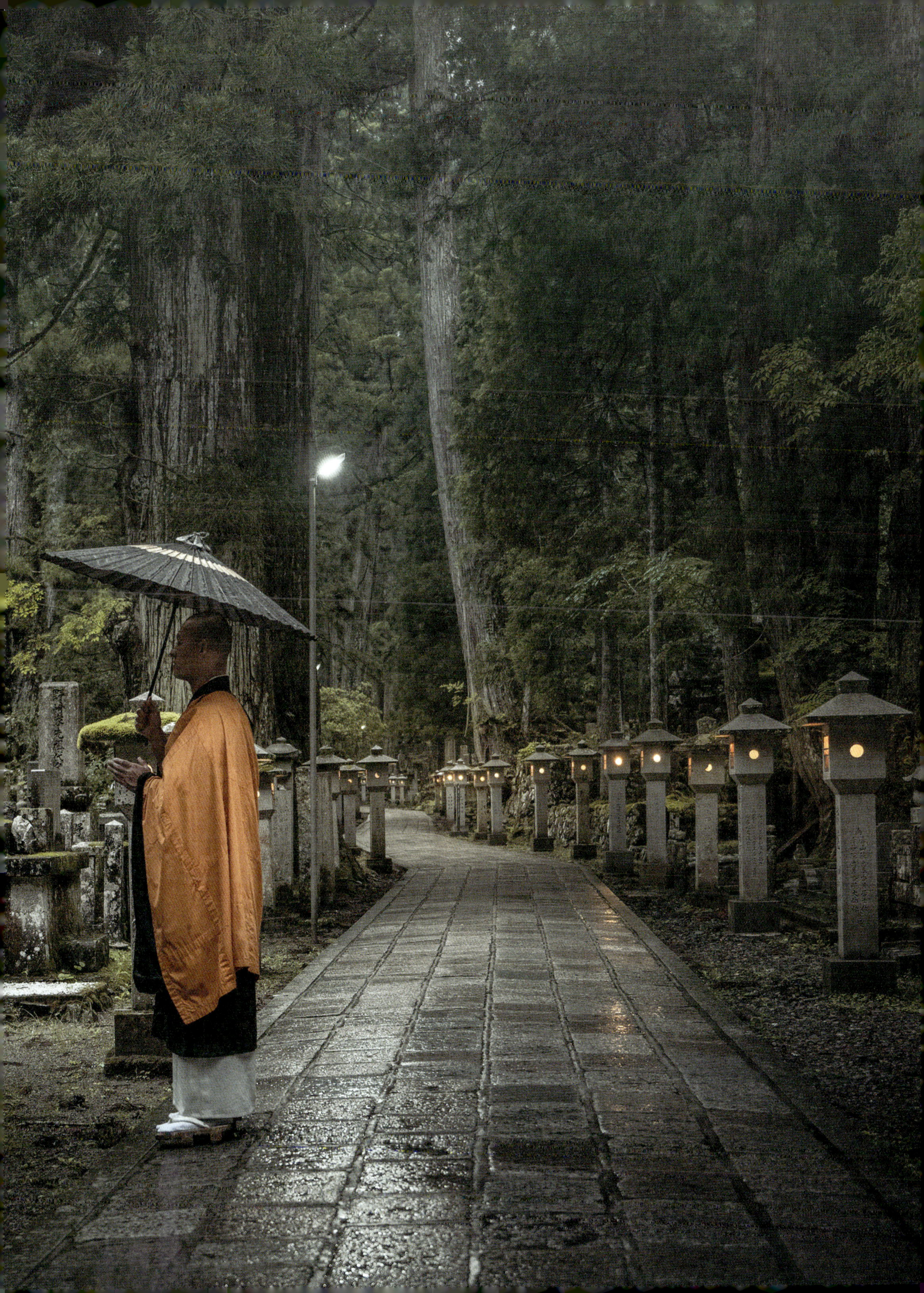

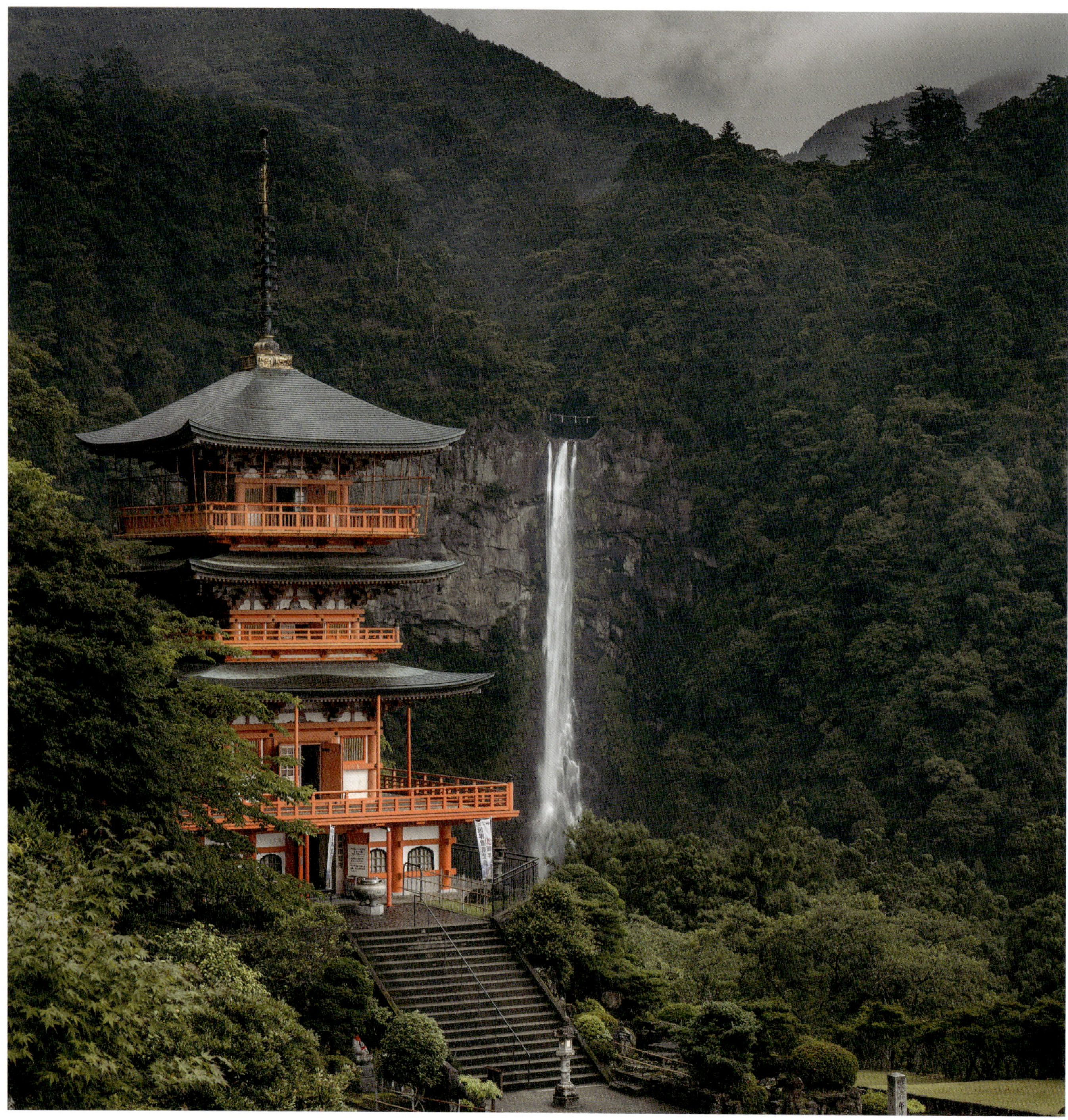

Nachi no Taki Falls.

Nachi no Taki Falls: Nachi Falls, located in Wakayama Prefecture, are Japan's tallest waterfalls, featuring an awe-inspiring 133-metre cascade. Surrounded by a dense, sacred forest, they create a majestic landscape crowned by the silhouette of the Kumano Nachi.

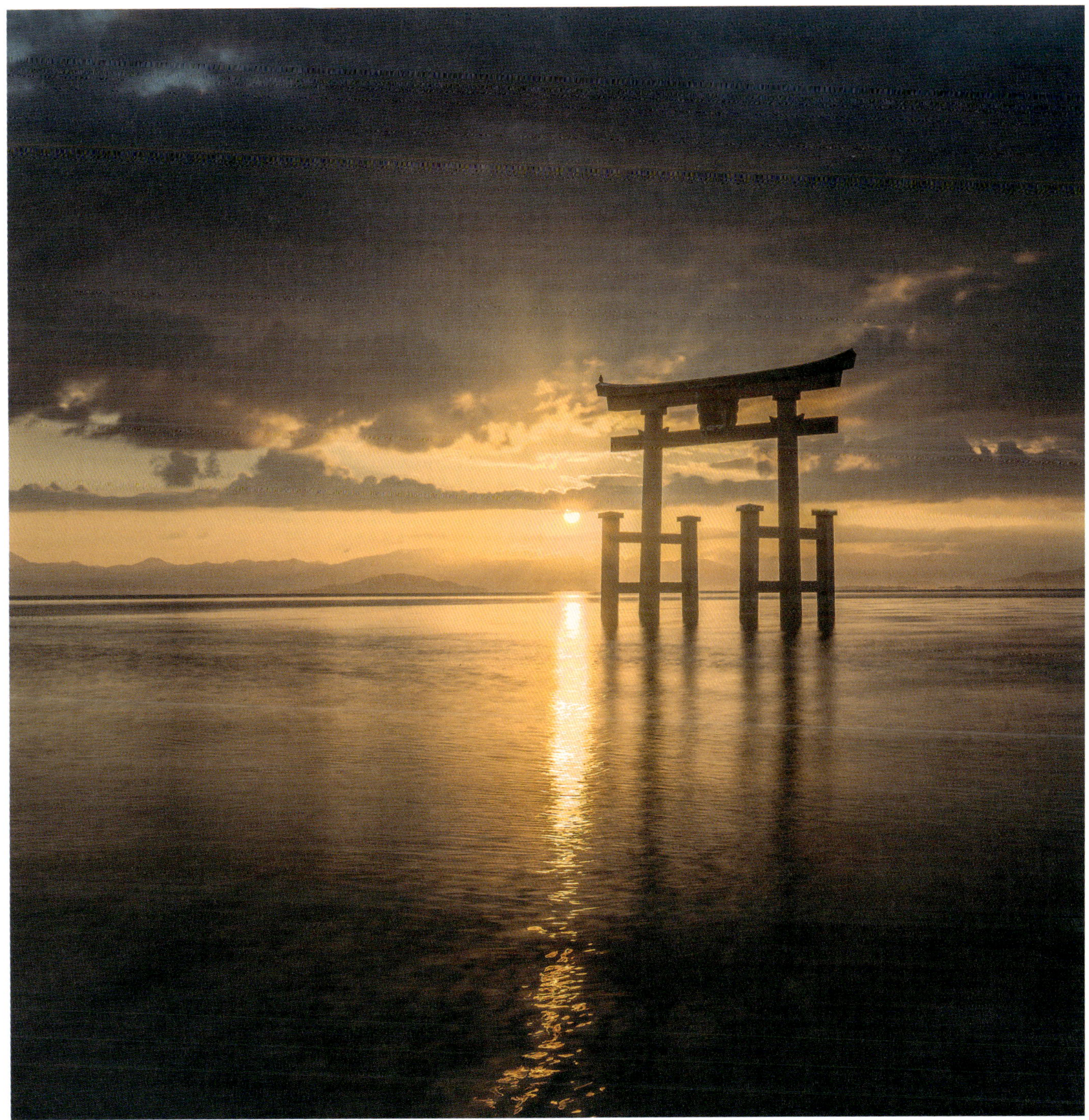

Shirahige Shrine Torii.

Rising from the serene waters of Lake Biwa, the Shirahige Shrine *Torii* stands as a mystical gateway between the world of humans and the realm of deities. Resembling the famous *torii* at Itsukushima, this sacred structure appears to float on the water, offering a breathtaking sight at sunrise and sunset. Symbolising longevity and protection, it serves as a silent guardian over pilgrims and travellers seeking tranquillity.

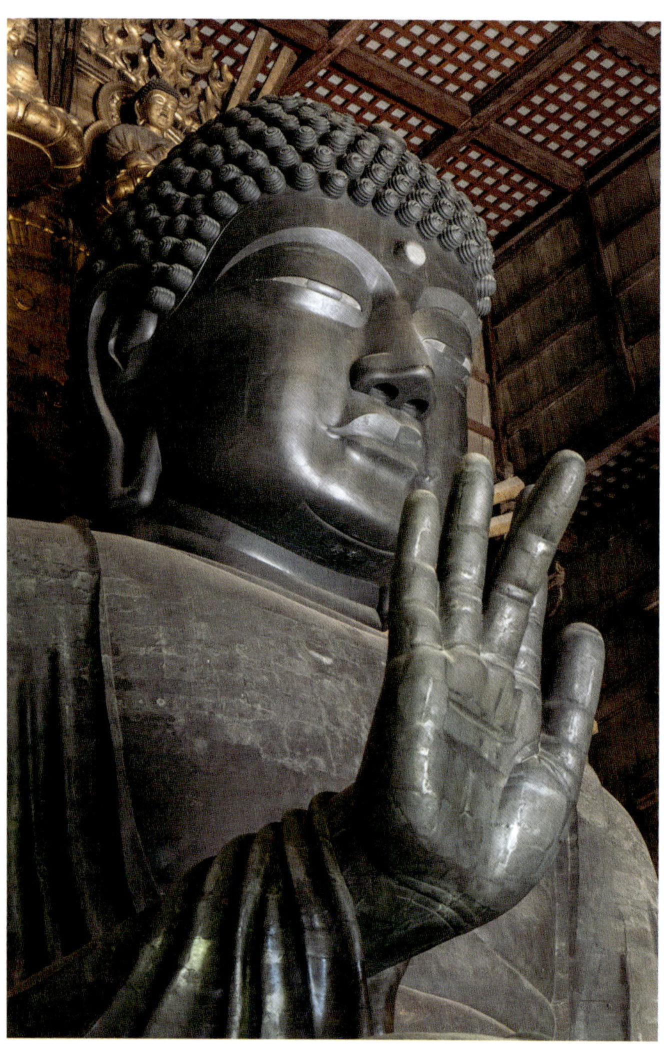

Kegon-shū Daihonzan Tōdai-ji.
The Kegon-shū Daihonzan, home to the Great Buddha of Nara, has stood in majestic serenity within the Tōdai-ji Temple since its consecration in 752. This towering bronze statue, which stands 15 metres tall, is one of the largest representations of the Vairocana Buddha in the world and a powerful symbol of spiritual grandeur.

Hasedera Temple.
In Nara Prefecture, Hasedera Temple, founded in 686, is a sacred site renowned for its traditional architecture and enchanting landscapes. Nestled deep within the mountains, it is famous for its breathtaking seasonal blooms, such as the vibrant hydrangeas in summer. It is also home to an imposing statue of Kannon, Japan's most revered Buddhist deity, Hasedera.

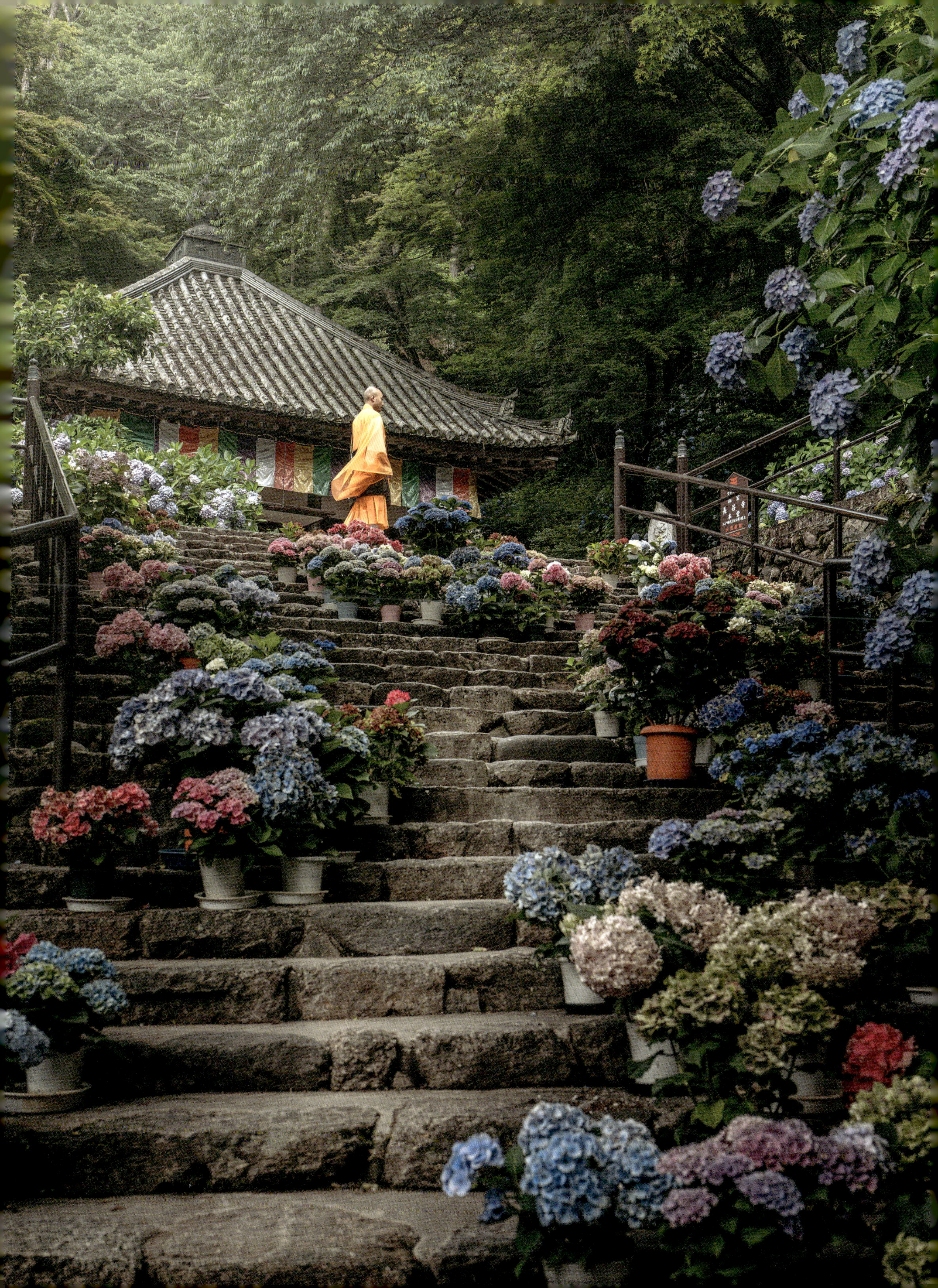

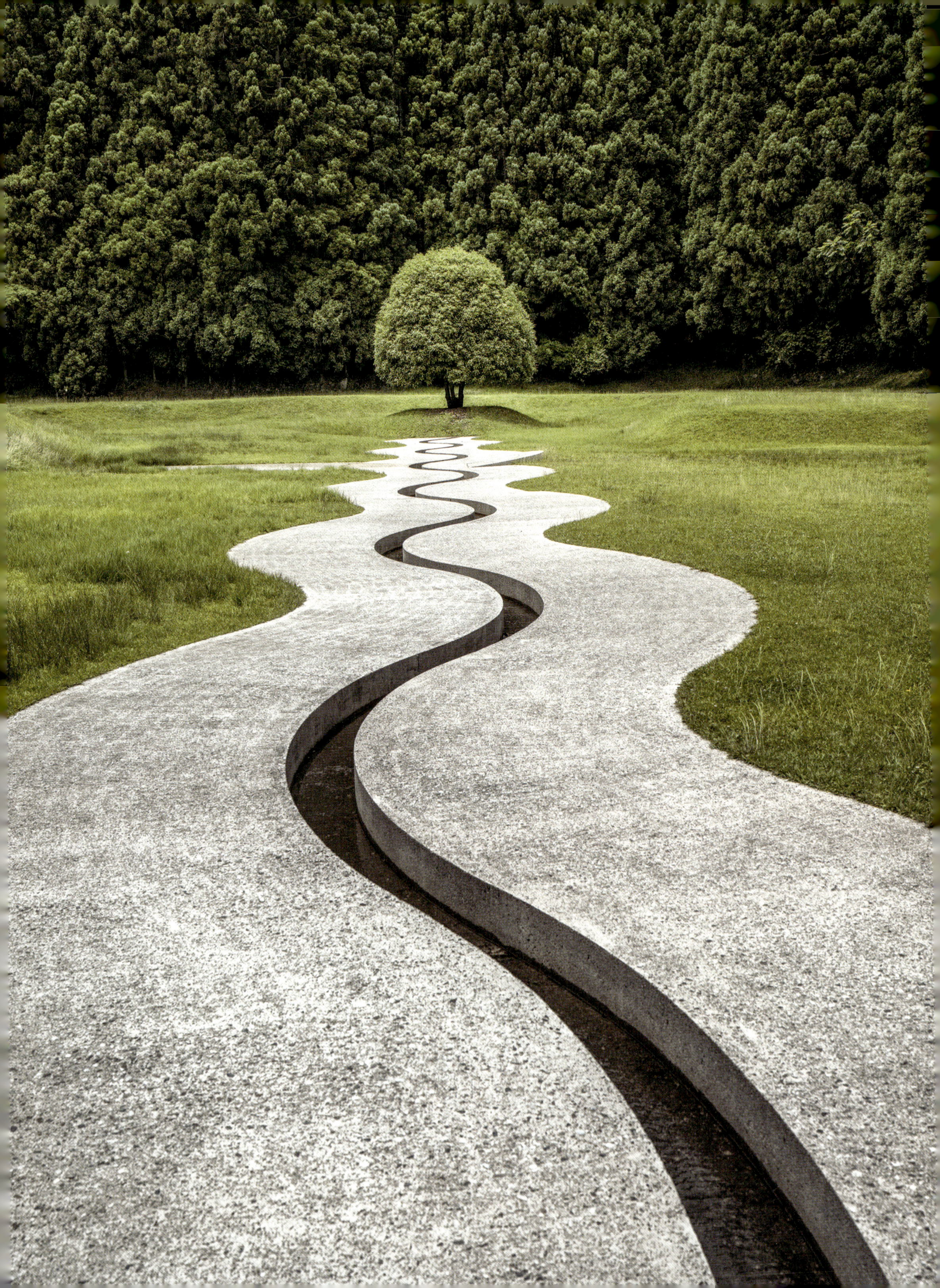

Murou Art Forest.
Murou Art Forest is a unique space where nature and architecture blend seamlessly. This verdant landscape, dotted with towering trees, features winding concrete paths that mimic the flow of water. Every element of the park is crafted to encourage reflection and foster a dialogue between humanity and the natural world.

Himeji Castle.
Towering over the town that bears its name, Himeji Castle is a striking example of Japanese feudal architecture at its finest. Constructed in the early 17th century, this UNESCO World Heritage Site is affectionately known as the "White Heron Castle" due to its pristine white walls and graceful, wing-like rooftops. Remarkably preserved through centuries of war and natural disasters, it stands as a testament to the splendour and strategic brilliance of medieval Japan. >

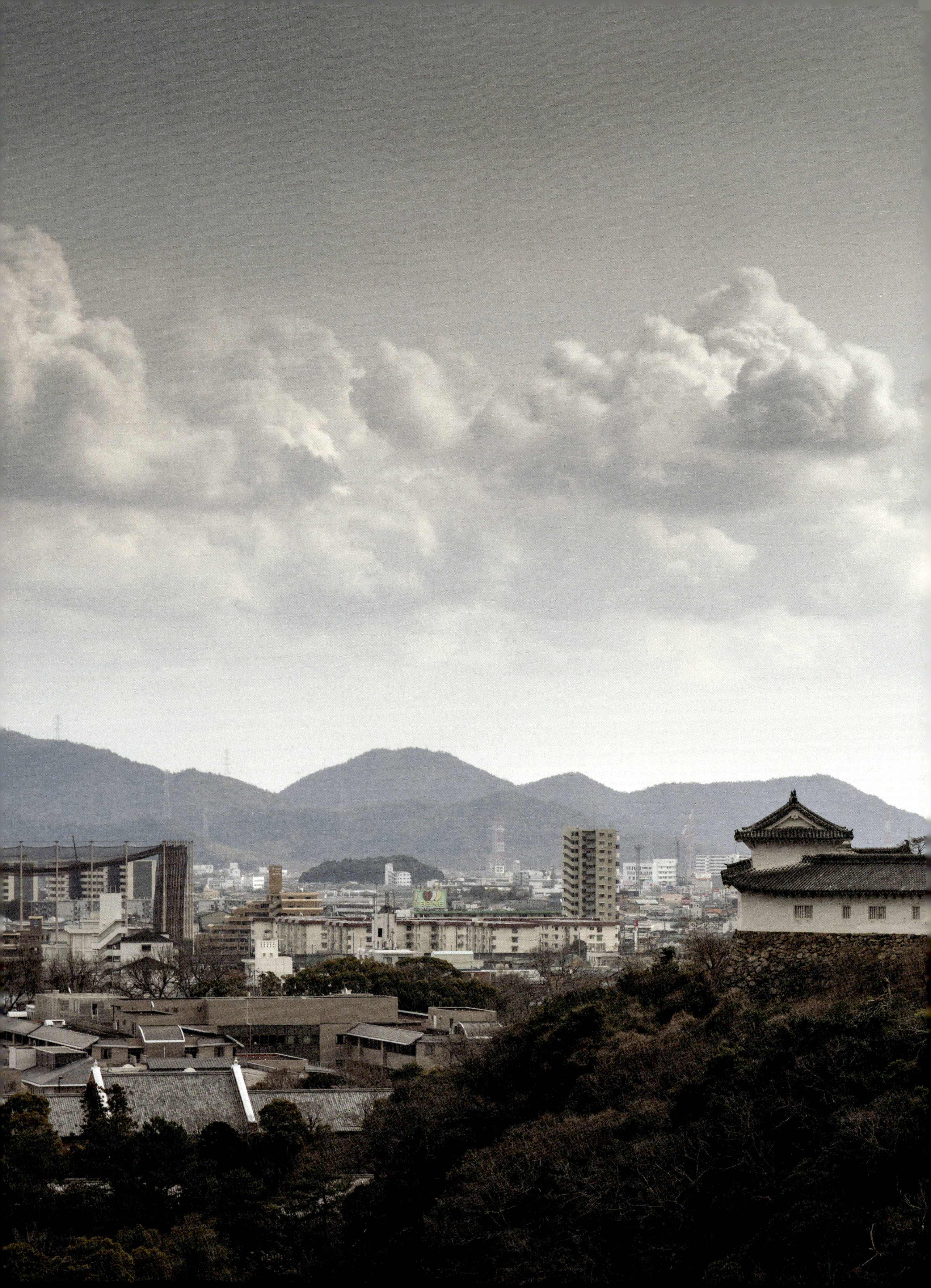

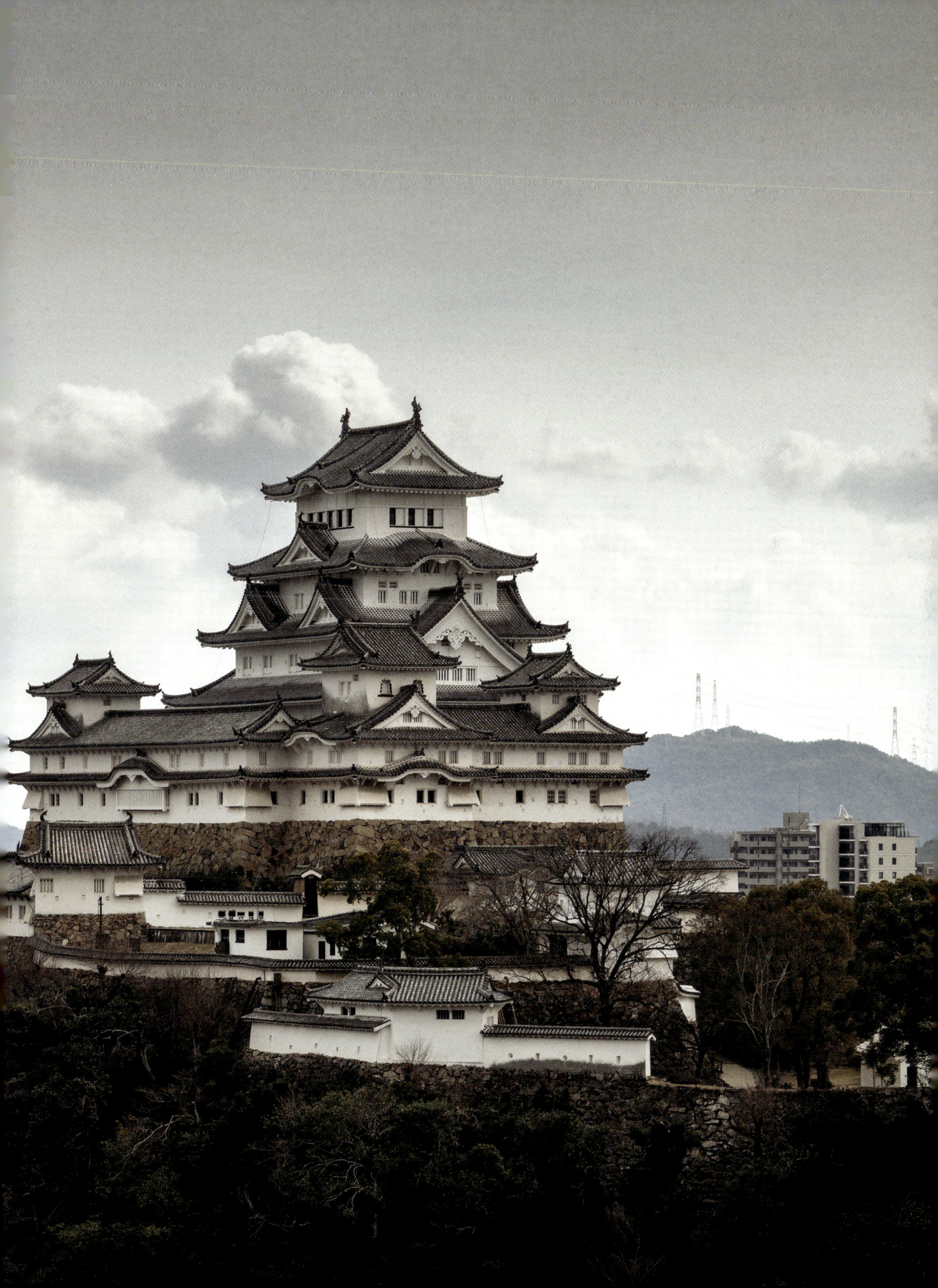

Geisha.
In the bewitching alleyways of Kyoto's Gion district, this geisha embodies Japanese elegance and tradition. As guardians of Japanese culture, geishas preserve an ancestral savoir-faire, seamlessly blending dance, music, and the art of conversation into a living heritage. Today, Gion remains one of the last districts where this tradition lives on, offering a precious testimony to the Japan of yesteryear.

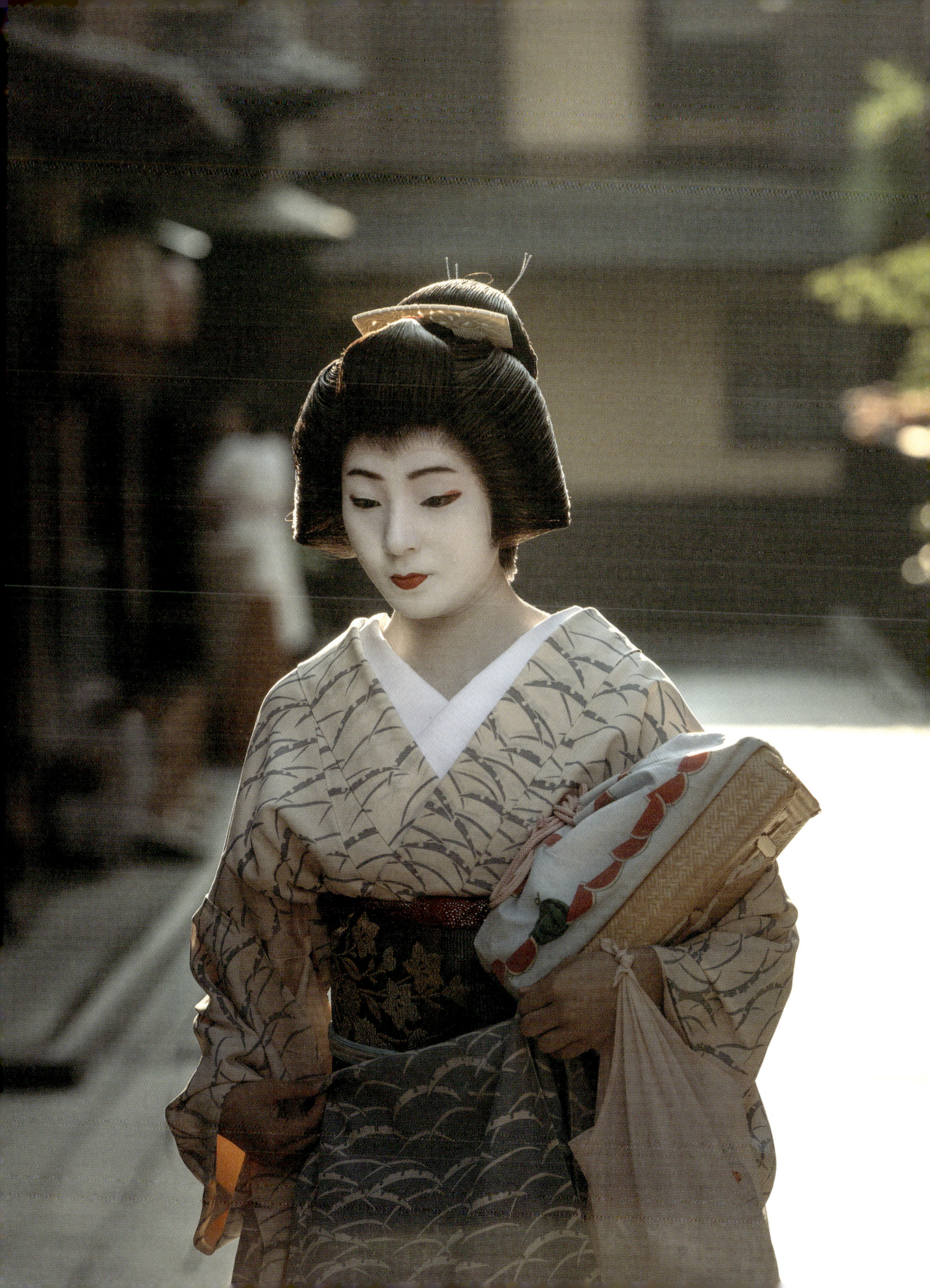

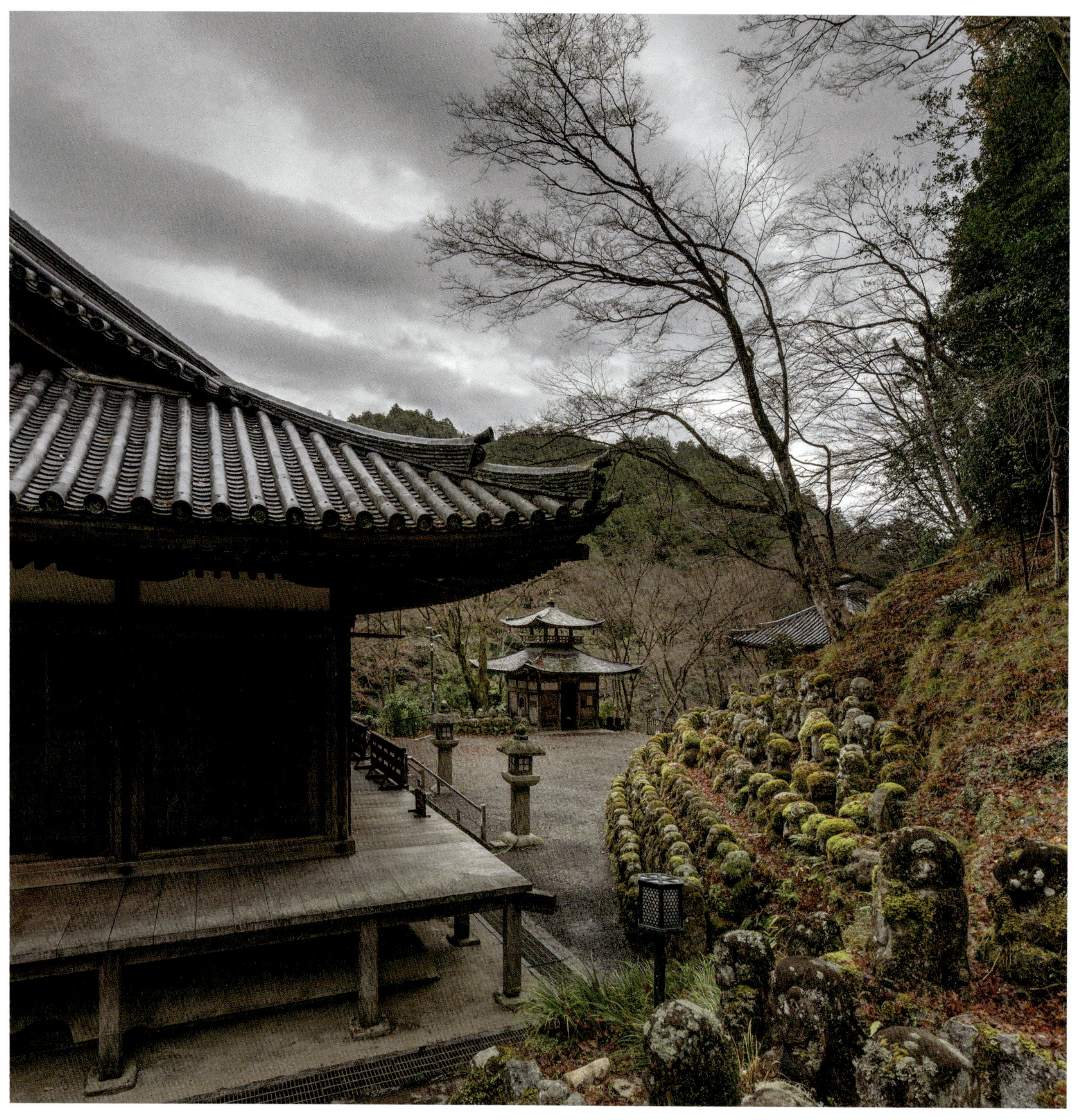

Otagi Nenbutsu-ji.
Nestled in the hills west of Kyoto, Otagi Nenbutsu-ji Temple is home to nearly 1,200 stone statues of rakan – enlightened disciples of the Buddha – carved between 1981 and 1991 by amateur artists under the guidance of monk Kocho Nishimura. Moss-covered and full of character, each figure is unique, contributing to a serene, almost whimsical atmosphere that the graceful architecture surrounding them enhances.

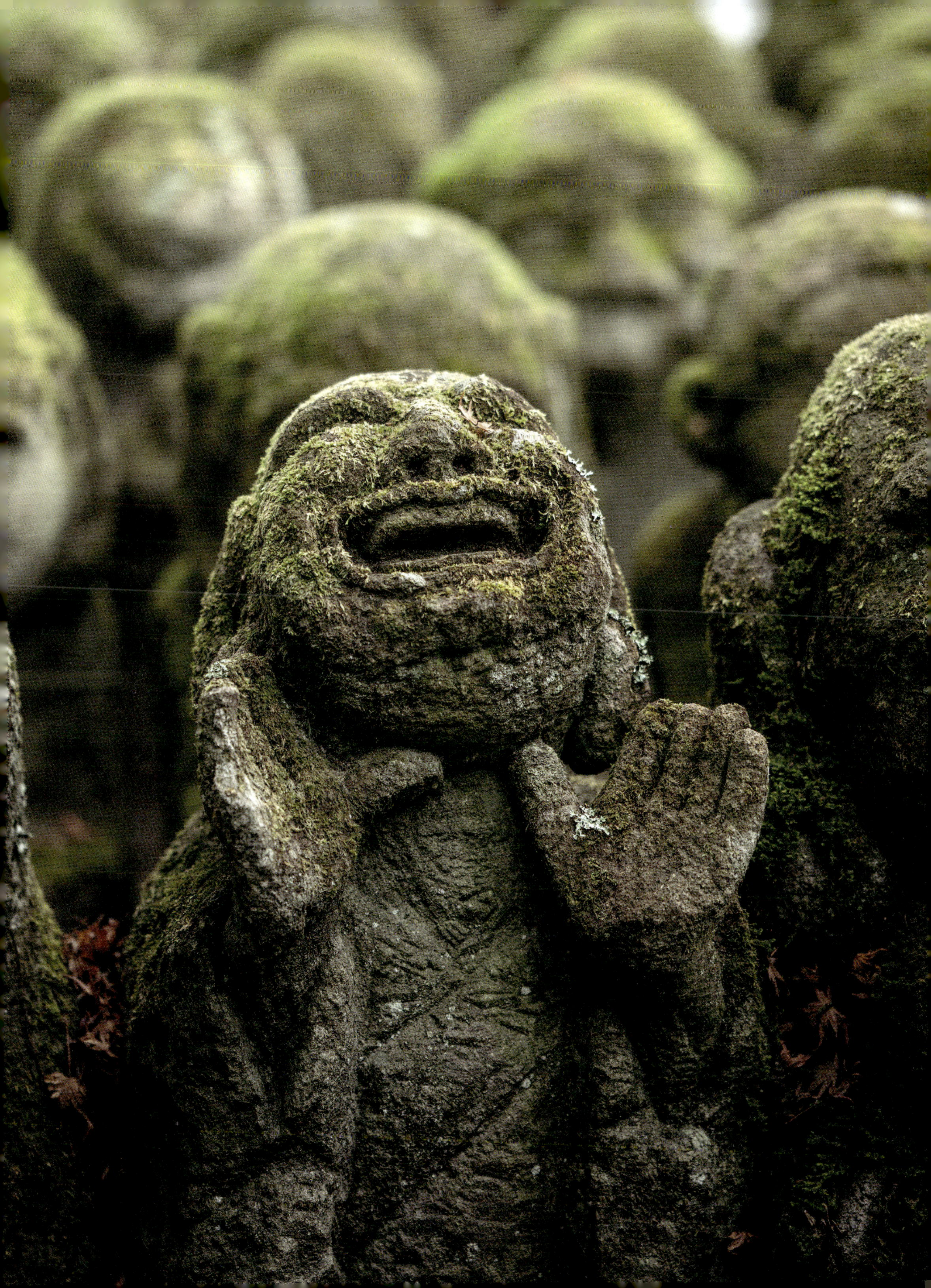

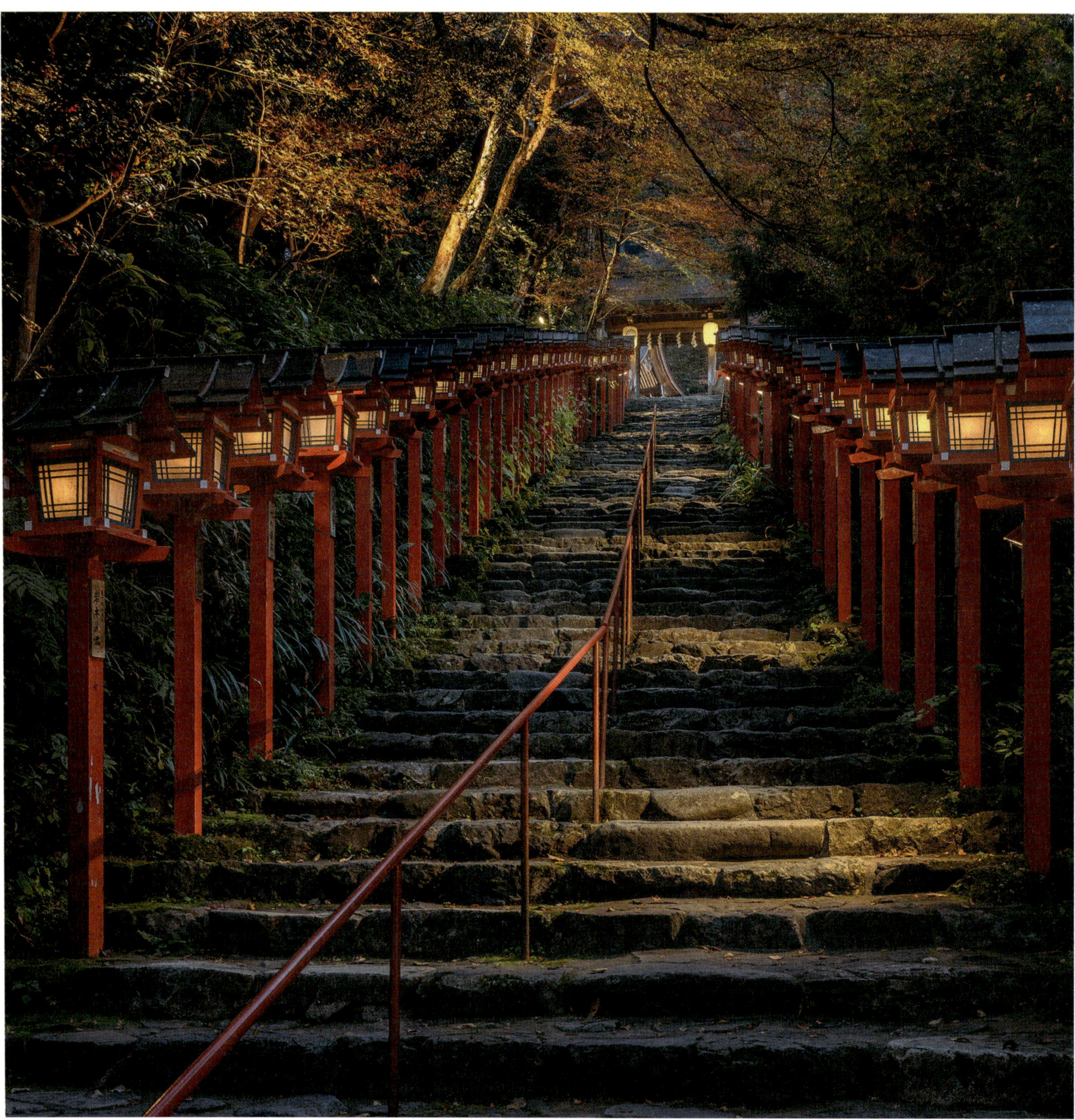

Kifune-jinja.
Tucked away in the mountains north of Kyoto, Kifune-jinja Shrine, founded over 1,300 years ago, is dedicated to the deity of water and rain. Its iconic path, lined with red lanterns glowing softly at dusk, leads visitors to a mystical sanctuary. Revered as an important spiritual site, it is also famous for its *omikuji* (fortune slips), which float on the water as a tribute to the shrine's sacred connection with this elemental force..

Pagoda Hōkan-ji.
Overlooking the picturesque lanes of Higashiyama, the Hōkan-ji Pagoda, also known as the Yasaka Pagoda, serves as an iconic symbol of Kyoto. Constructed in the 6th century and reconstructed in 1440, its slender silhouette stands proudly against the backdrop of a setting sun.

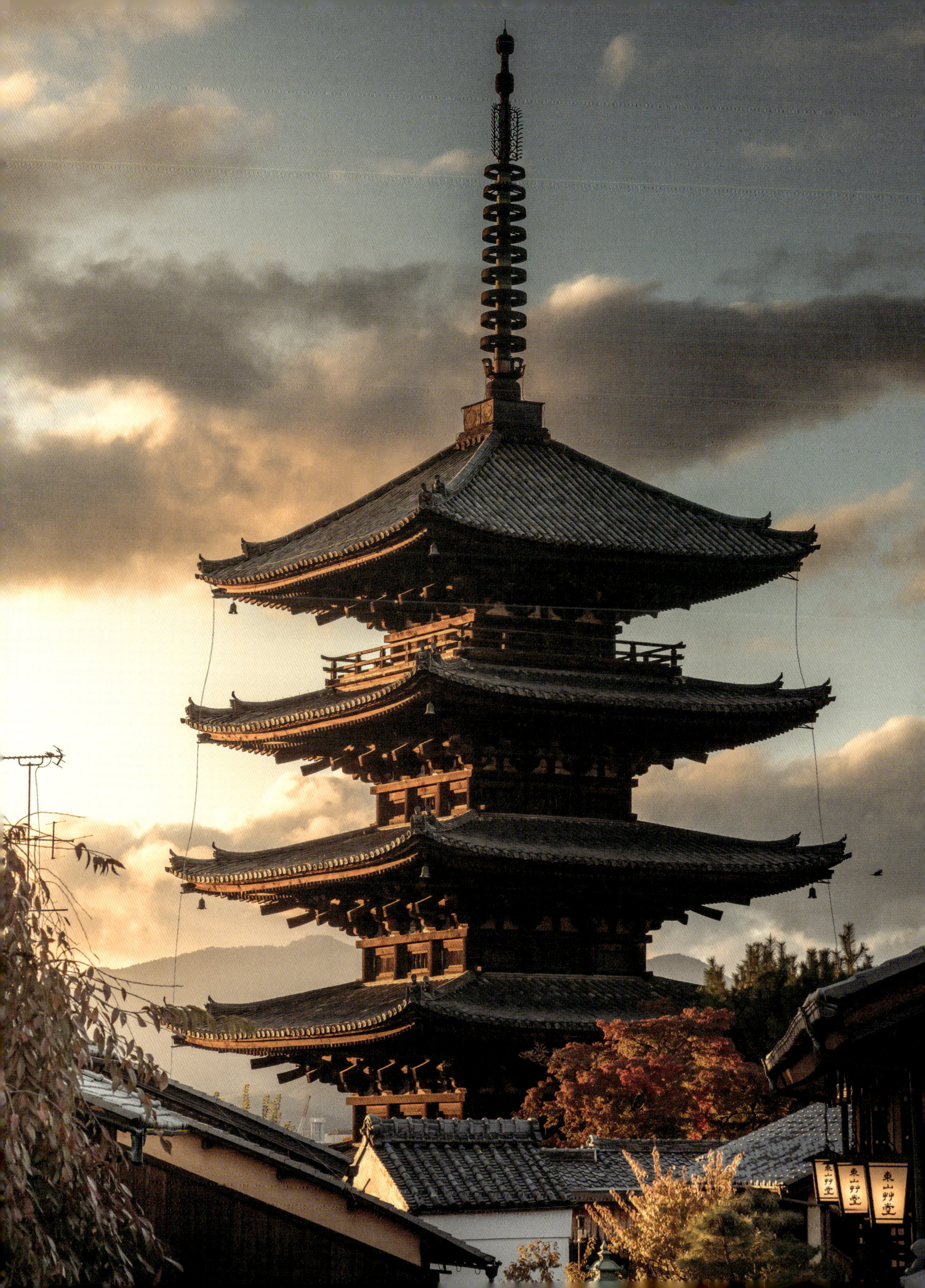
東山艸堂
東山艸堂
東山艸堂

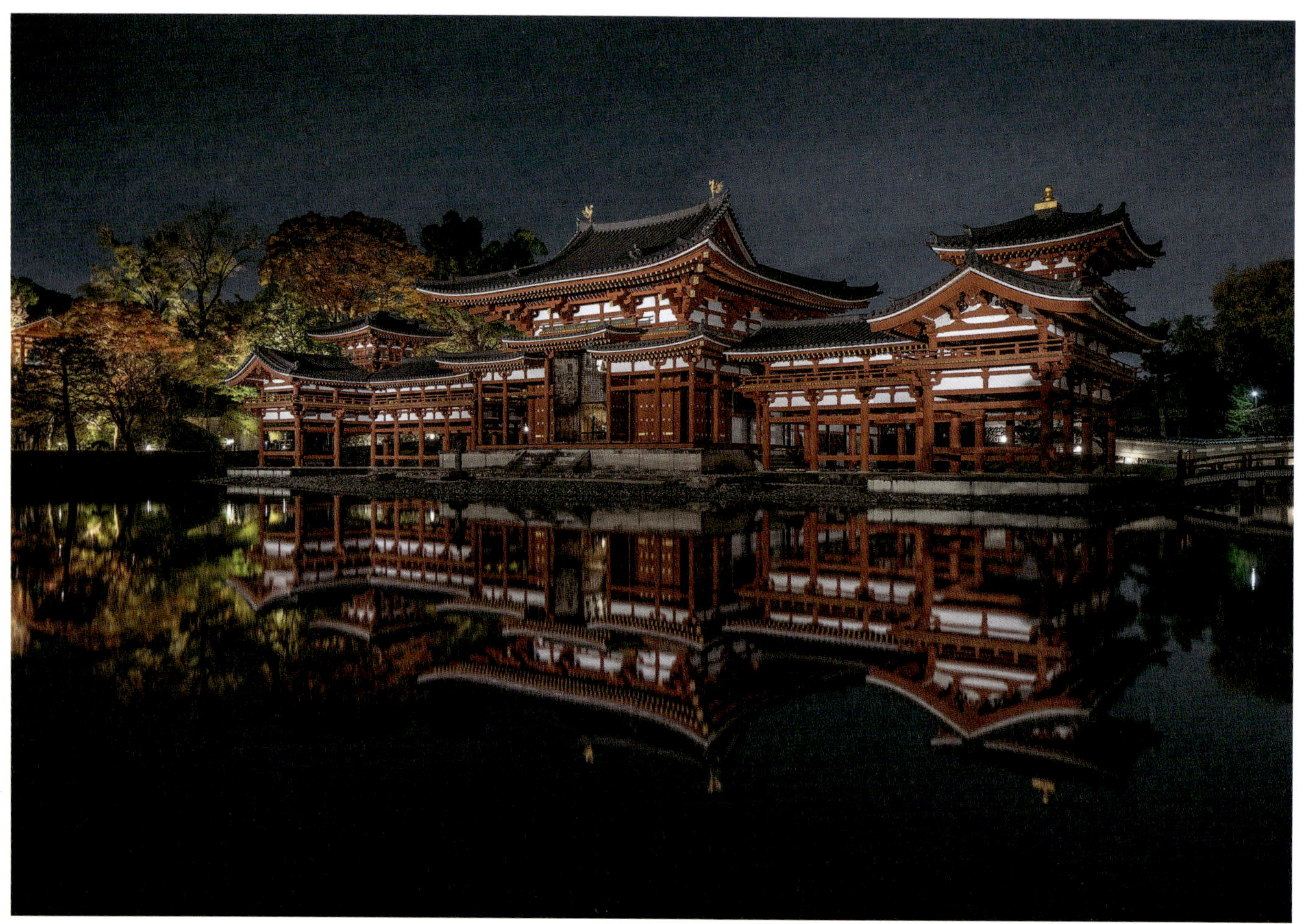

Byodo-in.
The Byodo-in Buddhist temple in Uji is beautifully reflected on the tranquil surface of its pond. The 11th-century structure, featuring its Phoenix Hall, radiates a serene light that seems to float between the heavens and the earth – an enchanting sight that captivates the soul.

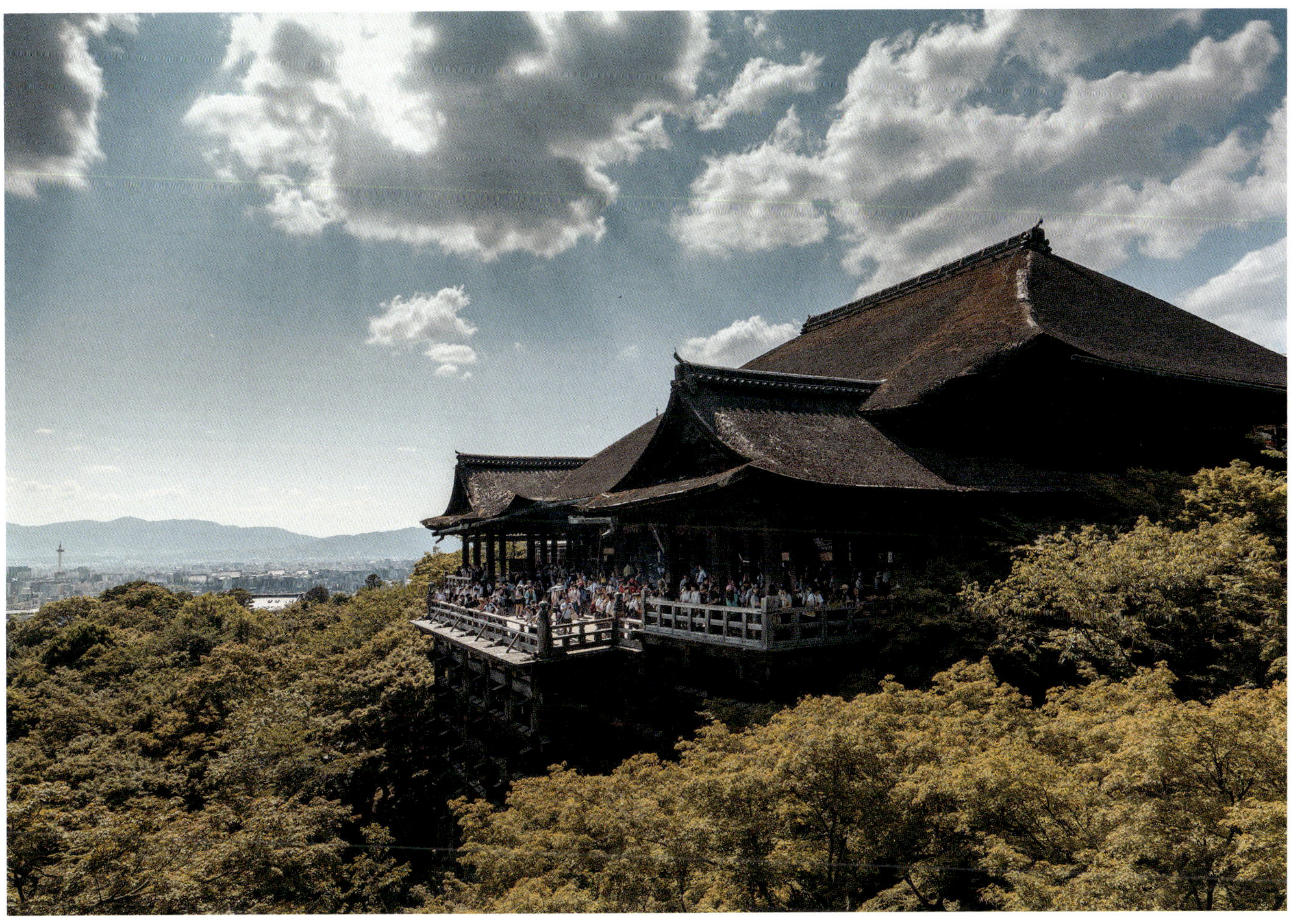

Kiyomizu-dera.
Perched high in the hills above Kyoto, the majestic Kiyomizu-dera temple commands the city below with its expansive wooden terrace, supported by towering 13-metre-high pillars. Founded in 778, this Buddhist shrine is dedicated to Kannon, the goddess of mercy, attracting pilgrims and visitors seeking blessings and fulfilled wishes. Strolling beneath the cherry and maple trees, visitors encounter not only the temple's grandeur but also several pagodas, a serene waterfall, and a Shinto shrine dedicated to love and human connection.

Arashiyama Bamboo Grove.
Kyoto's Arashiyama Bamboo Grove is a captivating green corridor where towering stalks of bamboo reach skyward, casting dappled light over the path below. The gentle rustling of leaves and the occasional creak of the swaying stems create a dreamlike, meditative atmosphere. So evocative is the soundscape that Japan's Ministry of the Environment has named it one of the country's "100 Soundscapes."

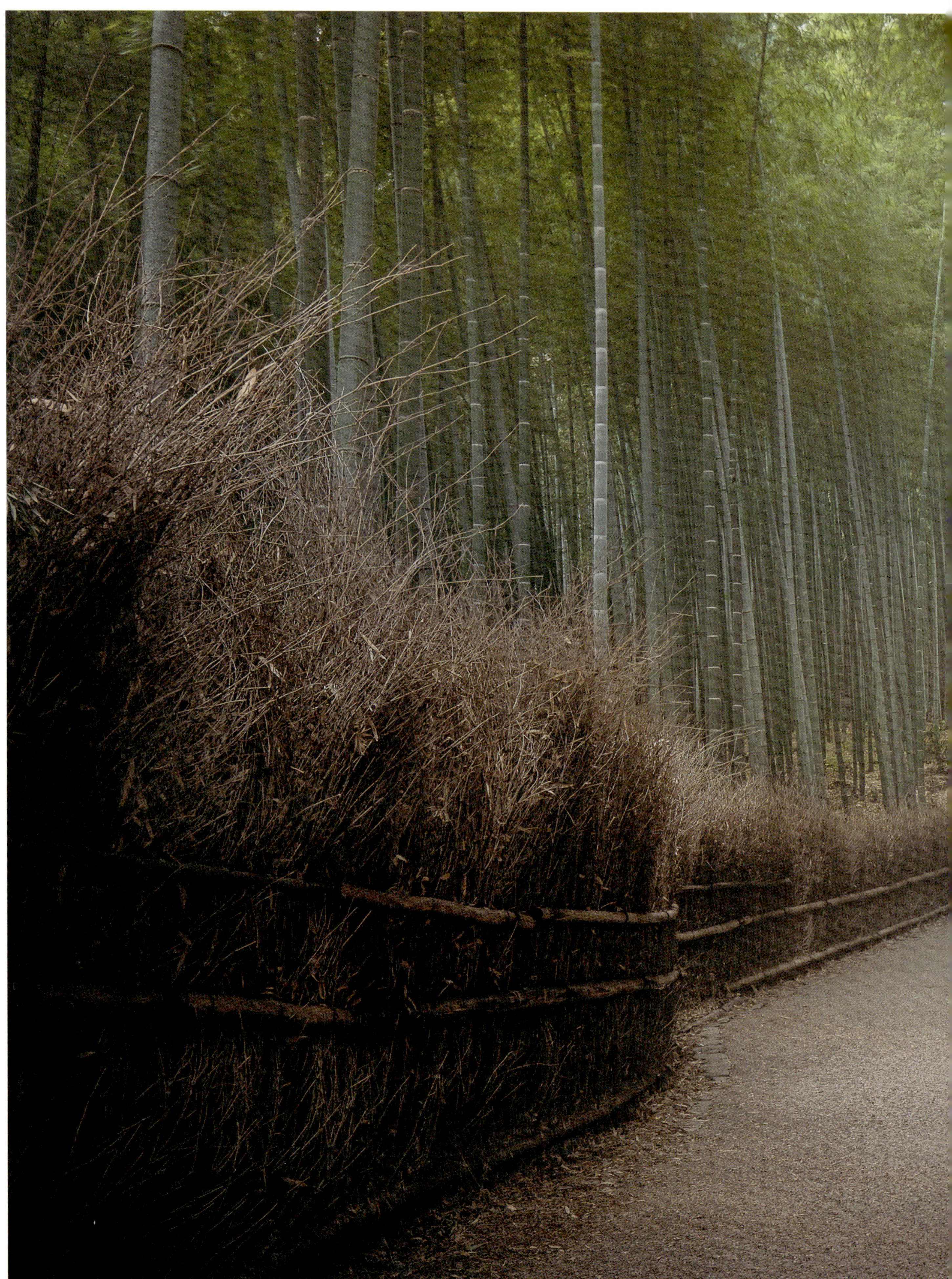

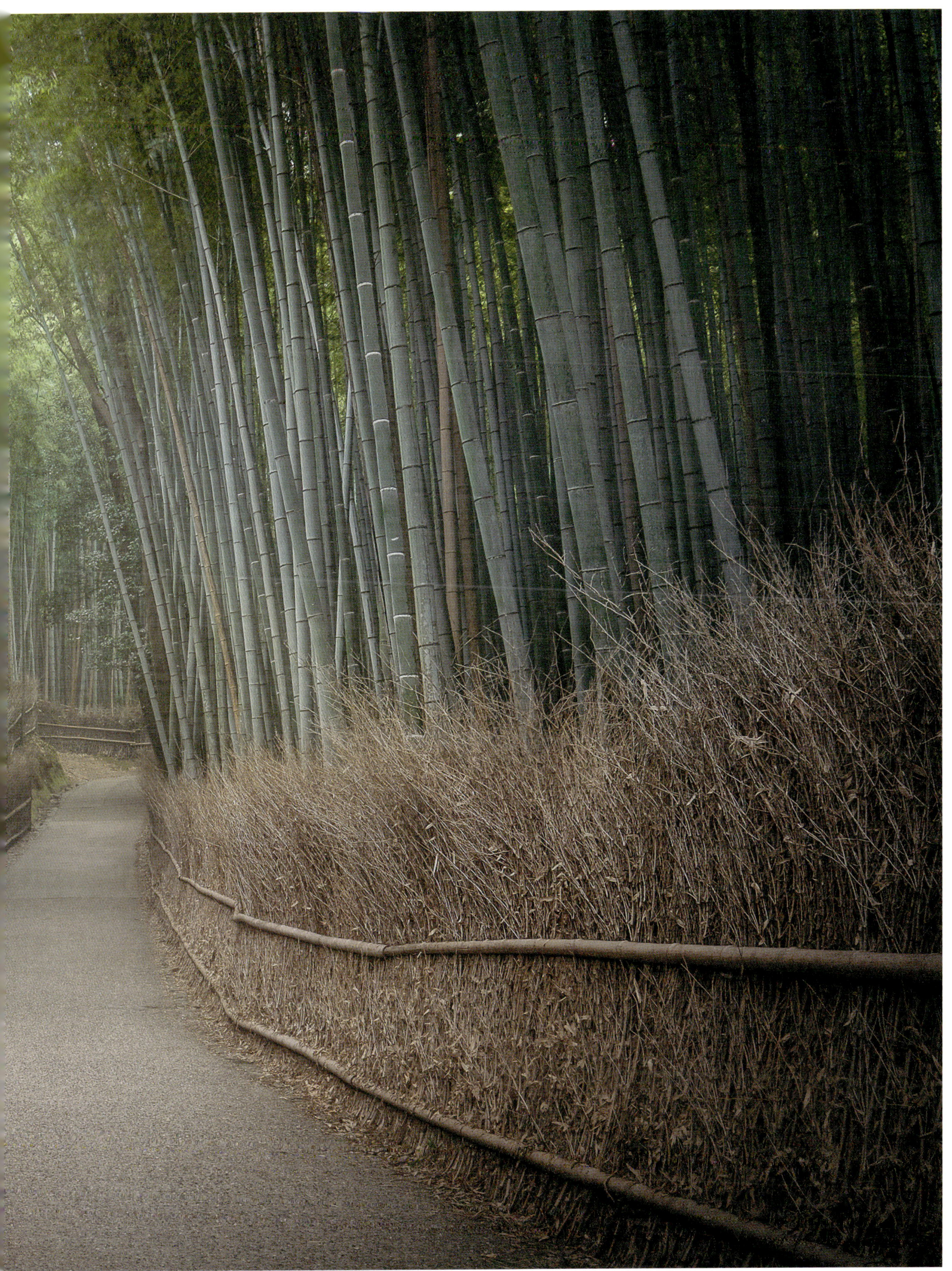

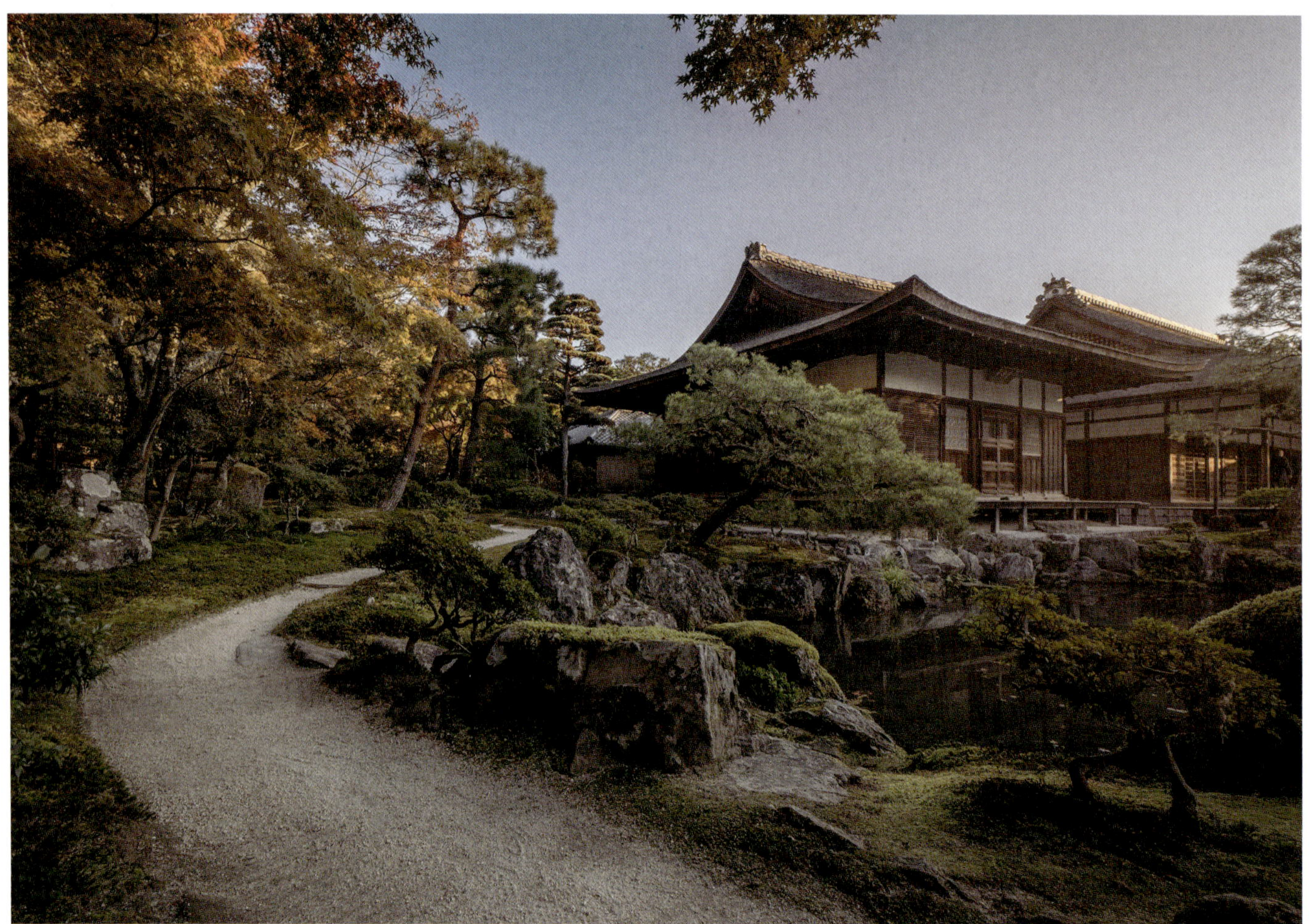

Ginkaku-ji.

Ginkaku-ji, the Silver Pavilion, is Kyoto's celebrated Zen temple, set within a tranquil garden characterised by winding paths, mossy banks, and peaceful ponds. Built in the late 15th century by Shogun Ashikaga Yoshimasa as his retirement retreat, it became a temple after his passing. Although the silver cladding was never realised, the understated beauty of the site embodies the Japanese aesthetic of wabi-sabi – the quiet charm of imperfection and transience.

Kinkaku-ji.

Also known as the Golden Pavilion, it is one of Kyoto's most iconic temples, renowned for its facades covered in gold leaf. Initially built in the 14th century as the retirement villa of Shogun Ashikaga Yoshimitsu, it was converted into a Buddhist temple after his death.

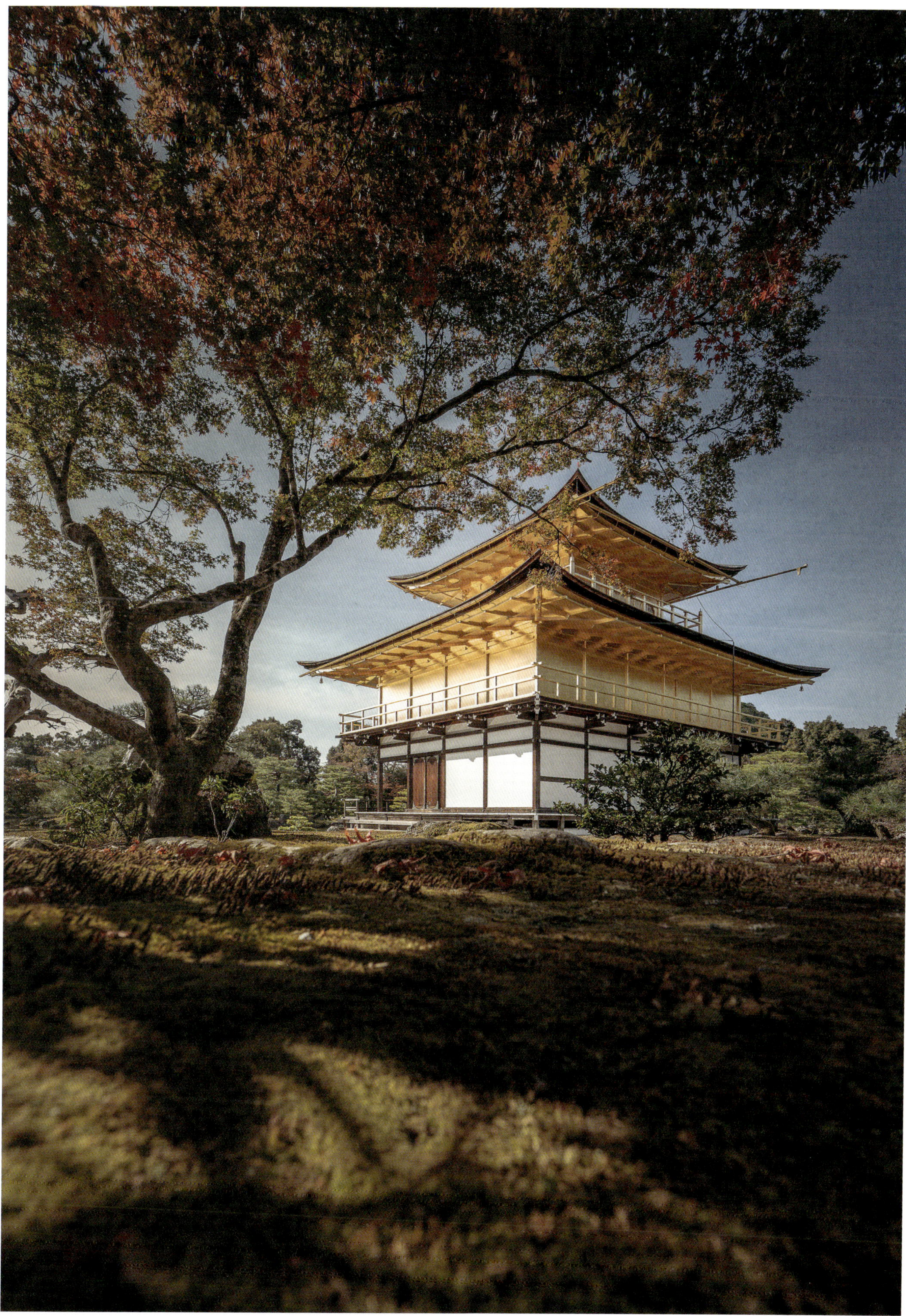

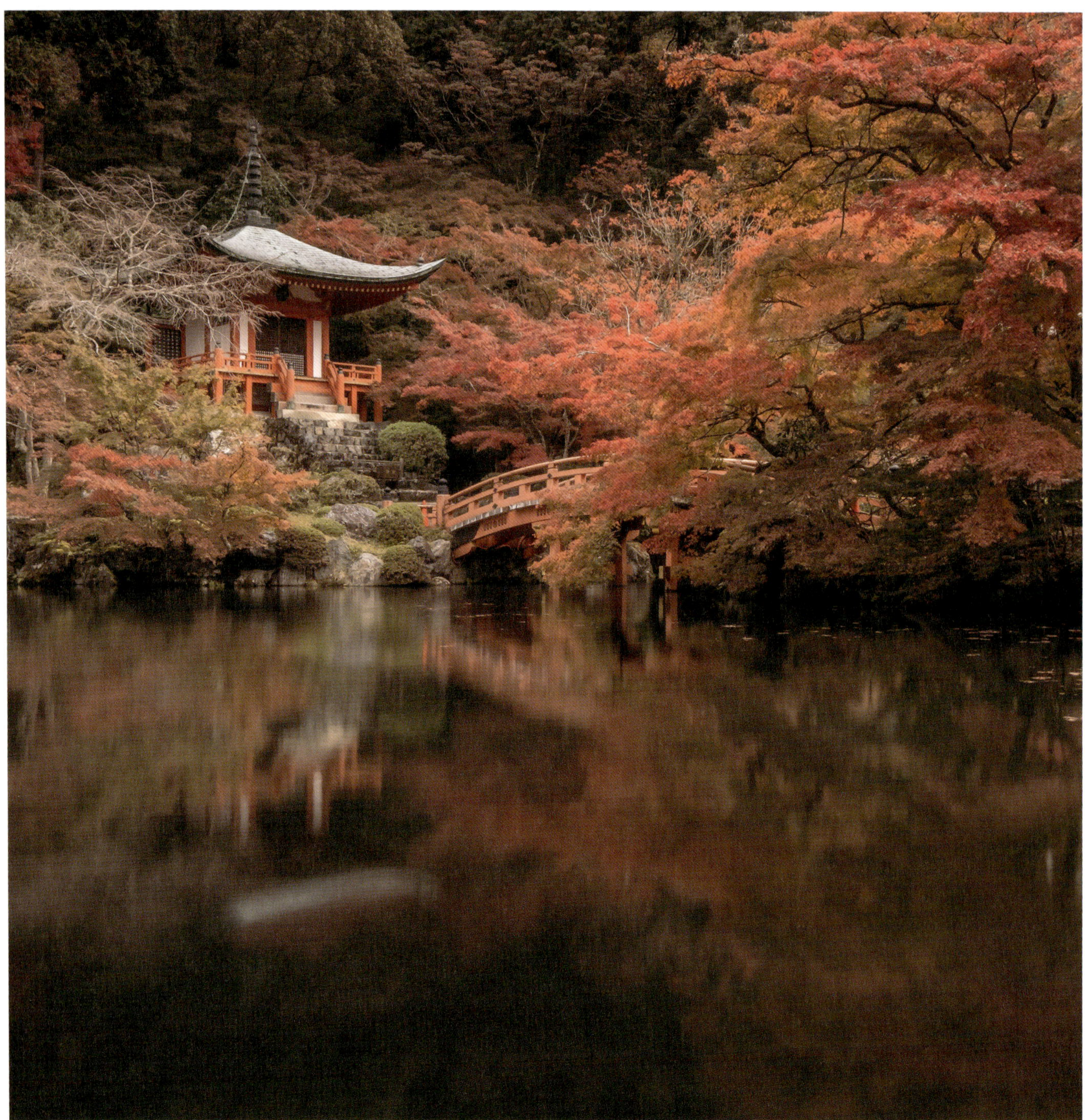

Daigo-ji.
Founded in 874, Daigo-ji Temple is one of Kyoto's Buddhist treasures and a UNESCO World Heritage Site. A pillar of Japanese culture, it was also the site of a famous *hanami* ceremony in 1598, organised by Toyotomi Hideyoshi, the mighty warlord and unifier of Japan, who celebrated the beauty of cherry blossoms in full bloom.

Nanzen-ji.
Beneath the fiery autumn maples, the grand Nanzen-ji temple reveals its imposing Sanmon Gate, a massive wooden structure built in 1628 that marks the entrance to its sacred grounds. Nestled amidst lush greenery at the foot of the Higashiyama mountains, east of Kyoto, this Zen Buddhist sanctuary houses numerous pavilions and features one of the city's most beautiful gardens.

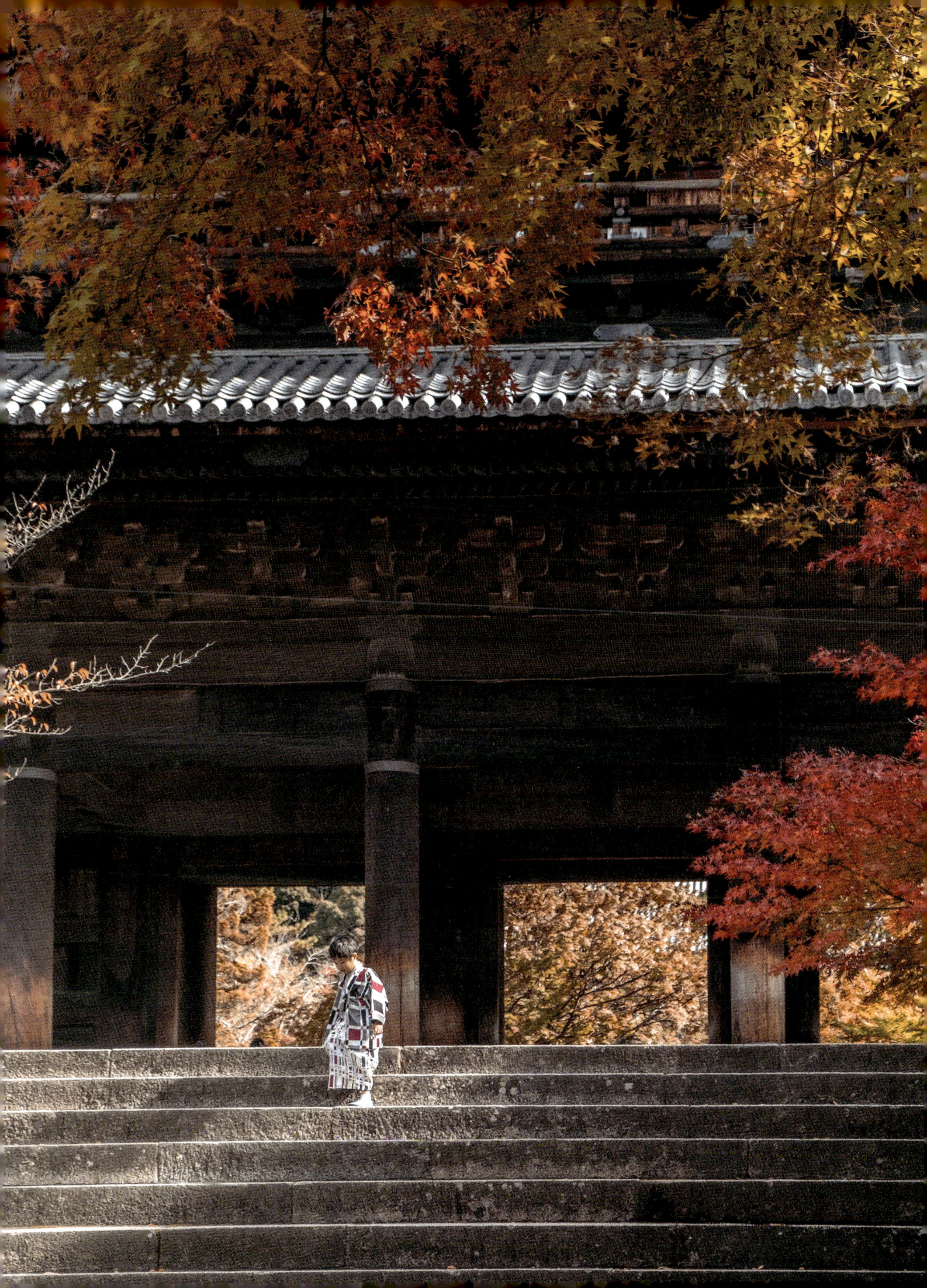

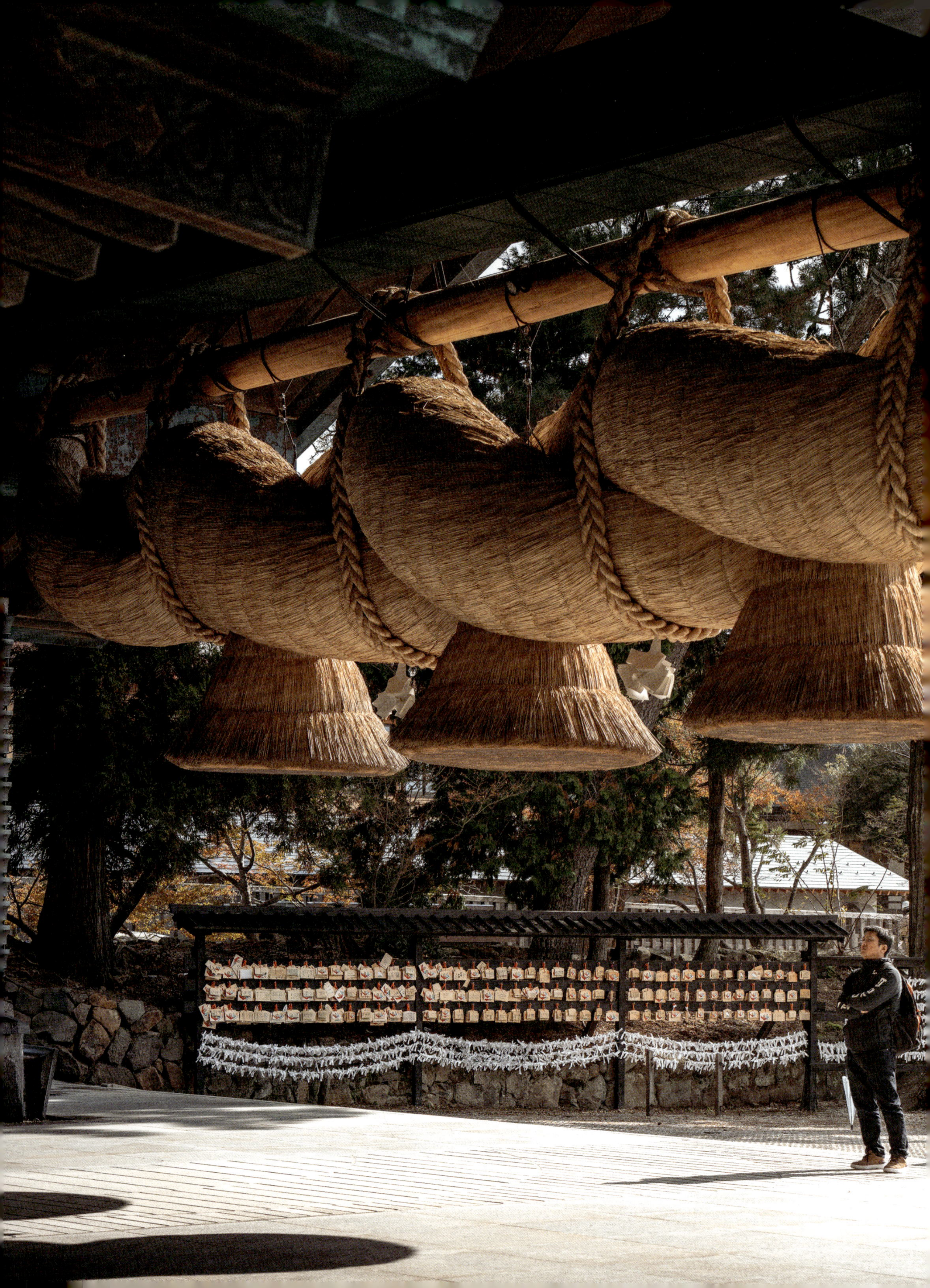

Izumo Taisha.
One of Japan's oldest and most revered Shinto shrines, Izumo Taisha is renowned for its massive *shimenawa* – the thick, braided straw ropes that hang dramatically beneath its roofs. Votive tablets and prayer strips left by worshippers illustrate the deep devotion of those seeking blessings from the shrine's deities.

中国地

Chūgoku

The Perfect Balance Between History and Nature

To the southwest of Japan's main island, Honshū, the Chūgoku region unveils a vibrant tapestry of landscapes and cultures, where sparkling seas, rugged mountains, and historic towns converge. Comprised of five prefectures – Hiroshima, Okayama, Shimane, Tottori, and Yamaguchi – Chūgoku is a land of striking contrasts, where the weight of history blends seamlessly with the serenity of nature. Less explored than Japan's major tourist hubs, this region offers a rare authenticity and diversity that truly captivates the hearts of travellers.

Surface Area.
The Chūgoku region covers approximately 31,922 km², accounting for around 8.4% of Japan's total land area.

Population and Demographics.
As of 2010, the region's population was around 7.6 million, with an average population density of 236.9 inhabitants per km².

Geographical Location.
Chūgoku comprises five prefectures: Hiroshima, Okayama, Shimane, Tottori and Yamaguchi. It borders the Kansai region to the east, the Seto Inland Sea to the south, the Kanmon Strait to the west (which separates it from Kyūshū), and the Sea of Japan to the north. The region is commonly divided into two subregions: San'in (along the Sea of Japan) and San'yō (along the Seto Inland Sea).

Climate and Seasons.
The climate varies between the northern and southern coasts. The San'in area, facing the Sea of Japan, experiences colder winters with snowfall, while the San'yō area, facing the Seto Inland Sea, enjoys a milder and sunnier climate. Summers are typically hot and humid, with the region affected by the rainy season in June and typhoons in September.

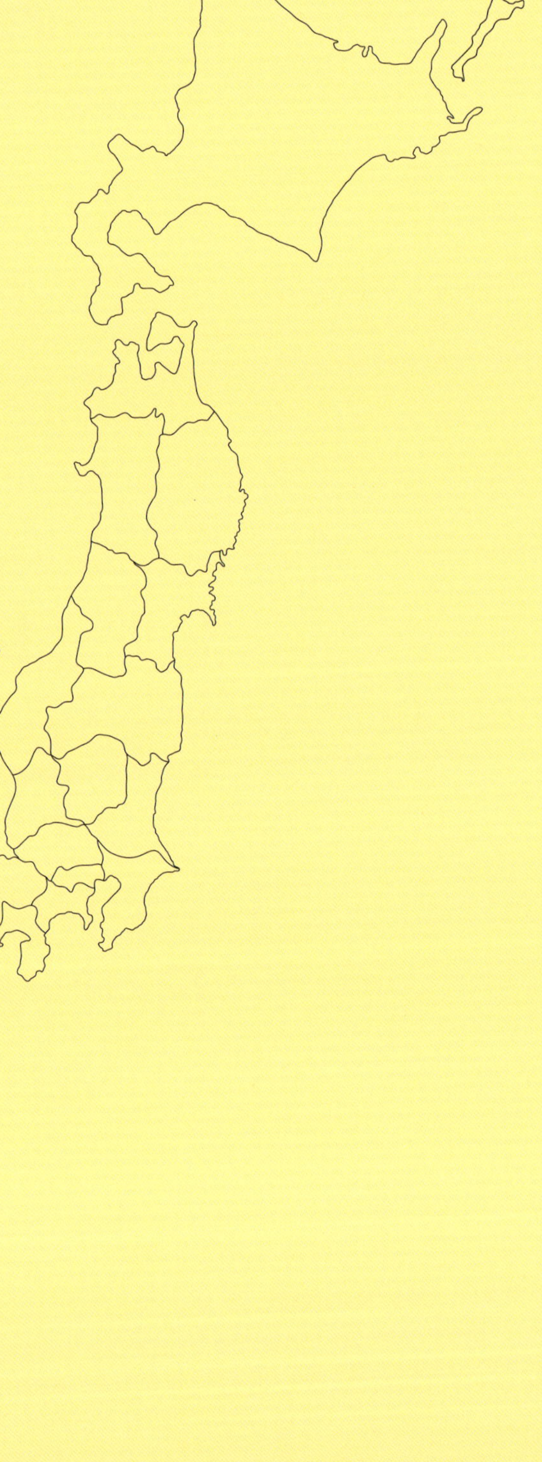

中国地

Hiroshima, A Call for Peace

One cannot mention Hiroshima without considering its sinister past, which embodies resilience and hope today. Located in the city's heart, Hiroshima Peace Memorial Park is a place of contemplation where the A-Bomb Dome stands as a silent witness to history. This UNESCO World Heritage Site is also home to the Peace Memorial Museum, a thought-provoking place that prompts reflection on the tragedies of war and the necessity of preserving peace.

Just a few kilometres off the coast of the city, the sacred island of Miyajima presents a striking contrast with its peaceful atmosphere. Itsukushima Shrine, renowned for its iconic red *torii* gate floating on the water, creates a magical scene, especially at sunset. Fallow deer roam freely, adding to the island's timeless allure. A hike to the summit of Mount Misen, Miyajima's highest peak, offers stunning panoramic views of the Seto Inland Sea.

Okayama, Gardens and Castles

Known as the "Land of the Sun", Okayama is a prefecture renowned for its stunning gardens and rich mythological heritage. Kōraku-en, one of Japan's three most beautiful gardens, is a true masterpiece of landscaping, where ponds, bridges, and pavilions blend together in perfect harmony.

Not far from there, Okayama Castle, often called "Crow Castle" due to its striking black exterior, stands proudly, its reflection shimmering in the waters of the Asahi River. The region is also famous for its connection to the legend of Momotarō, the fishing boy born from a giant peach, whose tale continues to inspire local imagination.

Nearby, Kurashiki is a hidden gem, with its historic Bikan district. Willow-lined canals and whitewashed warehouses, which now serve as museums and craft shops, create a charming, timeless atmosphere.

Shimane, Land of the Gods

Shimane is often described as a mystical land, deeply intertwined with the myths of Shintoism. The Izumo Taisha Shrine, dedicated to the god of marriages, is one of the oldest and most revered in Japan. Every November, it is said that Shinto deities from across the country gather here to discuss matters of human relationships.

Matsue Castle, classified as a "national treasure" and affectionately known as the "Black Castle", is one of the few remaining authentic castles in Japan. Perched on a hill, it offers sweeping views of the city and Lake Shinji, where sunsets are considered some of the most breathtaking in the country.

Another gem of Shimane is the Adachi Museum of Art in Yasugi, famous for its beautifully manicured gardens and remarkable collection of traditional Japanese paintings.

Tottori, Dunes and Mysteries

Tottori, Japan's least populous prefecture, boasts breathtaking landscapes and captivating traditions. The Tottori Sand Dunes, the largest in the country, span over 16 kilometres along the coast, resembling a miniature desert. Visitors can enjoy camel rides, paragliding, or simply take in the beauty of this unique environment.

The nearby Sand Museum features stunning sand sculptures created by artists from around the world, showcasing new themes each year.

Mount Daisen, often dubbed the "Mount Fuji of the West", is a popular hiking destination. Its pristine beech forests and towering peaks, the highest reaching 1,730 metres, offer panoramic views and complete immersion in nature. Close by, the Daisen-ji Temple, an ancient centre of esoteric Buddhism, invites visitors seeking peace and serenity.

Yamaguchi, The Bridge Between Two Worlds

Located at the western tip of Honshū, Yamaguchi is a prefecture where Japanese tradition and international influences blend seamlessly. Hagi, once the capital of one of Japan's most powerful samurai clans, remains one of the country's best-preserved castle towns. It is renowned for its UNESCO World Heritage Sites and the distinctive *hagi-yaki* pottery.

Shimonoseki, a bustling port city, is famous for its Karato Fish Market, where visitors can taste fugu (pufferfish), a delicate and cherished local delicacy.

The Kintai Bridge in Iwakuni is a true architectural marvel, with its five wooden arches spanning the Nishiki River. The scene is particularly enchanting in spring when cherry blossoms frame the landscape in a burst of colour.

Motonosumi Inari Shrine, with its 123 red *torii* gates leading to the sea, offers a striking and spiritual visual experience. Often regarded as one of the most beautiful shrines in Japan, it leaves a lasting impression on all who visit.

The Seto Inland Sea, A Shared Treasure

The Seto Inland Sea, bordered by several prefectures in Chūgoku, is a natural gem dotted with islands and small coastal communities. This maritime region is a haven for those who appreciate breathtaking coastal views and maritime traditions.

Naoshima, which is technically part of the neighbouring Shikoku region, is easily accessible from Chūgoku and is known for its contemporary art. The island's museums and art installations, set against stunning natural backdrops, draw visitors from around the globe

The Legacy of Ancient Roads

Chūgoku is crisscrossed by historic roads that once connected ancient capitals to rural villages. The San'in Road, stretching along the Sea of Japan, offers rugged landscapes and pristine fishing villages, while the San'yō Road, facing the Seto Inland Sea, reflects a rich history of trade and commerce.

The mountains, shrines, castles, and traditional villages along these ancient routes narrate the story of a region where time appears to stand still.

中国地

Best Times to Visit

– Spring (March to May).
Ideal for viewing cherry blossoms and enjoying mild weather.

– Autumn (September to November).
Perfect for admiring colourful autumn leaves and benefiting from a pleasant climate.

Top 5 Must-See Destinations

1. Hiroshima Peace Memorial.
A historic site honouring the victims of the atomic bomb and symbolising the call for world peace.

2. Miyajima Island.
Famous for its Itsukushima Shrine and floating *torii* gate, offering stunning vistas.

3. Tottori Dunes.
Japan's largest sand dunes, providing opportunities for activities such as sandboarding and camel rides.

4. Izumo Taisha Shrine.
One of Japan's oldest and most sacred Shinto shrines, located in Shimane.

5. Kintai Bridge.
A five-arched wooden bridge in Iwakuni, offering picturesque views and striking architecture.

中国地

Gastronomy

The Chūgoku region, located in the western part of Honshū, is renowned for its varied culinary traditions, which were shaped by the influences of the Sea of Japan and the Seto Inland Sea. Below is a comprehensive list of Chūgoku's culinary specialities, organised by city, with detailed descriptions.

広島
Hiroshima

[広島風お好み焼き]
Hiroshima Okonomiyaki
Hiroshima-style okonomiyaki differs from the Osaka version: it is layered rather than mixed, with noodles (*yakisoba* or *udon*), cabbage, pork and sometimes seafood. It is grilled on a hot plate and topped with a special sweet sauce.

[牡蠣の土手鍋]
Kaki no Dote Nabe
A Japanese hot pot featuring fresh oysters from Hiroshima simmered in a miso-based broth. Hiroshima is Japan's largest oyster-producing region.

[穴子飯]
Anago Meshi
A bowl of rice topped with grilled saltwater eel (*anago*), drizzled with a sweet soy-based sauce. This dish is a specialty of Miyajima.

[しゃっかりかん]
Shakkarikan
A traditional frozen dessert from Hiroshima, made with condensed milk and local citrus fruits.

岡山
Okayama

[ばら寿司]
Barazushi
A festive sushi dish with vinegared rice mixed with prawns, mackerel, vegetables and egg. Once reserved for special occasions.

[吉備団子]
Kibi Dango
A sweet *mochi* from Okayama, made with millet flour and sugar. Famous thanks to the folk tale of Momotarō.

[ままかり寿司]
Mamakari-zushi
Sushi made with *mamakari*, a small, pickled sprat. The name means "borrow rice" — it's said to be so delicious that one needs to borrow extra rice to enjoy it all!

[デミカツ丼]
Demi-Katsu Don
A variation of katsudon in which breaded pork cutlet is topped with a demi-glace sauce instead of the typical egg-based version.

松江
Matsue

[出雲そば]
Izumo Soba
This darker soba noodle variety is served in stacked bowls (wariko soba), and it is often enjoyed cold with a special soy dipping sauce.

[しじみ汁]
Shijimi Jiru
A delicate soup made with freshwater clams (*shijimi*) from Lake Shinji, reputed for their flavour and health benefits, particularly for the liver.

[ぼてぼて茶]
Botebotecha
A traditional tea dish where hot tea is poured over rice with vegetables and red beans, then eaten by mixing with chopsticks.

鳥取
Tottori

[鳥取和牛]
Tottori Wagyu
Tottori's wagyū beef is prized for its tenderness and rich flavour. Typically served grilled or as steak.

[松葉ガニ]
Matsuba Gani
Snow crab caught in the Sea of Japan during winter, served grilled, as sashimi, or in soups.

[鳥取カレー]
Tottori Curry
Tottori is well known for its local-style curries, with many unique variations including crab curry.

[砂だんご]
Suna Dango
A ball-shaped sweet inspired by Tottori's iconic dunes.

山口
Yamaguchi

[ふぐ料理]
Fugu Ryōri
Yamaguchi, particularly Shimonoseki, is Japan's pufferfish capital. This delicacy is served as sashimi, fried or in hot pot, and must be prepared by licensed chefs due to its toxicity.

[瓦そば]
Kawara Soba
A distinctive soba noodle dish served on a heated roof tile (kawara), accompanied by beef, egg, and dipping sauce.

[山口ういろう]
Yamaguchi Uiro
A lightly sweet rice cake with a soft texture, distinct from Nagoya's firmer *uiro*.

[シロウオの踊り食い]
Shiro-uo no Odorigui
A unique culinary experience involving the consumption of live whitebait (*shiro-uo*) dipped in vinegar.

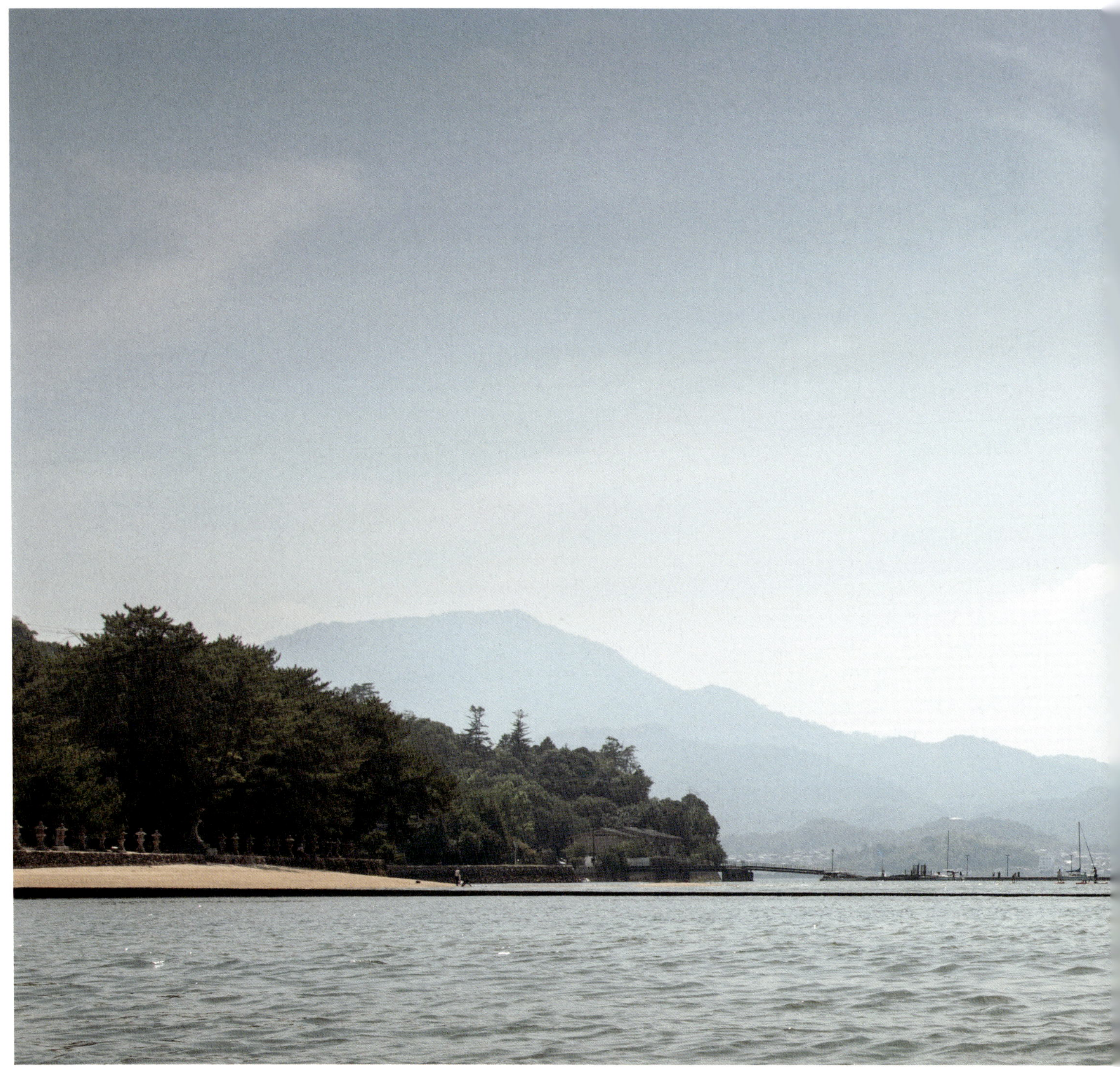

Itsukushima Shrine Torii.
Rising gracefully from the serene waters of Hiroshima Bay, the Itsukushima Shrine *Torii* is one of Japan's most iconic landmarks. Located on the island of Miyajima, this striking vermilion gate appears to float at high tide, creating a truly magical sight. As a UNESCO World Heritage Site, it attracts countless visitors each year who come to marvel at its spellbinding beauty.

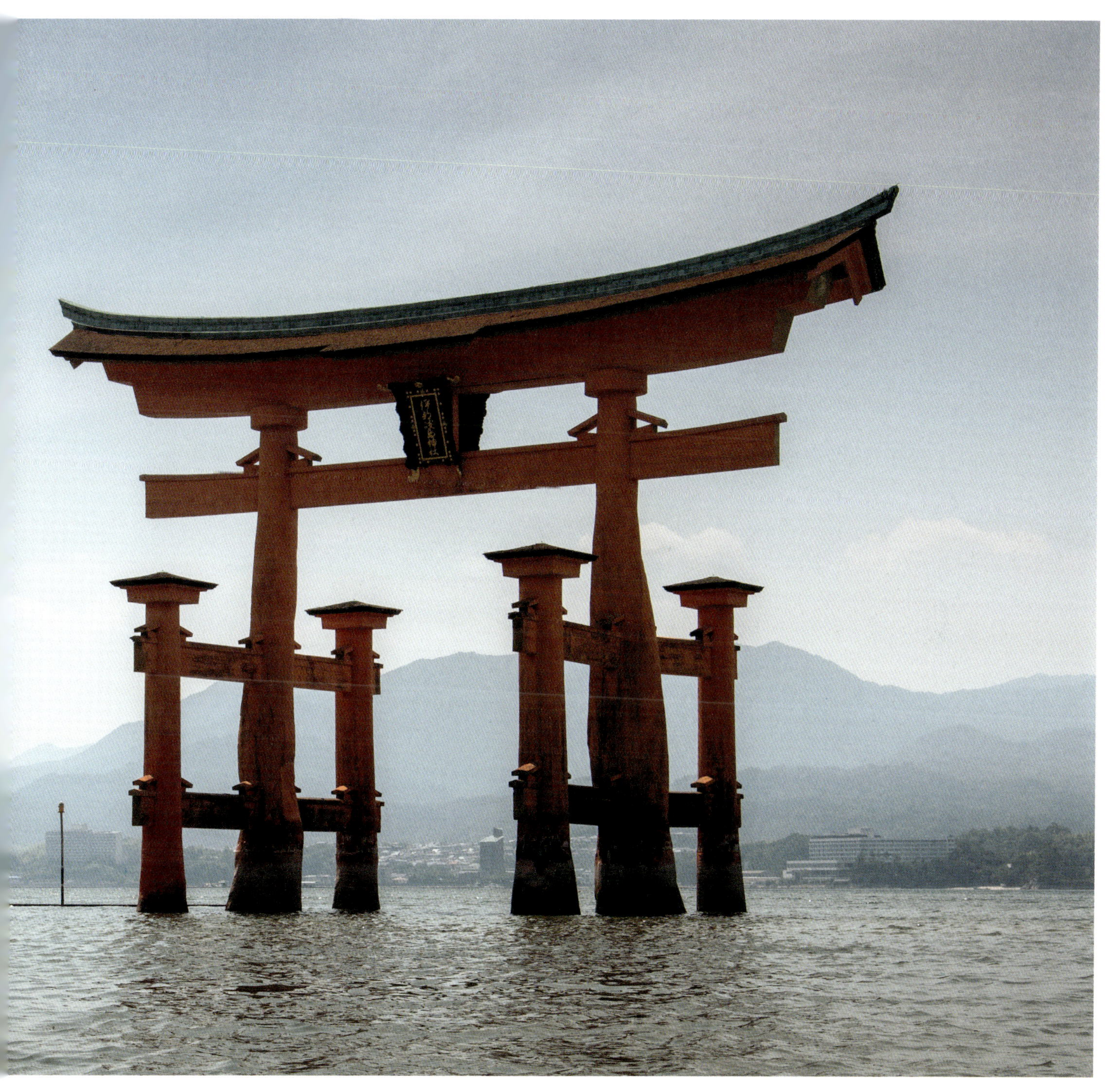

Kyūdō.
The traditional Japanese art of archery, kyūdō, is a practice steeped in discipline and self-mastery. Clad in traditional attire and wielding a long bamboo bow, the archer moves deliberately, each gesture infused with focus and harmony. More than a sport, kyūdō represents a spiritual journey – where the true aim lies not only in hitting the target but also in achieving inner balance. >

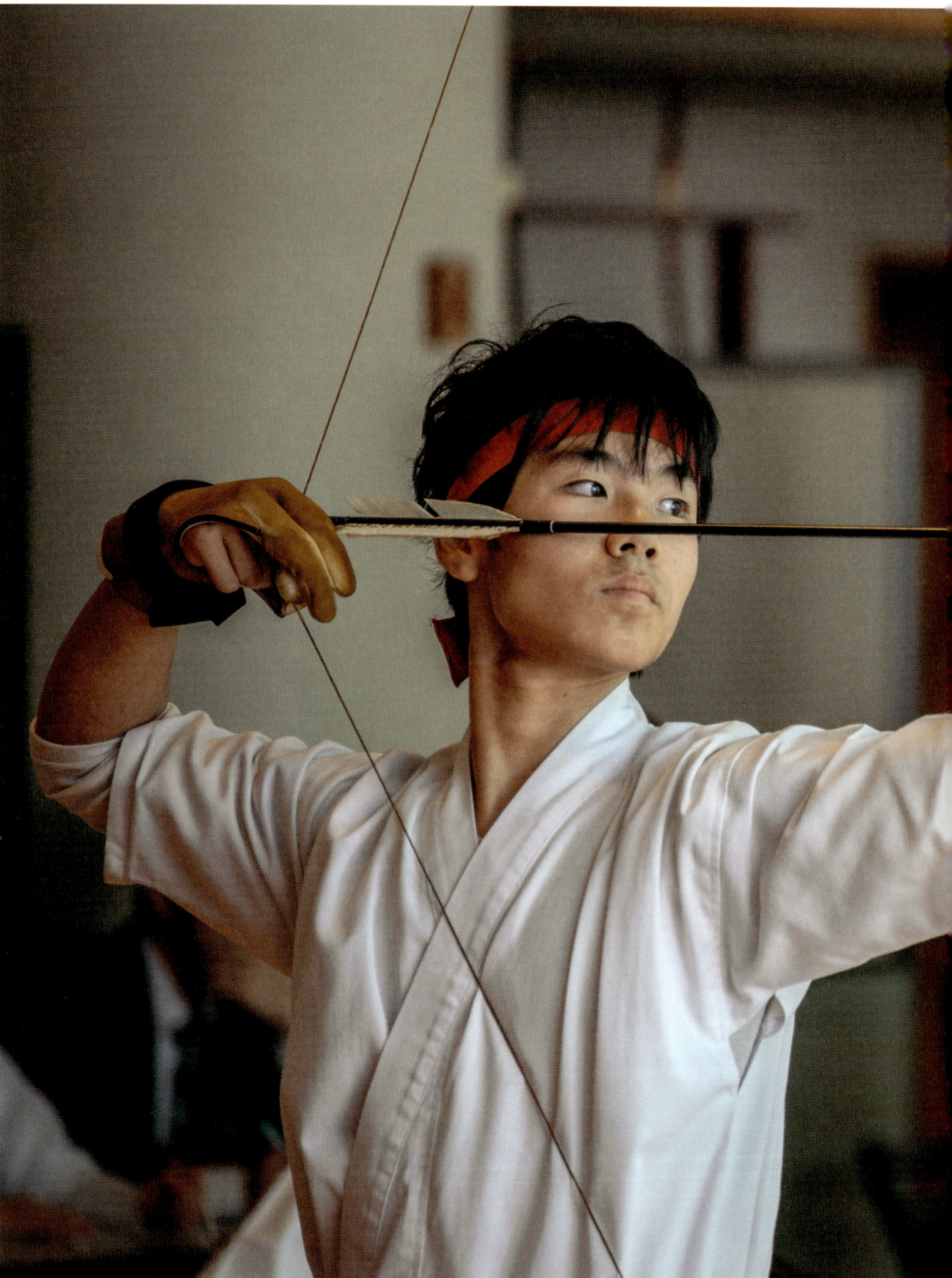

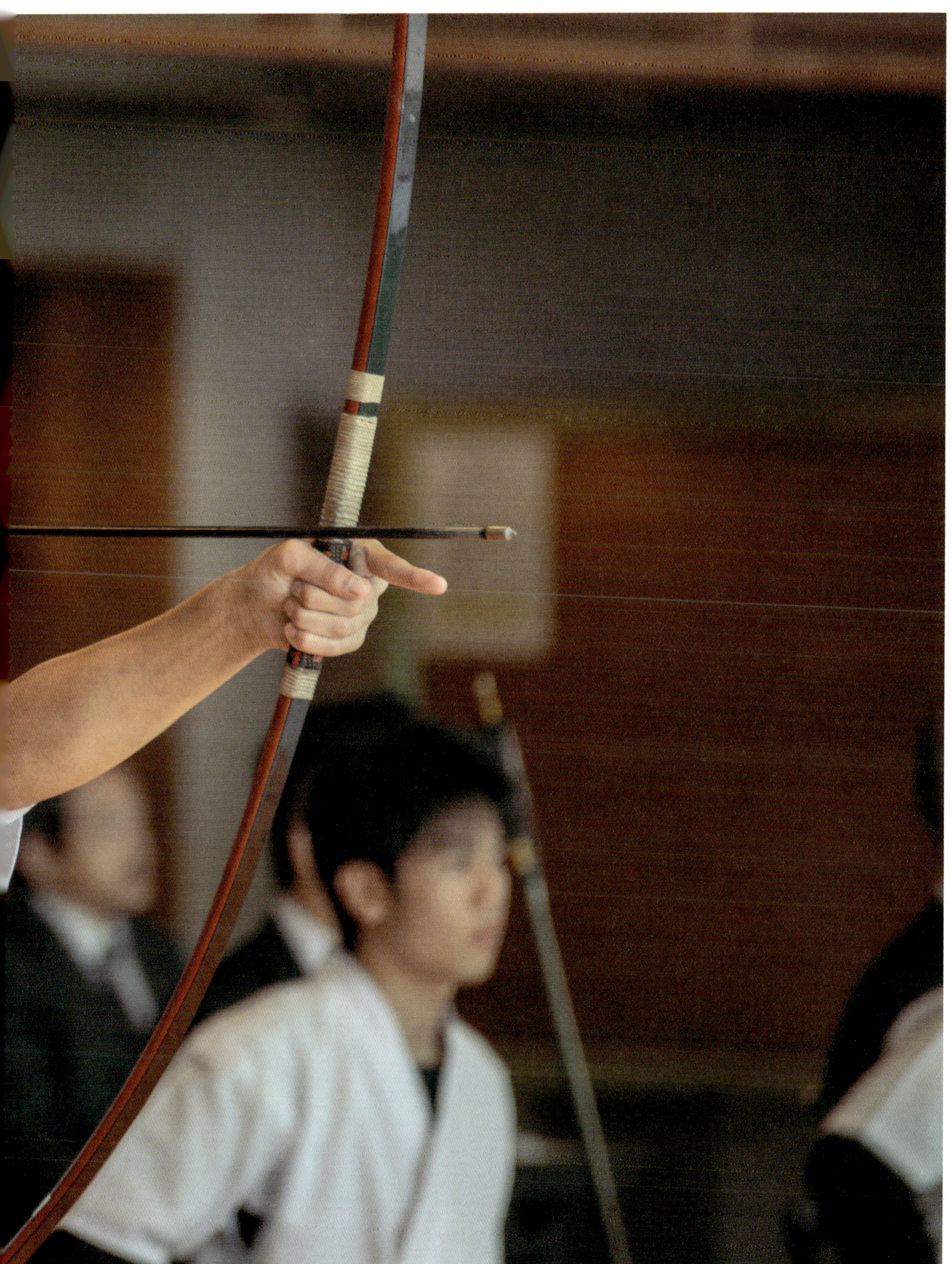

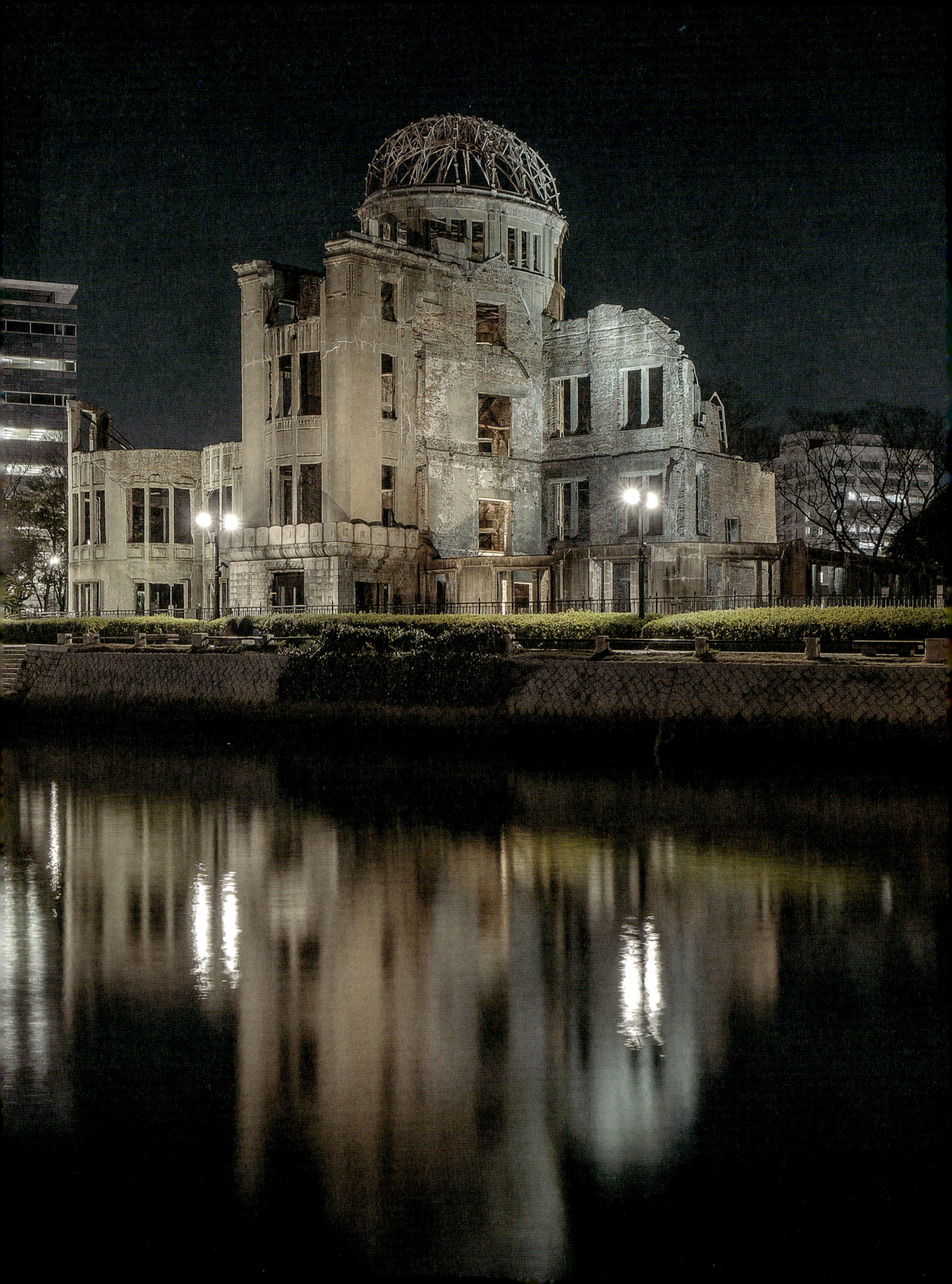

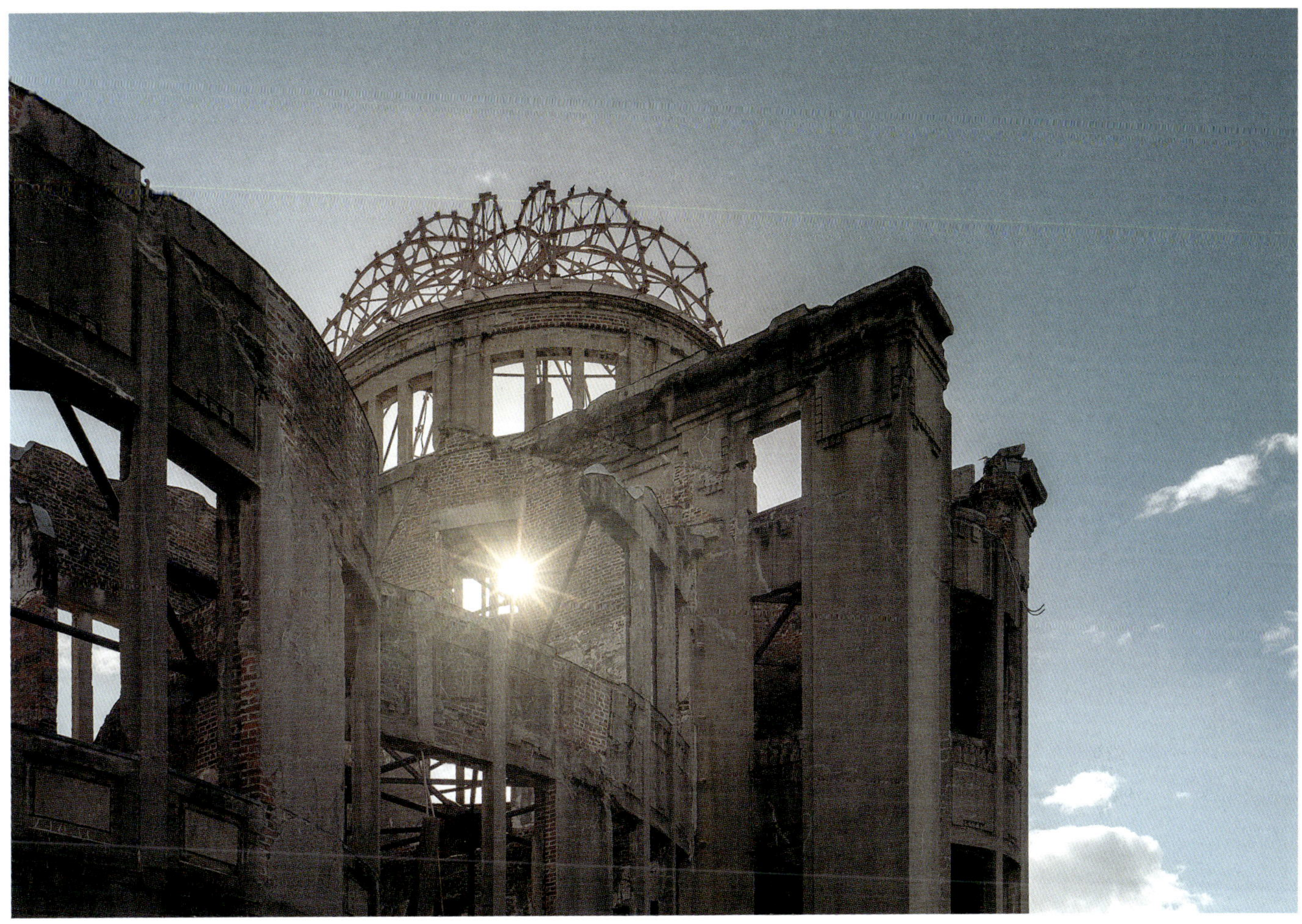

Genbaku Dome.

The Genbaku Dome, also known as the Atomic Bomb Dome, stands as a powerful symbol of peace and remembrance in Hiroshima. As one of the few structures to survive the 1945 atomic bombing, this haunting ruin is beautifully illuminated at night, casting a quiet reflection on the Motoyasu River. Now a UNESCO World Heritage Site, it honours the resilience of the Japanese people and the enduring call for a peaceful world.

Onomichi.

Nestled between rolling green hills and the Seto Inland Sea, Onomichi is renowned for its winding streets, historic temples, panoramic views, and picturesque waterfront. The suspension bridge connecting the nearby islands showcases the city's maritime heritage, while its artistic atmosphere continues to draw creatives and travellers from around the world.

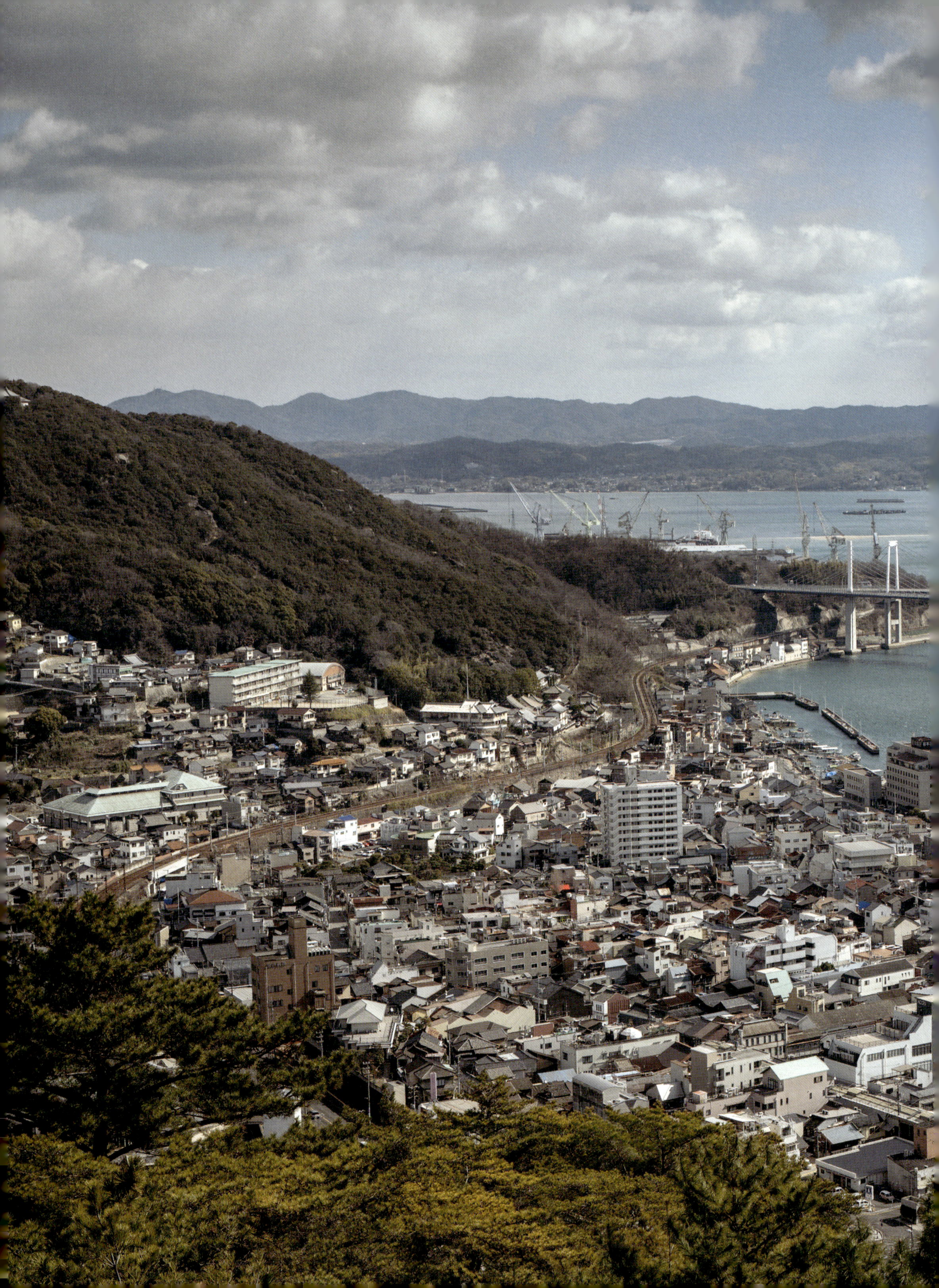

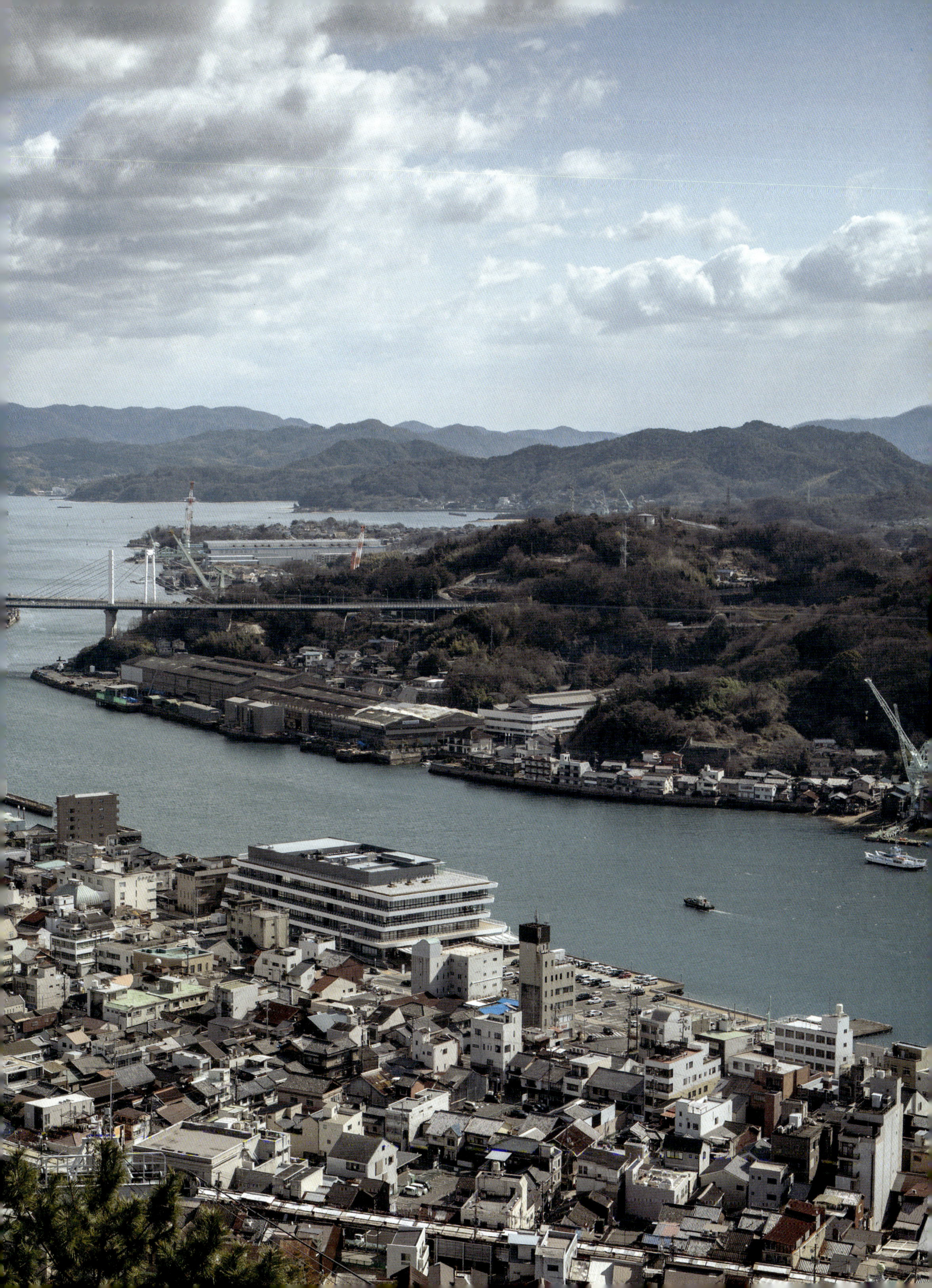

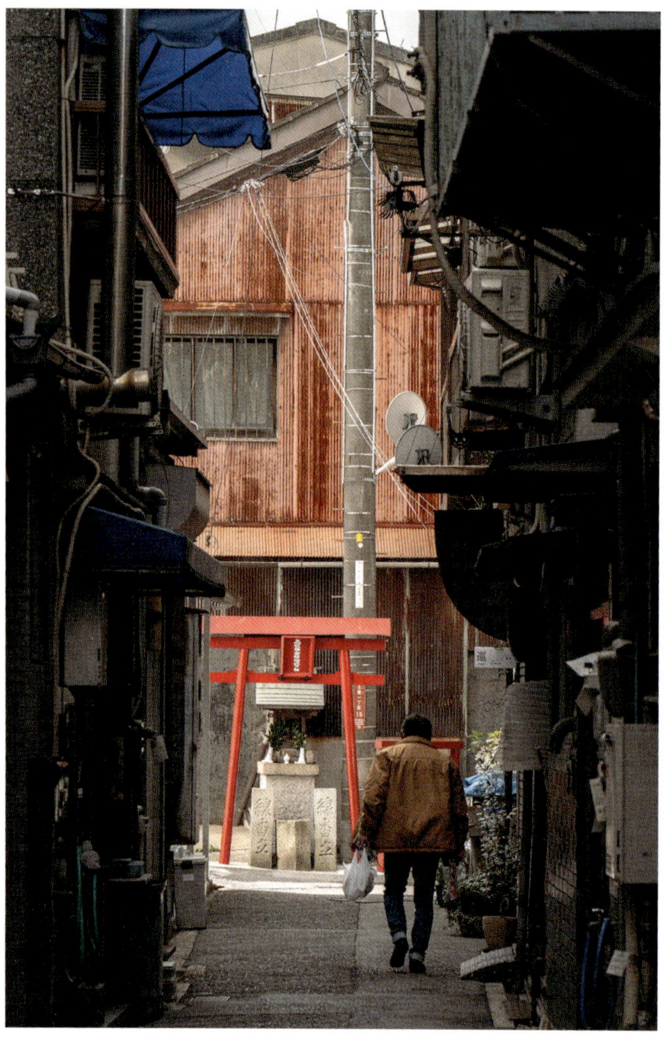

Onomichi Lanes.
The narrow lanes of Onomichi exude timeless charm, where old and new coexist in quiet harmony. Traditional homes sit alongside modern buildings, while the alleyways are full of character – crisscrossing power lines, subtle signage, and everyday objects that tell the story of daily life. Around one quiet corner, a vivid red *torii* stands tall, a gentle reminder of the spiritual thread running through this coastal town.

Jeans Street.
Located in Okayama, Jeans Street serves as a symbolic destination for denim enthusiasts, showcasing the region's internationally acclaimed craftsmanship. The street is lined with specialised boutiques such as "RIVETS" and adorned with hanging denim pieces that highlight the area's distinctive character and cultural identity.

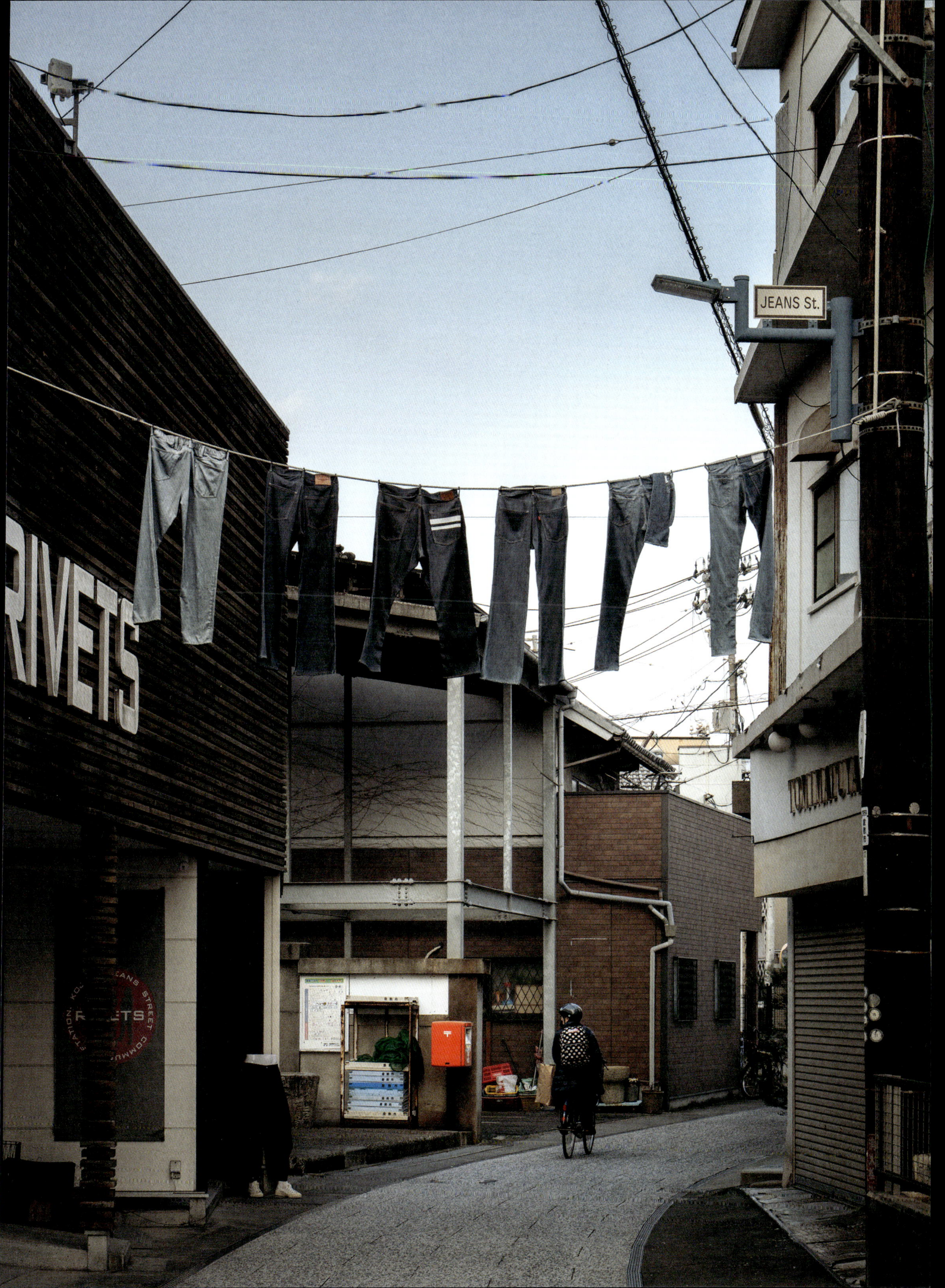
JEANS St.
RIVETS

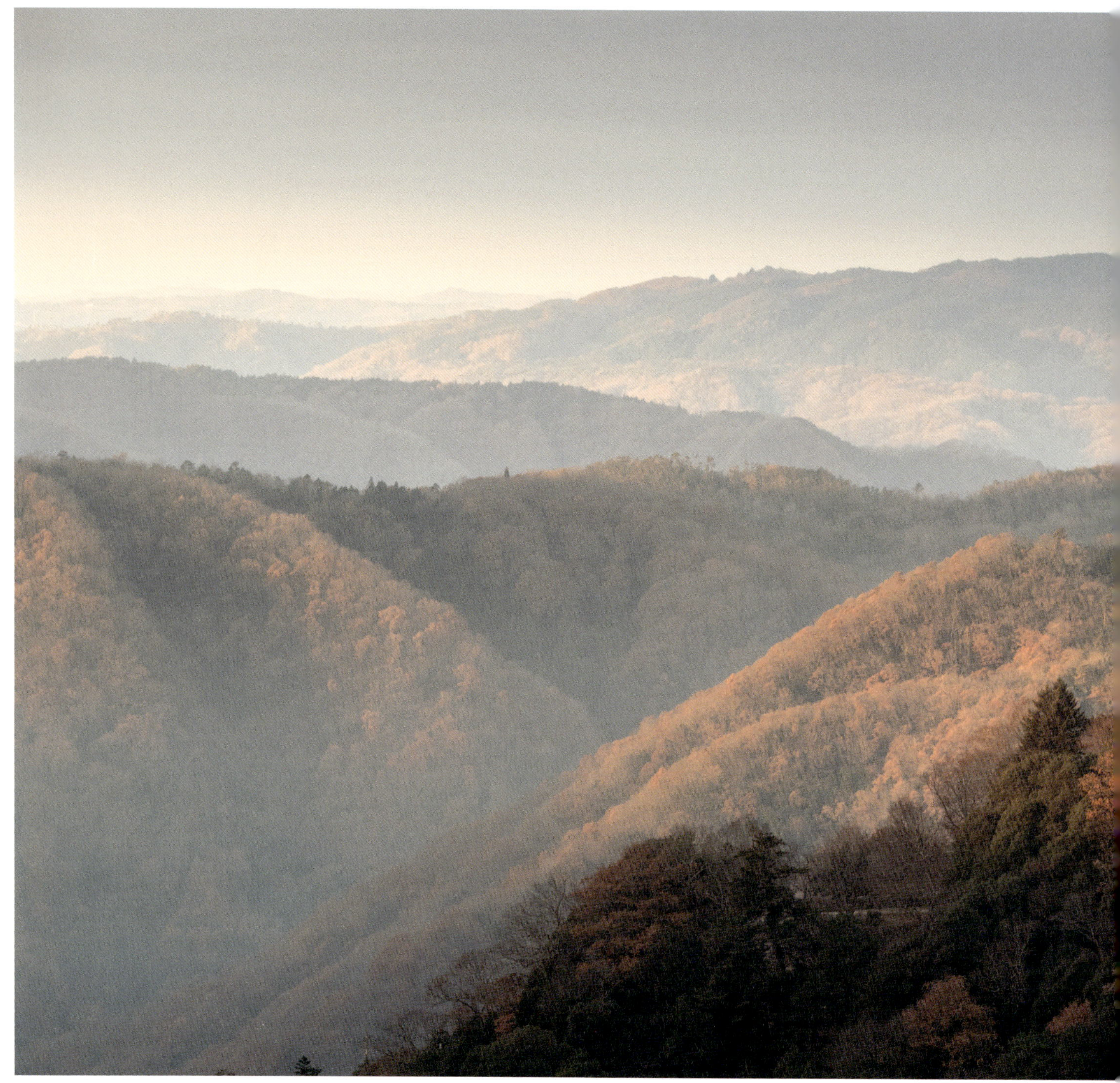

Bitchu Matsuyama Castle.
Rising high in the mountains of Okayama Prefecture, Bitchū Matsuyama Castle commands breathtaking views of the mist-covered hills below. Believed to be the highest-altitude feudal castle still standing in Japan, it provides a rare glimpse into the country's medieval past amid a serene, natural setting.

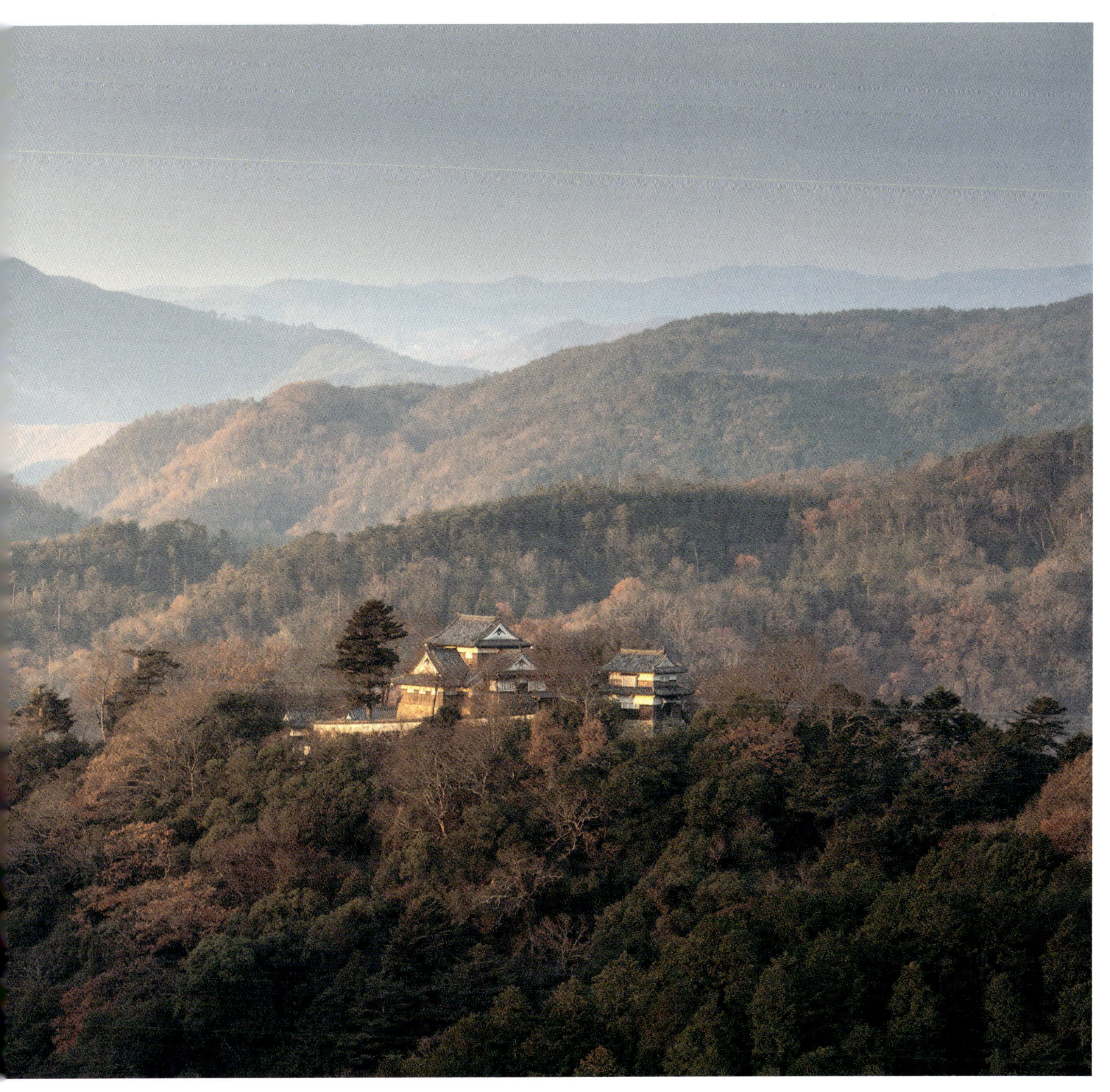

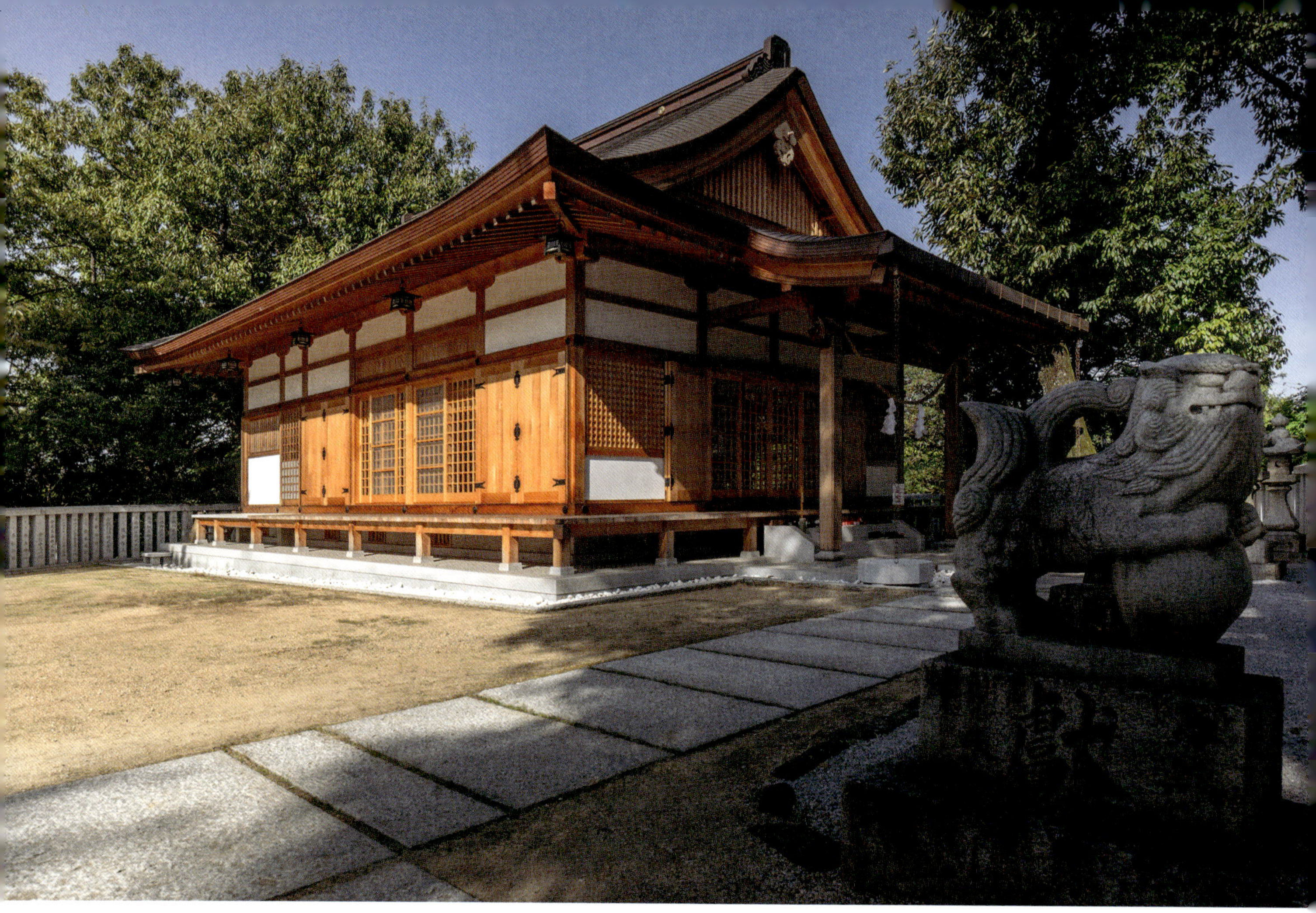

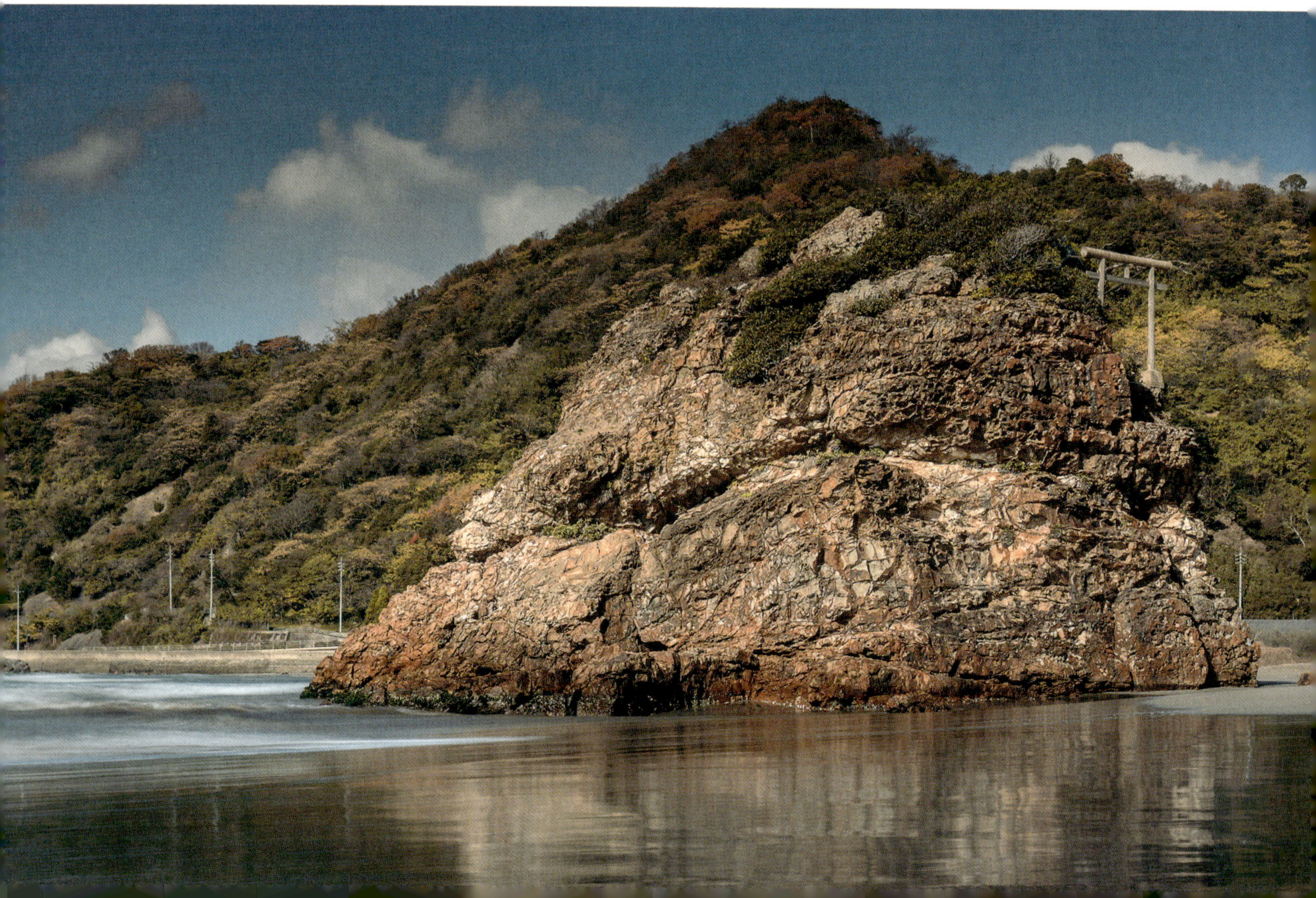

Achi Shrine.

Nestled high above Kurashiki, Achi Shrine has watched over the city and its people since its founding in 720 by the Korean monk Achi. This Shinto sanctuary, with its traditional wooden architecture, offers a tranquil retreat surrounded by lush greenery. A stone *komainu* – guardian lion-dog – stands proudly at the entrance, symbolising spiritual protection.

Inasa Beach & Bentenjima Island.

Framed by forested hills, Inasa no Hama Beach offers a stunning view of Bentenjima Island. This remarkable rock formation, shaped by time, is crowned with a solitary *torii* gate – an emblem of sacred space.

Motonosumi Inari Shrine.

Motonosumi Inari Shrine: Perched in Yamaguchi Prefecture, Motonosumi Inari Shrine is famous for its striking path of 123 vivid red *torii* gates, which wind their way up to a dramatic cliffside overlooking the Sea of Japa.

>

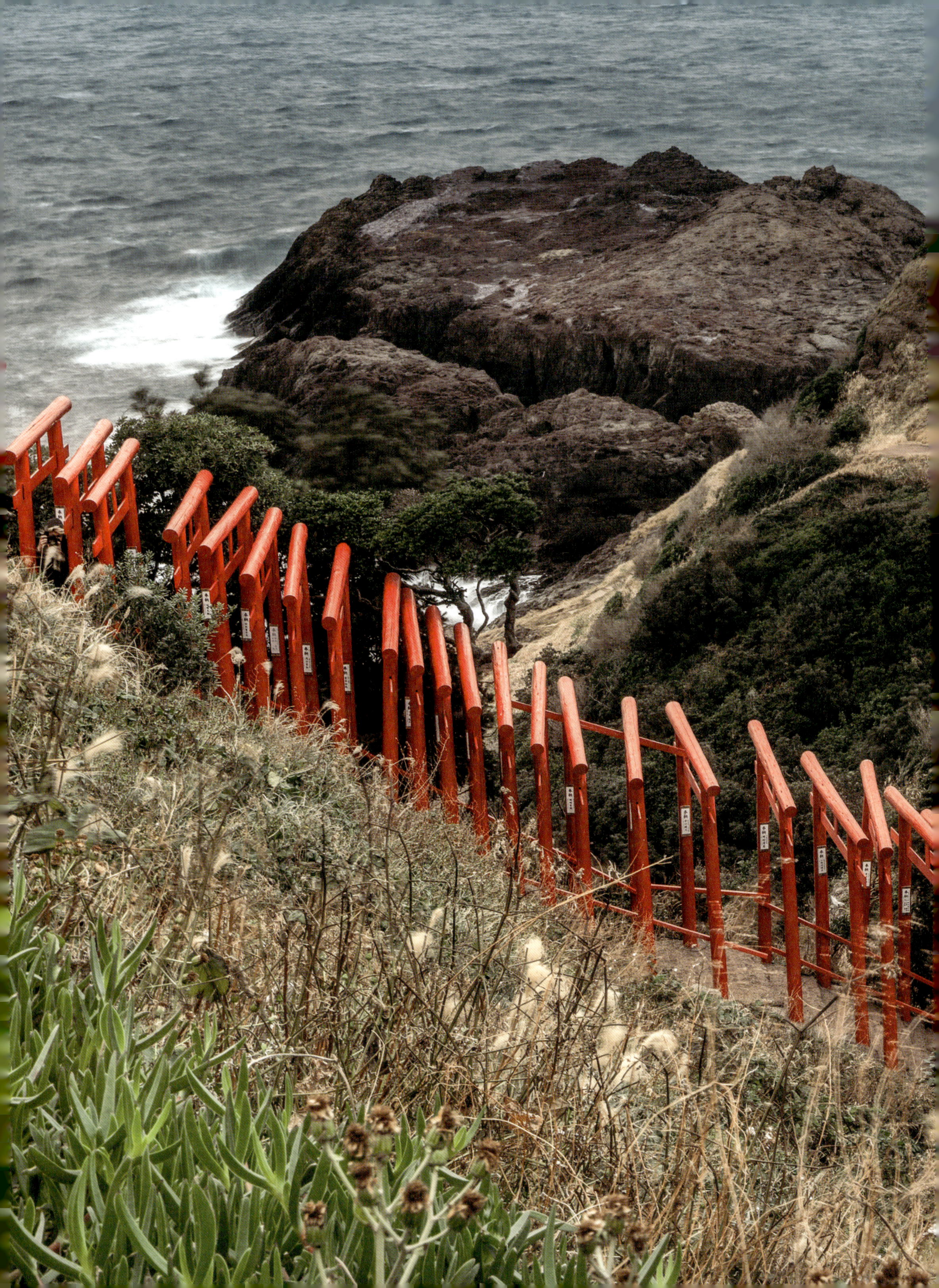

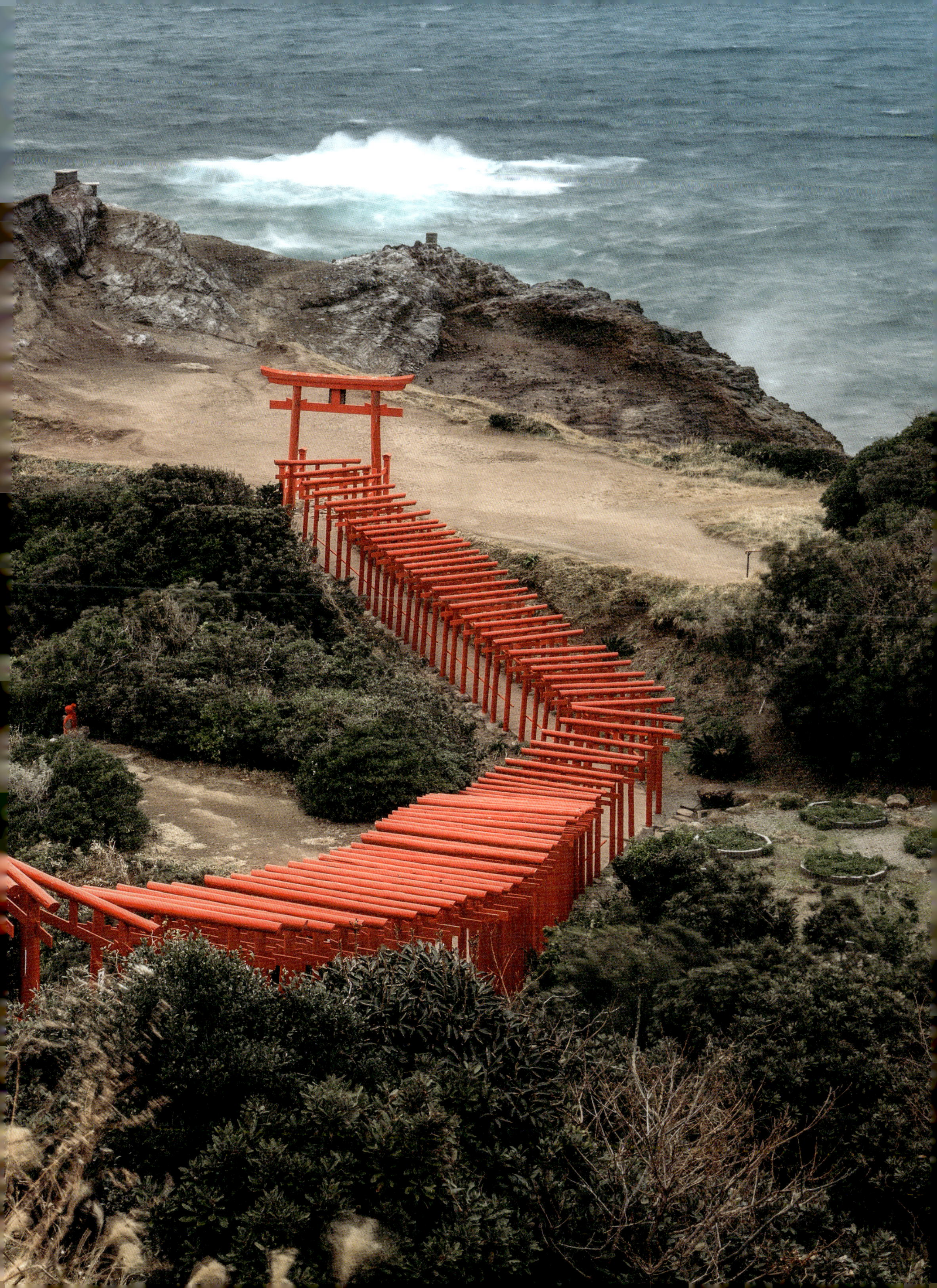

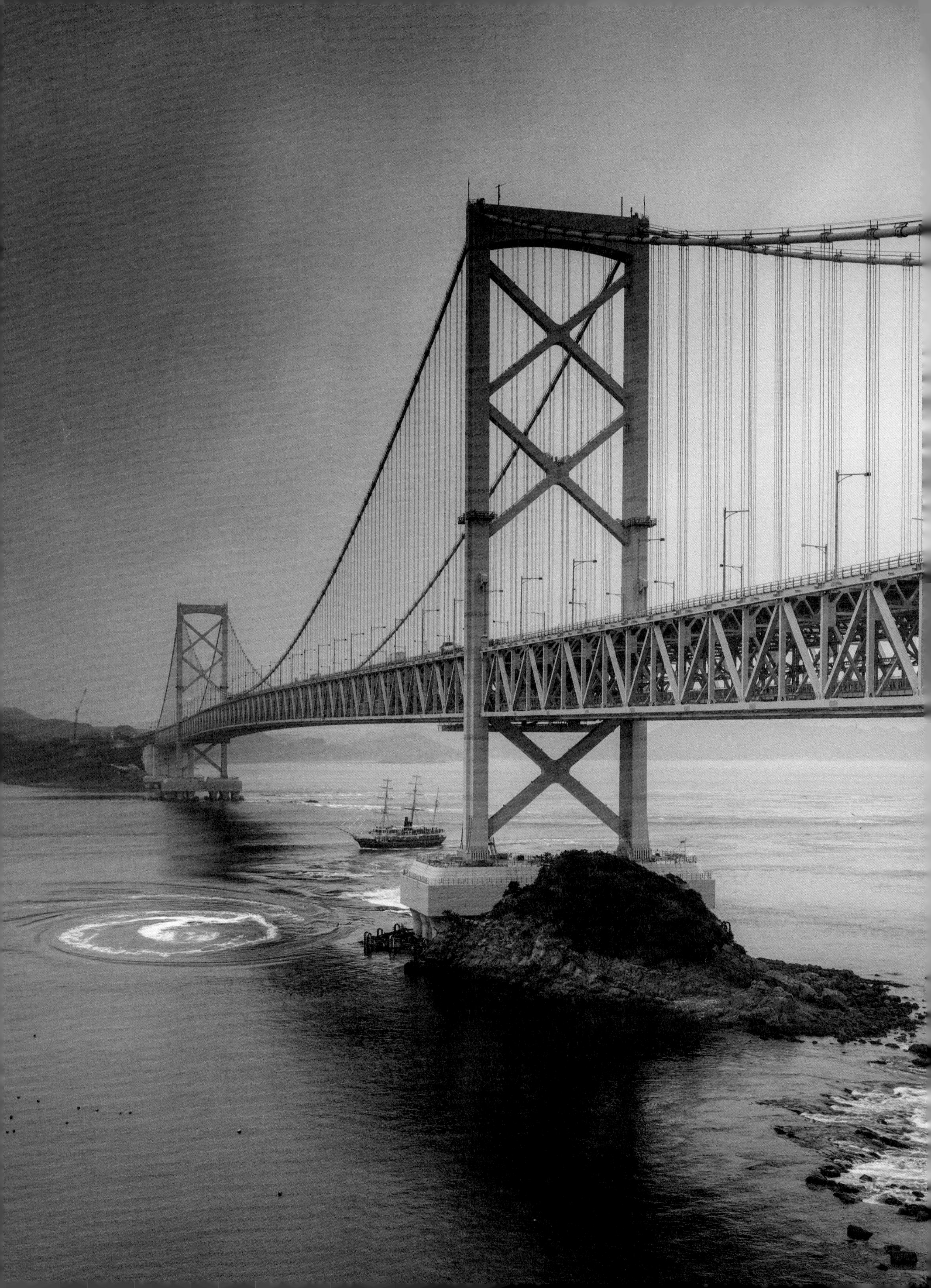

Naruto Whirlpools.
Beneath the grandeur of Ōnaruto Bridge, the Naruto whirlpools twist and churn with mesmerising force. This captivating natural phenomenon, caused by the tidal flows between the Seto Inland Sea and the Pacific Ocean, creates powerful vortexes that are visible during high tide

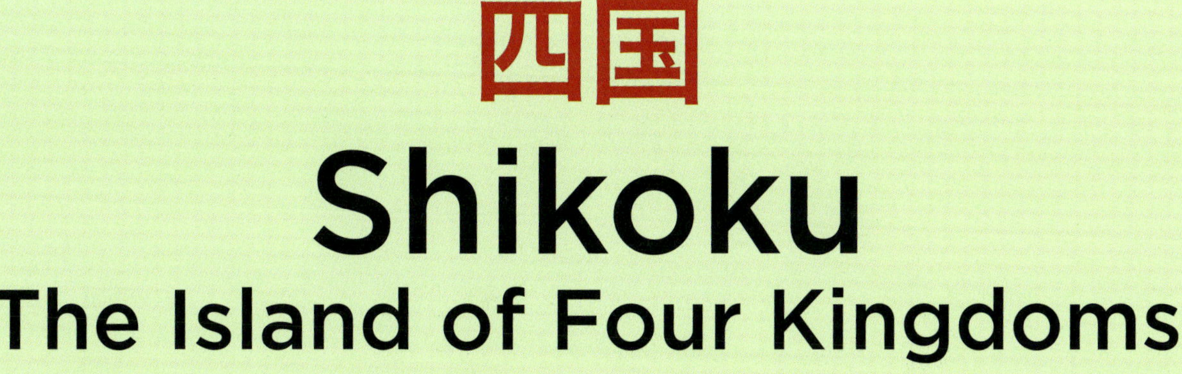

Shikoku

The Island of Four Kingdoms

Divided into four prefectures – Ehime, Kagawa, Kōchi, and Tokushima – the island's name, meaning "Four Provinces", harks back to its feudal past. Less visited than the larger Honshū, Kyūshū, or Hokkaidō islands. With its natural landscapes, historic sites, and spiritual essence, it is a region that truly encapsulates the richness and diversity of Japan, Shikoku offers a pilgrimage where every step uncovers a unique facet of Japan.

Area.
Shikoku spans an area of about 18,800 km², making it the smallest of Japan's four main islands.

Demographics and Population.
The island has approximately 4.5 million inhabitants.

Geographical Location.
Nestled between the Seto Inland Sea to the north and the Pacific Ocean to the south, Shikoku is connected to the main island of Honshu by multiple bridges, making it easily accessible from cities such as Kobe and Okayama. The region consists of four prefectures: Tokushima, Kagawa, Ehime, and Kōchi.

Climate and Seasons.
Shikoku enjoys a temperate climate. April, May, October, and November are particularly favourable for exploring the island, offering pleasant weather with infrequent rainfall.

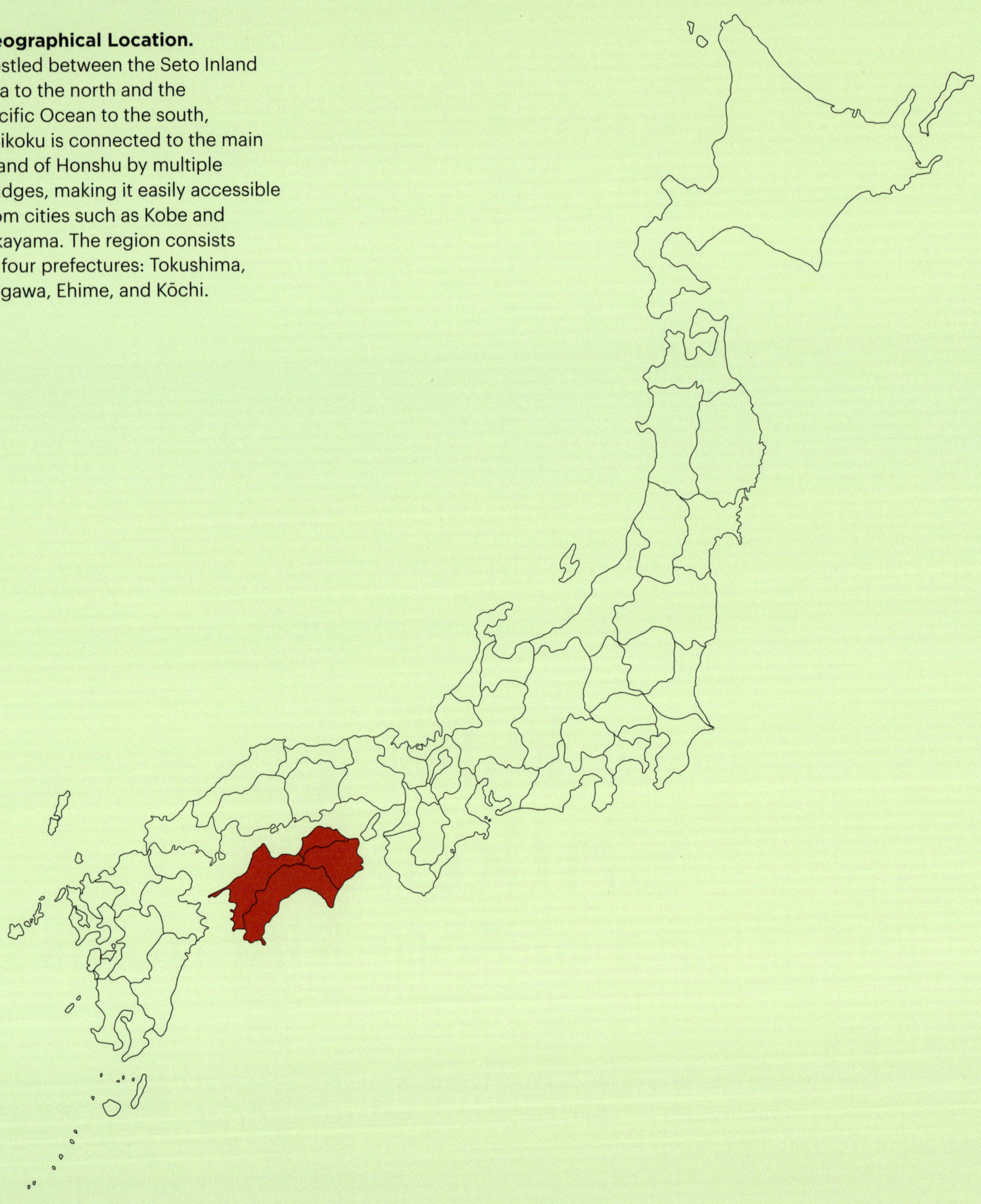

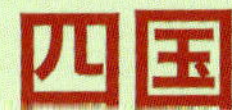

The Pilgrimage of the 88 Temples

The Shikoku Pilgrimage, or *Shikoku Henro*, is a spiritual journey that attracts pilgrims and travellers from around the globe. Spanning nearly 1,200 kilometres, this sacred route connects 88 Buddhist temples, each filled with history and symbolism. Founded by Kūkai, known as Kōbō Daishi, a renowned monk from the Heian period, this pilgrimage is much more than just a religious journey – it is an exploration of the soul and the island's natural beauty.

From temples perched in the mountains, such as Tairyūji, reached by a cable car through dense forests, to coastal sanctuaries like Kōnomineji, which overlooks the sea, each site offers a unique atmosphere. Even those who don't embark on the whole pilgrimage can visit iconic temples like Ryōzenji (the first on the route) or Zentsū-ji, the birthplace of Kūkai.

Tokushima, The Naruto Whirlpools and Awa Dances

To the east of Shikoku, Tokushima is a prefecture where water and culture converge with vibrant energy. The Naruto Whirlpools, spectacular natural phenomena created by the tides in the Naruto Strait, attract curious visitors who can admire them from bridges or from specially adapted boats.

Tokushima is also the birthplace of the Awa Odori, one of Japan's most famous traditional dance festivals. Each summer, the city's streets come alive with the rhythm of drums, *shamisen*, and lively songs, as dancers in traditional costumes perform graceful movements in a festive atmosphere.

Mount Bizan, which dominates Tokushima, offers panoramic views of the city and the Seto Inland Sea. For outdoor enthusiasts, the Iya Valley, with its vine bridges and crystal-clear waters, provides an adventure into the wild heart of Shikoku.

Kagawa, The Sanctuary of Flavours and Art

Kagawa, the smallest prefecture in Japan, is full of hidden treasures. Known as the "Udon Prefecture", it is famous for its *Sanuki udon* noodles, a regional speciality that can be savoured in countless local restaurants.

Takamatsu, the gateway to Kagawa, is home to the renowned Ritsurin Garden – a masterpiece of Japanese landscaping where ponds, hills, and pavilions blend harmoniously.

A short ferry ride from Takamatsu leads to Naoshima, known as the "Art Island". Naoshima is a paradise for contemporary art lovers, featuring its museums and outdoor installations integrated into the natural landscape. Yayoi Kusama's iconic yellow pumpkin symbolises the island's fusion of tradition and modernity.

Ehime, The Majesty of Matsuyama and Dōgo's Onsen

Ehime, located northwest of Shikoku, is a prefecture that is rich in history and hot springs. The city of Matsuyama is dominated by Matsuyama Castle, one of the last 12 Japanese castles that still retains its original keep, which sits atop a hill. The view over the city and the Seto Inland Sea is breathtaking from its ramparts.

Dōgo Onsen, one of Japan's oldest hot spring resorts, has welcomed visitors for over a thousand years. Its main building, featuring traditional architecture and healing waters, is said to have inspired Hayao Miyazaki's animated film *Spirited Away*.

For literature lovers, Matsuyama is also linked to Natsume Sōseki, one of Japan's greatest authors, whose novel Botchan is partly set in this city.

Kōchi, Wild Shores and the Spirit of Freedom

To the south of Shikoku, Kōchi is a prefecture where nature reigns supreme. Bordering the Pacific Ocean, it is famous for its wild beaches, crystal-clear rivers, and tranquil atmosphere.

Kōchi is dominated by Kōchi Castle, an original castle known for its well-preserved keep and tranquil gardens. The Hirome Market, located in the city's heart, is a must-visit for sampling local delicacies like *katsuo no tataki* (seared bonito) in a friendly, laid-back atmosphere.

Kōchi's coastline is renowned for Cape Ashizuri, where steep cliffs plunge into the ocean, offering breathtaking panoramic views. The Shimanto River, often called "Japan's last clear stream", meanders through picturesque landscapes and offers activities such as canoeing and fishing.

The Bridges and Seto Inland Sea

The Seto Inland Sea surrounds Shikoku and is dotted with islands and bridges connecting it to the rest of Japan. The *Shimanami Kaidō*, a route linking Shikoku to Honshū through a series of spectacular bridges, is a haven for cyclists. Passing through picturesque islands and peaceful villages, the trail offers a unique immersion in the region's coastal landscapes.

The surrounding islands, such as Shōdo-shima, known for its olive groves and Kankakei Gorge, enhance the allure of this maritime region.

The Flavours and Heritage of Shikoku

Shikoku is a land of culinary delights and traditional crafts. In addition to the famous Sanuki *udon* from Kagawa, visitors can savour the *sake* from Ehime, *Kōchi* beef, and the region's local citrus fruits, such as *sudachi* and *mikan*.

The island's craft traditions include Tosa washi paper, local ceramics, and the centuries-old Awa indigo dyeing techniques that all thrive to this day.

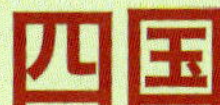

Best Times to Visit

– Spring (Mars to May). Temperatures
Cherry blossoms create stunning landscapes and offer comfortable Temperatures.

– Autumn (September to November).
Perfect for admiring colourful autumn leaves and benefiting from a pleasant climate.

Top 5 Places to Visit

1. The Shikoku 88 Temple Pilgrimage.
An iconic spiritual journey across the island.

2. Iya Valley.
Spectacular landscapes with traditional vine bridges.

3. Matsuyama Castle.
One of the best-preserved castles in Japan.

4. Dōgo Onsen.
One of the oldest hot spring resorts in the country.

5. Naruto Bridge.
Famous for its impressive marine whirlpools.

四国

Gastronomy

The region of Shikoku, which consists of the prefectures of Tokushima, Kagawa, Ehime, and Kōchi, is an island renowned for its culinary specialities, featuring seafood, citrus fruits, and noodles. Below is a list of Shikoku's culinary delights, organised by city, along with detailed descriptions.

徳島
Tokushima

[徳島ラーメン]
Tokushima Rāmen
A unique type of *rāmen* with a soy sauce and pork-based broth, often rich and slightly sweet. It is topped with braised pork, a raw egg, and spring onions.

[祖谷そば]
Iya Soba
Soba noodles made with a high proportion of buckwheat flour, giving them a crumblier texture. They are often served with a simple hot broth.

[すだち]
Sudachi
An iconic citrus fruit from Tokushima, used to flavour fish dishes, soups, and even desserts.

[鮑丼]
Awabi-don
A rice bowl topped with steamed abalones (*awabi*), served with a slightly sweet soy sauce.

[鳴門金時]
Naruto Kintoki
A variety of sweet potatoes from Naruto, known for their intense sweetness, often used in desserts or grilled.

高松
Takamatsu

[讃岐うどん]
Sanuki Udon
Sanuki *udon* are thick, elastic, and firm noodles. They are served in various ways: in hot soup, cold with dipping sauce, or *tempura*.

[しっぽくうどん]
Shippoku Udon
A winter *udon* soup where root vegetables, mushrooms, and meat accompany the noodles.

[骨付鳥]
Honetsukidori
A dish of whole roasted chicken leg with crispy skin and juicy meat. It is often served with potatoes and local beer.

[オリーブ牛]
Olive Beef
Wagyū beef fed on olives, giving it a sweet flavour and an exceptionally tender texture.

松山
Matsuyama

[じゃこ天]
Jakoten
A fried fish cake made from small whole fish pounded together, giving it a soft texture and a strong umami flavour.

[鯛めし]
Taimeshi
A rice dish prepared with sea bream.There are two styles:
1. Style Uwajima : The fish is marinated in soy sauce and served with rice.
2. Style Matsuyama : lThe sea bream is cooked with the rice in a broth.

[坊っちゃん団子]
Botchan Dango
This iconic dessert from Matsuyama consists of three coloured mochi balls (green tea, red bean, and egg), inspired by the novel Botchan by Natsume Sōseki.

[伊予みかん]
Iyo Mikan
These mandarins from Ehime are known for their sweetness and abundant juice. They are eaten fresh or turned into sweets and beverages.

高知
Kōchi

[鰹のたたき]
Katsuo no Tataki
An emblematic dish from Kōchi where *bonito* (*katsuo*) is lightly grilled over an open flame, then sliced and served with salt, sudachi vinegar, and garlic.

[皿鉢料理]
Sawachi Ryōri
A large celebratory dish combining *sashimi*, *tempura*, *sushi*, and other foods, typically shared in groups during special occasions.

[土佐寿司]
Tosa Zushi
A type of pressed sushi made with mackerel, bonito, or other local fish, often served with yuzu or *sudachi*.

[芋けんぴ]
Imo Kenpi
Sweet potato sticks that are deep-fried and caramelised, crunchy and sweet, very popular in Kōchi.

[とさこい汁]
Tosakoi Jiru
A local soup made with miso, vegetables, and fish, mainly eaten in winter.

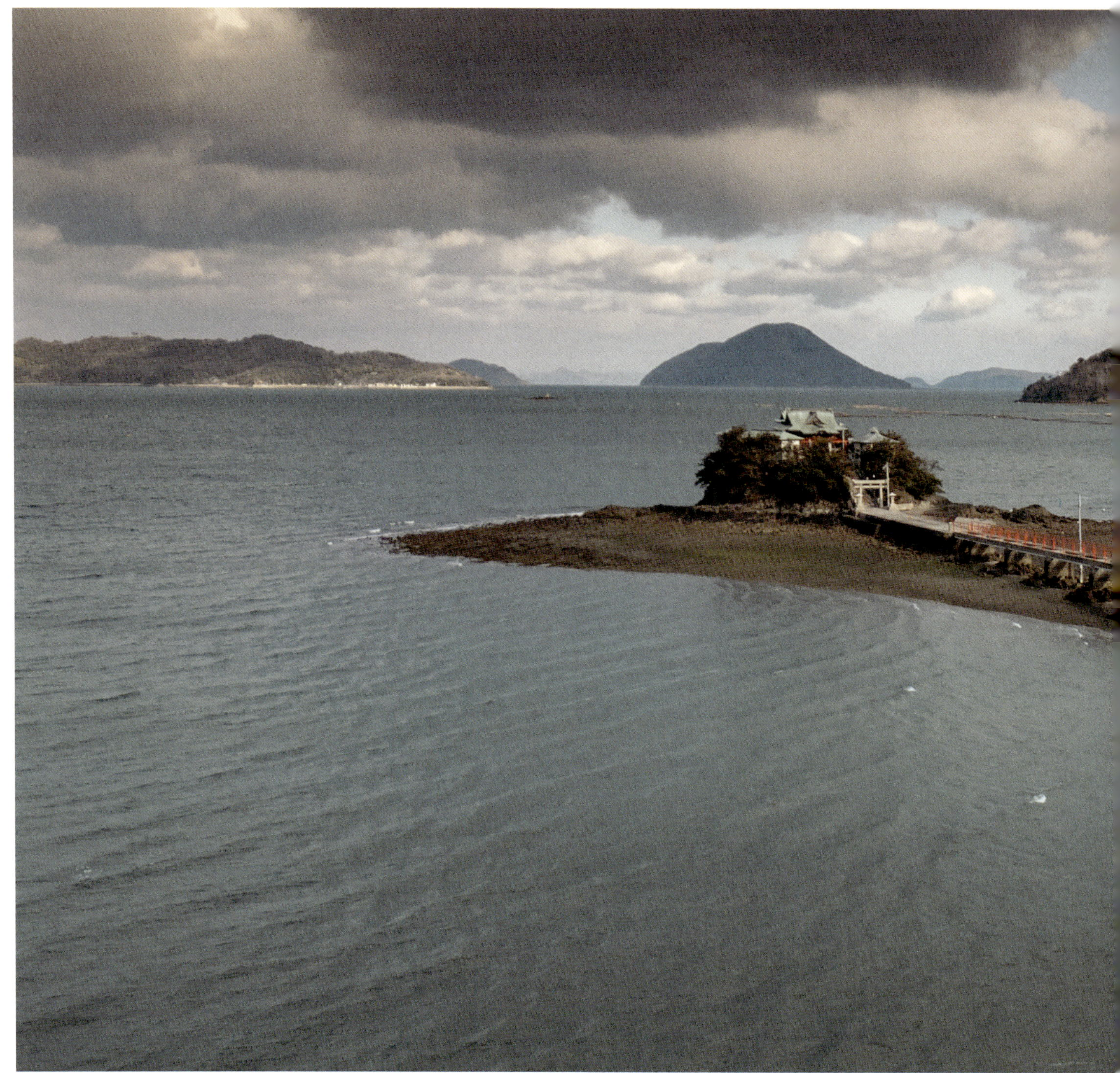

Tsushima Shrine.
Located on a small island in Kagawa Prefecture, Tsushima Shrine is accessible via an elegant red footbridge that connects it to the mainland. Surrounded by the tranquil waters of the Seto Inland Sea, the shrine offers a constantly changing vista, at times isolated from the shore and at times linked by the ebb and flow of the tides. Open only twice a year for its grand summer festival, the shrine transforms into a place of pilgrimage, where families gather to pray for the protection and well-being of their children.

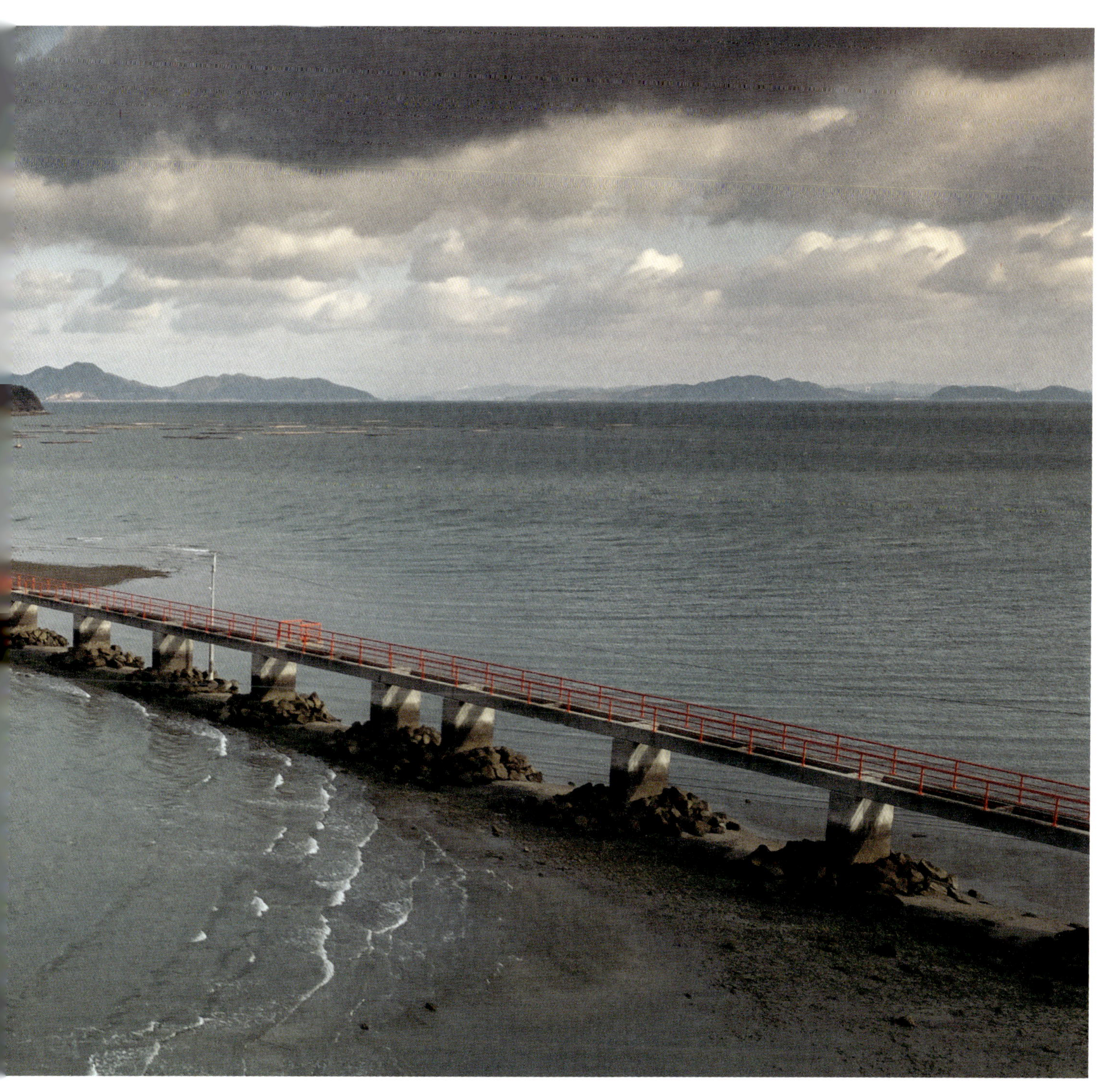

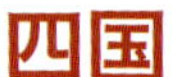

Public Bath "I Love Yu".
With its eclectic design and vibrant colours, "I Love Yu" is more than just a public bath; it is an immersive piece of art. Located on Naoshima Island, this one-of-a-kind *sento*, created by artist Shinro Ohtake, blends mosaics, found objects, and whimsical installations into a unique artistic experience.

Naoshima Pumpkin.
Yayoi Kusama's iconic yellow pumpkin, adorned with black polka dots, stands proudly on the quay of Naoshima Island and has become a defining symbol of contemporary art in Japan. Blending nature with surrealism, this striking sculpture reflects the artist's childhood and obsession with repetitive patterns.

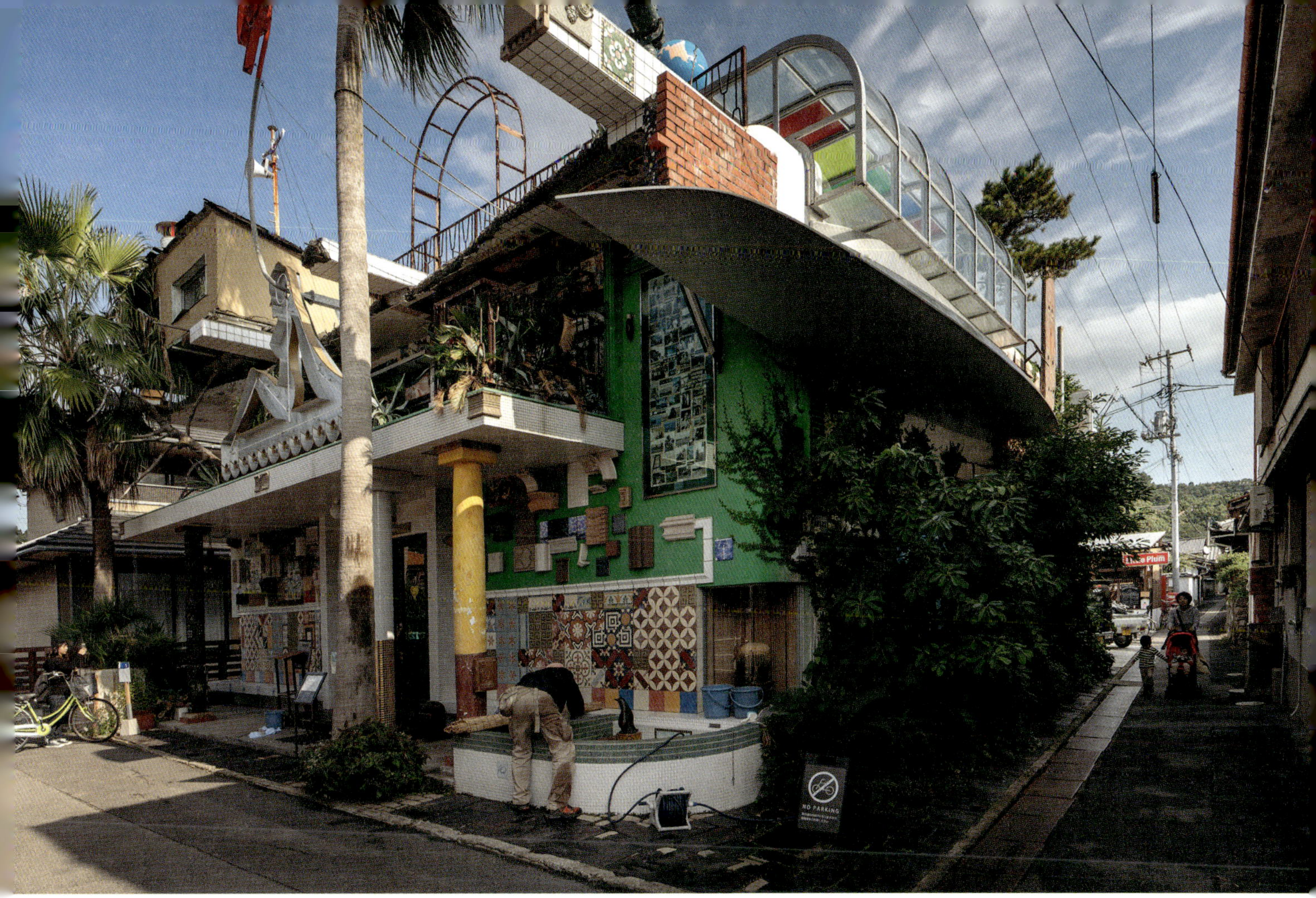

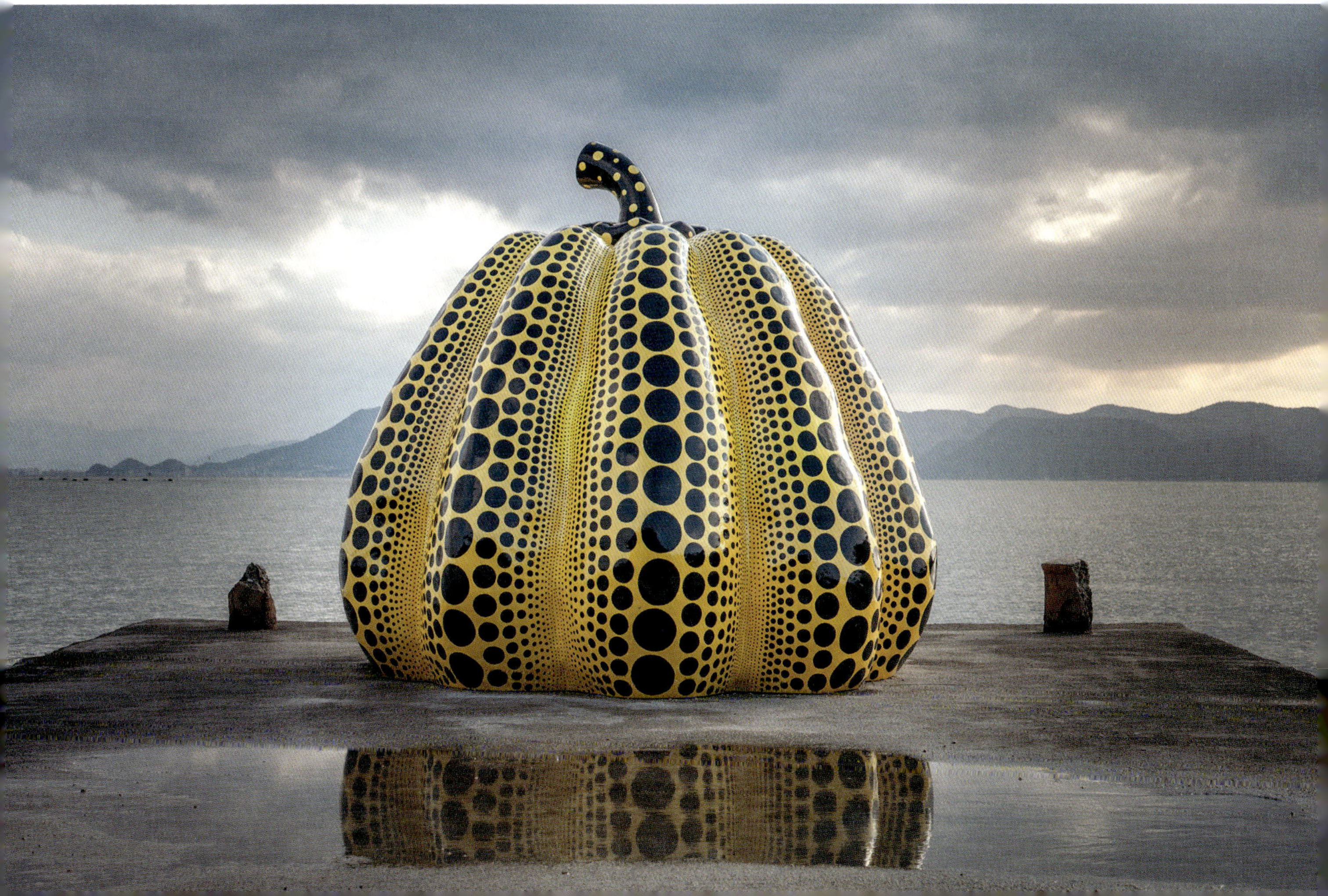

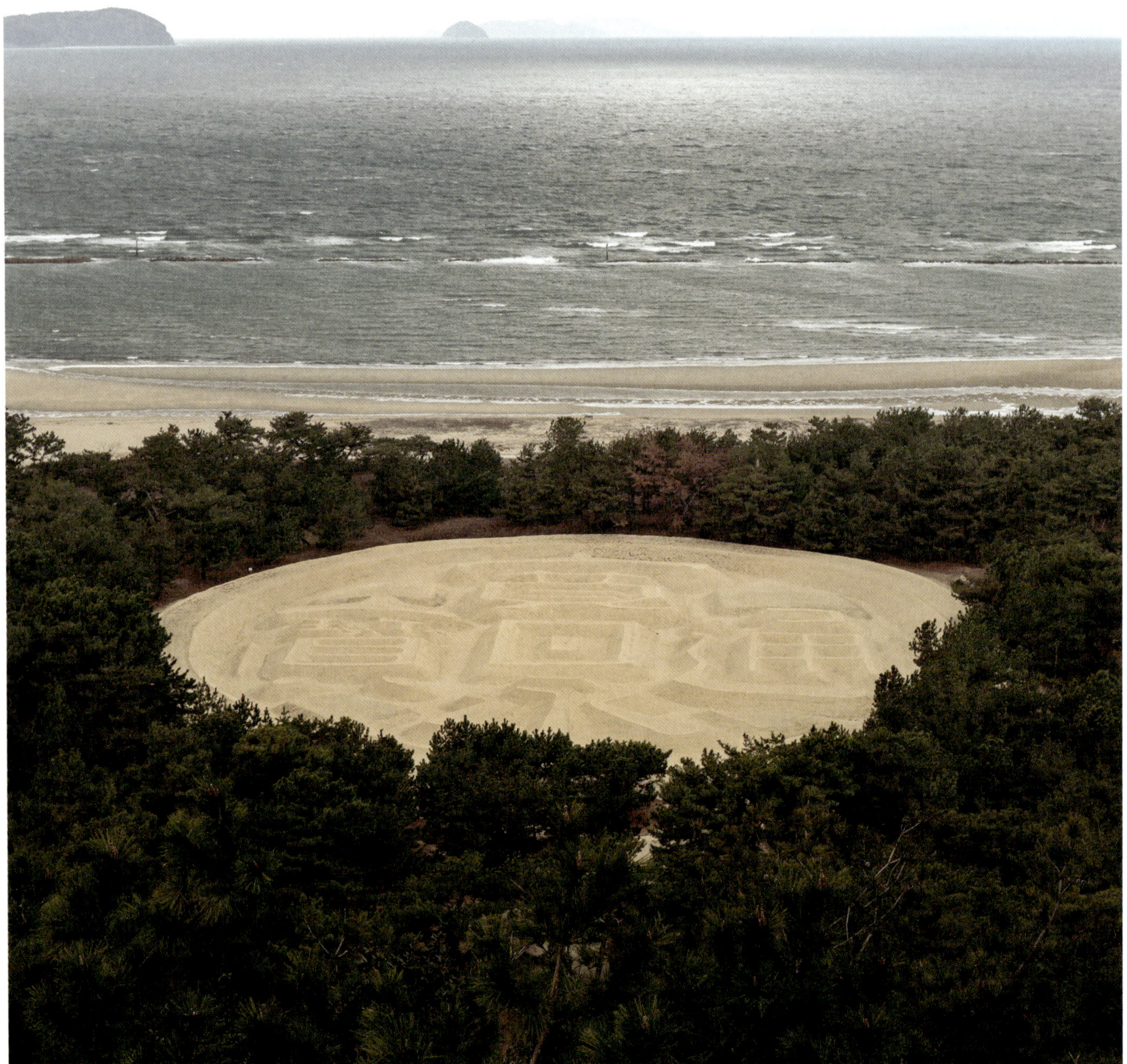

Zenigata.
Set against a backdrop of pine trees and overlooking the Seto Inland Sea, Zenigata is an immense sand sculpture shaped like an ancient coin, unfurling near Kotohiki Beach. Created overnight in 1633 to impress a feudal lord, this symbol of prosperity has since become a cherished good-luck charm, believed to bring fortune and longevity to those who glimpse its vast form.

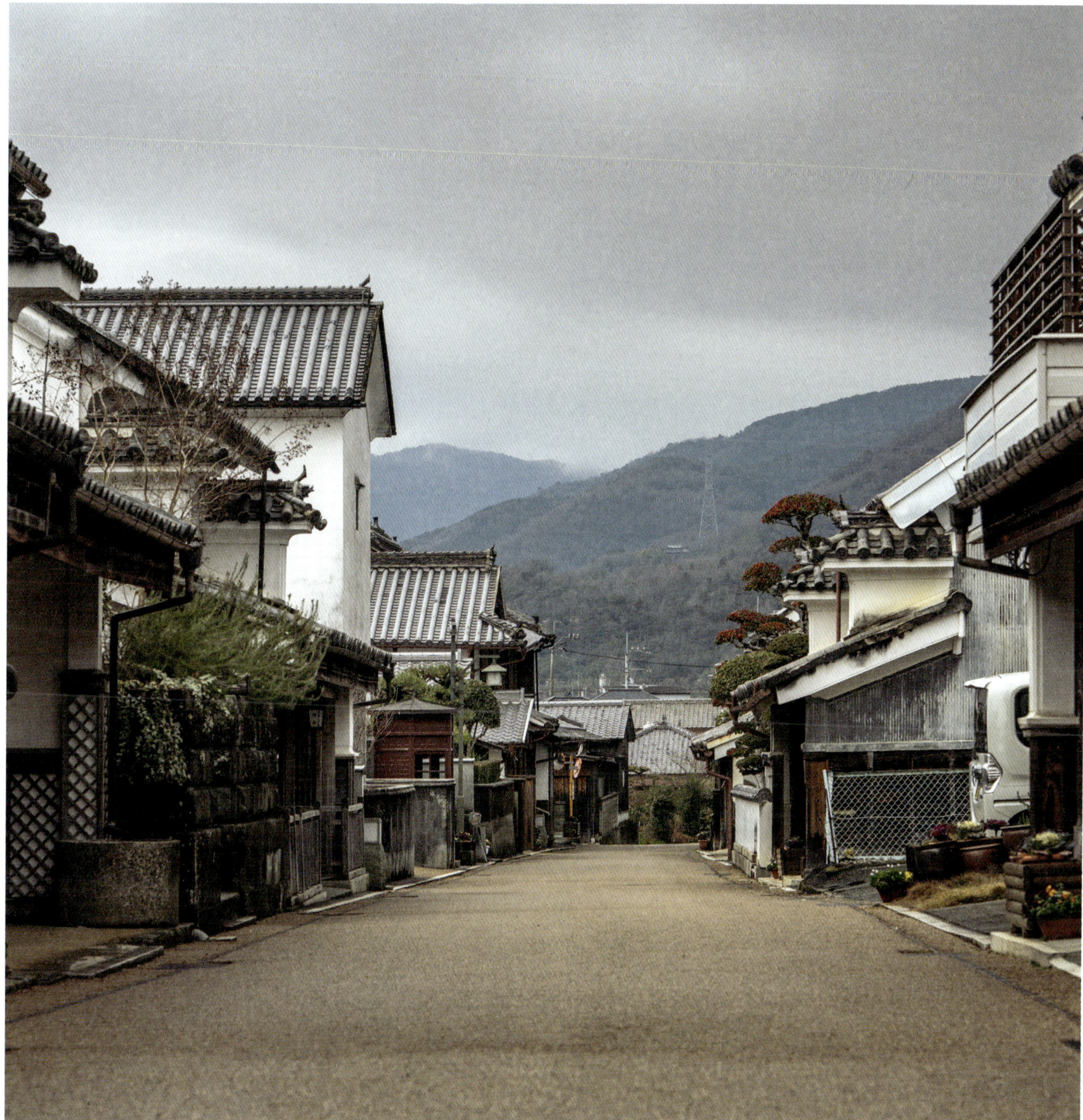

Udatsu.
In the heart of the old village of Udatsu, traditional houses with distinctive *udatsu* fireproof elevations transport travellers back to a bygone era. This well-preserved street, lined with whitewashed facades and intricate wooden carvings, reflects the region's rich trading history.

Hongaku-ji Temple.
Nestled along the serene banks of a river and encircled by mountains, Hongaku-ji Temple features a stone garden that exemplifies the harmony of the elements. >

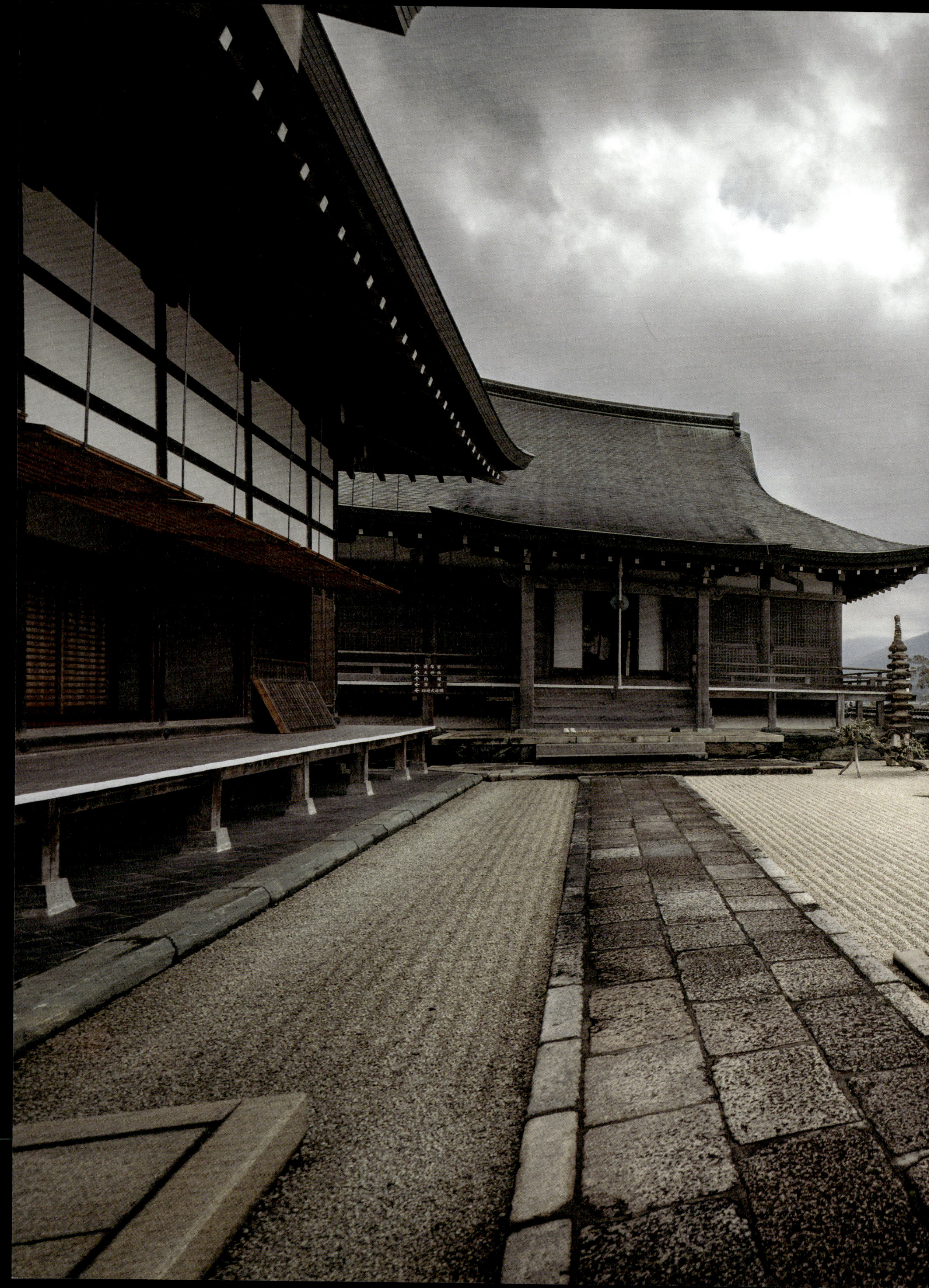

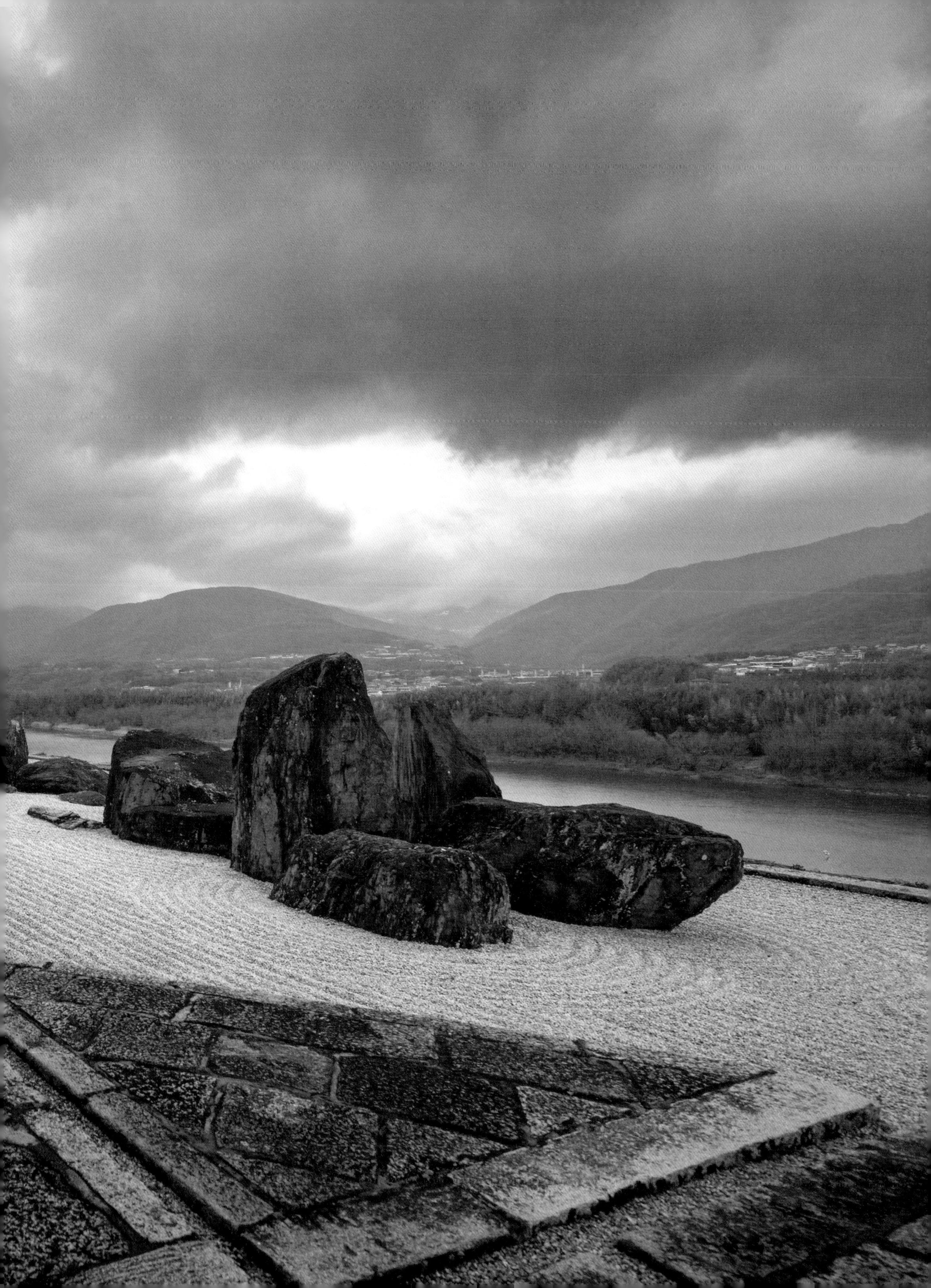

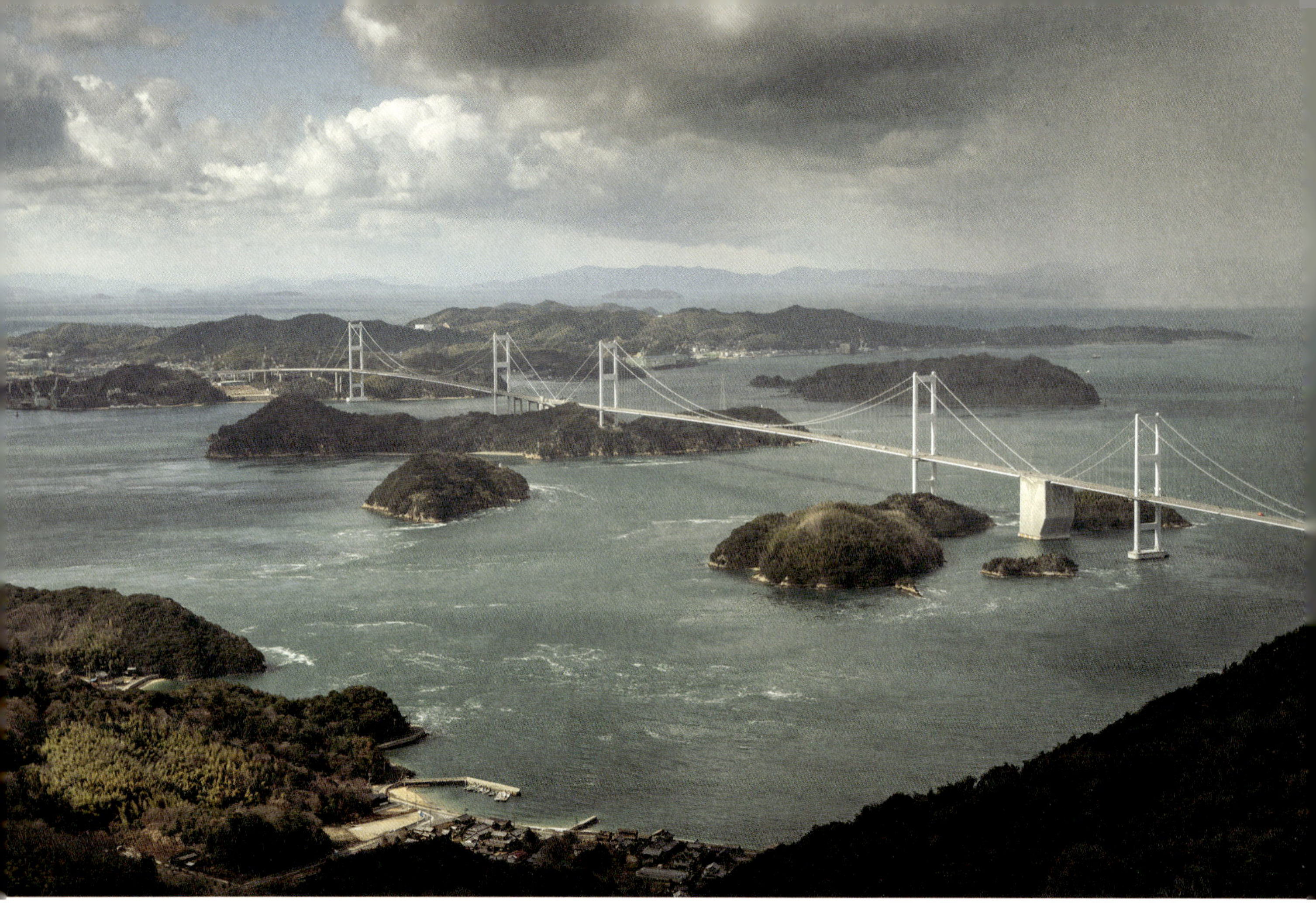

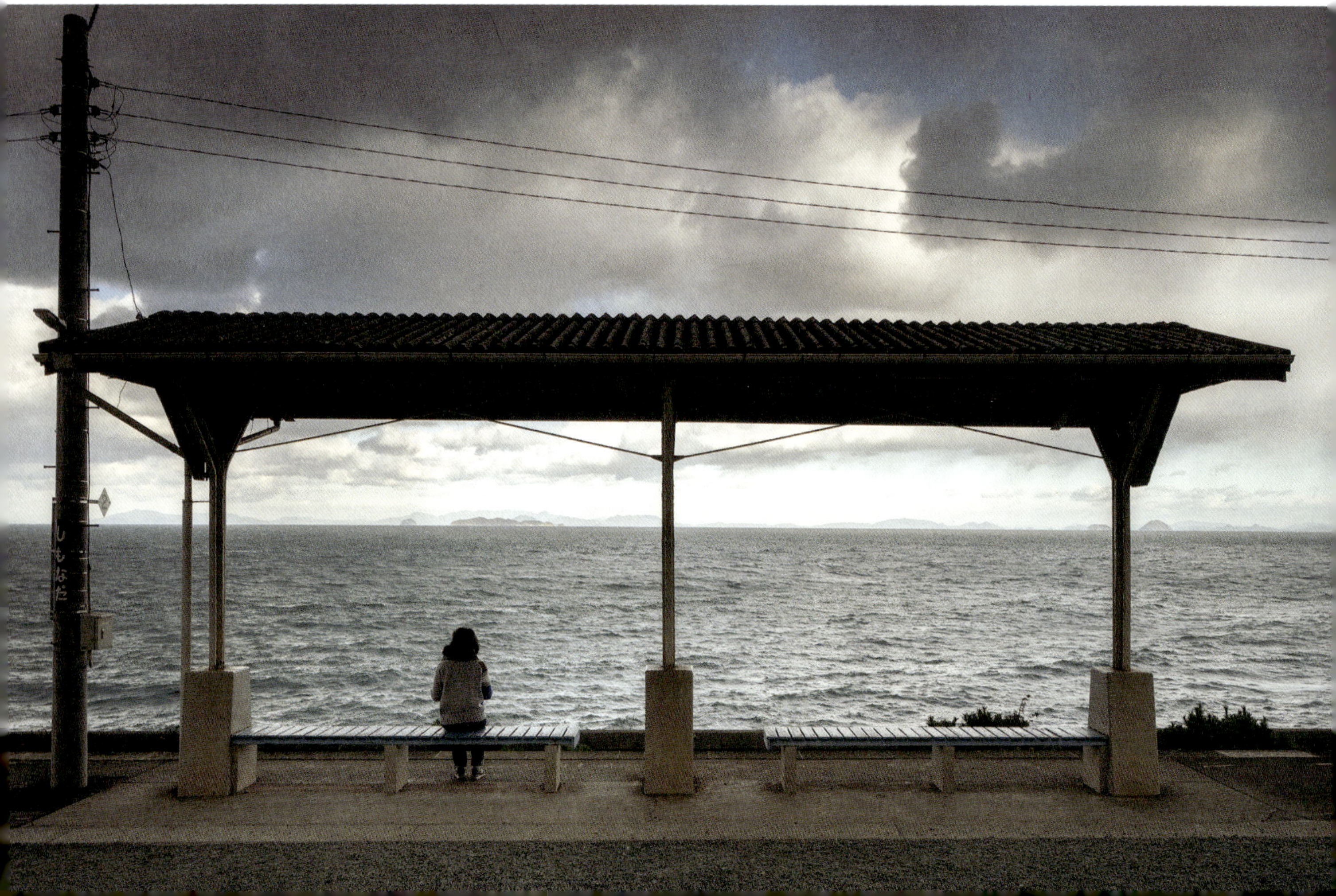

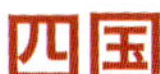

Kurushima Strait Bridge.
Stretching over the swirling waters of the Seto Inland Sea, the Kurushima Strait Bridge is a remarkable feat of engineering and part of the Shimanami Kaidō Highway that connects Honshū to Shikoku. As the world's first triple-span suspension bridge, it blends seamlessly with the island landscape.

Shimonada Station.
Nestled in Ehime Prefecture, Shimonada Station is one of Japan's most picturesque train stations, offering a stunning view of the Seto Sea. Secluded and tranquil, the station exudes a poetic melancholy, with its simple shelter and benches facing the endless horizon.

Matsuyama Castle.
Perched atop a hill, Matsuyama Castle commands a sweeping view of the town below. Its traditional tiled roofs stand in striking contrast to the modern buildings beneath. Built in 1603, this majestic fortress, one of the best-preserved in the country, was once the residence of the powerful Matsudaira clan.

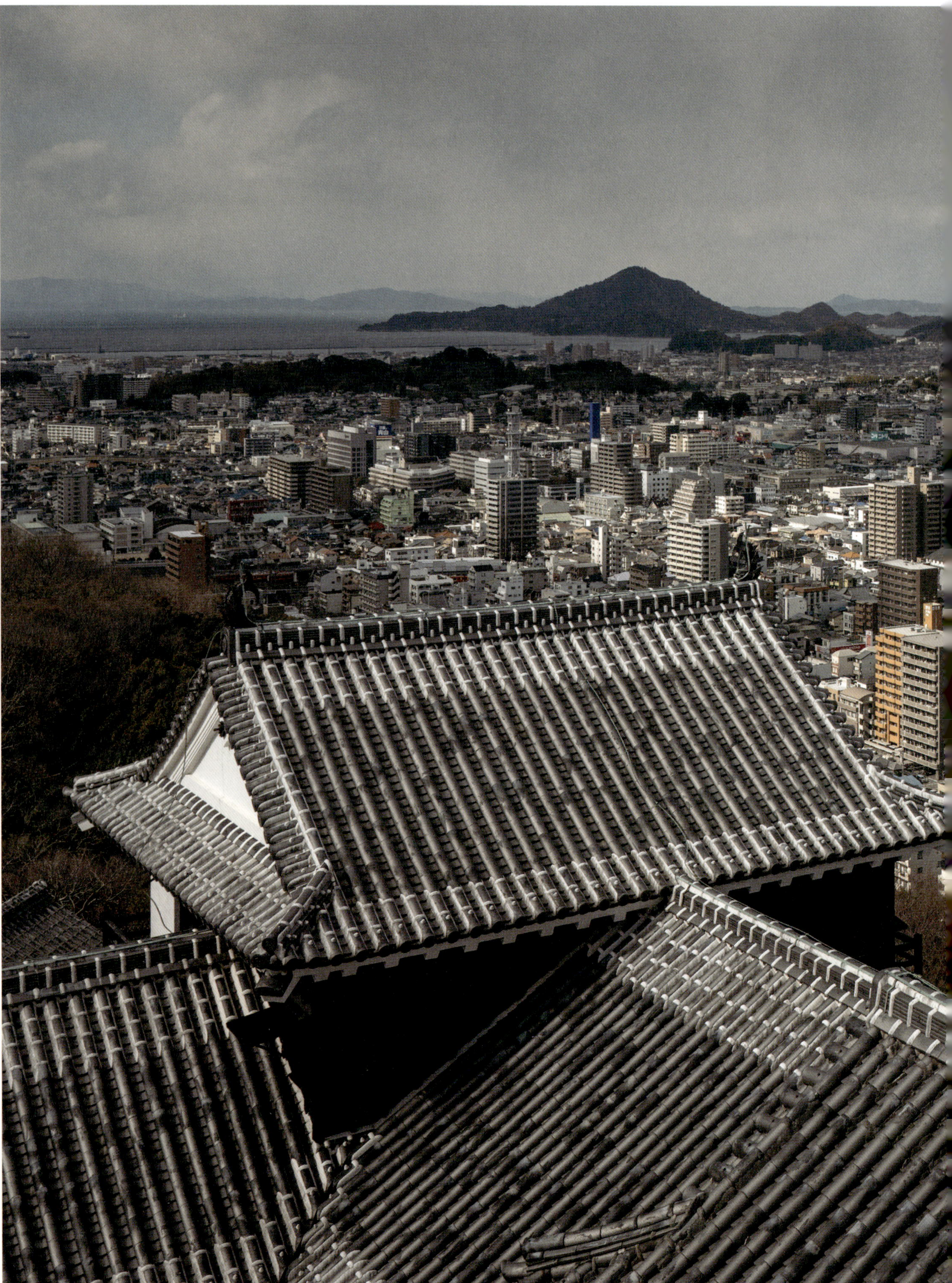

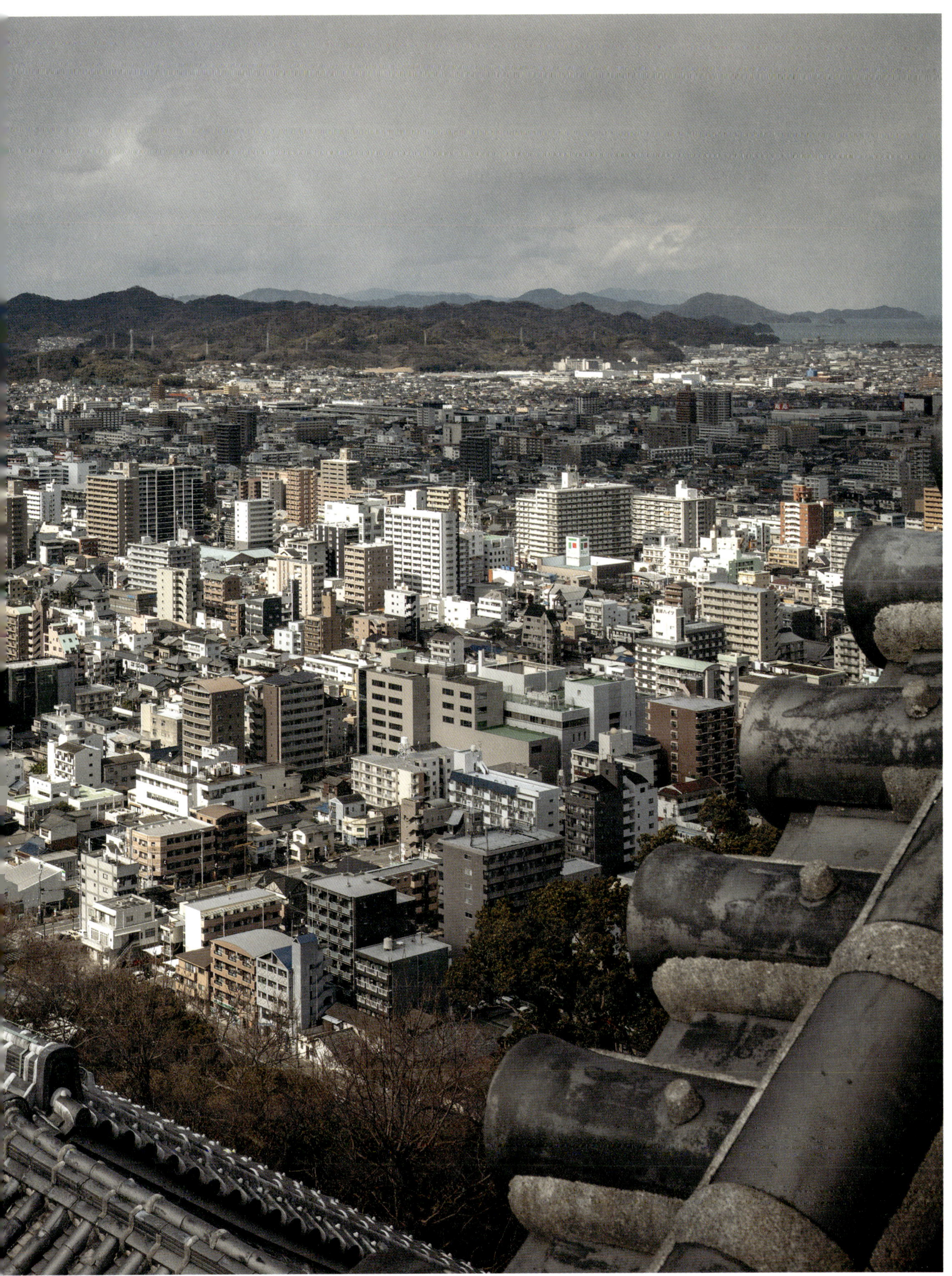

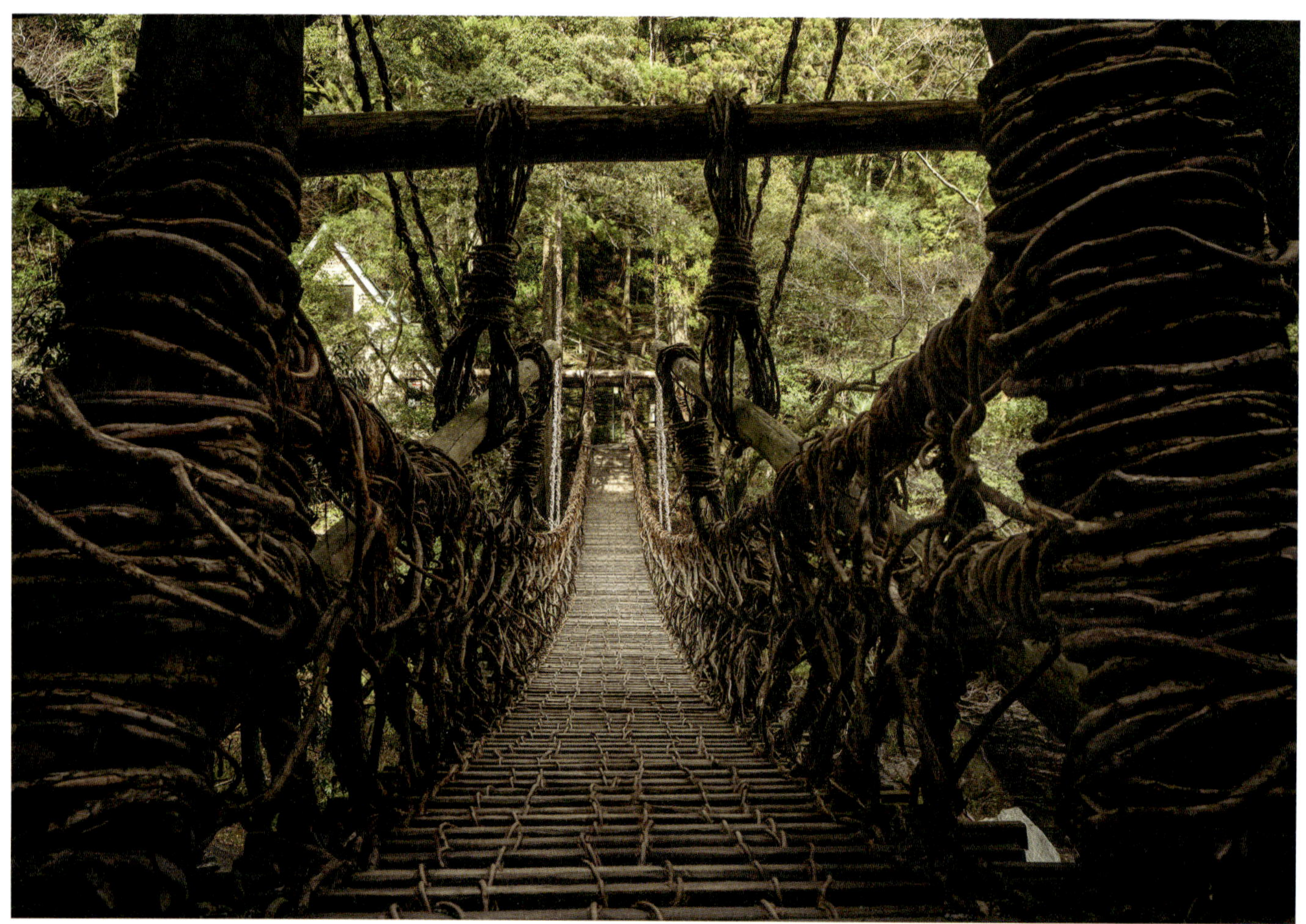

Kazurabashi Bridge.
Suspended high above the Iya Valley, the Kazurabashi Bridge is a stunning marvel handwoven from thick lianas. Nestled in the lush wilderness of Shikoku, this legendary bridge was once used by fleeing samurai.

Pilgrim at Ryozen-ji.
Ryozen-ji, located in Tokushima Prefecture, marks the beginning of the 88-temple pilgrimage of Shikoku, a spiritual journey dedicated to Kūkai, the founder of Shingon Buddhism. As the first temple on this sacred path, it symbolises the start of an inward journey for the pilgrims (*henro*), who don their white robes in search of enlightenment across the 1,200 kilometres of the island.

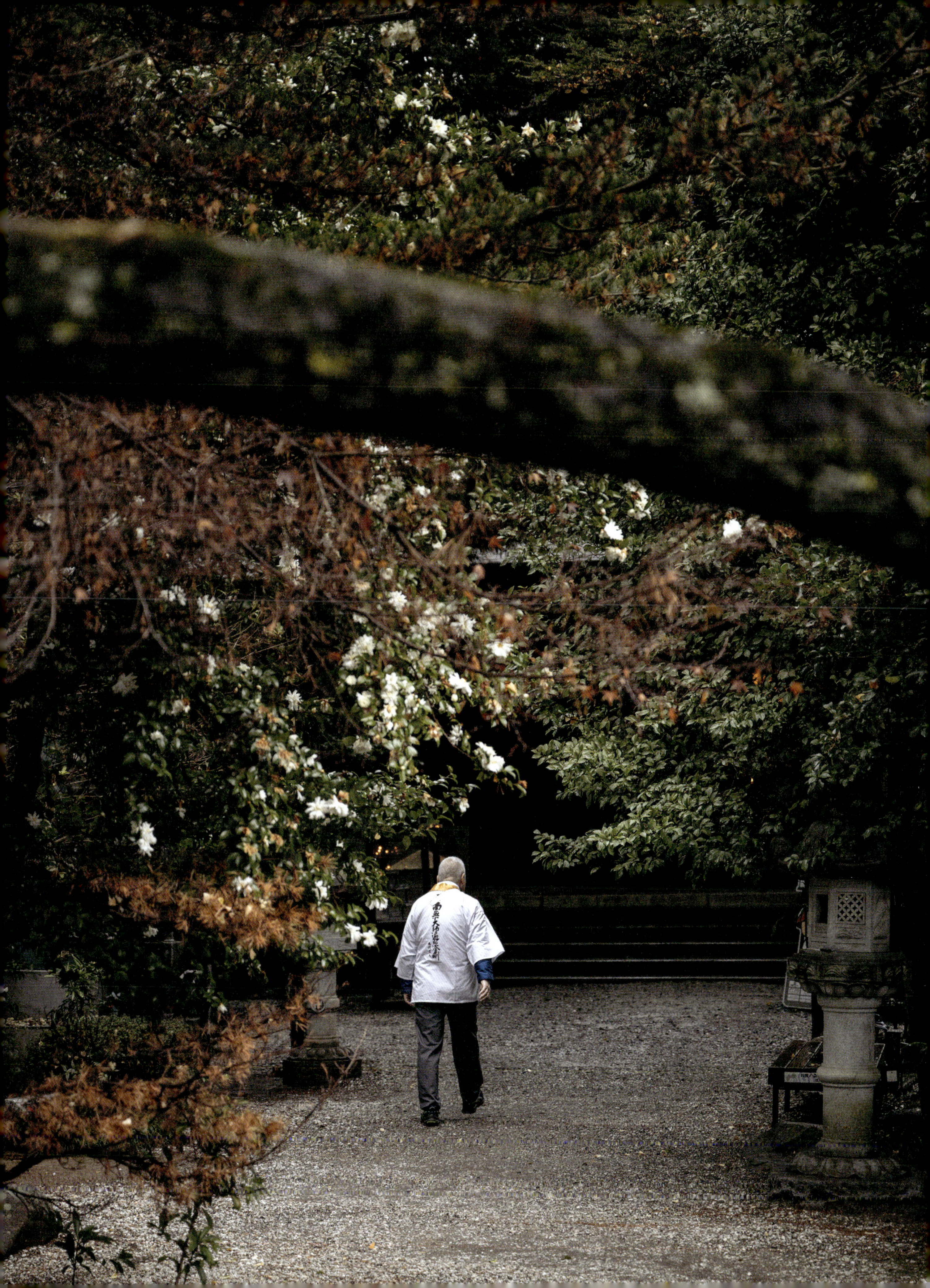

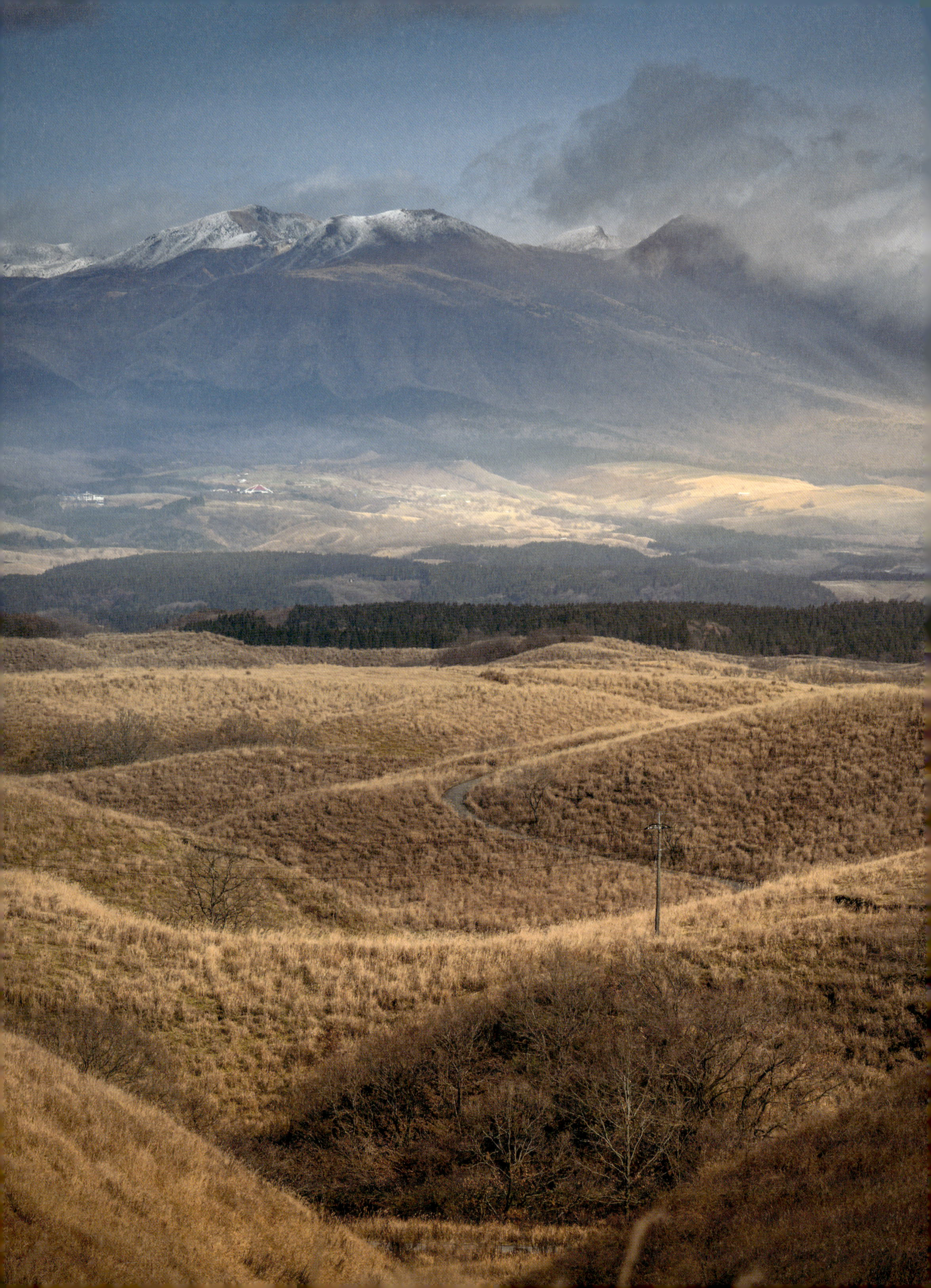

Mount Aso.
At the heart of Kyūshū lies Mount Aso National Park, which is home to one of the world's largest active volcanoes.

九州 / 沖縄
Kyūshū and Okinawa
Japan's Southern Soul

In the south of the Japanese archipelago, where mountains gently fade into the sea and ancient traditions blend with lush landscapes, lie the captivating lands of Kyūshū and Okinawa. Although united by their southern location and mild climate, each of these islands offers a unique experience: Kyūshū, with its active volcanoes, temples, and hot springs, represents a vibrant, living portrait of Japan; while Okinawa, surrounded by the turquoise waters of the East China Sea, provides an island atmosphere steeped in tranquillity and a distinctive cultural heritage.

Area.

Kyūshū. Covering an area of about 37,000 km², Kyūshū is the third-largest island in Japan.

Okinawa. Including the main island and many surrounding islands, Okinawa covers approximately 2,281 km².

Demographics and Population.

Kyūshū has a population of approximately 14.3 million people, while Okinawa has about 1.45 million residents.

Geographical Location.

Kyūshū. Located to the southwest of the main island, Honshū, Kyūshū is surrounded by the Sea of Japan to the west, the East China Sea to the south, and the Pacific Ocean to the east.

Okinawa. An archipelago situated to the south of Kyūshū, Okinawa is the southernmost prefecture of Japan, lying between the Japanese mainland and Taiwan.

Climate and Seasons.

Kyūshū. This region has a humid subtropical climate characterised by hot, humid summers and mild winters. Rainfall is abundant, especially during the rainy season in June and July.

Okinawa. This area features a subtropical climate, with warm temperatures throughout the year. The typhoon season occurs from June to September, bringing heavy rains and strong winds.

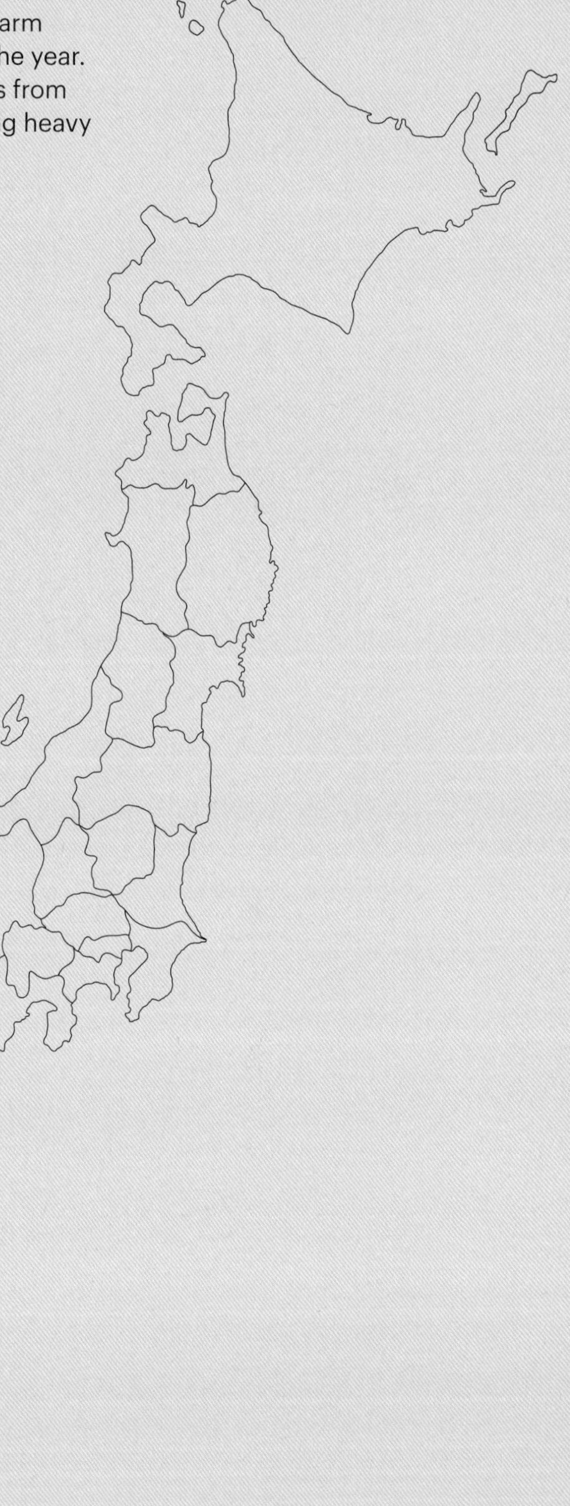

九州 / 沖縄

Kyūshū, Land of Fire and History

Kyūshū, Japan's third-largest island, is shaped by volcanic forces and features stunning landscapes formed by the earth's raw power. Its seven prefectures – Fukuoka, Kumamoto, Kagoshima, Nagasaki, Ōita, Saga, and Miyazaki – are abundant in natural beauty, history, and cultural treasures.

Fukuoka, A Dynamic Gateway

Located in northern Kyūshū, Fukuoka is often regarded as the gateway to the island. Vibrant and modern, this bustling port city serves as a crossroads between Japan and mainland Asia, a role reflected in its rich history and cuisine.

The city is renowned for its *yatai* – small open-air food stalls where visitors can sample signature dishes like *tonkotsu* rāmen (noodle soup with a rich pork broth). The Dazaifu Tenman-gū Shrine, dedicated to the god of knowledge, attracts students and visitors who pray for academic success.

Not far from the city, the ruins of the fortified town of Dazaifu offer a glimpse into the region's historical significance as an administrative and cultural hub during the Heian period.

Kumamoto, The Majestic Black Castle

Kumamoto is dominated by its castle, one of the most impressive in Japan. Although it was damaged in the 2016 earthquake, the castle still exudes a sense of grandeur, standing as a symbol of the region's resilience.

Not far from the city, Mount Aso, Japan's largest active volcano, showcases a dramatic, almost lunar landscape, offering breathtaking panoramas from its smoking crater. The expansive grassy plains surrounding the volcano make it a favoured destination for hiking and horseback riding.

Kagoshima, The Sakurajima Volcano

To the south of Kyūshū, Kagoshima is a prefecture where nature reigns supreme. The city is dominated by Mount Sakurajima, an active volcano that regularly sends ash plumes into the sky. Accessible by ferry, the volcanic island features hiking trails and natural hot springs, all of which provide breathtaking sea views.

Kagoshima is also the gateway to Yakushima, a UNESCO World Heritage Site. Here, ancient forests are home to thousand-year-old cedar trees and an extraordinary range of biodiversity. The island's mystical atmosphere is said to have inspired the renowned Studio Ghibli film *Princess Mononoke*.

Nagasaki, Memory and Tolerance

As a historic port city, Nagasaki has long served as Japan's primary point of contact with the West. Having welcomed Portuguese missionaries and Dutch merchants, among others, this city, open to the world, boasts a unique cultural heritage.

Peace Park and the Atomic Bomb Museum serve as solemn reminders of the tragic events of 1945, while also symbolising the city's resilience and hope. Glover Garden, a collection of colonial-era residences perched on a hill, offers stunning views of the harbour and stands as a testament to the era of international trade.

Ōita, Beppu Hot Springs

Ōita is a prefecture renowned for its *onsen*, with Beppu as its undisputed hot spring capital. This spa town is famous for its "Hell Tour", a series of hot springs showcasing spectacular colours and features, from bright blue bubbling pools to pools of volcanic mud steaming in the air.

Further north, the town of Yufuin is a renowned hot spring destination, offering a more intimate atmosphere with *ryokan* (traditional inns) set in a charming natural setting.

Miyazaki, Beaches and Mythology

Miyazaki, located on the east coast, is a prefecture where Japan's mythological history feels vibrant. The *Udo-jingū* shrine, situated in a cave overlooking the ocean, is dedicated to *Yamasachihiko*, an important figure in Japanese mythology.

The region is also renowned for its beaches, including Nichinan, perfect for surfing, and Florante Miyazaki Park, where tropical landscapes evoke a Southern atmosphere.

Saga, A Land of Handcrafted Treasures

Although frequently overlooked, Saga is a prefecture abundant in traditional crafts. The town of Arita is the birthplace of Japanese porcelain, celebrated worldwide for its delicate patterns and exceptional quality.

Karatsu, known for its seaside castle and the *Karatsu Kunchi Festival*, offers a glimpse into local traditions, while the hot springs at Takeo Onsen provide a peaceful retreat in a historic setting.

Okinawa, Pearls of the Pacific

Further south, Okinawa feels like a world of its own. This archipelago, consisting of over 150 islands, is surrounded by the turquoise waters of the East China Sea and exudes a unique atmosphere, rich in Ryūkyū culture.

The Main Island, Naha and Shuri

The city of Naha, Okinawa's capital, serves as the gateway to exploring this captivating archipelago. Once the political and cultural heart of the Ryūkyū Kingdom, Shuri Castle stands as a symbol of the region's rich heritage.

The Makishi Market, located in the heart of Naha, offers a genuine taste of local gastronomy. It features distinctive products such as *goya* (bitter melon) and vibrant coral reef fish.

Paradise Islands

The Okinawa Islands are a true paradise for nature and beach lovers. Ishigaki, with its crystal-clear waters and vibrant coral reefs, is ideal for diving and snorkelling. Kabira Bay, renowned for its emerald waters, is one of the most photographed spots in the archipelago.

Miyako Island offers a serene escape with its powdery white sandy beaches and the Ikema Bridge linking the surrounding islands. Additionally, Zamami Island, accessible by ferry from Naha, is known for its tranquil waters, where whales can be spotted during winter.

Ryūkyū Culture and Traditions

Once a territory of the Ryūkyū Kingdom, an independent state that was a vassal of China's Qing dynasty from the 14th to the 19th century, Okinawa remains a unique cultural stronghold. The island is renowned for its music, cuisine, and dances, which all stand apart from the rest of Japan. The *sanshin*, a traditional three-stringed instrument, accompanies folk songs at local festivals. Dishes such as Okinawa *soba* and pork flavoured with *shikuwasa* (a local citrus fruit) reflect a fusion of Japanese and Chinese influences due to centuries of maritime trade.

九州 / 沖縄

Best Times to Visit

Kyūshū.
Spring (March to May) and autumn (September to November) offer comfortable temperatures and beautiful landscapes.

Okinawa.
The months from April to June and September to November are perfect for avoiding the intense summer heat and typhoon season.

Top 5 Places to Visit

1. Kumamoto Castle.
One of Japan's most impressive castles, located in Kumamoto.

2. Beppu Onsen.
A renowned spa town famous for its numerous hot springs and sand baths.

3. Yakushima.
A UNESCO World Heritage island, famed for its ancient forests and thousand-year-old cedars.

4. Okinawa Churaumi Aquarium.
One of the world's largest aquariums, showcasing the region's rich marine life.

5. Shuri Castle.
The former royal residence of the Ryūkyū Kingdom, located in Naha, Okinawa.

九州 / 沖縄

Gastronomy

Kyūshū and the Okinawa Archipelago are rich in culinary specialities, influenced by their warm climate, proximity to the sea, and historical exchanges with China and Southeast Asia. Below is a list of Kyūshū and Okinawa specialities, sorted by city, along with detailed descriptions of each dish.

福岡
Fukuoka

[博多ラーメン]
Hakata Rāmen
A *tonkotsu* (pork bone) rāmen with a creamy, rich broth, served with thin, firm noodles. It is typically topped with *chāshū* (braised pork), green onions, and pickled ginger.

[もつ鍋]
Motsunabe
A hot pot dish made from beef or pork offal, simmered with cabbage, leeks, and chilies in a soy or miso broth. This dish is popular in winter.

[明太子]
Mentaiko
Spicy cod roe marinated in chilli and salt. It is often enjoyed on its own, with rice, or as a topping for dishes like pasta.

[鉄鍋餃子]
Tetsunabe Gyoza
Pan-fried gyoza served directly in a cast iron pan, giving them a crispy, savoury texture.

北九州
Kitakyūshū

[焼きカレー] Yaki Curry
A Japanese curry, gratinated in the oven with cheese, typical of the Mojikō district.

[瓦そば]
Kawara Soba
Soba noodles served on a hot tile (*kawara*), accompanied by beef, eggs, and a slightly sweet soy sauce.

長崎
Nagasaki

[ちゃんぽん]
Champon
A noodle dish in a broth made from pork and seafood, topped with vegetables, meat, and shrimp. This dish is influenced by Chinese cuisine.

[皿うどん]
Sara Udon
Crispy noodles topped with a thick stew made from vegetables, seafood, and meat.

[カステラ]
Kasutera
A fluffy, slightly sweet cake of Portuguese origin, introduced to Nagasaki in the 16th century.

[卓袱料理]
Shippoku Ryōri
A banquet-style meal that blends Chinese, Japanese, and European influences, with various dishes served at once, including fish, duck, and stewed vegetables.

熊本
Kumamoto

[熊本ラーメン]
Kumamoto Rāmen
A *tonkotsu rāmen* similar to Hakata's, albeit with a milder taste, often enhanced with fried garlic and black garlic oil.

[馬刺し]
Basashi – Horse Sashimi
Raw horse meat, thinly sliced and served with ginger, garlic, and soy sauce.

[太平燕]
Taipien
A Chinese-origin glass noodle soup (vermicelli), with vegetables, shrimp, and sometimes hard-boiled eggs.

大分
Ōita

[とり天] Toriten
Tempura-style fried chicken pieces, often served with *ponzu* sauce.

[だんご汁] Dangojiru
A thick soup with homemade dumplings, root vegetables, and *miso*.

[豊後牛] Bungo Gyu
Wagyū beef reared in Ōita, renowned for its tenderness and umami flavour.

宮崎
Miyazaki

[宮崎地鶏] Miyazaki Jidori
Local chicken grilled over charcoal, giving it a unique smoky flavour.

[チキン南蛮]
Chicken Nanban
Fried chicken coated in a vinegar-based sauce and topped with tartar sauce.

[冷や汁] Hiyajiru
A cold miso soup with sesame, cucumber, and grilled fish, poured over hot rice.

鹿児島
Kagoshima

[黒豚とんかつ]
Kurobuta Tonkatsu
A breaded pork cutlet made with *kurobuta* (black pork from Kagoshima), known for its tender and juicy meat.

[鶏刺し]
Torisashi
Raw chicken served as *sashimi*, accompanied by ginger and soy sauce.

[さつま揚げ]
Satsuma-age
A deep-fried fish cake, which is often served alongside noodles or rice.

[焼酎]
Shōchū de Kagoshima
A spirit made from sweet potatoes, typical of Kagoshima, that can either be drunk hot or cold.

那覇
Naha

[ゴーヤーチャンプルー]
Gōyā Champurū
A stir-fry dish made with gōyā (bitter melon), tofu, eggs, and pork or Spam.

[ラフテー]
Rafute
Pork braised in soy sauce, sugar, and *awamori* (local alcohol).

[ソーキそば]
Sōki Soba
Thick noodles served in a clear broth made from pork and bonito, topped with simmered pork spare ribs.

[タコライス]
Taco Rice
A dish inspired by Mexican tacos, with seasoned beef served on rice, topped with lettuce, cheese, and tomato sauce.

[紅芋タルト]
Beni Imo Tart
A tart made with *beni imo* (purple sweet potato), a hallmark of Okinawa.

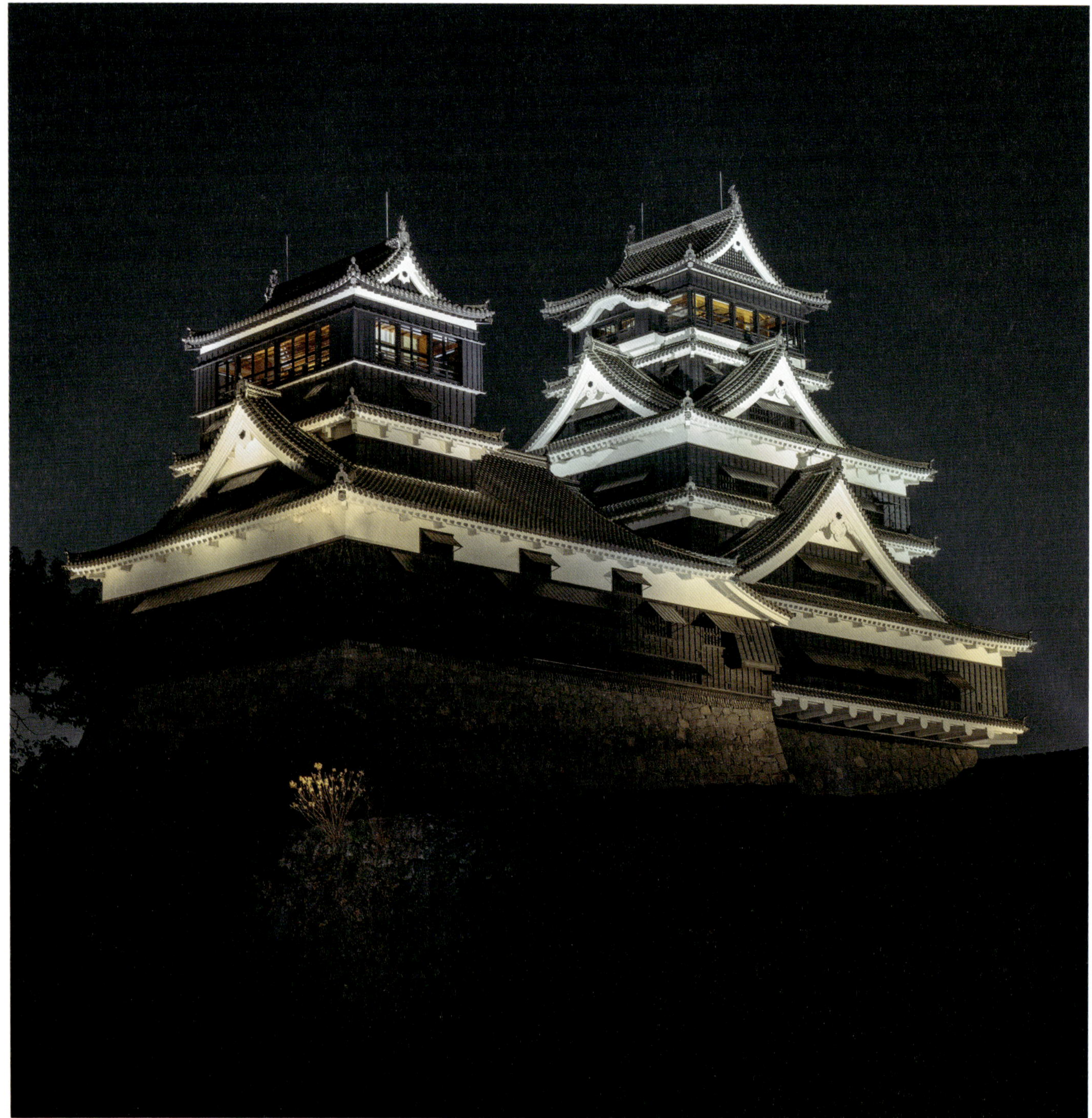

Kumamoto Castle.
Bathed in light at night, Kumamoto Castle stands as one of Japan's most magnificent and historic structures. Built in 1607 by the renowned warrior Kato Kiyomasa, it once served as a formidable fortress and a symbol of feudal power. Although it was set ablaze during the Satsuma Rebellion in 1877 and severely damaged by the 2016 earthquake, the castle has been meticulously restored.

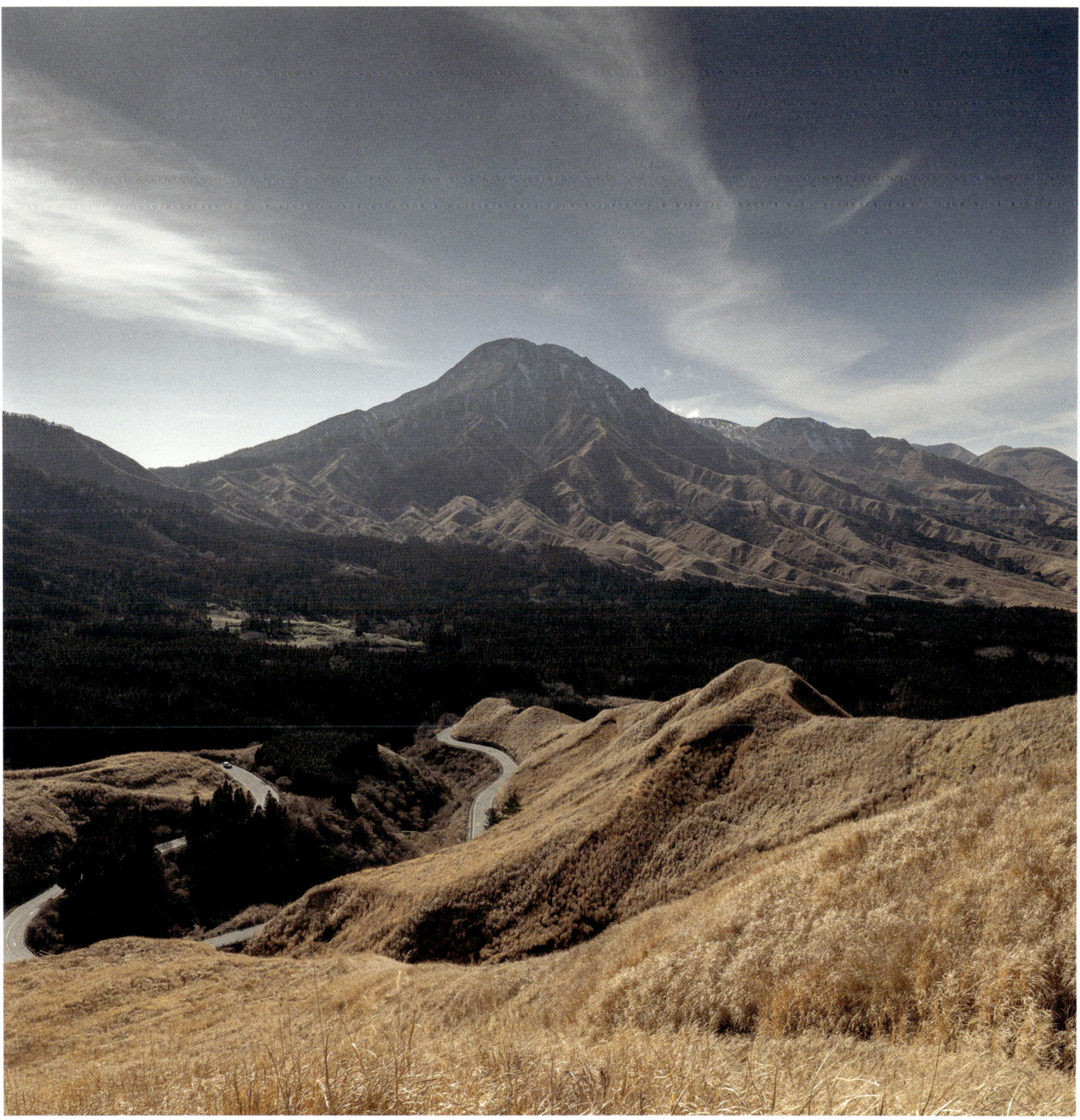

Mount Aso.
Mount Aso is one of Japan's most active and awe-inspiring volcanoes. Its expansive landscape, with rolling ridges and golden plains, stands in striking contrast to the dark forests that embrace the valley below. The towering summit, commanding the horizon, offers a breathtaking display of nature's raw power and beauty.

Einoo Tsurugi Shrine.
Rising from the tranquil waters, the Einoo Tsurugi Shrine has captivated visitors since its establishment in 713. Its sacred *torii* gate, facing the horizon, appears to float with the ebb and flow of the Yatsushiro Sea's tides, guarded by two elegant stone lanterns. As dusk falls, the golden light of the setting sun enhances the spiritual atmosphere, inviting deep contemplation and inner peace. >

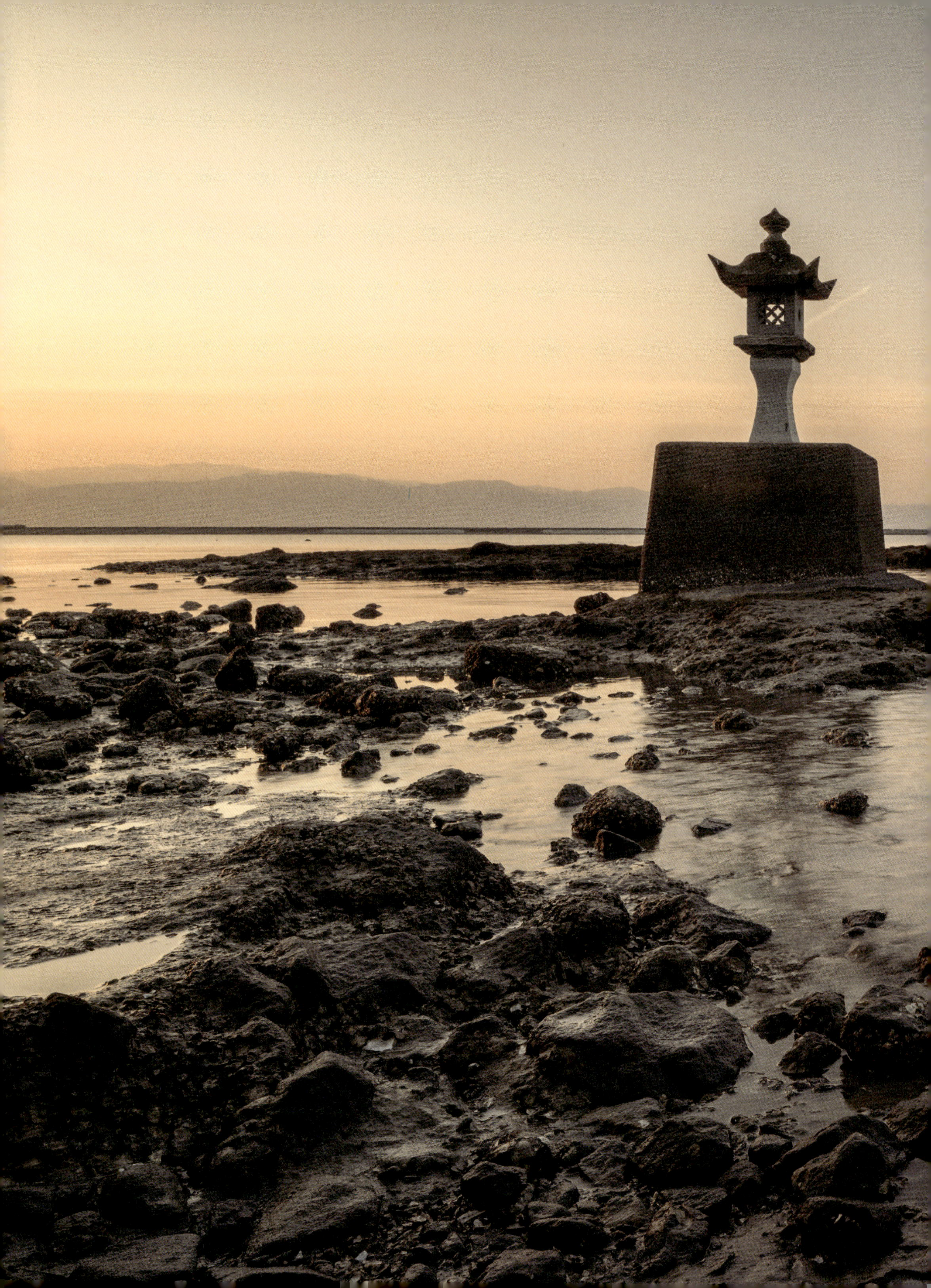

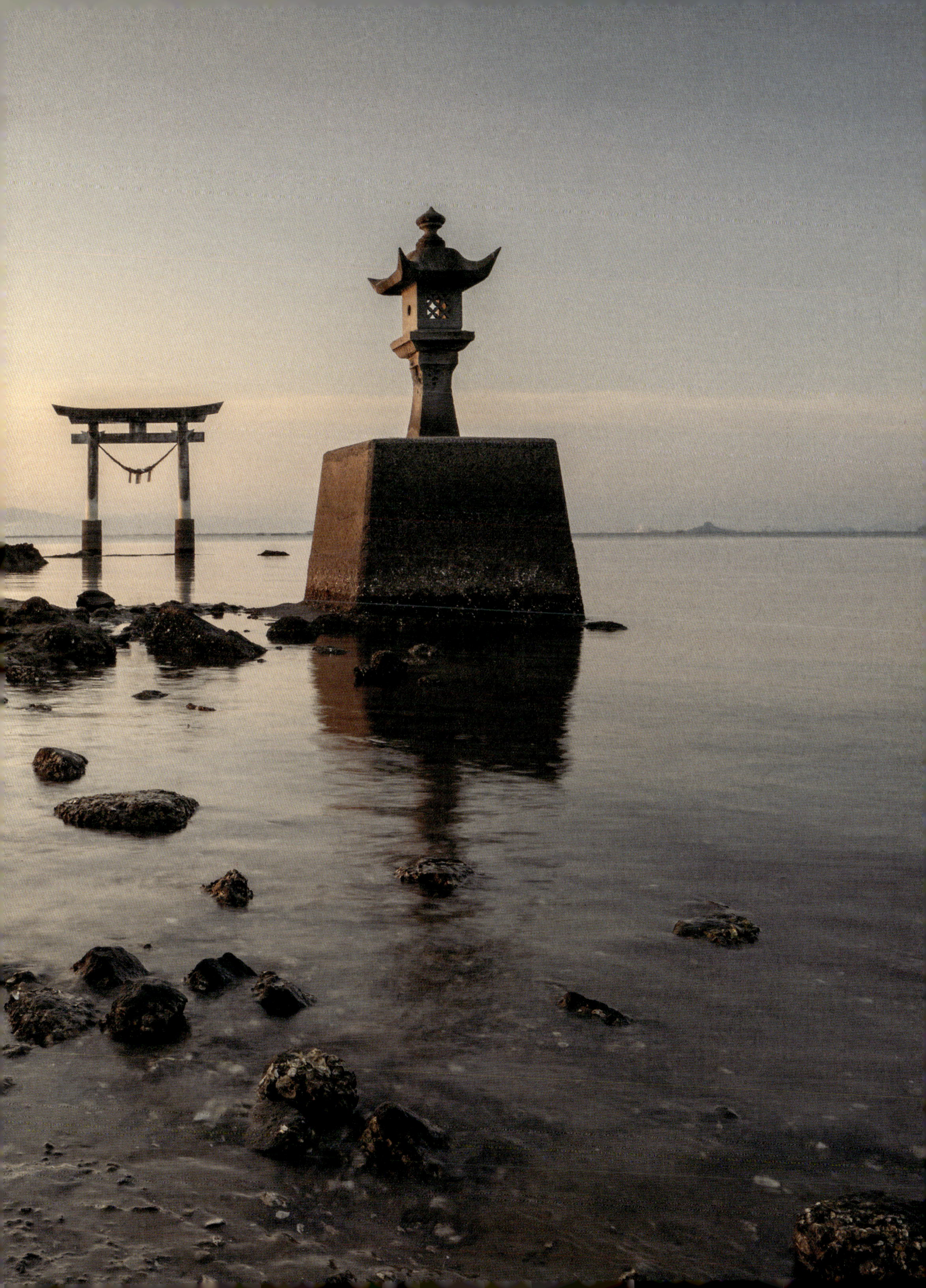

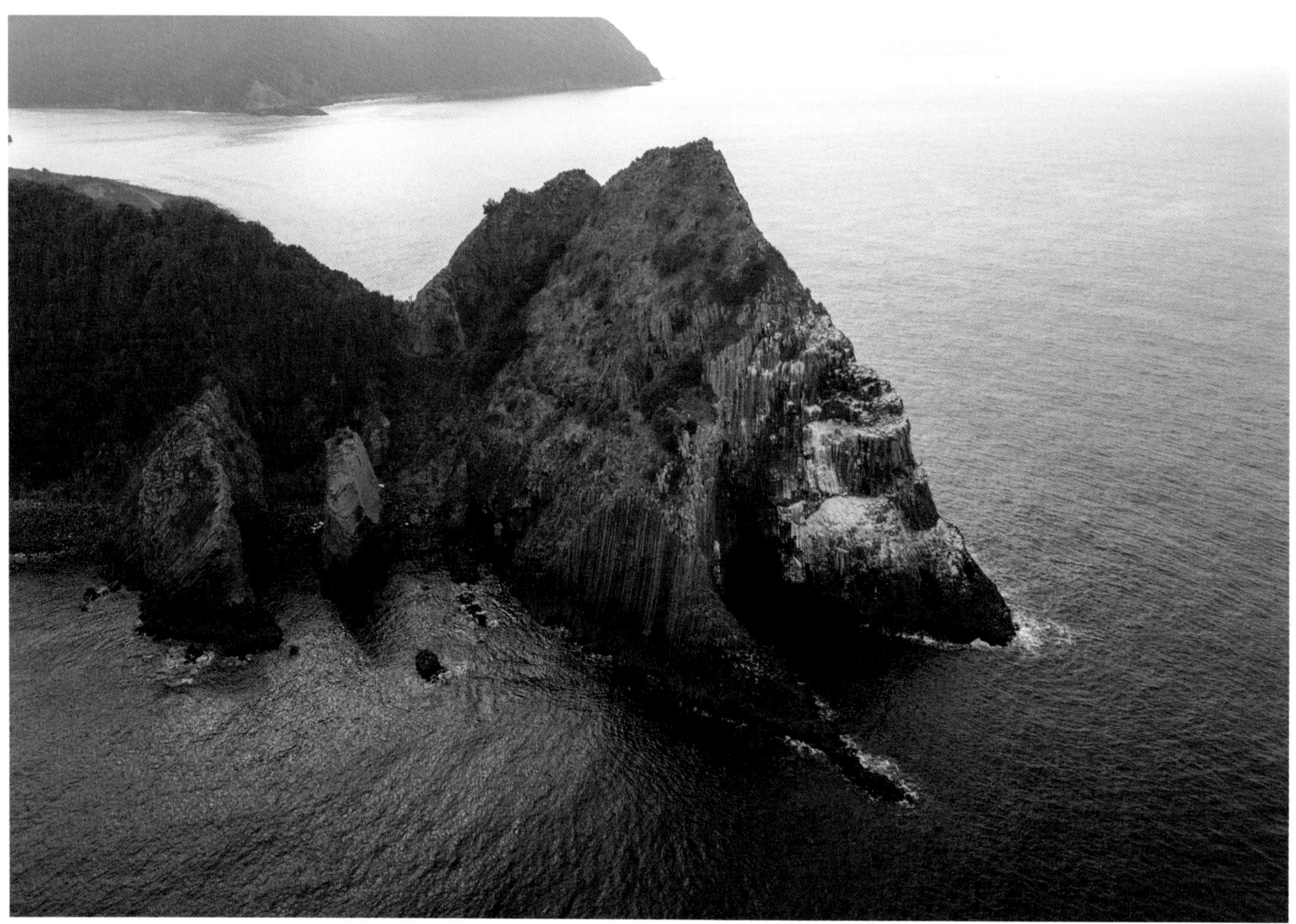

Keya no Oto.
Keya no Oto, a natural masterpiece on the Fukuoka coast, is an awe-inspiring rock formation shaped over centuries by the relentless forces of wind and sea. Towering basalt cliffs, adorned with vertical columns, shelter a vast sea cave that can be explored by boat.

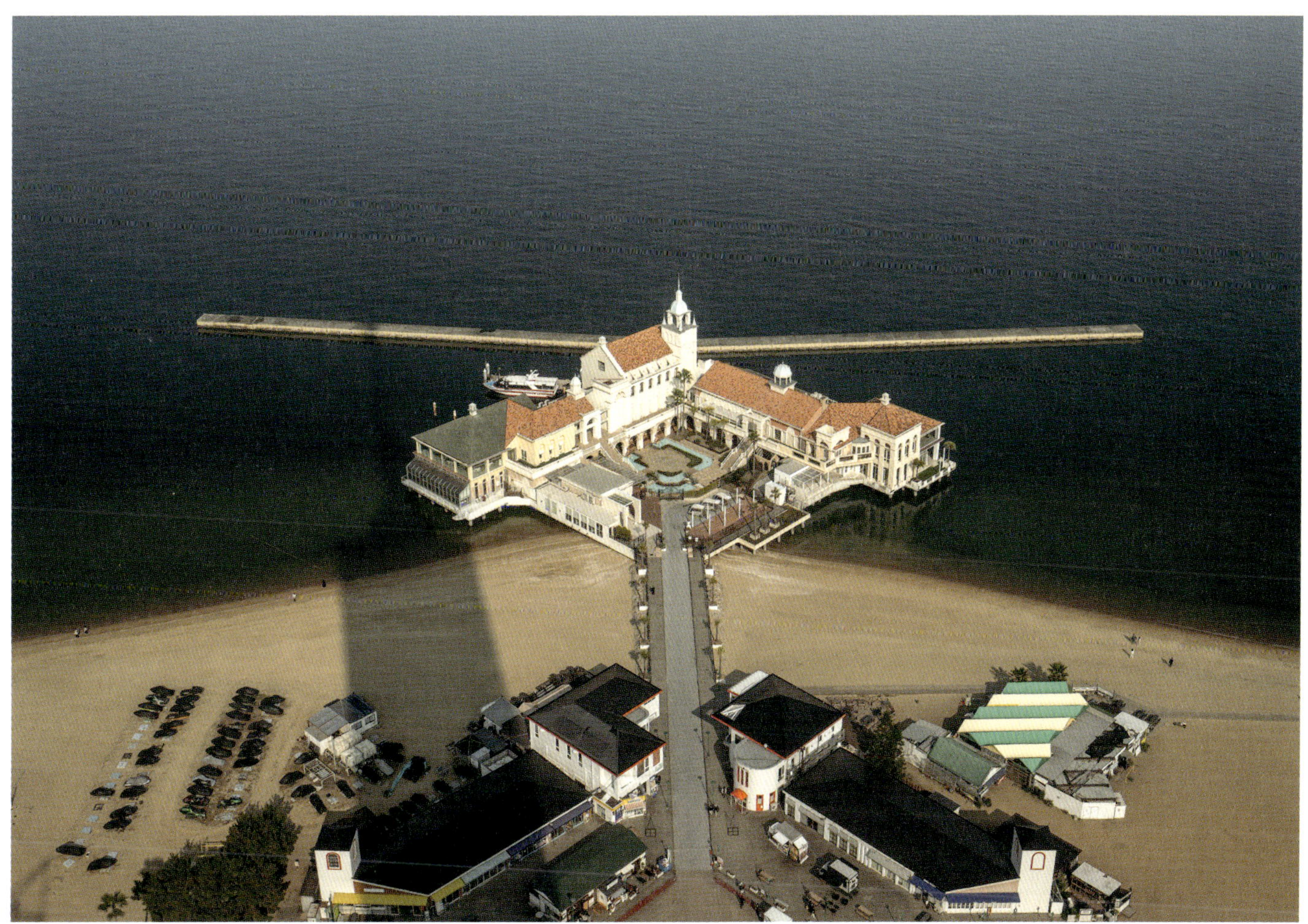

Marizon.
Nestled along Momochi Beach in Fukuoka, Marizon is a sophisticated complex that seems to float gracefully on the tranquil waters of the bay. Its Mediterranean-inspired architecture, featuring charming, red-tiled roofs and elegant arcades, makes it a favoured destination for weddings and seaside retreats.

Futamigaura Shrine Torii.
Rising from the waves against a backdrop of a golden beach, the Futamigaura Shrine *Torii* serves as a striking gateway between the sky and the sea.

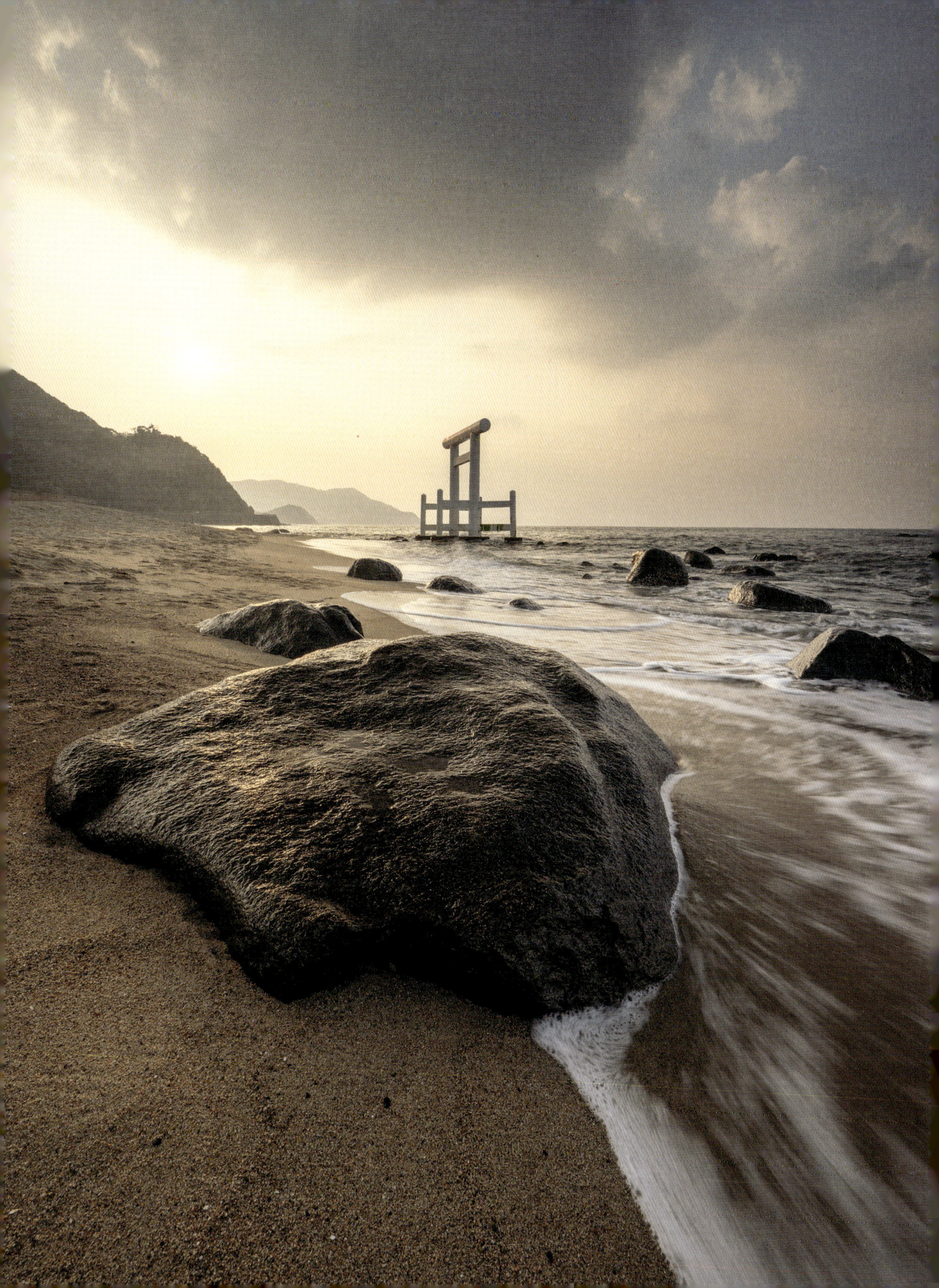

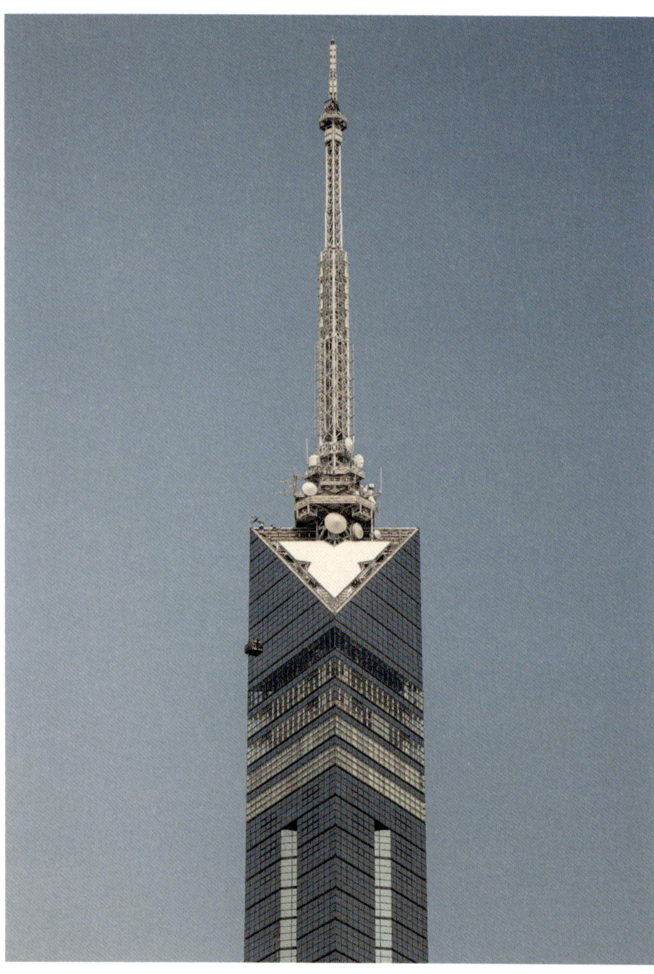

Fukuoka Tower.
Sleek and futuristic, it commands the skyline with its impressive 234-metres glass and steel structure. As Japan's tallest coastal tower, it offers an observation platform with sweeping panoramic views of the city and the serene Hakata Bay.

View of Fukuoka.
As night descends, Fukuoka awakens, unveiling a dazzling skyline illuminated by lights. Dominated by the shimmering Fukuoka Tower, the city extends towards the sea, intersected by vibrant corridors of light.

Wakato Bridge.
Bathed in a red glow, Wakato Bridge spans the waters between the Wakamatsu and Tobata districts. It perfectly embodies the dynamic energy of Kitakyushu.

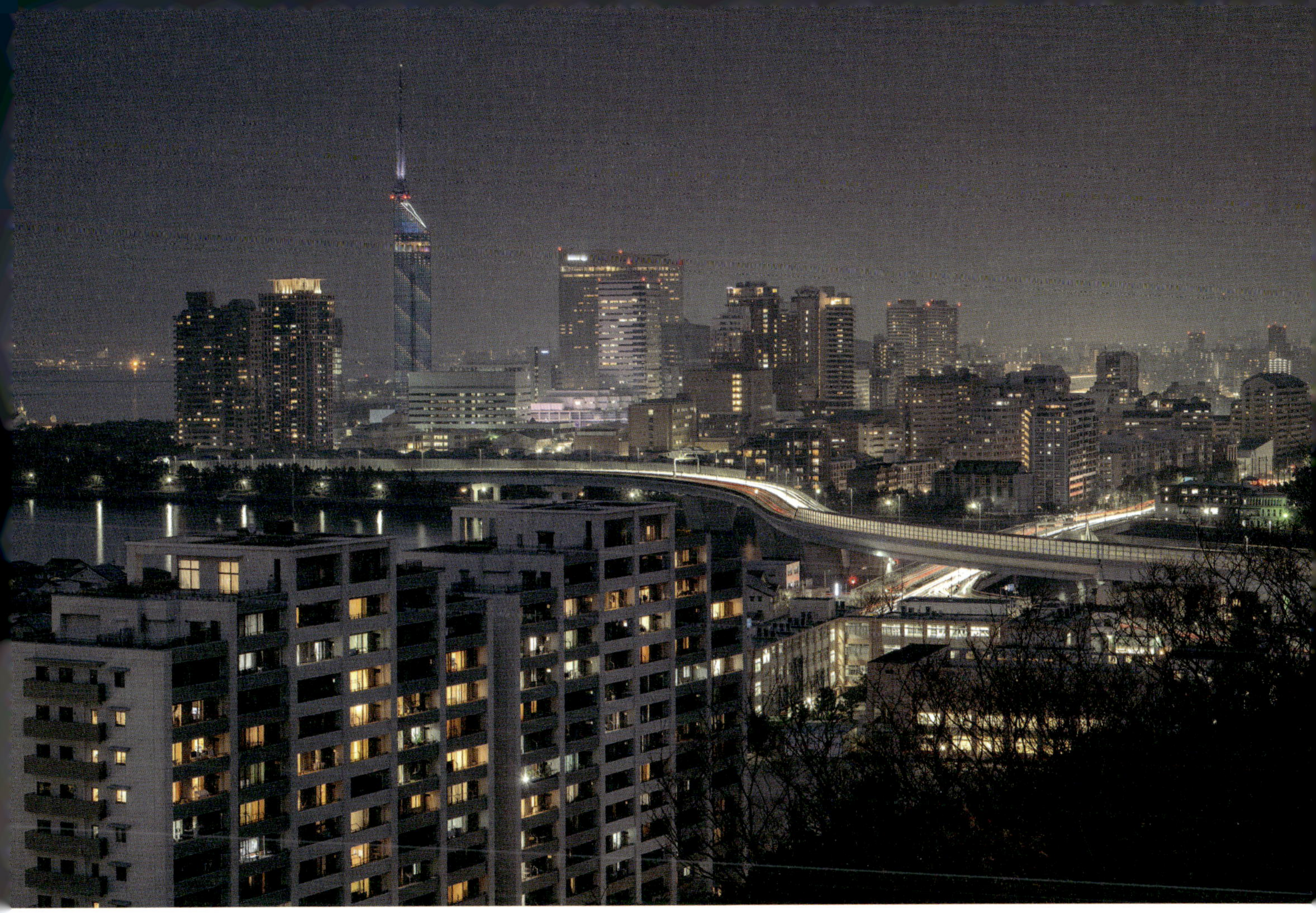

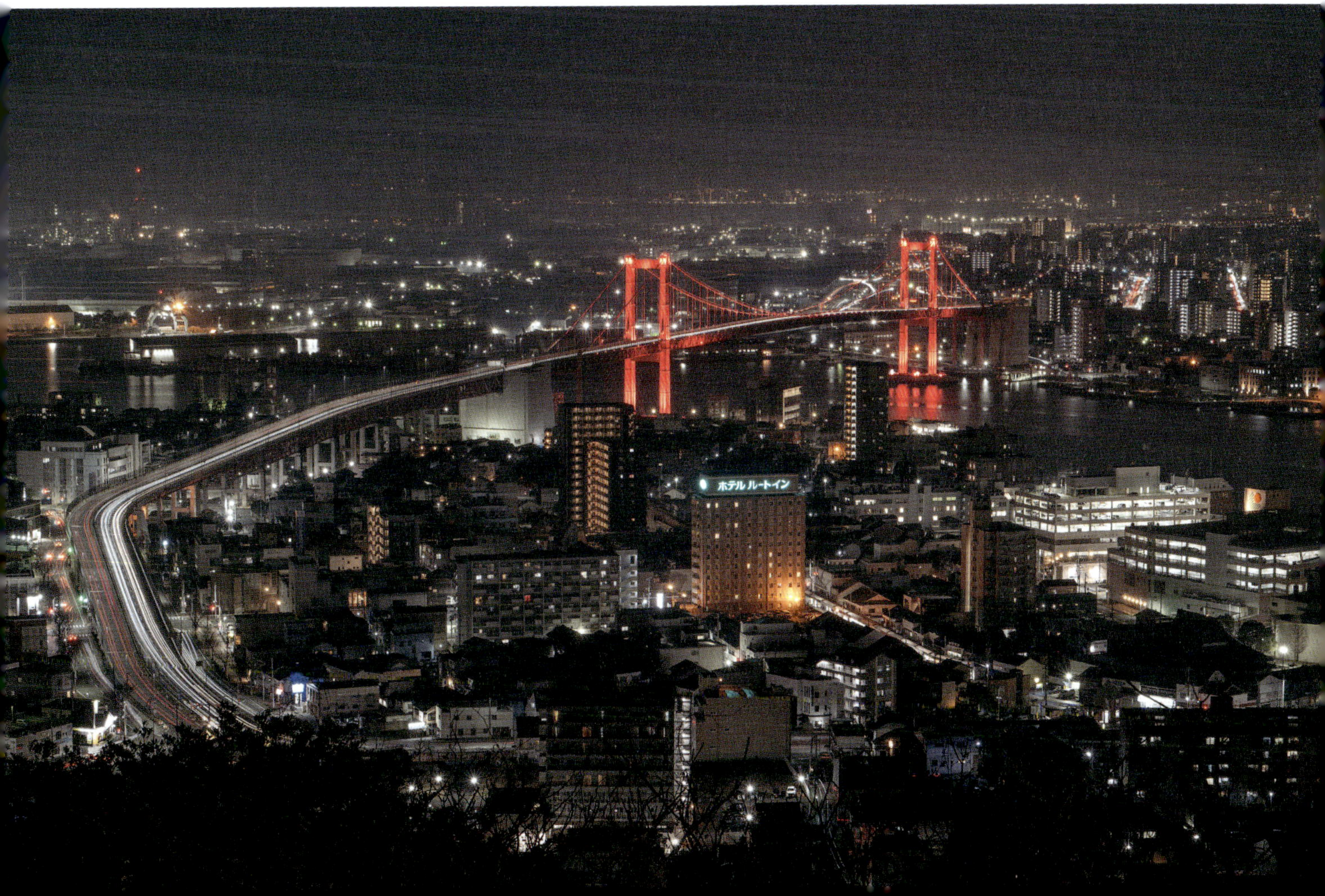

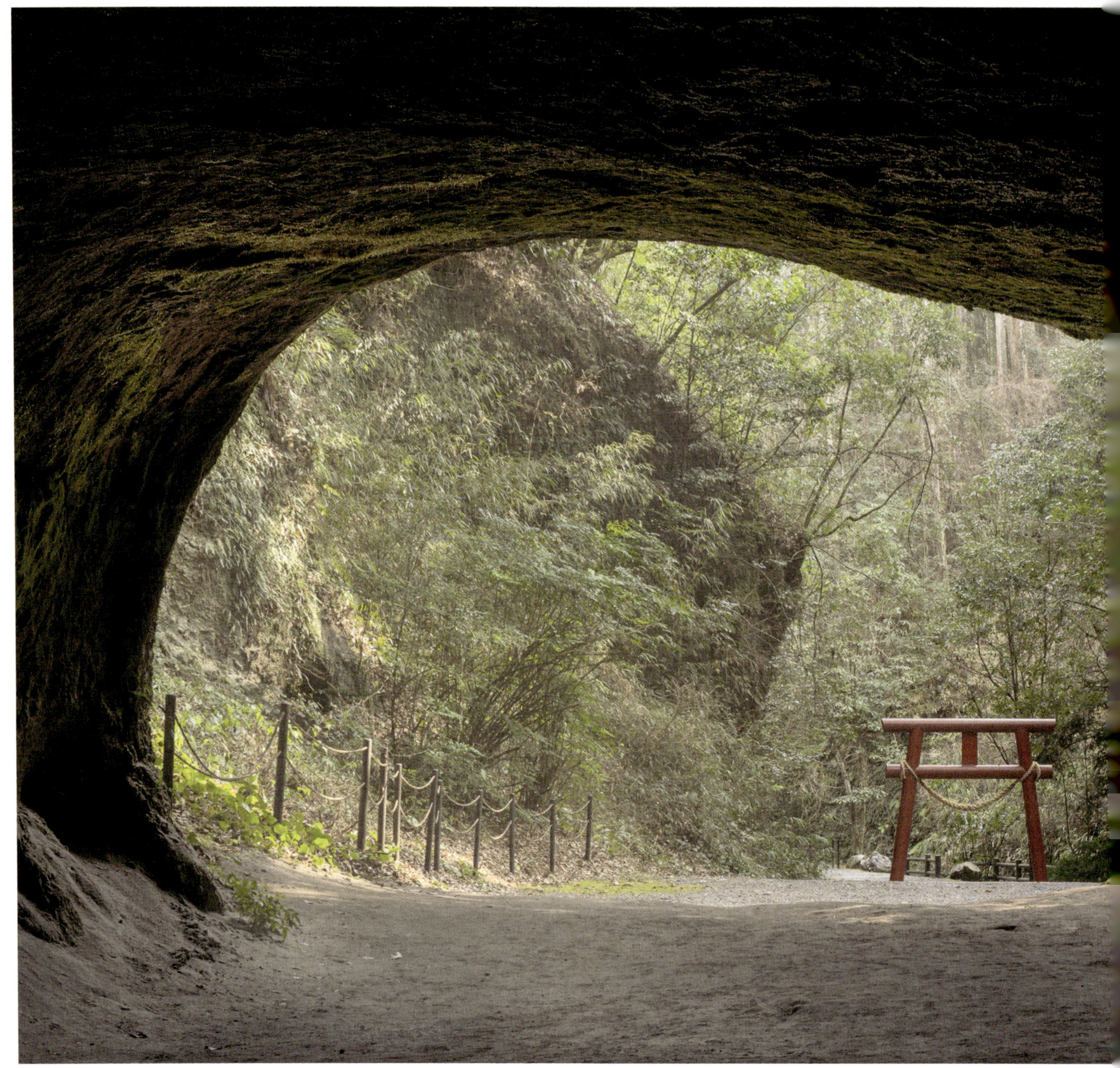

Mizonokuchi Caves.
Hidden within the heart of a lush forest, the Mizonokuchi Caves open to a serene sanctuary. A vibrant red *torii* marks the threshold between the earthly realm and the sacred.

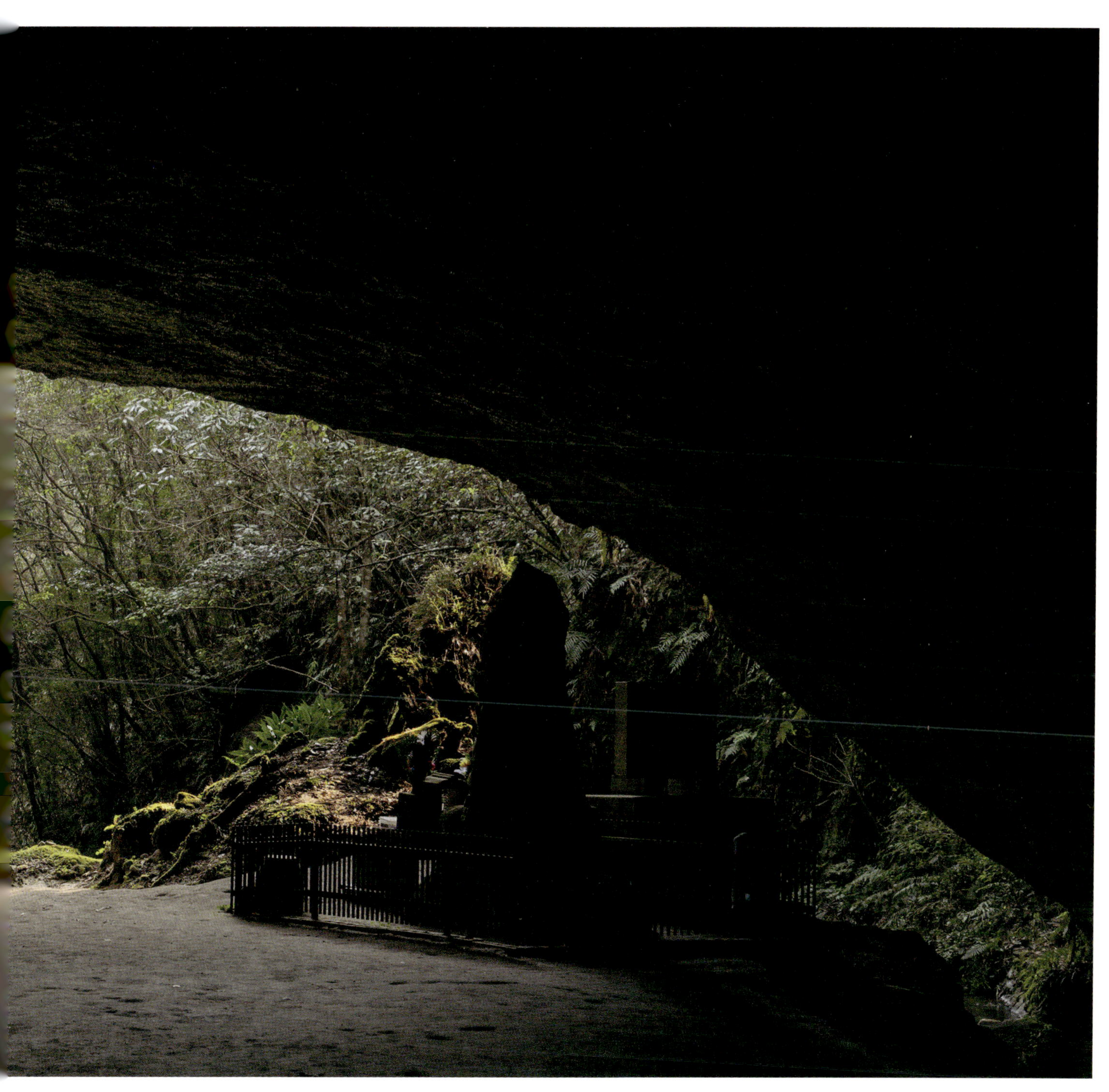

Fishermen.
In the southern part of Kyūshū, this aerial view captures the graceful choreography of Japanese fishermen deploying their nets in the turquoise waters. The boats, surrounded by a network of buoys and nets, testify to traditional fishing techniques passed down through generations.

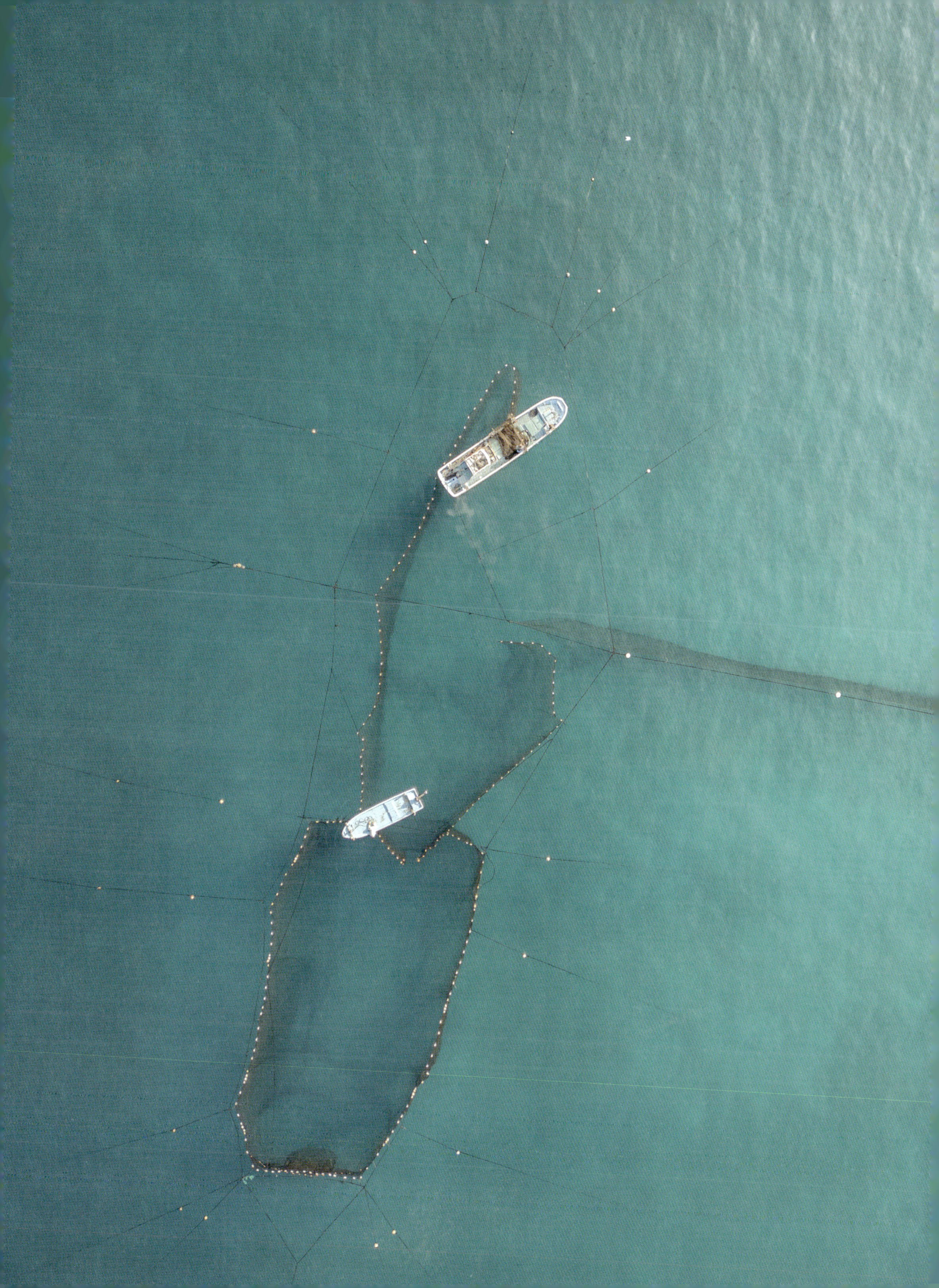

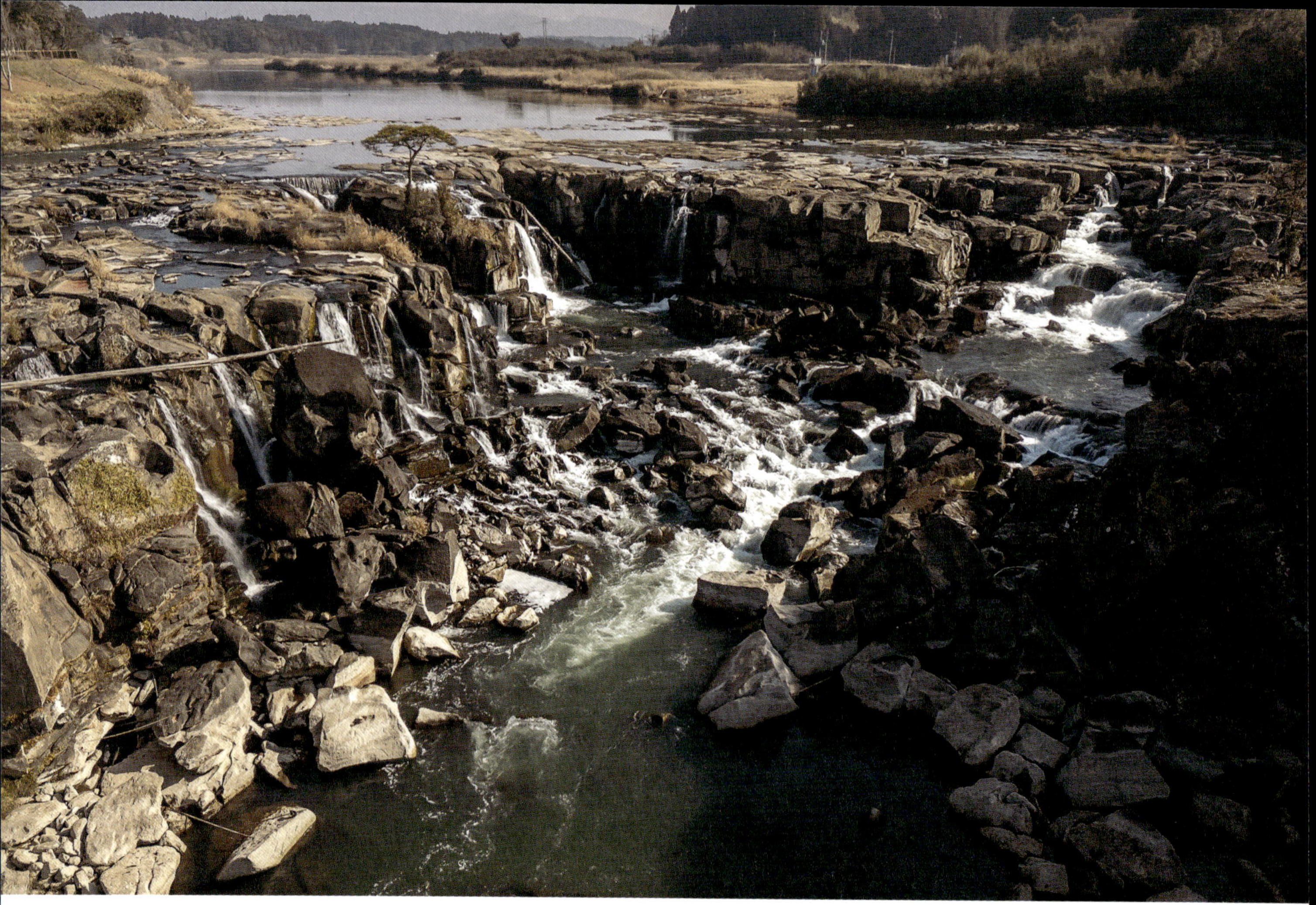

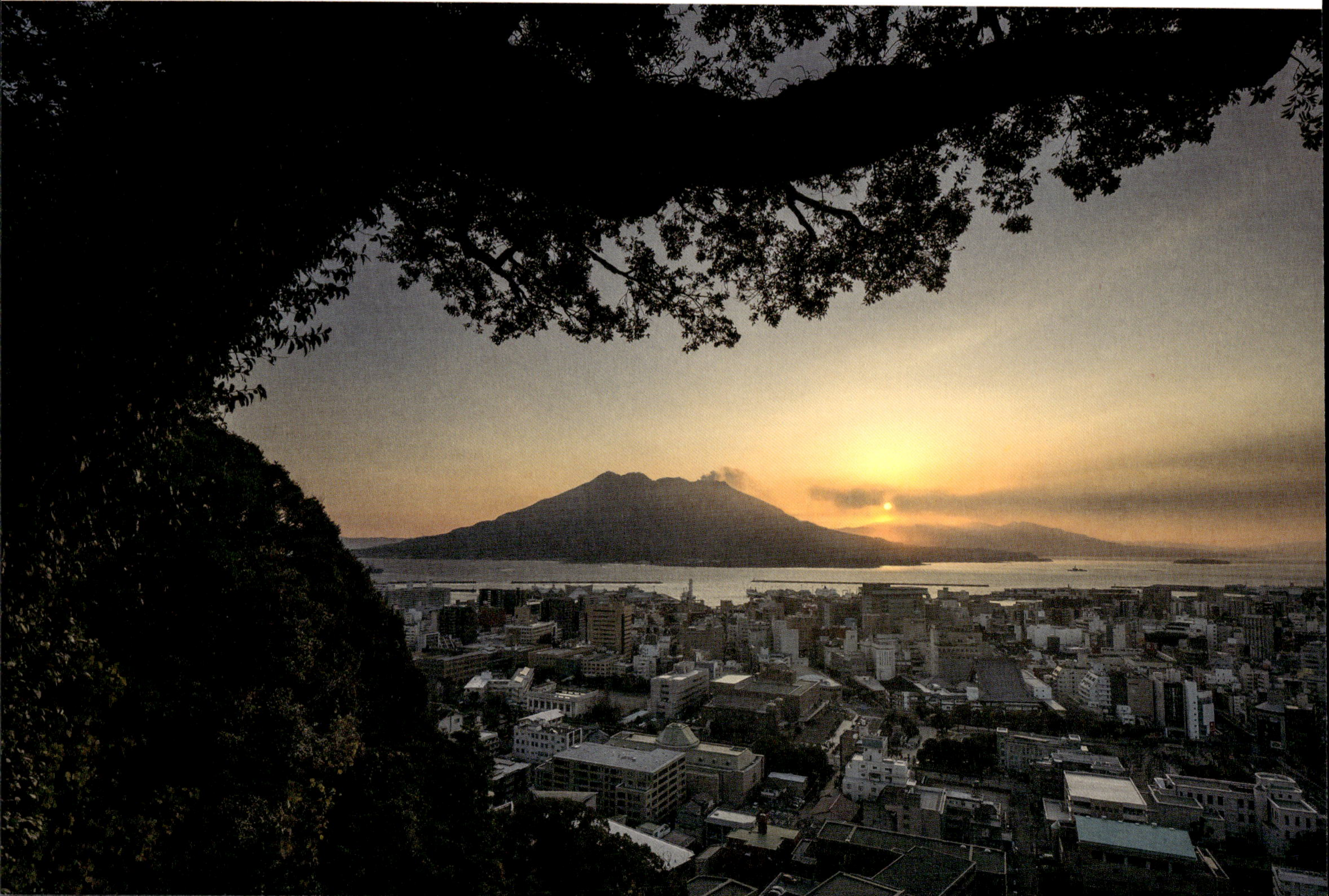

Sogi Falls.
Known as the "Niagara of the Orient", Sogi Falls presents a breathtaking panorama of water cascading gracefully over dark, imposing rocks. In daylight, the waterfalls shimmer and sparkle as they stretch across a width of more than 100 metres, creating a dramatic display.

Kagoshima & Sakurajima.
From the summit of Mount Shiroyama, the city of Kagoshima peacefully stretches out at the base of the towering Sakurajima volcano, with fumaroles gently rising into the sky.

Oouo Shrine.
The Oouo Shrine, located in Saga Prefecture, presents a captivating sight, with its towering red *torii* gate rising from the water. A stone path emerges at low tide, allowing visitors to walk towards and reflect upon this iconic spiritual site in serene solitude. >

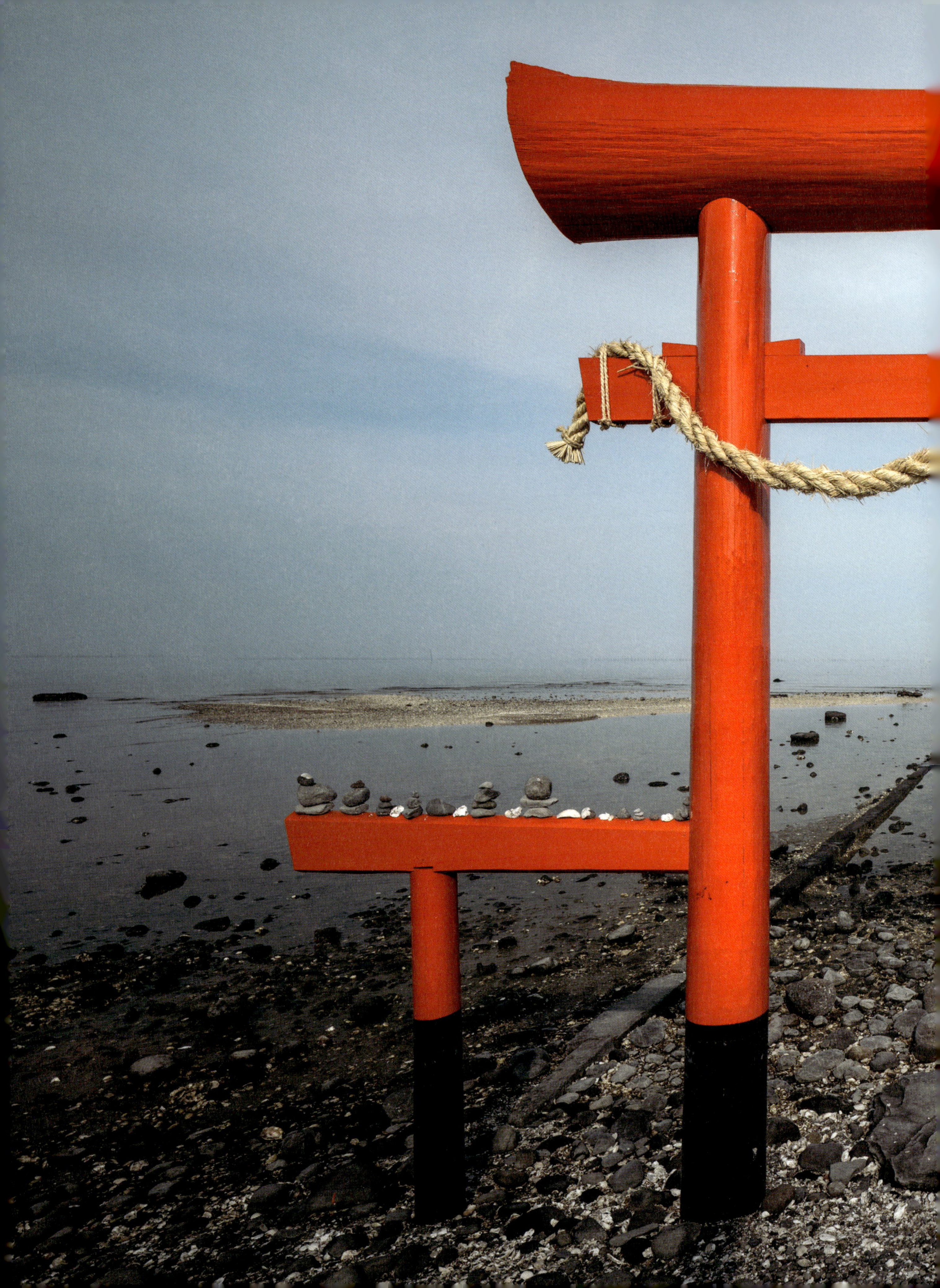

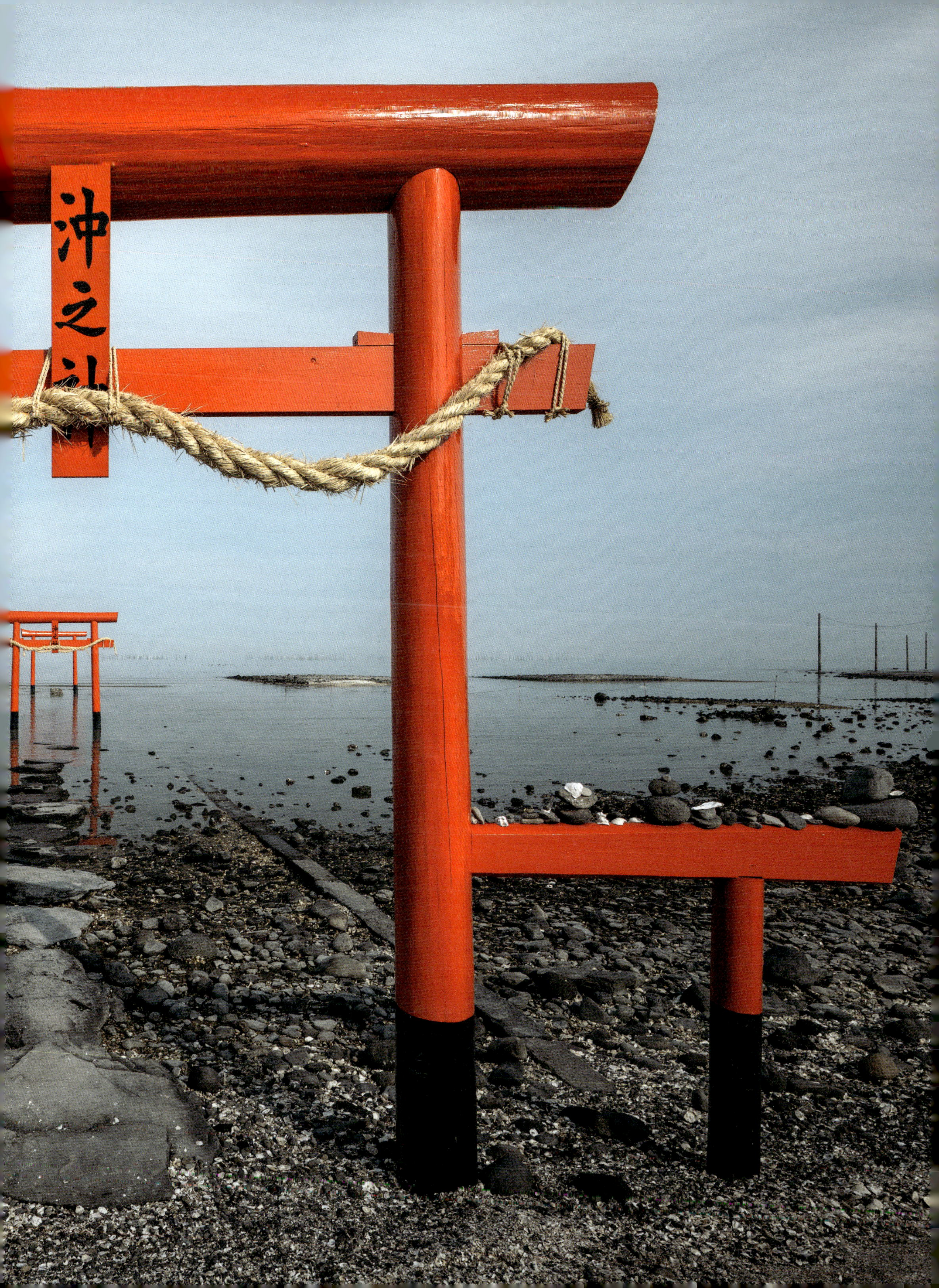
沖之

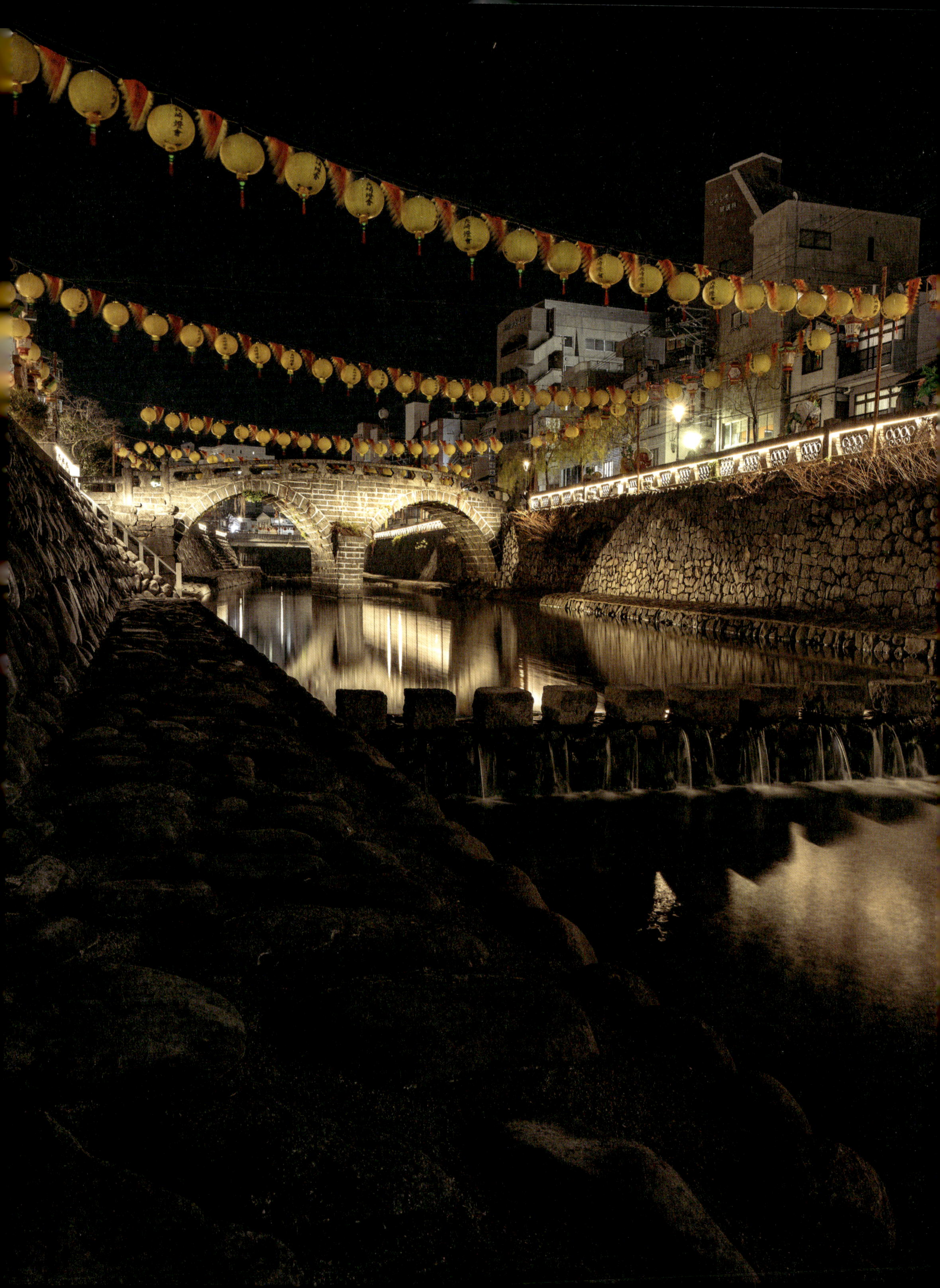

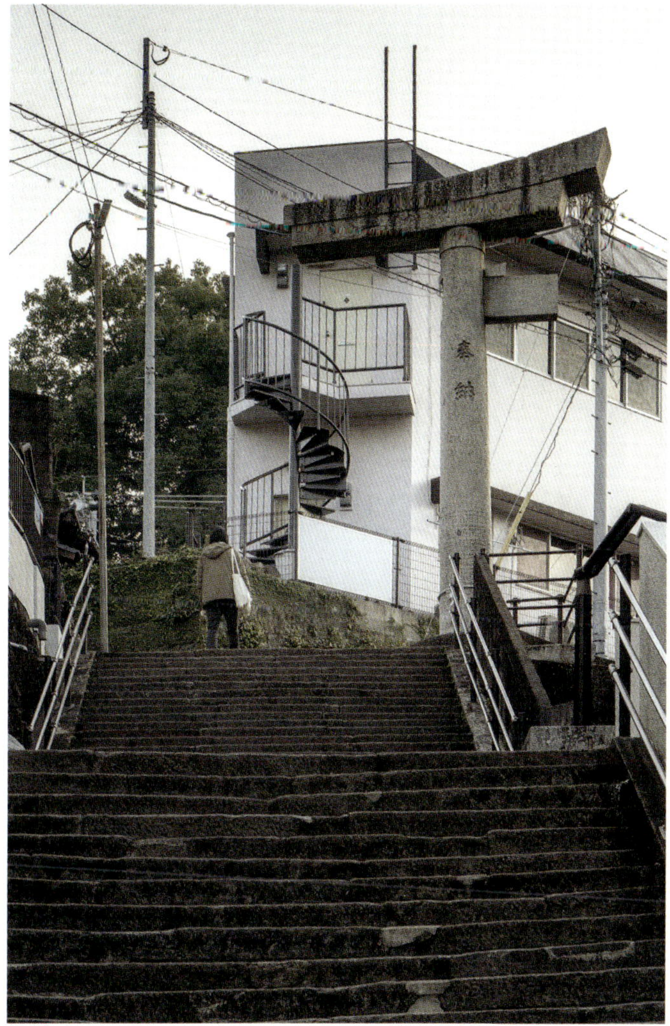

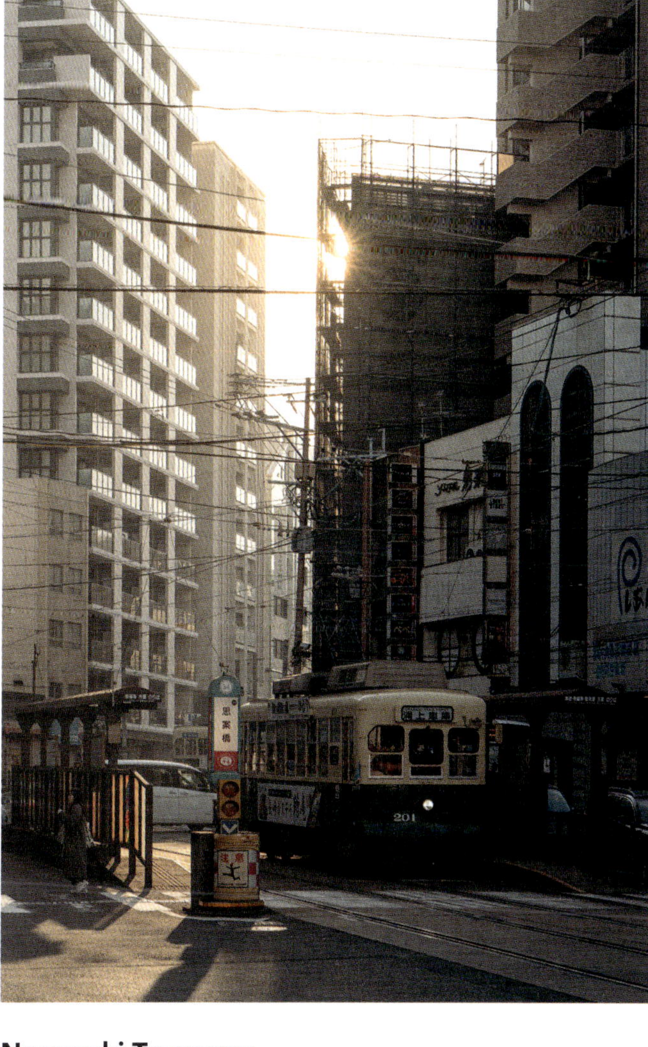

Nagasaki's Broken Torii.
A poignant relic of history, Nagasaki's broken *torii* symbolises resilience and survival. Bearing the scars of the atomic blast on August 9, 1945, it remains a testament to the city's endurance and rebirth. Situated at the bend of an urban staircase, it serves as a quiet reminder of the past's strength and the ongoing spirit of reconstruction.

Nagasaki Tramway.
In the heart of Nagasaki, the vintage tramway winds its way through a blend of modern buildings and vibrant alleyways. These colourful trams, living links to the past, carry both locals and visitors on a nostalgic journey through time.

Megane Bridge.
Ideal for walks, Nagasaki's Megane Bridge gracefully arches over the tranquil waters of the Nakashima River. Known as the "Spectacles Bridge" for its flawless reflection on the water's surface, it becomes even more enchanting during the Lantern Festival, when golden lanterns illuminate its elegant stone structure.

Nagasaki.
From the observatory atop Mount Nabekanmuri, Nagasaki spreads out like a jewel in a case of light.

Glover Sky Road.
Nestled in the rolling hills of Nagasaki, Glover Sky Road winds through a blend of traditional and modern houses, terraced along the steep slopes. This charming vista presents a glimpse into the city's unique character, where narrow lanes and tiled rooftops weave a narrative of rich cultural heritage and historical depth.

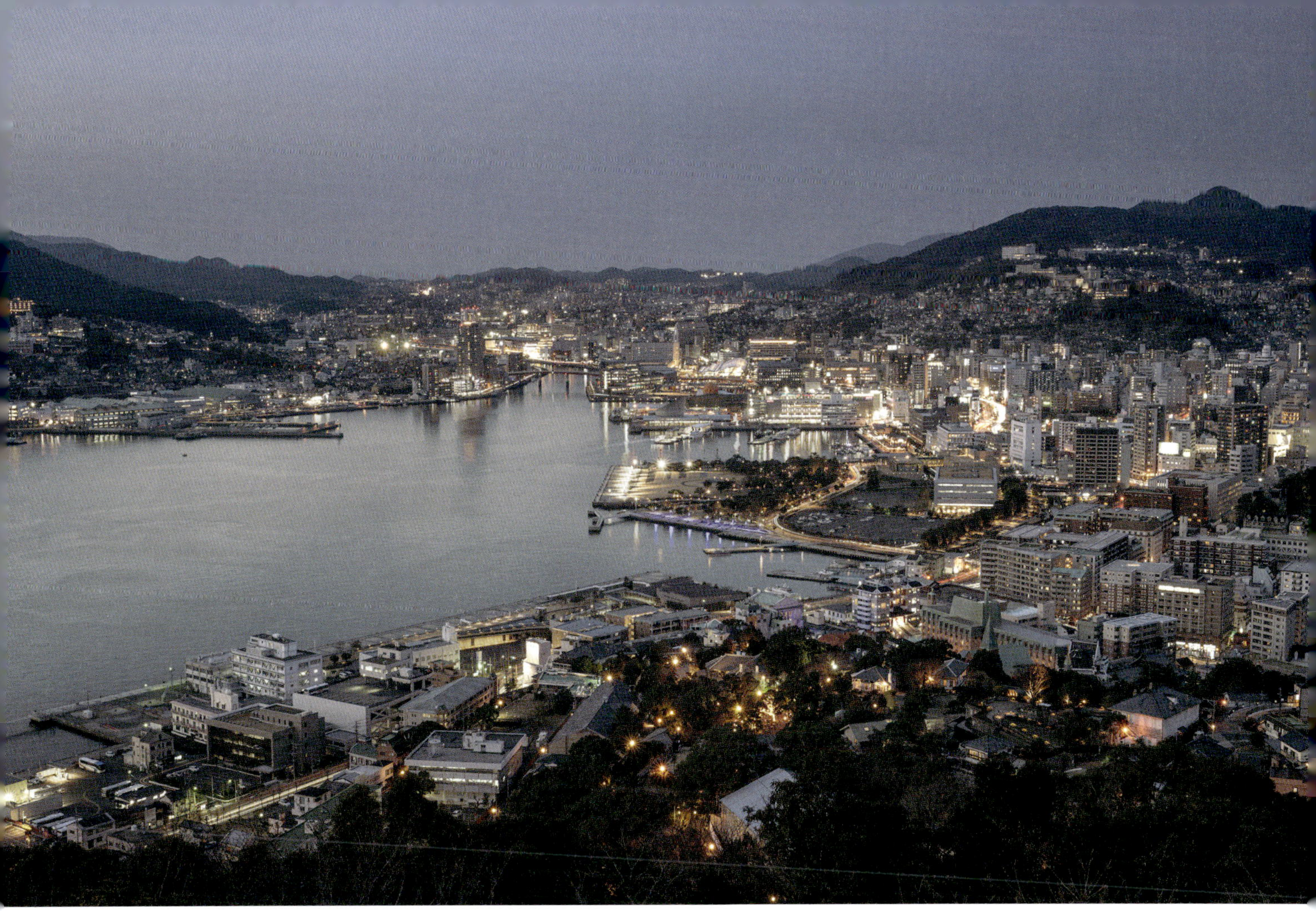

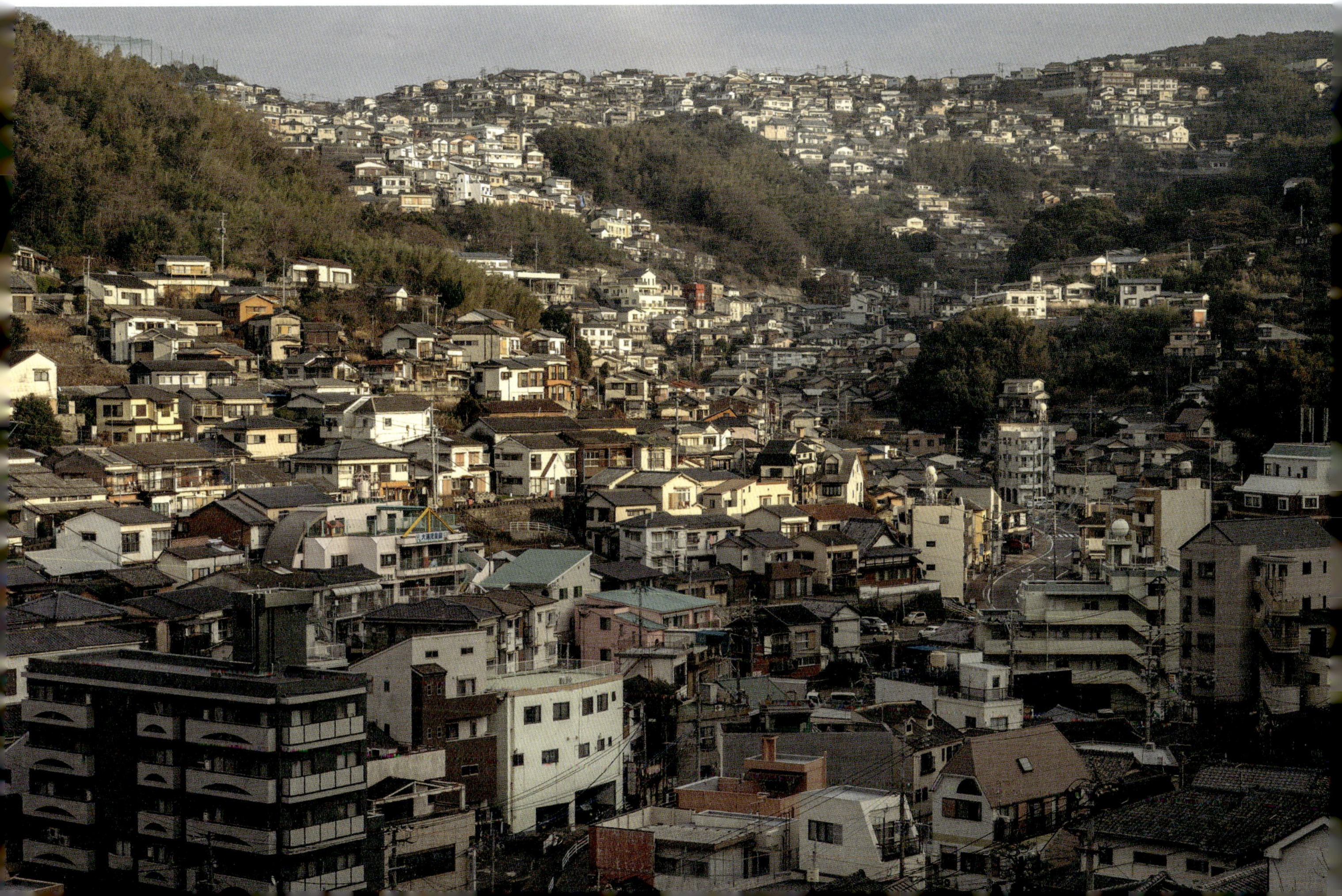

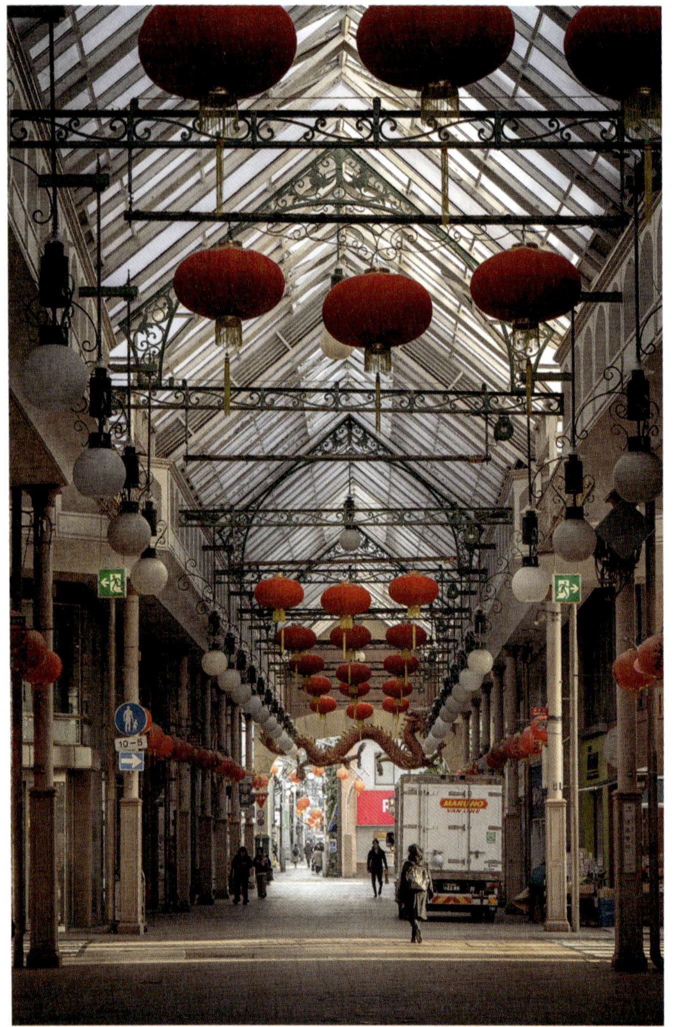

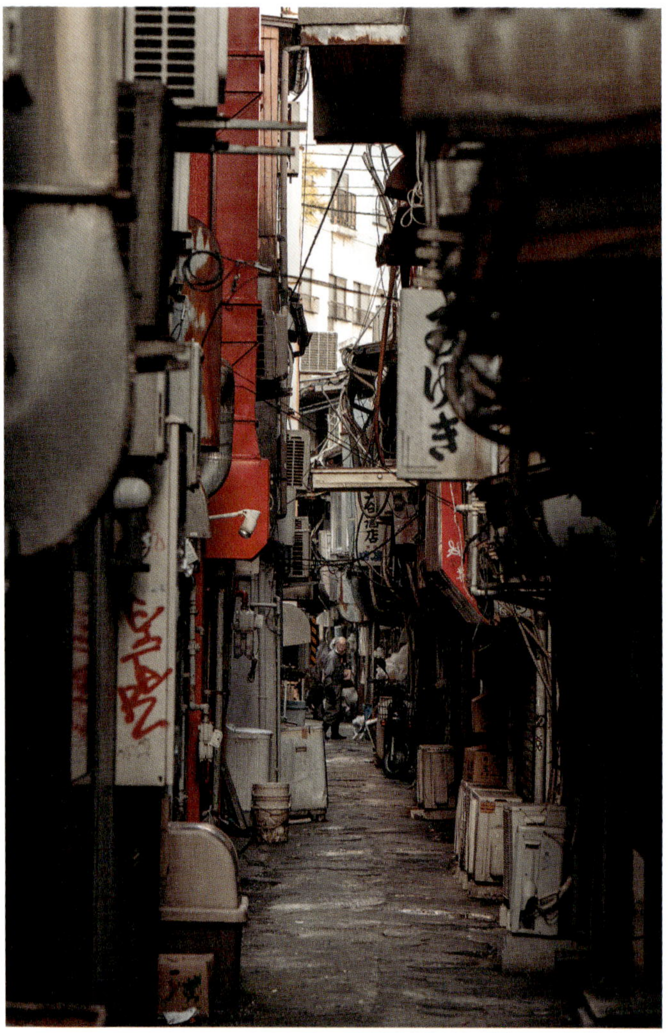

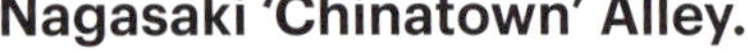

Nagasaki 'Chinatown' Alley.
This covered alleyway in Nagasaki, adorned with vibrant red lanterns and traditional Chinese motifs, stands as a testament to the city's profound Chinese cultural influence. Beneath its elegant glass canopy, visitors meander through a lively space, where bustling shops and festive decorations create an energetic atmosphere.

Nagasaki Alley.
This narrow alley in Nagasaki unveils a more intimate and authentic side of the city.

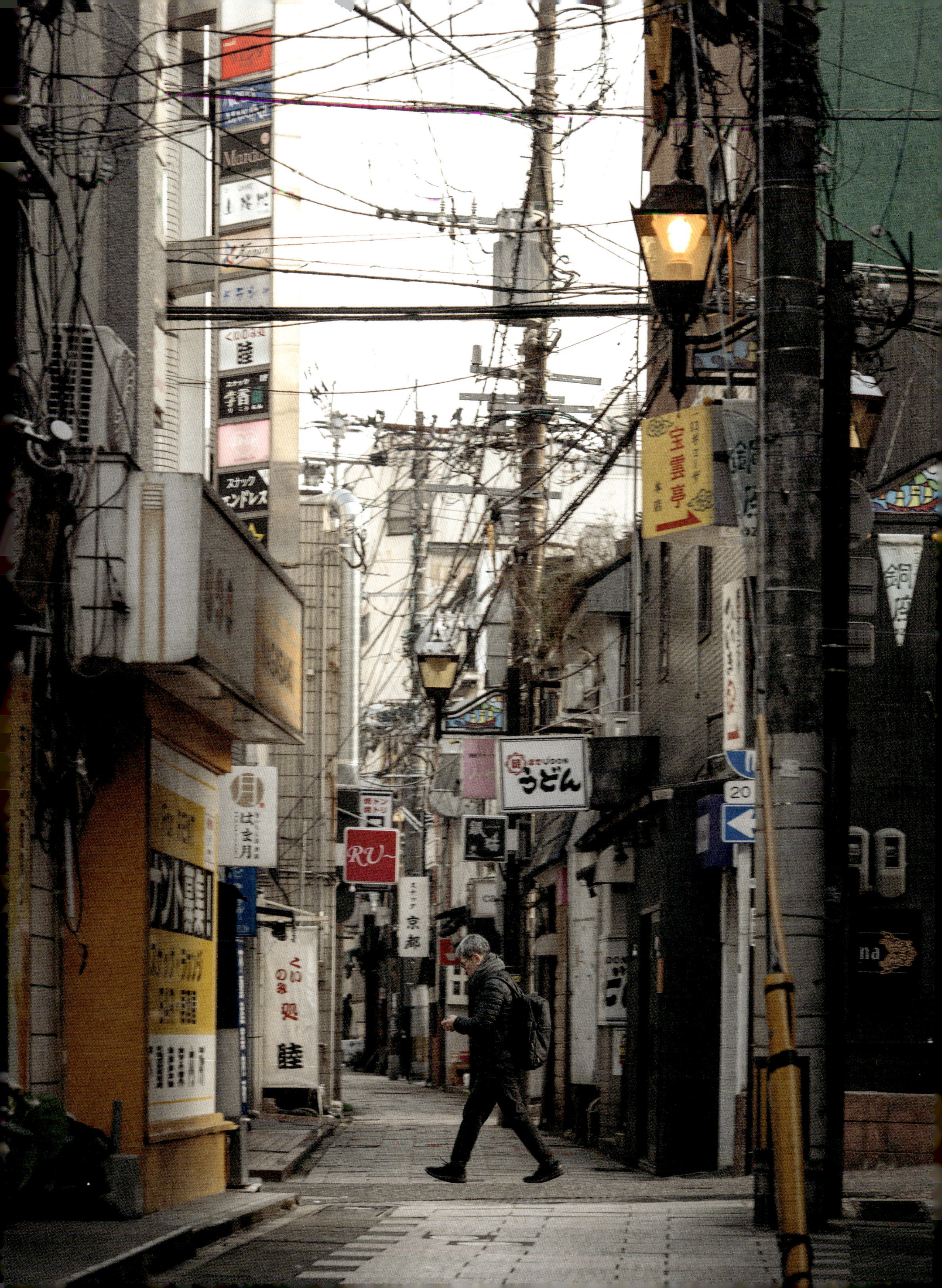

宝雲亭
本店
うどん
はま月
RU~
京都
20

Takachiho.
Nestled deep within a volcanic gorge and flanked by dramatic basalt cliffs, the magnificent Takachiho Falls offers a mesmerising spectacle. Visitors can approach this emblematic waterfall of Miyazaki prefecture by boat, surrounded by crystal-clear waters and verdant nature.

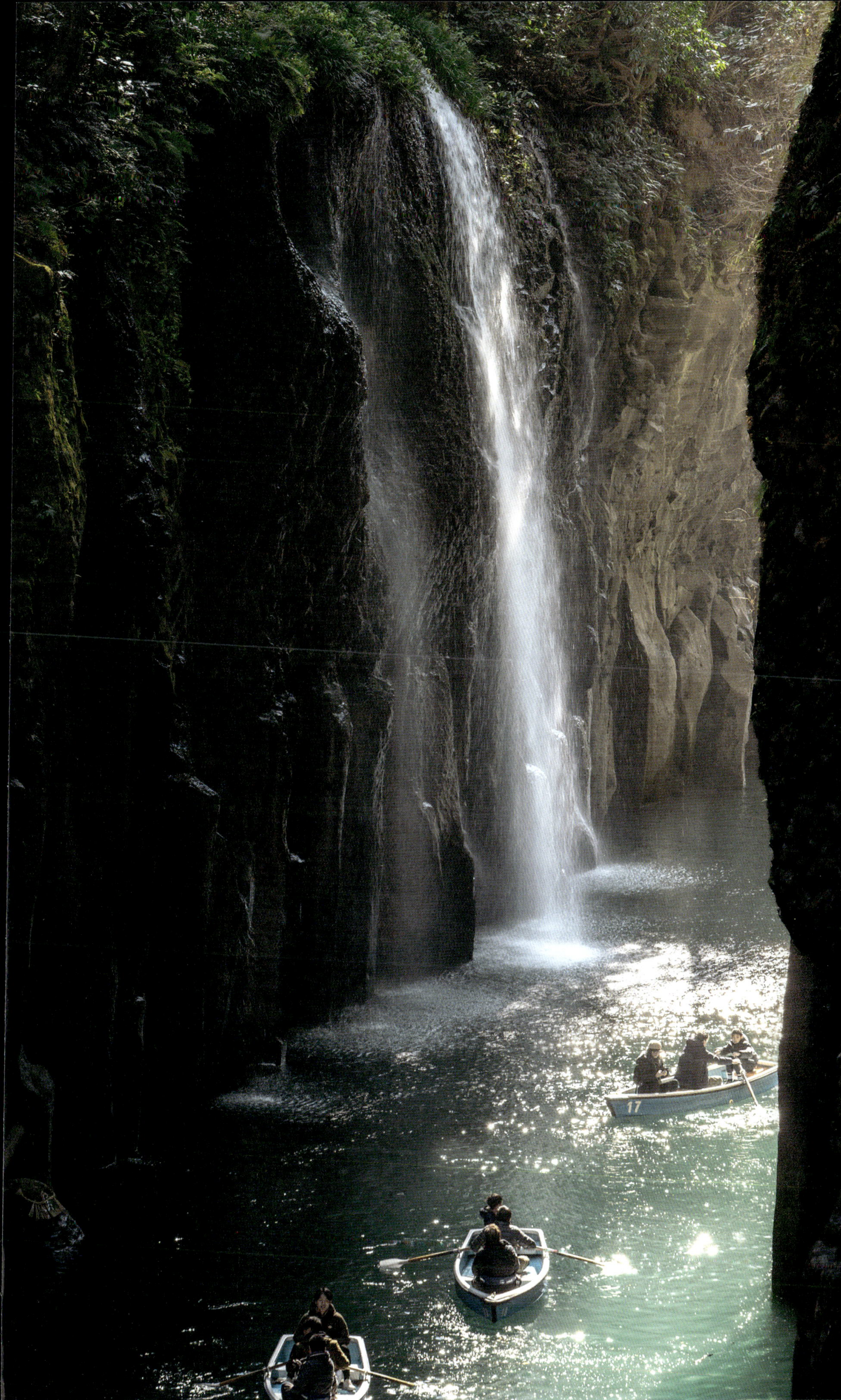
17

謝辞

I would like to express my heartfelt gratitude to all those who have contributed to the creation of this photo book on Japan.

To my beloved wife, Midori Iwama, my constant source of inspiration and unwavering support since my arrival in Japan. It is through her boundless love and encouragement that I have found the strength and motivation to capture the beauty of this remarkable country.

To my parents, France and Eric Wauters, whose belief in me and unwavering support have given me the energy to chase my dreams.

To Fabian San Martin, my colleague and fellow photographer. His shared passion for Japan has not only enriched this journey but also opened the doors to unforgettable places.

Lastly, to Léopold and Charlotte, my two faithful canine companions. Since 2013, they have been by my side on countless explorations, bringing joy, curiosity, and companionship at every turn. Their presence has enabled me to form lasting and unique connections with many wonderful people in Japan.

Author
Nicolas Wauters

Pictures
Nicolas Wauters
https://www.nicolaswauters.com/

Graphic design and layout
Dominique Hambÿe

Translation
Olivier Grégoire

Proofreading
Paula Cook, Olivier Grégoire, Elise Nogues

Éditions Racine /
Lannoo Publishers
https://www.lannoopublishers.com/en

Tour & Taxis – Entrepôt royal
Avenue du Port, 86C / bte 104A
B-1000 Brussels
Tel. +32 (0)2 646 44 44
www.racine.be

ISBN : 978-23-902-5351-8
Legal deposit : D/2025/6852/21
Printed in Europe